THE SECRET SENTRY

The Untold History of the National Security Agency

MATTHEW M. AID

BLOOMSBURY PRESS
New York • Berlin • London

Published by Bloomsbury Press, New York

All papers used by Bloomsbury Press are natural, recyclable products made from wood
grown in well-managed forests. The manufacturing processes conform to the environ-
mental regulations of the country of origin.

LIBRARY OF CONGRESS CATALOGING-IN-PUBLICATION DATA

Aid, Matthew M., 1958–
The secret sentry : the untold history of the
National Security Agency / Matthew M. Aid.
p. cm.
Includes bibliographical references and index.
ISBN 978-1-59691-515-2 (alk. paper hardcover)
1. United States. National Security Agency—History. 2. Intelligence service—
United States. 3. Electronic surveillance—United States. 4. United States—
History—1945– I. Title. II. Title: Secret sentry, the untold history of the NSA.
III. Title: Untold history of the National Security Agency.
UB256.U6A53 2009
327. 1273—dc22
2008037442

First published by Bloomsbury Press in 2009
This paperback edition published in 2010

Paperback ISBN: 978-1-60819-096-6

1 3 5 7 9 10 8 6 4 2

Typeset by Westchester Book Group
Printed in the United States of America by Worldcolor Fairfield

To Harry, Rita, and Jonathan Aid
My Family, My Best Friends, and My Staunchest Supporters
Gratis eternum

Happy Birthday
to Doug
2010
from Dad & Pat

*Know your enemy and know yourself, find
naught in fear for 100 battles.
Know yourself but not your enemy, find level of
loss and victory.
Know thy enemy but not yourself, wallow in
defeat every time.*

—SUN TZU

*There are no secrets except the secrets that keep
themselves.*

—GEORGE BERNARD SHAW,
BACK TO METHUSELAH

Contents

The Origins of the American Cryptologic Effort Against Russia

Another man's soul is darkness. Does anybody
ever really know anybody else?
——RUSSIAN PROVERB

The consensus of historians (and the overwhelming burden of evidence) dates the initial stages of the Cold War to well before the end of World War II. The United States would emerge from the war as a superpower with arguably the world's strongest armed forces, sole possession of the atomic bomb, a vastly expanded industrial base, and an infrastructure untouched by the ravages of war. But on the negative side, the country had at best a rocky relationship with one of its wartime allies, the Soviet Union. By the time Nazi Germany and Japan had surrendered, Russia was on a collision course with both the United States and Britain. It was not long before the Soviet Union was regarded as "the main enemy" by the Western nations. Since it remained a rigidly closed society under Joseph Stalin's regime, the lack of transparency was a major factor driving the Cold War. Because the United States had only a very limited idea of what was going on in the Soviet Union, its satellite countries in Eastern Europe, and communist China, the emerging confrontation became all the more dangerous. But one of the most secret resources that had greatly contributed to the victory of the Allied Powers—the United States and Britain's ability to intercept and read the communications of our former enemies Germany, Japan, and Italy, both in the clear and encoded—would be quickly redirected to the task of gathering communications intelligence about the new Sino-Soviet threat.

It is difficult to imagine, many decades later, just how mortal that threat was perceived to be, particularly after the Soviet Union detonated its first atomic device in the summer of 1949. The prospect of a "nuclear Pearl Harbor" meant that the United States would rely heavily on an increasingly large and expensive communications intelligence effort.

Carter Clarke Declares War on Russia

In a certain sense, Brigadier General Carter Clarke was the founding father of the National Security Agency (NSA). A blunt, often profane, hard-drinking, and demanding individual, Clarke lacked the polish of his fellow officers who had gone to West Point. He began his career as an enlisted man and worked his way up through the ranks. Despite a lack of previous intelligence experience and a file drawer full of bad fitness reports (Clarke was a real maverick), he was the man the U.S. Army selected to run the analytic side of SIGINT Army G-2, the Special Branch. A college dropout (he joined the army and served under General John Pershing chasing Pancho Villa in Mexico), he was a highly intelligent man and an autodidact.

Clarke was described by many who worked with him as being a tough, impatient, no-nonsense workaholic who abhorred conformity and was intolerant of bureaucracy. When things did not get done to his satisfaction, Clarke's volatile temperament usually took over. Former colleagues recall that his temper tantrums were legendary. A former army officer said, "I knew that Clarke had an explosive temper. Although quite a decent person, he laced his language with frequent bursts of profanity." His detractors, who were many, described him as loud, uncouth, brash, and argumentative, with a tendency toward overstatement when trying to make a point or win an argument. And yet, despite his brashness, gruff talk, and stern demeanor, Clarke earned the respect (and fear) of virtually all the U.S. Army intelligence officials he dealt with. A former senior NSA official, Frank B. Rowlett, described Clarke as "a very unconventional man and a man of considerable moral courage [who] would spit in your face and laugh at you."[1]

Clarke's Special Branch was a component of Army G-2 in the Pentagon created after Pearl Harbor, the unit to which all intercepts were sent for analysis and reporting to consumers. It only worked on SIGINT materials, while the rest of Army G-2 worked on more mundane materials, like military attaché reports. The army's SIGINT organization, the Signal Security Agency (SSA), commanded by Brigadier General W. Preston Corderman, was a separate field agency that was (until 1944) part of the Army Signal Corps. As noted above, all its intercept material went to Clarke's G-2 Special Branch.

When Clarke took command of the Special Branch of Army G-2 (intelligence) in May 1942, the United States was able to read the top Japanese diplomatic and military encoded communications (which enabled U.S. forces to win the Battle of Midway in 1942, the turning point of the war in the Pacific) and the British were reading the German codes generated by the Enigma machine. Despite his rough edges, Clarke worked well with his British counterparts in the Bletchley Park code-breaking center. Deep down, however, he trusted no man and no nation. According to Rowlett, "Clarke was a good man to have in the intelligence business in our line of command [the communications intelligence, or COMINT, field] because he didn't trust any nation. He just said, 'They're your friends today and they're your enemies tomorrow, and when they're on your side find out as much as you can about them because you can't when they become your enemy.' "[2]

The United States was not only reading the codes of the three Axis Powers; it was reading the encrypted diplomatic and military traffic of more than forty other countries—including our allies and neutral states. Well before the end of the war, Clarke, like many in the American military and government, decided that the Soviet Union would become our next "main enemy" after the war, and he issued an order in January 1943 to begin cracking Russian codes. So secret and delicate was this operation that very few people were allowed to even know it existed, and since virtually nothing was put in writing, the paper trail today is virtually nonexistent. The U.S. Navy had its own code-breaking operation headquartered in Washington. Though the two cryptanalytic organizations shared code-breaking responsibilities, cooperation was the exception rather than the rule.[3]

The army code breaking operation was headquartered in a former girls' preparatory school named Arlington Hall, located in Arlington, Virginia. The main building on its large and beautifully landscaped campus housed the administrative offices. Tacked onto it, once the army took over and fenced it off from the world, were two wings that housed large open bays crammed with code breakers, linguists, and analysts, crowded together and forced to endure the scorching and humid Washington summers before the widespread use of air-conditioning. Hundreds of fans provided some relief—but unfortunately they blew working papers all over the place. The sole air-conditioning was reserved for the noisy and noxious IBM tabulating machines.[4]

Clarke had some supervisory authority over Arlington Hall Station (its official designation), but he largely worked out of a high-security area in the Pentagon. The intercepts of enemy communications that were picked up by a far-flung network of listening posts, some of them in remote areas like Ethiopia and Alaska, went to Arlington Hall, where they were decrypted and translated. Then they were sent on to Clarke's analytic organization. The intelligence product derived from intercepts was so sensitive that its distribution was extremely limited, reaching only a few hundred people with the highest security clearances. The paradox here is that in order to protect the sources and methods used to gather this invaluable signals intelligence (SIGINT) and not tip off the enemy that the United States was reading virtually all of its communications, the intelligence product often had to be "sanitized" (i.e., put in a form that would not disclose the source of the intelligence reporting) and sometimes did not reach those who needed it most. (Both Admiral Husband Kimmel and General Walter Short, who took the burden of blame for Pearl Harbor, were arguably deprived of information that could have made the events of December 7, 1941, a very different story.) Throughout the war, commanders in the field below a certain level of rank and responsibility were not furnished with this critical information, or got it in a very watered-down form, which tended to make the material not as useful as it should have been, particularly because these officers could not know just how definitive and reliable it was. The same complaints that were voiced back then are still heard today.

Because the British had developed a formidable code-breaking operation that was in many ways superior to the Americans', once the United States entered the war there was an almost complete sharing of information and coordination of efforts. But the British were not apprised of the U.S. attack on Russian codes. In any event, they were undertaking their own effort, which they also did not disclose to the United States.[5]

Well before Germany, Japan, and Italy surrendered, the Cold War was under way, setting our quondam ally, the Soviet Union, on a collision course with the United States, Great Britain, and, in time, the other nations that would become the North Atlantic Treaty Organization (NATO). Accordingly, before Germany surrendered, the United States and the United Kingdom decided that everybody's cards had to be put on the table. Prime Minister Winston Churchill and his commanders (particularly Brigadier General Sir Stewart Menzies, the head of the British spy agency MI-6) firmly believed that a concerted effort had to be made to penetrate what Churchill described as a "riddle wrapped up inside an enigma"—the essentially closed society of the Soviet Union. This belief was shared by General George Marshall, Admiral Ernest King, and just about everybody at senior levels of the U.S. government and military—with one exception, President Franklin Delano Roosevelt. FDR wistfully believed that the United States and Russia could "peacefully coexist" after the Allied victory. So it was decided that he not be informed that we were spying on our Russian ally. The Russians, of course, were doing the same thing to the United States and Britain and, unfortunately, as we know now, doing a much better job. The full extent of Russian espionage was made clear when we began to read their enciphered messages. One key early breakthrough came in October 1943, when a thirty-seven-year-old lieutenant named Richard Hallock, who before the war had been an archaeologist at the University of Chicago, made the first break into the Russian ciphers. Incredibly, the Soviets had reused the pages of their one-time pad cipher keys on a number of occasions in different kinds of message traffic.[6]

(A "one-time pad" used to encipher messages is a bound set of sheets, each one printed with randomly generated numbers—representing both words and numbers—organized as additive "keys" and a certain number of lines of numbers in separate "groups." No one sheet in a pad and no pad or set of sheets duplicates any other, except for the matching pad's sheets used for deciphering the encoded message. The sheets are to be used once only and then destroyed. If used properly, the pad provides a virtually unbreakable code.)

The German invasion of Russia in June 1941 and the chaos that followed had created a severe shortage of cipher materials at Russian overseas diplomatic establishments, leading the NKVD's* cryptographic department in Moscow, which produced all code and cipher materials, to take shortcuts to fill the increasing demand for cryptographic materials. As the German army drew ever closer to Moscow in the winter of 1941, the Russians apparently panicked, printing duplicates of twenty-five thousand pages of one-time pad keys during the first couple of months of 1942, then binding them into one-time pad books and sending them not only to their diplomatic and commercial establishments, but also to the various NKVD *rezidenturas* (or "stations") around the world, thus unwittingly compromising the security of all messages encrypted with these duplicated pads. Then, to make matters worse, the Russians could not get new cipher materials to their diplomatic establishments in the United States and elsewhere because of German U-boat activity in the North Atlantic, which hampered Soviet merchant shipping traffic between Murmansk and the United States.[7]

---

* The designation of the Soviet intelligence and security service changed on numerous occasions. After the postrevolutionary Cheka, it became the State Political Directorate, or GPU (1922–1923); the United State Political Directorate, or OGPU (1923–1934); the Main Directorate for State Security, or GUGB (1934–1943); the People's Commissariat for State Security, or NKGB (1943–1946); and the Ministry for State Security, or MGB (1946–1953). From 1953 to 1954, all intelligence and internal security functions were merged into the Ministry for Internal Affairs (MVD). Between March 1954 and October 1991, the principal Soviet intelligence and security service was the Committee for State Security (KGB). In October 1991, the KGB was dissolved following the collapse of the USSR and the abortive coup d'état against Mikhail Gorbachev.

SIGINT Comes of Age

Beginning in early 1943, the U.S. Army's SIGINT collection effort slowly began to shift from Axis military communications targets to the pre–Pearl Harbor focus on foreign diplomatic communications traffic, largely because of dramatic changes taking place in the global geopolitical balance of power, with the United States rapidly emerging as the world's top superpower. Senior U.S. government and military policy makers and intelligence officers alike fully understood that while military decrypts (Ultra) might be helping win World War II on the battlefield, diplomatic COMINT (Magic) would be essential to help the U.S. government "win the peace." There was a determination within the U.S. government that this time around America would not be bullied or manipulated by its now less powerful European allies or the Russians at the peace talks that would inevitably follow the end of the war. It would soon become clear that Clarke's suspicions about Soviet long-term intentions were not only widely shared by others in the military and the government—they would also become key factors in how the nations of the West would respond to and then counter Russia's postwar strategy.[8]

To achieve these goals, however, the United States had to become as self-sufficient as possible in the realm of SIGINT. This meant that it had to put some distance between itself and Great Britain and begin spying on those countries or organizations that might conceivably constitute a threat in the future. The secrecy of the Russian effort was particularly intense. When Corderman inquired whether Russian traffic had been deliberately omitted from a target list just received by his agency, he was told that "[reference to] Russian traffic was intentionally omitted with Clarke's approval."[9] But the accumulating intercepts of Russian traffic from 1943 on would yield one of the greatest U.S. COMINT harvests ever—the program code-named Venona. Begun immediately after the end of World War II, the decoding and analysis would stretch over many, many years (until the program formally ended in 1980). Venona material gradually and retrospectively revealed the astounding extent of Soviet intelligence activity in America and Mexico. (Among other things, it made clear why Stalin was not surprised by Truman's carefully vague reference to the atomic bomb at Potsdam.) As we will see, the ultimate irony was that Venona's access was so valuable that it could not be compromised by using the material gathered as evidence (or even for counterintelligence measures) against those Soviet sources (and methods) revealed by decryption over many years.

The critical importance of the initial SIGINT effort was underlined by the events that unfolded in the next few years—the Berlin Crisis and subsequent Berlin Airlift (June 1948 through July 1949) in response to Russia's attempt to cut off West Berlin from access by its former allies, the detonation of the first Soviet atomic bomb in August 1949, and the outbreak of the Korean War in June 1950. What Anglo-American code breakers could learn about Russian capabilities and intentions was frightening enough; what they could *not* learn about because too many Soviet codes proved resistant to solution was an even greater cause for worry. Clarke, Rowlett, their colleagues, and their successors found themselves on the front line of a secret and increasingly desperate struggle. And the U.S. military, which soon began drawing up plans for war with the Soviet Union, would find SIGINT even more vital than it was in World War II, largely because Russia (as well as its satellite nations and China) was highly resistant to penetration by human intelligence operations.

CHAPTER 1

Roller-Coaster Ride

The Travails of American Communications Intelligence: 1945–1950

*When troubles come, they come not as single
spies but in battalions.*
—WILLIAM SHAKESPEARE, *HAMLET*

On August 14, 1945, the day Japan formally surrendered, the American signals intelligence empire stood at the zenith of its power and prestige. The U.S. Army and Navy cryptologic organizations, the Signal Security Agency (SSA) and the Naval Communications Intelligence Organization (OP-20-G) respectively, together consisted of more than thirty-seven thousand military and civilian personnel manning thirty-seven listening posts and dozens of tactical radio intelligence units around the world. The reach of America's code breakers was extraordinarily deep, with the army alone able to read 350 diplomatic code and cipher systems belonging to sixty countries. Needless to say, the two American SIGINT organizations seemed to be in much better shape, both quantitatively and qualitatively, than the poorly funded three-hundred-man American cryptologic establishment that had existed when Japan bombed Pearl Harbor on December 7, 1941.[1]

Structural changes within army and navy COMINT organizations came quickly after the end of the war. On September 15, 1945, the SSA was redesignated as the Army Security Agency (ASA), which was given complete control over all U.S. Army COMINT activities.[2] On July 10, 1946, the U.S. Navy COMINT organization OP-20-G was deactivated and all navy COMINT intercept and processing units were merged into a new and much smaller organization called the Communications Supplementary Activities (CSA).[3]

The Terrible Peace

Within hours of Japan's surrender, the thousands of American radio inter-cept operators and intelligence analysts around the world suddenly found themselves unemployed as the few remaining Japanese radio transmitters went off the air. Listening posts around the world were given "make-work" projects until the intercept operators could be discharged and sent home.[4] The same was true at the army and navy SIGINT analysis centers in Wash-ington, D.C.[5]

President Harry Truman's order for rapid demobilization after Japan's sur-render took its toll on America's SIGINT capability. General Corderman was forced to dismantle the unit he had personally spent so much time and effort building, and he did so amid intense opposition from Army G-2 and his own top deputies, such as his operations chief, Frank Rowlett, who urged him to fight the demobilization order. Decades later, a still-angry Rowlett recalled that his boss "made a speech to them, and in essence what he said was, we'd like you to stay but here's your hat."[6]

Over the next 120 days, the army and navy COMINT organizations lost 80 percent of their personnel.[7] Desperate last-minute efforts to convince the best and the brightest of the departing staff to stay on were to no avail. America's SIGINT establishment would need many years to make up for the loss of so much talent and intellectual firepower.

The same evisceration was taking place at all of the army's and navy's lis-tening posts. By December 1945, the army's and navy's radio intercept efforts had shrunk to skeleton crews whose operational accomplishments were de-teriorating rapidly. Even more worrisome, the radio traffic that the two U.S. COMINT organizations could access plummeted, since most of the foreign military communications traffic that the United States had been listening to was shifted from radio to landlines, and the volume of foreign diplomatic message traffic dropped back to normal peacetime levels.[8]

There was now much less raw material for the few remaining American cryptanalysts to work on, which in turn led to a dramatic decline in the num-ber of foreign code and cipher systems that were being exploited. In particu-lar, work on South American, Balkan, and Chinese diplomatic codes and ciphers fell off sharply because of a lack of intercepts. Without the assistance of the British, U.S. efforts to maintain continuity coverage of Middle Eastern and Near Eastern communications traffic would have collapsed. By the end of 1945, the supply of radio intercepts had fallen to a point where code-breaking work had almost come to a complete standstill, including the joint Anglo-American operation code-named Bourbon, the intercepting and decoding of Soviet communications.[9]

The Customers Complain

During the months after the end of the war, the U.S. Army and Navy COMINT organizations were not producing much in the way of useful political intelligence. Among the few sensitive materials produced during this troubled time were decrypted telegrams concerning foreign work on atomic energy, such as a September 27, 1945, French message mentioning Norwegian heavy water supplies and a November 27, 1945, Chinese diplomatic message concerning Russian nuclear weapons research efforts; decrypted French foreign intelligence service message traffic; and messages that revealed secret U.S. diplomatic activities around the world that the British and other allies were not meant to be privy to, such as a December 2, 1945, Chinese diplomatic message concerning the planned construction of an American air base in Saudi Arabia.[10]

Then there was the super-secret intercept program known as Operation Gold. In May 1946, two years before the creation of the state of Israel, the U.S. Navy COMINT organization began intercepting the international telephone calls and international cable traffic of Jewish agents in the United States and elsewhere who were engaged in raising money and buying arms for the Jewish underground in Palestine. According to a former army intelligence official, the Gold intercepts proved to be highly informative. "We knew who was shipping the arms, who was paying for them, who was being paid in this country, every illegal thing that was going on in this country." But the official added, "Because of politics, very little was ever done with [this intelligence]."[11]

COMINT was also producing very little meaningful intelligence on foreign military targets. As of 1946, the Army Security Agency (ASA) was reading the encrypted military communications of Argentina, Czechoslovakia, France, Romania, Spain, and Yugoslavia. Decrypts of Soviet military traffic were notable by their absence.[12]

By January 1946, the quantity and quality of the intelligence reporting coming from COMINT had fallen to such a low level that the director of naval intelligence, Rear Admiral Thomas Inglis, wrote that "we have been getting disappointingly little of real value from [communications intelligence] since VJ day."[13]

Complaints from intelligence consumers about the dearth of intelligence coming from COMINT were rampant. For example, on December 22, 1945, former U.S. Army chief of staff General George Marshall went to China in a foredoomed effort to broker some sort of deal between Chiang Kai-shek and Mao Tse-tung. No useful decrypts were available to offer any insight into the thorny problems confronting Marshall, and only months later did the army begin producing the first useful translations of intercepted Chinese National- ist and Chinese Communist communications.[14]

Yet the harshest criticism coming from customers was over the paucity of intelligence about what was going on inside the Soviet Union. A senior U.S. Army officer who visited Europe in the spring of 1946 was told that it was un- likely that Washington would get any kind of meaningful advance warning of a Soviet attack on Western Europe because of a near total lack of reliable intel- ligence about "the main enemy."[15]

The BRUSA Agreement

Thus the American COMINT establishment desperately needed help from somewhere in order to remain a viable intelligence provider. As it turned out, relief for the battered U.S. COMINT community was to come from across the Atlantic.

On March 5, 1946, former prime minister Winston Churchill, at Truman's invitation, delivered his famous speech in Fulton, Missouri, in which he warned, "From Stettin in the Baltic to Trieste in the Adriatic, an Iron Curtain has descended across the continent." The "informal" wartime arrangements for co- operation between American and British COMINT organizations were formal- ized on the same day. At almost the exact same time that Churchill was delivering his memorable speech, in a heavily guarded conference room in downtown Washington, D.C., a group of senior American and British intelli- gence officials were signing a seven-page Top Secret intelligence-sharing agree- ment called the British–United States Communication Intelligence Agreement, which was referred to within the U.S. intelligence community as the BRUSA Agreement. This may be one of the most important and longest-lasting agree- ments among foreign intelligence services ever conceived. The product of six months of intense and often acrimonious negotiations, the agreement recog- nized that given the "disturbed" condition of the world, the American and British COMINT organizations needed to continue to work together in order to monitor the broad array of new threats, especially the Soviet Union.[16]

In its final form, rather than being a blueprint for action, BRUSA was a general statement of principles meant to "govern the relations" of the United States, Britain, and the British Dominions "in communication intelligence matters only."[17] Contrary to what has previously been written about it, it was strictly a bilateral agreement between the United States and Great Britain that standardized the day-to-day collaboration between the two countries' SIGINT organizations. There was to be a complete and free exchange of all forms of communications intelligence "product" between the U.S. organizations and the British cryptologic organization, the Government Communications Headquarters (GCHQ). Both the U.S. Army and Navy COMINT organizations were required under the terms of the BRUSA Agreement to send one copy of every finished COMINT report (excepting those deemed to be specifically exempt from the intelligence-sharing agreement) to GCHQ, and vice versa. There was also a sidebar agreement between the Americans and the British for cryptanalytic cooperation on selected intelligence problems, such as the continuation of the joint efforts involving Russian and French ciphers. Other key provisions of the BRUSA Agreement established procedures governing the two nations' handling, safe-keeping, and exchange of COMINT.[18]

America's other English-speaking wartime SIGINT allies—Canada, Australia, and New Zealand—were referenced, but not included as signatories. BRUSA recognized that these nations, as British Dominions, would continue to operate under the overall direction of the British SIGINT agency GCHQ. Were the United States to make arrangements with the SIGINT organizations of these countries, BRUSA required that Britain be informed ahead of time, which in effect meant that London had to agree to the arrangements and could nix them at any point. It was to take eight more years and thousands of hours of further negotiations before BRUSA would finally morph, in 1954, into what is now known as the United Kingdom–United States (UKUSA) Agreement.[19]

The first of the Dominion countries that the United States sought to establish bilateral SIGINT relations with was Canada. During World War II, the U.S. Army and Navy COMINT organizations had maintained close relations with their Canadian counterparts, although the level of cooperation between the two countries never came close to approaching the intimacy that characterized the Anglo-American COMINT relationship. After the end of the war, U.S. and Canadian officials held some preliminary discussions about continuing their wartime COMINT collaborative relationship. But on September 5, 1945, a twenty-six-year-old Russian cipher clerk by the name of Igor Gouzenko walked out the door of the Russian embassy in Ottawa and after many adventures succeeded in defecting to Canada. Information provided by Gouzenko helped the Royal Canadian Mounted Police identify seventeen spies working for the Soviet military intelligence service, the GRU, in Canada and Britain.[20] The sensational revelations stemming from the Gouzenko spy scandal—that the Russians had an agent network inside the Canadian government—naturally made U.S. intelligence officials extremely wary about restoring their cryptologic relationship with the Canadians. The result was that in October 1945 U.S. intelligence officials broke off their talks with their Canadian counterparts, with the head of the U.S. Navy COMINT organization, Captain Joseph Wenger, telling his Canadian counterpart, "The whole matter is awaiting a high policy decision so, of course, nothing can be done until this is settled."[21]

The talks resumed in mid-1946 but essentially went nowhere until a series of compromises were reached that permitted the Canadian government to agree to the terms of the CANUSA COMINT Agreement, signed in November 1949.[22]

Reaching an agreement that included the rather small Australian SIGINT organization was complicated because of mounting evidence emanating from the Venona intercepts (to be discussed later in this chapter), which strongly indicated that Soviet intelligence had spies inside the Australian government who were feeding Moscow highly classified documents concerning Anglo-American defense matters. In January 1948, the U.S. government cut off the Australian government from access to all American classified information, and the American COMINT organizations were specifically barred from cooperating with their Australian counterparts in any way. Only after a new conservative Australian government headed by Robert Menzies was elected in December 1949 did the U.S. government relent and resume SIGINT collaboration with Australia on a limited basis, in 1950, after it was clear that the Soviet spies inside the Australian government had been removed. Australia was not admitted to BRUSA until three years later, in September 1953. In May 1954, the BRUSA Agreement was renamed the UKUSA Agreement so as to reflect the addition of Australia and New Zealand as full members of the global Anglo-American SIGINT enterprise.[23]

A Brief Shining Moment: The Break Into the Soviet Ciphers

Almost immediately after the signing of the BRUSA Agreement, the U.S. intelligence community's knowledge about what was transpiring inside the USSR began to improve, as the joint Anglo-American code-breaking enterprise—Bourbon—made dramatic progress solving a number of Soviet cipher systems.[24]

The British end of Bourbon was run from a motley, drab collection of buildings hidden behind high walls in the nondescript London suburb of Eastcote, which was the new home of the GCHQ. (Better quarters would later be established in the somewhat more balmy climate of Cheltenham.)[25]

The man who ran the British end of the Bourbon project was the head of the 140-man GCHQ Russian Cryptographic Section, Richard Pritchard.[26] Pritchard, who had managed the secret British cryptanalytic attack on Russian codes and ciphers during World War II, was one of those rare people blessed with multiple gifts. He had extraordinary mathematical talent and a genius for music, and he was a natural cryptanalyst to boot. F. W. Winterbotham, author of *The Ultra Secret*, described Pritchard as "young, tall, clean-shaven, rather round of face, with a quiet voice, could talk on any subject with witty penetration. He, too, was deeply musical."[27]

Pritchard assembled a small but remarkably talented group of veteran code breakers to work on Bourbon, the two most important of whom were Conel Hugh O'Donel Alexander, an extraordinarily gifted cryptanalyst and former British chess grand master, and Major Gerry Morgan, a brilliant machine cryptanalyst and the head of GCHQ's Crypto Research Section, which contained the best of the British cryptanalysts who had chosen to remain on in government service after the war.[28]

The level of "customer satisfaction" would soon begin to rise rapidly. In the span of only a year, teams of code breakers on both sides of the Atlantic accomplished an astounding series of cryptanalytic breakthroughs that, for an all-too-brief moment in time, gave the leaders of the United States and Great Britain unparalleled access to what was going on inside the Soviet Union, especially within the Russian military.

In February 1946, less than a month before the signing of the BRUSA Agreement, ASA cryptanalysts at Arlington Hall Station in Virginia managed to reconstruct the inner workings of a Soviet cipher machine that they called Sauterne, which was used on Red Army radio networks in the Far East. On March 1, 1946, a veteran U.S. Army cryptanalyst at Arlington Hall named Robert Ferner managed to produce the first decrypted message from a Sauterne intercept. By the end of the month, U.S. Navy cryptanalysts had discovered a means of determining the daily rotor settings used to encipher all messages on the Sauterne cipher machine, with the result that on April 4, 1946, a regular supply of Sauterne decrypts began to be produced.[29] The translations of the

Sauterne decrypts provided a window into what the Russian army was up to in the Far East.[30]

At the same time that Sauterne was solved, GCHQ began producing the first intelligence derived from its solution of another Russian army cipher machine system, which the British called Coleridge and which was used to encrypt traffic on Russian army radioteletype networks in the European half of the Soviet Union.[31] Alexander led the cryptanalytic attack on Coleridge. He had returned to code-breaking work after a brief, unhappy stint working as a financier in London because he could not stand a job "that involved a black jacket and striped trousers."[32] Assisting Alexander on the other side of the Atlantic was a team of U.S. Navy code breakers led by one of the best machine cryptanalysts in America, Francis "Frank" Raven. A 1934 graduate of Yale University, Raven had worked as the assistant manager of the Allegheny Ludlum Steel Company in Pittsburgh before joining the navy COMINT organization in 1942. An incredibly talented cryptanalyst, during the war he had been instrumental in solving a number of Japanese navy cipher machine systems.[33] The Coleridge decrypts were found to contain reams of administrative traffic for the Soviet military, but when analyzed, they yielded vitally important information about its order of battle, training activities, and logistical matters.[34]

At about the same time, the Anglo-American cryptanalysts made their first entry into a third Russian cipher machine system, designated Longfellow. By July 1946, a copy of the Longfellow cipher machine had been constructed by U.S. Navy cryptanalysts in Washington, D.C., based on technical specifications provided by the British cryptanalysts who had solved the system, but the solution of the cipher settings used on the Longfellow machine required several more months of work. Finally, in February 1947 a team of British cryptanalysts led by Gerry Morgan and a team of U.S. Navy analysts in Washington, headed by Commander Howard Campaigne, together solved the encryption system used by the Soviet army's Longfellow cipher machine system.[35]

But the value of the decrypts of Longfellow traffic that were just beginning to be produced in the spring of 1947 was eclipsed by the ever-rising volume of translations being produced across the Atlantic at GCHQ through the exploitation of the Coleridge cipher machine. These decrypts proved to be so valuable that, according to a report by the U.S. Navy liaison officer assigned to GCHQ, Coleridge was "the most important, high-level system from which current intelligence may be produced and is so in fact regarded here."[36]

The net result was that by the spring of 1947, translations of decrypted messages from all three systems were being produced in quantity. At Arlington Hall, the ASA cryptanalysts alone were churning out 341 decrypts a day, seven days a week, 365 days a year, most of which were derived from Russian radio intercepts.[37] By early 1949, more than 12,500 translations of decrypted Russian army radio messages had been published by ASA and sent to intelligence consumers in Washington.[38]

The Anglo-American cryptanalysts were also experiencing considerable success in solving the cipher systems used by the Soviet navy. By early 1947, a number of Russian navy ciphers used in the Far East had been successfully solved, largely because the two Russian fleets operating in the Pacific were forced by geography to use radio to communicate with Moscow instead of secure teletype landlines. This allowed U.S. Navy listening posts in the Far East to easily intercept the radio traffic sent between these headquarters and Moscow. There was also some success in reading the cipher systems used by the Soviet fleets in the Baltic Sea, as well as the ciphers used by the Black Sea fleet and the Caspian Sea flotilla. By February 1949, U.S. Navy cryptanalysts had produced more than twenty-one thousand decrypts of Soviet naval message traffic, which was almost double the number of decrypts of Russian army traffic produced by ASA.[39]

A number of the Soviet air force's operational ciphers were also quickly solved. In 1947, ASA cryptanalysts solved one of the operational cipher systems used by the Soviet air force headquarters in Moscow to communicate with its subordinate commands throughout the Soviet Union and Eastern Europe, as well as several variants of this system.[40] In the Far East, U.S. Army cryptanalysts in Japan were reading the encrypted radio traffic of the Soviet Ninth Air Army at Ussurijsk/Vozdvizhenka and the Tenth Air Army at Khabarovsk.[41]

In room 2409 at Arlington Hall, a brilliant thirty-four-year-old former Japanese linguist and cryptanalyst named Meredith Knox Gardner was making spectacular progress solving the ciphers that had been used during World War II by the Soviet civilian intelligence service (its military counterpart was the GRU), then called the NKGB, to communicate with its *rezidenturas* in the United States. In later years, this work would be part of Venona program. In December 1946, Gardner solved part of a 1944 NKGB message that gave the names of some of the more prominent American scientists working on the Manhattan Project, the American wartime atomic bomb program. The decrypt was deemed so important that army chief of staff Omar Bradley was personally briefed on the contents of the message. Five months later, in May 1947, Gardner solved part of a message sent from the NKGB's New York *rezidentura* on December 13, 1944, which showed that an agent within the U.S. Army General Staff in Washington had provided the Soviets with highly classified military information. Unfortunately, Gardner was not able to deduce anything further as to the agent's true identity from the fragmentary decrypt. By August 1947, new decrypts provided the first evidence that an extensive Soviet spy ring was operating in Australia during World War II, which set off alarm bells in both Washington and London. Gardner was able to report that the decrypts contained the cryptonyms of dozens, perhaps hundreds, of Soviet agents operating in the United States, Australia, and Sweden during the war. But the report also clearly showed that Gardner had only made partial headway into the Soviet codebook, and that the results of his work were still very fragmentary.[42]

Taken together, these decrypts opened up a wide array of Soviet military and civilian targets for exploitation by the information-starved intelligence analysts in both Washington and London. An NSA historical monograph notes, "ASA in the post–World War II period had broken messages used by the Soviet armed forces, police and industry, and was building a remarkably complete picture of the Soviet national security posture."[43] This is confirmed by material obtained by researchers from the former KGB archives in Moscow, which reveals that the Anglo-American COMINT organizations were deriving from these decrypts a great deal of valuable intelligence about the strength and capabilities of the Soviet armed forces, the production capacity of various branches of Soviet industry, and even the super-secret work that the Soviets were conducting in the field of atomic energy.[44]

Former NSA officials have stated in interviews that the first postwar crisis in which COMINT played an important role was the 1948 Berlin Crisis.[45] Ultimately, it was COMINT that showed that the Soviets had no intention of launching an attack on West Berlin or West Germany. The initial stage of the Berlin Crisis was actually a Russian feint.[46] COMINT also provided valuable data during the second part of the crisis, when on June 26, 1948, the Soviet's cut off all access to West Berlin, forcing the United States and Britain to begin a massive airlift to keep West Berlin supplied with foodstuffs and coal for heating. Careful monitoring of Soviet communications indicated that the Russians would not interfere with the airlift.[47]

Black Friday

During President Truman's October 1948 nationwide whistle-stop train tour in his uphill battle for reelection against Governor Thomas Dewey, the U.S. government was at a virtual standstill. On the afternoon of Friday, October 29, just as Truman was preparing to deliver a fiery campaign speech at the Brooklyn Academy of Music in New York City, the Russian government and military executed a massive change of virtually all of their cipher systems. On that day, referred to within NSA as Black Friday, and continuing for several months there-after, all of the cipher systems used on Soviet military and internal-security radio networks, including all mainline Soviet military, naval, and police radio nets, were changed to new, unbreakable systems. The Russians also changed all their radio call signs and operating frequencies and replaced all of the cipher machines that the Americans and British had solved, and even some they hadn't, with newer and more sophisticated cipher machines that were to defy the ability of American and British cryptanalysts to solve them for almost thirty years, until the tenure of Admiral Bobby Ray Inman in the late 1970s.[48]

Black Friday was an unmitigated disaster, inflicting massive and irreparable damage on the Anglo-American SIGINT organizations' efforts against the USSR, killing off virtually all of the productive intelligence sources that were then available to them regarding what was going on inside the Soviet Union and rendering useless most of four years' hard work by thousands of American and British cryptanalysts, linguists, and traffic analysts. The loss of so many critically important high-level intelligence sources in such a short space of time was, as NSA historians have aptly described it, "perhaps the most significant intelligence loss in U.S. history." And more important, it marked the beginning of an eight-year period when reliable intelligence about what was occurring inside the USSR was practically nonexistent.[49]

The sudden loss of so many productive intelligence sources was not the only damage that can be directly attributed to the Black Friday blackout. In the months that followed, the Anglo-American code breakers discovered that they now faced two new and seemingly insurmountable obstacles that threatened to keep them deaf, dumb, and blind for years. First, there was far less high-level Soviet government and military radio traffic than prior to Black Friday because the Russians had switched much of their military communication to telegraph lines or buried cables, which was a simple and effective way of keeping this traffic away from the American and British radio intercept operators. Moreover, the high-level Russian radio traffic that could still be intercepted was proving to be nearly impossible to crack because of the new cipher machines and unbreakable cipher systems that were introduced on all key radio circuits. The Russians also implemented tough communications security practices and procedures and draconian rules and regulations governing the encryption of radio communications traffic, and radio security discipline was suddenly rigorously and ruthlessly enforced. Facing potential death sentences for failing to comply with the new regulations, Russian radio operators suddenly began making fewer mistakes in the encoding and decoding of messages, and operator chatter disappeared almost completely from the airwaves. It was also at about this time that the Russian military and key Soviet government ministries began encrypting their telephone calls using a newly developed voice-scrambling device called Vhe Che ("High Frequency"), which further degraded the ability of the Anglo-American SIGINT personnel to access even low-level Soviet communications. It would eventually be discovered that the Russians had made their massive shift because William Weisband, a forty-year-old Russian linguist with ASA, had told the KGB everything that he knew about ASA's Russian code-breaking efforts at Arlington Hall. (For reasons of security, Weisband was not put on trial for espionage.)

Decades later, at a Central Intelligence Agency conference on Venona, Meredith Gardner, an intensely private and taciturn man, did not vent his feelings about Weisband, even though he had done grave damage to Gardner's work on Venona. But Gardner's boss, Frank Rowlett, was not so shy in an interview before his death, calling Weisband "the traitor that got away."[50]

Unfortunately, internecine warfare within the upper echelons of the U.S. intelligence community at the time got in the way of putting stronger security safeguards into effect—despite the damage that a middle-level employee like Weisband had done to America's SIGINT effort. Four years later, a 1952 review found that "very little had been done" to implement the 1948 recommendations for strengthening security practices within the U.S. cryptologic community.[51]

The Creation of the Armed Forces Security Agency

At the same time that the U.S. and British intelligence communities were reeling from Black Friday, several new institutional actors shoved their way into the battered U.S. cryptologic community. On October 20, 1948, the newly independent U.S. Air Force formally activated its own COMINT collection organization, the U.S. Air Force Security Service (USAFSS).[52] It immediately became responsible for COMINT coverage of the entire Soviet air force and air defense system, including the strategic bombers of the Soviet Long Range Air Force. But the ability of USAFSS to perform this vital mission was practically nonexistent at the time owing to a severe shortage of manpower and equipment, largely because the U.S. Air Force headquarters staff in Washington was slow to provide the necessary resources that the COMINT organization so desperately needed. As a result, by the end of 1949, USAFSS was only operating thirty-five COMINT intercept positions in the U.S. and overseas, which was far short of what was expected of it. By December 1949, the situation was so serious that the chief of

USAF Intelligence was forced to report that USAFSS's COMINT capability was "presently negligible and will continue to be negligible for an unwarranted period of time unless immediate steps are taken to change the present low priority on equipment and personnel assigned to the Air Force Security Services."[53]

Seven months later, on May 20, 1949, Secretary of Defense Louis Johnson issued a Top Secret directive creating the Armed Forces Security Agency (AFSA), which was given the responsibility for the direction and control of all U.S. communications intelligence and communications security activities *except* for tactical cryptologic activities, which remained under the control of the army, navy, and air force.[54]

AFSA was a fatally flawed organization from its inception. Its funding was grossly inadequate when compared with the significantly higher level of funding given to the CIA, which had been created two years earlier in 1947.[55] The military services then systematically stripped AFSA of virtually all of the authority that it had originally been granted. As a result, by the summer of 1950, AFSA found itself powerless and completely dependent on the military for all of its money, radio intercept facilities, personnel, equipment, communications, and logistical support.[56] Then, taking full advantage of AFSA's weakened state, the military services got key portions of their COMINT missions exempted from its authority. With no means of compelling the other services to comply, including no control over the budgets of the three military SIGINT units, AFSA was forced to humble itself and negotiate on bent-knee agreements with the services that gave even more power away to them.[57]

It is clear now that many of AFSA's problems can be traced directly to its first director, Rear Admiral Earl Stone, who did not possess the combative personality desperately needed to force the branches of the military to cooperate in order to make AFSA work. By the time he left office in July 1951, a standing joke among his subordinates was that Stone's authority extended only as far as the front door of his office, and even that was subject to debate.[58] Looking back on Stone's sad two-year tenure as director of AFSA, one of his senior deputies, Captain Wesley Wright, said that the decision to give the job to Stone in the first place "was a horrible thing to do."[59]

Jack Gurin's War

Declassified documents make clear that AFSA's legion of internal management woes, although serious, were the least of its problems. From the moment it was born, AFSA inherited, as a declassified NSA history puts it, "a Soviet problem that was in miserable shape."[60]

AFSA had only one source of intelligence left that offered any insight into what was going on inside the Soviet Union: intercepts of low-level, unencrypted Soviet administrative radio traffic and commercial telegrams, which were generally referred to as "plaintext" within the Anglo-American intelligence communities. A declassified NSA historical report notes, "Out of this devastation, Russian plaintext communications emerged as the principal source of intelligence on our primary Cold War adversary."[61] Outside of plaintext, the only other source for information on what was going on behind the iron curtain came from Traffic Analysis, where analysts studied the now-unreadable intercepts to try to derive intelligence from the message "externals."

Plaintext intercepts had been ignored as an intelligence source since the end of World War II; after Black Friday, everything changed. Since high-level Russian communications traffic could no longer be read, the previously deprecated Russian plaintext intercepts being processed in Arlington Hall's room 1501-B suddenly became of critical importance for U.S. SIGINT. Overnight, the twenty-seven-year-old chief of the AFSA plaintext unit, Jacob "Jack" Gurin, became a leading figure within the U.S. intelligence community.[62] Now the world was beating a path to his door.

The Blackout Curtain

In addition to focusing on plain text intercepts, the other principal problem that the newly created AFSA had to confront was how to revamp itself and at the same time try to repair the damage caused by the Black Friday blackout. The U.S. Communications Intelligence Board quickly conducted a study, which determined that an additional 160 intercept positions and 650 intercept operators were needed just to meet minimum coverage requirements. The study also found that "currently allowed personnel are not sufficient for these and other important tasks."[63]

The question became, how should the scarce COMINT collection resources available be reallocated? In early 1949, the U.S. Army and Navy COMINT organizations began systematically diverting personnel and equipment resources away from non-Soviet targets in order to strengthen the Soviet COMINT effort. By the summer of 1949, 71 percent of all American radio intercept personnel and 60 percent of all COMINT processing personnel were working on the "Soviet problem"—at the expense of coverage of other countries, including AFSA's

targets in the Far East, most significantly mainland China. Declassified documents show that the number of AFSA analysts and linguists assigned to Asian
problems had declined from 261 to 112 personnel by the end of 1949. Work on
all other nations in the Far East was either abandoned completely or drastically
reduced.[64]

Also in early 1949, personnel were pulled from unproductive Soviet cryptanalytic projects and put to work instead on translating and analyzing the
ever-mounting volume of Soviet plaintext teletype intercepts, which overnight
had become AFSA's most important intelligence source. There were dire consequences resulting from the shift to plaintext, however. The reassignment of
those working on Soviet cryptanalytic problems to plaintext processing badly
hurt the American cryptanalytic effort to solve Soviet ciphers and indirectly
contributed to the departure of a number of highly talented cryptanalysts.
By 1952, there were only ten to fifteen qualified cryptanalysts left at AFSA,
down from forty to fifty at the height of World War II.[65]

One Soviet-related cryptanalytic effort after another ground to a halt for
lack of attention or resources. For instance, the Anglo-American COMINT
organizations largely gave up on their efforts to solve encrypted Soviet diplomatic and military attaché traffic. These cipher systems, almost all of which
were encrypted with unbreakable one-time pad ciphers, had defied the best
efforts of the American and British cryptanalysts since 1945. As of August
1948, the principal Soviet diplomatic cipher systems had not been solved,
and available information indicates that they never were.[66] The ciphers used
on the Ministry of State Security (MGB) high-level internal security communications networks also consistently stymied the American and British
cryptanalysts.[67]

With their access to Soviet high-level cipher systems irretrievably lost,
SIGINT production on the USSR fell precipitously, and notable successes became few and far between. But it was during this bleak period that the most important retrospective breaks into the Venona ciphers were made. Between
December 1948 and June 1950, Meredith Gardner decrypted portions of
dozens of Soviet intelligence messages, which helped the Federal Bureau of Investigation identify Judith Coplon, Klaus Fuchs, Donald MacLean, David Greenglass, Julius Rosenberg, and the physicist Theodore Alvin Hall, among others,
as having spied for the Soviet Union during World War II.[68] However, Venona,
as noted earlier, sadly turned out to be an intelligence asset that could not be
used. While it is certainly true that the Venona decrypts allowed the FBI and its
counterparts in England and Australia to identify a large number of Soviet spies
during the late 1940s and the 1950s, they did not produce many criminal in-

dictments and convictions. Declassified FBI documents show that only 15 of the 206 Soviet agents identified in the Venona decrypts were ever prosecuted, in large part because the secrecy of these decrypts prevented them from being used in an American court of law.[69]

As a result, most of the "big fish" who spied for the Russians got away. For example, although her complicity in spying for the Soviet Union was proved by Venona decrypts, all of Coplon's criminal convictions were overturned on appeal because of mistakes made by the FBI and also because the SIGINT materials could not be used in court. Forty individuals identified in Venona as having spied for Russia fled before they could be prosecuted, including MacLean, Guy Burgess, and Kim Philby. But most of the agents who spied for Russia were never indicted because it might have revealed U.S. success in breaking Russian codes. For example, when in 1956 the FBI proposed prosecuting former White House aide Lauchlin Currie for espionage based on information developed from Venona, NSA's director, Lieutenant General Ralph Canine, strongly objected, telling the Justice Department that anything that might reveal NSA's success in breaking Russian codes would be "highly inadvisable."[70]

For the same reason, even the man whose treachery probably led to the Black Friday disaster, William Weisband, could be convicted only of contempt of court in 1950 for refusing to testify before a federal grand jury after the director of AFSA, Rear Admiral Earl Stone, refused to sanction a criminal indictment for espionage. Weisband worked for the rest of his life as an insurance salesman in northern Virginia and died of a heart attack in May 1967 at the age of fifty-nine.[71]

The State of American COMINT in June 1950

As of June 1950, AFSA and the three military cryptologic organizations were in a lamentable state. They were short of money, personnel, and equipment. Neither AFSA nor Britain's GCHQ were reading any Soviet or Chinese high-level code or cipher systems.[72] AFSA was deriving intelligence from low-level plaintext intercepts, and even that effort was not doing very well. As a result, high-quality intelligence about what was going on inside the USSR was minimal. A CIA history reveals that COMINT was only producing high-quality intelligence about Soviet foreign trade, internal consumer goods policies, gold production, petroleum shipments, shipbuilding activities, military and civilian aircraft production, and civil defense.[73] Not surprisingly, intelligence consumers were concerned that AFSA was not carrying out its mission, and a consensus began to emerge within the U.S. intelligence community that radical changes were probably needed in order to get it back on track.[74]

But perhaps the most prescient judgment on the state of American COMINT in 1950 comes from an NSA historian, who writes, "American cryptology was really just a hollow shell of its former self by 1950 . . . With slim budgets, lack of people, and lack of legal authorities, [AFSA] appeared set up for failure should a conflict break out."[75] And that is exactly what happened on June 25, 1950, in a country that Secretary of State Dean Acheson in a colossal gaffe had neglected to include in the U.S. "Asian defense perimeter"—Korea.[76]

CHAPTER 2

The Storm Breaks

SIGINT and the Korean War: 1950–1951

The hammer shatters glass, but forges steel.
—RUSSIAN PROVERB

The Shattered Frontier

At four A.M. on the morning of Sunday, June 25, 1950, over seven hundred Russian-made artillery pieces and mortars of the North Korean army opened fire on the defensive positions of the South Korean army deployed along the 38th parallel, which since the end of World War II had served as the demarcation line between communist North Korea and the fledgling democracy of South Korea. The impact of thousands of artillery shells landing in just thirty minutes shattered the morale of the green Republic of Korea (ROK) forces. Two hours later, over one hundred thousand combat-tested North Korean troops backed by more than 180 Russian-made T-34 medium tanks and self-propelled artillery guns surged across the 38th parallel. Within a matter of hours, the North Koreans had routed all but a few of the undermanned and poorly equipped South Korean army units along the border. The Korean War had begun.[1]

Why hadn't AFSA or any of the three service cryptologic agencies provided advance warning? The answer revealed by newly declassified documents is that there had been no COMINT coverage whatsoever of North Korea prior to the invasion. An NSA historical monograph admits that "the North Korean target was ignored."[2] The reason was that virtually all of AFSA's meager collection resources were focused on its customers' primary target, the Soviet Union. Virtually all other target countries were being ignored or given short shrift by AFSA. The result, according to Colonel Morton Rubin, a former

Army G-2 official, was that: "North Korea got lost in the shuffle and nobody told us that they were interested in what was going on north of the 38th parallel."[3]

This meant AFSA's capabilities against North Korea were nonexistent. Nobody at AFSA was working on North Korean codes and ciphers. The AFSA Korean Section existed only on paper; the two civilians on its nominal staff were actually assigned to the Chinese Section and tasked with working on the codes and ciphers of both North and South Korea only in their limited spare time. Neither one had any degree of expertise on the North Korean military. In addition, the AFSA Korean Section possessed no Korean dictionaries or Korean-language reference books; no North Korean traffic analytic aids; no Korean-language typewriters, necessary for transcribing intercepts; and virtually no knowledge of North Korean military terminology and radio working procedures because there had not been any serious intercept coverage of North Korea since 1946.[4]

The Thirty-Day Miracle

On June 28, 1950, three days after the invasion began, the South Korean capital of Seoul fell to the North Koreans without a fight. Over the next month, the news from Korea became increasingly grim. Every day the American troops in Korea lost more ground against the numerically superior and better equipped North Korean forces. On July 3, the port of Inchon fell, followed by the key railroad junction at Suwon on July 4. On July 20, the North Koreans captured the city of Taejon, wiping out an entire American infantry regiment. Five days later, on July 25, the North Koreans destroyed a regiment of the First Cavalry Division that was trying to defend the Korean towns of Kumch'on and Yongdong.

But what the public did not know was that only a few days after the North Korean invasion began, the intercept operators at the U.S. Army listening post outside the city of Kyoto, Japan, began intercepting North Korean military Morse code radio traffic coming from their forces inside South Korea. On the morning of June 29, 1950, the first intercepted North Korean radio traffic from Kyoto began arriving at AFSA's SIGINT processing center at Arlington Hall Station over the teletype links from the Far East. Because there were so few Korean linguists available, it took AFSA a week before the first translated North Korean message was completed on July 3, the same day that the port of Inchon fell to the North Koreans. A quick scan of the intercepts revealed that the North Korean army was transmitting highly classified information, such as daily situation reports, battle plans, and troop movement orders, in the clear. The analysts were amazed that the North Koreans were not bothering to encode this incredibly valuable material.[5] It took another week before the first Top Secret Codeword traffic analysis report based on intercepts of NKPA plaintext radio traffic was published and distributed by AFSA to its consumers in Washington and the Far East on July 11, just two weeks after the North Korean invasion began. Three days later, on July 14, AFSA cryptanalysts at Arlington Hall broke the first encrypted North Korean military radio message. In the days that followed, the AFSA cryptanalysts solved several more cipher systems then being used by the North Korean combat divisions and their subordinate regiments, as well as some of the cipher systems used by North Korean logistics units.[6]

The upshot was that in a mere thirty days, AFSA's cryptanalysts had achieved the cryptologic equivalent of a miracle—they had succeeded in breaking virtually all of the North Korean military's tactical codes and ciphers, which must rank as one of the most important code-breaking accomplishments of the twentieth century. The result was that by the end of July 1950, AFSA was solving and translating over one third of all intercepted North Korean enciphered messages that were being intercepted. Only a severe shortage of Korean linguists kept them from producing more.[7]

The net result was that AFSA's spectacular code-breaking successes gave the commander of the Eighth U.S. Army in Korea, Lieutenant General Walton Walker, what every military commander around the world secretly dreams about—near complete and real-time access to the plans and intentions of the enemy forces he faced. James H. Polk, who was a senior intelligence officer on General MacArthur's G-2 staff in Tokyo at the time, recalled, "We had the North Korean codes down pat. We knew everything they were going to do, usually before they got the orders from Pyongyang decoded themselves. You can't ask for more than that." A young army field commander attached to Eighth U.S. Army headquarters at Taegu named James K. Woolnough, who would later rise to the rank of general, had this to say about the importance of the SIGINT available to General Walker: "They had, of course, perfect intelligence. It all funneled in right there. They knew exactly where each platoon of North Koreans were going, and they'd move to meet it . . . That was amazing, utterly amazing."[8]

These code-breaking successes were to prove to be literally lifesaving over the forty-five days that followed as the vastly outnumbered American and South Korean infantrymen of the Eighth U.S. Army tried desperately to hold on to a tiny slice of South Korea around the port city of Pusan in a series of battles that are referred to today collectively as the Battle of the Pusan Perimeter. Declassified documents reveal that between August 1 and September 15, 1950, SIGINT was instrumental in helping General Walker's Eighth Army beat back a half-dozen North Korean attacks against the Pusan Perimeter.[9] By the end of August, SIGINT revealed that the North Korean army had been reduced to a shadow of its former self. The North Korean Thirteenth Division could only muster a thousand men for combat, while some battalions of the North Korean Fifth Division had lost more than 80 percent of their troops, with one battalion reporting that it had only ten soldiers left on its muster rolls.[10] SIGINT also showed that under relentless air attacks, the North Korean supply system had almost completely stopped functioning. Ammunition shortages were so severe that it was severely affecting the combat capabilities of virtually all frontline NKPA units deployed around the Pusan Perimeter. For example, an intercept revealed that ammunition shortages in the North Korean Thirteenth Division east of Taegu were so severe that it could not fire its few remaining artillery pieces.[11]

The Inchon Landing

In one of the greatest gambles of the Korean War, on the morning of September 15, 1950, units of the U.S. Tenth Corps staged an amphibious landing, planned by General MacArthur, behind the North Korean lines at the port of Inchon, west of Seoul.

Recently declassified documents reveal that the Inchon landing would not have been successful without the SIGINT coming out of AFSA. Thanks to SIGINT, MacArthur and his intelligence chief, Major General Charles Willoughby, had a fairly clear picture of the North Korean army order of battle, including the locations, strengths, and equipment levels for all thirteen infantry divisions and a single armored division deployed around the Pusan Perimeter. Most important, the SIGINT data showed that there were no large North Korean units deployed in the Inchon area.[12] In the month prior to the Inchon landing, MacArthur's intelligence analysts in Tokyo, thanks to the decrypts, were able to track the locations and movements of virtually every unit in the North Korean army. In mid-August, SIGINT revealed that the North Koreans were taking frontline combat units from the Pusan Perimeter and moving them to defensive positions along both the east and west coasts of South Korea, suggesting that the North Korean general staff was concerned about the possibility of a U.N. amphibious landing behind North Korean lines. By early

September, decrypted high-level North Korean communications traffic showed that the North Korean army's senior commanders were concerned that the United States might attempt an amphibious landing on the west coast of South Korea, but had incorrectly guessed that the landing would most likely occur to the south of Inchon at either Mokpo or Kunsan port.[13]

Despite SIGINT indications that the North Koreans knew a U.S. amphibious operation was imminent, MacArthur went ahead with the landing at Inchon on September 15. It was a stunning success, with little North Korean resistance. The sole attempt by the North Koreans to mount a major counterattack against the Inchon bridgehead was picked up by SIGINT well before it began, and mauled by repeated air strikes. In a matter of just a few hours, the entire North Korean force was destroyed.[14]

With the collapse of the Inchon counterattack, there were no more organized North Korean forces standing between the U.S. forces and Seoul. On September 28, Seoul fell to the Americans. With that, all thirteen North Korean combat divisions around the Pusan Perimeter abandoned their positions and fled to the north. By the end of the month, all of the rest of South Korea up to the old demarcation line at the 38th parallel had been recaptured.

The Chinese Intervention

Newly declassified documents have revealed that at the time of the Inchon landing, AFSA had very few SIGINT resources dedicated to monitoring what was occurring inside the People's Republic of China, North Korea's huge communist neighbor, because, as a declassified NSA history put it, AFSA had "employed all available resources against the Soviet target." The only SIGINT resources available were a few intercept positions at the U.S. Army listening post on the island of Okinawa, Japan, which were monitoring low-level Chinese civil communications traffic, primarily unencrypted Chinese government cables and the communications traffic of the Chinese Railroad Ministry. A small team of Chinese linguists at Arlington Hall Station, headed by a twenty-nine-year-old New Yorker named Milton Zaslow, was able to derive a modicum of intelligence about the state of the Chinese economy, transportation and logistics issues, and even the movements of Chinese military units inside China from these telegrams. It was not a very impressive effort, but it was all that the overstretched AFSA could afford at the time.[15]

Beginning in July 1950, and continuing through the fall, Zaslow's team picked up indications in these low-level intercepts that the Chinese were shifting hundreds of thousands of combat troops from southern and central China to Manchuria by rail.[16] But according to Cynthia Grabo, then an intelligence analyst at the Pentagon, the U.S. Army's intelligence analysts refused to accept the reports of a Chinese military buildup in Manchuria, arguing instead that the Chinese intended to invade Taiwan.[17]

But there were other SIGINT sources that were indicating that China intended to take forceful action in Korea. AFSA's principal source for intelligence on China was its ability to read the cable traffic of arguably the best informed foreign diplomat based in Beijing, Dr. Kavalam Madhava Panikkar (sometimes spelled Pannikar), India's ambassador to China. Panikkar had the ear of Premier Chou En-lai and other senior Chinese leaders, which made him AFSA's best source for high-level diplomatic intelligence about what was going on in Beijing.[18] For example, intercepts of Panikkar's cables to New Delhi in July and August 1950 revealed that he had been told by Chou En-lai that the Chinese would *not* intervene militarily in Korea.[19]

But diplomatic decrypts revealed that the position of the Chinese leadership changed dramatically following the amphibious landing at Inchon. The decrypted cables of the Burmese ambassador in Beijing, whose government also maintained generally friendly relations with China, warned that China now intended to become involved militarily in Korea.[20] A week later, decrypts of Ambassador Panikkar's cable traffic to New Delhi revealed that on September 25, Chou En-lai had warned the Indian ambassador that China would intervene militarily in Korea if U.N. forces crossed the 38th parallel.[21] But Panikkar's reporting was either discounted or ignored completely by policymakers in Washington because of his alleged pro-Chinese leanings.[22]

But the Chinese were not bluffing. On October 1, South Korean troops crossed the 38th parallel and marched into North Korea. The next day, the Chinese Communist Party's Politburo decided to intervene militarily in the Korean War, with Mao Tse-tung ordering 260,000 Chinese troops to begin crossing the Yalu River on October 15.[23]

The Chinese leadership in Beijing made one last final effort to head off war with the U.S. Shortly after midnight on the morning of October 3, 1950, Chou En-lai called in Ambassador Panikkar and told him that if U.S. troops crossed the 38th parallel, China would send its forces across the Yalu River to defend North Korea. On the same day, the Dutch chargé d'affaires in Beijing cabled his foreign ministry in the Hague quoting Chou En-lai to the effect that China would fight if U.N. forces crossed the 38th parallel.[24] But Washington refused to pay heed to these warnings, which were dismissed in their entirety as being nothing more than a bluff. On October 5, the first American combat troops were ordered to cross the 38th parallel and advance on the North Korean capital of Pyongyang. By this singular act, General MacArthur committed U.S. and U.N. forces to a course of action that was to have dire consequences for everyone involved.[25]

On the morning of October 15, Mao sent a cable to his military commander in Manchuria, General Peng Dehuai, ordering him to send the first Chinese army units across the Yalu River into North Korea. On the night of October 15–16, the 372nd Regiment of the Chinese 42nd Army secretly crossed the Yalu. The die had been cast. China had entered the Korean War.[26]

Declassified documents confirm that AFSA failed to detect the movement of the more than three hundred thousand Chinese soldiers into Korea, largely because the Chinese forces operated in complete radio silence.[27] But SIGINT did pick up a number of changes in Soviet, Chinese, and North Korean military activities indicating that something significant was happening across the border in Manchuria. On October 20, the CIA sent President Truman a Top Secret Codeword memo (which the CIA has steadfastly refused to fully declassify) revealing that SIGINT and other intelligence sources indicated that the Chinese intended to intervene militarily in the Korean War to protect their interests in the Suiho hydroelectric complex in North Korea. According to the report, SIGINT "noted the presence of an unusually large number of fighter aircraft in Manchuria."[28] The next day, October 21, AFSA reported that intercepts of Chinese radio traffic showed that during the first three weeks of October, three Chinese armies had been deployed to positions along the Yalu River. Also on October 21, AFSA reported that during the previous week, twenty troop trains carrying Chinese combat troops had been sent from Shanghai to Manchuria and more were on their way.[29]

Sadly, all of this intelligence data was again ignored or discounted because it ran contrary to the prevailing wisdom of the U.S. intelligence community. For example, the October 18, 1950, edition of the CIA's *Review of the World Situation* stated, "Unless the USSR is ready to precipitate global war, or unless for some reason that Peiping leaders do not think that war with the U.S. would result from open intervention in Korea, the odds are that Communist China, like the USSR, will not openly intervene in North Korea."[30] In Tokyo, MacArthur chose to ignore the SIGINT. One of MacArthur's senior intelligence officers, Lieutenant Colonel Morton Rubin, remembered personally briefing the general and his intelligence chief, General Charles Willoughby, on the Chinese troop movements appearing in SIGINT, but the intelligence reports apparently did not convince either man that the Chinese threat was real. Lieutenant General Matthew Ridgway, who later was to replace MacArthur as commander of

U.S. forces in the Far East, recalled that "the great fault over there was poor evaluation of the intelligence that was obtained. They knew the facts, but they were poorly evaluated. I don't know just why that was. It was probably in good part because of MacArthur's personality. If he did not want to believe something, he wouldn't."[31]

The result was that when the Chinese launched their first offensive in Korea, it achieved complete surprise. Striking without warning, between October 25 and November 2, 1950, three PLA armies decimated the entire South Korean 2nd Corps and a regiment of the U.S. 1st Cavalry Division near the North Korean town of Unsan. The Chinese troops then quietly withdrew back into the hills to prepare for the next phase of their offensive.[32]

After the Unsan fiasco, the entire U.S. intelligence community went into a state of denial, refusing to accept the fact that the Chinese military was in Korea. In Washington, the CIA's intelligence analysts concluded, "There has been no definitive evidence of Soviet or Chinese intervention in Korea." On October 30, the CIA's *Daily Summary* opined that "the presence of Chinese Communist units in Korea has not been confirmed. CIA continues to believe that direct Chinese Communist intervention in Korea is unlikely at this time." In Korea, the Eighth Army reported that despite the fact they held seven Chinese POWs, they were "not inclined to accept reports of substantial Chinese participation in North Korean fighting."[33]

What is curious is that all the assessments coming out of the intelligence staffs in Washington and Tokyo were directly contradicted by what the chatty Chinese POWs captured at Unsan were telling their interrogators, which was that whole Chinese combat divisions were then operating inside Korea.[34] When CIA officers in Korea had the temerity to cable Washington with the results of the interrogations of the Chinese prisoners, Willoughby barred CIA personnel from further access to the POW cages, telling the Eighth Army's intelligence chief to "Keep him [the CIA station chief in Korea] clear of interrogation." It was the prototypical case of shooting the messenger.[35]

In the weeks that followed, an increased volume of disquieting intelligence came out of AFSA indicating that the Chinese military was preparing to attack. In early November, AFSA reported that the Chinese had just moved three more armies by rail to Manchuria, and that the security forces guarding Beijing had just been placed on a state of alert.[36] On November 24, the CIA issued a report based on COMINT, which revealed that an additional one hundred thousand Chinese troops had just arrived in Manchuria and that the Chinese were shipping thirty thousand maps of North Korea to its forces in Manchuria.[37] AFSA also produced intelligence indicating that MacArthur was looking for a fight with the Chinese. On November 11, Army chief of staff J. Lawton Collins sent a Top Secret Codeword "Eyes Only" message to MacArthur containing the text of a decrypted message from the Brazilian ambassador in Tokyo, Gastão P. Do Rio Branco, to his home office in Rio de Janeiro. According to the decrypt: "Speaking with . . . frankness, he [MacArthur] told the President that it would be better to face a war now than two or three years hence, for he was certain that there was not the least possibility of an understanding with the men in the Kremlin, as the experience of the last five years has proved. He felt, therefore, that in order to attain peace it is necessary to destroy the focus of international bolshevism in Moscow."[38]

The general got his wish. At 8:00 P.M. on the night of November 25, 1950, the Chinese army struck once again, this time with even greater force, decimating the combined U.S. and South Korean forces stretched out along the Yalu River, sending the allied forces reeling backward in retreat. The final word appropriately goes to MacArthur, who sent a panicky Top Secret cable to Washington on November 28 including the now-famous line: "We face an entirely new war."[39]

World War III Cometh

On the night of November 30, General Walker's Eighth U.S. Army broke contact with the Chinese People's Liberation Army (PLA) forces along the Yalu River and began a two-week-long, 120-mile retreat south to the Imjin River, north of Seoul. During this critically important two-week period, there was no contact whatsoever between the Eighth Army and the pursuing Chinese forces, which resulted in the entire U.S. intelligence community being left almost completely in the dark concerning the PLA forces.

Declassified documents show that during the Eighth Army's hasty retreat southward, SIGINT was not able to provide much in the way of substantive intelligence information about the strength, locations, or movements of the three hundred thousand Chinese troops following them. Apart from exploiting intercepted low-level railroad traffic, AFSA had devoted virtually no resources to monitoring Chinese military communications prior to the Chinese intervention in Korea. Even if the U.S. military SIGINT units in the Far East were intercepting Chinese radio traffic, they didn't have any Chinese linguists who could translate the intercepts. The result was that as of mid-December 1950, senior U.S. military commanders found themselves in the embarrassing position of having to admit that information from all sources was "vague and indefinite on the exact disposition of CCF [Chinese Communist Forces] in Korea."[40]

On December 23, Lieutenant General Walker was killed in a jeep accident. He was replaced by Lieutenant General Matthew Ridgway, one of the U.S. Army's best field commanders, who flew in from Washington on December 26 and discovered that the intelligence situation map at his Eighth Army headquarters in Seoul showed only "a large red goose egg" north of his front lines, indicating an estimated 174,000 PLA troops—which was all that army intelligence then knew about the estimated strength and position of the Chinese forces. While American units had obtained some intelligence from two captured Chinese soldiers, everything else that Eighth Army G-2 believed to be true about Chinese PLA troop dispositions was pure speculation.[41]

But while AFSA was producing no intelligence about the Chinese forces, it continued to generate vast amounts of data about the North Korean military forces because of its continued ability to read all major North Korean ciphers. According to a declassified NSA history, as of December 1950 AFSA was solving and translating 90 percent of the encrypted North Korean messages it was intercepting.[42] For example, SIGINT derived from these communications was instrumental in allowing the U.S. Navy to successfully evacuate by December 24 the entire U.S. Tenth Corps plus tens of thousands of refugees from the North Korean port of Hungnam. SIGINT also confirmed that the Chinese and North Koreans did not intend to disrupt the evacuation by air attack.[43]

The Chinese January 1951 Offensive in Korea

On New Year's Eve, December 31, 1950, seven Chinese armies launched a major offensive across the 38th parallel, which shattered the Eighth U.S. Army's defensive positions along the Imjin River. Seoul fell for a second time on January 4, 1951, the last U.S. forces having fled the city the night before.[44]

As American forces struggled to keep a foothold in Korea, there was little SIGINT to offer by way of intercepts of Chinese military radio transmissions because of a lack of Chinese linguists, and also because almost all available radio intercept resources were focused on the more productive North Korean military target. As a result, the SIGINT organizations were producing virtually nothing in the way of usable tactical intelligence on the Chinese military at a time when U.S. field commanders in Korea were desperate for *any* tidbit of information.[45]

Despite these inherent weaknesses, SIGINT performed brilliantly during the month of January, helping Lieutenant General Ridgway's Eighth Army decimate the newly rebuilt North Korean Second and Fifth Corps as they strove to break through the American–South Korean defensive lines in the Korean central highlands. When the South Korean Second Corps collapsed, it was SIGINT that revealed the North Korean attack plans, with a decrypted January 2 message from the North Korean general staff in Pyongyang ordering the commander of the North Korean Fifth Corps to push through the breach and "pursue the enemy, not giving them time to rest."[46] By January 15, Eighth Army G-2 was convinced from an accumulation of information derived from SIGINT that the Chinese and North Koreans were readying themselves for yet another major offensive. But SIGINT revealed that the enemy forces had taken murderously heavy losses in the fighting up to that point, and that certain key units were barely combat ready. Another critically important piece of intelligence provided by SIGINT was a January 23 decrypted message revealing that the entire Chinese Ninth Army Group was reforming near the North Korean port of Wonsan and would "take a rest until the end of February." Ridgway now knew that three Chinese armies would not be taking part in the upcoming Chinese–North Korean offensive.[47]

Acting on this intelligence, on January 24, Ridgway launched a counterattack called Operation Thunderbolt, which by January 31 had forced the Chinese forces back toward Seoul. By the end of January, SIGINT revealed that the Chinese and North Korean forces were exhausted, short of ammunition and supplies, and decimated by battlefield casualties and infectious diseases.[48]

The Ides of March: The Russians Are Here!

In late March 1951, an event took place that literally overnight changed the way the entire U.S. intelligence community thought about the war in Korea. According to declassified documents, on March 30 the U.S. Air Force radio intercept unit in Japan, the 1st Radio Squadron, Mobile, commanded by Major Lowell Jameson, "made one of the most important contributions to Air Force Intelligence in its history." Intercepts of MiG radio traffic confirmed the long-held suspicion that the Russians were controlling the air defense of North Korea and Manchuria, not the Chinese or the North Koreans.[49] As a former air force Russian linguist stationed in the Far East recalled, "we were actually monitoring the Soviet Air Force fighting the American Air Force and we were listening to the Soviet pilots being directed by Soviet ground control people to fight the Americans. We were fighting our own little war with the Soviets."[50]

The decision was made to keep this revelation out of all widely circulated intelligence publications, such as the CIA's National Intelligence Estimates (NIEs), in order to prevent the leakage of this highly sensitive intelligence to right-wing members of Congress, such as Senator Joseph McCarthy, who would no doubt have used (or misused) the information to drum up public support for war with the USSR at a time when the U.S. government was trying to prevent that from happening.[51] While President Truman had made a bold decision to resist communist aggression in Korea, the war effort (or "police action," as he described it) was facing decreasing support from the public even as American paranoia about communist threats from abroad and subversion within began to create great difficulties for the administration. Amid this poisonous atmosphere at home and the fraught situation in the Far East, the U.S. military prepared for Armageddon.

General MacArthur's Dismissal

On April 11, 1951, just as the U.S. Armed Forces reached a maximum state of readiness for nuclear war, without any prior public warning President Truman fired General MacArthur from his post as commander in chief of U.S. forces in the Far East.[52]

The president's decision stunned the nation. As it turned out, the AFSA code breakers at Arlington Hall had a great deal to do with Truman's decision to fire America's most popular military commander. Throughout 1950 and 1951, AFSA was intercepting and decrypting the telegrams of the various foreign diplomats based in Tokyo. Among the most prominent targets being exploited were the diplomatic cables of the ambassadors from Spain, Portugal, and Brazil.[53] Both MacArthur and Major General Charles Willoughby made the mistake of candidly disclosing their extreme political views on Russia and China to these three ambassadors. Among the comments that MacArthur made was that he hoped the Soviets would intervene militarily in Korea, which he believed would give the United States the excuse to destroy once and for all Mao Tse-tung's communist regime in Beijing. MacArthur also told the foreign ambassadors that he thought war with Russia was inevitable.[54]

In mid-March 1951, Truman's naval aide, Admiral Robert Dennison, handed him a batch of four decrypted messages sent the preceding week by the Spanish ambassador in Tokyo, Francisco José del Castillo, summarizing his private conversations with MacArthur. The late Ambassador Paul Nitze, who was then head of the State Department's Policy Planning Staff, said in an interview, "From those communications, it was perfectly clear that what MacArthur had in mind was that either he would have a complete victory in North Korea or, if the Chinese Communists got involved, then the war would be spread to the Chinese mainland as a whole and the object of the game would then be the unseating of Mao Tse-tung and the restoration of Chiang Kai-shek. In the course of doing that you had your nuclear weapons if you needed them. This would then enable one to do what was strategically important and that was to defeat the Chinese Communists. That was clearly what was on MacArthur's mind. Part of the reason he took these excessive risks was to create a situation in which we would be involved in a war with the Chinese Communists."[55]

Given the overwhelming preponderance of evidence that MacArthur was deliberately ignoring orders from Washington, and with the SIGINT intercepts indicating that he was secretly hoping for an all-out world war with the Soviets and the Chinese, Truman fired him. In retrospect, it was almost certainly the right thing to do. But it had a catastrophic effect on Truman's standing with the American people. His poll numbers sank like a stone in the months that followed. By mid-1951, his approval ratings had plummeted to 23 percent, the lowest ever recorded by the Gallup Poll for a sitting American president.

General Ridgway's Crisis

The man chosen by the Pentagon to replace General Douglas MacArthur as commander in chief, Far East, was General Matthew Ridgway, who before moving into MacArthur's office suite in the Dai Ichi Building in downtown Tokyo had commanded the Eighth U.S. Army in Korea since December 1950. The hard-nosed former paratrooper took command at a moment when the intelligence picture in the region was bleak—and would only become grimmer as the months went on.

Intelligence reporting convinced Ridgway that a storm was about to break on his forces. All intelligence, including that extracted from POWs as early as February 1951, indicated that the Chinese and North Koreans were about to launch their massive Spring "Fifth Phase" Offensive in Korea. SIGINT revealed that there had been two major conferences attended by all Chinese and North Korean army and corps commanders, as well as Russian military advisers, to work out the details of the offensive. Additional intelligence reports received in

March indicated that D-day for the Chinese–North Korean offensive was expected to be some time in April. Then on April 1, the North Koreans changed their codes, a sure sign that something dramatic was in the offing. But thanks to the efforts of the U.S. Army code breakers in Korea, within a week the new North Korean ciphers were solved.[56]

Over the next two weeks, the SIGINT analysts in Washington and Tokyo laid bare the plans for the upcoming Chinese–North Korean offensive. Thanks in large part to SIGINT, Ridgway was able to discern weeks in advance that the brunt of the offensive would come in the mountainous central portion of the front, and not along the flat west coast of Korea north of Seoul. SIGINT also provided a fairly complete picture of the enemy forces committed, specifically four newly arrived Chinese armies plus two North Korean corps. And most important, it provided relatively clear indications about when the offensive would start. SIGINT also detailed the massive buildup of Russian, Chinese, and North Korean combat aircraft in Manchuria, plus attempts by the North Koreans to repair their airfields. When the enemy offensive finally commenced on April 22, Ridgway knew virtually everything about it except the exact time that it was due to begin.[57]

By the middle of June, SIGINT intercepts of North Korean radio traffic would reveal that the Chinese–North Korean offensive, which had sputtered to a halt earlier that month, had cost the communists a staggering 221,000 Chinese and North Korean casualties. COMINT also provided hard evidence of the communists' substantial logistical difficulties, which required that tens of thousands of frontline PLA forces be employed behind the lines to keep supply lines open, and documented the severe food shortages being experienced by Chinese forces at the front, which the Chinese commanders blamed for the collapse of the offensive.[58]

The War Clouds Darken

The shocker came on April 25, three days after the Chinese–North Korean offensive in Korea began, when SIGINT revealed that Soviet air force flight activity throughout the USSR and Eastern Europe had ceased completely. American and British radio intercept operators around the world began cabling urgent reports to Washington and London stating that they were picking up virtually no radio chatter coming from any Soviet military airfields in Eastern Europe or the Soviet Far East. Alarm bells sounded all over Washington.

Soviet air force radio silence was regarded as one of the key indicators that the Soviets were preparing for a military offensive.[59]

This ominous silence convinced General Ridgway that the Russians were about to launch their much-anticipated air assault against his forces in Korea and Japan. SIGINT showed that the enemy had 860 combat aircraft in Manchuria, 260 of which were modern MiG-15 jet fighters. SIGINT also showed that 380 of the 860 combat aircraft were "controlled" by the Soviet air force, including all of the MiG-15 jet fighters. And SIGINT confirmed that there had been a significant increase in radio traffic between Moscow and the headquarters of the three Long Range Air Force (LRAF) air armies; that there had been an increase in operational flight-training activities by LRAF TU-4 Bull nuclear-capable bombers in the European portion of the USSR; and that a new Soviet air defense fighter interceptor command headquarters had just been established at Vladivostok and Dairen.[60] Fortunately, the Soviet air attack never took place.

The Lights Go Out

In the first week of July 1951, just as cease-fire truce talks were getting started at Kaesong, disaster struck the American cryptologic effort in Korea yet again. In a massive shift in their communications and cipher security procedures, the North Korean military stopped using virtually all of the codes and ciphers that the Americans had been successfully exploiting since August 1950, and they replaced them with unbreakable one-time pad cipher systems on all of their high-level and even lower-level radio circuits. Radio frequency changes were now made more often, radio call signs were encrypted, and unencrypted plaintext radio traffic virtually disappeared from North Korean People's Army (NKPA) radio circuits. Moreover, the North Koreans shifted a significant portion of their operational communications traffic to landline circuits that blocked it from being intercepted.

This move by the North Koreans effectively killed off the sole remaining productive source of high-level COMINT that was then available to American intelligence in the Far East, leaving AFSA and the service cryptologic organizations with only low-level tactical voice communications left as a viable source of intelligence. Today, NSA officials believe that this move was prompted by Soviet security advisers with the North Korean forces, who were alarmed at the shoddy communications security (COMSEC) procedures utilized by the North Korean forces.[61]

The Good, the Bad, and the Really Ugly

On the positive side for the COMINT community, during the first and most per-
ilous year of the Korean War, AFSA and the military COMINT units in the Far
East were virtually the only source of timely and reliable intelligence for American field commanders in Korea about North Korean military activities. But the
agency's cryptanalysts were never able to solve any of the high-level ciphers used
by the Chinese military in Korea, which meant that American commanders in
the Far East never truly understood their principal enemy's intentions or capabilities.

A former NSA historian concluded, "There were successes, there were failures, but the failures tended to overshadow the successes."[62] The net result was
that SIGINT did not provide anywhere near the quantity or quality of high-level
strategic intelligence that it had during World War II. According to a declassified NSA study, there were numerous successes during the Korean War; "to
most intelligence consumers, however, the results still looked extremely thin,
especially with the lack of COMINT from [high-level] communications."[63]

CHAPTER 3

Fight for Survival

The Creation of the National Security Agency

And what rough beast, its hour come round
at last,
Slouches towards Bethlehem to be born?
—W. B. YEATS, "THE SECOND COMING"

The Dog Has Teeth: The Arrival of
General Ralph Canine

Among those inside the U.S. intelligence community who were privy to AFSA's secrets, the announcement of fifty-five-year-old army major general Ralph Canine's appointment as AFSA director in July 1951 came as a huge surprise, but it didn't cause even a ripple in the newspapers because few members of the press or public had any idea of what the agency did. Not only was General Canine (pronounced keh-NINE) not a West Point graduate, but he also had very little prior experience in intelligence (he had only served as the deputy chief of Army G-2 for ten months before being named to the post at AFSA), and he knew nothing whatsoever about codes and ciphers.[1] He was promoted to lieutenant general and became the second—and last—AFSA director.

Intelligence insiders had expected that Brigadier General Carter Clarke, a veteran intelligence officer with long experience with SIGINT, would be appointed to the position. But Clarke, then commanding a logistics unit in Japan, wanted nothing to do with the deeply troubled AFSA and nixed his own nomination, as did virtually every other senior army and air force intelligence officer qualified for the post. So Canine got the job by default. He told friends that he had initially been "violently against" becoming the head of AFSA, preferring instead to take retirement after thirty-five years of military service, including combat duty in two world wars. But he had been convinced by colleagues in Army G-2 to take the job against his better judgment.[2]

Canine was "old army"—a tough and efficient chief of staff of a corps in General George Patton's Third Army, where he was famous for "kicking the ass" of recalcitrant division and regimental commanders. And that is exactly what Canine did at AFSA. In much the same way that his counterpart at the CIA, General Walter Smith, rebuilt and reinvigorated his dormant intelligence organization, so too did General Canine. In the six years (1951 to 1956) that he served as the director of AFSA and then the National Security Agency, the hard-charging Canine made his organization a force to be reckoned with inside the U.S. intelligence community.[3]

But even the resourceful Canine could not overcome the myriad problems that bedeviled his organization. Among other things, SIGINT produced by AFSA still did not provide U.S. forces in Korea and its other customers with the intelligence (in quantity and quality) they needed. The squabbling and feuding within AFSA itself was causing no end of problems for the agency's managers, who were struggling to help win the war in Korea as well as handle a series of potentially explosive international crises. Senior army and navy officers at AFSA fought vicious internal bureaucratic battles with one another as well as their air force counterparts. And all three of the military services refused to cooperate with the agency's civilian customers at the FBI, CIA, and State Department. To say that AFSA was dysfunctional would be an understatement.[4]

Canine had a real fight on his hands. Internally, he made sweeping changes in the agency's management in January 1952. One of those who would leave in the middle of this reorganization was Frank Rowlett. Like many of his colleagues, he found this radical housecleaning to be the proverbial final straw. Angry and frustrated, in a fit of spite Rowlett accepted the offer of a job helping the CIA build its own SIGINT organization.[5]

Canine fought off attacks from the military services and tried to defend the agency against the increasingly hostile criticism of its customers, but ultimately he lost the battle. In November 1951, CIA director Smith struck a mortal blow. Smith knew that the armed services would try to seize their shares of control of SIGINT if AFSA were to be dismantled, and he believed that SIGINT had to be consolidated in the form of an entirely new entity. His bureaucratic masterstroke was instigating the creation of an "outside" committee to evaluate and, hopefully, doom AFSA. The committee was headed by George Brownell, a New York corporate lawyer and a good friend of the CIA's deputy director, Allen Dulles. The military services were completely shut out. The only representation on the Brownell Committee the military got was Canine, who held the nominal position of consultant but was not a voting member. From the makeup of the committee, senior military officials knew that they were not going to like what came out of its work.[6]

Rain of Devastation: The Brownell Committee Report

At ten forty-five A.M. on the morning of Friday, June 13, 1952, President Truman welcomed CIA director Smith and James Lay Jr., executive secretary of the National Security Council (NSC), into the Oval Office at the White House for a regularly scheduled meeting. Smith, however, was the bearer of bad tidings. He reached into his briefcase and gave Truman a copy of a 141-page Top Secret Codeword report on the state of health of the U.S. national SIGINT effort. It was the much-anticipated Brownell Report on AFSA.[7]

It is clear in reading between the lines of the Brownell Committee's report that all of the managerial sins of the agency's leadership would have been forgiven if AFSA had been producing decent intelligence. But it was not.

The Brownell Committee called for a complete overhaul and reorganization of AFSA. In effect, Brownell and his fellow committee members recommended scrapping it in its current form because it was unsalvageable. Instead, they recommended replacing it with a new unified SIGINT agency that would possess greater authority to operate a modern, centralized global SIGINT effort on behalf of the U.S. government.

Not surprisingly, Smith and Secretary of State Dean Acheson enthusiastically endorsed the committee's recommendations. Secretary of Defense Robert Lovett also approved the report's findings. By September 1952, the Joint Chiefs of Staff and the military services, under intense pressure from the Office of the Secretary of Defense, reluctantly accepted most of the recommendations. Throughout October, Canine tried unsuccessfully to negotiate some changes in the wording of a draft directive to be signed by Truman; that would have given the new agency more power to do its own analysis, but this proposal was summarily shot down. Canine was told in no uncertain terms that the deal was done and that it was time for him to take his seat and let events take their course.[8]

The Birth of the National Security Agency

At ten forty-five A.M. on Friday morning, October 24, 1952, Smith and Lay returned to the White House to meet with Truman only four months after Smith had given him his copy of the Brownell Report. After the usual handshakes and brief pleasantries, Lay placed on Truman's desk a buff file folder with a "Top Secret" cover sheet stapled to its front. Inside the folder was an eight-page document titled "Communications Intelligence Activities," which had a tab at the rear indicating where the president's signature was required. We do not know what, if anything, was said among the three men. All we know for certain is that Truman signed the document, and ten minutes later Smith and Lay walked out of the Oval Office with the file folder. Except for Truman, Smith, and Lay, very few people in Washington knew that the president had just presided over the creation of the National Security Agency (NSA).[9]

The eight-page directive that Truman had signed made SIGINT a national responsibility and designated the secretary of defense as the U.S. government's executive agent for all SIGINT activities, which placed NSA within the ambit of the Defense Department and outside the jurisdiction of the CIA. Truman gave NSA a degree of power and authority above and beyond that ever given previously or since to any American intelligence agency, placing it outside the rubric of the rest of the U.S. intelligence community. Truman also ordered that the new agency's powers be clearly defined and strengthened through the issuance of a new directive titled National Security Council Intelligence Directive No. 9 "Communications Intelligence."[10] The creation of NSA got in just under the wire. November 4, 1952, was Election Day in America. That evening, Dwight Eisenhower won in a landslide, decisively beating Adlai Stevenson to become the next president of the United States.

CHAPTER 4

The Inventory of Ignorance

SIGINT During the Eisenhower Administration: 1953–1961

In the land of the blind, the one-eyed man is king.
—Desiderius Erasmus

The Unhappy Inheritance

Dwight Eisenhower was sworn in as the thirty-fourth president of the United States on Tuesday, January 20, 1953. As supreme allied commander in Europe and a top customer for Ultra decrypts during World War II, he understood more about the value of intelligence (and its limitations) than any president since Ulysses S. Grant. But nothing could have prepared Eisenhower for what he confronted when he took office.

Five weeks after his inauguration, on March 4, the Soviet dictator Joseph Stalin suddenly died. Eisenhower was not happy that the first news that he got of Stalin's death came from Associated Press and United Press International wire service reports from Moscow. Like the rest of the U.S. intelligence community, NSA had provided no indication whatsoever that Stalin was ill. In fact, in the month before Stalin's death NSA had sent to the White House decrypted messages from the Argentinean and Indian ambassadors in Moscow detailing their private audiences with the Russian dictator, which tended to suggest to the intelligence analysts that the Russian dictator's health was good. In the chaotic days after Stalin's death, the only SIGINT that NSA could provide the White House with were decrypted telegrams concerning the reactions of Western leaders and a number of foreign Communist Party chiefs to the death of Stalin. All in all, it was not a very impressive performance.[1]

Concern inside Washington about NSA's performance mounted when on June 16, rioting broke out in East Berlin as thousands of civilian protesters took to the streets en masse to register their pent-up anger at the continued occupation of their country by the Russians. Within twenty-four hours, the rioting had spread to virtually every other city in East Germany. NSA's performance during the early stages of the Berlin Crisis was viewed in Washington as disappointing because most of the early intelligence reaching the White House about what was transpiring in East Berlin came from the CIA's Berlin station and from wire service news reports, with very little coming from NSA.[2]

Trying to Peer Behind the Iron Curtain

Regrettably, the reason SIGINT provided no warning was because Soviet high-grade ciphers remained "an unrevealed mystery."[3] Despite the commitment of massive numbers of personnel and equally massive amounts of equipment to this critically important target, there is little discernible evidence that any progress was made in this area. And as the years passed and the Russian ciphers continued to elude NSA's ability to solve them, the pressure on the agency inexorably mounted to do whatever it took for a breakthrough. A Top Secret report sent to Eisenhower in May 1955 recommended, "This is of such great importance that monetary considerations should be waived and an effort at least equal to the Manhattan Project should be exerted at once." But Frank Rowlett, who was now the head of the CIA's own SIGINT organization, Staff D, was not impressed with the increasingly urgent recommendations coming out of the multitude of blue-ribbon panels, study groups, review panels, and committees created during the 1950s to find a solution to NSA's code-breaking problems, telling an interviewer decades later, "Most of the people on these panels would not have known a Russian cipher if it hit them on the head . . . Rule by committee is a terrible way to run a spy agency."[4]

NSA's SIGINT effort against mainland China was even more frustrating than the Russian problem. Unlike the attack on the Russian ciphers, which received unlimited attention and resources, the NSA cryptanalytic attack on Chinese codes and ciphers was hampered by perpetual shortages of manpower and equipment. The result was that virtually no progress was being made in solving any of the high-grade Chinese cipher systems and NSA had to be content with exploiting low-level Chinese plaintext radio traffic and traffic analysis for information about what was going on inside China. And as if this situation was not bad enough already, after the signing of the July 1953 armistice agreement in

Korea, NSA lost most of its access to Chinese and North Korean military communications when these forces switched from radio to landlines. A February 1954 report to the NSC conceded the result: that relatively little was known about what was going on inside China. And a recently declassified CIA report bluntly states, "The picture for the major target area in Asia, i.e. Communist China, is very dark."[5]

1956—The Year of Crisis

As NSA was in the process of moving from Arlington Hall to its new headquarters at Fort Meade, in Maryland, in the fall of 1956, NSA was struck nearly simultaneously by three international crises that stretched the agency's resources to the limit.

The first was the violent worker riots that took place in the Polish city of Poznan in late June 1956. The riots were crushed by Polish troops using live ammunition, and at least fifty civilians were killed. The events precipitated a political crisis within the hard-line Polish government. When the Polish Communist Party met in Warsaw on October 19, it elected a progressive-minded reformer named Wladyslaw Gomulka, who had just been released from prison for having been a "counterrevolutionary," as Poland's new leader. NSA immediately picked up indications that the Russians were preparing to use military force against Poland. The crisis was defused on October 24, when Gomulka reaffirmed Poland's political and military ties with the USSR, leading the Russians to order their troops to return to their barracks.[6]

On the afternoon of October 23, the day before Gomulka ended the Polish crisis, peaceful anti-Soviet demonstrations in downtown Budapest escalated into a full-blown armed insurrection against the Soviet-backed, hard-line communist Hungarian government. Hungary immediately called for Soviet military assistance in putting down the riots, which by the end of the day had spread from Budapest to a number of other major Hungarian cities. Within hours of the rioting's breaking out in Budapest, the twenty-seven thousand Russian troops based inside Hungary began to move. Early on the morning of October 24, intercept operators at the U.S. Army listening post at Bad Aibling Station, in West Germany, began noting all four Russian combat divisions based in Hungary rapidly converging on Budapest. At ten twenty-eight A.M., the Bad Aibling listening post intercepted an order passed in the clear from the commander of the Russian Second Guards Mechanized Division authorizing his troops to use their tank cannons and heavy artillery to "disperse the rioters" in

Budapest. It marked the beginning of a bloody day of street fighting between Russian troops and Hungarian civilians throughout the city. By the end of the day 24, radio intercepts reaching NSA had revealed that selected Soviet Long Range Air Force bomber units in the western USSR had been placed on a heightened state of alert, as had selected Russian ground, air, and naval forces stationed in Eastern Europe, especially in East Germany.[7]

By October 27, SIGINT had confirmed that there were now four full-strength Russian combat divisions totaling forty thousand troops deployed in and around virtually all major Hungarian cities, with especially high numbers in Budapest. SIGINT showed that the Russian Second Guards Mechanized Division and the Thirty-second Mechanized Division had borne the brunt of the fighting up until that point in downtown Budapest, with the intercepts reflecting heavy personnel and equipment losses among those troops as well as severe ammunition shortages in some units. Intercepts also showed that large numbers of seriously wounded Russian military personnel were being airlifted from the Budapest-Tokol airport to the city of L'vov in the USSR. The problem for Russia was that the Hungarian rioters still controlled large portions of Budapest and other major Hungarian cities.[8]

Then two days later, on the morning of October 29, Israeli forces attacked Egyptian forces based in the Sinai Peninsula and the Gaza Strip. Tensions in the Middle East had been building since June, when Egypt forced the British to remove the last of their forces from the Suez Canal, which had been nationalized. Since early October, NSA and the rest of the U.S. intelligence community had been intensively tracking the buildup of Israeli forces along the border with Egypt, as well as a comparable buildup of French and British forces on Cyprus. By October 27, all signs pointed to an imminent Israeli attack on Egypt. A report was sent out by the CIA that afternoon stating, "The likelihood has increased of major Israeli reprisals, probably against Egypt, in the near future." The next day, SIGINT reports coming out of NSA confirmed that Israel was about to attack Egypt, with fragmentary SIGINT reports indicating that British forces based on Cyprus appeared ready to strike Egypt as well. Later that afternoon, NSA reported to the White House that it had monitored a massive jump in diplomatic communications traffic passing between Tel Aviv and Paris. This led CIA analysts to conclude, correctly as it turned out, that "France [might] be planning [military] actions in conjunction with Israel against Egypt."[9]

The following morning, October 29, the deputy director of the CIA's Office of Current Intelligence, Knight McMahan, was about to brief Democratic presidential candidate Adlai Stevenson at his hotel in Boston. According to

McMahan's recollection, the previous day "the Watch Committee was reviewing newly available intelligence confirming that Israel, with British and French support, was completing its mobilization and would attack Egypt. *Because the evidence came from intercepted communications, this sensitive information was not included in the written briefing materials prepared for Stevenson.*" Instead, McMahan intended to handle this breaking story orally. But before McMahan could utter a word, one of Stevenson's aides rushed into the room to announce that according to wire service reports, Israeli troops had launched their offensive against Egyptian forces in the Sinai.[10] A furious Eisenhower, reacting to the invasion, called British prime minister Anthony Eden and asked his old friend if he had gone out of his mind.

Six days later, on November 4, while the fighting in the Sinai was still raging, Soviet military forces in Hungary moved to crush once and for all the uprising in Budapest and other cities. Two days before the Soviets moved, SIGINT showed that they were up to something. Beginning on the evening of November 2, SIGINT detected massive Soviet troop movements inside Hungary, as well as troop reinforcements crossing into the country from the western USSR. Clearly, the Soviet military was preparing to attack. On the morning of November 4, Soviet troops attacked Budapest and other Hungarian cities that had risen up in revolt. By eight A.M., Soviet troops had captured the Hungarian parliament building in downtown Budapest and had arrested virtually the entire Hungarian government and parliament, including the newly elected reformist prime minister Imre Nagy. The battle for Budapest was over even before it started. An estimated twenty-five thousand Hungarians were killed in the uprising. Again, Soviet casualty figures are unknown, but were probably heavy.[11] (There is an ongoing debate about the extent of the CIA's role in encouraging the uprising. In any event, Eisenhower decided not to intervene in Hungary, disavowed any involvement in or approval of the Suez invasion, and effectively forced Israel, France, and Britain to put an end to it.)

On the afternoon of November 4, NSA declared an alert and placed all its assets in a heightened state of readiness. The alert, which was designated Yankee, was prompted by a series of bombastic threats issued by senior Soviet leaders threatening to intervene militarily in the Middle East, as well as some fragmentary intelligence indicating that Soviet military forces in Eastern Europe and the western USSR had dramatically increased their readiness levels. There was also some intelligence indicating that between two and four Soviet attack submarines had been sent into the Mediterranean. But SIGINT confirmed that Soviet military forces, such as their crack airborne troops, had not been placed on alert, and there were no indications of Soviet forces being redeployed in preparation for intervention in the Middle East conflict. A declassified NSA history notes, "Timely reporting over a period of months could have left no doubt within the [Eisenhower] administration that Soviet diplomacy consisted of posturing. They were not going to go down to the Middle East to bail out anyone. Forces just weren't moving."[12]

The output that NSA produced during these crises indicates that the agency performed creditably. In the weeks leading up to the 1956 Arab-Israeli War, SIGINT proved to be a critically important source of intelligence indicating that war was imminent. A declassified 1957 CIA postmortem evaluation of U.S. intelligence performance prior to the Israeli-British-French attack on Egypt notes that "the Watch Committee, in October 1956, provided several days of advance warning of the imminent possibility of Israeli-Egyptian hostilities and 24 hours' specific warning of Israel's intention to attack Egypt with French and (initially) tacit British support."[13] During the Soviet military intervention in Hungary, an NSA history notes, SIGINT "provided fairly complete indicators concerning Soviet military unit movements throughout the crisis." The NSA history also makes clear that SIGINT was the only reliable intelligence source available to the U.S. intelligence community on Soviet military movements and activities in Hungary.[14]

Despite providing timely intelligence, NSA's overall performance revealed that the agency's hidebound bureaucracy had trouble reacting rapidly to extraordinary circumstances. NSA was roundly criticized for the intelligence material that it produced. A declassified NSA history notes, "As for crisis response, all was chaos. The cryptologic community proved incapable of marshaling its forces in a flexible fashion to deal with developing trouble spots. The events of the year did not demonstrate success—they simply provided a case study to learn from."[15]

The Samford Era at NSA

On November 23, 1956, General Ralph Canine retired after almost forty years in the U.S. Army. His replacement as NSA director was Lieutenant General John Samford of the U.S. Air Force. Born in tiny Hagerman, New Mexico, on August 29, 1905, Samford graduated from West Point in 1928 and joined the U.S. Army Air Corps. During World War II, he served as the chief of staff of the Eighth Air Force from 1942 until 1944, then at the Pentagon as a senior intelligence officer. After the war, Samford held a series of senior intelligence billets, becoming the chief of U.S. Air Force intelligence in 1951. He held this position until becoming NSA's vice director in July 1956, then director four months later, in November 1956.[16]

As head of air force intelligence, Samford was well known as a defense hawk and one of the primary proponents within the air force of the idea that the Soviets were seeking strategic nuclear superiority over the United States. Many senior NSA staff also remembered Samford's strident opposition to the formation of NSA in October 1952. When he was announced as the new director, many of the civilian staff at Fort Meade were alarmed about what his appointment would mean for the agency.[17]

But Samford proved to be a pleasant surprise. Polished and thoughtful, he quickly became a convert to the idea that the rapidly growing NSA would someday be a superpower within the American intelligence community. His quiet but diligent work on behalf of the agency earned him the informal moniker Slamming Sammy among his staff. Samford also moved rapidly to heal the gaping wounds that had developed in the relationship between NSA and the CIA during Canine's tumultuous tenure. A declassified NSA history notes, "Samford was a consummate diplomat, and he probably gained more by soft-soaping the downtown intelligence people than Canine could have done through head-on collisions."[18]

Forward! Ever Forward!

Just as his predecessor had, Samford found that the Soviet Union ate up the vast majority of NSA's SIGINT collection resources. But like his predecessor's, Samford's tenure was marked by the continuing failure of the agency's cryptanalysts to break into the Soviet high-grade ciphers. Just as in baseball, NSA's senior leadership tried to shake up the management of their cryptanalytic effort to see if that would produce results, but to no avail.

By 1958, a whopping 54 percent of NSA's SIGINT collection resources were dedicated to monitoring military and civilian targets inside the Soviet Union. But NSA's cryptanalysts had actually lost ground since the Korean War. The Russians put a series of new and improved cipher machines into service, each of which was harder to solve than the machines they replaced. And the communications traffic generated by these machines remained impenetrable. The Soviets also continued to shift an ever-increasing percentage of their secret communications from the airwaves to telegraph lines, buried cables, and microwave radio-relay systems, which was a simple and effective way of keeping this traffic away from NSA's thousands of radio intercept operators.[19]

NSA and the U-2 Overflight Program

Even if NSA's cryptanalysts were stymied by the Russian high-grade ciphers, other branches of NSA were producing intelligence. One of the most important, albeit unheralded, missions performed by NSA during General Samford's tenure was providing SIGINT support to the CIA's U-2 reconnaissance aircraft that were engaged in secretly overflying the USSR. Declassified documents show that between April 1956 and May 1960, the CIA conducted twenty-four U-2 overflights of the USSR, which produced some of the most important intelligence information about what the Russians were up for the information-starved American intelligence analysts back in Washington.[20]

Although it is not recognized in CIA literature on the U-2 program, newly declassified documents show that over time a close and symbiotic relationship developed between NSA and CIA. NSA derived incredibly valuable intelligence about Soviet military capabilities by monitoring how the Soviets reacted to each U-2 overflight. And over time, the CIA increasingly came to depend on intelligence information collected by NSA in order to target the U-2 overflights, with a declassified NSA history noting that as time went by SIGINT "became more and more a cue card for U-2 missions."[21]

The genesis of the NSA-CIA relationship regarding the U-2 program dates back to a Top Secret May 1956 agreement between the CIA and NSA, whereby NSA's listening posts situated around the Soviet periphery were tasked with closely monitoring Soviet air defense reactions to each U-2 overflight mission by intercepting the radio transmissions of Soviet radar operators as they tracked the CIA reconnaissance aircraft flying deep inside their country. The American radio intercept operators could copy the radio transmissions of Soviet radar operators deep inside the USSR, in some cases thousands of miles away. This meant that American radio intercept operators in England and Germany could listen to Soviet radar operators in the Urals or deep inside Kazakhstan as they excitedly tracked the flight paths of the U-2s. A former U.S. Air Force intercept operator recalled, "We could track our U-2s using the Soviet's own radar, long after our U-2s were out of the range of our own long range radar stations."[22]

The intercepts stemming from the U-2 overflights proved to be an intelligence bonanza for the analysts in NSA's Soviet Air Division, headed by a veteran U.S. Air Force SIGINT officer named Colonel Harry Towler Jr. Between 1956 and 1960, Towler's division produced reams of reports detailing the strength, readiness, and capabilities of the Soviet air defense forces. Intercepts collected during the early U-2 overflights in the summer of 1956 revealed that the accuracy of the Soviet radars was not very good, but over time their accuracy improved markedly as new systems were introduced. The intercepts also revealed that the command and control network of the huge Soviet air defense system was cumbersome, and oftentimes very slow to react to extraordinary situations. A former NSA analyst involved in the program recalled that by correlating intercepts of Soviet radar tracking transmissions with intercepts of Russian early-warning radars, he could literally "time with a stopwatch" how fast the Russians reacted to each individual U-2 overflight. SIGINT also revealed that the Soviet air defense fighter force was larger than previously believed. Every time a U-2 conducted an overflight of the USSR, the Soviets scrambled dozens of fighter interceptors from different bases to try to shoot the aircraft down. By monitoring the air-to-ground radio traffic between the fighters and their home bases, NSA was able to identify dozens of previously unknown Soviet air defense fighter regiments throughout the USSR.[23]

The U-2 intercepts also revealed how poor the operating capabilities of the Soviet fighters and their pilots sometimes were. While in training in the U.S. during the 1960s, a former USAFSS Russian linguist listened to a training tape of intercepted PVO air-to-ground radio transmissions during an attempt by Russian MiG fighters to shoot down a CIA U-2 reconnaissance aircraft flying over Russia. The linguist recalled that one of the MiG fighters flew too high, which resulted in the plane's jet engines flaming out. The pilot could not restart his engine at such a high altitude, and his plane plummeted to the earth. As caught on the tape, the Russian MiG pilot spent his last seconds alive screaming "Beda! Beda!" (Mayday! Mayday!) into his radio set before his plane crashed and the radio transmission abruptly went dead.[24]

The Fool's Errand: NSA and the 1960 U-2 Shootdown

At eight thirty-six on the morning of May 1, 1960, a Russian SA-2 Guideline surface-to-air missile (SAM) fired by a battery of the Fifty-seventh Anti-Aircraft Rocket Brigade, commanded by Major Mikhail Voronov, shot down a CIA U-2 reconnaissance aircraft piloted by Francis Gary Powers deep inside Russia near the city of Sverdlovsk.[25]

NSA was deeply involved in all aspects of Gary Powers's ill-fated mission. Many of the top targets that the mission was supposed to cover had been identified by SIGINT, including suspected Soviet intercontinental ballistic missile (ICBM) launch sites at Polyarnyy Ural, Yur'ya, and Verkhnyaya Salda and an alleged missile production facility in Sverdlovsk. But one of the main targets of Powers's overflight mission was to confirm reports received from NSA that the Russians were building an ICBM launch site in northern Russia somewhere along the Vologda-Arkhangel'sk railroad in the vicinity of the frigid village of Plesetsk. As it turned out, the SIGINT reporting was correct: The Russians had begun building their first operational ICBM site at Plesetsk in July 1957 and had completed construction in mid-1959. Between December 1959 and February 1960, Norwegian listening posts in northern Norway had intercepted Russian radio traffic suggesting that Soviet missile activity was then being conducted at Plesetsk, which Power's mission was supposed to confirm.[26]

As with all previous U-2 overflights of the USSR, NSA was able to monitor Soviet air defense reactions to the mission. The man at NSA headquarters responsible for running this operation was Henry Fenech, who headed NSA's Soviet Air Defense Branch. Well before Powers's U-2 took off from Peshawar airfield in northern Pakistan, Fenech had become concerned about the safety of the U-2 aircraft. There were clear signs appearing in SIGINT that the Soviet air defenses were getting better, and that they were getting close to being able to shoot down a U-2.[27]

Powers's mission did not begin well. Even before his U-2 reached the Soviet border on May 1, intercepted Soviet air defense tracking communications showed that his plane had been detected and was being closely tracked by Russian early-warning radars. While the U-2 streaked northward into the heart of Russia, NSA intercept operators in Karamursel, Turkey, listened intently as Soviet radar operators continued to track the plane. Then something went terribly wrong. The intercepts of Soviet air defense radar tracking showed that just north of Sverdlovsk, Powers's aircraft descended from over sixty-five thousand feet to somewhere between thirty thousand and forty thousand feet, changed course to head back toward Sverdlovsk, then disappeared completely off the Soviet radar screens thirty-five minutes later. Fenech could only report to the CIA that the U-2 "had been lost due to unexplained causes." But in a follow-up report, Fenech's analysts stated that based on intercepts of Soviet radar tracking communications, they believed that Powers's aircraft might have been hit by the SAM at an altitude of between thirty thousand and forty thousand feet while descending, and not at an altitude of sixty-five thousand feet as Powers claimed.[28]

The downing of the U-2 was a major diplomatic disaster. It took place just two weeks before Eisenhower (who had to authorize all such overflights and had very reluctantly allowed this one—to take place no later than May 2) was to meet with Soviet leader Nikita Khrushchev for a crucial summit meeting in Geneva. Not only did the Soviets capture Powers after he parachuted from his doomed aircraft, but they also displayed pieces of the latter (along with Powers) in public. The summit meeting, like the U-2, was shot down by the Russians. And a very unhappy Eisenhower wanted an explanation of what had gone wrong.

Fenech's report stirred up a hornet's nest of controversy, with CIA officials vehemently denying its conclusions. But it was not until Powers returned to the United States in February 11, 1962, after being traded for convicted Soviet spy Rudolph Abel, that NSA "got its day in court." Admiral Laurence Frost— who had replaced General Samford as director of NSA in November 1960— and his analysts attended a contentious CIA board of inquiry, convened on February 19, at which Fenech was grilled for hours by board member John Bross, a former lawyer and a veteran CIA officer, about his conclusions, and Fenech continued to insist that the intercepted Soviet air defense tracking showed that Powers was flying much lower than he claimed. The CIA board maintained, however, that the Soviet radar operators had been mistaken about the altitude. So on February 27, 1962, the board sent a Top Secret report to CIA director John McCone and President John Kennedy that cleared Powers of any culpability or negligence, concluding that "the evidence establishes overwhelmingly that Powers' account was a truthful account."[29]

Louis Tordella, NSA's deputy director, was incensed, telling CIA general counsel Lawrence Houston that "the markedly hostile nature of much of the questioning indicated that the Board had already decided on a course of action which was not supported by the NSA produced materials." But the politically astute Tordella ultimately conceded that the board had arrived at the "best" decision—i.e., one that protected the reputation of the CIA and the rest of the U.S. intelligence community.[30]

CHAPTER 5

The Crisis Years

SIGINT and the Kennedy Administration: 1961–1963

It may not be war, but it sure as hell ain't peace.
—MAJOR GENERAL STEVEN ARNOLD

Jack Frost's 600 Days

On January 20, 1961, John Kennedy was sworn in as the thirty-fifth president of the United States. His national security advisers quickly discovered that NSA was the most important, the largest, and the most expensive component of the U.S. intelligence community. With a budget of $654 million and employing 59,000 military and civilian personnel, NSA was truly a behemoth. By way of comparison, the CIA consisted of only 16,685 personnel, with a budget of $401.6 million.[1]

Leaders in the intelligence community had worried about the tendency of NSA's director, Lieutenant General John Samford, to focus on meeting the demands of the Pentagon rather than on making NSA a strong national intelligence organization. A search had been mounted to find a successor who could do just that.[2]

Vice Admiral Laurence "Jack" Frost seemed to have the requisite qualifications for the job. Quiet and soft-spoken, Frost had replaced Samford as the director of NSA on November 24, 1960. A native of Fayetteville, Arkansas, Frost was a 1926 graduate of the U.S. Naval Academy. He spent his formative years in the navy as a gunnery and communications officer, and he was in command of the destroyer USS *Greer* when it was attacked on September 4, 1941, by a German U-boat in the North Atlantic while on a mail run to Iceland, a seminal event that helped propel the United States into World War II. During the war, Frost commanded a destroyer and served as a communications officer in the Pacific. He returned to Washington in September 1945 and became an intelligence officer, commanding the unit of the Office of Naval Intelligence (ONI) that managed the navy's SIGINT processing and reporting efforts, then ONI's Intelligence Estimates Division. After more sea duty, Frost served as NSA's chief of staff from 1953 to 1955, then became the director of ONI on May 16, 1956. He remained at the helm until becoming NSA director in 1960.[3]

But Frost turned out to be a disaster as head of NSA. During his twenty-month tenure, the vice admiral, used to naval discipline and unquestioning obedience to orders, soon found that his civilian staffers would not toe the line, so he surrounded himself with some naval officers who would. Senior civilian managers dubbed them the Navy Cabal and saw Frost as a threat to their management control over the agency. In response, his senior civilian staff fought him on policy issues and began sabotaging many of his initiatives behind his back.[4]

Frost also never developed a good rapport with the Kennedy administration, which made it difficult for him to protect NSA's independence from the encroachment of Secretary of Defense Robert McNamara and his top deputies as well as the CIA, headed by John McCone. By the spring of 1962, McNamara was fed up with Frost and fired him. Today it is hard to find former NSA officials who have anything good to say about Vice Admiral Frost.

NSA Enters the War in Vietnam

At the time the Kennedy administration entered the White House, in January 1961, NSA was devoting few resources to monitoring events in Asia. Of the agency's total SIGINT collection resources, 50 percent were devoted to the Soviet Union, 8.4 percent to Asian communist targets, and 7.6 percent to noncommunist countries elsewhere around the world, which in NSA parlance were known as the ALLO (all other) nations. The remaining 34 percent was working staff positions and other esoteric collection functions, such as electronic intelligence.[5]

The man heading NSA's SIGINT collection operations in the Far East was Dr. Lawrance Shinn, who had been chief of NSA's Office of Asiatic Communist Countries (ACOM) since 1959. Like many of his colleagues at the time, Larry Shinn was not a professional cryptologist. The holder of a B.S. degree in chemistry from the University of Chicago and a Ph.D. in bacteriology from the University of Pittsburgh, Shinn had joined the U.S. Navy cryptologic organization during World War II. He quickly demonstrated a modest talent for code breaking but even more impressive skills as a manager, which led to his meteoric rise after the war within AFSA, then NSA.[6]

As of 1961, the vast majority of Shinn's SIGINT collection and analytic resources were focused on mainland China, with a smaller effort targeting North Korea. NSA had a small number of SIGINT intercept positions at its two listening posts in the Philippines covering North Vietnam and Viet Cong guerrilla activities in South Vietnam, though those facilities devoted more of their resources to China traffic. Back at Fort Meade, what SIGINT reporting was being produced conclusively showed that the Viet Cong insurgency was being directed and supported by North Vietnam through a clandestine radio network that extended from Hanoi to 114 Viet Cong radio stations spread throughout South Vietnam.[7]

Until 1960, NSA was able to read with relative ease the high-level diplomatic and military cipher systems of North Vietnam. But the agency's window into these communications closed quickly. In the fall of that year, the North Vietnamese began changing all of their codes to a new unbreakable cipher system called KTB. The first systems to "go black" were all of the high-level North Vietnamese government and military ciphers, and over the next two years North Vietnam converted all of the ciphers used by its military to KTB. The first changes in Viet Cong cipher usage came in the fall of 1961, and then on April 14, 1962, all one-hundred-plus Viet Cong radio transmitters in South Vietnam "executed a major, nearly total communications and cryptographic change on their military and political-military networks." All high-level North Vietnamese and Viet Cong ciphers became unreadable to the cryptanalysts at NSA, forcing the agency to rely, for the rest of the Vietnam War, on the exploitation of low-level North Vietnamese and Viet Cong cipher systems, plaintext intercepts, and traffic analysis.[8]

In the summer of 1960, the increasing intensity of the Viet Cong insurrection in South Vietnam forced the U.S. intelligence community to devote more resources to monitoring Viet Cong activity. Since existing security regulations barred the United States from giving direct SIGINT support to the South Vietnamese government, the CIA chief of station in Taiwan, Ray Cline, was asked by Washington to see if the Taiwanese intelligence services "would assist the South Vietnamese in methods for collecting intelligence, including signals interception and the flying of clandestine missions behind enemy lines."[9] But the Taiwanese personnel ultimately sent to South Vietnam spent most of their time intercepting Chinese military radio traffic, at which they excelled, and made no real contribution to the war effort. Efforts by the commander of the U.S. Military Assistance Group (MAAG) in Vietnam, Lieutenant General L. C. McGarr, to convince the newly installed Kennedy administration of the need to provide the South Vietnamese with SIGINT equipment were met by stiff resistance from the U.S. intelligence community, especially NSA, which was naturally reluctant to provide the South Vietnamese with sensitive American SIGINT technology.[10]

In March 1961, the U.S. Intelligence Board (USIB) approved a wide range of new clandestine intelligence collection and covert action programs, including a classified CIA program to drop large numbers of agents into North Vietnam, as well as a sizable expansion of NSA's SIGINT collection program for both Viet Cong and North Vietnamese communications. The USIB also approved a parallel program that authorized the ASA to train South Vietnamese military personnel in SIGINT collection. On April 29, 1961, President Kennedy and the NSC approved the plan, including giving limited intelligence information derived from SIGINT to the South Vietnamese military.[11]

On May 12, 1961, McGarr, Ambassador Frederick Nolting Jr., and the CIA's Saigon chief of station, William Colby, obtained South Vietnamese president Ngo Dinh Diem's approval to deploy American SIGINT troops to South Vietnam. The next day, the first contingent of ninety-three ASA personnel, calling themselves the Third Radio Research Unit under the command of Lieutenant Colonel William Cochrane, flew into Tan Son Nhut Air Base outside Saigon and moved its Morse intercept operators into vans parked alongside the runways. Their presence was to be kept top secret. The army SIGINT troops wore civilian clothes and were barred from carrying military ID cards in order to provide cover, which must have deceived very few, since all of them wore sidearms and carried M-1 rifles everywhere they went. For additional cover, their medical records were stamped, "If injured or killed in combat, report as training accident in the Philippines."[12] To preserve security as well as cover, Washington tactfully declined to give in to the South Vietnamese government and military's demands for full access to the unit's operations spaces and the intelligence information that it produced.[13]

But as of the fall of 1961, the SIGINT effort was producing virtually no hard intelligence about the strength, capabilities, and activities of the Viet Cong guerrillas in South Vietnam. A Top Secret November 1961 report to the White House by General Maxwell Taylor recommended that NSA "adjust its priorities of effort and allocations of personnel and material, both in Washington and Vietnam, as required to break Viet Cong communications codes." His findings, coupled with the rapidly deteriorating military situation in South

Vietnam, led President Kennedy to authorize yet another dramatic increase in the number of American troops and advisers in South Vietnam. As part of the buildup, an additional 279 ASA personnel were ordered to be deployed to South Vietnam by January 14, 1962, to augment the Third Radio Research Unit.[14]

Operation Mongoose

Pursuant to a November 30, 1961, directive from Kennedy, the CIA began planning a large-scale covert operation called Mongoose, whose purpose was to overthrow the Fidel Castro regime in Cuba through a combination of guerrilla attacks by CIA-trained Cuban exiles and the judicious use of political, economic, and psychological warfare.[15] This regime change plan naturally had the full support of the Pentagon and the U.S. intelligence community, with the chairman of the Joint Chiefs of Staff going so far as to write, "The United States cannot tolerate [the] permanent existence of a communist government in the Western Hemisphere."[16]

Between January and March 1962, all branches of the U.S. intelligence community, including NSA, were tasked with increased coverage of Cuba to support the CIA's Mongoose covert action operations. NSA's initial intelligence collection effort was relatively small. Then, in response to White House demands that "special intelligence [i.e., SIGINT] assets be exploited more fully," the agency sent a plan to Secretary of Defense McNamara in November 1961, calling for additional intercept positions to monitor Cuban communications. This required placing the newly commissioned NSA spy ship USS *Oxford* off the northern coast of Cuba and hiring a dozen anticommunist Cuban exiles to translate the intercepted message traffic. This plan and another, more expansive version submitted in February 1962 were quickly approved by McNamara.[17]

Juanita Morris Moody, chief of the Office of Non-Communist Nations (B1), had the responsibility of running SIGINT collection operations against Cuba. As a woman holding a senior management position, with no college degree or advanced technical background, she was a rarity in that era at NSA. Born in Morven, North Carolina, she attended Western Carolina College in 1942–1943 but never graduated. She left school in April 1943 and volunteered to join the war effort. Within a month, she found herself assigned to SSA at Arlington Hall Station as a code clerk. While waiting for her security clearance to come through, she took a number of unclassified courses in cryptanalysis, in which she demonstrated her flair for code breaking, and she subsequently excelled in breaking complex cipher systems, such as a high-level German one-time pad cipher system. By the end of the war, she had risen from code clerk to office head. At the urging of her supervisor, she decided to stay on with the ASA. In only three years, she advanced to the position of chief of operations for one of ASA's most important operational units. In subsequent years, she headed a number of important operational units at NSA, including the division that specialized in the solution of Soviet manual cipher systems.[18]

Much of NSA's early effort against Cuba was driven by the intelligence requirements of the CIA, not only for its own analytic purposes but also to support Operation Mongoose.[19] For example, declassified documents show that the CIA's Clandestine Service was anxious to detect dissension within the Castro regime or the Cuban populace through NSA's monitoring of Cuban police and internal security force communications.[20] In February 1962, a small team of SIGINT analysts belonging to ASA were sent to the CIA's newly opened interrogation center at Opa-Locka, Florida, the Caribbean Admissions Center, to gather intelligence information needed to support the SIGINT effort against Cuba by interrogating Cuban refugees and defectors.[21] Then there were the requirements of the FBI, which in 1962 wanted NSA to send it copies of all Western Union telegrams between the United States and Cuba, particularly those that identified which U.S. companies were still doing business with Cuba or revealed the names of Americans traveling there illegally.[22]

NSA began diverting collection resources from other targets in order to cover Cuba. By April 1962, the number of NSA radio intercept positions dedicated to copying Cuban radio traffic had increased from thirteen to thirty-five, and the number of intelligence analysts and reporters working on the Cuban mission at NSA headquarters at Fort Meade had risen to eighty-three personnel. The number of aerial SIGINT collection flights around Cuba was dramatically increased, and in February 1962 the USS *Oxford* made another visit to the international waters off Havana to monitor Cuban communications traffic. The presence of the *Oxford*, with its 116 U.S. Navy SIGINT operators, outside Havana harbor so infuriated the Cuban government that on February 22, 1962, Fidel Castro publicly charged that the *Oxford* had violated Cuban territorial waters, and he handed out to journalists grainy photos of the antenna-studded ship, which could be seen clearly as it cruised nearby.[23]

NSA's SIGINT production on Cuba quickly dwarfed the reporting coming from all other agencies. During the six-month period from April 1962 to October 1962, NSA provided fifty-seven hundred reports on what was going on inside Cuba.[24] Intercepts in April and May confirmed that the Cubans were receiving new Soviet-made radars, part of the rapid construction of a modern air defense system. In June, NSA reported that MiG-21 fighters, the most modern Soviet-made jets, were in Cuba. At the same time, American radio intercept operators in southern Florida caught Russians talking in heavily accented Spanish on Cuban air force radio frequencies, teaching Cuban pilots and ground controllers fighter interception tactics. By July 1962, SIGINT showed that the Cuban MiG fighters were now routinely conducting ground-controlled intercept (GCI) air defense exercises, and on two occasions NSA intercept operators in southern Florida detected Cuban MiG fighters intercepting intruding aircraft, probably CIA resupply planes, clear evidence that the Cuban air force was fast becoming combat ready.[25]

By mid-July 1962, Secretary McNamara had become quite concerned about these capabilities, as well as about intelligence reports indicating the presence of Soviet military advisers on the island. NSA concurred and once again requested permission from the Pentagon to divert collection resources from other targets in order to augment its SIGINT coverage of Cuba. In his response, on July 16, McNamara ordered NSA to dramatically increase its coverage as "a matter of the highest urgency."[26]

NSA had one hugely important asset, which allowed it to listen in on what was happening inside Cuba—it could tap right into the Cuban national telephone system. This was possible because the American telecommunications giant RCA International had built the system in 1957, and it used a vulnerable microwave relay system rather than invulnerable landlines to carry virtually all telephone traffic between Havana and all major towns and cities in Cuba.[27]

Miffed by the seizure of its Cuban holdings by Castro's government in 1959, RCA willingly provided the CIA and NSA with the schematics of the Cuban communications system as well as details about the operating parameters of the equipment. But in 1960, the Soviets began to replace the American-made equipment with Russian communications and cryptographic equipment as part of their military aid program to Cuba. NSA estimated that it would take the Cuban government about two years to phase out the American equipment and replace it with the Russian equipment, by which time, it was believed, the lack of spare parts and poor maintenance would take its toll on the latter, forcing the Cubans to continue to use the American-built communications network for the foreseeable future. They were right.[28]

To intercept the Cuban telephone traffic, NSA needed to park a ship equipped with special intercept equipment off the Cuban coast. So on July 19, 1962, the

USS *Oxford* was diverted from a scheduled cruise around Latin America and ordered to proceed at flank speed to undertake another intelligence-gathering cruise around Cuba.[29] The *Oxford* arrived off the northern coast of Cuba on July 21 and began to cruise at a leisurely five knots within its assigned operations area in international waters twelve miles off Havana and the port of Mariel, monitoring Cuban communications traffic and radar emissions. The *Oxford*'s most productive target was the easily intercepted message traffic sent over the Cuban microwave telephone network.[30]

On July 31, a Cuban navy patrol boat circled the *Oxford* while crewmen photographed the ship. Electronic intelligence (ELINT) operators aboard the *Oxford* nervously watched as the Cubans used their shore-based surveillance radars to continuously track the ship's movements and no doubt associated its position relative to the sites of contemporaneous CIA Operation Mongoose commando raids along the Cuban coastline. On August 30, Cuban newspapers prominently reported on the presence of the *Oxford* off the Cuban coast. Observers standing on the Malecón seawall around Havana harbor could, once again, clearly see the spy ship as it slowly cruised back and forth just outside Cuban territorial waters.[31]

Change in Command

After its disastrous experience with Admiral Laurence Frost, the Pentagon selected a fifty-two-year-old U.S. Air Force communications officer with little intelligence experience named Lieutenant General Gordon Blake to head up NSA. But his past experience might well have sold him on the importance of SIGINT. On the morning of December 7, 1941, Blake was serving as the base operations officer at Hickham Field, in Hawaii, when the Japanese attacked Pearl Harbor. He was awarded the Silver Star for gallantry for his actions during the attack. After World War II, Blake held a series of command positions on the air staff in Washington, where he helped plan the Distant Early Warning (DEW) Line radar network across Alaska and Canada. In 1961, he was named commander of the Continental Air Defense Command, attaining the rank of lieutenant general on October 1, 1961, and he remained there until being named NSA director on July 1, 1962.[32]

It was a precarious time for NSA. The agency was still battered by the bad feelings generated by Frost's contentious relationship with Robert McNamara's Pentagon. Frost and Blake had been friends since World War II, which helped ease the transition somewhat, but Blake later confessed that he "felt badly about coming in over [Frost's] prostrate form."[33]

Blake was to serve as the director of NSA for three years, until May 31, 1965. His impact on the agency, though little publicized, was important and far-reaching. He was at the helm during the 1962 Cuban Missile Crisis, and he managed the agency during a period of dramatic expansion brought on by the war in Vietnam. NSA's personnel numbers and budget figures reached record highs under his command, and he was instrumental in getting funding for an intensified research and development program needed to develop new SIGINT collection and computerized processing systems. Personable and easygoing, Blake went out of his way to try to forge closer links between NSA and the Pentagon, developing a close working relationship with Frost's archnemesis, Assistant Secretary of Defense John Rubel, and his successor (and a future secretary of state during the Carter administration), Cyrus Vance. Blake also restored a more harmonious relationship with the CIA and patched up NSA's virtually nonexistent relationship with the National Reconnaissance Office, which Frost had left in tatters because of a fight over NSA's lack of control over SIGINT satellite collection. By the time Blake departed, NSA had eclipsed all other agencies comprising the U.S. intelligence community, with SIGINT becoming the "predominant source" used by American intelligence analysts and policy makers.[34] But the outcome of the struggle for control of future increasingly sensitive SIGINT satellites and amazingly high-resolution reconnaissance satellites would be crucial to NSA's maintaining intelligence primacy.

Monitoring the Russian Surge

It was not until the first in a new flow of Soviet cargo and passenger ships headed for Cuba in mid-July 1962 that NSA intelligence analysts concluded that something unusual was happening. NSA routinely intercepted all Soviet naval and commercial shipping radio traffic in the North Atlantic in conjunction with GCHQ in Britain and the Canadian SIGINT agency, the Communications Branch of the National Research Council (CBNRC). As a result, virtually everything that the U.S. intelligence community knew about Soviet shipments of men, weapons, and material to Cuba came from SIGINT. The importance of this NSA coverage to the CIA was so high that, as a report prepared by the CIA notes, "SIGINT provided information on daily positions, tonnages, destinations, and cargoes, as well as Soviet attempts to deny or falsify this information. On sailings from the Baltic, SIGINT often provided the initial information."[35]

The first indication that something untoward was occurring resulted from the analysis of the manifests for these ships, which NSA was routinely intercepting. Beginning on July 15, fully laden Soviet cargo ships began sailing for Cuba from Russian ports in the Black Sea. As they passed through the Dardanelles strait, the captains of these merchant ships gave false declarations to Turkish authorities in Istanbul as to their destinations and the cargoes they were carrying. They also lied about the cargoes' weight, which was well below what the ships were capable of carrying. NSA analysts at Fort Meade quickly figured out that the false declarations indicated that the ships were secretly carrying military cargoes.[36]

Declassified intelligence reports show that in July 1962, NSA detected twenty-one Russian merchant ships docking in Cuba, including four passenger ships, which was a single-month record for Soviet ships docking in Cuba. Among the passenger ships detected by NSA as soon as they left Russian ports were the *Maria Ulyanova* and the *Latvia*, which brought key staff components of the Soviet Group of Forces to Cuba. In August, NSA detected thirty-seven Soviet merchant ships, eleven tankers, and six passenger ships docking in Cuba. Little intelligence was available about what exactly the Russians were shipping there until mid-August, when imagery analysts at ONI identified crates for Komar missile patrol boats sitting on the deck of a Soviet merchant ship on its way to Cuba. In September, forty-six Soviet merchant ships were detected docking in Cuba by SIGINT, along with thirteen tankers and four passenger ships.[37]

These ships secretly carried thousands of Russian air defense troops and construction workers to Cuba. Despite attempts to disguise the newly arrived Russian troops in Cuba as civilian "agricultural technicians," refugees and defectors who found their way to Miami told their CIA interrogators that these "agricultural technicians" were young, wore matching civilian clothing, had military haircuts, marched in formation, and carried themselves like soldiers. In late July, the Russian military construction personnel had begun building launch sites for six SA-2 Guideline surface-to-air missile (SAM) regiments, whose 144 missile launchers were to be deployed throughout Cuba. The first SA-2 SAM sites were concentrated in the San Cristóbal area, in western Cuba. By the end of August, construction on the first SA-2 SAM site had been completed.[38]

Recently declassified documents reveal that despite the preponderance of evidence from SIGINT that these Soviet cargo ships were carrying weapons to Cuba, the Pentagon and its intelligence arm, the Defense Intelligence Agency (DIA), refused to accept this interpretation of the intelligence material. DIA's performance during the Cuban Missile Crisis was, according to the CIA, disgraceful. For instance, DIA blocked an attempt by the CIA to insert an item in the August 3, 1962, edition of the *Central Intelligence Bulletin* noting that "an unusual number of suspected arms carriers were enroute to Cuba." A watered-down version of this report was carried the next day, but in the month that followed, DIA blocked four more attempts by CIA analysts to publish reports that the Russians were shipping weapons to Cuba, with DIA analysts taking the following position: "The high volume of shipping probably reflects planned increases in trade between the USSR and Cuba." As late as the end of August, the chairman of the Joint Chiefs of Staff, General Maxwell Taylor, was telling President Kennedy that the surge in Soviet shipping traffic to Cuba "reflected an increased flow of economic aid" rather than weapons. DIA did not acknowledge that the Soviets were sending large quantities of weapons until September 6, a week after a U-2 reconnaissance mission confirmed that Russian-made SA-2 SAMs were operational in Cuba.[39]

On August 20, 1962, CIA director John McCone wrote a memorandum to President Kennedy reporting that a significant and worrisome surge in the number of Soviet merchant ships docking in Cuba had been detected and that an accumulation of human intelligence (HUMINT) reports strongly indicated that a contingent of about five thousand Russian troops was now in Cuba. The memo incorporated intelligence that had been received from the French intelligence service's chief of station in Washington, Thyraud de Vosjoli, who had just returned from a visit to Havana. According to de Vosjoli, between four thousand and six thousand Soviet military personnel had arrived in Cuba since July 1, 1962, although no Russian military units per se were included in this group.[40]

Intelligence information regarding the shipments was passed to the Special Group at a meeting at the State Department on August 21, and President Kennedy was briefed at the White House the following day. Confirmation of these reports by U-2 aerial reconnaissance was immediately ordered.[41] On August 23, NSA reported that nineteen Soviet freighters or passenger ships were then en route to Cuba, most of which appeared to be carrying weapons.[42] The next day, the CIA issued another intelligence report based on HUMINT, noting that on August 5–6 large numbers of Soviet personnel and equipment had arrived at the Cuban ports of Trinidad and Casilda, and that the Soviet personnel and equipment had departed from the ports in large convoys in the direction of the town of Sancti Spíritus.[43]

But it was not until the U-2 reconnaissance overflight of Cuba conducted on August 29 that the U.S. intelligence community received confirmation of the presence of Soviet-made SAMs in Cuba. The U-2 found a total of eight SA-2

Guideline SAM sites in various stages of construction throughout western Cuba, as well as five MiG-21 crates being unpacked at San Antonio de los Baños Air Base outside Havana, guided missile patrol boats, and the construction site of a coastal defense cruise missile base near the port of Banes in eastern Cuba. A report sent to McCone noted ominously that more Russian-made military equipment was on its way to Cuba, with SIGINT confirming that sixteen Russian freighters were then en route, ten of which were definitely carrying military equipment.[44]

At this critical juncture, disaster struck. NSA's ability to generate intelligence about the cargoes being carried by Soviet shipping to and from Cuba was publicly revealed by the State Department, in an effort to generate negative publicity about the increasing volume of Soviet weapons shipments to third world countries, such as Indonesia and Cuba. The CIA complained in a memo that State had released information "covered by this classification [Top Secret Codeword]. Said material appeared in part in the *Washington Post* within 12 hours of the time we gave it to State." The result of the unauthorized release was devastating. By mid-September, NSA had lost its ability to provide the U.S. intelligence community with details concerning what weapons Soviet merchant ships were carrying to these countries.[45]

The September Buildup

The U-2's discovery of SA-2 SAMs in Cuba on August 29 shocked the White House and set off alarm bells throughout the entire U.S. intelligence community.

The subsequent discovery of the Soviet surface-to-surface coastal defense missile site at Banes marked the beginning of a concerted effort by the entire U.S. intelligence community, including NSA, to try to find any indications that the Russians had deployed, or intended to deploy, offensive nuclear weapons to Cuba. But an NSA study of the Cuban Missile Crisis states unequivocally that "signals intelligence did *not* provide any direct information about the Soviet introduction of offensive missiles into Cuba."[46] The comprehensive security measures that the Soviets used to hide the shipment and placement of offensive ballistic missiles worked completely. An NSA history ruefully admits, "Soviet communications security was almost perfect."[47]

Across the Straits of Florida in Cuba, Major General Igor Dem'yanovich Statsenko, the commander of the Soviet missile forces there, was busy trying to get his nuclear-armed missiles operational. Construction of the missile

launch sites had begun in August 1962, but it was not until mid-September
that the Soviet merchant ships *Poltava* and *Omsk* arrived in Cuba carrying in
their holds thirty-six SS-4 medium-range ballistic missiles and their launchers. After their arrival, Soviet personnel moved sixteen of the missile launchers to four sites around the town of San Cristóbal, while eight more were
deployed to two sites around the town of Sagua la Grande, in central Cuba.[48]

The Soviet military went to extraordinary lengths to deny NSA access to any
form of communications traffic that might have given away the deployment of
Soviet troops and missiles to Cuba. Communications between Moscow and the
Russian merchant ships at sea and Soviet troops in Cuba were handled by
the Soviet merchant marine, with each ship reporting every morning to Moscow
on its location and status using a special one-time cipher system that NSA could
not crack. During the early phase of the Russian deployment to Cuba, all communications between Russian field units and the Soviet headquarters at Managua, outside Havana, were oral and delivered personally—never by radio or
telephone. Other than a few start-up tests of their communications equipment,
the Russian troops in Cuba maintained strict radio silence until October in order
to defeat the American listening posts located seventy miles away in southern
Florida.[49]

Having found no sign whatsoever of Soviet offensive weapons in Cuba, by
late September CIA intelligence analysts had concluded, on the basis of the
SIGINT they were getting from Juanita Moody's B1 shop at Fort Meade, plus
collateral material from other intelligence sources outside of NSA, that the Soviets were only engaged in an effort to establish, on a crash basis, modern
Soviet-style air defense and coastal defense systems in Cuba.[50]

On these subjects, NSA was continuing to produce plentiful amounts of
high-quality intelligence, almost entirely based on intercepts of Cuban radio
traffic and telephone calls, the most useful dealing with Cuban air force activity, including MiG training flights.[51] SIGINT reporting coming out of NSA
took on an ominous tone when the agency reported that on September 8 two
Cuban MiG fighters had attempted to intercept two U.S. Navy patrol aircraft
flying in international airspace off the coast of Cuba.[52] In late September, NSA
reported that Cuban MiG fighters were now routinely challenging American
reconnaissance aircraft flying off the coast of Cuba, and that multiple intercepts clearly showed that the ground controllers directing the Cuban fighters
to their targets were Russians.[53]

NSA was also producing a fair amount of intelligence reporting on the operational readiness of Soviet SA-2 SAMs in Cuba and the overall readiness of
the Cuban air defense system. The first radar signal, from an SA-2 SAM site

three miles west of the port of Mariel, was intercepted on September 15, 1962, although NSA's intercept operators could not find any radio traffic servicing the SAM sites. Five days later, a Fan Song radar tracking signal from another SA-2 SAM site in the Havana-Mariel area was intercepted, indicating that at least one of the twelve SAM sites in Cuba had become operational.[54]

NSA was also continuing to maintain a close watch on Russian merchant shipping traffic between the Soviet Union and Cuba. On September 13, CIA director McCone reported to the White House that according to COMINT and collateral maritime surveillance data, there were at least twenty-six Russian merchant ships on the high seas headed for Cuba.[55] On September 17, the CIA reported that since late July, Russian passenger ships had made nine un-scheduled and unpublicized round-trips to Cuba, and that two more Russian passenger ships were then en route there. The CIA estimated that these ships carried some forty-two hundred Russian military technicians.[56] On September 25, NSA reported that another thirteen Soviet merchant ships had been confirmed by COMINT as being en route to Cuba.[57]

Then in late September, the first indications began to appear in NSA's intelligence reporting that there were Soviet military personnel in Cuba above and beyond the trainers and military advisers that the Russians had maintained in Cuba since 1960. A declassified study of the Cuban Missile Crisis notes, "An intercept of the Soviet Air Force link in Hungary on 14 September stated that 'volunteers for the defense of Cuba' " were expected to "hand in applications [to volunteer]." Another message on the same link requested the number of volunteers who had applied. Similar intercepted calls for volunteers went out to Soviet military units stationed in Eastern Europe.[58]

The Missiles of October

On Thursday, October 4, 1962, Attorney General Robert Kennedy convened a special meeting of the team of CIA and other U.S. government officials who were running Operation Mongoose. Bobby Kennedy lit into the assembled officials, telling them that he had just discussed the efforts to unseat Castro with his brother, President Kennedy, who was "dissatisfied with [the] lack of action in the sabotage field" inside Cuba. The attorney general was angry that "nothing was moving forward" and demanded that the CIA redouble its efforts to cause havoc inside Cuba.[59]

Against this backdrop, NSA continued to plug away at what it could hear inside Cuba. On October 8, General Blake told Secretary McNamara that NSA was making excellent progress in its efforts to exploit Soviet and Cuban communications traffic inside Cuba.[60] The next day, an air force radio intercept unit in southern Florida intercepted the first Cuban radar tracking broadcasts, which indicated that the Cuban radar network and air surveillance system was now operational.[61] On October 10, NSA reported that Cuban radar stations had just begun passing radar tracking data to higher headquarters and to the various MiG air bases in Cuba in exactly the same manner as the Soviet air defense system.[62] And on October 11, NSA reported that thirteen more Soviet cargo ships were en route to Cuba.[63]

But on October 14, everything changed literally overnight. A CIA U-2 reconnaissance aircraft conducted a high-altitude overflight of Cuba and brought back the first clear pictures of six Russian SS-4 medium-range ballistic missiles at a launch site outside the town of San Cristóbal.[64] NSA played no part in launching this recon mission. Declassified documents show that it was a combination of CIA agent sources inside Cuba and interrogations of refugees in Florida that triggered the flight.[65] As incredible as it may sound, on October 16, the same day that President Kennedy and his top policy advisers were briefed on the presence of Soviet ballistic missiles in Cuba, Attorney General Kennedy, in a meeting at the Justice Department, again lambasted the men running Operation Mongoose. Opening the meeting by telling them of the "general dissatisfaction of the President" with their progress (or lack thereof), he announced that he was taking personal command of Mongoose to ensure that operations against Cuba were stepped up dramatically.[66]

At Fort Meade, the discovery of the SS-4 missiles in Cuba led to a week of unadulterated hell for the intelligence analysts. Every one of the agency's consumers was screaming for more information on the missiles in Cuba. "I could not believe all the demands for information that were coming in from everywhere," a former manager who worked in Juanita Moody's office recalled. "The U-2 had just discovered the damned missiles inside Cuba, and everyone expected us to have somewhere in our filing cabinets the answers to why they were there, what their targets were, how were they protected . . . But we had nothing in our files, zip, which was very hard for us to admit."[67]

To handle the massive new workload, on October 19 the head of NSA's Production Directorate, Major General John Davis, transferred over one hundred veteran Russian linguists and intelligence analysts from Herbert Conley's A Group, which handled the "Soviet problem," to Moody's office. Among them was Lieutenant Colonel Paul Odonovich, the deputy chief of the Office of Soviet Ground Forces Problems, who was ordered to take charge of Moody's Latin American Division, which was responsible for Cuba. Odonovich was not happy about his new job because, as he later admitted, he "didn't know [Cuba] from scratch." After the arrival of Odonovich and the dozens of analysts sent down from A Group's offices on the third floor of the NSA operations building, all of the elderly ladies who had run the Cuban shop since the end of World War II "kind of disappeared and went off to the side," recalled Harold Parish, one of the newly arrived A Group analysts.[68]

The *Oxford* was ordered to remain on station, monitoring Cuban internal telephone traffic around the clock. The USAF was ordered to increase the number of airborne reconnaissance missions it was flying off the coast of Cuba to monitor the rising volume of Soviet and Cuban air force and air defense radio traffic.[69]

But despite the added staff and increased collection resources at their disposal, Odonovich's analysts were still unable to find any communications links coming from inside Cuba that could be clearly identified as supporting the Russian ballistic missiles, which was what U.S. war planners desperately needed if they were ordered by the White House to destroy the Soviet missile launchers. This lack of success meant that the U.S. Intelligence Board's Guided Missile and Astronautics Intelligence Committee was compelled to report to President Kennedy and his advisers on October 18 and 19 that the command-and-control communications links for the Soviet ballistic missiles in Cuba had "not yet been found."[70]

Senior U.S. military commanders, who were preparing air strikes against military targets inside Cuba, were also asking NSA for any information about whether the air defense system in Cuba had become operational. When Joint Chiefs of Staff chairman General Taylor asked CIA director McCone at a White House meeting on October 18 whether NSA had detected any electronic emissions from the Soviet SA-2 SAM radars in Cuba, the answer he got was a qualified no, although the CIA's analysts believed that some of the SAMs in Cuba would become operational in a week. Unfortunately, this guesstimate was wrong. The very next day, an American reconnaissance aircraft orbiting off the northern coast of Cuba intercepted emissions from a Russian Fan Song radar associated with the SA-2 SAM—the first of the Soviet SAM air defense sites was now operational. General Taylor had to bring the bad news to President Kennedy.[71]

On October 21, the day before Kennedy publicly announced the presence of Soviet ballistic missiles in Cuba, NSA's General Davis declared a formal SIGINT alert, SIGINT Readiness Condition BRAVO, the equivalent of the U.S. military's DEFCON-2 . Moody and Odonovich shifted immediately to a sleepless 24-7 work schedule. For the next several weeks, nobody went home

except to shower or occasionally catch a meal before heading back to their office in the Ops 1 building at Fort Meade. Even that was a rarity. Odonovich recalled, "For six weeks I never had supper at home, everything was sent up
here." Moody said that she managed to catch a few hours of sleep every day on
a cot that was set up in her office. When General Blake came to her and asked
if he could help, she requested some additional staff to bear the crushing
workload. The next thing she heard was Blake on the telephone talking to off-
duty employees: "This is Gordon Blake calling for Mrs. Moody. Could you
come in to work now?"[72]

Maximum Effort

At seven P.M. on Monday, October 22, 1962, President Kennedy, in a nationally
televised broadcast, informed the American people that the Soviet Union had
placed offensive nuclear-armed missiles in Cuba that were capable of striking
targets throughout most of the United States. The president also declared an
immediate quarantine of Cuba and ordered the U.S. Navy to stop and search
any ships suspected of carrying weapons there. At the same moment that
Kennedy began his speech, all U.S. armed forces around the world went to
DEFCON-3 alert status. For the next two days, the world seemed to teeter on
the brink of nuclear disaster.

October 23 was a day that no one who was then working at NSA would ever
forget. Within hours of Kennedy's speech, the Russian military forces in Cuba
began to communicate openly among themselves and with Moscow.[73] Shortly
after midnight on the morning of October 23, NSA detected two high-level enciphered radioteletype links carrying communications traffic for the first time
between the Soviet Union and a Russian military radio station in Cuba located
near the town of Bauta, outside Havana. The first link appeared to be primarily associated with Russian naval radio traffic, while the second link, the analysts concluded, was reserved for high-level communications between
Moscow and the commander of the Soviet forces in Cuba.[74] At almost the
same time, a Soviet air defense radio network inside Cuba suddenly appeared
on the airwaves, which intercepts showed linked the commander of the Soviet
air defense forces in Havana with all Soviet radar stations, SA-2 Guideline
SAM sites, and AAA batteries throughout Cuba.[75] NSA also intercepted a
high-precedence message from the Soviet air force headquarters in Moscow
asking if the navigational beacons at a number of Soviet strategic-bomber dispersal bases in the Arctic were in proper working order. The intercept caused

chills in Washington, because the Russians never deployed strategic bombers to the Arctic dispersal bases except for exercises or during periods of heightened alert, and this was definitely not an exercise.[76] There was also a sudden and dramatic increase in Cuban military radio traffic immediately following the president's speech, with one intercepted message confirmed that the Cuban armed forces had just been placed on the "highest degree of alert."[77]

At one fifty-seven A.M., the Morse intercept operators at the U.S. Navy listening post in Cheltenham, Maryland, intercepted the first of a series of high-precedence messages sent by the Soviet merchant marine's main radio station, outside Odesa, to each of the twenty-two Soviet merchant ships or tankers heading for Cuba. The messages were apparently a warning for the ship captains to stand by to receive an extremely important message from Moscow. Twenty-five minutes later, at two twenty-two A.M., the intercept operators heard the first Morse code preamble of a high-priority enciphered message being sent from Moscow to all twenty-two ships. After finishing copying the lengthy message, the intercept operators immediately put it on the teletype and sent it to NSA headquarters at Fort Meade to see if the analysts could read it. Unfortunately, NSA's cryptanalysts could not read the cipher used with the message, but given that this particular cipher system was only used in emergencies, it appeared that whatever Moscow had told the Russian ships approaching the quarantine line that the U.S. Navy was manning around Cuba was important. So the American, Canadian, and British radio intercept operators at listening posts around the Atlantic periphery, together with the intelligence analysts at Fort Meade, got themselves ready for what they knew was going to be a very eventful day to come.[78]

They did not have long to wait. Starting at about five A.M., NSA's listening posts situated around the periphery of the Soviet Union began reporting that the level of Soviet military communications traffic throughout Russia and Eastern Europe was rising rapidly, indicating that the Soviet military had moved to a higher alert status. That afternoon, the U.S. Navy listening post in Key West, Florida, intercepted an order from the commander of Cuban naval forces instructing patrol boats to immediately take up patrol stations off the eastern Cuban coast at Banes and Santiago Bay.[79]

As the day progressed, the two dozen or so U.S. Navy, British, and Canadian direction-finding stations ringing the Atlantic continuously monitored every radio transmission going to or from the twenty-two Soviet merchant ships approaching the Cuba quarantine line, in order to track the movements of the Russian ships. By twelve noon, the U.S. Navy's direction-finding stations began reporting to NSA that their tracking data indicated that some of the Russian merchant ships had stopped dead in the water, and that it seemed that at least eight of the ships had reversed course and were headed back toward Russia. The SIGINT data, however, had not yet been confirmed by visual observation, so ONI did not forward the information to the White House, the Pentagon, or the CIA.[80]

The information about the Soviet ships would have certainly affected the discussion at a six P.M. meeting at the White House between President Kennedy and his national security advisers. As far as an increasingly apprehensive Kennedy and his advisers knew, the Soviet merchant ships were all still sailing straight for Cuba. But thanks to NSA, the president knew that something was afoot. Attorney General Kennedy later wrote in his memoirs, "During the course of this meeting, we learned that an extraordinary number of coded messages had been sent to all the Russian ships on their way to Cuba. What they said we did not know then, nor do we know now, but it was clear that the ships as of that moment were still straight on course."[81]

Later that evening, the director of ONI, Rear Admiral Vernon Lowrance, was informed of the latest intelligence about the courses of the Soviet merchant ships approaching Cuba, but for reasons not easily explained he decided not to inform the White House, the Pentagon, or the CIA until the reports had been verified by U.S. Navy warships and reconnaissance aircraft. CIA director McCone was awakened in the middle of the night by a telephone call from the CIA duty officer and was told that ONI was sitting on unconfirmed intelligence indicating that the Russian freighters had turned about before reaching the quarantine line.[82]

Wednesday, October 24, did not start well. At two thirty A.M. the Morse intercept operators at Cheltenham and other intercept stations began picking up the first parts of an extremely urgent message being sent from the Soviet merchant fleet's primary radio station at Odesa to all twenty-two Soviet cargo vessels and tankers sailing toward Cuba. A few minutes after the message ended, the captains of the Soviet vessels received another message from Odesa telling them that from that point onward "all orders would come from Moscow."[83]

At about the same time that this was happening, U.S. Navy listening posts picked up a series of burst radio transmissions from Moscow to a number of Soviet submarines operating in the North Atlantic, along with the replies from the submarines themselves. A "burst transmission" is one in which the message is compressed electronically and the information packed into the "burst" takes only seconds to be transmitted and received. NSA had been tracking the radio transmissions of these submarines since September 27, when SIGINT detected four Soviet Foxtrot-class attack submarines departing Northern Fleet naval bases on the Kola Peninsula for what was then thought to be a naval exercise in the Barents Sea.[84] But three weeks later, the subs reappeared. Not in the Barents Sea, but several hundreds of miles to the south, in the North Atlantic, escorting the Soviet merchant vessels approaching Cuba. Although NSA could not unscramble the transmissions, by examining the taped signals and direction-finding data, a team of analysts in NSA's Soviet Submarine Division headed by a talented cryptanalyst, Lieutenant Norman Klar, were able to ascertain that there were three or four Russian attack submarines operating in close proximity to the Soviet ships.[85]

At nine A.M., ONI finally informed the chief of naval operations, Admiral George Anderson, that preliminary direction-finding data coming from NSA indicated that some of the Russian merchant ships in the North Atlantic had either stopped dead in the water or reversed course. As incredible as it may sound, Anderson decided *not* to tell Secretary McNamara of this new intelligence for the same reason given earlier by Rear Admiral Lowrence of ONI—it had not been confirmed by visual sightings. A declassified Top Secret U.S. Navy history of the Cuban Missile Crisis states, "About 0900Q, [Secretary of Defense McNamara] received a standard merchant ship briefing. At the same time, Flag Plot in the Pentagon received the first directional fix report that some Soviet vessels bound for Cuba had reversed course. This information was inconclusive and Mr. McNamara was not informed."[86]

At President Kennedy's ten A.M. meeting at the White House with his senior national security advisers, the news delivered by CIA director McCone was not good. New U-2 imagery showed that the Russians had accelerated their work on completing the ballistic missile sites in Cuba, and the latest intelligence showed that twenty-two Russian merchant ships were still steaming toward the quarantine line. Inside the USSR and Eastern Europe, all indications appearing in SIGINT showed that the Russians were still bringing some but not all of their military forces to a higher state of readiness. NSA intercepts showed that Soviet air force flight activity was at normal peacetime levels, although Soviet strategic bomber flight activity was significantly below normal operating levels, and there were additional indications that the Russians were about to deploy a unit of strategic bombers to Arctic forward staging bases. Earlier that morning, a U.S. Navy listening post in southern Florida intercepted a directive from Cuban armed forces headquarters in Havana to all Cuban air defense units instructing them not to fire on American aircraft flying over Cuban airspace except in self-defense.[87]

It was not until noon that Admiral Anderson finally told Secretary McNamara that the latest direction-finding tracking data coming out of NSA had revealed that fourteen of the twenty-two Soviet merchant ships bound for Cuba had suddenly reversed course after receiving extended high-precedence enciphered radio transmissions from Moscow. By the end of the day, SIGINT and aerial surveillance had confirmed that all of the Soviet merchant ships bound for Cuba either had come to a dead halt in the water or had reversed course and were headed back to the Soviet Union.[88] When McNamara was told that the navy had sat on this critically important information for more than twelve hours without telling anyone, an NSA history reports, the secretary of defense "subjected Admiral Anderson, the Chief of Naval Operations, to an abusive tirade." Why the navy did not pass on this vital information remains a mystery. But the retreat of the Soviet merchant ships did not end the crisis.[89]

On Friday, October 26, NSA confirmed that all Soviet and Warsaw Pact ground and air forces in Eastern Europe and throughout the European portion of the Soviet Union had been placed on an increased state of alert. SIGINT also confirmed that some Soviet army units had suddenly left their barracks in East Germany and moved to concentration points closer to the border with West Germany; Soviet military exercises and training activity in East Germany had been stepped up; and even more Soviet tactical aircraft based in East Germany had been placed on five-minute-alert status. COMINT confirmed that an unknown number of ships and submarines from the Soviets' North and Baltic Sea Fleets had hastily sortied from their home ports, and that Soviet naval units had stepped up their surveillance of the entrance to the Baltic Sea.[90]

As the level of tension and apprehension increased, NSA director Blake became increasingly concerned about the close proximity of the *Oxford* to the Cuban shoreline, which left the unarmed ship highly vulnerable to attack by Cuban or Russian forces if war broke out. The Cubans had vigorously complained to the U.N. Security Council about the *Oxford*'s continued presence off Havana.[91] At a ten A.M. meeting with President Kennedy on October 26, the question of what to do with the *Oxford* came up, and Secretary McNamara urged the president to pull the ship back so as to prevent a possible incident. He later noted, "The Navy was very much concerned about the vulnerability of this ship and the loss of security if its personnel were captured . . . It seemed wise to draw it out 20, 30 miles to take it out of range of capture, at least temporarily."[92] The *Oxford* was ordered to pull back to a distance of thirty miles from the Cuban coastline until further notice.[93]

The Cuban Missile Crisis hit its peak on Saturday, October 27, which many NSA staffers remember as the scariest of the entire crisis, particularly for those at NSA headquarters, where the agency's intelligence analysts knew how dire the situation really was. NSA official Harold Parish, who was then working on the Cuban problem, recalled, "The [Soviet] ships were getting close to the [quarantine] lines . . . It was a scary time for those of us who had a little bit of access to information which wasn't generally available."[94] The news coming out of Fort Meade was ominous. NSA reported that its listening posts had detected the Cuban military mobilizing at a "high rate," but that these forces remained "under orders not to take any hostile action unless attacked." In East Germany, intercepted radio traffic showed that selected Russian combat units were continuing to increase their readiness levels, although no significant troop movements had been noted in SIGINT or other intelligence sources.[95]

Throughout Washington, there was heightened concern about the possibility of an armed incident taking place involving an American reconnaissance aircraft. On August 26 and 30, U-2 reconnaissance aircraft had accidentally penetrated Soviet airspace, the latter incident resulting in Russian MiGs scrambling to intercept the errant American plans. Then on September 8, a U-2 had been shot down by a Chinese SAM while over the mainland. Its Chinese Nationalist pilot was killed.[96]

On the afternoon of October 27, everyone's worst fears came true. At twelve noon, intercepts of Cuban radio traffic confirmed that a Soviet SA-2 SAM unit near Banes had shot down a U.S. Air Force U-2 reconnaissance aircraft. The U-2's pilot, Major Rudolf Anderson Jr., had been killed instantly. At six P.M., the Joint Chiefs of Staff were told, "Intercept says the Cubans have recovered body and wreckage of the U-2."[97] In April 1964, an analysis of traffic on that day suggested that the SAM site that brought down Anderson's aircraft might have been manned by trigger-happy Cubans. But no definitive conclusion was ever reached.[98]

However, SIGINT confirmed that within hours of Anderson's U-2 being shot down, the Soviets took over the entire Cuban air defense system lock, stock, and barrel. From that evening onward, only Russian-language commands, codes, call signs, and operating procedures were used on the air defense radio links. Intercepts also showed that within forty-eight hours Russian air defense troops physically took over all of the SA-2 SAM sites in Cuba. The same thing happened to the Cuban air force, whose voices overnight disappeared from the airwaves and were replaced by those of Russian pilots flying more advanced MiG-21 fighters.[99]

On Sunday, October 28, fresh U-2 reconnaissance imagery showed that all twenty-four medium-range ballistic missile launchers in Cuba were now fully operational. And on the same day, NSA intercepted a number of messages from

the Cuban Ministry of Armed Forces addressed to all Cuban air defense and antiaircraft units, reminding them to continue to obey an edict from October 23
"not to open fire unless attacked." NSA also intercepted a radio transmission
made by the head of the Las Villas province militia ordering that "close surveillance be maintained over militiamen and severe measures be taken with those
who demonstrate lack of loyalty towards the present regime." On the other side
of the Atlantic, intercepted radio traffic showed that Soviet forces in East Germany remained in a state of "precautionary defensive readiness." Intelligence
from NSA's Soviet Submarine Division at Fort Meade showed that the number
of Soviet attack submarines at sea was higher than normal, but none were detected leaving Soviet home waters and heading for Cuba.[100]

Meanwhile, the Cubans struck back. On the night of October 28, saboteurs
blew up four electrical substations in western Venezuela that were owned by
the American oil company Creole Corporation, resulting in the temporary
loss of one sixth of Venezuela's daily oil production of three million barrels.
The previous afternoon, an NSA listening post had intercepted a radio transmission from a clandestine transmitter located somewhere near Havana ordering a number of unknown addressees in South America to destroy "any
kind of Yankee property." The same directive was also broadcast on October
28 and 30. CIA analysts soberly concluded, "Further attempts at sabotage elsewhere in Latin America can be expected." They were right. On October 29 in
Santiago, Chile, a bomb that was meant to blow up the U.S. embassy exploded
prematurely, killing the bomb maker.[101]

Conclusions

The bomb blasts marked, at least from NSA's perspective, the end of the
Cuban Missile Crisis. Despite the agency's many important contributions, it is
now clear that the crisis was in fact anything but an intelligence success story.
Because NSA was unable to read high-level Soviet cipher systems, it was not
able to give an advance warning of Soviet intentions before the first Soviet
merchant ships carrying the missiles headed for Cuba. According to a former
NSA intelligence analyst, the agency failed to detect the disappearance, in internal Soviet communications traffic, of the Fifty-first Rocket Division before
it appeared in Cuba in October 1962. Moreover, NSA failed to detect the disappearance of five complete medium-range and intermediate-range missile
regiments from their peacetime home bases inside the Soviet Union before
they too were detected inside Cuba in October. The agency intercepted only

one low-level Russian message that vaguely suggested that the Russians were thinking of deploying missiles to Cuba.[102]

But most important of all, SIGINT did not pick up any indication whatsoever that the Russian ballistic missiles were in Cuba before they were detected by the CIA's U-2 spy planes. A recently declassified NSA history concludes that the Cuban Missile Crisis "marked the most significant failure of SIGINT to warn national leaders since World War II."[103]

CHAPTER 6

Errors of Fact and Judgment

SIGINT and the Gulf of Tonkin Incidents

*Behold, how great a matter a little fire
kindleth.*

—JAMES 3:5

The 1964 Gulf of Tonkin Crisis is an important episode in the history of both NSA and the entire U.S. intelligence community because it demonstrated all too clearly two critical points that were to rear their ugly head again forty years later in the 2003 Iraqi weapons of mass destruction scandal. The first was that under intense political pressure, intelligence collectors and analysts will more often than not choose as a matter of political expediency *not* to send information to the White House that they know will anger the president of the United States. The second was that intelligence information, if put in the wrong hands, can all too easily be misused or misinterpreted if a system of analytic checks and balances are not in place and rigidly enforced.[1]

OPLAN 34A

Between 1958 and 1962, the CIA had sent a number of agents into North Vietnam. The first agents were assigned just to collect intelligence. Then, starting in 1960, teams of South Vietnamese agents trained by the CIA were infiltrated into North Vietnam to conduct sabotage as well as collect intelligence. With very few exceptions, these agent insertion operations were complete failures. The North Vietnamese security services captured the agents almost as soon as they arrived. Between 1961 and 1968, the CIA and the Defense Department lost 112 agents who were parachuted into North Vietnam, as well as a number of the C-54, C-123, and C-130 transport aircraft used to drop them.

Secretary of Defense Robert McNamara's typically understated comment on the agent drop program was "Nothing came of any of it."[2]

After this dismal performance, in July 1962 the management of all covert operations against North Vietnam was transferred from the CIA to the Defense Department. On January 1, 1963, control of the conduct of covert action operations inside North Vietnam was given to the U.S. Army's super-secret clandestine intelligence unit in Vietnam, the Military Assistance Command Vietnam Studies and Observation Group (MACVSOG). Pursuant to a Top Secret operations plan designated OPLAN 34-63, put together by the staff of the Commander in Chief, Pacific (CINCPAC), in Hawaii, U.S.-backed raids against the North Vietnamese coastline by South Vietnamese commandos commenced in the fall of 1963. But the results produced by these raids were disappointing, and in December 1963 MACVSOG went back to the drawing board and devised a new plan, OPLAN 34A, which included an even greater level of South Vietnamese participation and U.S. Navy support. In January 1964, the U.S. Navy set up a secret base in Da Nang to train South Vietnamese military personnel to conduct maritime commando raids against the North Vietnamese coastline with two PT boats provided by MACVSOG.[3]

Incredibly, virtually no one in NSA's Office of Asian Nations (B2), which was responsible for monitoring developments in North Vietnam, was cleared for access to details of OPLAN 34A, including its head, Milton Zaslow. Years later, Zaslow would tell a group of NSA historians, "None of us had been cleared for 34A, and we did not know that there were actions underway."[4]

But a few officials within NSA knew about OPLAN 34A and were tasked with secretly providing SIGINT support for the MACVSOG commando raids under the name Project Kit Kat. Inside South Vietnam, some 130 army, navy, and air force SIGINT operators were engaged full-time in monitoring North Vietnamese communications as part of Kit Kat, including a highly secretive unit at Tan Son Nhut Air Base, outside Saigon, called the Special Support Group, whose job was to feed SIGINT reporting concerning North Vietnamese reactions to the OPLAN 34A raids to MACVSOG headquarters in Saigon.[5]

In Washington a fierce debate was raging within the U.S. intelligence community about whether to release to the public information, including SIGINT, "demonstrating to the world the extent of control exercised by Hanoi over the Viet Cong in SVN [South Vietnam] and Pathet Lao forces in Laos." The available intelligence showed that Hanoi was supplying and equipping the guerrillas both by sea and by the Ho Chi Minh Trail. But the U.S. intelligence community refused to even consider releasing any SIGINT, warning, "Should it become public knowledge that we are successfully exploiting North Vietnamese communications, not only the Vietnamese but the [Chinese] can be expected to take additional security measures."[6]

Back in Southeast Asia, the second round of MACVSOG commando raids on the North Vietnamese coast was proving to be no more successful than the first round. During the spring of 1964, North Vietnamese security forces inflicted severe losses on the OPLAN 34A maritime commando forces and bagged the few remaining agents left in North Vietnam. Testifying in a closed session before the House Armed Services Committee, CIA director John McCone admitted that there had been "many disappointments with these operations with a number of teams rolled up" and that sabotage efforts had "not been too significant."[7]

In fact, as a declassified NSA history reveals, these commando raids had only served to piss the North Vietnamese off and "raised Hanoi's determination to meet them head on." The volume of North Vietnamese naval radio traffic went through the roof every time there was a commando raid, with the intercepts indicating a determination by the North Vietnamese to annihilate the attackers. But the pressure from Washington for quick results meant that the intelligence warnings of North Vietnamese resolve were ignored, and new, larger, and more aggressive commando raids were immediately planned for the summer. Looking back at these events, it is clear that both sides were charging rapidly toward an inevitable clash that would lead to war.[8]

In Harm's Way

On July 3, 1964, the new commander of U.S. forces in South Vietnam, General William Westmoreland, cabled Washington with his intelligence requirements in support of OPLAN 34A. Westmoreland urgently requested more intelligence collection regarding North Vietnamese coastal defense and naval forces, which had been plaguing the American-led 34A Special Operations Forces. Westmoreland also required details concerning North Vietnamese coastal radars that could detect and track the 34A patrol and speed boats operating along the North Vietnamese coast. In particular, intelligence coverage was requested for those areas in North Vietnam scheduled as targets for OPLAN 34A commando raids in July, specifically the area around the city of Vinh and the islands of Hon Me, Hon Nieu, and Hon Matt, further up the coast.[9]

The principal means available in the Far East at the time to gather this kind of intelligence was to use U.S. Navy destroyers carrying a SIGINT detachment and special radio intercept gear to slowly cruise off the enemy's coastline ferreting out secrets. These secret destroyer reconnaissance patrols were known by the code name Desoto.[10] The first of these Desoto destroyer reconnaissance patrols was conducted off the coast of China in April 1962. By July 1964, the Navy had conducted sixteen Desoto patrols without serious incident, all but two of which were focused on the Soviet and Chinese coastlines.[11]

Responding to Westmoreland's request, on July 10, Admiral Ulysses S.G. Sharp Jr., the newly appointed commander of CINCPAC in Hawaii, approved a destroyer reconnaissance patrol of the North Vietnamese coast and forwarded the request to the 303 Committee, the secret committee in Washington that then supervised all sensitive covert and clandestine intelligence activities conducted by the U.S. intelligence community. After a perfunctory review, the 303 Committee approved the patrol on July 15 and a host of other sensitive reconnaissance operations proposed for initiation in August, with the Desoto patrol getting under way no later than July 31, to determine the nature and extent of North Vietnam's naval patrol activity along its coastline.[12]

On July 18, CINCPAC selected the destroyer USS *Maddox* (DD-731), then in port at Keelung, to conduct the August Desoto patrol off North Vietnam. The twenty-two-hundred-ton *Maddox* was a World War II–vintage Alan M. Sumner–class destroyer built in Bath, Maine, and commissioned on June 2, 1944. She served with distinction during World War II in the Pacific, taking a hit from a Japanese kamikaze on January 21, 1945, which kept her out of action for two months. She served in support of U.N. forces during the Korean War and continued operating in various parts of the Pacific until 1974. She carried a crew of 336 officers and enlisted men, and her main armament were six twin-mounted five-inch guns and four twin-mounted three-inch antiaircraft guns mounted on raised platforms behind the rear smokestack, which had been added in the mid-1950s in place of her original complement of forty-millimeter and twenty-millimeter AA guns. The *Maddox* was chosen for the mission because her old torpedo tubes, which had taken up the entire 0-1 deck between the two smokestacks, had been removed in the 1950s and replaced by two antisubmarine "hedgehogs" located on either side of the bridge. This meant that the entire torpedo deck was free for modules that housed electronic surveillance equipment and the military and NSA personnel who operated them, in what was known as a SIGINT COMVAN.[13]

The primary mission of the *Maddox* was to collect intelligence on North Vietnamese naval forces, monitor North Vietnamese coastal radar stations, and try to ascertain whether junks based in North Vietnam were helping infiltrate supplies and equipment into South Vietnam. Only four officers on board were cleared for access to SIGINT: the task force commander, Captain John Herrick; the ship's captain, Captain Herbert Ogier Jr.; Herrick's flag lieutenant; and Ogier's executive officer. All four officers were briefed in general terms about the OPLAN 34A commando operations then taking place against North Vietnam, but they were deliberately not told about the forthcoming 34A raids that would coincide with their mission. As with the *John R. Craig*'s patrol in the Gulf of Tonkin four months earlier, CINCPAC ordered that the destroyer come no closer than eight miles from the North Vietnamese coastline, but the *Maddox* was permitted to come within four miles of islands off the coast, which as it turned out were key targets of the forthcoming raids.[14]

Captain Norman Klar, the commander of the U.S. Navy SIGINT unit in Taiwan—Naval Security Group Activity, Taipei—gave Captains Herrick and Ogier, as well as their staff officers, a pre-mission intelligence briefing on the North Vietnamese order of battle. At the end of the briefing, Ogier asked Klar only one question: "Will my ship be attacked?" This, according to Klar's memoirs, written years later, was his response: "I said 'No.' You are not the first DESOTO patrol in the Gulf. There has been absolutely no hostile action taken by the Vietnamese in the past, and I believe that will continue." Klar went on to admit that his assessment turned out to be horribly incorrect, saying, "Talk about being wrong!"[15]

The "business end" of the *Maddox*'s secret intelligence mission arrived on July 24, when a massive shipyard crane lifted a ten-ton SIGINT COMVAN off the deck of the destroyer USS *George K. MacKenzie*, which had just returned to Keelung from an intelligence collection mission off the Soviet coastline, and placed it on the torpedo deck of the *Maddox* between the ship's two smokestacks. The *Maddox*'s crew, who had watched with undisguised interest as the heavily guarded van was lowered onto their ship, were ordered not to enter the restricted area around the COMVAN or to ask any questions about what it was there for. Inside the air-conditioned gray van were three radio intercept positions and a communications position linking the van with NSA and local listening posts. Several intercept antennae were mounted on the roof of the van, while other antennae were hastily strung between the van and the *Maddox*'s smokestacks. Accompanying the COMVAN was a fifteen-man detachment of navy and marine intercept operators under the command of a twenty-eight-year-old Texan named Lieutenant Gerrell "Gary" Moore, a Chinese linguist whose regular billet was assistant operations officer at the U.S. Navy listening post in Taiwan at Shu Lin Kou Air Station, west of Taipei. Their job was to warn the *Maddox* of any danger to the ship and to collect SIGINT concerning North

Vietnamese naval activity of interest to theater of operations and national intelligence consumers.[16]

At eight in the morning on July 28, the *Maddox* departed from Keelung. For three days it steamed southward along the southern Chinese coast and around the Chinese island of Hainan in the Gulf of Tonkin. The embarked Naval Security Group personnel used the time to check their equipment and monitor Chinese radio traffic and radar emissions from the east coast of Hainan as the *Maddox* headed for "Yankee Station," off the coast of North Vietnam.[17]

Unbeknownst to the men on the *Maddox*, shortly before midnight on the evening of July 30, four South Vietnamese "Nasty"-class patrol boats working for MACVSOG attacked North Vietnamese coastal defense positions on Hon Me and Hon Nieu Islands.[18] Although the damage inflicted by the patrol boats was slight, the North Vietnamese reacted violently to the attack, with SIGINT showing that the four patrol craft were pursued for a time by as many as four North Vietnamese Swatow-class patrol vessels. The captain of the North Vietnamese Swatow vessel T-142 later radioed that the boats had been unable to catch the South Vietnamese craft, had ceased the pursuit, and were returning to base. This encrypted message, sent in Morse code, was intercepted by the U.S. Navy listening post at San Miguel in the Philippines, decrypted, translated, and sent via teletype to NSA headquarters at Fort Meade.[19]

At seven twenty A.M. on Friday, July 31, only a few hours after the OPLAN 34A attack on Hon Me and Hon Nieu Islands had taken place, the *Maddox* refueled from the tanker USS *Ashtabula* east of the demilitarized zone (DMZ), then steamed northward along the North Vietnamese coast on its assigned patrol track. During the refueling, lookouts on the *Maddox* spotted the South Vietnamese patrol craft that had attacked Hon Me and Hon Nieu moving south at maximum speed toward their base at Da Nang.[20]

For the next two days, the *Maddox* sailed northward at a leisurely pace, spending most of July 31 off Hon Gio Island near the DMZ, then the morning of August 1 off the port of Vinh Son, before reaching its third orbit point ("Point Charlie") off Hon Me Island just as the sun was setting, at seven P.M. As noted above, Hon Me had been attacked by South Vietnamese Nasty patrol boats two nights earlier. Up to this point, the two-day cruise along the North Vietnamese coast had been uneventful. But unbeknownst to the *Maddox*, North Vietnamese radar stations were closely following the ship's movements.[21]

Shortly before midnight (eleven twenty-seven P.M.) on August 1, U.S. Navy radio intercept operators at San Miguel and Phu Bai, in South Vietnam, intercepted a North Vietnamese radio message. It took almost three hours to decrypt, then translate the message. When fully translated, it turned out to be a high-priority message from the North Vietnamese Southern Fleet headquarters at Ben Thuy to an entity designated only as "255," stating that it had "decided to fight the enemy tonight." The San Miguel analysts were pretty sure the "enemy" referred to was the *Maddox*.[22] A few minutes later, a second message was intercepted by the San Miguel listening post that confirmed it. Shortly after that, at one fifty-five A.M. on August 2, San Miguel intercepted a third message revealing that three Russian-made P-4 PT boats had been dispatched from nearby Thanh Hoa naval base to reinforce the three Swatow-class patrol boats already operating in the Hon Me–Hon Nieu area, where the *Maddox* was cruising.[23]

At two twenty-four A.M., San Miguel forwarded a summary of the translated "fight the enemy tonight" intercept to the COMVAN on the *Maddox*. A few minutes later, Lieutenant Moore, the commander of the COMVAN, woke Captains Herrick and Ogier in their staterooms and informed them of the new intelligence. The report unsettled Herrick, who concluded that the *Maddox* was about to be attacked. At two fifty-four A.M., Herrick sent a FLASH-precedence message to the commander of the U.S. Seventh Fleet in Japan stating, "Contemplate serious reaction my movements [vicinity] Pt. Charlie in near future. Received info indicating possible hostile action." Without waiting for a reply from the Seventh Fleet, Herrick ordered general quarters sounded on the *Maddox* and shifted course to the east. While the crew took up battle stations, the destroyer sped away from the North Vietnamese coast and the threatened attack at flank speed.[24]

Despite the urgent request from the on-scene commander to cancel the remainder of the patrol because of "unacceptable risk," Herrick was directed to resume the patrol by the commander of the Seventh Fleet. The *Maddox* reached "Point Delta," off the port and naval base of Thanh Hoa, at nine forty-five A.M. and prepared for an eight-hour orbit just off Hon Me Island. But the cautious Herrick refused to allow the *Maddox* to come as close to the North Vietnamese coastline as he had the previous day, keeping his ship out of harm's way as best he could.[25]

At two past ten A.M. as the *Maddox* sailed toward Hon Me Island, an urgent message titled "Possible Planned Attack by DRV Navy on Desoto Patrol" was sent from NSA to CINCPAC and the Seventh Fleet—but strangely enough, the COMVAN on the *Maddox* was not on the distribution list. The NSA message noted that an intercepted July 31 North Vietnamese message detailing the damage caused by the OPLAN 34A attack on Hon Me also "indicated DRV [North Vietnamese] intentions and preparations to repulse further such attacks." As a result, NSA concluded that the North Vietnamese "reaction to Desoto patrol might be more severe than would otherwise be anticipated" because the North Vietnamese had connected the July 31 commando raid with the presence of the *Maddox*. The problem was that the *Maddox* did not know this.[26]

At eleven thirty A.M., an hour and a half after the NSA warning message was issued, three North Vietnamese P-4 PT boats (T-333, T-336, and T-339 from Division 3 of PT Squadron 135) were spotted by the *Maddox*'s lookouts arriving at Hon Me Island. A few minutes later, the *Maddox* spotted two Swatow patrol boats (T-142 and T-146) entering Hon Me cove. In response to the arrival of these vessels, at eleven thirty-eight the *Maddox* shifted course to the northeast and moved toward its next patrol orbit point, designated "Point Echo," in order to put some distance between it and the five North Vietnamese boats. By two P.M., the *Maddox* was fifteen miles from the North Vietnamese coastline on course for Point Echo, moving northward at a leisurely ten knots.[27]

At two sixteen P.M., Lieutenant Moore raced to the bridge of the *Maddox* carrying yet another single slip of paper. It was a CRITIC message just issued by the listening post at San Miguel, and it reported that two and a half hours earlier the North Vietnamese navy headquarters had ordered the five warships at Hon Me Island to attack "the enemy and use torpedoes."[28] Despite the fact that this was the second attack order that had been intercepted that day, Captains Herrick and Ogier concluded that an attack on the *Maddox* was indeed imminent, and at two twenty-three Ogier ordered the *Maddox* to shift course to the east and make best speed for the safety of the open waters at the mouth of the Gulf of Tonkin.[29]

The veracity of the information contained in the intercept was confirmed seven minutes later when the *Maddox*'s radar operators detected three North Vietnamese torpedo boats thirty miles to the southwest headed directly toward the *Maddox* at thirty knots. At the time, the *Maddox* was twenty-two miles off the coast of North Vietnam and moving at eleven knots to the east away from the coastline. When the torpedo boats came within twenty miles of the *Maddox*, at two thirty, P.M., Ogier ordered general quarters sounded and increased the ship's speed to twenty-five knots, moving the destroyer's course further to the southeast so as to present a smaller target to the torpedo boats directly behind him. At two forty P.M., Herrick sent a FLASH precedence message to the commander of the Seventh Fleet reporting, "I am being approached by high-speed craft with apparent intention of torpedo attack. Intend to open fire if necessary in self-defense."[30]

By three P.M., the North Vietnamese PT boats were only five miles from the *Maddox* and continuing to close at their maximum attack speed of fifty knots.

At five past three, as the PT boats moved into attack formation at a distance of 9,800 yards from the destroyer to begin their torpedo runs, the *Maddox* fired three warning shots from her five-inch guns across the bow of the lead PT boat. When the boats continued on their attack run, at seven past three the *Maddox* radioed that it was under attack and opened fire on the attackers with all its main batteries.[31]

Two of the PT boats launched their torpedoes from a distance of 2,700 yards, forcing the *Maddox* to take evasive action while continuing to fire on the attackers with its main batteries. Just as the third PT boat launched its torpedoes, it took a direct hit from one of the *Maddox*'s five-inch guns and was reduced to a fiery furnace. At about the same time, four U.S. Navy F-8E Crusader fighters from the aircraft carrier USS *Ticonderoga* arrived on the scene and attacked the PT boats, which were damaged and retiring from the battle. Under the cover of the air attack, the *Maddox* took the opportunity to withdraw from the scene and make for the mouth of the Gulf of Tonkin.

When the thirty-seven-minute battle was over, the *Maddox* had fired more than 250 five-inch and three-inch shells. One of the North Vietnamese PT boats was dead in the water and burning fiercely. The other two torpedo boats had withdrawn back to Hon Me after having suffered extensive damage. For its part, the *Maddox* had been hit by only a single machine gun bullet.

News of the North Vietnamese attack on the *Maddox* began rolling across the teletypes in the communications centers at the White House, the CIA, and the State and Defense Departments shortly after five A.M. Eastern Daylight Time (EDT) on Monday, August 2. President Lyndon Johnson was informed of the attack before he sat down to breakfast at nine. At a meeting with his national security advisers in the Oval Office at eleven thirty A.M., senior NSA officials briefed Johnson, Secretary of Defense McNamara, Secretary of State Dean Rusk, and the chairman of the Joint Chiefs of Staff (JCS), General Earle Wheeler, on the available SIGINT concerning the attack. CIA director McCone was notably but mystifyingly not invited to attend the meeting. A review of the evidence convinced those present that the attack had probably been ordered by overzealous North Vietnamese naval commanders, leading Johnson not to opt for retaliation despite pressure from the South Vietnamese government and the American ambassador in Saigon to do so. Instead, Johnson decided on a more restrained response. Seeking to show strength and resolve, he ordered the *Maddox* to resume its patrol, this time reinforced by the destroyer USS *C. Turner Joy*, but both ships were instructed to stay at least eleven miles from the North Vietnamese coastline at all times. Continuous air cover for the patrol was to be supplied by the carrier *Ticonderoga*, stationed nearby in the Gulf of Tonkin, and the aircraft carrier USS *Constellation* was ordered from Hong Kong to rein-force the *Ticonderoga*. Johnson then called news reporters into the Oval Of-fice and announced that the United States intended to continue the Desoto patrol, and that any repetition of the August 2 attack would have "dire con-sequences."[32]

Johnson's national security officials had already come to the conclusion that the North Vietnamese had attacked the *Maddox* because, as SIGINT showed, Hanoi had connected the presence of the destroyer off the coast with the OPLAN 34A commando raids. With more raids scheduled for that night and the next three days, and despite suggestions from a few officials at the State Department that the raids be temporarily suspended to defuse the situation, Johnson and his key national security advisers concluded that the raids should continue because they were "beginning to rattle Hanoi and [the] *Maddox* inci-dent [was] directly related to their effort to resist these activities." Determined to show resolve, Johnson and his advisers ordered the Desoto patrol to con-tinue and the tempo of the OPLAN 34A attacks to be intensified.[33]

At twelve fifteen P.M. EDT (eleven fifteen P.M. Gulf of Tonkin, or GOT, time), NSA headquarters issued orders to the headquarters of NSA Pacific in Hawaii and to all army, navy, and air force listening posts in the western Pa-cific, declaring a SIGINT Readiness Condition BRAVO, which was a height-ened state of alert comparable to the DEFCON alert system utilized by the JCS. Under this elevated SIGINT Readiness Condition, which was designated Lantern, all NSA intercept stations in the Pacific were ordered to intensify their collection efforts against North Vietnamese communications in support of the ongoing Desoto patrol and were directed to report immediately by CRITIC-priority message any reflections appearing in COMINT of North Vietnamese or Chinese military reactions to the Desoto patrol.[34]

The events of August 2, 1964, showed NSA at its most impressive. The offi-cial NSA history of the affair reports, "The SIGINT community could be proud of its efforts during the day. The field sites and NSA had intercepted, pro-cessed, and reported North Vietnamese naval communications in such a rapid and clear way that everyone in the Pacific command was aware of the approach-ing attack."[35] But it was at the tactical level that NSA's efforts mattered most. Dr. Edwin Moïse, a historian at Clemson University who has studied the Gulf of Tonkin incident for almost ten years, concluded that the interception of the North Vietnamese attack order gave the *Maddox* a crucial advantage over the North Vietnamese, since it allowed the destroyer's captain to change course in time, forcing the Vietnamese PT boats to attack the destroyer from the rear.

This minimized the target that the unfortunate North Vietnamese commander could hit and at the same time presented the PT boats with the full force of the destroyer's weaponry.[36]

Interregnum: August 3, 1964

At six thirty A.M. local time on Monday, August 3, the *Maddox*, accompanied by the newly arrived destroyer *C. Turner Joy*, resumed its patrol in the Gulf of Tonkin, heading once again for Point Charlie off the island of Hon Me. Captain Herrick's recommendation that the patrol be canceled because of the likelihood of a North Vietnamese attack was rejected by higher authorities, and he was ordered to resume the patrol. The cruise northward was uneventful except for the interception of Skinhead radar emissions at two twenty P.M. Ensign Frederick Frick, who was the watch officer in the *Maddox*'s combat information center, recalled, "We knew there was a bad guy [Swatow patrol boat] out there. And we knew there were three or four more of them."[37]

Two hours later, a North Vietnamese Swatow patrol boat (T-142) began shadowing the two American destroyers, periodically reporting the positions of the *Maddox* and the *Turner Joy* to headquarters by radio, messages that were intercepted by NSA listening posts in South Vietnam and the Philippines. After completing his assigned patrol orbit off Hon Me, at four twenty-seven P.M. Herrick ordered the *Maddox* to retire to the mouth of the Gulf of Tonkin for the night before resuming its patrol along the coastline in the morning.[38]

That night, from ten fifty-two to two past eleven P.M., South Vietnamese PT boats belonging to MACVSOG bombarded North Vietnamese coastal installations, specifically a radar site at Vinh Son and a coastal defense installation at Mui Ron. These OPLAN 34A attacks were sure to elicit a military response from the North Vietnamese. On their return to Da Nang, the South Vietnamese boats were pursued for an hour by a North Vietnamese patrol boat.[39]

Early the next morning, COMINT began picking up the first North Vietnamese military reactions to the Vinh Son–Mui Ron raids that had taken place a few hours earlier. Radio intercepts collected by Marine Corps intercept operators at Phu Bai revealed that the North Vietnamese navy headquarters in Haiphong had connected the presence of the two American destroyers in the Gulf of Tonkin with the OPLAN 34A raids on Vinh Son and Mui Ron and that a response was anticipated.[40]

The Phantom Battle of August 4, 1964

After a long and sleepless night, at six A.M. on August 4 the *Maddox* and the *Turner Joy* resumed their patrol, making for the North Vietnamese coastline two hundred miles above the DMZ.

On the *Maddox*, Captain Herrick was decidedly unhappy about the position he had been placed in by his superiors, and he decided to take action to protect his command based on what had happened to the *Maddox* two days previously. Although unaware of the OPLAN 34A attacks that had taken place just a few hours earlier, Herrick was nevertheless concerned that the day's patrol track called for him to once again orbit off Hon Me Island, where he knew a force of North Vietnamese PT boats was based that could easily attack the destroyers with little or no warning. At eight forty A.M., Herrick sent the following message to Seventh Fleet headquarters in Japan:

> Evaluation of info from various sources indicates that the DRV considers patrol directly involved with 34A operations and have already indicated readiness to treat us in that category.
>
> DRV are very sensitive about Hon Me. Believe this PT operating base and the cove there presently contains numerous patrol and PT craft which have been repositioned from northerly bases.
>
> Under these conditions 15 min. reaction time for operating air cover is unacceptable. Cover must be overhead and controlled by DD's at all times.[41]

Admiral Thomas Moorer, the commander of the Pacific Fleet in Hawaii, read Herrick's message and fired off an angry cable of his own to CINCPAC, recommending the continuation of the Desoto patrol and arguing, "Termination of Desoto patrol after two days of patrol ops subsequent to Maddox incident . . . does not in my view adequately demonstrate United States resolve to assert our legitimate rights in these international waters." What had started out as a simple intelligence collection mission had now become a matter of asserting freedom of navigation on the high seas, as well as not showing any sign of weakness in the face of North Vietnamese belligerence.[42]

Herrick's sense of apprehension was heightened when at nine thirty A.M. the radar operators on the *Maddox* and the *Turner Joy* picked up a radar contact of a "bogey" (unidentified surface craft) paralleling the course of the two American destroyers, but then the target disappeared as quickly as it had appeared.

Herrick concluded that his task force of destroyers was being shadowed by at least one Swatow patrol boat.

The destroyers reached Point Delta, off Thanh Hoa, at eleven forty-five. They then shifted course to the south and followed a course parallel to the North Vietnamese coastline down to a point opposite Hon Me, coming no closer than sixteen miles from the coast. On the cruise southward, the radar operators on the two ships picked up a few contacts, but otherwise the patrol was uneventful. After a tension-filled day with little intelligence to show for the effort, a relieved Herrick called off the patrol at four P.M. and ordered a change of course to the east and the middle of the Gulf of Tonkin, well away from the coastline, with the intention of resuming the patrol the following morning.[43]

At six fifteen, a little more than two hours after Herrick had called it a day, the NSA listening post at Phu Bai sent to the COMVAN on the *Maddox* a CRITIC message stating, "Poss DRV naval operations planned against the Desoto patrol tonite 04 Aug[ust]. Amplifying data [follows]." Twenty-five minutes later, Phu Bai sent a follow-up report, which stated, "Imminent plans of DRV naval action possibly against Desoto mission," adding that intercept messages revealed that two hours earlier three North Vietnamese Swatow patrol boats had been ordered to "make ready for military operations the night of 4 August."[44]

Once again, Lieutenant Moore raced from the COMVAN to the bridge of the *Maddox* to hand-deliver the report to Captains Herrick and Ogier. Both men concluded that the intercept was an authentic order to attack the destroyers. At seven thirty P.M., Herrick ordered the two destroyers to increase speed from twelve to twenty knots in the hope of reaching the mouth of the Gulf of Tonkin before the pursuing North Vietnamese could catch up to them. Ten minutes later, Herrick radioed the captain of the aircraft carrier *Ticonderoga*, steaming nearby, that he had received "info indicating attack by PGM/P-4 imminent. My position 19-107N 107-003E [60 miles southeast of Hon Me]. Proceeding southeast at best speed." He described the source of this information as simply "an intelligence source."[45]

Less than a minute after Herrick's message to the *Ticonderoga* went out, the radar operators on the *Maddox* picked up an intermittent surface contact (or "skunk") forty-two miles to the northeast, which was where both destroyers had anchored the previous evening. Fearing a trap, at seven forty-six P.M. Herrick ordered the *Maddox* and the *Turner Joy* to shift course away from the reported radar contacts. But Herrick was unable to shake his pursuers.[46]

Four minutes after the *Maddox* and the *Turner Joy* changed course, at eight fifty A.M. EDT in Washington, Secretary McNamara and the chairman of the

JCS, General Wheeler, were briefed on the contents of the Phu Bai CRITIC message. At nine twelve A.M., McNamara informed President Johnson of the indications coming from Fort Meade that the North Vietnamese intended to attack the *Maddox* and the *Turner Joy*. Wheeler telephoned Admiral Sharp at CINCPAC headquarters and told him to ensure that the captain of the *Ticonderoga*, which was stationed off the coast fifteen minutes by air from the two destroyers, was apprised of the situation and to authorize the carrier commander to take "positive aggressive measures to seek and destroy attacking forces if the attack should occur."[47] McNamara did not waste any time beginning to plan a retaliatory strike. At nine twenty-five A.M. EDT, only thirteen minutes after he had spoken to Johnson, McNamara called a meeting in his office attended by his deputy, Cyrus Vance, and representatives of the JCS to discuss possible retaliatory measures if the North Vietnamese should attack the *Maddox* and the *Turner Joy*.[48]

In the Gulf of Tonkin, events moved with astonishing speed. At eight thirty-six P.M. (nine thirty-six A.M. EDT), Captain Herrick radioed that the radar operators on the *Maddox* and the *Turner Joy* were tracking two unidentified surface contacts and three unidentified aircraft. The unidentified aircraft disappeared from the radar screens, but the radar operators on the two destroyers reported that the surface contacts were coming ever closer at speeds of between thirty-five and forty knots. At nine thirty-nine P.M., the *Turner Joy* opened fire on a radar contact believed to have been a North Vietnamese PT boat that had closed to within seven thousand yards. She was joined almost immediately by the five-inch guns on the *Maddox*. During the three-and-a-half-hour "battle" that ensued, the *Maddox* and the *Turner Joy* fired more than 370 rounds from their three-inch and five-inch guns and dropped four or five depth charges, beating off an attack of what were believed to be six or more North Vietnamese PT boats and reportedly sinking two of the attackers—and amazingly without sustaining a single hit from enemy torpedoes or gunfire.[49]

The Day of Reckoning: August 5, 1964

The first FLASH-precedence messages about the naval engagement in the Gulf of Tonkin started coming across the teletypes at the National Military Command Center in the Pentagon at eleven A.M. EDT on August 4, less than twenty minutes into the engagement. The messages reported that the American destroyers were under attack and had evaded numerous enemy torpedoes.

At six past eleven A.M. (six past ten A.M. GOT time), Secretary McNamara called President Johnson to tell him that a sea battle was then under way in the Gulf of Tonkin. Four minutes later, McNamara convened a meeting in his third-floor conference room in the E Ring of the Pentagon with the members of the JCS, Secretary of State Rusk, and National Security Advisor McGeorge Bundy to discuss military retaliation against North Vietnam. At eleven thirty-five A.M., McNamara, Rusk, and Bundy left the Pentagon to attend a regularly scheduled NSC meeting at the White House, where they intended to recommend an immediate retaliatory air strike against North Vietnam, which had the blessing of the JCS. At twelve forty P.M., McNamara briefed Johnson and the NSC on the latest information available concerning what was occurring halfway around the world in the Gulf of Tonkin.

Within an hour of the meeting's breaking up, Admiral Sharp telephoned McNamara from Hawaii to personally recommend air strikes against the bases of the North Vietnamese torpedo boats. With this recommendation in hand, the JCS staff began selecting targets for the retaliatory air strike from a ninety-four-target list that had been secretly compiled earlier in 1964. At a one P.M. luncheon at the White House, Johnson, McNamara, Rusk, Bundy, and CIA director McCone unanimously agreed that retaliatory air strikes were required.[50]

At twelve twenty-seven A.M. on August 5 in the Gulf of Tonkin, Captain Herrick sent the following cautious message to Sharp: "Review of action makes many recorded contacts and torpedoes fired appear doubtful. Freak weather effects on radar and overeager sonarmen may have accounted for many reports. No actual visual sightings by Maddox. Suggest complete evaluation before any further actions." At twelve fifty-four, he sent a second message: "Joy also reports no actual visual sightings or wake of enemy . . . Entire action leaves many doubts except for apparent attempt at ambush at beginning."[51]

At one thirty-five P.M. EDT, August 4 (twelve thirty-five A.M. GOT time, August 5), the JCS informed McNamara that a list of targets had been compiled for air strikes, which could be executed if approved by the president. At a second NSC meeting that afternoon, Johnson ordered that the retaliatory air strikes be executed and said that he would seek to obtain as quickly as possible the support of the U.S. Senate for the strikes. As an NSA historical report notes, "Certainly none of the information coming out . . . either before or in the hours following the execution order was sufficiently persuasive to support such a momentous decision." At three P.M., Secretary McNamara returned to the Pentagon to approve the target list for the air strikes, leaving the preparation of the execute order to the JCS. He told the JCS that Johnson wanted the air strikes to begin promptly at seven that evening (six A.M. GOT time, August 5) so as to coincide with a planned prime-time televised address by Johnson to the nation.[52]

As the plans for the retaliatory air strike moved rapidly forward, Captains Herrick and Ogier on the *Maddox* were frantically trying to ascertain what exactly had occurred while battling exhaustion and fending off urgent demands for information from their superiors. When the two were told that during the engagement they had evaded a total of twenty-six torpedoes, they immediately knew that something was terribly wrong, since there were only twelve PT boats in the entire North Vietnamese navy, each carrying only two torpedo tubes that could not be reloaded at sea. What this meant was that even if every single North Vietnamese PT boat had been in the Tonkin Gulf that night (an impossibility to begin with), they could have fired only twenty-four torpedoes. Their suspicions were reinforced when they learned that all of the torpedoes had been heard by the *Maddox*'s inexperienced sonar operator, while the more experienced sonar operator on the nearby *Turner Joy* did not hear one torpedo in the water during the entire four-hour battle. Someone on the *Maddox* finally figured out that every torpedo warning issued by the ship's sonarman had followed a sharp change in course by the *Maddox*. A test proved that the sonar operator on the *Maddox* had mistaken the change in cavitation noises made by the destroyer when it changed course for the noise made by a torpedo.[53]

At one forty-eight A.M. GOT time, August 5, Herrick sent another message to Admiral Sharp at CINCPAC, which stated,

> Certain that original ambush was bonafide. Details of action following present a confusing picture. Have interviewed witnesses who made positive visual sightings of cockpit lights or similar passing near Maddox. Several reported torpedoes were probably boats themselves which were observed to make several close passes on Maddox. Own ship screw noises on rudders may have accounted for some. At present cannot even estimate number of boats involved. Turner Joy reports 2 torpedoes passed near her.[54]

Despite Herrick's more upbeat and confident report, Sharp became worried about the strength of the evidence, or lack thereof, regarding the purported engagement. The three after-action reports that Sharp had received from Herrick were far from definitive and clearly indicated doubts about what had actually happened. When McNamara called Sharp at eight past four P.M. EDT (eight past three A.M. GOT time, August 5), Sharp was forced to tell him that the latest messages from Herrick indicated "a little doubt on just what exactly went on." With the air strike preparations now nearing completion, this clearly was not what McNamara wanted to hear. He told Sharp that the air strike execution order would remain in force (the aircraft were expected to launch from their carriers in three hours), but ordered him to confirm that an attack had indeed taken place before the navy fighter-bombers were launched.[55]

At four forty-seven P.M. EDT, McNamara met with the JCS "to marshal the evidence to overcome lack of a clear and convincing evidence showing that an attack on the destroyer had in fact occurred." Based on the information then available to CINCPAC, Sharp concluded that an attack had taken place, an opinion that carried great weight with McNamara and the JCS. From Herrick's reports, which were a mixed bag at best, McNamara and the JCS were able to extract some evidence to support their belief that the attack had occurred, including sightings of ship wakes by navy pilots; sonar reports of torpedoes being fired at the American destroyers; a report from the captain of the *Turner Joy* that his ship had been illuminated by what was believed to be a searchlight while taking automatic weapons fire; and the fact that one of the destroyers had observed cockpit lights on an unidentified ship. Finally, and most important, there were a number of SIGINT intercepts that appeared to buttress the case for an attack having occurred, the contents of which were apparently briefed to McNamara and the JCS, though hard copies of the intercepts were not provided to those attending the meeting.[56]

Among the five evidentiary items then available indicating that an attack had taken place, the only two reliable pieces of information were SIGINT reports from NSA. One was an intercept of a statement that a North Vietnamese patrol boat had shot at U.S. aircraft. The other, received via teletype two hours earlier, at two thirty-three P.M., contained the text of a report by an unidentified North Vietnamese command authority who stated that his forces had "shot down two planes in the battle area" and that "we have sacrificed two ships and all the rest are okay." At the end of the intercept was a report that "the enemy ship could also have been damaged."[57]

McNamara and the JCS knew from Herrick's reports from the Gulf of Tonkin that there were numerous problems with the evidence cited above. Admiral James Stockdale, then a navy pilot who flew from the *Ticonderoga* that night, later disputed the navy's official position that pilots had seen the wakes of enemy torpedo boats and gun flashes. A navy reconnaissance mission flown the morning after the supposed battle found no evidence of one, particularly oil slicks or debris that would have supported the claim that the destroyers had sunk one or more of the attacking North Vietnamese ships. The sonar evidence was highly dubious. Detailed examination of the reports of visual sightings turns up numerous inconsistencies that in aggregate render these reports less than reliable, especially since they were "firmed up" after the JCS demanded conclusive proof that an attack had taken place.[58]

The Fruit of the Poisoned Tree

This left the NSA intercepts as the sole remaining credible evidence to support McNamara and the navy's contention that an attack had taken place. A declassified NSA history notes, "The reliance on SIGINT even went to the extent of overruling the commander on the scene. It was obvious to the president and his advisors that there really had been an attack—they had the North Vietnamese messages to prove it."[59]

But we now know that Johnson and McNamara got it badly wrong in their headlong rush to launch the retaliatory air strikes. The former head of the State Department's Bureau of Intelligence and Research (INR), Dr. Ray Cline, recalled that NSA fed the White House and the Defense Department raw intercepts, which were analyzed and evaluated by civilian officials and military commanders with little or no background in intelligence, much less SIGINT analysis. At no point were the SIGINT specialists at NSA called upon to provide the benefit of their deep knowledge of North Vietnamese communications, nor were CIA intelligence analysts called upon to provide an assessment of the intelligence concerning the alleged August 4 naval engagement. Cline later told an interviewer, "Everybody was demanding the SIGINT; they wanted it quick, they didn't want anybody to take any time to analyze it."[60]

McNamara's proceeding solely on the basis of *his* analysis of the available SIGINT may go down in history as one of the most serious mistakes made by a senior U.S. government official. He ended up seeing what he wanted to believe. Like a future secretary of defense named Donald Rumsfeld, the intellectually gifted McNamara made no secret of the fact that he thought he was a better intelligence analyst than the men and women at the CIA who had done it all their adult lives, a situation exacerbated by his intense distrust of intelligence professionals in general. In another interview, Cline said, "I of course never had a lot of faith in Bob McNamara's judgment about intelligence. I think, like many policy makers, he was too persuaded of his own ability to analyze things correctly and he didn't feel that intelligence officers were very likely to tell him anything he didn't already know. Now, this is a congenital disease among high-level policy makers."[61]

If McNamara and the JCS had taken the time to look long and hard at the intercepts on the afternoon of August 4, 1964, maybe history would be different, because there were some significant problems with the intercepts if they were to be taken as the most conclusive proof that an attack had occurred that night.

For example, a halfway decent SIGINT analyst looking at the scanty evidence would have immediately noticed that there were no intercepts of North Vietnamese radio traffic or radar emissions, such as one would expect to find during the course of a heated naval battle, and such as had been intercepted by NSA during the first Gulf of Tonkin battle two days earlier. For the August 4 "Phantom Battle," there were no comparable intercepts to be found anywhere.[62] Former NSA officials indicated that the traffic analysis reports produced by B Group at NSA headquarters at Fort Meade after the battle showed only routine radio activity within the North Vietnamese navy radio grid on the night of August 4. North Vietnamese naval traffic showed a heightened state of alert along the coastline, almost certainly because of the continuing OPLAN 34A raids, but the NSA analysts could find no indications of any spike in radio traffic that would have been indicative of combat activity by North Vietnamese naval units.[63]

In the absence of any other reliable SIGINT information, the only piece of tangible evidence left was the report by the unidentified North Vietnamese command authority, which McNamara thought was an after-action report on the August 4 naval battle. The substance of the NSA translation is this:

> We shot down two planes in the battle area, and one other plane was damaged. We sacrificed two ships and all the rest are okay. The combat spirit is very high and we are starting out on the hunt and [are waiting to] receive assignment. Men are very confident because they themselves saw the enemy planes sink. The enemy ship could also have been damaged.[64]

But in fact the NSA translation does not reflect what the navy listening post at San Miguel intercepted. In fact, the San Miguel intercept reads as follows:

> We shot at two enemy airplanes and at least one was damaged. We sacrificed two comrades but all are brave and recognize our obligation.[65]

It would seem that some unidentified person or persons in the reporting unit of B Group, for reasons we can only speculate about, not only changed the wording of the translation and, in doing so, the import and meaning of the text, but also changed the call signs used by the North Vietnamese transmitter and recipient and reformatted the message to include material not contained in the original intercept. Sadly, the section of the NSA historian's report on how this could conceivably have happened at Fort Meade was redacted by the NSA FOIA office. But more important, the intercept could not have been an after-action report because it was intercepted only an hour after the destroyer *Turner Joy* opened fire, and the "battle" raged for another two and a half hours. The only reason McNamara thought it was an after-action report was because he got it off the teletype from Fort Meade two and a half hours after the battle in the Gulf of Tonkin was over. Apparently McNamara did not bother to look at the times contained in the intercept itself.[66]

The Rush to Battle

In retrospect, it is clear that everyone in the White House was in a hurry to act, and nobody seemed to want to take the time to scrutinize the evidence that was available to see if it justified going to war. After reviewing the intelligence material for all of two full minutes, Secretary McNamara and the JCS agreed that the evidence, in their opinion, clearly indicated that an attack had taken place in the Gulf of Tonkin on the night of August 4. At five nineteen P.M. EDT (four nineteen A.M. GOT time, August 5), without waiting for additional information from Captain Herrick in the gulf or conducting a detailed assessment of the COMINT intercepts, McNamara ordered that the air strikes be launched within two and a half hours.[67]

At CINCPAC headquarters in Hawaii, a harried Admiral Sharp was still trying to figure out what had happened in the gulf from Herrick and the commander of the Seventh Fleet in Japan when McNamara's strike execute order arrived on his desk. Finally, at about five P.M. EDT, Sharp was given the COMINT intercepts described above. After quickly scanning them with his intelligence staff, at five twenty-three P.M. EDT Sharp telephoned General David Burchinal at the Pentagon and told him that the intercept concerning the "sacrifice of two ships" had convinced him that the attack had taken place. Sharp told Burchinal that the intercept ". . . pins it down better than anything so far." Burchinal asked Sharp, "Indicates that [the North Vietnamese] were out there on business, huh?" Sharp's response was "Oh, yes. Very definitely." Burchinal agreed with Sharp's assessment, despite the fact that he had not yet seen the intercepts that Sharp was referencing. The only "hot" item that Burchinal had to pass on to Sharp from the Washington end was that McNamara was "satisfied with the evidence."[68]

At five thirty-four P.M. EDT, Sharp sent a FLASH-precedence message to Herrick demanding a categorical and unambiguous answer as to whether he could "confirm absolutely" that the attack had taken place and that two North Vietnamese vessels had been sunk during the engagement.[69]

While Sharp was waiting for a reply from the Gulf of Tonkin, a FLASH-precedence message from NSA arrived in the Pentagon communications center. A report based on intercepted Chinese air force radio traffic, it ominously stated that the Chinese were in the process of sending a unit of MiG fighters from an air base in southern China to the North Vietnamese airfield at Dien Bien Phu.[70]

Twenty minutes later, Herrick sent Sharp a radio message containing a qualified answer to his inquiries:

> Turner Joy claims sinking one craft and damage to another with gunfire. Damaged boat returned gunfire—no hits. Turner Joy and other personnel observed bursts and black smoke from hits on this boat. This boat illuminated Turner Joy and his return fire was observed and heard by T.J. personnel. Maddox scored no known hits and never positively identified a boat as such.
>
> The first boat to close Maddox probably fired torpedo at Maddox which was heard but not seen. All subsequent Maddox torpedo reports are doubtful in that it is suspected the sonarman was hearing the ship's own propeller beat reflected off rudders during course changes (weaving). Turner Joy detected 2 torpedo runs on her, one of which was sighted visually passed down port side 3 to 5 hundred yards.
>
> Weather was overcast with limited visibility. There were no stars or moon resulting in almost total darkness throughout action.[71]

Herrick's report was filled with so many inconsistencies that it served only to further muddy the waters, rather than clear them up. Herrick knew when he sent it that his report conflicted with a message sent by the captain of the *Turner Joy*, which claimed to have sunk one enemy vessel and damaged another. But in sum, Herrick told Sharp that based on the information available to him, he believed that the attack had taken place, subject to the qualifications contained in the body of his report, but that he would investigate further and provide more conclusive proof if he could. After reading Herrick's message, at six P.M. EDT Sharp again called McNamara to tell him that Herrick now was convinced that the attack had taken place, but that there remained serious questions as to whether the engagement had, putting in jeopardy the retaliatory air strike.[72]

At six forty-five P.M. EDT, thirty-eight minutes after McNamara had sent the air strike execute order to CINCPAC, President Johnson met with sixteen senior congressional leaders from both parties and briefed them for ninety minutes, informing them that he had authorized retaliatory air strikes against North Vietnam and would seek a congressional resolution in support of his action.[73]

But the conflicting reports sent by the *Maddox* and the *Turner Joy* had created consternation at the Pentagon and at CINCPAC, both of which desperately wanted uniform and consistent reports from both ships as to what had occurred the previous night. Sharp sent a message to Herrick asking, "Can you confirm that you were attacked by PT or Swatow?" Herrick did not respond to the request, but the captain of the *Turner Joy* radioed at six ten A.M. local time (seven ten P.M. EDT, August 4) that he was convinced that an attack had taken place because a lookout had reported seeing a torpedo wake.[74]

The mounting number of conflicting reports from the *Maddox* and the *Turner Joy* only created more concern at higher headquarters. At eight A.M. GOT time, August 5, the commander of the Seventh Fleet, Admiral Roy Johnson, asked the captain of the *Turner Joy* for the names of the witnesses to the attack and an evaluation as to their reliability. Thirty minutes later, Johnson ordered the captains of the *Maddox* and the *Turner Joy* to initiate a search for debris that would prove that there had been a battle on the night of the 4th. After a twenty-minute search, both ships were forced to report that they had found no debris at the alleged site of the sea battle.[75]

At ten thirty P.M. EDT on August 4, while navy commanders in the Pacific were still furiously trying to collect and collate the evidence, President Johnson went on television to announce, "Air action is now in execution against gunboats and certain supporting facilities in North Vietnam." As he spoke, sixty-four U.S. Navy fighter-bombers from the aircraft carriers *Ticonderoga* and *Constellation* struck North Vietnamese naval bases, surface units, and oil storage depots, destroying or damaging twenty-five patrol and torpedo boats and more than 90 percent of North Vietnam's petroleum storage capacity. The toll for America, however, was heavy. North Vietnamese antiaircraft gunners shot down two navy fighter-bombers, resulting in the first American prisoner of war (POW) and the first pilot confirmed dead in the Vietnam War.

In the White House and the Pentagon's haste to execute the air strikes, nobody bothered to tell NSA that it was happening. As NSA director Gordon Blake told an interviewer, "the retaliation took everyone by surprise. NSA wasn't warned that there would be a retaliation. We weren't even able to read-just our [SIGINT] coverage in order to see the effects of the retaliation."[76]

On August 7, 1964, Congress nearly unanimously approved what became known as the Gulf of Tonkin Resolution, which authorized the president of the United States to "take all necessary measures to repel any armed attack against the forces of the United States," thus allowing the Johnson adminis-tration to expand the role of American military forces in Southeast Asia.

Postscript

This was an intelligence disaster of epic proportions. After all the available in-formation is carefully reviewed and the arguments on both sides given careful consideration, the overwhelming weight of the evidence now strongly indi-cates that there was no naval engagement in the Gulf of Tonkin on the night of August 4, 1964.

Declassified documents reveal that President Johnson secretly doubted whether a naval battle had actually taken place. On September 19, he kicked off a meeting of his national security advisers by telling them that he had "some doubt as to whether there had in fact been any vessels of any kind in the area." Despite his doubts, that afternoon the White House issued an un-equivocal statement that there had indeed been a naval battle that fateful night.[77] As time went by, though, Johnson exhibited increasing doubt as to the veracity of the NSA radio intercepts that had been critically important in justifying America's entry into the Vietnam War. Years after the Gulf of Tonkin incidents, Johnson would occasionally tease Secretary McNamara about the intercepts, chiding him with sarcastic jabs such as "Well, those fish [certainly] were swimming," or "Hell, those dumb stupid sailors were just shooting at flying fish."[78]

This opinion is now shared by the two on-scene U.S. Navy commanders, Captains Herrick and Ogier (both retired), and even by a repentant Robert Mc-Namara.[79] Experts such as NSA deputy director Louis Tordella and INR's Ray Cline have concluded that the intercepts were more likely puffed-up North

Vietnamese postmortem reports concerning the August 2 battle, rather than descriptions of the events that allegedly took place on August 4.[80]

Even at NSA, there was much skepticism at the time about the veracity of the intelligence that the agency had provided that justified America's entering the Vietnam War. Frank Austin, the chief of NSA's B Group, which was responsible for all communist Asian targets, was, according to a declassified NSA history, "skeptical from the morning of 5 August," as was Colonel John Morrison, the head of NSA Pacific in Hawaii, who wrote a lengthy and critical analysis of the NSA reporting, questioning whether an attack had taken place.[81] A declassified agency history of the affair notes, "The NSA analyst who looked at the traffic believed that the whole thing was a mistake. The [intercepted] messages almost certainly referred to other activity—the 2 August attack and the Desoto patrols. The White House had started a war on the basis of unconfirmed (and later-to-be-determined probably invalid) information."[82]

It was not until 2000 that NSA historian Dr. Robert Hanyok wrote a detailed study of the Gulf of Tonkin incidents for an internal NSA publication; it concludes, on the basis of a review of over one hundred NSA reports that somehow never found their way to the White House, that the August 4, 1964, Gulf of Tonkin incident never happened. Hanyok's conclusions are sobering: "Through a compound of analytic errors and an unwillingness to consider contrary evidence, American SIGINT elements in the region and at NSA [headquarters] reported Hanoi's plans to attack the two ships of the Desoto patrol. Further analytic errors and an obscuring of other information led to publication of more 'evidence.' In truth, Hanoi's navy was engaged in nothing that night but the salvage of two of the boats damaged on 2 August." Hanyok's controversial top-secret report alleges that NSA officials withheld 90 percent of the SIGINT about the Gulf of Tonkin attacks in their possession, and instead gave the White House only what it wanted to hear. He concludes that "only SIGINT that supported the claim that the communists had attacked the two destroyers was given to administration officials."[83]

But whatever doubts may have existed in August 1964 about the credibility of the evidence provided by NSA about the Gulf of Tonkin naval engagement, in the end it really did not matter. It was no secret that, wanting to "look tough" in an election year, Johnson administration officials were looking for a casus belli for attacking North Vietnam. So President Johnson, Secretary of Defense McNamara, and the JCS appear to have cherry-picked the available intelligence, in this case SIGINT from NSA, in order to justify a decision they had already made to launch air strikes against North Vietnam. Ray Cline stated that Johnson and McNamara "were dying to get those air attacks off and did finally send them off with a pretty fuzzy understanding of what had really happened."[84] The final word goes to an NSA historian, who concluded, "The administration had decided that expansion of American involvement would be necessary. Had the 4 August incident not occurred, something else would have."[85]

CHAPTER 7

The Wilderness of Pain

NSA and the Vietnam War: 1964–1969

A man's judgment is no better than his information.
                                        —LYNDON JOHNSON, 1968

Flying Blind

Recently declassified documents make clear that everything we thought we knew about the role of NSA in the Vietnam War needs to be reconsidered. One fact kept a secret until now was that after the North Vietnamese and Viet Cong converted all their communications to unbreakable cipher systems in April 1962, as described in chapter 5, NSA was never again able to read any high-level enemy communications traffic except for very brief periods of time. Throughout the war, the North Vietnamese and Viet Cong constantly changed and improved their high-level diplomatic and military cipher systems, in the process killing off the few cryptanalytic successes that NSA enjoyed. As a declassified NSA history notes, "it was not the sophistication of Hanoi's cryptography that hindered cryptanalysis, but the short shelf-life of its systems. Even then, the time between intercept and decryption was still months."[1] At some point in the mid-1960s, NSA made the controversial decision to give up altogether on its efforts to crack the high-level North Vietnamese ciphers and instead focus its resources on solving lower-level enemy military codes used on the battlefield in South Vietnam and on traffic analysis.[2]

Since NSA could not provide any high-level intelligence about the strategic intentions of Ho Chi Minh and the rest of the North Vietnamese leadership, the U.S. government found itself repeatedly and unpleasantly surprised by the actions of the North Vietnamese and Viet Cong. Failing to forecast the North

Vietnamese–Viet Cong 1968 Tet Offensive was perhaps the worst U.S. intelligence failure, one that occurred in part because, per a 1968 CIA postmortem report, *"high-level Communist communications"* were *"for the most part unreadable"* (italics added).[3]

NSA's best intelligence was derived from reading the diplomatic traffic of foreign countries like Brazil and Indonesia, which maintained embassies in Hanoi. The cable traffic of foreign journalists visiting Hanoi was also a useful source of information. For example, in 1968 NSA intercepted a message from a Japanese journalist in Hanoi to his home office in Tokyo reporting that he had interviewed and photographed a number of American POWs held by the North Vietnamese.[4]

The North Vietnamese Enter the War in the South

Immediately after the Gulf of Tonkin incidents, the U.S. intelligence community tasked NSA with intensifying its SIGINT coverage of both Viet Cong (VC) radio traffic inside South Vietnam and North Vietnamese Army (NVA) communications north of the DMZ. The agency's monitoring of VC Morse code communications traffic quickly identified a number of major enemy corps and division-size headquarters staffs covering all of South Vietnam. NSA also began closely monitoring the radio traffic of the NVA unit that ran the entire army logistics infrastructure in North Vietnam and Laos, the General Directorate of Rear Services (GDRS). GDRS was a critically important target because it was responsible for moving men and supplies down the Ho Chi Minh Trail from North Vietnam through southern Laos and Cambodia into South Vietnam.[5]

Within weeks of initiating intercept coverage of GDRS, NSA began intercepting message traffic suggesting that elements of a regular North Vietnamese Army unit, the 325th NVA Division, had begun preparing to cross into southern Laos from their home base in Dong Hoi in North Vietnam. In November 1964, SIGINT confirmed that an enemy radio station operating along the Ho Chi Minh Trail in southern Laos had suddenly converted its radio operating procedures to those used by regular NVA units. A few weeks later, in December, CIA "road watch" teams in southern Laos spotted several battalions of regular North Vietnamese troops moving down the Ho Chi Minh Trail in the direction of South Vietnam. In the ensuing months, traffic analysis coming out of NSA tracked the movement of the 325th NVA Division through the Mu Gia Pass and southern Laos and into South Vietnam. Although U.S. Army direction-finding assets confirmed the presence of this division in the Central Highlands of South Vietnam in January 1965, the Military Assistance Command Vietnams' (MACV) intelligence staff in Saigon refused to accept the presence of NVA regular forces in the country because it had not been confirmed by POWs or captured documents. It was not until early February that MACV finally agreed that the headquarters of the 325th NVA Division plus a subordinate regiment were in the Central Highlands.[6]

The Opening of the Ground War in South Vietnam

In South Vietnam, the ground war was moving into a new and more lethal phase. The initial landing of U.S. Marines took place in March 1965, and by June the entire Third Marine Amphibious Force was operating in the northern part of South Vietnam, based in the city of Da Nang. In July 1965, the first U.S. Army combat unit, the First Cavalry Division (Airmobile), arrived in South Vietnam. As the number of U.S. combat troops in South Vietnam rose steadily, so did the number and intensity of North Vietnamese and Viet Cong attacks. Forces on both sides began maneuvering for advantage, shadowboxing while waiting for the other side to make the first decisive move.

The first battle of the new "American phase" in the Vietnam War began in August. Early that month, U.S. Army airborne radio direction finding (ARDF) aircraft flying routine SIGINT collection missions over the northern portion of South Vietnam picked up a heavy volume of Viet Cong Morse code radio messages coming from just south of the Marine Corps base at Chu Lai. By mid-August, the ARDF aircraft had discovered the source of the Morse code transmissions and the identity of the Viet Cong unit sending the messages. The transmitter belonged to the headquarters of the two-thousand-man First Viet Cong Regiment, which was secretly concentrating its forces on the Van Tuong Peninsula, fifteen miles south of Chu Lai. The information was fed to General Lewis Walt, commander of the Third Marine Amphibious Force, who immediately initiated a search-and-destroy operation against the VC regiment. Designated Operation Starlight, it commenced on August 18. A marine battalion quickly penned the VC regiment up against the sea, while another marine battalion landed on the peninsula and began wiping out the trapped Viet Cong forces. By August 24, the marines reported that they had destroyed two battalions of the VC regiment, killing an estimated seven hundred Viet Cong troops. On the negative side, over two hundred marines had been killed or wounded in the fierce fighting. Despite the heavy casualty toll, NSA officials considered the success of Operation Starlight to be SIGINT's most important accomplishment in Vietnam up until that point.[7]

Unfortunately, as was too often the case during the war, the use of body count metrics to measure success during Operation Starlight produced a chimera. In fact, SIGINT showed that the majority of the First Viet Cong Regiment had somehow managed to escape from the Van Tuong Peninsula. According to a declassified NSA history, radio intercepts showed that "within two days of the battle, the First Regiment's radio network was back on the air."[8]

Two months later, in October, three regiments of the 325th NVA Division launched an offensive in the Central Highlands with the objective of cutting the country in half. In this first offensive in the south, NVA regulars scored a quick victory at the Plei Mei Special Forces camp, twenty-five miles south of the city of Pleiku, but then were forced to retreat up the nearby Ia Drang Valley when confronted by a strong force of American infantrymen belonging to the newly arrived First Cavalry Division (Airmobile), commanded by Major General Harry Kinnard.

As the 325th NVA Division retreated deeper into the Ia Drang Valley, it was shadowed by five ARDF aircraft tracking the locations of the radio signals of the division's commander and his subordinate regimental commanders, which enabled Kinnard's forces to leapfrog up the valley in their Huey helicopters, harrying the retreating division every chance they got. At about four thirty A.M. on November 14, a tactical SIGINT intercept team attached to the First Battalion, Seventh Cavalry, intercepted a transmission indicating that a battalion of the 325th NVA Division (the Ninth Infantry Battalion of the Sixty-sixth NVA Regiment) was trapped at the base of the Chu Pong Massif. Acting on this intelligence, at eleven A.M. helicopters dropped the 450 men of the First Battalion, Seventh Cavalry, commanded by Lieutenant Colonel Harold Moore, at landing zone (LZ) X-Ray, in front of the Chu Pong Massif, to destroy the enemy force.[9]

But SIGINT can sometimes be wrong. As immortalized in the book and movie *We Were Soldiers Once . . . and Young*, Hal Moore discovered almost immediately that he was facing not an NVA battalion, but rather two full regiments of the 325th NVA Division. Two days of fierce and bloody fighting ensued, much of it hand-to-hand. When it was over, both of the NVA regiments had for all intents and purposes been destroyed, with the survivors retreating across the border into Cambodia. But the Battle of LZ X-Ray, the first engagement of the Vietnam War between American and North Vietnamese troops, showed that the North Vietnamese could stand and fight against the better-armed Americans.

As in Operation Starlight, SIGINT's performance during the Battle of the Ia Drang Valley was not a complete success, with a declassified NSA history reporting, "At least four times during the struggle, South Vietnamese and American units had been ambushed by large communist units—twice during helicopter landings—and SIGINT had been unable to detect the traps." The lesson learned from these two battles was that SIGINT was an imperfect intelligence source if used all by itself, without supporting intelligence from agents, POWs, and captured documents. Sadly, as we shall see, this simple truth was forgotten by later generations of senior U.S. field commanders in Vietnam.[10]

SIGINT Successes in the Ground War in South Vietnam

While the Rolling Thunder bombing campaign in North Vietnam continued into 1966, in South Vietnam NSA was beginning to rack up some impressive gains. The list of the agency's targets grew rapidly in response to customers' demands for more and better intelligence, including information on the deployments and movements of North Vietnamese and Viet Cong forces down to the tactical level, North Vietnamese fighter activities and surface-to-air missile locations and readiness levels, Soviet and Chinese weapon and supply shipments to North Vietnam, North Vietnamese weather forecasts, civil aviation flights, and on and on.

And despite its inability to crack the North Vietnamese military's high-level ciphers, NSA was increasingly able to produce vast quantities of intelligence about the North Vietnamese and to a lesser degree the Viet Cong forces operating inside South Vietnam by cracking their low-level cipher systems, as well as making use of increasingly expert traffic analysis and direction-finding data obtained by army and air force ARDF aircraft. Throughout the war, according to a declassified NSA history, "American and Allied cryptologists would be able to exploit lower level communist cryptographic systems, that is, more precisely, ciphers and codes used by operational and tactical-level units, usually regiment and below, on an almost routine basis. In fact, the volume of the so-called low-to-medium-grade systems exploited by NSA was so great that by 1968 the exploitation had to be automated."[11]

This success quickly translated into better intelligence about the strength and capabilities of the enemy. A declassified May 1966 Defense Intelligence Agency (DIA) order of battle estimate of the North Vietnamese military shows that SIGINT was able to identify the locations of virtually every major North Vietnamese combat unit stationed in North and South Vietnam, as well as the

locations and complete aircraft inventory for every regiment in the North Vietnamese air force.[12]

On the battlefield in South Vietnam, SIGINT quickly outstripped other intelligence sources in its ability to find and accurately track the movements of
the ever-elusive North Vietnamese and Viet Cong forces, which made destroying them immeasurably easier. Jim Lairson, an army Morse intercept operator
based at the huge Phu Bai listening post, in northern South Vietnam, recalled
an incident in February 1966, when the intercepts of the Viet Cong combat
unit he was assigned to monitor began moving inexorably toward his post. He
remembered, "The [enemy] operator I was copying got frustrated with [his]
control and switched from coded to plain text. Our translator was standing behind me and as I typed Phu Bai on the paper. I got the word. There were three
battalions of Viet Cong coming at us." The approaching enemy force was immediately hit by dozens of bombs dropped by an on-call force of U.S. Air Force
fighter-bombers, and the threat to the base passed.[13]

One of the most skilled users of SIGINT in Vietnam was Major General
William DePuy. Commander of the First Infantry Division, based north of
Saigon, he owed his skills largely to his experience in the intelligence field before coming to Vietnam. In July 1966, army ARDF aircraft located the headquarters of the 272nd Regiment of the Ninth Viet Cong Division near the village
of Minh Thanh, in Tay Ninh Province near the Cambodian border. In the resulting battle, troops belonging to DePuy's division surprised the Viet Cong regiment, killing three hundred VC soldiers and putting the entire Ninth VC
Division out of action for the next three and a half months.[14]

Three weeks later, in August, U.S. Air Force EC-47 ARDF aircraft flying
over Quang Tri Province, in the northernmost part of South Vietnam, intercepted the largest number of NVA transmitter fixes found in the DMZ since
America's entry into the war. The radio emitters belonged to the North Vietnamese 324B Division, which was in the process of trying to flee back across
the DMZ into North Vietnam after being mauled by U.S. Marine Corps units
earlier that month. B-52 bombers were called in to plaster the locations of the
324B Division with carpet bombing. Hundreds of NVA troops died in the resulting conflagration of high-explosive ordnance and napalm. The director of
intelligence of U.S. Pacific Command reported on September 29, "Without
[EC-47's] work and that of more sensitive intelligence [SIGINT], we would be
completely in the dark about the enemy situation in the DMZ."[15]

But getting better at finding the enemy was just one of NSA's big successes
that year. After months of dissecting intercepted North Vietnamese and Viet
Cong radio traffic, in early 1966 NSA SIGINT analysts figured out that prior to

every enemy attack, the North Vietnamese and Viet Cong radio operators made significant changes to their transmitting procedures, including changing their radio frequencies, cipher systems, and call signs, as well as establishing special backup radio centers and forward command centers that only appeared in North Vietnamese radio traffic just prior to attacks. Radio traffic volumes also shot up dramatically, as did the number of high-precedence messages being sent and received. With this analytic breakthrough, the SIGINT analysts could predict, sometimes weeks in advance, when and where the enemy intended to launch an offensive, which units were going to participate in the attack, and even what their objectives were. It would prove to be a hugely important development that would cost the North Vietnamese and Viet Cong forces dearly in the years that followed, as American combat forces were able to parry the enemy blow and frustrate enemy commanders time after time.[16]

For example, in March 1966 SIGINT detected radio transmitters associated with a high-level North Vietnamese command unit plus intelligence units moving toward the cities of Pleiku and Kontum, in the Central Highlands, suggesting that the North Vietnamese were gearing up for an attack on the cities. The U.S. Twenty-fifth Infantry Division was sent into the region to preempt the attack, forcing the North Vietnamese units to retreat back to their base areas in Cambodia after two months of battle. Then in June 1966, another radio transmitter belonging to a North Vietnamese high-level headquarters was detected approaching the highlands city of Dak To. This time, units of the 101st Airborne Division were sent in to clear out the North Vietnamese, who were forced to withdraw in July. In October 1966, SIGINT detected the arrival of the NVA 324B Division in Quang Tri Province, south of the DMZ. By November, elements of the NVA 341st Division had crossed the DMZ into Quang Tri. The North Vietnamese intended either to launch a major offensive or to create a stronghold in the region south of the DMZ. In the battle that followed, U.S. Marine units badly mauled the North Vietnamese division with the help of massive B-52 Arc Light air strikes.[17]

As exemplified by the above, SIGINT proved to be instrumental in foiling virtually every North Vietnamese offensive during 1966 and in the years that followed, with some notable exceptions, such as the 1968 Tet Offensive, which is discussed later in this chapter. The North Vietnamese offensive efforts in 1966 resulted in no tangible ground gains, but yielded massive casualties among their troops. One has to wonder if the North Vietnamese military leadership ever stopped to question how the Americans always seemed to know what their plans were. This may also have been the high point of the American SIGINT effort in Vietnam.

Pound Them into the Dirt

For NSA, the year 1967 was marked by one resounding success after another on the Vietnamese battlefield. In April, SIGINT detected a large North Vietnamese troop buildup in northern Quang Tri Province, south of the DMZ, with radio intercepts confirming that the entire North Vietnamese 325C Division had moved into the region. Other data appearing in SIGINT indicated that the NVA intended to launch an offensive to liberate Quang Tri and neighboring Thua Thien Province as early as June. Guided to their targets with unerring accuracy by NSA information, B-52 bombers and navy and air force fighter-bombers smashed the North Vietnamese troop buildup. The bombers were followed by a large force of U.S. Marine Corps infantry backed by tanks, artillery, and air support. The 325C Division was for all intents and purposes wiped out as an effective military unit in the fighting.[18]

Beginning in September, SIGINT detected another dramatic increase in the number of North Vietnamese radio transmitters operating along the DMZ and in the A Shau Valley, just to the south. New North Vietnamese combat units were quickly identified in the area south of the DMZ by SIGINT. This material, when matched with captured documents and information received from POWs and defectors, led intelligence analysts in Washington to conclude that rates of North Vietnamese infiltration into these two areas had reached invasion levels. The State Department's intelligence staff issued a highly classified report warning that SIGINT showed that four new North Vietnamese regiments had just arrived, or were about to arrive, in the area just south of the DMZ. But MACV refused to accept the presence of these new units because, once again, the SIGINT data had not been confirmed by captured documents or by prisoners.[19]

Despite the nagging doubts of General William Westmoreland's intelligence chief, General Phillip Davidson, about the validity of much of the intelligence data he was getting from Fort Meade, SIGINT continued to rack up more impressive successes. In October, SIGINT collected by the U.S. Army listening post in Pleiku revealed that the North Vietnamese First Division had just crossed into South Vietnam from Laos and had massed near Dak To, a key garrison located northwest of Pleiku. In late October, an accumulation of radio intercepts showed that an attack on Dak To was imminent, as evidenced by a dramatic surge in the volume of North Vietnamese radio transmissions coming from the Dak To area from normal twice-a-day contacts to once an hour. On November 1, elements of the U.S. Fourth Infantry Division and the 173rd Airborne Brigade were moved to Dak To so as to preempt the anticipated North Vietnamese attack. The enemy offensive began on November 7. The battle raged for ten days, after which the battered First NVA Division broke off the engagement and retreated into Cambodia. The casualty counts on both sides were massive, with 280 American paratroopers killed and 500 wounded in the battle. No one knows for sure how many North Vietnamese soldiers were killed or wounded, but MACV estimated that 2,100 North Vietnamese were killed.[20]

The Battle of Dak To was considered by many senior American military commanders in Vietnam to have been SIGINT's brightest-shining moment up until that point in the war. But it was almost instantly eclipsed by an even more significant cryptologic breakthrough.

The "Vinh Window"

In October 1967, while the Battle of Dak To was still raging, radio intercept operators aboard a U.S. Air Force C-130 SIGINT aircraft orbiting over the Gulf of Tonkin intercepted a new North Vietnamese radio net carrying what seemed to be routine voice communications. The intercept tapes were brought back to the U.S. Army listening post at Phu Bai, where Vietnamese linguists pored over them. Their analysis of the tapes showed that the North Vietnamese radio operators were passing mundane information concerning low-level logistical matters over a newly constructed microwave radio-relay system linking the North Vietnamese coastal cities of Thanh Hoa and Vinh. Situated just above the DMZ, Vinh was the location of a huge North Vietnamese logistics center supplying the entire Ho Chi Minh Trail. From that point onward, C-130 SIGINT aircraft began regularly flying orbits off the North Vietnamese coast targeting these en clair radio transmissions. Then in November, the nature of the traffic being carried on this radio net changed, with intercepts revealing that the North Vietnamese radio operators were now sending complete run-downs on the number of infiltration groups about to be sent down the Ho Chi Minh Trail from the Vinh base area. It was an incredible find. NSA's analysts now could determine how many NVA infiltration packets were traversing the Ho Chi Minh Trail, as well as the size of the infiltration groups and their destination inside South Vietnam. In short, what NSA called the "Vinh Window" appeared to be an intelligence bonanza of unprecedented proportions.[21]

President Lyndon Johnson and his national security advisor Walt Rostow were euphoric when they were briefed about the breakthrough by NSA officials in early 1968. Everyone from the president on down suddenly believed that at last the United States could attack the North Vietnamese infiltration route down the Ho Chi Minh Trail. A declassified NSA history states, "At the White House, there was a sense that this intelligence breakthrough was the key [to the strategy of stopping infiltration]."[22]

But sadly, the Vinh Window ultimately proved in many respects to be a bust. NSA oversold the value of this SIGINT product to its customers, promising them that the agency would be able to give them exact locations for the North Vietnamese infiltration groups moving down the Ho Chi Minh Trail. NSA's air force and navy customers complained when the agency was unable to produce this kind of intelligence from the intercepts. In addition, the thousands of hours of intercepted North Vietnamese voice traffic produced every month by American SIGINT reconnaissance aircraft orbiting over Laos and the Gulf of Tonkin swamped NSA's small cadre of Vietnamese linguists, and a proposal to use South Vietnamese personnel to transcribe the tapes was rejected for security reasons. As a result, a massive backlog of hundreds of Vinh Window intercept tapes quickly built up, which, by the time they were finally transcribed, analyzed, and reported, were already obsolete. As a declassified NSA history puts it, "Whatever tactical advantage that could have been gotten from the exploitation of the GDRS voice communications would never be realized. Like the proverbial children at the candy store, American intelligence could only press its face against the Vinh Window and imagine the opportunity . . . the true goodies remained beyond our touch."[23]

A Victim of Its Own Success

Despite the widespread disappointment that the Vinh Window intercepts did not allow the U.S. military to shut down the Ho Chi Minh Trail, by the end of 1967 NSA had become a superstar, albeit a secret one, in Vietnam. U.S. military field commanders in Southeast Asia were gushing in their praise of SIGINT. General Bruce Palmer Jr., the army's vice chief of staff, told a gathering of senior officers that SIGINT was for his commanders in Vietnam "the backbone of their intelligence effort. They could not live or fight without it." Palmer was not overstating the case. Declassified documents reveal that SIGINT was the primary driver of U.S. Army combat operations in Vietnam, providing anywhere from 40 to 90 percent of the intelligence available to U.S. forces about the strength and capabilities of the enemy forces facing them. Over half of all major U.S. Army offensive operations launched in 1965 and 1966 had been triggered by intelligence coming from SIGINT.[24]

With each new success, senior army commanders in Vietnam became increasingly enamored of this seemingly magical fount of knowledge, and in the process cast aside the more conventional sources of intelligence, such as POW interrogations and agent operations. The result was that by 1967 dependence on SIGINT was so high that an American intelligence officer who served in Vietnam told a congressional committee that American military commanders in Vietnam were "getting SIGINT with their orange juice every morning and have now come to expect it everywhere."[25]

But hidden behind the scenes, a tide of discontent was rising within the U.S. military and intelligence communities regarding this source, among both those officials who had access to the material and those who did not. Meanwhile, there was also a rising tide of antiwar sentiment in the United States, creating an increasingly intractable problem for the Johnson administration. By 1966, public opinion had begun to turn against the war, even though the military continued to insist that the United States was winning. Army and marine casualties were mounting, and by the end of 1966 almost five hundred American aircraft had been lost and hundreds of pilots and crew killed or captured and held as POWs under terrible conditions. The next year saw an increase in public demonstrations against the war and less than 50 percent of Americans supporting the way the war was being conducted. Time was not working in favor of Johnson. Nevertheless, he continued to believe what he heard from his top commander in Vietnam, General Westmoreland. Apart from the metric of body count, the military increasingly depended on various forms of intelligence—above all SIGINT—to know whether or not the United States really was winning, and to anticipate and counter relentless enemy pressure, from both the VC and the NVA.

Among the select few senior U.S. government officials and top American commanders with unfettered access to SIGINT, many were worried that the U.S. military in Vietnam had become far too dependent on SIGINT. General Palmer, who valued it so highly at the time, years later wrote that by 1968 MACV was largely reliant on SIGINT as its primary source of intelligence on enemy movements and activities, and consequently placed less importance on HUMINT, POWs, and captured documents.[26] NSA historians generally agree with Palmer's assessment; one writes, "SIGINT had only part of the picture, and intelligence analysts relied too heavily on the single source. In hindsight, it is clear that too little attempt was made to flesh out the rest of the picture through interrogations, captured documents, and the like. SIGINT became the victim of its own success."[27]

SIGINT generated so much information that the overworked intelligence analysts in Washington and Saigon were buried by the mass of intercepts being produced every day, and as time went by, it became increasingly difficult to ascertain what was important and what was not. In addition, the military command bureaucracy in Southeast Asia was so dense and multilayered that critical intelligence reporting oftentimes failed to make it from the SIGINT collection units in the field to the military commanders they were supposed to support in a timely manner, or fashioned in such a way that it could be immediately acted upon by field commanders.[28]

And army and marine field commanders at the corps and division levels who did have access to SIGINT failed to use it properly. Many had little or no knowledge of, or prior experience with, SIGINT and therefore were suspicious of a source that they did not control, much less understand. The list of senior army commanders who went to Vietnam knowing next to nothing about SIGINT is staggering. General Creighton Abrams Jr. admitted, "It has been my feeling in years past that we did not know too much about ASA [Army Security Agency]." The military services were largely to blame for failing to educate their senior officers in the fundamentals of this vitally important battlefield intelligence source, especially given how crucial SIGINT had proved to be during the Korean War. But NSA also bears a large part of the blame because of the agency's insistence that all aspects of SIGINT "sources and methods" be kept a secret from all but those few officers deemed to have a need to know.[29]

The Tet Offensive

Back at NSA's Indochina Office (B6) at Fort Meade, while the Battle of Dak To was raging and the Vinh Window was just opening up, a number of disturbing signs were beginning to appear in intercepts arriving via teletype from Southeast Asia. Beginning in late October 1967 and continuing through November, SIGINT detected elements of two crack North Vietnamese divisions, the 304th and the 320th, and three independent regiments departing their home bases in North Vietnam and moving onto the Ho Chi Minh Trail in southern Laos. This was the first time ever that NSA analysts had seen two North Vietnamese divisions moving onto the trail at the same time. By mid-December, the troops had been tracked by SIGINT to staging areas around the southern Laos city of Tchepone, just across the border from the U.S. Marine Corps firebase at Khe Sanh.[30]

Then during the first week of January 1968, radio transmitters belonging to two regiments of a third North Vietnamese division, the 325C, were detected operating north and west of Khe Sanh. At the same time, SIGINT monitored the first two divisions surging across the border into South Vietnam and taking up positions south and east of the firebase. The marines inside the base were now surrounded by vastly superior enemy forces. Everyone from President Johnson down to General Westmoreland in Saigon immediately assumed that the North Vietnamese were about to launch a major offensive to take the base.[31]

But the ominous portents continued to build in the days that followed. By mid-January, SIGINT showed that there were three NVA division headquarters and at least seven regiments totaling more than fifteen thousand enemy troops deployed around the Marine Corps firebase. To the south of Khe Sanh, in the Central Highlands, an accumulation of intercepted radio traffic passing between the North Vietnamese B-3 Front headquarters and its subordinate divisions indicated that the North Vietnamese were preparing to attack a number of cities in Kontum, Pleiku, and Darlac Provinces. To the east along the coast, SIGINT detected the North Vietnamese Second Division moving southeast to staging positions outside the city of Hué, the largest urban center in northern South Vietnam. Within a matter of days, the huge NSA listening post at Phu Bai was monitoring North Vietnamese and Viet Cong radio transmissions coming from just outside Hué itself. Phu Bai and NSA's other listening posts in South Vietnam detected a dramatic increase in the volume of radio traffic passing along critical North Vietnamese and Viet Cong communications links throughout South Vietnam, much of it high-precedence messages. Unfortunately, NSA could not read the codes the messages were enciphered with. On January 17, NSA issued an intelligence report warning that there was now firm evidence that the North Vietnamese were preparing to launch an offensive in Pleiku Province, in the Central Highlands.[32] Westmoreland and the U.S. embassy in Saigon interpreted this as an indication that the offensive would target the Central Highlands and Khe Sanh, just south of the DMZ, an opinion shared by President Johnson and his senior advisers. But at this stage, there were no reliable indications whatsoever coming from SIGINT or any other intelligence source to suggest that the North Vietnamese and Viet Cong intended to mount any offensive operation south of the highlands.[33]

The suspicions of the White House and Westmoreland about the enemy's intentions were apparently confirmed when on January 21 three battalions of the North Vietnamese 325C Division launched a two-pronged assault on marine defensive positions to the north and south of the besieged Khe Sanh firebase. The North Vietnamese overran the village of Khe Sanh itself, but the attacks on the base were repulsed. In response, a marine battalion was hastily flown in along with much-needed supplies, bringing the size of the marine garrison to over six thousand combat troops.

But at the same time that NSA was reporting on the North Vietnamese military buildup in northern South Vietnam and the Central Highlands, SIGINT collected independently by the radio intercept units belonging to the ASA's 303rd Radio Research Battalion at Long Binh, outside Saigon, revealed a dramatic surge in the number of Viet Cong radio transmissions coming from the area surrounding Saigon, with many of the transmissions originating closer to Saigon than heretofore had been noted. By January 15, army intelligence analysts had concluded that three North Vietnamese and Viet Cong divisions, which had previously been noted in Cambodia in late December 1967, were now confirmed by SIGINT as being deployed in an arc around Saigon within easy striking distance of the South Vietnamese capital.[34]

During the ten-day period between January 15 and January 25, NSA listening posts in Southeast Asia intercepted what is described in a declassified report as an "almost unprecedented volume of urgent messages . . . passing among major [enemy] commands." There were other equally troubling portents appearing in intercepts of low-level North Vietnamese radio traffic. North Vietnamese units throughout South Vietnam were changing en masse their radio frequencies and cryptographic systems, activating forward command posts and emergency radio nets, and North Vietnamese intelligence teams were detected in SIGINT reconnoitering target areas *throughout* South Vietnam. The possibility of a major enemy offensive in South Vietnam had now become a probability. An internal NSA history notes, "Never before had the indicators been so ubiquitous and unmistakable. A storm was about to break over South Vietnam."[35]

On January 25, NSA sent a report to MACV titled *Coordinated Vietnamese Communist Offensive Evidenced in South Vietnam*, the lead conclusion of which was this:

> During the past week, SIGINT has provided evidence of a coordinated attack to occur in the near future in several areas of South Vietnam. While the bulk of SIGINT evidence indicates the most critical areas to be in the northern half of the country, there is some additional evidence that Communist units in Nam Bo [the southern half of South Vietnam] may also be involved. The major target areas of enemy offensive operations include the Western Highlands, the coast provinces of Military Region (MR) 5, and the Khe Sanh and Hue areas.[36]

Thanks to newly declassified documents, we now know that NSA's warning message was either ignored, misunderstood, or misapplied by the White House, the CIA, and MACV. The crux of the problem was that senior officials at

MACV, in General Bruce Palmer's opinion as expressed in a later declassified CIA study, "flatly did not believe that the enemy had either the strength or the command and control capability to launch a nationwide coordinated offensive." George Carver Jr., the CIA's special adviser for Vietnamese affairs, also refused to accept warnings from his junior analysts because, according to the study, he "did not fully buy the thesis that the coming offensive would be an all-out affair of great portent."[37] The January 28, 1968, edition of the CIA's *Central Intelligence Bulletin* commented, "It is not yet possible to determine if the enemy is indeed planning an all-out, country-wide offensive during, or just following, the Tet holiday period."[38]

General Westmoreland told Washington he was convinced that NSA's intelligence about possible widespread attacks merely reflected a North Vietnamese attempt to divert his attention from the real objective—Khe Sanh. Ultimately, however, the North Vietnamese never mounted a major attack on Khe Sanh coinciding with the launch of the Tet Offensive.[39]

In the days that followed, NSA intercept sites in Southeast Asia continued to pick up further "hard" indications that the North Vietnamese offensive was about to be unleashed, including one intercept on January 28, which revealed that "N-day" for the kickoff of the North Vietnamese offensive in the Central Highlands was going to be January 30, at three A.M., less than forty-eight hours away. This report was deemed to be so important that it went straight to President Johnson.[40]

But the Defense Intelligence Agency believed that the North Vietnamese and Viet Cong would wait until after the end of the Tet holiday to launch their offensive. So DIA too discounted NSA's warnings, and its analysts wrote in the January 29, 1968, daily DIA summary, "Indications point to N-Day being scheduled in the Tet period, *but it still seems likely that the Communists would wait until after the holiday to carry out a plan*" (italics added).[41]

Then, on the night of January 29–30, a U.S. Army SIGINT specialist named David Parks and his partner were manning a radio direction-finding post at Bien Hoa air base, outside Saigon, just as the Tet holiday began. Parks later recounted, "About midnight, every VC/NVA radio in the country went silent, 'Nil More Heard' for sure! We could not raise a ditty bop for love nor money. It was the damnedest thing I ever *didn't* hear. Complete radio silence."[42]

Three hours later, at three A.M. on January 30, 1968, over one hundred thousand North Vietnamese and Viet Cong troops launched a massive and coordinated offensive against virtually all cities, towns, and major military bases throughout South Vietnam, attacking thirty-eight of the country's forty-four provincial capitals and seventy district capitals, capturing the city of Hué, seizing large portions of Saigon, and even managing briefly to seize portions of the American embassy in downtown Saigon.

Postmortem on Tet

After a month of unrelenting seesaw fighting, the Tet Offensive finally concluded by the end of February 1968. From a purely military standpoint, the Tet Offensive turned out to be a clear-cut victory for the United States. The North Vietnamese and Viet Cong lost an estimated thirty thousand troops in the battle. The enemy forces in South Vietnam were badly battered, with SIGINT picking up signs of demoralization in the ranks of the North Vietnamese Army. According to General Daniel Graham, then an intelligence officer in Saigon, "We could read the communications along the Ho Chi Minh Trail, and it was perfectly obvious that they were having one terrible time because people from South Vietnam were going to go back up that trail come hell or high water. All discipline had broken down and they were going back up the trail. Even some of the people who were operating the radio stations along the trail had bugged out."[43]

But while Tet may have been a military victory, it produced a political firestorm back in the United States. It shattered American political resolve and devastated the Johnson administration. From a political standpoint, Tet was an unequivocal strategic victory for North Vietnam and the turning point in the Vietnam War—the defining moment when the U.S. government and the American populace finally decided that they could not win the bloody conflict in Southeast Asia and that it was time to leave. On March 31, 1968, only two months after the beginning of the Tet Offensive, Lyndon Johnson went on national television and told his fellow countrymen that he had decided not to run for reelection. This signaled the beginning of the end of America's involvement in the Vietnam War.

Not surprisingly, the postmortem reviews of the U.S. intelligence community's performance prior to the Tet Offensive praised NSA. A CIA study states unequivocally, "The National Security Agency stood alone in issuing the kinds of warnings the U.S. Intelligence Community was designed to provide."[44] A declassified Top Secret Codeword report submitted to the President's Foreign Intelligence Advisory Board notes,

> Despite enemy security measures, communications intelligence was able to provide clear warning that attacks, probably on a larger scale than ever before, were in the offing . . . These messages, taken with

such nontextual indicators as increased message volumes and radio direction-finding, served both to validate information from other sources in the hand of local authorities and to provide warning to senior officials. The indicators, however, were not sufficient to predict the exact timing of the attack.[45]

But recently declassified material reveals that prior to the launch of the Tet Offensive, NSA only had definitive information that indicated imminent North Vietnamese and/or Viet Cong attacks in eight South Vietnamese provinces, all in the northern part of the country or in the Central Highlands. The provinces around Saigon and the Mekong Delta were never mentioned in any of the NSA reports. Except for the January 25 message detailed above, the NSA intelligence reporting provided no indication of the enemy's intent to undertake a major nationwide offensive, including attacks on virtually every major South Vietnamese city, including Saigon itself. It was not until years later that NSA admitted, "SIGINT was unable to provide advance warning of the true nature, size, and targets of the coming offensive."[46]

And last (but not least), despite the fact that NSA was the only U.S. intelligence agency to issue *any* warning that the North Vietnamese and Viet Cong intended to launch a major offensive in South Vietnam, NSA's official history of the Vietnam War sadly notes that "the [NSA] reports failed to shake the commands in Washington and Saigon from their perception of the communist main threat centered in the north, especially at Khe Sanh, and in the Central Highlands."[47]

The Battle of Khe Sanh

As vicious as the fighting would often be, the battle for Khe Sanh was not the decisive event that Johnson and Westmoreland had anticipated—or the American equivalent of the 1954 Battle of Dien Bien Phu (where the French army lost an entire garrison to the Viet Minh) that the White House was so anxious to avert.

As noted above, the Battle of Khe Sanh had commenced a week before the beginning of the Tet Offensive when the North Vietnamese 325C Division launched an unsuccessful three-battalion assault on marine defensive positions in the hills outside the firebase. Then for the next three weeks there was a surprising hiatus while the Communist Tet Offensive raged over the rest of South Vietnam. Newly declassified documents suggest that SIGINT played a major role in this delay. On the weekend before the Tet Offensive began, army and air force ARDF aircraft pinpointed the location just inside Laos of the NVA "Front" headquarters directing operations in the Khe Sanh area. On January 29, the day before the Tet Offensive began, forty-five B-52 bombers dumped 1,350 tons of bombs on the site of the North Vietnamese headquarters, and the radio transmissions that had been originating from the site disappeared for almost two weeks, indicating that the bombers had destroyed the enemy headquarters.[48]

It took the North Vietnamese several weeks to get reorganized. On February 7, NVA troops and tanks overran the nearby Green Beret base at Lang Vei. But rather than presage a massive assault on Khe Sanh, the attack on Lang Vei marked the beginning of almost three months of desultory North Vietnamese attacks on the firebase, which finally petered out in April. During this three-month period, the marines beat off repeated small-scale North Vietnamese ground assaults, in many cases, only after fierce hand-to-hand fighting, but no major attack on the firebase itself ever occurred. In fact, after the fall of Lang Vei evidence appearing in SIGINT indicated that the North Vietnamese had stripped troops from the front lines around Khe Sanh and sent them south. As a result, President Johnson and General Westmoreland's fears that Khe Sanh would become the "American Dien Bien Phu" never materialized. The embarrassment felt by U.S. government and military officials in Washington and Saigon was palpable. The decisive battle with the best units in the NVA that they had hoped for never happened.

According to a declassified NSA history, the Battle of Khe Sanh was "one of the greatest SIGINT success stories ever." Much of the success can be credited to a tiny U.S. Marine Corps SIGINT detachment belonging to the First Radio Battalion and an attached South Vietnamese SIGINT unit, which had been operating a radio intercept site inside Khe Sanh since August 1967. Once the NVA attacks against Khe Sanh began, the marines started intercepting North Vietnamese artillery communications, which allowed the unit to warn the marine commander of the base every time the NVA planned to bombard the base. The marine SIGINTers also became expert in predicting when the North Vietnamese planned to attack the base. A declassified NSA document notes, "SIGINT predicted some 90 percent of all ground assaults during the siege."[49]

Throughout the battle, one or more army or air force ARDF aircraft continually orbited over Khe Sanh, pinpointing the sites of NVA radio transmissions, enabling the marines to direct air strikes and artillery fire toward the North Vietnamese commanders as they spoke on the radio. The process of locating

NVA radio transmitters became so smooth that within ten minutes of a North Vietnamese radio operator going on the air, his location was being plastered by artillery fire or tons of bombs dropped by orbiting fighter-bombers.[50]

The casualties that the North Vietnamese suffered thanks to SIGINT were considerable. Daniel Graham, then a colonel serving on the MACV intelligence staff in Saigon, said, "We knew . . . from intelligence that we had got our direction-finding equipment going so well up around Khe Sanh that whenever they'd hit the [Morse] key for a minute, boom, they'd get hit. We'd get gripes; here were [North Vietnamese] commanders on their telephones, saying, 'I need a radio operator. My people won't man the radios.' Every time they'd open up with a radio, boom! There comes shot and shell . . . Oh hell, you know, you got to the point where you kind of sympathized with these poor bastards out there under that kind of shot and shell."[51]

The Invasion of Cambodia

By early 1970 the Nixon administration was secretly planning to expand the war into neighboring Cambodia. In February, President Richard Nixon authorized a massive secret bombing campaign against North Vietnamese base camps and supply depots there. On March 18, Cambodian leader Prince Norodom Sihanouk was overthrown in a coup d'état led by the Cambodian defense minister, General Lon Nol.[52]

On April 30, Nixon ordered U.S. troops to cross into Cambodia and wipe out the vast network of North Vietnamese military headquarter complexes and base camps inside the country. Demonstrations immediately erupted across America, which led to the tragic encounter between Ohio Army National Guard troops and student protesters at Kent State University, which left four students dead.

So secret were the administration's plans that neither NSA nor the military SIGINT units in Vietnam were sufficiently forewarned. Lieutenant Colonel James Freeze, the commander of the ASA's 303rd Radio Research Battalion at Long Binh, did not find out about the invasion until April 28, two days before it was due to begin. There was not a lot that NSA and the military SIGINT units in Vietnam could do in forty-eight hours to prepare for the invasion.[53]

One of the main objectives of the invasion was to capture or destroy the headquarters of all North Vietnamese and Viet Cong forces fighting in South Vietnam, which was known as the Central Office, South Vietnam (COSVN). SIGINT collected prior to the invasion showed that the COSVN headquarters

complex was located somewhere just inside Cambodia opposite Tay Ninh
Province in South Vietnam. Throughout the incursion, U.S. Army and Air
Force ARDF aircraft were able to track the movements of COSVN by listening
to its radio transmissions as it retreated deeper into Cambodia, always well
ahead of the slow-moving U.S. and South Vietnamese forces, which, SIGINT
showed, never came close to capturing the headquarters.[54]

The invasion of Cambodia prompted the North Vietnamese to expand their
control over eastern Cambodia. By the end of May 1970, all U.S. and South Vietnamese forces had retreated back across the border into South Vietnam, and the
North Vietnamese military was left with complete control over all of northeastern Cambodia. As an NSA historian put it, "few operations in American military history had such dismal consequences."[55]

This Is the End

On January 27, 1973, Secretary of State William Rogers and his North Vietnamese counterpart, Le Duc Tho, signed the Paris Peace Agreement, and the last remaining U.S. forces were withdrawn from South Vietnam two months later,
including the last remaining U.S. military SIGINT collection units. After the
U.S. troop withdrawal was completed, in late 1973, the only remaining NSA
presence in the country was the agency's liaison staff in Saigon, as well as several hundred U.S. Army advisers who were engaged in trying to train and equip
the South Vietnamese SIGINT service.[56]

Things remained relatively peaceful until the fall of 1974, when SIGINT
reporting coming out of NSA began indicating that the North Vietnamese were
openly building up the strength of their military forces inside South Vietnam.
SIGINT clearly showed that huge numbers of North Vietnamese troops and
supplies, including tanks and armored vehicles, were flowing down the Ho Chi
Minh Trail, and they were no longer being hindered by American air strikes. By
January 1975, SIGINT showed that the North Vietnamese military buildup in
South Vietnam had been completed. Everyone in Washington knew that the "fi-
nal offensive" was coming soon.[57]

The collapse of South Vietnam began with the North Vietnamese conducting a probing attack in January 1975 in Phuoc Long Province, in southern
South Vietnam. After a short fight, the province swiftly fell, a preview of what
was to come. Despite all SIGINT indications of a continued North Vietnamese
military buildup throughout the south, on February 5 the CIA's intelligence analysts made this prediction: "While we expect localized heavy fighting to re-

sume soon, there are no indications of Communist plans for an all-out offensive in the near future." On February 18, the CIA predicted, "heavy North Vietnamese attacks" by the end of the month, with the expected focus of the new offensive to be Tay Ninh City, north of Saigon.[58]

The CIA analysts could not have been more wrong. In March, the all-out North Vietnamese offensive commenced, not around Tay Ninh but across northern South Vietnam and the Central Highlands. NSA and South Vietnamese SIGINT somehow failed to detect the presence of at least three North Vietnamese divisions in the Central Highlands until the attacks began. City after city fell in rapid succession, and by the end of March the entire Central Highlands had been abandoned to the North Vietnamese. The NSA representative at the South Vietnamese SIGINT intercept center in Pleiku barely managed to get out of the city before it fell. As North Vietnamese forces streamed south virtually unopposed, the old imperial capital of Hué fell on March 22. In mid-March, SIGINT had detected a number of North Vietnamese strategic reserve divisions being hastily moved into South Vietnam for the final push.[59]

As the North Vietnamese forces pushed southward toward the city of Da Nang, on March 26 NSA ordered the sole agency officer assigned to the South Vietnamese listening post in the city to get out immediately. The NSA officer drove to the Da Nang airport and managed to talk his way on board one of the last Boeing 727 aircraft to get out of the city. An NSA history notes, "He rode the overloaded airplane to Saigon with a Vietnamese child on his lap." Da Nang fell to the North Vietnamese four days later.[60]

As the North Vietnamese brought up reinforcements and supplies for the final push to take Saigon, a few hundred miles to the west the forces of the Cambodian government were rapidly collapsing. Since the U.S. invasion of Cambodia in April 1970, the North Vietnamese–backed Khmer Rouge forces had methodically captured most of the country from President Lon Nol's poorly led government forces. By January 1975, Lon Nol's troops held only a tiny island of territory surrounding the capital of Phnom Penh, and SIGINT reporting coming out of NSA and from U.S. military units based in neighboring Thailand showed that the Khmer Rouge were inching closer to the besieged capital. On April 11, a U.S. Air Force SIGINT unit in Thailand intercepted a message from the Khmer Rouge high command ordering the final assault on Phnom Penh. Ambassador John Gunther Dean was immediately ordered to evacuate all employees of the U.S. embassy and any other Americans remaining in Cambodia. U.S. military helicopters had completed the evacuation by the end of the day on April 12. The city fell to the Khmer Rouge the next day.[61]

In Saigon, Ambassador Graham Martin refused to believe the SIGINT reporting that detailed the massive North Vietnamese military buildup taking place all around the city. He steadfastly disregarded the portents, even after the South Vietnamese president, Nguyen Van Thieu, and most of his ministers resigned and fled the country. An NSA history notes that Martin "believed that the SIGINT was NVA deception" and repeatedly refused to allow NSA's station chief, Tom Glenn, to evacuate his forty-three-man staff and their twenty-two dependents from Saigon. Glenn also wanted to evacuate as many of the South Vietnamese SIGINT staff as possible, as they had worked side by side with NSA for so many years, but this request was also refused. NSA director Lieutenant General Lew Allen Jr., who had taken over the position in August 1973, pleaded with CIA director William Colby for permission to evacuate the NSA station from Saigon, but even this plea was to no avail because Martin did not want to show any sign that the U.S. government thought Saigon would fall. So Glenn disobeyed Martin's direct order and surreptitiously put most of his staff and all of their dependents onto jammed commercial airlines leaving Saigon. There was nothing he could do for the hundreds of South Vietnamese officers and staff members who remained at their posts in Saigon listening to the North Vietnamese close in on the capital.[62]

By April 24, 1975, even the CIA admitted the end was near. Colby delivered the bad news to President Gerald Ford, telling him that "the fate of the Republic of Vietnam is sealed, and Saigon faces imminent military collapse."[63]

Even when enemy troops and tanks overran the major South Vietnamese military base at Bien Hoa, outside Saigon, on April 26, Martin still refused to accept that Saigon was doomed. On April 28, Glenn met with the ambassador carrying a message from Allen ordering Glenn to pack up his equipment and evacuate his remaining staff immediately. Martin refused to allow this. The following morning, the military airfield at Tan Son Nhut fell, cutting off the last air link to the outside.

A massive evacuation operation to remove the last Americans and their South Vietnamese allies from Saigon began on April 29. Navy helicopters from the aircraft carrier USS *Hancock*, cruising offshore, began shuttling back and forth, carrying seven thousand Americans and South Vietnamese to safety. U.S. Air Force U-2 and RC-135 reconnaissance aircraft were orbiting off the coast monitoring North Vietnamese radio traffic to detect any threat to the evacuation. In the confusion, Glenn discovered that no one had made any arrangements to evacuate his remaining staff, so the U.S. military attaché arranged for cars to pick up Glenn and his people at their compound outside Saigon and transport them to the embassy. That night, Glenn and his colleagues boarded a U.S. Navy helicopter for the short ride to one of the navy ships off the coast.[64]

But the thousands of South Vietnamese SIGINT officers and intercept operators, including their chief, General Pham Van Nhon, never got out. The North Vietnamese captured the entire twenty-seven-hundred-man organization intact as well as all their equipment. An NSA history notes, "Many of the South Vietnamese SIGINTers undoubtedly perished; others wound up in reeducation camps. In later years a few began trickling into the United States under the orderly departure program. Their story is yet untold." By any measure, it was an inglorious end to NSA's fifteen-year involvement in the Vietnam War, one that still haunts agency veterans to this day.[65]

CHAPTER 8

Riding the Whirlwind

NSA During the Johnson Administration: 1963–1969

> Sic gorgiamus allos subjectatos nunc
> (*We gladly feast on those who would subdue us*).
> —Morticia Addams, *The Addams Family*

The State of the SIGINT Nation

Between 1961 and 1969, NSA grew from 59,000 military and civilian person-nel, with a budget of $654 million, to a staggering 93,067 men and women, 19,300 of whom worked at NSA headquarters at Fort Meade, in Maryland. The agency's budget stood at over $1 billion.[1]

As it quickly became larger than all the other U.S. intelligence agencies combined, it was developing and deploying cutting-edge technology that radi-cally transformed how it collected and produced intelligence. Beginning in 1960, NSA's highly classified Boresight project employed special equipment at Naval Security Group high-frequency direction-finding (HFDF) listening posts that could locate the source of the burst transmissions of Soviet sub-marines in the Atlantic and the Pacific.[2] Later in the 1960s, a new worldwide ocean surveillance SIGINT system was brought online called Classic Bullseye. An automated, larger, faster, and more capable HFDF system than previous manual versions, Classic Bullseye merged and modernized the naval SIGINT intercept and HFDF resources of all five UKUSA member nations. It enabled the United States and its SIGINT partners to track in near real time the move-ments and activities of Soviet warships and submarines around the world. By the early 1970s, the Naval Security Group Command was operating twenty-one

Classic Bullseye stations around the world, which were integrated with eight stations operated by NSA's UKUSA partners.[3]

NSA also fitted out seven spy ships under the rather transparent cover description of "Technical Research Ships." In June 1956, NSA director General Ralph Canine had recommended putting NSA intercept gear on U.S. Navy ships as a rapid-reaction force to cover contingencies in parts of the world where NSA did not have listening posts. Under pressure from the CIA in the late 1950s, NSA increased its SIGINT coverage of areas it had long neglected, particularly Latin America and Africa, where events commanded greater U.S. intelligence attention following the granting of independence to former colonies by European nations. Small but bloody guerrilla wars, many communist-backed, broke out throughout Latin America, Africa, and Asia. To monitor all these developments, NSA built its own fleet of spy ships—patterned after the Russian spy trawlers that had lurked off American territorial waters since the early 1950s—which were to be manned by U.S. Navy officers and crews but used exclusively for NSA.[4]

With the launch of the first "ferret" electronic intelligence satellites by the National Reconnaissance Office (NRO) in the early 1960s, NSA also played an increasingly important role in space, its ELINT collection exponentially expanding what the U.S. intelligence community knew about the Soviet Union. Between 1963 and 1967, American ferret satellites mapped the locations and ascertained the capabilities of virtually every Soviet radar site in Eastern Europe and the Soviet Union, as well as all Chinese, North Korean, and North Vietnamese radar systems. By 1967, the ELINT database had enabled the CIA to issue its first truly comprehensive National Intelligence Estimate on the state of Soviet air defenses, an assessment based almost entirely on SIGINT.[5]

Beginning in 1966, the U.S. intelligence community became alarmed about the nascent Soviet antiballistic missile (ABM) system that was then being constructed around Moscow. Given a November 17, 1966, U.S. Intelligence Board mandate, CIA director Richard Helms ordered his agency to develop—in a year or less—a new ELINT satellite to collect intelligence about Soviet ABM work. It was developed, produced, and launched by the NRO, and the first of the new ABM-intercept satellites went into orbit in early 1968. Colonel John Copley, head of the NSA division processing the satellite intercepts, later recounted, "By 1968 data from these payloads and the follow-on systems had identified early ABM-associated radars, greatly reducing the uncertainty associated with the Soviet strategic threat."[6]

To exploit the cornucopia of intercepted SIGINT data, NSA's basement computer complex expanded dramatically in the 1960s, particularly with the advent of IBM's development in the late 1950s of a revolutionary new data processor called Stretch, which was one hundred times more powerful than any other existing computer system. NSA's deputy director, Louis Tordella, immediately ordered the computer. The first one, christened Harvest by NSA, was delivered in early 1962. With the capacity to read three million characters per minute, Harvest could do in minutes what older computers had taken weeks to accomplish. For example, in 1968 Harvest took only three hours and fifty minutes to scan seven million intercepts to see if they contained any of seven thousand words and phrases on a watch list, which equated to over thirty thousand intercepts scanned per minute. This huge computer system, the agency's workhorse for the next fifteen years, is generally credited with helping NSA stay competitive in the code-breaking game throughout the 1960s and was reportedly instrumental in helping NSA solve a number of important Soviet cipher systems during the 1970s.[7]

By 1968, NSA's inventory of computers dwarfed the computing power of the rest of the U.S. government combined, with the exception of the somewhat smaller computer complex used by the nuclear weapons designers of the Atomic Energy Commission. NSA's director, General Marshall Carter, boasted, "NSA had over 100 computers occupying almost 5 acres of floorspace."[8]

I Get the Sense You Are Disappointed

But despite all of the new technology at NSA's command, it was becoming increasingly difficult to produce against its primary targets. To NSA's frustration, a new generation of computerized cipher machines were being introduced around the world, which taxed the ability of NSA's cryptanalysts to the limit, making it even more difficult for NSA to produce meaningful intelligence. As this increasingly worrisome decline continued, senior U.S. intelligence officials began to question whether SIGINT was worth all of the time, effort, and money allotted to it. The greatest problem was that twenty years after the end of World War II, NSA still could not read high-level enciphered Russian traffic. By 1965, there was a widespread belief within the U.S. intelligence community that the decline in NSA's intelligence production had reached worrisome proportions, with a declassified CIA memo admitting that "SIGINT, striving for breakthroughs, is struggling against the growing security barriers that increasingly prevent readout of wanted information from signals."[9]

A special unit called A5 was created in 1961 to mount an all-out assault on Soviet codes, headed by one of NSA's best cryptanalysts, William Lutwiniak, who in his spare time was also the editor of the *Washington Post* crossword puzzle. He had been hired by the legendary William Friedman in February 1941 and worked on Japanese codes during the war. After that, he turned his attention to Russian ciphers, including some groundbreaking work on the solution of the Venona material. He would head A5 for the next twelve years. Unfortunately, he came in at a time when the hugely expensive cryptanalytic effort against Russian high-level ciphers remained stalled, with only one Soviet high-grade cipher machine system then being partially readable. According to a confidential source, the two Russian cipher machine systems that NSA was partially exploiting at the time—Silver and Mercury—yielded a trickle of intelligence rather than a flood.

Concerned about the declining value of NSA's cryptanalytic product, and in particular the agency's lack of progress against Soviet cipher systems, in 1965 the CIA asked the former chief of the agency's Clandestine Service, Richard "Dick" Bissell, to take a long, hard look at NSA's cryptanalytic efforts. Working largely by himself, Dick Bissell examined the long-term prospects for success against Soviet cipher systems. Bissell concluded that there should be no reduction in NSA's overall cryptanalytic effort, but recommended that many of the NSA personnel then working on Soviet systems might be better employed working on the ciphers of "softer" non-Soviet targets.[10]

This meant that NSA's most productive sources during the 1960s remained low-level signals sources that still had to be harvested and analyzed en masse in order to derive even a modicum of useful intelligence. For example, NSA was able to locate a few Soviet ICBM launch sites and missile test and production facilities by carefully monitoring the flight activity of special transport aircraft belonging to a number of special Soviet air force transport units based in and around Moscow whose function was to transport senior military officials and scientists and engineers involved in the missile program throughout the country.[11] In a similar vein, virtually all of the intelligence that NSA was producing in the 1950s and early 1960s concerning Soviet nuclear weapons testing activities was based almost entirely on intercepts of low-level radio traffic relating to special transport aircraft flight activity and weather reporting relating to Russian nuclear weapons tests, as well as exploiting the unencrypted communications traffic of the Soviet nuclear test detection system.[12]

But declassified documents show that it was becoming increasingly difficult for NSA to get at these low-level targets because beginning in the early 1960s, the Russians moved important chunks of their telephone and telegraph traffic to new telecommunications systems which the agency could not intercept, such as buried coaxial cable links and microwave radio-relay systems. According to former senior CIA official Albert Wheelon, by 1963 "communications intelligence against the USSR was helpful but eroding as the Soviets moved their traffic to landlines and microwave links." This meant that NSA's collection specialists spent the entire decade of the 1960s trying as best they could to"reestablish COMINT access to Soviet and Chinese communications traffic."[13]

Pat's House

In April 1965, Lieutenant General Gordon Blake retired and was replaced as NSA's director by his 1931 West Point classmate Lieutenant General Marshall "Pat" Carter, who was to become one of the most important men ever to head the agency, for better and for worse.

Carter served in a variety of antiaircraft artillery postings in the United States, Hawaii, and Panama before the army recognized his considerable intellect and sent him to study at the Massachusetts Institute of Technology, from which he graduated in 1936. From 1946 to 1947, he was the executive assistant to General George Marshall when the latter served as Truman's special envoy to China. To everyone's surprise, the taciturn Marshall and the jovial bon vivant Carter got along so well that when Marshall was named secretary of state in January 1947, he asked the Pentagon if he could keep Carter on as his assistant. After graduating from the National War College in June 1950, Carter moved over to the Pentagon to return to his old job as executive assistant to Marshall, who was now the secretary of defense. From that point onward, Carter served in a number of significant command positions. In March 1962, President Kennedy named him the deputy director of the CIA despite the fact that he had no prior intelligence experience. The job came with a promotion to the rank of lieutenant general. At the CIA, he was intimately involved in Operation Mongoose, the Cuban Missile Crisis, and the Gulf of Tonkin incidents, which brought him into close contact with Presidents Kennedy and Johnson and their cabinet members on a daily basis. Carter remained at the CIA until he was named director of NSA.[14]

Bald and pudgy, and not particularly imposing, Carter was bright, shrewd, and an extremely capable administrator, which, coupled with his lengthy exposure to high-level policy making in Washington, made him formidable. He also had a wicked sense of humor that was infamous throughout Washington.

When the aloof CIA director John McCone sealed up the connecting door to Carter's adjacent office at the agency's Langley, Virginia, headquarters in the dead of night, Carter affixed a fake hand to the wall where the door used to be, a less than subtle way of making fun of McCone's action, but also leaving Carter's visitors to wonder if McCone was trying to get out of his office. When McCone asked that perfumes and special toilet paper be placed in his private bathroom at Langley to accommodate the needs of his new wife, Carter responded by installing a container in his private bathroom to hold, among other things, a selection of corncob pipes and a well-worn copy of the Sears catalog.[15]

Despite the fact that he had never before commanded anything as large or complex as NSA, in a matter of months Carter began transforming the agency to fit his own personal vision, and he launched an intensive lobbying campaign to promote NSA within the U.S. intelligence community. This instantly brought him into conflict with senior officials at the CIA, who were inherently fearful of NSA's growing power within the community, and with Secretary of Defense Robert McNamara's Pentagon, which wanted a docile agency that would do as it was told. Rather than bend or compromise, Carter, as a declassified NSA history puts it, "fell on a startled national defense community like a bobcat on the back of a moose."[16]

The years 1965 through 1969 were marked by a never ending series of brawls that pitted Carter and NSA against virtually everybody else in official Washington. In short order, the director managed to alienate McNamara, the entire Joint Chiefs of Staff, and most of the other senior military commanders, which "poisoned the atmosphere and led to a confrontational relationship between NSA and the military it was sworn to support." To many of his subordinates, it seemed as if Carter was deliberately picking fights with anyone who stood in his way.[17]

If anything, NSA's relationship with the U.S. intelligence community was worse. As the agency's influence inside the Johnson White House increased, so too did fear and resentment within the intelligence community. In a series of running battles, the CIA charged that NSA was producing finished intelligence in violation of NSC guidelines; that NSA deliberately sat on intelligence that the CIA needed so that it could look good with the White House; that the analysts at Fort Meade were not getting material to the intelligence community fast enough; and that NSA was flouting the authority of the director of central intelligence to manage the entire U.S. intelligence community.[18]

The Six-Day War and the Attack on the USS Liberty

Well before the start of the June 1967 Arab-Israeli War, NSA listening posts around the Middle East detected a substantial increase in Egyptian, Syrian, Jordanian, and Israeli military activity along the first three countries' borders with Israel, including troop and equipment concentrations, intensified military exercises, and increased Israeli reconnaissance overflights of the other countries. The Naval Security Group (NSG) listening post in Morocco also picked up clear indications of impending hostilities from its intercepts of Egyptian military radio traffic.[19]

On April 7, 1967, a border clash between Israeli and Syrian troops in the Golan Heights escalated into a pitched battle, with the Israeli air force conducting dozens of air strikes on Syrian military positions deep inside Syria. This prompted NSA to declare a SIGINT Readiness Alfa alert for all Middle East targets. The alert was terminated three days later after the fighting ceased.[20]

But the situation in the region continued to deteriorate. On April 22, NSA intercepted radio traffic revealed that Egyptian TU-16 Badger bombers were dropping mustard gas bombs on Yemeni royalist positions in North Yemen. Between May 11 and May 14, the bombers struck a number of towns in southern Saudi Arabia, prompting NSA to increase its SIGINT coverage of Egyptian military activity in Yemen because of the threat it posed to America's ally in the region, Saudi Arabia.[21]

More ominously, NSA intercepted and decrypted a message sent on May 13 by the Egyptian ambassador in Moscow to Cairo that, according to a CIA report, stated "Soviet Deputy Foreign Minister Semenov had told the Egyptians that Israel was preparing a ground and air attack on Syria—to be carried out between 17 and 21 May. It stated that the Soviets had advised the UAR [United Arab Republic] to be prepared, to stay calm, and not to be drawn into fighting with Israel." The Russian warning was totally wrong, but it gave Egyptian president Gamal Abdel Nasser an excuse to ratchet up the tension level, with a CIA report dryly noting, "The Arabs were to take the information but not the advice."[22] The next day, radio intercepts arriving at NSA confirmed that the Egyptians had just placed their entire air defense force on alert and sortied a number of warships out to sea. With this move, NSA extended its SIGINT alert to all Middle Eastern targets.[23]

Nasser's intentions were clearly indicated by his demand, on May 19, for the removal of all U.N. peacekeeping forces in the Sinai Peninsula, which had been in place since the end of the 1956 Arab-Israeli War. After the United Nations withdrew, fifty thousand Egyptian troops along with five hundred tanks streamed across the Suez Canal. SIGINT reporting from the U.S. Air Force listening post at Iráklion, on the island of Crete, showed that the majority of the Egyptian armored and infantry units in the Sinai were now deployed from east to west between the city of Khan Yunis, in the Gaza Strip, and the town of El-Arish, on the north coast of the Sinai.[24] On May 22, Egyptian naval forces imposed a blockade on the Strait of Tiran and closed the Gulf of Aqaba to Israeli shipping, prompting the full-scale mobilization of the Israeli Defense Forces. NSA SIGINT revealed that an Egyptian coastal artillery unit had taken up positions at Sharm al-Sheikh, at the mouth of the Gulf of Aqaba, and that Egyptian torpedo boats were now patrolling the Strait of Tiran, giving the Egyptians the means to attack any ship attempting to sail to the Israeli port of Eilat. The following day, the CIA's Office of Current Intelligence (OCI) formed a Middle East task force in order to monitor the increasingly tense situation in the region, and on May 23, NSA raised its alert status to SIGINT Readiness Bravo Crayon for all Middle East targets, its highest non-wartime alert readiness level.[25] All NSA-controlled listening posts capable of Middle East intercepts were ordered to intensify coverage of military targets in the region, especially the U.S. Army's huge listening post outside Asmara, Ethiopia, known as Kagnew Station; the U.S. Air Force intercept station at Iráklion; and the U.S. Navy listening posts at Yerolakkos on Cyprus, Sidi Yahia in Morocco, and Rota, Spain. NSA also had a few small clandestine listening posts hidden inside U.S. embassies in places like Beirut, which were operated by ASA through an intensely secretive 337-man unit whose oblique cover name was the U.S. Army Communications Support Unit. NSA feared that in the event of war, Egypt and its Arab allies would break diplomatic relations and force the closure of the embassies, shutting down those listening posts. Accordingly, on May 23, NSA ordered the U.S. Navy SIGINT ship USS *Liberty* to sail for the eastern Mediterranean at top speed.[26]

Until its arrival, only a few U.S. Air Force and Navy reconnaissance aircraft equipped for SIGINT collection, based outside Athens, were available for close-up monitoring of the situation, so they were given daily missions off the coast of the Sinai to collect increased intercepts of very high frequency (VHF) and ultrahigh frequency (UHF) Arab and Israeli military radio traffic. These missions yielded full confirmation that Arab and Israeli military forces were on a state of high alert.[27]

During the first weeks of June, radio intercepts revealed that Egyptian antiaircraft batteries deployed around Sharm al-Sheikh had opened fire on Israeli Mirage fighters patrolling the area. COMINT also showed that Egyptian air force aircraft were conducting aerial reconnaissance missions along the border with Israel, and that Egyptian navy torpedo boats had intensified their patrolling activities in the Strait of Tiran.[28] By June 3, COMINT revealed that Egyptian transport aircraft had flown several elite commando battalions to Jordan.[29]

Intercepts by NSA and Great Britain's GCHQ of French diplomatic communications confirmed these and other developments at a time when the United States did not have diplomatic relations with Egypt (hence no firsthand intelligence reporting). The French ambassadors in Cairo and Tel Aviv were trying to broker a peaceful settlement between Egypt and Israel over the Sinai before it erupted in war. NSA was also intercepting and reading Soviet diplomatic radio traffic between Moscow and its military representatives in Cairo, which indicated that the Soviets believed that war between Israel and Egypt was imminent. In April, NSA issued a CRITIC warning after COMINT detected Russian military preparations for this eventuality.[30]

On Sunday morning, June 4, NSA decoded an intercept (whether from French or Israeli communications is still unknown), which revealed that the Israelis intended to attack Egypt within twenty-four hours. One of the very few U.S. government officials cleared for access to this material was a State Department intelligence analyst named Philip Merrill, who was the duty officer in the State Department INR unit that handled SIGINT. Merrill later recalled, "I checked this one morning and a certain word we were looking for, let's just call it *Geronimo*, came in at 5:00 a.m. This was the jump-off word [for the Israeli attack] and there was some limited associated material with it." Merrill raced upstairs to Secretary of State Dean Rusk's office, but Rusk was closeted in a meeting on the crisis with Secretary of Defense McNamara, National Security Advisor Walt Rostow, and others. Of those attending, only Rusk, McNamara, and Rostow were cleared for access to the NSA material, so Rusk's executive secretary devised a pretext for getting those not cleared out of the room so that Merrill could pass on the message. Merrill found it all somewhat amusing but says that it was "an indication for the record of history, how tightly held much of this was."[31]

Monday morning, June 5, started normally for the radio intercept operators at the U.S. Army's huge Kagnew Station, in Ethiopia. At eight A.M. local time (two A.M. Washington time), operators were waiting to be relieved by the day shift when, a former army intercept supervisor recalled years later, one of the night shift's French linguists announced that "some guy was screaming in French and there were clearly bombs exploding in the background. It turned out that the source of the commotion was a French reporter at the Cairo airport, who was yelling into a telephone describing the bombing of the airport while Israeli bombs rained down around him." The 1967 Arab-Israeli War had just begun.[32]

The majority of the four hundred combat aircraft belonging to the Israeli air force were busy destroying virtually all of the Egyptian air force's airfields. A smaller number of Israeli fighter-bombers were at the same time attacking key military airfields in Jordan, Syria, and western Iraq. As a declassified NSA history notes, "by nightfall Israel had complete mastery of the sky having virtually destroyed four Arab air forces."[33]

Around three A.M. Eastern Standard Time (EST) NSA placed all of its units in the Middle East on SIGINT Readiness Alfa, and some of them intercepted the following Egyptian radio message: "Cairo has just been informed at least five of its airfields in Sinai and the Canal area have suddenly become unserviceable." Less than an hour later, the NSA listening post at Iráklion intercepted a Jordanian air force message indicating that a number of its airfields were also being attacked by Israeli fighter-bombers.[34]

National Security Advisor Walt Rostow, reading forwarded raw transcripts of these intercepts in the White House Situation Room (the first reached him shortly after nine A.M.), phoned President Johnson with summaries as soon as they came in. The SIGINT reporting convinced Rostow and Johnson that the Israelis had just launched a massive first strike against the opposing Arab air forces. By midafternoon, it was clear that the Israelis had almost completely wiped out the Egyptian and Jordanian air forces, leading Rostow to send a memo to Johnson later that afternoon titled "The first day's Turkey Shoot."[35]

Chaos within the Egyptian military command structure, as reflected in the COMINT intercepts, was so pervasive that Egyptian military communications personnel stopped enciphering their communications and talked in the clear, giving an unexpected gift to American, British, and Israeli radio intelligence personnel.[36] SIGINT during the war also revealed that Iraq, which had promised to provide the Syrians fighting the Israelis in the Golan Heights with a full combat division, had in fact not moved any units toward its border with Syria.[37]

Beginning on June 6, the day after the Israeli offensive began, and continuing for the next three weeks, NSA listening posts in Europe and the Middle East monitored over 350 flights of Russian military transport aircraft from the Soviet Union to Syria and Egypt carrying military equipment and supplies.[38]

But the Russian shipments were all for naught. By the end of June 7, virtually all the Egyptian army units in the Sinai had been destroyed, and the survivors were fleeing back to Egypt as fast as they could. Robert Wilson, an Arabic linguist on the NSA spy ship the *Liberty*, which had finally arrived off the north coast of the Sinai on June 7, recalled, "Once we got on station, the Egyptians were dead, practically. There was no voice communications at all that we could pick up, except for the Israelis." Unfortunately, as recently declassified NSA material reveals, the *Liberty* had sailed without any Hebrew linguists aboard, since NSA had not tasked it to intercept Israeli communications before it sailed.[39]

SIGINT was able to show that the Egyptian general staff was desperately trying to extricate what was left of its decimated forces from the Sinai. By the end of June 8, NSA analysts knew that the war was for all intents and purposes over, having intercepted a message from the commander of Israeli forces in the Sinai telling Tel Aviv that his forces were "camping on the banks of the Suez Canal and the Red Sea."[40]

But that afternoon, Israeli fighter-bombers and motor torpedo boats attacked the *Liberty* as it sailed in international waters off the north coast of the Sinai. The attack killed 34 members of the ship's crew, including 25 navy, marine, and NSA civilian cryptologists in its research spaces, and wounded a further 171 crew members. This incident represents the single worst loss of SIGINT personnel in NSA's history, something for which, understandably, many former NSA personnel and most crewmen who were on the *Liberty* have never forgiven the Israelis.[41]

While the *Liberty* was unable to read the communications in Hebrew of the attacking Israeli warplanes and torpedo boats, a U.S. Navy EC-121M SIGINT aircraft flying out of its base in Greece was able to intercept the radio traffic between Israeli helicopter pilots scouting the ship and their ground controller at Hatzor Air Base, near Tel Aviv, shortly after the attacks took place.[42] These intercepts confirmed that Israeli forces had attacked the *Liberty*, and that the Israelis had failed to identify it as an American ship before or during the attack. One intercept caught the pilot of one of the Israeli helicopters radioing that the attacked ship was "definitely Egyptian."[43]

Thirty years later, a raging controversy continues to swirl around the Israeli attack on the *Liberty*. The Israeli government admitted that its forces had attacked the ship, but claimed that it had been an accident. Although the U.S. government accepted the Israeli government's finding and reparation payment, this explanation was rejected by most of the *Liberty*'s surviving crew members, who wonder how the Israeli fighter pilots and torpedo boat captains who attacked the ship could not have noticed the huge American flag flying from the ship's masthead. Former NSA officials and *Liberty* crew members have, more recently, alleged that NSA is withholding from the public transcripts of intercepted Israeli communications that allegedly show that the Israelis knew they were attacking an American ship. But current NSA officials deny this claim, although they acknowledge that NSA continues to withhold from public release a number of documents relating to the attack, for reasons as yet unknown.

In the days after the attack on the *Liberty*, the Israeli military captured the Golan Heights and threatened to extend its advance toward the Syrian capital of Damascus. But the Russians were not about to let Syria be humiliated in the same way as its Egyptian ally. At eight forty-eight A.M. on Saturday, June 10, the Washington-Moscow Hot Line teletype machine in the White House Situation Room printed out a message from Soviet premier Aleksey Kosygin for President Johnson, one of the most ominous ever transmitted via this communications link. It read, in part, "A very crucial moment has now arrived which forces us, if military actions are not stopped in the next few hours, to adopt an independent decision. We are ready to do this. However, these actions may bring us into a clash, which will lead to a grave catastrophe . . . We propose to warn Israel that, if this is not fulfilled, necessary actions will be taken, including military." In other words, if the Israeli military's advance on Damascus was not stopped immediately, the Soviets would intervene militarily. Kosygin's threat set off alarm bells all over Washington. CIA director Richard Helms, who was in the Cabinet Room at the White House when Kosygin's message was delivered, recalled, "The atmosphere was tense. The conversation was conducted in the lowest voices I have ever heard." The entire U.S. intelligence community was immediately placed on alert, with NSA's director of operations, Oliver Kirby, declaring a SIGINT Readiness Bravo Crayon alert for all Soviet communications targets.[44]

Shortly after Kosygin's message, SIGINT revealed that a number of Soviet airborne divisions and their associated military transport aircraft had been placed on alert inside the Soviet Union. SIGINT also confirmed that at least some of Russia's strategic nuclear forces had been placed on alert. A month later, in July, SIGINT detected the largest integrated exercise of Soviet strategic nuclear forces ever witnessed by the U.S. intelligence community. Not only were all units of the Soviet Strategic Rocket Forces (SRF) tested in a series of high-level command post and communications exercises, but the Russians sortied an unusually high number of submarines from their home bases and even sent a portion of Russia's small strategic bomber force to conduct simulated nuclear strikes on American targets from their Arctic staging bases. To put it mildly, the unannounced exercise caused a fair amount of apprehension in Washington.[45]

Fortunately for all concerned, the Israeli army stopped its advance into Syria, and the Israeli government accepted an immediate U.N.-sponsored ceasefire.

The war officially came to an end at six thirty P.M. on June 10, 1967, and everyone in the U.S. intelligence community breathed a deep sigh of relief.

The USS Pueblo

In February 1965, the commander of the U.S. Pacific Fleet recommended to the chief of naval operations that the navy acquire at least one dedicated spy ship of its own to perform the kinds of SIGINT collection missions that NSA's Liberty-class spy ships were doing. The navy was frustrated that NSA's fleet of "Technical Research Ships" such as the USS Liberty were oriented exclusively toward national SIGINT targets, making them next to useless for gathering the kind of tactical intelligence on Soviet naval activities that the navy wanted but that NSA tended to ignore. So in 1965, the navy approved the conversion of not one but three naval vessels into intelligence collection ships, designated AGERs, which would collect intelligence solely for navy commanders. NSA very reluctantly agreed to allow this, because of fears that the navy had far more ambitious objectives than the ones it cited as grounds for carrying out its own sea-based SIGINT operations.[46]

The navy selected three mothballed World War II–era cargo ships (AKs). The first was the USS Banner, a light cargo ship (AKL-25), chosen in July 1965 because it was "the least unsuitable hull that could be made immediately available." Seven weeks and $1.5 million later, the conversion was complete. Eight SIGINT antennae were bolted to the ship's superstructure and masthead; below the main deck just forward of the pilothouse, a SIGINT operations center nicknamed the Sod Hut (where a twenty-seven-man SIGINT detachment was to work) was added. It was small and extremely cramped, measuring only about thirty feet in length and eleven feet in width, and was configured with five SIGINT intercept positions and a separate communications position, which was less than one quarter the number of intercept positions on NSA's much larger Liberty-class spy ships.[47]

As soon as the conversion was completed, the Banner sailed to her new home port in Yokosuka, Japan, without undertaking any sea trials; arriving in Japan on October 17, she commenced her first operational patrol on October 30. Over the next two years, the Banner provided valuable SIGINT about Soviet, Chinese, and North Korean fleet activities and antisubmarine warfare techniques.[48]

In November 1965, the navy was authorized to modify two more ships into AGER intelligence collection vessels. These ships were the USS Pueblo and the USS *Palm Beach*. On April 12, 1966, the *Pueblo* was reactivated and taken to the Puget Sound Naval Shipyard, where it was converted into an AGER between June 1966 and September 1967 at a cost of $4.5 million. The *Pueblo* departed Bremerton, Washington, in September, and, after a brief shakedown cruise off San Diego, sailed for Japan, arriving at the port of Yokosuka on December 1. She sailed from the port of Sasebo, Japan, on her maiden voyage on January 11, 1968, on what was supposed to be a routine three-and-a-half-week intelligence collection mission off the east coast of North Korea.[49] Twelve days later, on January 23, the *Pueblo* was attacked and seized by North Korean warships in international waters twenty-five miles off the North Korean port of Wonsan. One crewman, Duane Hodges, was killed during the attack.[50]

Weeks before the *Pueblo* sailed, on December 23, 1967, NSA had sent out a message to the U.S. intelligence community warning about the possibility that the spy ship might be attacked by an increasingly belligerent North Korea and suggesting that "ship protective measures"—i.e., air cover and/or a naval escort—be seriously considered. But a congressional investigation after the ship's seizure found that the NSA message "never reached responsible authorities" and observed that "the incredible handling of the NSA warning message on the *Pueblo* mission is hardly looked upon with pride by responsible authorities in the Pentagon." On January 2, 1968, nine days before the *Pueblo* sailed into history, the CIA's deputy director for intelligence wrote a memo to CIA director Helms also warning that the North Koreans "might choose to take some sort of action against these ships."[51]

Intercepts of North Korean naval radio traffic indicated that the North Koreans were well aware of the *Pueblo*'s presence off their coast at least twenty-four hours before the attack, suggesting to American intelligence analysts that the attack was premeditated.[52] NSG listening posts in Japan intercepted radio transmissions from the North Korean warships during the attack that showed that the ship was in international waters when she was seized, although intercepted North Korean radar tracking transmissions reportedly indicated that she had violated North Korean territorial waters.[53]

The damage to U.S. national security caused by the capture of the *Pueblo* was massive and, in most respects, irreparable. An NSA history notes, "It was everyone's worst nightmare, surpassing in damage anything that had ever happened to the cryptologic community."[54]

The problem was that the U.S. government could not admit this because, at the time, the Johnson administration was still sticking to the cover story that the *Pueblo* was an "oceanographic research ship" engaged in routine scientific research. NSA and the rest of the U.S. intelligence community initially believed that the ship's crew had managed to destroy all of the classified documents and equipment on the ship before it was boarded by the North Koreans. Then a few days later, NSA was stunned when it received word that North Korean state television had just broadcast photographs of a large number of Top Secret Codeword documents that had been captured on the *Pueblo*, including the titles of the documents. A few months later, the North Koreans published a book in French that included photographs and the full text of many of the same NSA documents (some of which the agency still holds to be classified), demonstrating what the *Pueblo*'s true mission was.[55]

Then, to make matters even worse, on January 27, 1968, four days after the *Pueblo* was seized, NSA intercepted the radio transmissions of a Vladivostok-based Russian navy AN-12 military transport plane as it landed at the military airfield serving the port of Wonsan. American intelligence analysts were forced to assume the worst case—that Russian experts had flown in and been allowed to examine the *Pueblo*'s SIGINT spaces and captured documents. Shortly afterward, a U.S. Air Force listening post in northern Japan, which was monitoring the Pyongyang-to-Moscow facsimile link, detected that many of the classified documents captured on the *Pueblo* were being sent to Moscow.[56]

In the months that followed, several important SIGINT sources that NSA had been successfully exploiting in the Soviet Union and North Korea dried up without any warning. The loss of these sources made the disaster complete. A January 24 Top Secret Codeword cable from the director of NSA admitted that the capture of the ship was "a major intelligence coup without parallel in modern history." According to the report, the damage to U.S. SIGINT collection operations was deemed to be "very severe."[57]

The White House, the Pentagon, senior U.S. military officers, and even the CIA and NSA all concluded that the mission had been not only dangerous but also unnecessary. When asked by an army interviewer years later whether the *Pueblo* mission had been worth the risk, the commander of U.S. military forces in Korea at the time, General Charles Bonesteel III, said, "No . . . the degree of risk was totally unnecessary. Now, I wanted intelligence. I didn't have any damned intelligence, real intelligence that could provide early warnings against a surprise attack from the North. But we didn't need it in superfluous COMINT. This was the intelligence tail wagging the dog."[58]

The Invasion of Czechoslovakia

SIGINT proved to be valuable and effective in covering the Soviet military buildup for the invasion of Czechoslovakia that began on August 20, 1968. The purpose of the Soviet invasion was to topple the Czech government headed by a progressive-minded Communist Party official named Alexander Dubček. Immediately upon being elected in April 1968, Dubček earned the ire of Moscow by firing all of the hard-line Communists from the Czech government, then instituting a series of popular political and social reforms that caused even more consternation in Moscow.

Within days of Dubček taking power, SIGINT detected the movement of eight Soviet combat divisions from their barracks in East Germany, Poland, and the western military districts of the Soviet Union to points around the periphery of Czechoslovakia. By the end of June, SIGINT and satellite reconnaissance revealed that the Soviets now had thirty-four combat divisions deployed along the Czech border, and that the Soviets were rapidly moving hundreds of combat aircraft to airfields within striking distance of targets inside Czechoslovakia. On July 17, SIGINT detected the first signs that the Soviet military had begun mobilizing its forces in the western USSR for a potential invasion of Czechoslovakia. Three days later NSA reported that a newly activated high-level Soviet headquarters was now operating inside the Soviet military bunker complex at Legnica in southern Poland. On August 3 and 4, NSA listening posts detected the movement of large numbers of Soviet, East German, and Polish troops to the Czech border, and further large-scale troop movements were detected within the Soviet Baltic and Belorussian Military Districts toward the Polish and Czech borders.[59]

But sadly, despite the numerous indicators turning up in SIGINT and from other intelligence sources, the CIA's intelligence analysts at Langley stuck by their judgment that the Soviets would not intervene militarily in Czechoslovakia until after a special meeting of the Czech Communist Party scheduled for September 9, 1968. As it turned out, the Kremlin had already decided that they had to intervene before the Czech Party Congress meeting for fear that the gathering of Czech officials might conceivably endorse a stronger anti-Soviet political platform than that already advocated by the Dubček government.

The best potential source available to the U.S. intelligence community as to whether the Soviets intended to invade Czechoslovakia came from the supersecret joint CIA-NSA listening post located on the tenth floor of the American embassy in Moscow that had been intercepting the telephone calls of key Politburo members since at least the early 1960s. There was also a separate intercept operation hidden inside the British embassy in Moscow. Both sites monitored a wide range of radio and telephone communications inside the Russian capital, including KGB, GRU, Soviet government, and police radio messages, as well as the car phone conversations of Soviet premier Nikita Khrushchev and his successors.[60]

Despite the public disclosure of the Moscow embassy SIGINT operation by the *New York Times* in 1966, the Russian leaders continued to talk away on their car phones in the years that followed, and the CIA and NSA continued to tape and translate them as fast as they came in. The highly sensitive intelligence reports derived from these intercepts, code-named Gamma Guppy, were deemed to be so secret that they were distributed to a very select few in the entire U.S. government. But Gamma Guppy proved not to be a definitive source on the question of Czechoslovakia. According to Ambassador David Fischer, who in 1968 was a senior intelligence analyst at the State Department:

> We had an interesting system called Guppy. Guppy was very compartmentalized special intelligence. It was basically intercepts of the mobile phone lines of the Russian leadership in Moscow. The reason I tell this story is that on the eve of the invasion of Czechoslovakia, the then head of the Warsaw Pact, Marshal [Andrei Antonovich] Grechko, had gone around to all the Warsaw Pact members to canvas them whether or not they were going to invade. And when he arrived back at Moscow airport, we were able to intercept a telephone call Grechko made to Brezhnev. The problem was they were no fools and spoke in a word code—you know, the moon is red or some silly phrase—and we didn't have the faintest idea whether that meant the invasion was on or off.[61]

Back in Washington, an accumulation of new SIGINT convinced NSA intelligence analysts that the Soviets intended to invade Czechoslovakia. On August 19, NSA issued an alert message to the entire U.S. intelligence community that warned that all signs appearing in intercepted Soviet radio traffic indicated that the Russians were about to invade Czechoslovakia. Later that morning, NSA official David McManis, who was serving at the time as the deputy chief of the White House Situation Room, sent a brief note to National Security Advisor Rostow, telling him that "the invasion they both thought would happen appeared to be imminent."[62]

The warnings out of NSA proved to be correct. A few hours later, shortly after midnight on the morning of August 20, a fresh batch of intercepts revealed that fifteen to sixteen Soviet combat divisions and supporting Warsaw Pact forces had crossed the border into Czechoslovakia. In a matter of hours they had occupied most of the largest cities and almost all key government military installations inside Czechoslovakia.[63]

The October Surprise

One of the great secrets of the Vietnam War era was that some of NSA's best SIGINT product came from the agency's ability to read virtually all of the high-level military and diplomatic traffic of the government of South Vietnam as early as the October 1963 coup d'état that overthrew South Vietnamese president Ngo Dinh Diem.[64]

NSA's intelligence continued to improve as the Vietnam War intensified, largely because NSA had supplied all of the South Vietnamese government's communications and encryption equipment to begin with. The most important SIGINT materials coming out of NSA were decrypts of the cable traffic between South Vietnamese president Nguyen Van Thieu and his ambassador in Washington, Bui Diem, which covered the full gamut of U.S.–South Vietnamese relations. By the fall of 1968, these NSA decrypts were deemed to be so sensitive that they were placed in a separate reporting compartment designated Gamma Gout, which limited access to only a select few officials in Washington. Thanks to the NSA decrypts, President Johnson knew virtually everything about the South Vietnamese government's attitudes toward the Paris peace talks with the North Vietnamese, as well as President Thieu's negotiating positions.[65]

It was no secret that an unwilling and angry Thieu felt that Johnson had forced his government to participate in the Paris talks. But Thieu knew that since Johnson was not running for reelection, Thieu stood a pretty good chance of being able to abandon the talks, depending on who won the election in November—the Democrat Hubert Humphrey or the Republican Party's candidate, Richard Nixon.

A little more than a week before the U.S. presidential election, between October 23 and 27, NSA intercepted several "eyes only" messages from Diem to Thieu. Senior members of the Nixon entourage, Diem reported, including longtime Republican political activist Anna Chennault, who was the vice chair of the Republican National Finance Committee, had asked that Thieu stand firm until after the election, when a Republican administration could offer the South Vietnamese government more favorable terms than an administration headed by Humphrey. The Nixon campaign didn't want Thieu to do anything that might help Humphrey get elected, so Nixon wanted Thieu to stall the Paris peace talks by not attending until after the election.[66]

One of Johnson's senior aides, Arthur Krim, recalled in an interview, "The President told me very much off the record . . . they had this cable that Madame [Anna] Chennault had sent I guess it was [Nguyen Van] Thieu or somebody in South Vietnam saying, 'Don't cooperate in Paris. It will be helpful to Humphrey.' I'm not giving you the words, but the gist was wait for Nixon."[67]

The substance of these NSA decrypts was repeatedly confirmed by taps placed in Thieu's office in Saigon by the CIA, which gave the CIA station in Saigon unparalleled access to Thieu's thinking and the machinations of the South Vietnamese government in general.[68] An October 26 CIA memo to National Security Advisor Rostow contained a bombshell derived from the taps: "Thieu sees a definite connection between the moves now underway and President Johnson's wish to see Vice President Humphrey elected. Thieu referred many times to the U.S. elections and suggested to his visitors that the current talks are designed to aid Humphrey's candidacy. Thieu has said that Johnson and Humphrey will be replaced and then Nixon could change the U.S. position."[69]

On October 29, a week before Election Day, Rostow wrote a memo to Johnson that began, "I have been considering the explosive possibilities of the information that we now have on how certain Republicans may have inflamed the South Vietnamese to behave as they have been behaving. There is no evidence that Mr. Nixon himself is involved . . . Beyond that, the materials are so explosive that they could gravely damage the country whether Mr. Nixon is elected or not. If they get out in their present form, they could be the subject of one of the most acrimonious debates we have ever witnessed."[70]

In late October, Johnson ordered FBI assistant director Cartha "Deke" DeLoach to immediately place Anna Chennault under surveillance and put wiretaps on all of the telephone lines servicing the South Vietnamese embassy in Washington. DeLoach recalls that he asked Johnson, "Mr. President, please call the Attorney General and instruct him to tell us to do this." Shortly thereafter, Attorney General Ramsey Clark instructed the FBI to wiretap the South Vietnamese embassy. According to DeLoach, the taps picked up no firm evidence that American political figures were trying to influence South Vietnamese politics.[71]

But in the end, Thieu followed the advice he had gotten from Chennault. On November 2, he reneged on his agreement to sit down in Paris at the same table with the Viet Cong, dashing Johnson's hopes of negotiating a last-minute deal.

For reasons not yet known, Johnson chose not to publicly divulge what Nixon's supporters had done, perhaps because he knew that revealing it would cause political carnage in Washington. Even if he had disclosed the material, it probably would not have helped. Three days later, on November 5, Humphrey was decisively defeated, and on January 20, 1969, Richard Nixon became the new president of the United States.

CHAPTER 9

Tragedy and Triumph

NSA During the Nixon, Ford, and Carter Administrations

The light shines in the darkness, and the
darkness has not overcome it.

—JOHN 1:5

The Post-Vietnam Blues

On the day that Richard Nixon was sworn in as the president of the United States, January 20, 1969, NSA was a billion-dollar colossus, consisting of a staggering 93,067 military and civilian personnel in the United States and seventeen foreign countries. This meant that NSA accounted for 62 percent of the 153,800 military and civilian personnel then engaged in intelligence activities for the Defense Department.[1]

The six years of the Nixon presidency (1969–1974) were anything but a happy time for NSA. As America's involvement in the Vietnam War wound down, the U.S. intelligence community's resources were dramatically slashed. It lost 40 percent of its budget and 50 percent of its people. NSA fared worst of all. Its budget was cut by one third and its manpower fell from 95,000 military and civilian employees in 1969 (19,300 of whom worked at NSA headquarters at Fort Meade) to approximately 50,000 by 1980, of whom 16,500 worked at Fort Meade.[2] The cohesion and discipline of the agency's draftee military personnel deteriorated rapidly. Marijuana usage among military SIGINT personnel increased dramatically. Courts-martial and other forms of disciplinary action involving SIGINT personnel rose dramatically, as did desertion and AWOL rates. Radio intercept operators staged work slowdowns to protest American military operations in Southeast Asia, and NSA personnel even participated in antiwar protests at home against the Vietnam War.[3] The result, according to an NSA historian, was "a scarcely mitigated disaster."[4]

The agency's relationship with the Nixon White House was oftentimes strained. Nixon's national security advisor from 1969 to 1973, Henry Kissinger, established a precedent followed by many of his successors by centralizing control over the entire U.S. government's national security apparatus in his office in the West Wing of the White House, including control of key intelligence assets, especially the super-sensitive SIGINT product coming out of NSA. Kissinger ordered that all NSA intercepts mentioning him or Nixon by name be routed to him exclusively and to nobody else in the U.S. intelligence community. According to former CIA deputy director for intelligence Ray Cline, the CIA objected strongly to this practice, stating that "it made a very serious impact, adverse to the efficient workings of the intelligence community." Kissinger also ordered that certain particularly sensitive NSA intercepts not be shared with the secretaries of state and defense. Colonel Robert Pursley, assistant to Secretary of Defense Melvin Laird, recalled that Laird "always had the feeling we weren't getting all the [NSA] stuff the White House was. Very little intercept mail was going to Mel and most of what we got was so innocuous." When Kissinger became secretary of state in September 1973, he continued the practice of maintaining a back-channel flow of intelligence from NSA.[5] Senior NSA officials who dealt with the White House, such as David McManis, the head of the White House Situation Room, walked a fine line trying to keep on the right side of the law, and not always successfully. As a declassified NSA history admits, "It was not good for SIGINT, and it was deadly for the presidency."[6]

The Shootdown of the EC-121

On April 14, 1969, two North Korean MiG-21 fighters shot down a U.S. Navy EC-121M SIGINT aircraft ninety miles southeast of the North Korean port of Chongjin, over international waters. The aircraft and its crew of thirty-one, including nine navy and marine SIGINT operators, were lost.[7]

The EC-121M took off from Atsugi Naval Air Station, in Japan, at seven A.M. local time on what was supposed to be a routine Beggar Shadow SIGINT collection mission over the Sea of Japan. The mission had been flown more than 190 times without incident by U.S. Navy and Air Force reconnaissance aircraft during the first three months of 1969 alone, so local navy commanders thought there was no reason that this mission should be any different.[8]

The U.S. Air Force listening post at Osan followed every moment of the North Korean attack until one forty-nine P.M., when intercepted North Korean radar tracking intercepts showed the North Korean MiGs returning to base and the stricken EC-121 descending rapidly in a spiral toward the sea.[9]

Radio operators at the EC-121's home base at Atsugi initially hoped that the aircraft's pilot had "hit the deck" to evade the MiGs. But when the plane did not answer repeated calls, at two forty-four P.M. a CRITIC message was issued noting only that the EC-121 was missing and its fate was unknown. An hour and fifteen minutes later, North Korean state radio announced that its fighters had shot down an American "spy plane."[10]

On April 18, an angry President Nixon revealed at a press conference that NSA had read the North Korean air defense radar tracking codes, stating, "What is even more important, they knew [that the aircraft was over international waters] based on their radar. Therefore this attack was unprovoked. It was deliberate. It was without warning." Officials at NSA fell off their chairs when they heard this astounding compromise of a critical NSA capability. A former senior NSA official recalled, "I know it was wrong, but I wanted to take Nixon across my knee and give him the paddling of his life for what he had done. It was inexcusable."[11]

Exit Carter, Enter Gayler

In August 1969, NSA director General Marshall "Pat" Carter retired from active duty. To put it mildly, there were very few tears shed in Washington when Pat Carter stepped down after four years running the agency. Champagne corks popped throughout CIA headquarters in Langley, Virginia, on Carter's last day in office. His subdued retirement ceremony at the Pentagon lasted only ten minutes, with an NSA historian dryly noting, "The Pentagon was [sic] happy to see the last of Marshall Carter as Carter was to leave the wars."[12]

Carter's replacement was a distinguished fifty-four-year-old navy vice admiral named Noel Gayler (pronounced "guy-ler"), who got the job because he was a protégé of Admiral Elmo Zumwalt, the new chief of naval operations. Gayler was considered by many in the Pentagon to be a perfect fit because he was one of the brightest and most capable officers in the military. The son of a career navy officer, he had graduated from the U.S. Naval Academy in 1935 and spent most of his career as a naval aviator. During World War II, he had been a fighter pilot flying off the aircraft carrier USS *Lexington*, winning three Navy Crosses,

the first naval aviator to achieve this distinction. He was also the third navy officer to have flown a jet aircraft and had piloted the longest flight to date launched
from an aircraft carrier. Prior to joining NSA, Gayler had overseen the selection
of nuclear attack targets inside the USSR. But unlike his recent predecessors at
NSA, he had no prior intelligence experience.[13]

The job was a stepping-stone to higher office, Gayler had been assured, but it
came with a price tag. Secretary of Defense Laird approved the selection of
Gayler and his counterpart at the Defense Intelligence Agency (DIA), General
Donald Bennett, because, as Laird later recalled, he could count on their loyalty.
As Laird told them in a meeting in his office, they would *have* to be loyal to him
if they expected to "get four stars after four years. And goddam it, they were
loyal."[14]

Gayler was not an easy man to get to know, much less like. Described by an
NSA historian as "dynamic, mercurial, and high-strung," he was a strict, by-the-
book naval officer who ran a tight ship and did not tolerate dissent.[15]

Because he did not have a technological background Gayler was never able
to fully grasp the details of the important work that his agency performed. "We
were told to 'dumb-down' our briefings," a former NSA official recalled.[16] Frequently frustrated by the complexity of NSA's mission, Gayler later told a congressional staff member, "I often felt like a fire hose was held to my mouth."
He spent most of his three years as director trying to understand the mechan-
ics of how his agency worked, and he wondered why a more experienced navy
intelligence officer had not been selected for the post. Like so many directors
before him, Gayler depended heavily on his civilian deputy, Louis Tordella, to
run the agency while he handled high-level policy matters, especially NSA's
testy relations with the U.S. military.[17]

SIGINT and SALT I

NSA played an enormously important role in the negotiations that led up to the
signing, on May 26, 1972, in Moscow of two Strategic Arms Limitation Treaty
agreements (collectively known to posterity as SALT I). The first agreement was
the Anti-Ballistic Missile (ABM) Treaty, which limited both the United States
and the USSR to a set number of ABM launchers. The second agreement set
firm limits on the total number of strategic nuclear weapons that the two nations could deploy and established strict guidelines for what new strategic nuclear weapons could be developed in the future.

The covert intercept posts inside the American and British embassies in Moscow, code-named Broadside and Tryst, had collected highly valuable intelligence, code-named Gamma Guppy, since at least the early 1960s, by listening in on the Soviet leadership as they talked over the mobile phones in their Chaika limousines. These intercepts were deemed to be so sensitive that their distribution was limited to a very small number of American and British government officials. Then, in 1972, the Canadian SIGINT organization, CBNRC, opened its own small clandestine SIGINT intercept facility in Moscow (code-named Stephanie), hidden inside the military attaché's office in the Canadian embassy. The Stephanie intercept equipment, which was supplied by NSA, was able to intercept many of the radio and telephone signals that were being broadcast from the top of the huge Ostankino radio and TV tower, which loomed over downtown Moscow.[18]

The Gamma Guppy intercepts provided a window, albeit a narrow and imperfect one, into what was going on inside the Kremlin, including decision-making processes, as well as details on the organization of the Soviet Politburo and the personalities and behavior of key Politburo figures.[19] The current director of national intelligence, Rear Admiral John "Mike" McConnell, who served as director of NSA from 1992 to 1996, recalled:

> In the mid-1970s, NSA had access to just about everything the Russian leadership said to themselves and about one another . . . we knew Brezhnev's waist size, his headaches, his wife, his wife's problems, his kids' problems, his intentions on the Politburo with regard to positions, his opinion on the American leadership, his attitude on negotiations, and on and on and on it goes.[20]

But in September 1971, nationally syndicated newspaper columnist Jack Anderson revealed in an article that "for years, the CIA has been able to listen to the kingpins of the Kremlin banter, bicker, and backbite among themselves." According to Anderson's column, the intercepts revealed that "the Soviet leaders gossip about one another and complain about their ailments like old maids." After Anderson's column appeared, the Russians reportedly shut off NSA's access to their car telephone traffic. According to Admiral McConnell, "Jack Anderson published it on Tuesday and it was gone on Thursday, never to be recovered."[21]

Despite the fact that Gamma Guppy had been compromised, the Soviet leaders continued to use this insecure form of communications. The Gamma Guppy intelligence continued to roll in. For example, on May 22, 1972, four days before SALT was signed, National Security Advisor Kissinger informed President Nixon that "very recent developments in Moscow indicate that [General Secretary Leonid] Brezhnev has encountered certain problems regarding his foreign policy . . . There is a suggestion in a sensitive intercept that Brezhnev used his friend [Soviet Defense Minister Andrei] Grechko to justify his military policies, including SALT."[22] On May 26, the embassy listening post intercepted a crucial radio-telephone conversation between Brezhnev and Grechko about the Soviet negotiating position on the last day of the summit meeting with President Nixon before the signing of SALT I. Grechko assured Brezhnev that the huge SS-19 ICBM then being tested could be placed inside the existing SS-11 ICBM silo, thus bypassing the provision of article 2 of SALT I, which limited increases in silo dimensions to 15 percent. According to publicly available information, American negotiators "maneuvered with [the SIGINT intercepts] so effectively that they came home with the agreement not to build an antiballistic missile defense system." A senior U.S. intelligence official who read the intercepts was quoted as saying, "That's the sort of thing that pays NSA's wages for a year."[23]

But after more U.S. news reports (many of them inaccurate) during the early 1970s revealed the role played by the Gamma Guppy intercepts, the Soviets apparently decided to take action. In 1973, they began installing powerful jamming equipment in apartment buildings surrounding the U.S. embassy, and then periodically bombarded the building with microwave signals. U.S. intelligence officials believed the Russians were trying to interfere with or block American eavesdropping equipment. But it was not until May 1975 that the Russians began a continuous microwave bombardment that, according to a declassified CIA report, was done because of "Soviet embarrassment and dismay caused by US press accounts . . . alluding to a US capability to intercept microwave communications in Moscow."[24]

Lew Allen Takes the Helm

In June 1972, Admiral Gayler left NSA—and got his fourth star when Nixon promoted him to the post of heading up CINCPAC, in Hawaii.

His replacement as director of NSA was Air Force Lieutenant General Samuel Phillips, fifty-one, who like Gayler had no intelligence experience before arriving at Fort Meade. Phillips was an accomplished research engineer, holding a master's degree in electrical engineering from the University of

Michigan. He worked on nuclear delivery systems (aircraft and missiles) and the Apollo project, and just prior to his appointment to NSA he had been responsible for launching missiles and satellites into space.[25]

Phillips did not remain at NSA long enough to leave an imprint, much less a legacy. According to his successor, Lieutenant General Lew Allen, shortly after arriving at NSA, Phillips became aware of his agency's involvement in a number of peripheral issues relating to the escalating Watergate scandal, which "influenced his determination to move on."[26] The one significant decision Phillips made that was to have a long-term impact was to begin "civilianizing" many SIGINT collection functions formerly performed by the military, as well as automating many of NSA's SIGINT processing, analytic, and reporting functions so as to reduce the agency's huge civilian payroll.[27]

On August 19, 1973, Phillips was replaced by Allen, a forty-eight-year-old U.S. Air Force officer who was a rare individual for the U.S. military—a certifiable genius who also had a talent for management and a deep understanding of, and interest in, technical matters. He started his air force career as a nuclear weapons ordnance officer with the Strategic Air Command, but his intellect predestined him for greater things. The air force sent him to the University of Illinois, where he obtained both a master's degree and a Ph.D. in nuclear physics. Upon graduating, he was ordered to the Los Alamos nuclear weapons laboratory, where he worked from 1954 to 1957 as a physicist in the nuclear weapons test division studying the effects of high-altitude nuclear detonations on missiles. He then moved into the field of satellite reconnaissance, serving for eight years with the U.S. Air Force component of the National Reconnaissance Office in Los Angeles, from 1965 to 1973. After a brief tenure as the assistant to the director of the CIA for the Intelligence Community Staff, Allen's benefactor in Washington, Secretary of Defense James Schlesinger, arranged for him to become director of NSA.[28]

Perhaps one of the brightest men ever to sit in the NSA director's office, Allen proved to be the perfect man to hold the post during what would be one of the most difficult periods in the agency's history. Some of Allen's subordinates at NSA recalled that the highly focused and businesslike director's face didn't reveal much about what he was thinking. Those who got to know him quickly warmed to him, even those who were not necessarily friends of NSA. L. Britt Snider, who in 1975 was the chief counsel of the Church Committee, which was investigating NSA's domestic activities, described Allen as "a man of impeccable integrity," seemingly a rare virtue in those troubled days in Washington.[29]

Allen's four-year tenure as NSA director was marred by controversy, with NSA being forced to admit publicly in August 1975 that it had engaged in illegal domestic eavesdropping since 1945. Allen was compelled to testify before Congress, the first time ever that an NSA director testified in public session about the activities of the agency.[30]

NSA Enters the Space Race

Unbeknownst to the American public, Allen's tenure was also marked by a number of secret cryptologic successes, many of them brought on by the introduction of new high-tech spying systems, such as a new generation of satellites placed into orbits chosen specifically to facilitate the monitoring of Soviet communications traffic.

Three new types of SIGINT satellites, whose classified nicknames were Canyon, Jumpseat, and Chalet, were put into orbit starting in the late 1960s and continuing throughout the 1970s. These satellites gave NSA access for the first time to high-level telephone traffic deep inside the USSR that was being carried over microwave radio-relay networks.[31] The level of detail obtained from the intercepts produced by these satellites was so high that a former American intelligence officer stated "We could hear their teeth chattering in the Ukraine."[32]

The CIA's brand-new Rhyolite SIGINT satellite revolutionized the U.S. intelligence community's knowledge of Soviet strategic weapons development by intercepting previously unheard telemetry data coming from Soviet strategic ballistic missile and bomber test sites deep inside the Soviet Union. The former CIA deputy director for science and technology Albert Wheelon was to later write that thanks to this satellite, "the intelligence community eventually had almost the same data on each ICBM flight as that available to Soviet engineers. It was immediately clear from the telemetry what type of missile had been flown. When test launches failed, the reason was usually apparent in the telemetry data and the missile's reliability could be established with some confidence. As the Soviets changed from single warhead missiles to multiple warhead reentry vehicles, that change was apparent in the data."[33]

Then, in the fall of 1976, the U.S. Navy ELINT organization launched into orbit the first of its brand-new ocean surveillance satellites, whose classified nickname was Parcae. The system had the unclassified designation of White Cloud, and its clusters of satellites continuously orbited the earth, allowing the navy to track the movements of virtually every warship—Russian, Chinese, or otherwise—on a real-time basis and to a degree that heretofore had not been possible or even imagined.[34] According to an Office of Naval Intelligence

(ONI)–sponsored historical study, "ELINT collection and analysis improved to such an extent that individual Soviet units could be tracked through entire deployments by following the radiation emitted by their navigation and surface-search radar sets."[35]

The 1973 Arab-Israeli War

On October 6, 1973, one hundred thousand Egyptian troops backed by one thousand tanks launched a surprise attack on Israel across the Suez Canal, and fifty thousand Syrian troops advanced into the Golan Heights. Not only were the Israelis caught entirely by surprise, but so was the U.S. intelligence community. Postmortem studies conducted by the community revealed that NSA's reporting on Egypt and Syria's preparations for attacking Israel either had been rejected out of hand by the CIA's intelligence analysts or had been so secret that the vast majority of the analysts at Langley had not been cleared to see it.[36]

The Top Secret Codeword daily and weekly SIGINT summaries prior to the attack from NSA's Office of the Middle East, North Africa, Cuba, Central and South America (G6), then headed by navy captain Dwane Yoder, were chock-full of high-quality intelligence reporting about political, military, and economic activities in the Arab world. Not only did NSA have particularly deep and comprehensive insights into the capabilities of the Egyptian army, the Arab world's largest, but it also had detected the arrival of North Korean fighter pilots and air defense personnel as well as Iraqi Hawker Hunter and Libyan Mirage fighters. The CIA and NSA clandestine listening posts hidden inside the U.S. embassies in Cairo and Damascus were also providing Washington with excellent intelligence from their coverage of local government, military, and police radio traffic. A former CIA operations officer who was in Cairo in 1973 recalled, "We even knew what [Egyptian president Anwar] Sadat was telling his ministers on the phone."[37]

The problem was that since 1967, CIA intelligence analysts back in Washington had formed a distinctly negative impression of the readiness and overall combat capabilities of the Egyptian and Syrian militaries, a view encouraged by reports supplied by Israeli intelligence. When Sadat kicked his Russian military advisers out of Egypt in July 1972, DIA and CIA intelligence analysts further downgraded their estimates of Egyptian combat capabilities, particularly those of Sadat's air force, an estimate that was, unfortunately, reinforced by some NSA SIGINT intelligence sent to Langley.[38]

And yet, starting in the summer of 1973, accumulating NSA SIGINT data clearly indicated that Egypt and Syria were preparing to attack Israel, and in late September NSA reported that it would be "a major offensive." The SIGINT evidence for these preparations was voluminous and highly detailed, including the fact that the Egyptian military had canceled leaves and mobilized its reserves, and that a special command post outside Cairo that in the past had been used only for crisis situations had been activated. Extremely sensitive NSA Top Secret Gamma intercepts also revealed that "a major foreign nation [the Soviet Union] had become extremely sensitive to the prospect of war and concerned about their citizens and dependents in Egypt." All this led NSA intelligence analysts to conclude that war was imminent.[39]

The CIA postmortem study noted, "The information provided by those parts of the Intelligence Community responsible for intelligence collection [NSA] was sufficient to prompt such a warning. Such information (derived from both human and technical sources) was not conclusive but was plentiful, ominous, and often accurate."[40]

But the CIA analysts responsible for the Middle East rejected the intelligence reporting and warnings coming from NSA. Navy captain Norman Klar, who in 1974 took over as head of the NSA's G6 office, recalled, "the NIO [the CIA's national intelligence officer] refused to accept SIGINT information that an attack was imminent. He insisted it was an exercise, because the Arabs wouldn't be 'stupid enough' to attack Israel."[41] Both DIA and the CIA ignored or paid scant heed to the NSA warnings, and the CIA Watch Committee chose to ignore the data completely and reported to the White House that war in the Middle East was *not* imminent. The CIA postmortem study concluded, "Those elements of the Intelligence Community responsible for the production of finished intelligence [notably the CIA!] did not perceive the growing possibility of an Arab attack and thus did not warn of its imminence."[42]

The CIA protested, after the fact, that its analysts had been swamped by hundreds of unintelligible SIGINT summaries, but NSA fired back, arguing that if it had been able to get its unvarnished SIGINT summaries through to the White House without the CIA's intelligence analysts putting their "spin" on the material, it would have been clear that Egypt and Syria were about to attack.[43]

NSA director Lew Allen "resolved that in the future [he] would ensure that a separate view be presented when the judgment of SIGINT analysts [differed] from the common [i.e., CIA, DIA, and other agencies'] view." Allen and his successors fought furiously to ensure that in future the White House would be fully informed about their agency's views, *especially* if they conflicted with those of the CIA.[44]

Norm Klar's Tour de Force

In February 1974, Frank Raven, head of NSA's G Group, which was responsible for SIGINT coverage of all noncommunist countries around the world, gave Norman Klar command of his group's largest and most important unit, the 400-man G6 office. Klar was one of NSA's best cryptanalysts. Trained as a Chinese linguist, he had spent much of his career in the Far East, serving tours of duty in Japan, Taiwan, and the Philippines before returning to Fort Meade in 1971. Raven had initially given him the task of running the part of G Group that broke the codes and ciphers of India and Pakistan. Much of the intelligence reporting produced by Klar's division during the December 1971 war between India and Pakistan had ended up on the desks of President Nixon and Henry Kissinger.[45]

Over the next six years, Klar's unit handled a half-dozen wars and untold numbers of smaller conflicts, including the Turkish invasion of Cyprus in 1974, the Cuban military interventions in Angola and Ethiopia, the bloody civil war in Lebanon, the 1976 Israeli hostage rescue mission at Entebbe, Uganda, the fall of the Somoza regime in Nicaragua, the collapse of the shah of Iran's regime and his replacement by the radical cleric Ayatollah Khomeini, the seizure of the U.S. embassy in Tehran and the resulting hostage crisis, and, finally, the Soviet invasion of Afghanistan in 1979. Klar later joked that his unit was NSA's "crisis management shop," since nothing that G6 handled was ever routine. "We operated under a microscope . . . sometimes we were handling two or three high profile crises at the same time with everything we were producing going straight to the White House."[46]

Klar's unit became the hub of the U.S. intelligence community's first counterterrorism effort, in 1972, and made the first breaks into the communications of Yasser Arafat's Palestine Liberation Organization (PLO) and the host of competing Palestinian terrorist organizations in places like Lebanon. In 1973, the unit's SIGINT helped thwart a plot to bomb Israeli diplomatic establishments and businesses in New York City, and G6 was instrumental in warning that Palestinian terrorists intended to assassinate Secretary of State Kissinger during a 1974 visit to Damascus. By 1979, NSA was reading some of Arafat's most sensitive cable traffic and listening in on his international telephone calls to great effect.[47]

Klar's unit performed well during the civil war in Angola that raged from 1975 through the late 1980s. When the first Cuban combat troops were sent there in September 1975 to prop up the Soviet-supported Angolan regime, the cryptanalysts in G6 made daily, highly detailed reports on the Cuban troops and their Soviet military advisers, including information on Cuban combat losses suffered while they fought with South African forces in late 1975 and early 1976.[48]

When civil war erupted in Lebanon in 1975, followed almost immediately by Syrian military intervention in the country, NSA stepped up its SIGINT coverage of what was going on there, including the redeployment of a MiG-21 fighter regiment to Al Qusayr, in northeastern Syria, where it could be used in Lebanon.[49]

SIGINT and the Panama Canal Negotiations

In 1974, President Gerald Ford opened negotiations with Panamanian strongman General Omar Torrijos over transferring control of the Panama Canal from the United States to Panama. By 1976, the two countries were beginning to make significant headway in their negotiations, despite the fact that Torrijos had sought added leverage by having Lieutenant Colonel Manuel Noriega, the head of the Guardia Nacional G-2, Panama's foreign intelligence organization, stage demonstrations and attacks on Americans.

Virtually everything Torrijos said over the telephone from his office and from his home in Farallón, outside Panama City, was carried over an easily intercepted and American-built microwave network. His conversations were secretly sucked up by a nondescript U.S. Army antenna array at Albrook Air Force Station, which overlooked Panama City. Torrijos's calls were immediately forwarded to U.S. Army intercept operators at Fort Clayton, inside the U.S.-controlled Panama Canal Zone, who taped the calls and urgently forwarded all the processed material to NSA headquarters.[50] Klar's Spanish linguists and analysts in the G6 office, on the third floor of the NSA operations building, sent hastily made translations and analysts' comments via teletype to the State Department and the NSC "within 24 hours after their Panamanian counterparts got them."[51]

This continued from 1975 to 1977, providing the United States with not only salacious material about Torrijos's extracurricular love life, but also vital details on the protracted canal negotiations. The White House and State Department customers effusively commended NSA for this invaluable information, and in 1978, NSA awarded the annual Travis Trophy, denoting the best strategic SIGINT unit working for NSA, to the U.S. Army's 470th Military Intelligence Group in Panama.[52]

But in the spring of 1976, U.S. Army intelligence officials picked up the first indications that Colonel Noriega had penetrated the American SIGINT operation in Panama, and they soon discovered that a twenty-year-old sergeant and Spanish linguist assigned to the 408th ASA Company at Fort Clayton had passed classified information to Noriega's Guardia Nacional G-2. A full-scale inquiry, designated Canton Song, was launched into the sergeant's activities on April 23, 1976.[53]

After an intensive investigation of, and a grant of immunity to, the sergeant (who also implicated another linguist in his unit), it was determined that vital intelligence, including details on how the U.S. Army intended to defend the Panama Canal, had been betrayed to the Panamanians. For his work, the sergeant received only sixteen thousand dollars, much of which he quickly blew on local prostitutes. In January 1976, he tried to sell the same information to the Cuban embassy in Panama City, but the Cubans threw him out, believing that he was a CIA agent provocateur.[54]

Though the two sergeants were guilty of espionage, the army decided that, because they had been immunized, it would be too difficult to prosecute them and dropped the case. But senior officials at NSA demanded that the Ford administration not let these men go unpunished, and in late 1976, NSA director Allen sent a memo to CIA director George H. W. Bush recommending that both sergeants be prosecuted for espionage. Bush declined Allen's request, arguing that he had no authority to overturn the army's decision, but the real reason for not doing so was that it would have exposed the ongoing intelligence operations in Panama, and even possibly derailed negotiations over the draft Panama Canal Treaty.[55]

In January 1977, Gerald Ford left office and was replaced by President Jimmy Carter. The Carter administration felt that it had to inform the House and Senate intelligence committees about the compromise of the NSA operation, but asked the committees not to do anything about it because the matter "was still under investigation."[56] In the end, the two sergeants were given honorable discharges, the case was closed, and on September 7, 1977, the Panama Canal Treaty was signed.

Bobby Ray Inman

On July 5, 1977, Lieutenant General Allen stepped down as director of NSA, was given another star, and was appointed commander of the U.S. Air Force Systems Command. A year later, he became the air force chief of staff, serving until his retirement in June 1982.

His replacement as NSA director was forty-six-year-old Vice Admiral Bobby

Ray Inman, the youngest man ever to hold the position. The son of a gas station owner in tiny Rhonesboro, Texas, Inman was a childhood prodigy, graduating from the University of Texas with honors at nineteen. After graduation, he taught school for a year, then joined the navy in 1951, never intending to do more than a single three-year tour of duty. But Inman chose to remain in the navy, and over a thirty-year career he rose rapidly through the ranks, holding a series of increasingly important positions in naval intelligence. He was a protégé of Admiral James Holloway III, who first got Inman the job of chief of intelligence at Pacific Fleet. When Holloway became chief of naval operations in July 1974, he got Inman promoted to rear admiral and the position of director of ONI, which Inman held from September 1974 to July 1976, before becoming vice director of DIA, a position he held from 1976 to 1977.[57]

Agency veterans were stunned by the torrid pace that the workaholic Inman set; he got up at four A.M. every day except Sunday to read the stack of intelligence reports that had come in overnight and was usually in his office at Fort Meade by six. He drove his senior managers and support staff nuts as they tried to keep up with their demanding boss. A typical workday was ten to twelve hours, six days a week and half a day on Sunday after church services. But Inman was perpetually late for appointments and required a bevy of executive assistants to help him keep track of all the meetings he needed to attend and the papers that required his signature. An NSA historian has written of him, "He appeared perpetually calm, but in reality was about as stable as high voltage across an air gap."[58]

Charming and possessing a dry sense of humor, Inman was infamous within NSA for his awkwardness and clumsiness, earning himself the nickname the Blue Klutz. But those who worked for him, almost without exception, liked and respected him.[59]

Inman proved to be a relentless and vociferous advocate for his agency, which immediately put him at odds with the CIA. Antagonism between the two agencies' top brass had been growing since the 1973 Arab-Israeli War debacle, leading one senior CIA official to recall the days when "NSA looked respectfully and appreciatively to CIA for guidance as to what it should collect and produce. It also depended frequently on the Agency for support in its annual quests for funds . . . As time passed and its budget doubled, tripled, and quadrupled, NSA began to swell its corporate chest and develop a personality and style of its own. An organization which began with a serious inferiority complex gradually developed a feeling that it has 'a corner on the market' in terms of intelligence fit to print."[60]

When the CIA's new director, Admiral Stansfield Turner, tried to rein NSA in by cutting its $1.3 billion budget, Inman went around the CIA and began intensively lobbying on behalf of his agency at the White House. In the process, he made a number of important friends, particularly President Carter's crusty national security advisor, Zbigniew Brzezinski, and Brzezinski's deputy, Colonel William Odom, who would become the director of NSA in 1985. Inman also became a one-man public relations firm trumpeting NSA's accomplishments, even giving on-the-record press interviews, something that previous NSA directors had never done.[61]

After a somewhat rocky start, Inman's relationship with Brzezinski became increasingly close, even though "Zbig" sometimes wanted, according to Inman, "to push me to do things that I think the Agency should not be involved in."[62] Like Henry Kissinger, Brzezinski insisted that NSA send him, on an "eyes only" basis, any decrypts containing his name or the name of any other senior Carter administration official. Inman was only too happy to oblige. His brilliant performances before the Senate and House intelligence committees are legendary. During his tenure at NSA, Inman assiduously courted Congress, established an NSA Legislative Affairs Office, and, for the first time, sent reports detailing NSA's highly sensitive SIGINT activities to the two congressional intelligence oversight committees.[63]

He needed all the friends on Capitol Hill he could get. Upon moving into the director's office at Fort Meade, Inman discovered that NSA, with a staff of forty thousand soldiers and civilians, needed money—lots of money—to deal with a number of major problems that he inherited from Allen. Before taking over at NSA, Allen gave Inman a report on the Soviet cryptanalytic effort, which was on the verge of major success but in desperate need of more money and personnel, which were needed to achieve the anticipated breakthroughs. Another briefing paper given to him in 1977 noted that the new generation of SIGINT satellites in orbit over the Earth had "achieved outstanding performance in a number of areas." But the report noted that more could be done and a rationale was needed for the next generation of huge SIGINT satellites due to be launched into space in the late 1970s. The most pressing problem he inherited was an old one— NSA's analysts were drowning in a sea of intercepts that was growing incrementally every day. A report noted that NSA had "not developed capabilities to efficiently deal with the increased amount of raw data generated by new collection systems."[64]

Inman got $150 million in 1977 to modernize NSA's worldwide operations, with huge appropriations in the following years to expand NSA's SIGINT coverage to previously ignored areas of the world, build new and improved SIGINT satellites, and develop and build a host of new high-tech systems to gain access to a new generation of Soviet communications systems. Inman's advancement of NSA's interests earned him the enmity of many within the U.S. intelligence community, particularly CIA director Turner.[65]

Inman's numerous battles with Turner still reverberate in the halls of NSA and the CIA. Turner was determined to gain a greater degree of control over NSA. Years later, he would describe it as "the largest agency in the intelligence community; a top command of some general or admiral; and a proud, highly competent organization that does not like to keep its light under a bushel . . . a pretty remote member of the [intelligence] community. The physical remoteness [from Washington] is compounded by the fact that the NSA deals in such highly secret materials that it is often reluctant to share them with others lest a leak spoil their ability to get that kind of information again. It is a loner organization."[66]

Inman struggled to get NSA out from under the control of the CIA's National Intelligence Tasking Center, Turner's creation designed to coordinate intelligence tasking and requirements within the U.S. intelligence community. The two men were soon no longer on speaking terms, forcing Frank Carlucci, the deputy director of the CIA, into the uncomfortable position of acting as go-between. But most of all, Inman fought to dismantle Turner's proposed APEX code word classification system, because NSA feared that it would ultimately give the CIA control over the dissemination of NSA-produced intelligence. Inman and his deputies managed to stall implementation of the APEX system until the Reagan administration came into power in January 1981 and promptly killed the plan.[67]

Under Inman's direction, by the late 1970s, NSA had become the top U.S. producer of hard, usable intelligence. During Inman's watch, the agency broke into a series of high-level Soviet cryptographic systems, giving the U.S. intelligence community high-level access to Soviet military and political thinking for the first time in years.[68]

The Soviet Target

Going into the 1970s, NSA and its British partner, GCHQ, were deriving a moderate degree of high-level intelligence about the USSR from sources like the Gamma Guppy intercepts from Moscow, and another program that enabled NSA to read communications traffic between Moscow and the Soviet embassy in Cairo in the months leading up to the October 1973 Arab-Israeli War.[69] In the United States, Project Aquarian gave NSA the ability to tell which U.S. government telephone calls the Soviets were intercepting from inside their diplomatic establishments in Washington, New York, and San Francisco. One intercept caught the KGB listening in on Attorney General Griffin Bell discussing classified information on an unsecure telephone line.[70]

But according to some sources, the overall importance of SIGINT within the U.S. intelligence community continued to decline in the 1970s, particularly with regard to the USSR. This was due in part to a GCHQ official named Geoffrey Arthur Prime, a Russian linguist at Cheltenham from 1968 to 1977, who was arrested in 1982 and charged with spying for the Soviet Union. NSA officials confirmed that while Prime was working at GCHQ headquarters, NSA and GCHQ lost their ability to read a number of important Soviet systems when the Russians abruptly and without warning changed their codes or modified their communications procedures in order to make them impenetrable to the American and British cryptanalysts. In November 1982, Prime pleaded guilty and was sentenced to thirty-eight years in prison.[71]

A 1976 study of U.S. intelligence reporting on the Soviet Union, however, found that virtually all of the material contained in the CIA's National Intelligence Estimates about Soviet strategic and conventional military forces came from SIGINT and satellite imagery. A similar study found that less than 5 percent of the finished intelligence being generated by the U.S. intelligence community came from HUMINT.[72] Moreover, rapid changes in intelligence-gathering and information-processing technology proved to be a godsend for NSA. In 1976, NSA retired its huge IBM Harvest computer system, which had been the mainstay of the agency's cryptanalysts since February 1962. It was replaced by the first of computer genius Seymour Cray's new Cray-1 supercomputers. Standing six feet six inches high, the Cray supercomputer was a remarkable piece of machinery, capable of performing 150–200 million calculations a second, giving it ten times the computing power of any other computer in the world. More important, the Cray allowed the agency's cryptanalysts for the first time to tackle the previously invulnerable Soviet high-level cipher systems.[73]

Shortly after Bobby Inman became the director of NSA in 1977, cryptanalysts working for the agency's Soviet code-breaking unit, A Group, headed by Ann Caracristi, succeeded in solving a number of Soviet cipher systems that gave NSA access to high-level Soviet communications. Credit for this accomplishment goes to a small and ultra-secretive unit called the Rainfall Program Management Division, headed from 1974 to 1978 by a native New Yorker named Lawrence Castro. Holding bachelor's and master's degrees in electrical engineering from the Massachusetts Institute of Technology, Castro got into the SIGINT business in 1965 when he joined ASA as a young second lieutenant. In 1967, he converted to civilian status and joined NSA as an engineer in the agency's Research and Engineering Organization, where he worked on techniques for solving high-level Russian cipher systems.[74]

By 1976, thanks in part to some mistakes made by Russian cipher operators, NSA cryptanalysts were able to reconstruct some of the inner workings of the Soviet military's cipher systems. In 1977, NSA suddenly was able to read at least some of the communications traffic passing between Moscow and the Russian embassy in Washington, including one message from Russian ambassador Anatoly Dobrynin to the Soviet Foreign Ministry repeating the advice given him by Henry Kissinger on how to deal with the new Carter administration in the still-ongoing SALT II negotiations.[75]

The Iranian Revolution

NSA was successful in deciphering the most sensitive communications traffic and high-level thinking of the Iranian government prior to the fall of the shah in February 1979, but there is little indication that the intelligence analysts at the CIA took much note of this material. Instead, Langley seems to have relied on the daily reporting of the U.S. military attachés in Tehran, who generally presented a more optimistic view of the viability of the shah's regime than most other experts.[76]

When the February 1979 revolution brought the Islamic fundamentalist cleric Ayatollah Khomeini to power, the CIA's Tacksman intercept bases in Iran, which monitored Russian missile telemetry signals, were shut down. However, NSA continued to exploit high-level Iranian diplomatic and military communications traffic, the best intercepts coming from the Rhyolite SIGINT satellites parked over North Africa, which were retargeted to intercept Iranian military tactical radio traffic.[77]

The 1979 Sino-Vietnamese War

After Vietnamese forces invaded Cambodia in late December 1977, Beijing ratcheted up a war of words directed at Vietnam, forcing it to withdraw its troops in January 1978. The first signs that China had begun preparing for a potential war with Vietnam came in October 1978, when SIGINT detected Chinese army units leaving their garrisons in and around the southern Chinese city of Kunming and taking up positions along China's border with Vietnam. The buildup of troops and aircraft continued until, by January 1, 1979, the Chinese troops deployed along the Vietnamese border outnumbered the Vietnamese troops four to one. War was imminent. It was just a question of when it would break out.[78]

On the morning of January 4, over one hundred thousand Vietnamese troops invaded Cambodia, and in a matter of a few weeks they destroyed the military forces of the brutal Khmer Rouge regime and forced its despotic ruler, Pol Pot, and his minions to flee to neighboring Thailand. The next day, NSA and the Australian SIGINT agency, the Defence Signals Directorate (DSD), declared a SIGINT alert, anticipating that the invasion would almost certainly provoke a forceful Chinese response.[79]

NSA and DSD watched and listened as the Chinese ultimately positioned 320,000 ground troops and 350 combat aircraft in the area adjacent to the Vietnamese border by early February, as well as activating special communications circuits connecting Beijing with a special Chinese general staff command post at Duyun, in southern China, one that had previously been activated only in time's of hostilities. On January 19, the CIA had reported, "The manner of the buildup, its timing and the mix of forces involved suggest offensive rather than defensive preparations." CIA and Australian intelligence analysts in Washington and Canberra also believed that outright war between the two countries was unlikely. So it came as a shock to many policy makers in Washington when seven Chinese armies surged across the border into Vietnam at dawn on the morning of February 17.[80]

NSA's performance during the run-up to the Chinese offensive appears to have been a mixed bag, largely because its overall collection efforts were hampered by communications security measures taken by both the Chinese and the Vietnamese militaries, such as extensive use of landlines instead of radio.[81]

The Fall of Somoza and the Russian Brigade in Cuba

On July 17, 1979, the longtime Nicaraguan dictator Anastasio "Tacho" Somoza fled Nicaragua for Miami, but was denied entry to the United States by President Carter. Two days later, the Sandinista guerrillas who had battled Somoza for a decade entered the Nicaraguan capital of Managua and declared themselves the new rulers of the country.

The Carter administration ordered intensified intelligence coverage of the new regime because it was supported by the Soviet Union and Cuba. In particular, the White House wanted to know if the Sandinistas were providing material or financial support to the Marxist guerrillas operating in neighboring El Salvador, who called themselves the Faribundo Martí National Liberation Front (FMLN). As part of the "surge" effort, Norman Klar's G6 stepped up SIGINT reporting on Nicaragua. U.S. Navy SIGINT reconnaissance aircraft were deployed to Guantánamo Bay, Cuba, to monitor developments in Nicaragua, and NSA's listening posts in the region were tasked with greater coverage of Sandinista communications.[82]

By 1980, Klar's cryptanalysts had solved and were reading some high-level Nicaraguan diplomatic communications traffic, but much less SIGINT was being obtained from the Salvadoran FMLN guerrillas, who communicated by radio far less often than their Nicaraguan counterparts.[83]

Administration officials, particularly Zbigniew Brzezinski, were convinced that the Sandinista victory in Nicaragua and the growing power of FMLN in El Salvador were being directed by Fidel Castro in Havana, almost certainly with backing from the Soviet Union, so NSA and the rest of the U.S. intelligence community were ordered to intensify their reporting on Cuban military and clandestine activity in Central America as well as Soviet activities in Cuba itself. Accordingly, in July and August 1979, NSA dramatically stepped up its SIGINT coverage of Cuba.[84]

The U.S. intelligence community knew the Russians had maintained a sizable military training mission in Cuba since 1962, and the CIA reported to President Carter in May 1979 that there were two thousand Soviet military personnel serving as advisers to the Cuban military and conducting SIGINT collection at a large listening post in Lourdes, outside Havana. The report stated that, according to some fragmentary SIGINT, Soviet pilots were flying Cuban MiG fighters, but it made no mention of Soviet combat troops being in Cuba.[85]

Based on a few intercepts, some CIA agent reports, and some satellite imagery, during the period from April to July 1979 Klar's G6 office came to the conclusion that a Soviet combat unit of brigade size was stationed in Cuba. As former CIA director Stansfield Turner notes in his memoirs, this "was a big inference from a sparse fact or two." Without the approval of the CIA, NSA published its findings in the July 13 edition of the "Green Hornet," as NSA's daily compendium of SIGINT "news," the *SIGINT Summary*, was widely known in Washington.[86]

The U.S. intelligence community, already concerned about the Cuban military's role in Angola and Ethiopia, as well as the increasingly unstable political situation in Central America, was upset by NSA's action, and an incensed

Stan Turner informed the White House that NSA's actions constituted a direct violation of the prohibition against its producing finished intelligence reports for the president, a function reserved for the CIA.[87]

On July 19, the CIA and the rest of the U.S. intelligence community issued a report that tentatively concluded "that a Soviet ground forces brigade was *possibly* stationed in Cuba, but that its size, location(s), and mission were uncertain." Then, triggered by an intercepted message, on August 17, a CIA reconnaissance satellite passed over Cuba and found the brigade, engaged in a routine military exercise, which led to the CIA's issuing a report on September 18 (basically confirming the original NSA missive) stating that a twenty-six-hundred-man Soviet combat brigade was then in Cuba and had probably been there since at least 1964, if not since the 1962 Cuban Missile Crisis.[88]

When this leaked out to the press, it touched off a political firestorm in Washington that almost destroyed whatever gains had been made since the signing of SALT I in 1972 in terms of improving U.S.-Soviet relations, which was perhaps the reason the report was leaked in the first place.[89]

The Soviet Invasion of Afghanistan

Since there have been so few success stories in American intelligence history, when one comes along, it is worthwhile to examine it to see what went right. NSA's performance in the months prior to the Soviet invasion of Afghanistan in December 1979 was one of these rare cases. Not only did all of the new high-tech intelligence-collection sensors that NSA had purchased in the 1970s work as intended, but the raw data that they collected was processed in a timely fashion, which enabled Bobby Ray Inman to boast that his agency had accurately predicted that the Soviets would invade Afghanistan.[90]

As opposition to the Soviet-supported Afghan regime in Kabul headed by President Nur Mohammed Taraki mounted in late 1978 and early 1979, the Soviets continued to increase their military presence in the country, until it had grown to five Russian generals and about a thousand military advisers.[91] A rebellion in the northeastern Afghan city of Herat in mid-March 1979 in which one hundred Russian military and civilian personnel were killed was put down by Afghan troops from Kandahar, but not before an estimated three thousand to five thousand Afghans had died in the fighting.[92]

At this point, satellite imagery and SIGINT detected unusual activity by the two Soviet combat divisions stationed along the border with Afghanistan. The CIA initially regarded these units as engaged in military exercises, but these "exercises" fit right into a scenario for a Soviet invasion. On March 26–27, SIGINT detected a steady stream of Russian reinforcements and heavy equipment being flown to Bagram airfield, north of Kabul, and by June, the intelligence community estimated that the airlift had brought in a total of twenty-five hundred personnel, which included fifteen hundred airborne troops and additional "advisers" as well as the crews of a squadron of eight AN-12 military transport aircraft now based in-country. SIGINT revealed that the Russians were also secretly setting up a command-and-control communications network inside Afghanistan; it would be used to direct the Soviet intervention in December 1979.[93]

In the last week of August and the first weeks of September, satellite imagery and SIGINT revealed preparations for Soviet operations obviously aimed at Afghanistan, including forward deployment of Soviet IL-76 and AN-12 military transport aircraft that were normally based in the European portion of the USSR.[94]

So clear were all these indications that CIA director Turner sent a Top Secret Umbra memo to the NSC on September 14 warning, "The Soviet leaders may be on the threshold of a decision to commit their own forces to prevent the collapse of the Taraki regime and protect their sizeable stake in Afghanistan. Small Soviet combat units may have already arrived in the country."[95]

On September 16, President Taraki was deposed in a coup d'état, and his pro-Moscow deputy, Hafizullah Amin, took his place as the leader of Afghanistan.

Over the next two weeks, American reconnaissance satellites and SIGINT picked up increased signs of Soviet mobilization, including three divisions on the border and the movement of many Soviet military transport aircraft from their home bases to air bases near the barracks of two elite airborne divisions, strongly suggesting an invasion was imminent.[96]

On September 28, the CIA concluded that "in the event of a breakdown of control in Kabul, the Soviets would be likely to deploy one or more Soviet airborne divisions to the Kabul vicinity to protect Soviet citizens as well as to ensure the continuance of some pro-Soviet regime in the capital."[97] Then, in October, SIGINT detected the call-up of thousands of Soviet reservists in the Central Asian republics.[98]

Throughout November and December, NSA monitored and the CIA reported on virtually every move made by Soviet forces. The CIA advised the White House on December 19 that the Russians had perhaps as many as three airborne battalions at Bagram, and NSA predicted on December 22, three full days before the first Soviet troops crossed the Soviet-Afghan border, that the Russians would invade Afghanistan within the next seventy-two hours.[99]

NSA's prediction was right on the money. The Russians had an ominous Christmas present for Afghanistan, and NSA unwrapped it. Late on Christmas Eve, Russian linguists at the U.S. Air Force listening posts at Royal Air Force Chicksands, north of London, and San Vito dei Normanni Air Station, in southern Italy, detected the takeoff from air bases in the western USSR of the first of 317 Soviet military transport flights carrying elements of two Russian airborne divisions and heading for Afghanistan; on Christmas morning, the CIA issued a final intelligence report saying that the Soviets had prepared for a massive intervention and might "have started to move into that country in force today." SIGINT indicated that a large force of Soviet paratroopers was headed for Afghanistan—and then, at six P.M. Kabul time, it ascertained that the first of the Soviet IL-76 and AN-22 military transport aircraft had touched down at Bagram Air Base and the Kabul airport carrying the first elements of the 103rd Guards Airborne Division and an independent parachute regiment. Three days later, the first of twenty-five thousand troops of Lieutenant General Yuri Vladimirovich Tukharinov's Fortieth Army began crossing the Soviet-Afghan border.[100]

The studies done after the Afghan invasion all characterized the performance of the U.S. intelligence community as an "intelligence success story."[101] NSA's newfound access to high-level Soviet communications enabled the agency to accurately monitor and report quickly on virtually every key facet of the Soviet military's activities. As we shall see in the next chapter, Afghanistan may have been the "high water mark" for NSA.[102]

Postscript

By the end of the 1970s, NSA had been largely rebuilt thanks to the efforts of Lew Allen and Bobby Ray Inman. Despite the dramatic cuts in its size, the agency remained, as a former senior NSA official, Eugene Becker, put it, "a several billion dollar a year corporation, with thousands of people operating a global system."[103] It had, thanks to a new generation of spy satellites and other technical sensors, once again gained access to high-level Soviet communications. It did not take long before NSA was producing reliable intelligence on what was going on behind the iron curtain. According to a declassified NSA history, "even with decreased money, cryptology was yielding the best information that it had produced since World War II."[104]

CHAPTER 10

Dancing on the Edge of a Volcano

NSA During the Reagan and Bush Administrations

"My name is Ozymandias, king of kings:
Look on my works, ye Mighty, and despair!"
—PERCY BYSSHE SHELLEY, "OZYMANDIAS"

General Lincoln Faurer: April 1981–April 1985

On April 1, 1981, Admiral Bobby Inman became the deputy director of the CIA. He was replaced at the helm of NSA by Lieutenant General Lincoln Faurer of the U.S. Air Force. A 1950 graduate of West Point, Faurer had a résumé filled with intelligence experience, including DIA vice director for production and director of intelligence of U.S. European Command in West Germany.[1]

Amiable and easy to get along with, Linc Faurer seems to have been liked by virtually everyone, including his predecessor and six former senior NSA officials interviewed for this book, who felt he was a man to whom you could take problems without fear of recrimination. He was fortunate to have as his deputy Ann Caracristi, an extremely capable NSA cryptanalyst, who served as deputy director of NSA from April 1, 1980, to July 31, 1982. Caracristi's successor, Robert Rich, who served from August 1, 1982, to July 1986, was a Far East expert. Caracristi and Rich handled internal management while Faurer focused on NSA's relations with Washington and foreign collaborating agencies.[2]

Faurer's four years at NSA were tumultuous. Shortly after President Ronald Reagan took office, Faurer persuaded Congress to allocate a huge amount of funding for a dramatic expansion of NSA's workforce, which grew by 27 percent, to twenty-three thousand personnel, between 1981 and 1985; the agency was forced to lease space in nearby office buildings to temporarily house the staff overflow. In 1982, Congress funded two new large buildings adjacent to NSA headquarters, Operations 2A and 2B, and NSA expanded its mission to include operations security and computer security.[3]

When Faurer became director, 58 percent of the agency's resources were devoted to covering the Soviet Union and its Eastern European allies. The remainder was dedicated to some twenty "hard target" countries, including China, North Korea, Vietnam, Cuba, Nicaragua, El Salvador, Egypt, Syria, Jordan, Iran, Iraq, and Libya. But within the first months of his tenure, NSA's SIGINT operations took on new directions as innovative high-tech collection systems came online—while new crises erupted and targets of opportunity presented themselves.[4]

The Gulf of Sidra

In July 1981, President Reagan ordered the U.S. Navy to conduct a naval exercise in the Gulf of Sidra, which Libya claimed as its territorial waters but which all other nations held to be international waters. The CIA warned the White House and the Pentagon, "The Libyan Government is likely to view the exercise as a conspiracy directed against it. The possibility of a hostile tactical reaction resulting in a skirmish is real. Even without such a skirmish, the Libyan Government may view the penetration of its claimed waters and airspace as 'an incident' and that Syrian pilots operating Libyan MiG fighters at Benina Air Base were the most likely to attack U.S. aircraft if the Libyans chose to initiate combat."[5]

Despite the CIA's warning, the exercise proceeded as planned, and on August 19 a Libyan SU-22 Fitter fighter fired an air-to-air missile at two U.S. Navy F-14 Tomcat fighters from the aircraft carrier USS *Nimitz* over the Gulf of Sidra. The missile missed its target, but the Tomcats shot down the Libyan jet. U.S. Navy radio intercept operators on a nearby SIGINT EA-3B aircraft and aboard the destroyer USS *Caron* monitored all of the radio traffic of the Libyan fighter pilot during the engagement, which showed that the Libyans had deliberately sought a fight with the American planes.[6]

Unbeknownst to Libyan leader Colonel Muammar Qaddafi, the cryptanalysts in NSA's G Group had for years been able to read the most sensitive Libyan diplomatic and intelligence ciphers. The agency was also listening to all of Qaddafi's telephone calls, which proved to be an important source of intelligence about the Libyan leader's intentions. A day or two after the Gulf of Sidra shootdown, an American listening post intercepted a phone call from an enraged Qaddafi to Ethiopian leader Mengistu Haile Mariam, in which Qaddafi swore that he would kill President Reagan to avenge the insult. As a result of this warning, the U.S. Secret Service increased the level of its protection of President Reagan, but no tangible threat surfaced and the security alert was called off in December 1981.[7]

The CENTAM Conundrum

In August 1981, the Reagan administration began to publicly assert that the United States now had firm intelligence showing that Nicaragua's Sandinista government had intensified its covert arms supply to the FMLN guerrillas inside El Salvador. NSA had been reading Nicaragua's diplomatic codes for months, as well as intercepting most of the radio traffic between Managua and the rebels in El Salvador. At the request of the White House, in November the agency increased its SIGINT coverage of the Sandinista regime and began tracking the movements of the FMLN guerrilla units, who were now powerful enough to threaten the stability of the newly elected Salvadoran government of José Napoleon Duarte.[8]

NSA threw a vast amount of SIGINT collection resources at the FMLN guerrillas. In July 1981, huge RC-135 reconnaissance aircraft flying from Offutt Air Force Base in Nebraska began conducting SIGINT collection missions off the coast of El Salvador, followed by other airborne intercept operations through October, enabling U.S. intelligence to monitor FMLN activities and share the take with the Salvadoran military. If the locations of FMLN radio transmitters were triangulated, U.S. Air Force AC-130 gunships were called in from Panama to destroy the guerrilla bases, all of which was done in complete secrecy. It was a very serious and very secret war that was being fought in El Salvador.[9]

In December, the U.S. Navy began stationing a SIGINT-equipped destroyer off the coast of El Salvador as part of Jittery Prop, an operation to intercept radio traffic related to arms shipments and to pinpoint the locations of Nicaraguan military and Salvadoran guerrilla radio transmitters. When the U.S. press broke the story about Jittery Prop in February 1982, the FMLN guerrillas switched radio frequencies, and NSA temporarily lost its ability to listen to the transmitters, but by the early summer of 1982 Jittery Prop ships had restored their SIGINT coverage of the Nicaraguan and Salvadoran guerilla radio nets.[10]

Virtually all of the best evidence available was coming from SIGINT, including NSA's almost daily intercepts containing status reports from almost all FMLN units operating inside El Salvador. But the Reagan administration chose not to make the evidence provided by the intercepts public, apparently to avoid compromising the source.[11]

Beginning in late 1983, however, NSA's access began to drop off dramatically as the Nicaraguan regime began to tighten up its communications security. New Russian-made cipher machines were put into use on all major Nicaraguan communications circuits, and communication between Managua and the FMLN was converted to unbreakable one-time pad systems.[12]

KAL 007

At three twenty-six A.M. (local time) on September 1, 1983, Major Gennadiy Nikolayevich Osipovich, a veteran SU-15 fighter pilot assigned to the Soviet 777th Fighter Aviation Regiment at Dolinsk-Sokol Air Base on Sakhalin Island, fired two AA-3 Anab missiles at a Korean Airlines Boeing 747 as it was exiting Soviet airspace west of the island. The airliner, whose flight number was KAL 007, was flying from New York to Seoul via Anchorage. Both of Osipovich's missiles hit the passenger aircraft. For the next twelve minutes, the 747 spiraled downward, before impacting on the water below. All 269 passengers and crew were killed, including U.S. congressman Lawrence "Larry" McDonald.[13]

U.S. Air Force radio intercept operators working the night shift at the NSA listening post at Misawa, Japan, had monitored the entire sequence of events from the moment the Korean airliner had veered off course and entered Soviet airspace over the Kamchatka Peninsula. An hour before KAL 007 was shot down, the intercept operators at Misawa had noted an increased volume of Soviet air defense radio transmissions as the Korean airliner crossed Kamchatka. Russian radar tracking activity throughout the Far East increased dramatically, and several MiG fighters were detected in intercepts taking off from Petropavlovsk-Yelizovo Air Base on Kamchatka. SIGINT analysts in the Far East concluded at the time that in all likelihood the activity was part of an unannounced air defense exercise.[14]

As the 747 crossed Sakhalin Island, unaware of the chaos going on around it, a highly classified thirty-man NSA radio intercept facility at Wakkanai on the northernmost tip of the Japanese island of Hokkaido, called Project Clef, began intercepting, at two fifty-six A.M. (thirty minutes before the shootdown took place), highly unusual radio transmissions from four Russian fighter interceptors who appeared to be conducting live intercept operations just across the La Perouse Strait (between Sakhalin Island and Hokkaido) against an unknown target. One of the intercept operators at Wakkanai happened to be sitting on the air-to-ground radio frequency of Major Osipovich's fighter regiment at Dolinsk-Sokol, which proved to be providential because as he sat listening to the Russian fighter pilot's radio transmissions he heard the fateful transmissions at three twenty-six A.M. indicating that Osipovich had fired his missiles ("I have executed the launch"), followed two seconds later by the Russian fighter pilot reporting to his ground controller that "the target is destroyed." It was this tape recording that was to figure so highly in the days and weeks that followed.[15]

When the first CRITIC report from Misawa hit Washington early on the morning of September 1, it set into motion a chain of events that would have severe repercussions for U.S.-Soviet relations. Secretary of State George Shultz pushed hard to get NSA and the rest of the U.S. intelligence community to agree to allow him to release to the public the tape-recorded intercept of Major Osipovich shooting down the airliner, later telling an interviewer, "It's a pretty chilling tape. It seemed to me that was a critical thing to get out. With the President's support I managed to get the intelligence people to release it. It was hard because they didn't want to release it."[16]

At ten forty-five A.M. (Washington time), Shultz walked to the podium in the Press Briefing Room at the State Department and laid out the facts about the shootdown, such as they were known at the time. But in doing so, he revealed a great deal about NSA's role in the affair, something which the astute reporters in Washington quickly picked up on, to the intense chagrin of senior agency officials at Fort Meade.[17]

But it turned out that in their rush to pillory the Soviets, much of what Shultz told the press about the incident turned out to be flat-out wrong. NSA analysts were still trying to put together a complete and accurate translation at the same time the Reagan administration was releasing selected extracts from the intercepts to buttress their case that the Soviets had committed an act of mass murder. It was not until late on the afternoon on September 1 that NSA completed its "scrub" of the intercept tapes and found that, according to former CIA deputy director for intelligence Robert M. Gates, "the story might be a little more complicated." The new NSA-produced translation showed that the Russians thought they were tracking an American RC-135 reconnaissance aircraft, not a Boeing 747 airliner, and that Major Osipovich, the SU-15 pilot who fired the fatal missiles, never identified the aircraft as a civilian airliner, believing that the "bogey" he was trailing was actually an American military aircraft. All of this information ended up in the next day's edition of the CIA's *President's Daily Brief*, as well as in a briefing for the National Security Council by CIA director William Casey.[18]

Everyone is familiar with the age-old adage "Never let the facts get in the way of a good story." That is exactly what Reagan administration officials did. On September 5, President Reagan went on national television and delivered a harsh and uncompromising attack on Moscow's actions, describing the KAL 007 shootdown as a "crime against humanity." He played carefully selected extracts of the NSA intercepts, then forcefully argued that the Russian fighter pilot must have known that he was shooting down a civilian airliner despite the fact that he had been told four days earlier that the tapes indicated otherwise. The next day, the U.S. ambassador to the United Nations, Jeane Kirkpatrick, played three carefully selected extracts from the NSA tapes before a standing-room-only session of the U.N. Security Council, again using the occasion to accuse the Soviets of having committed mass murder.[19]

The crux of the problem was that Reagan's and Kirkpatrick's presentations were only half true. Gates later admitted that much of what they had said was not entirely factual, writing in his memoirs that "the administration's rhetoric outran the facts known to it."[20] Alvin Snyder, the former head of television for the U.S. Information Agency, whose staff was given the job of producing the slick audio-video presentation given by Ambassador Kirkpatrick at the United Nations, later admitted that he was given only selected portions of the NSA intercept tapes. He only learned later that the complete, unabridged version of the NSA intercept tape showed that the Russians had tried to warn the Korean airliner by firing tracer bullets in front of the aircraft, but the Korean pilots never saw them.[21]

The fact that the Reagan administration played "fast and loose" with the NSA intelligence product only became known years later. According to Raymond Garthoff, a respected Soviet affairs analyst with the Brookings Institute in Washington,

> Secretary Shultz's statement had been made as soon as American intelligence had ascertained beyond any doubt that the airplane had been shot down. Unfortunately, many of the allegations about the incident made by him, by President Reagan, and by other administration spokesmen even days later were based on unfounded assumptions or incorrect information. It later became clear that, contrary to the confident American charges, the Soviets had not known that it was a civilian airliner and indeed had believed (as shown in other taped interceptions not played by the President) that it was an American military reconnaissance aircraft. Moreover, the U.S. government had information on the real situation before these inaccurate charges were

hastily made—although at least in some cases not known by those who made them . . . The facts were not important; what was important was the opportunity to savage the Soviet leaders.[22]

At Fort Meade, NSA officials were furious about how their intelligence information was being abused. The White House's selective release of the most salacious of the NSA material concerning the shootdown set off a firestorm of criticism inside NSA. Among the most vociferous of the critics was Walter Deeley, NSA's deputy director for communications security, who before he died in 1989 said that "releasing the KAL material just for propaganda purposes cost us sources and gained nothing tangible in the long run." Former NSA director Admiral Bobby Ray Inman agreed that the release of the tapes was counterproductive because it irretrievably broke down the wall of secrecy that had long surrounded NSA's operations, but he understood why some NSA officials chose to talk to reporters about the KAL incident because "they were so offended by the way they thought that material had been used for political purposes."[23]

Arguably the most significant revelation coming out of the KAL 007 shootdown was the fact that the massive Soviet national air defense system had not performed well at all. Intercepts showed that the Soviet's radar tracking data had been inaccurate, and that the data had not been transmitted in a timely manner from the radar stations to the Russian air defense command centers in the Far East. The intercepts also showed that Soviet fighter interceptors did not respond quickly, repeatedly failing to intercept the lumbering 747 airliner as it slowly traversed the Kamchatka Peninsula and Sakhalin Island. The normally staid and tightly disciplined Soviet command and control system degenerated into something bordering on chaos. Intercepted air-to-ground radio messages between Osipovich and his ground controller on Sakhalin Island revealed conflicting instructions being radioed from the ground. According to a declassified CIA report, "The pilot [Osipovich] was agitated and clearly indicated that he considered this instruction to be belated. 'It should have been earlier. How can I chase it? I'm already alongside the target.' "[24]

Lebanon

On August 25, 1982, U.S. Navy landing craft deposited eight hundred marine combat troops on the beaches of Beirut. Their mission was to supervise the evacuation of PLO forces from Lebanon, along with military contingents from France and Italy. The marines stayed only sixteen days in Beirut, but were forced to return on September 29 after President-elect Bashir Gemayel was killed when a car bomb destroyed his headquarters in East Beirut. In the days that followed, Israeli forces took advantage of the chaos that ensued and captured most of West Beirut. In East Beirut, Lebanese Christian militia forces besieged and eventually captured the Sabra and Shatila refugee camps, massacring hundreds of Palestinians.

A truce was hastily worked out, and the Israeli forces withdrew from Beirut. In order to protect a fragile cease-fire between Druze and Shi'ite Muslim militias and the Christian-dominated Lebanese army, the American and European forces stayed in Lebanon. The militias soon concluded that the U.S. forces were allied with the Lebanese army, and soon the marines came under fire as Muslim forces attacked the weakened Lebanese army troops guarding Beirut.

The marines had SIGINT support from their own Second Radio Battalion, which set up a listening post in Yarze, a town located in the Christian-controlled zone southeast of the city. During the next year and a half, the marine SIGINT detachment monitored the command nets of the various Palestinian factions around Beirut, as well as the radio communications of the Shi'ite Amal and Druze militias. On May 6, 1983, the marine SIGINT operators at Yarze intercepted an order being sent to a Druze artillery battery to shell the Beirut International Airport, where U.S. Marine ground forces were deployed. Fortunately, the artillery strike never took place, but the marines at the airport were placed on a higher state of alert because of the intercepts.[25]

But the fatal blow came from the Iranians, who had a large presence in Lebanon that was actively planning and financing attacks on American targets there. NSA was routinely decoding the secret cables sent from Tehran to Ali Akbar Mohtashami-Pur, the Iranian ambassador in Damascus, Syria, in which they repeatedly urged him to find ways to attack American targets in Lebanon. Most ominous were NSA decrypts revealing that the radical Shi'ite group Hezbollah in Lebanon routinely reported on its activities to Mohtashami-Pur, and that some (but not all) Hezbollah activities in Lebanon were directly controlled by the Iranian Ministry of Intelligence and Security (MOIS) and the Iranian Revolutionary Guard Corps in Tehran.[26]

NSA intercepts of Mohtashami-Pur's communications traffic revealed that the Iranians were providing financial and logistical support to a group of Shi'ite terrorists in the Bekaa Valley. On April 18, 1983, a member of this group drove a nondescript van next to the U.S. embassy in Beirut and detonated a bomb consisting of two thousand pounds of high explosives, killing sixty-three people, including seventeen Americans. Among the casualties were most of the staff of the embassy's CIA station, including the CIA's top Middle East expert, Robert Ames, and the CIA station chief, Kenneth Haas. Decrypted Iranian diplomatic cables showed that Mohtashami-Pur had been aware that an attack was being planned, that senior Iranian intelligence officials in Tehran had approved the attack, and that Tehran had transferred twenty-five thousand dollars to the Iranian embassy in Damascus to finance the operation. Other NSA intercepts showed that the Iranian government had sent one million dollars to the embassy in Damascus, which was used to buy the explosives used in the car bomb attack.[27]

Five months later, on September 24, an NSA listening post in the Middle East intercepted a message from the headquarters of MOIS in Tehran to Mohtashami-Pur in Damascus, directing the ambassador to "contact Hussein Musawi, the leader of the terrorist group *Islamic Amal*, and to instruct him . . . 'to take a spectacular action against the United States Marines.'" The intercept did not, however, provide any specifics about the time and place of the planned attack. On September 27, NSA sent an urgent warning message to the White House, the CIA stations in Beirut and Damascus, and the Second Marine Radio Battalion SIGINT detachment in Lebanon, indicating that a terrorist attack might be mounted against the United States in the near future.[28]

But amazingly, neither the Pentagon nor the commander of the U.S. Marine contingent in Beirut, Colonel Timothy Geraghty, seems to have reacted to this warning, which may well have gotten lost in the maze of the U.S. military's bureaucracy. We do know that Geraghty did not put his forces on alert, nor did he or any of his subordinate commanders take any additional measures to ensure the safety of their troops. Senior officials at the Pentagon also did nothing to prevent the attack. Less than a month later, the disaster that NSA had warned was coming finally came to pass.[29]

At six twenty-two A.M. on October 23, a terrorist named Ismalal Ascari drove a yellow Mercedes-Benz truck laden with explosives into the marine barracks complex at the Beirut International Airport and detonated it. The resulting explosion was massive, the equivalent of twenty thousand pounds of TNT detonating, giving it the sorrowful distinction of being the largest nonnuclear explosion in history. The casualty toll was appalling. When the body count was finally tallied, 241 marines and sailors were dead and 60 more badly wounded. Twenty seconds after the first attack, a second suicide bomber attempted to drive a truck laden with explosives into the nearby headquarters of the French peacekeeping force in Beirut. Although alert French sentries killed the driver, the bomb detonated, killing 58 French soldiers.[30]

After the bombing of the marine barracks, NSA unleashed the full range of its SIGINT assets on the Muslim militias now openly firing on the marine positions at the airport. Air force and navy SIGINT aircraft orbited over the Mediterranean twenty-four hours a day intercepting Druze, Shi'ite, and Syrian military radio traffic. SIGINT from the marine detachment at Bayt Miri began to be used for offensive purposes. Intercepts and direction-finding data from the Second Radio Battalion detachment were used to direct marine artillery and naval gunfire to the locations of artillery batteries and their firing-direction centers, manned by Druze gunners belonging to Walid Jumblatt's Progressive Socialist Party (PSP), in the hills above Beirut.[31]

Interviews with marine SIGINTers who served in Lebanon between 1982 and 1984 reveal that the problems experienced by the SIGINT detachment from the Second Radio Battalion in Beirut were huge. Not only had NSA not briefed the personnel of the marine SIGINT detachment about the signals environment in Lebanon before they deployed to Beirut, but the agency also did not provide them with any working aids or computerized databases related to the targets they were being tasked with copying. And once they arrived in Lebanon, they discovered that they did not have any access to NSA's databases, nor were they given copies of reports detailing what NSA was learning about the situation in Lebanon from its other SIGINT sources. But the biggest shock was the discovery, once they got to Beirut, that they were not properly equipped to conduct SIGINT operations in the low-tech signals environment that was Beirut. A former marine SIGINT operator stationed in Lebanon recalled, "We were trained and equipped to intercept conventional Soviet military radio communications, not the walkie-talkies used by the Shi'ites and Druze in the foothills overlooking our base . . . Initially we couldn't hear shit." The Shi'ite and Druze militiamen who were their principal targets did not use fixed radio frequencies or regular call signs, or follow standardized radio procedures, which made monitoring their communications extremely difficult. The differing Arabic dialects spoken by the militiamen were also extremely hard for the school-trained marine intercept operators to understand, as was the West Beirut street slang the militiamen used. Taken together, this meant that the marine radio intercept operators and analysts had to improvise (oftentimes under fire) to do their job. A former marine SIGINT detachment commander recalled, "It was a hell of a way to learn your job, but that's what Marines are good at. Adapt and improvise. I just wish we didn't have to. So many lives were lost because we weren't prepared for the enemy that we faced."[32]

General Odom at NSA: April 1985–August 1988

NSA's increasingly close relations with the White House infuriated Secretary of Defense Caspar Weinberger and his deputy, William Taft IV, who wanted to reestablish Defense Department control over the agency, which some Pentagon officials had begun to view as a "rogue elephant." This battle for control of NSA came to a head when agency director Faurer and Taft disagreed over NSA's role as national manager for telephone and computer security pursuant to National Security Decision Directive 145, particularly draft provisions that would have placed NSA under the authority of the NSC, not the Defense Department. Although NSA won this battle, the worst was yet to come. During budget negotiations before the Defense Resources Board in late 1984, Faurer hotly disputed a plan by the Defense Department to cut the part of NSA's funding earmarked for a large computer complex called the Supercomputing Research Center. Faurer appealed the board's decision in a memorandum to Secretary Weinberger and sent copies of the memo to several NSA allies at the White House. When Taft learned of this end run, he called Faurer into his office on January 3, 1985, for a meeting that was subsequently described as heated and acrimonious. Faurer was brusquely informed that he was through as NSA director. CIA director William Casey tried to intervene on his behalf, but to no avail. Faurer submitted his letter of resignation on March 19 and left NSA on April 1.[33]

On April 19, President Reagan nominated Lieutenant General William Odom, of the U.S. Army, to succeed Faurer as NSA director. Odom became NSA's eleventh director on May 8, the first army officer to head the agency since Lieutenant General Marshall Carter in 1969.[34]

Born in Cookeville, Tennessee, on June 23, 1932, Odom grew up in the nearby tiny farming community of Crossville, where his father ran an agricultural research station for the University of Tennessee. Odom graduated from West Point in 1954, and after several years as a platoon and company commander he obtained a master's degree in Russian studies from Columbia University, in 1962. From this point onward, most of Odom's career was spent in either academia or intelligence. He taught at West Point from 1966 to 1969, then earned a Ph.D. in political science from Columbia in 1970. Following graduation, he served a tour in Vietnam with the CIA-led pacification organization Civil Operations and Rural Development Support, then went to Moscow as the assistant military attaché, a position he held from April 1972 to June 1974. Following an assignment teaching political science at West Point, Odom served on the NSC as the military assistant to Jimmy Carter's national security advisor, Zbigniew Brzezinski, from 1977 to 1981, where he handled matters relating to crisis management, nuclear targeting, civil defense, terrorism, and third world military planning. His hard-line attitude toward the Soviet Union earned him the sobriquet Zbig's Super-hawk during his tour in the White House. From November 1981 to April 1985, Odom served as the army's assistant chief of staff for intelligence, where he promoted technical intelligence collection systems. Odom was also instrumental in saving the army's controversial clandestine intelligence unit, the Intelligence Support Activity, from extinction.[35]

Washington Post journalist Bob Woodward described Odom, perhaps politely, as "an intense, thin, stony man." Former NSA officials frequently used the words "acerbic," "fractious," "combative," and "hardheaded" in interviews to describe his personality, along with more colorful descriptions that cannot be printed here.[36]

Given these descriptions, it should come as no surprise that Odom's tenure as NSA director, from 1985 to 1988, was not a happy one. In a matter of months, he dismantled virtually all of the internal reform mechanisms put in place by former director Bobby Ray Inman, including the system designed to identify and promote talented managers. Commenting on this, Inman said, "I think much of it [the reform initiatives] died with Bill Odom, who had his strong likes and dislikes and zero interest in systems."[37]

A polarizing figure, Odom had an autocratic style that instantly put him at odds with many of NSA's senior civilian officials. There were resignations by key senior personnel and a minirevolt in 1988 after Odom's censure and demo-tion of the number-three man in NSA's Communications Security Organiza-tion, John Wobensmith, for assisting Lieutenant Colonel Oliver North, which was regarded as making Wobensmith the scapegoat for the agency's involve-ment in North's Iran-Contra scheme.[38] By mid-1988, many of Inman's protégés were fighting what they regarded as a purge of their ranks by Odom and his supporters. Things got so bad that Inman actually testified against Odom's ac-tions at a personnel hearing at Fort Meade.[39]

Odom made few friends in Washington and plenty of enemies because of his lobbying to increase the independence and power of NSA at the expense of the CIA and other intelligence agencies, which were already concerned about the burgeoning power of NSA. When CIA director Casey was told that Odom had been spotted on Capitol Hill leaving the office of a senator on the intelli-gence committee, Casey erupted in anger, telling one of his deputies, "This S.O.B. is incredible!"[40]

The Spy Satellites

NSA's SIGINT effort against the USSR during the 1980s was radically improved by a constellation of four new spy satellites parked in geosynchronous orbit twenty-two thousand miles above the earth called Vortex (previously known as Chalet), which was designed to suck up a huge amount of Russian communications traffic. Vortex was created in the early 1970s to replace the older Canyon as NSA's primary means of intercepting vast quantities of telephone traffic deep inside the Soviet Union. Sporting a huge parabolic receiving antenna, the eleven-foot long, eight-foot wide, 3,087-pound Vortex satellites were equipped with state-of-the-art intercept receivers that had the capacity to simultaneously intercept over eleven thousand telephone calls and faxes carried on Soviet microwave radio-relay circuits; the satellites then chose which signals to beam back to NSA-operated mission ground stations at Menwith Hill, in northern England, and Bad Aibling, in West Germany, in near real time based on a sophisticated "watch list" maintained by its onboard computers.[41]

The quantity and quality of intelligence coming from the Vortex satellites was impressive. Vortex intercepted to great effect the operational and tactical radio traffic of Soviet military forces deep inside Afghanistan throughout the 1980s, and it monitored the radio circuits used by Russian SS-20 mobile intermediate-range ballistic missile firing units and SS-24 mobile ICBM batteries to communicate with their operating bases. The best intelligence coverage of the April 1986 disaster at the Russian Chernobyl nuclear reactor available to the U.S. intelligence community came from intercepts supplied by Vortex satellites, which listened in on the Russian government's reaction to the disaster, including the telephone traffic of the Soviet general staff and the KGB. Two years later, in May 1988, a Vortex satellite picked up radio traffic indicating that a huge explosion had taken place at a Russian fuel propellant plant at Pavlograd, which made fuel components for Soviet ICBMs.[42]

Ronald Pelton

Arguably the worst damage that has ever been inflicted on NSA was not done by an enterprising journalist or a White House official leaking information. Rather, this dubious honor is held by a former NSA official named Ronald Pelton, who had worked in NSA's A Group, which was responsible for all SIGINT operations against the Soviet Union and Eastern Europe, for his entire career.

As chief of a key staff unit within A Group, Pelton had complete access to the details of all the unit's sensitive compartmented programs.

In July 1979, Pelton was forced to resign from NSA after filing for bankruptcy three months earlier. Desperate for money, on January 15, 1980, Pelton got in touch with the Russian embassy in Washington, and in the months that followed, he sold them, for a paltry thirty-five thousand dollars, a number of Top Secret Codeword documents and anything else he could remember. For the Soviets this was pure gold, and a bargain at that.[43]

The damage that Pelton did was massive. He compromised the joint NSA–U.S. Navy undersea-cable tapping operation in the Sea of Okhotsk called Ivy Bells, which was producing vast amounts of enormously valuable, unencrypted, and incredibly detailed intelligence about the Soviet Pacific Fleet, information that might give the United States a clear, immediate warning of a Soviet attack. In 1981, a Soviet navy salvage ship lifted the Ivy Bells pod off the seafloor and took it to Moscow to be studied by Soviet electronics experts. It now resides in a forlorn corner of the museum of the Russian security service in the Lubyanka, in downtown Moscow.[44]

Even worse, Pelton betrayed virtually every sensitive SIGINT operation that NSA and Britain's GCHQ were then conducting against the Soviet Union, including the seven most highly classified compartmented intelligence operations that A Group was then engaged in. The programs were so sensitive that Charles Lord, the NSA deputy director of operations at the time, called them the "Holiest of Holies." He told the Russians about the ability of NSA's Vortex SIGINT satellites to intercept sensitive communications deep inside the USSR that were being carried by microwave radio-relay systems. Pelton also revealed the full extent of the intelligence being collected by the joint NSA-CIA Broadside listening post in the U.S. embassy in Moscow. Within months of Pelton being debriefed in Vienna, the Soviets intensified their jamming of the frequencies being monitored by the Moscow embassy listening post, and the intelligence "take" coming out of Broadside fell to practically nothing. Pelton also told the Russians about virtually every Russian cipher machine that NSA's cryptanalysts in A Group had managed to crack in the late 1970s. NSA analysts had wondered why at the height of the Polish crisis in 1981 they had inexplicably lost their ability to exploit key Soviet and Polish communications systems, which had suddenly gone silent without warning. Pelton also told the Russians about a joint CIA-NSA operation wherein CIA operatives placed fake tree stumps containing sophisticated electronic eavesdropping devices near Soviet military installations around Moscow. The data intercepted by these devices was either relayed electronically to the U.S. embassy or sent via burst transmission to the United States via communication satellites.[45]

In December 1985, Pelton was arrested and charged in federal court in Baltimore, with six counts of passing classified information to the Soviet Union. After a brief trial, in June 1986 Pelton was found guilty and sentenced to three concurrent life terms in prison.[46]

Gulf of Sidra II and La Belle Disco

The year 1986 was one of dangerous confrontation between Muammar Qaddafi and the Reagan administration. In January, the U.S. Sixth Fleet's Freedom of Navigation exercises off the Libyan coast (designated Operation Attain Document) gave NSA an opportunity to monitor the reactions of Libyan MiG-23 and MiG-25 fighters. On January 13, two MiG-25s attempted to intercept a U.S. Navy EA-3 SIGINT reconnaissance aircraft flying over international waters southwest of Sicily. The Libyan aircraft retreated when a pair of navy F-18 fighters from the aircraft carrier USS *Coral Sea* arrived on the scene.[47]

A month later, on February 28, the Joint Chiefs of Staff requested NSA SIGINT support for enlarged navy exercises in the Gulf of Sidra, a move sure to produce a violent Libyan reaction. Pursuant to the request, NSA quickly reallocated otherwise dedicated resources for monitoring Libyan military communications traffic, among them one of the Vortex SIGINT satellites, a number of navy warships with embarked SIGINT intercept detachments, and a number of air force and navy SIGINT reconnaissance aircraft. In March, the increased tempo of American reconnaissance flights triggered an attempted intercept by two Libyan MiG-25s of a navy EA-3B reconnaissance aircraft flying from the aircraft carrier USS *Saratoga* 120 miles north of Tripoli. No shots were fired, but it became clear that the Libyans were serious about stopping American eavesdropping activities.[48]

Since NSA could read the Libyan cipher systems, the agency knew virtually everything worth knowing about the capabilities and locations of Libyan air and ground units, including the Libyan air defense system's radar and fire control systems. In early 1986, NSA learned that Qaddafi had ordered his tiny navy out onto the high seas to avoid being destroyed in port and had told his air force to increase the number of sorties being flown. But Libyan warships were prone to mechanical difficulties caused by poor maintenance, their crews were hindered by a lack of blue-water experience, and there were also operational difficulties, including an inability to replenish and refuel ships at sea. And the Libyan air force, NSA discovered, had serious problems operating its complex Russian-made fighters. Nevertheless, NSA monitored more than two hundred sorties by Libyan fighter aircraft trying to engage their more capable U.S. Navy counter-parts over the Gulf of Sidra. An air force radio intercept operator at Iráklion, Crete, later recalled that "a fistfight with Qaddafi was coming. It was just a mat-ter of when and where."[49]

On March 23, a Libyan SA-5 SAM battery launched four missiles at U.S. Navy aircraft that had deliberately flown across Qaddafi's so-called Line of Death over the Gulf of Sidra. The missile launch was detected by a U.S. Air Force RC-135 Burning Wind reconnaissance aircraft, which warned the navy fighters in time for them to do evasive maneuvers. The next day, U.S. Navy fighter-bombers de-stroyed the Libyan SAM battery and two Libyan guided missile patrol boats.[50]

Qaddafi demanded retaliation for the humiliation visited on his forces. On March 25, an NSA listening post intercepted a three-line telex message from the head of the Libyan Intelligence Service in Tripoli to eight Libyan embassies (called "People's Bureaus") in Europe, including East Berlin, instructing them to target places in which American servicemen congregated. An intercepted March 23 message from Tripoli to the People's Bureau in East Berlin had de-manded an attack "with as many victims as possible." This was followed by an intercepted message from East Berlin reporting that "an operation would be undertaken shortly and that Libyan officials would be pleased with it."

At one forty-nine A.M. on April 5, a bomb went off inside La Belle discotheque in West Berlin, killing two American servicemen and a Turkish woman and wounding 230 others. Shortly after, an intercepted message from Libya's East Berlin outpost reported that "the operation had been successfully completed, and that it would not be traceable to the Libyan diplomatic post in East Berlin." According to the files of the former East German secret service, the intercepted message stated, "At 1:30 this morning one of the acts was carried out with suc-cess, without leaving a trace behind."[51]

On the evening of April 7, President Reagan went on national television to announce that the U.S. government had incontrovertible evidence proving that the Libyan government was behind the La Belle Disco bombing. The Libyans immediately changed all of their codes and ciphers and purchased a new cipher machine from a Swiss company, negating many of NSA's gains made since the first Libyan cipher systems were solved in 1979.[52]

On April 14, eighteen U.S. Air Force F-111 fighter-bombers took off from air bases in England for a twenty-four-hundred-mile flight to bomb targets in Libya. The American air strikes hit selected targets in Tripoli and Benghazi, killing at

Brigadier General Carter Clarke, U.S. Army, and Mrs. Carter Clarke. Considered by some to be the founding father of NSA, while serving as a senior official in army intelligence during and after World War II, Clarke advocated a strong, unified SIGINT effort against America's friends and enemies. (National Archives and Records Administration [NARA])

British and American participants in the signing of the March 5, 1946, British–United States (BRUSA) Communications Intelligence Agreement in Washington, D.C., the Top Secret postwar agreement that formalized Anglo-American SIGINT cooperation. The 1946 BRUSA Agreement is discussed in chapter 1. (U.S. Army)

Rear Admiral Earl Stone. Director of the Armed Forces Security Agency (AFSA) from July 1949 to July 1951. Stone's two-year tenure as head of the deeply troubled AFSA was marked by a series of operational failures in Korea. His ability to command the fractious American cryptologic system was so limited that senior officers joked that his authority extended as far as the door of his office in Washington, D.C. (NARA)

General Douglas MacArthur during the Korean War. President Harry Truman's decision to fire MacArthur was prompted in part by cable intercepts of European ambassadors in Tokyo that suggested MacArthur wanted to widen the Korean conflict into a major war on the Chinese mainland in order to destroy Mao Tse-tung's communist regime. (NARA)

Major General Ralph Canine, U.S. Army. Director of AFSA from July 1951 to November 1952, then director of NSA from November 1952 to November 1956. Referred to by his colleagues as the "Great Unifier," General Canine presided over the creation of NSA and its dramatic expansion during the mid-1950s. He is credited with single-handedly making his agency a major force in the U.S. intelligence community. (NARA)

U.S. Army listening post, Sinop, Turkey, circa 1955. (U.S. Army)

Lieutenant General John Samford, U.S. Air Force. Director of NSA from November 1956 to November 1960. Samford continued the expansion of NSA started by his predecessor, General Canine, improving the agency's SIGINT capabilities in order to cover a host of new targets, such as the growing threat posed by Soviet ballistic missiles. (NARA)

Louis Tordella, deputy director of NSA from 1958 to 1974, who appears at several points in the book. His significance was his sixteen-year tenure running NSA as the agency's top civilian. (NARA)

Rear Admiral Laurence Frost, U.S. Navy. Director of NSA from November 1960 to January 1962. Considered to have been one of the worst of NSA's directors, Frost lasted only fifteen months at the helm before being fired by senior Defense Department officials in the Kennedy administration. (NARA)

Lieutenant General Gordon Blake, U.S. Air Force. Director of NSA from January 1962 to June 1965. Blake commanded NSA during the Cuban Missile Crisis and during the early years of American military involvement in Vietnam, including the Gulf of Tonkin incidents in August 1964. (NARA)

Juanita M. Moody, who directed
NSA's SIGINT operations during
the Cuban Missile Crisis in 1962, as
described in chapter 5. (NARA)

NSA spy ship USS *Oxford* after commissioning in New York City, 1961. (U.S. Navy)

Lieutenant General Marshall Carter, U.S. Army. Director of NSA from June 1965 to August 1969. At the helm of NSA at the height of the Vietnam War, including the 1968 Tet Offensive, Carter is remembered today for presiding over the dramatic expansion of NSA during the late 1960s, as well as for the many enemies he made within the U.S. intelligence community as he strove to further the interests of his agency. (NARA)

During the Six-Day War of 1967, Israeli fighter-bombers and torpedo boats attacked the spy ship USS *Liberty* as it sailed in international waters off the coast of the Sinai Peninsula, killing and wounding scores of crew members. This photo shows a huge hole caused by an Israeli torpedo blast that killed twenty-five U.S. Navy, Marine, and NSA SIGINT personnel who were working next to where the torpedo hit. (U.S. Navy)

U.S. Marines in Hué, South Vietnam, where some of the most bitter fighting of the Tet Offensive took place. NSA was the only branch of the U.S. intelligence community that provided any warning of a major North Vietnamese and Viet Cong offensive in South Vietnam during the Tet holiday in January 1968. But the warning was ignored by the White House, the commander of U.S. forces in Vietnam, and the rest of the U.S. intelligence community. (NARA)

Lieutenant General Lew Allen Jr., U.S. Air Force. Director of NSA from August 1973 to July 1977. One of the most intelligent men ever to command NSA, Allen presided over the agency in the troubled post-Vietnam era. It was during his tenure that the quantity and quality of NSA's intelligence reporting on the USSR began to improve noticeably, thanks to a host of new, high-tech SIGINT collection systems, such as a new generation of SIGINT satellites. (NARA)

Vice Admiral Bobby Ray Inman, U.S. Navy. Director of NSA from July 1977 to April 1981. Brilliant and unconventional, Admiral Inman is credited with reforming the agency, as well as restoring it to its former position of power within the U.S. intelligence community. New SIGINT satellites were sent into space on his watch, and NSA cryptanalysts made important breaks into Soviet communications, allowing NSA to correctly predict that the USSR was going to invade Afghanistan in December 1979. Inman also made a number of important enemies within the U.S. intelligence community, especially the director of the CIA, Admiral Stansfield Turner. (NARA)

Lieutenant General Lincoln Faurer, U.S. Air Force. Director of NSA from April 1981 to May 1985. Quiet and personable, General Faurer was at the helm of NSA during the host of international incidents that marked the first term of the Reagan administration, including the Gulf of Sidra incidents with Libya, the wars in Central America, and America's abortive military intervention in Lebanon. (NARA)

Lieutenant General William Odom, U.S. Army. Director of NSA from May 1985 to August 1988. A hardheaded and uncompromising leader, General Odom's three-year tenure at NSA was marred by internal controversy and internecine warfare with the rest of the U.S. intelligence community. For example, in the late 1980s a number of high-level agency officials were purged or resigned in protest in the aftermath of the Iran-Contra scandal. (NARA)

U.S. Army listening post, Teufelsberg West Berlin, circa 1989. (U.S. Army)

Vice Admiral William Studeman, U.S. Navy. Director of NSA from August 1988 to May 1992. The quiet and unassuming Studeman was a popular director at NSA, leading the agency through the invasion of Panama in 1989, Operation Desert Storm in 1990–1991, and the collapse of the Soviet Union. Studeman also recognized that NSA needed to reform and modernize itself, but his recommendations were, for the most part, not followed by subsequent directors. (NARA)

U.S. Air Force cryptologists manning radio intercept stations aboard an RC-135 aircraft, sometime in 2000. These reconnaissance planes would provide critically important SIGINT information about the strength and capabilities of the Iraqi air defense system both before and during the U.S. invasion of Iraq in March 2003. (Dave Nolan, U.S. Air Force)

Bad Aibling listening station, Germany, circa 2001. (U.S. Army)

General Michael V. Hayden, U.S. Air Force. Hayden was director of NSA from March 1999 to April 2005. He was then named principal deputy director of national intelligence before becoming director of the Central Intelligence Agency in 2006. (NARA)

Vice President Dick Cheney was the moving force inside the White House behind NSA's warrantless domestic eavesdropping program, largely running from his office in the West Wing. (Denny C. Cantrell, U.S. Navy)

Secretary of State Colin Powell displays a vial of anthrax at the United Nations Security Council on February 5, 2003. In his speech, Powell used a number of NSA SIGINT intercepts of Iraqi communications to bolster the U.S. government's case that Iraq was trying to hide its arsenal of weapons of mass destruction. Some NSA analysts had warned that the intercepts were fragmentary and ambiguous, and with hindsight Powell's interpretation was proved dramatically wrong. (U.S. Department of State)

NSA headquarters complex, Fort Meade, Maryland. (NSA)

least fifteen people, including Qaddafi's adopted daughter, and wounding more than one hundred others. But they did not succeed in killing Qaddafi.[53]

Admiral William Studeman, who would become director of NSA two years later, recalled that the entire intelligence community was scooped by CNN: "When we bombed Libya . . . we got more bomb damage assessments and a sense of what was going on inside Tripoli around those targets listening to the CNN guy talking on the balcony of a hotel in Tripoli than we did from all the electronic surveillance devices that we had focused on the problem."[54]

Admiral William Studeman: August 1988–January 1992

On August 1, 1988, General Odom retired from the military after the Joint Chiefs of Staff unanimously recommended against extending his three-year tour of duty as director of NSA. Despite support from the Pentagon's number-two man, William Taft, Odom's abrasive personality and autocratic style had rubbed too many people in the Defense Department and the intelligence community the wrong way.[55]

Odom was replaced by career naval intelligence officer Rear Admiral William Studeman. Bill Studeman was born in Brownsville, Texas, on January 16, 1940, the son of an American aviation pioneer who had flown during World War I and helped build Pan American Airways. He graduated from the University of the South in Sewanee, Tennessee, in 1962 with a B.A. in history, then joined the navy to become a pilot. Studeman's subsequent advance through the navy's ranks was meteoric, taking him from ensign to rear admiral in only twenty years. His big break came when he was assigned to be the executive assistant to the director of the Office of Naval Intelligence, Rear Admiral Bobby Ray Inman. Inman took Studeman under his wing and helped guide him through the ranks of naval intelligence. In September 1985, he became the fifty-third director of ONI and remained there until his assignment as director of NSA.[56]

Quiet and thoughtful, during his career in the navy Studeman had earned a reputation for blunt honesty and candor that had occasionally bruised some of his colleagues in naval intelligence, some of whom derisively referred to him as "the Boy Scout." It had fallen to Studeman, as director of ONI, to deal with the fallout of the Walker-Whitworth spy ring, which he had handled with aplomb despite the fact that it was arguably the worst intelligence disaster in U.S. history before the 2002 Iraqi weapons of mass destruction scandal.[57]

He was pleasantly surprised to get the nod to head NSA. Former agency officials who served under him believe that Studeman's three-year tenure there is underappreciated. He is credited with "righting the ship" after Odom's bruising and contentious tenure, restoring the shaken morale at the agency, and renewing NSA's sense of purpose and mission at a time when it needed it most.[58]

And most important, the agency was regarded as far more effective by its consumers after scoring some important intelligence coups, such as information concerning the Chinese military's bloody suppression of the democracy movement in Beijing's Tiananmen Square in June 1989. Intercepts collected by NSA detailed the reluctance of the commander of the Chinese Thirty-eighth Army in Beijing to attack the student protesters camped out in the square. When the Thirty-eighth Army would not move, SIGINT tracked the Chinese Twenty-seventh Army and the elite parachute divisions of the Fifteenth Air Army being brought into Beijing to put down the student-led movement. The intercepts confirmed that units of the Twenty-seventh and Thirty-eighth Armies had clashed with each other and that casualties had been sustained by both forces. The clandestine listening posts inside the American, British, Australian, and Canadian embassies also showed that the Chinese army had deployed forces around the Zhongmanhai Leadership Compound in Beijing to protect the Chinese Politburo.[59]

Then, in December 1989, SIGINT coming out of the joint NSA-CIA listening post inside the U.S. embassy in Bucharest proved to be vitally important during the military coup d'état that overthrew Romanian dictator Nicolae Ceauşescu. According to the late Ambassador Warren Zimmermann, once the coup began, "the CIA station started giving the ambassador intercepts which were of course, tremendously valuable to letting him make up his mind about how the coup was going and the direction it was going in and what would happen to Ceauşescu."[60]

Operation Just Cause: The Invasion of Panama

In the late 1980s, relations between the United States and the Panamanian regime led by Manuel Noriega, formerly the darling of the Reagan and Bush administrations, deteriorated rapidly. In June 1987, the chief of staff of the Panamanian Defense Forces (PDF) publicly accused Noriega of having engaged in drug trafficking and other assorted criminal enterprises. In 1988, Noriega was indicted by a federal grand jury in Tampa, Florida, for narcotics trafficking. As a result of the increasing tension between the United States and Panama, NSA was ordered to intensify its intelligence coverage of the country beginning in 1988, but this effort was hampered by the fact that Noriega had constructed a secure internal communications system, which NSA could not penetrate. Making matters even worse, as a 1994 paper written by a U.S. Army intelligence officer later revealed, Noriega's frequent purges of the PDF officer corps, which removed dozens of unreliable men from command positions, "had eliminated most of SOUTHCOM's [U.S. Southern Command's] and the CIA's HUMINT capability." Events continued to spin out of control during 1988 and 1989. In March 1988, there was an unsuccessful coup attempt to oust Noriega. In April 1989, a CIA operative in Panama was arrested. The following month, Noriega won a rigged national election. This was followed by another unsuccessful coup attempt in October 1989. By the late fall of 1989, U.S. intelligence resources, including those of NSA, were heavily committed to closely monitoring events in Panama.[61]

When the United States invaded Panama on December 20, 1989 (an action designated Operation Just Cause), NSA had been providing intelligence to its customers through a special "Panama Cell."[62] The agency's primary target was Noriega, who proved to be an elusive target, moving around "many times during the day and night" and sending "false radio and telephone traffic to further conceal his whereabouts." On December 19, the day before the invasion was due to begin, NSA lost Noriega because, according to a report written by an army intelligence officer, he "took an unexpected trip to Torrijos/Tocumen airport to visit one of his prostitutes." NSA informed the U.S. Army Ranger battalion whose mission it was to capture Noriega of the latest information, but the intelligence came too late. According to the report, the rangers "missed him by the narrowest of margins."[63]

As it turned out, Noriega's sudden disappearance may well have been due to a warning he had just received. While Noriega was visiting Colón, NSA intercepted a telephone call from an unknown person in Washington to Noriega warning him that, according to a State Department source, the United States was about to invade Panama. At ten P.M. on December 19, shortly before the invasion, NSA intercept operators listened as the radio station servicing the PDF general staff in Panama City began urgently transmitting messages to all Panamanian military units, warning them that the U.S. invasion was to start in three hours. The warning message ordered all troops to "report to their barracks, draw weapons and prepare to fight." Looking at the intercept, the commander of the American assault force, Lieutenant General Carl Stiner, advanced the time that the attack was to begin by fifteen minutes in the hope that he would be able to achieve some degree of surprise, but resistance from PDF forces was still heavier than expected.[64]

Postscript

The 1980s saw NSA grow from more than fifty thousand military and civilian personnel to seventy-five thousand in 1989, twenty-five thousand of whom worked at NSA headquarters at Fort Meade. In terms of manpower alone, the agency was the largest component of the U.S. intelligence community by far, with a headquarters staff larger than the entire CIA.[65]

As the agency's size grew at a staggering pace, so did the importance of its intelligence reporting. The amount of reporting produced by NSA during the 1980s was astronomical. According to former senior American intelligence officials, on some days during the 1980s SIGINT accounted for over 70 percent of the material contained in the CIA's daily intelligence report to President Reagan.[66] Former CIA director (now Secretary of Defense) Robert Gates stated, "The truth is, until the late 1980s, U.S. signals intelligence was way out in front of the rest of the world."[67]

But NSA's SIGINT efforts continued to produce less information because of a dramatic increase in worldwide telecommunications traffic volumes, which NSA had great difficulty coping with. It also had to deal with the growing availability and complexity of new telecommunications technologies, such as cheaper and more sophisticated encryption systems. By the late 1980s, the number of intercepted messages flowing into NSA headquarters at Fort Meade had increased to the point that the agency's staff and computers were only able to process about 20 percent of the incoming materials.[68] These developments were to come close to making NSA deaf, dumb, and blind in the decade that followed.

CHAPTER 11

Troubles in Paradise

From Desert Storm to the War on Terrorism

*The surest guarantee of disappointment is an
unrealistic expectation.*
—THOMAS PATRICK CARROLL

For NSA, the 1990s started with a resounding explosion and ended with a
barely discernible whimper. 1989 will forever be remembered as the year that
marked the beginning of the collapse of the Soviet Union and the Communist
regimes in Eastern Europe. In an event that most people alive at the time remember well, on November 9, 1989, the Berlin Wall came crashing down,
and what was left of the shell-shocked East German government succumbed
and allowed its people to leave the country for the first time. By June 1, 1990,
the Berlin Wall had ceased to exist and all crossing points between East and
West Berlin had been opened. Four months later, East and West Germany
were united as a single country on October 1. Soviet premier Mikhail Gorbachev radically changed course and adopted *perestroika* and *glasnost* as the by-
words of his government. Gorbachev's reforms set forth a chain reaction of
events that were to dramatically change the face of the world. Over the next
two years, all Soviet troops were withdrawn from Eastern Europe, the Warsaw
Pact was disbanded, all Eastern European nations became democracies, and
the Soviet Union disintegrated into sixteen separate countries. In the blink of
an eye, the Cold War was over, and with it, all of NSA's principal targets since
the end of World War II vanished. But despite the collapse of the Soviet
Union, there was to be no respite for NSA.[1]

Desert Storm

The invasion of Kuwait on August 2, 1990, by Iraq's Saddam Hussein caught the U.S. intelligence community by surprise once again. In a familiar but worrisome pattern, intelligence indicating the possibility of the invasion was not properly analyzed or was discounted by senior Bush administration officials, including then–secretary of defense Dick Cheney, who did not think that Hussein would be foolish enough to do it. General Lee Butler, the commander of the Strategic Air Command, was later quoted as saying, "We had the warning from the intelligence community—we refused to acknowledge it."[2]

It took five months for the United States to move resources by land and sea to implement Desert Storm's ground attack by three hundred thousand coalition troops. The operation began at three A.M. Baghdad time on January 17, 1991, with a massive series of air strikes and cruise missile attacks. The air campaign lasted thirty-eight days, battering the Iraqi military into a state of submission. On February 24, the much-anticipated ground offensive was launched. One hundred hours later, the war was over. President George H. W. Bush, who had no intention of "driving on to Baghdad," declared a cease-fire on February 27, and the Iraqi forces signed a formal agreement for cessation of hostilities on March 3.

Operation Desert Storm was a military victory of historic proportions—one whose like would probably never be seen again. In the span of only forty-three days, forty-two Iraqi combat divisions were destroyed and 82,000 prisoners taken, the entire Iraqi navy was sunk, and 50 percent of Iraq's combat aircraft were destroyed or fled to Iran to avoid destruction. The total number of Iraqi dead and wounded, including civilians, will probably never be known.[3] The cease-fire proved to be premature; despite the annihilation of Iraq's navy and combat aircraft, significant remnants of its military, including the Republican Guard, were never destroyed.

However, the crushing victory by U.S. and coalition forces would not have been possible without the benefit of NSA's flood of intelligence, which was particularly successful in helping to neutralize the huge Iraqi air defense system—over 700 radars, almost 3,700 SAMs, and 970 antiaircraft artillery sites spread throughout Iraq and occupied Kuwait, which was denser than the Soviet air defenses on the Kola Peninsula at the height of the Cold War. In the five-month interval after the Iraqi invasion of Kuwait, NSA's SIGINT satellites, ground-based listening posts, and reconnaissance aircraft mapped the locations of all Iraqi SAM sites, radar stations, and command centers, analyzed the system's capability—and figured out how the system worked and how to defeat it. Within hours of the initial attack against it, the system was reduced to rubble, giving the coalition un-challenged air supremacy.[4]

Most of the Iraqi command-and-control targets hit during the air campaign were based on SIGINT information. NSA coverage of Iraqi government and military strategic communications helped the U.S. Air Force to target virtually all key radio stations and fiber-optic communications nodes inside Iraq and Kuwait. The monthlong air strikes, according to future NSA director Rear Admiral John "Mike" McConnell, "prevented communications up and down the Iraqi chain of command and contributed to the confusion and lack of cohesion among Iraqi ground forces as coalition ground forces moved into Kuwait and Iraq."[5]

But four sites were spared—ones that the surviving Iraqi commanders in Kuwait would be forced to use to communicate with their superiors in Basra and Baghdad. The gamble succeeded. An army intelligence history notes, "Just before the ground war [began] allied intelligence agencies . . . left four [signal nodes] intact . . . leading to valuable NSA intercepts which, in conjunction with JSTARS [the army radar surveillance aircraft], brought into view a vivid picture of their movements and intentions."[6]

NSA's interception of messages to and from Nazar Hamdoon, Iraq's U.N. ambassador, showed that Hussein really believed his army could inflict heavy losses on the allied forces and repel any attempt to liberate Kuwait. The intercepts also revealed that Hussein refused to concede defeat until virtually the end of the war, suggesting to American intelligence analysts that the Iraqi dictator was delusional and/or operating in an information vacuum.[7]

But many senior American intelligence officials and military commanders found NSA's performance disappointing. First, the agency was unable to gain access to the communications of the Iraqi army and Republican Guard in Kuwait and southern Iraq until the very end of the war because of tight and doggedly maintained Iraqi communications security discipline until the air offensive began on January 17—to the extent that Iraqi commanders were "even pronouncing death sentences for those who used two-way radios or telephones."[8] Not even the Russians had been able to maintain such discipline at the height of the Cold War. As a result, the Iraqis effectively neutralized much of NSA and the U.S. military's ability to collect intelligence on enemy forces before and during Desert Storm.[9] According to David McManis, NSA's representative at the Pentagon during the war, Hussein "learned what his vulnerabilities were, and, boy, I'll tell you he's played it right. We've never faced a tougher partner in terms of [SIGINT] access."[10]

SIGINT did not become a significant factor in the ground war until it began on February 24, when the Iraqis hurriedly began redeploying their elite Republican Guard divisions from their reserve positions to face the U.S. and allied invasion force. This meant that they had to stop using their buried landlines. After that, NSA's SIGINT intercept operators had a field day. For example, NSA provided critical intelligence about the movements of three key Republican Guard divisions on February 26, which revealed that the commander of the Iraqi Third Corps had ordered his units to withdraw as rapidly as possible from Kuwait, a withdrawal that quickly turned into a rout.[11]

The greatest threat, at least psychologically, was presented by the limited-range Iraqi Scud missiles, which after the invasion of Kuwait were dispersed to presurveyed bases throughout Iraq. On January 18, the day after the U.S. air campaign began, the Iraqi missile batteries began lobbing Scud at Israel and later at Saudi Arabia. While none hit any military targets, public anxiety in the United States and Israel about these attacks forced the White House to order NSA and U.S. Central Command (CENTCOM) to dedicate a significant amount of their SIGINT collection resources to locating the missiles so that they could be destroyed by air strikes.[12]

This proved to be virtually impossible. A study written by a U.S. Army intelligence officer who served in Operation Desert Storm notes. "The quick nature of Iraqi 'shoot and scoot' tactics made detection extremely difficult, if not near impossible. The Iraqi missile units maintained excellent radio security, only infrequently communicating target data and fire commands with higher headquarters." The net result was that SIGINT, despite intensive efforts, did not find a single Scud missile launcher during the entire Persian Gulf War.[13]

Because of the limited use of radio communications by the Iraqis, U.S. Army and Marine Corps tactical SIGINT collection units produced virtually no intelligence during the war, which came as a nasty shock to U.S. military intelligence officials. Moreover, army and marine field commanders below the corps level confirmed that they received no SIGINT support from NSA during Operation Desert Storm. Apart from onerous security limitations on the dissemination of SIGINT material to the commanders who needed it the most, NSA tried to disguise the SIGINT origins of what intelligence it did provide, and generated reports that were so chopped up that they were virtually useless.[14]

But the greatest problem for SIGINT was the perpetual shortage of Arabic linguists, which forced NSA and the U.S. military to grant emergency security clearances to a number of Iraqi Americans serving in the military when Kuwait was invaded and ship them to the Persian Gulf to become instant radio intercept operators. In addition, three hundred Kuwaiti students were recruited from U.S. universities. They were given a crash course in the rudiments of SIGINT collection, flown to Saudi Arabia wearing the uniforms of sergeants in the Kuwaiti army, and then parceled out to various U.S. Army SIGINT units in the region. The commander of all U.S. Army intelligence forces in the gulf later wrote of the service provided by these young Kuwaiti volunteers: "Their performance and contribution was magnificent and immeasurable . . . we couldn't have done it without 'em."[15]

The net result, however, was that in the opinion of senior military field commanders and intelligence officials who served in the Persian Gulf, SIGINT and HUMINT did not perform particularly well during Operation Desert Shield/Storm. Instead, photo reconnaissance satellites, unmanned reconnaissance drones (referred to within the military as unmanned aerial vehicles, or UAVs), and airborne radar surveillance aircraft all proved to be more important to the successful prosecution of the war.[16]

Retrenchment and Debasement

Even before the defeat of Iraq was completed, back at Fort Meade NSA's director, Admiral William Studeman, had become concerned that the health of his agency was not good. Declassified documents reveal that the stifling, multilayered NSA bureaucracy had been allowed to grow unchecked during the 1980s because the agency's nominal watchdogs in the CIA, the Pentagon, and Congress had paid scant attention to what was going on, allowing the agency to become top-heavy and bloated. A February 1991 House intelligence committee report found "very limited internal oversight of Agency [NSA] programs," as well as no supervision of the agency by either the Defense Department Inspector General's Office or the congressional watchdog agency, the General Accountability Office (GAO).[17] A few months later, a report prepared by the Defense Department's inspector general confirmed, "NSA did not have sufficient oversight mechanisms to ensure the Agency efficiently accomplished its mission."[18]

An internal NSA study sent to Studeman before Iraq's surrender noted, "The Agency is effective, but it is not efficient . . . This inefficiency may waste money; it may waste technology; but the task force is convinced that it is surely wasting people." The agency's vast bureaucracy was strangling it. The report's key conclusion was this: "The Agency is in inchoate crisis, and if there is a single alarm to sound in this report, it is that the National Security Agency needs major fundamental change and needs it soon."[19]

This came as a shock at a time when NSA not only was the largest American intelligence agency, but also presented itself as the best organized, the most efficient, and the producer of the best intelligence available.[20] The agency's reputation inside the Bush White House and elsewhere in Washington had never been higher. But NSA was, in reality, a deeply troubled organization, suffering from a malaise that was very much of its own making.[21]

Shortly after the tearing down of the Berlin Wall and the subsequent demise of the Soviet Union, the rationale for maintaining a massive Cold War intelligence community was seen as questionable, and beginning in 1990, the Bush administration and Congress sharply cut the national intelligence budget. In late 1990, Studeman, faced with a shrinking budget, was forced to order substantial staff cuts, which were implemented shortly after the end of Desert Storm.[22]

The agency began to retire hundreds of its employees, many of whom had decades of experience and represented an irreplaceable institutional memory. One former NSA official who took early retirement in 1992 recalled one of his colleagues telling him with great sadness at his retirement party, "The good old days are gone forever."[23]

NSA's rapidly shrinking budget and workforce meant that reforming its bureaucracy was *not* the agency's top priority. In a 1994 study, an army intelligence officer noted, "Intelligence analysts must now consider an array of 160 nations and many other independent groups as separate entities without the simplicity of the East-West division."[24] In order to use its stretched resources to deliver intelligence product to its customers, NSA's two top priorities became (a) improving the quality of SIGINT support to the U.S. military and (b) maintaining NSA's access to the communications of its growing global target base.[25]

But owing to bureaucratic bungling, mismanagement, and faulty leadership, over the next eight years not only did NSA fail to effect any meaningful reforms to its management and financial practices, but it also failed to address the dramatic changes then taking place in global telecommunications technology. The agency's morale plummeted and its mission suffered. NSA's director of operations, James Taylor, wrote in a memo, "The mission should drive the budget process. In spite of our best efforts through the 1990s, the opposite has most often been the case. Our changes to deal with this have never gotten to the root of the problem. We have merely dressed up the problem in new clothes."[26]

Making matters worse, NSA simply did not have the ability to effectively cover the plethora of newly created nations holding nuclear weapons, such as Belarus, the Ukraine, and Kazakhstan.[27] Many of the so-called rogue nation states, such as Libya, Iraq, Iran, Syria, and North Korea, were already closing off SIGINT access by shifting from radio circuits to buried landlines and fiber-optic cables.[28]

The worst threat to NSA's fragile code-breaking capabilities came not from abroad but from a tiny computer software company in northern California called RSA Data Security, headed by Jim Bidzos. NSA was aware by the late 1980s that new encryption technologies being developed by private companies meant, according to a declassified internal NSA publication, that NSA's code breakers were falling behind: "The underlying rate of cryptologic development throughout the world is faster than ever before and getting faster. Cryptologic literature in the public domain concerning advanced analytic techniques is proliferating. Inexpensive high-grade cryptographic equipment is readily accessible on the open market."[29] The agency was still able to break the cipher systems used by a small number of key countries around the world, such as Libya and Iran, but this could change quickly as target nations began using commercially available and rapidly evolving encryption software packages. It would have a catastrophic impact on the agency's code-breaking efforts.[30]

In April 1992, Studeman stepped down as director of NSA to take the post of deputy director of the CIA. His last memorandum to the agency warned that given NSA's continually shrinking resources, "target technology will be tough, and many outsiders will want to rationalize a reduced threat dimension in order to further decrement intelligence for alternative agendas. There will be a trend to de-emphasize technical intelligence in favor of cheaper and historically less productive intelligence means." Studeman urged the agency to focus on "technical and operational innovation to deal with a changing and changed world . . . We cannot be layered, inefficient, bureaucratic, top heavy, isolated, or turf minded." Sadly, Studeman's warnings went largely unheeded, and his recommendations were not implemented by his successors. Six years after his departure, NSA was on the verge of going deaf, dumb, and blind.

The McConnell Years at NSA: 1992–1996

Admiral Studeman's replacement as NSA's director was another career navy intelligence officer, forty-eight-year-old Vice Admiral John "Mike" Mc-Connell. Born in Greenville, South Carolina, on July 26, 1943, McConnell joined the navy in 1966 after graduating from Furman College in Greenville with a bachelor's degree in economics. Over the next twenty-five years, he held a succession of increasingly important positions in naval intelligence, including deputy director of the DIA for joint staff support from 1990 until being nominated for the top job at NSA in 1992.[31] McConnell was chosen not because of his intelligence background, but rather for his superior communications skills, which he demonstrated while serving as the Joint Chiefs of Staff intelligence briefer during Operation Desert Storm. The chairman of the JCS, General Colin Powell, lobbied vigorously for McConnell's appointment.[32]

In a *New Yorker* article, Lawrence Wright describes McConnell as a man with "pale, thin, sandy hair, blue eyes, and skin as pink as a baby's. His back troubles him, and he walks with a slight stoop, which becomes more pronounced as the day wears on. His friends describe him as quick-minded and crafty, with an unusual ability to synthesize large amounts of information. A workaholic, he regularly lugged two briefcases home each night."[33]

McConnell was determined to give the U.S. military more and better intelligence and maintain NSA's access to the global communications infrastructure, as well as making the agency "leaner and more effective," despite shrinking budgets and declining manpower.[34] In September 1992, McConnell, aware that the Bush White House intended to impose more budget cuts on NSA, ordered a preemptive overhaul and reorganization of the entire agency coupled with deep personnel cuts. He knew that the "reduction in force" was going to hurt his agency badly, but he was convinced that reducing the size of NSA's huge and very expensive bureaucracy was the only way to find the money to develop and buy the new and very expensive SIGINT collection technology NSA desperately needed. McConnell dryly noted some years later, "The message that I took to the NSA bureaucracy was not warmly embraced."[35]

Between 1990 and 1995, the U.S. intelligence community's budget had been cut by 16 percent, and 20 percent of the community's workforce (20,559 men and women) had been forced into early retirement or laid off. NSA's budget was slashed by one third, which forced the agency to cut the size of its workforce by an equal amount and impose a freeze on hiring and pay raises. A declassified congressional study concluded, "One of the side effects of NSA's downsizing, outsourcing and transformation has been the loss of critical program management expertise, systems engineering, and requirements definition skills." Research and development on new collection and processing systems and technologies came to a near-complete standstill as NSA's money was diverted to keeping ongoing operations alive and producing intelligence.[36]

One Damn Crisis After Another

In November 1992, President Bush ordered American troops into Somalia to restore order and feed millions of starving Somalis in the famine-stricken, war-torn country. The intelligence that was available was so bad that General Anthony Zinni, the U.S. military's chief of operations there, was quoted as saying, "I don't know Somalis from salami."[37]

NSA played virtually no role in the U.S. military intervention because there was no Somali government and thus no diplomatic or military communications for it to monitor. The first army combat unit sent in, the Tenth Mountain Division, brought no SIGINT intercept gear with it. Because of this oversight, it was unable to "exploit the lucrative long-range radio communications between the warring factions" after discovering that the militia forces commanded by General Mohammed Farrah Aideed indeed used radios and walkie-talkies. The U.S. Marine Corps, however, sent a small SIGINT detachment to support the first marine combat units to land. So effective was the detachment's gathering of critically important intelligence that it was awarded the NSA's 1993 Director's Trophy.[38]

SIGINT played a relatively small but nonetheless important role during the U.S. invasion of Haiti, in September 1994. Prior to and during the invasion, NSA listening posts provided strategic SIGINT support for American forces by monitoring the shortwave communications traffic of the Haitian armed forces and intercepting the telephone calls of the Haitian strongman Lieutenant General Raoul Cédras as he negotiated his resignation and safe passage from the country with foreign intermediaries. NSA also monitored the communications of the Haitian exile leader and future president, Jean-Bertrand Aristide, as he waited in a hotel suite in Washington and provided insights into his intentions that were useful to the White House and State Department.[39]

Once U.S. Army ground troops had taken control of the country, army SIGINT intercept personnel (including a small number of newly recruited Creole linguists) were flown in from the United States to monitor the citizens' band radio communications and walkie-talkie traffic of what was left of the former regime's army and police forces, using portable radio scanners purchased from Radio Shack and other commercial vendors.[40]

But by far, the crisis that taxed NSA the most was the civil wars in the former Yugoslavia, especially the civil war in Bosnia. NSA had begun paying serious attention to Yugoslavia in 1990–1991 as the country disintegrated into six independent states, which became engulfed in an orgy of bloodshed and ethnic cleansing.

The best intelligence came from SIGINT, especially from the joint CIA-NSA listening post inside the U.S. embassy in Belgrade. Unfortunately, according to the late Warren Zimmermann, the U.S. ambassador to Yugoslavia from 1989 to 1992, in 1991 he was not provided with these "real time intercepts involving Serbian politicians, Yugoslav army, people we had a tremendous amount of interest in. It was information that would have been extremely useful to us in our dealings then."[41]

SIGINT coverage of the bitter civil war in Bosnia between Croatian, Serbian, and Bosnian Muslim militaries was intensified shortly after President Bill Clinton was inaugurated in January 1993. The newly reconstituted NSA Operations Analysis Group A, headed from 1992 to 1996 by William Black Jr., focused on identifying and tracking the command-and-control nets, the air defense networks, and the logistics structures supporting the Serbian-backed Bosnian Serbs, the Croatians, and the Bosnian Muslims as they struggled for control of Bosnia.[42]

NSA's SIGINT satellites were able to intercept much of the communications traffic coming in and out of the Bosnian Serb general staff headquarters, which was translated and processed in real time by NSA and military SIGINT personnel at NSA's Bad Aibling Station listening post, in southern Germany, then passed to consumers within the U.S. intelligence community. The information contained in these intercepts yielded vital intelligence about Serb military activities in Bosnia, as well as insights into the somewhat twisted personality of the Bosnian Serb military commander, General Ratko Mladic.[43] NSA's coverage of the telecommunications traffic of the Muslim Bosnian government in Sarajevo was also excellent. In 1996, SIGINT intercepts of Bosnian government communications traffic revealed that hundreds of Iranian Revolutionary Guard military personnel were still operating throughout the territory controlled by the Bosnian government, despite the government's promise to throw them out of the country under the terms of the 1995 Dayton Peace Accords.[44]

SIGINT played a key role in ensuring the effectiveness of the U.S. and NATO air strikes on Bosnian Serb military units and their air defense network in August and September 1995. Before the strikes, NSA's SIGINT assets allowed U.S. intelligence analysts to thoroughly map the Yugoslav and Bosnian Serb air defense systems in Bosnia. SIGINT also showed that Yugoslavian early-warning radars positioned inside Bosnian Serb territory were monitoring NATO air activity over Bosnia, and that the data from these radars was being fed in near real time to Bosnian Serb army commanders in northeastern Bosnia.[45]

After the Dayton Peace Accords were signed on November 21, 1995, American ground troops belonging to the First Armored Division were sent into Bosnia in early 1996 as part of a multinational peacekeeping force. They were accompanied by a host of American SIGINT collection assets, whose mission it was to warn the American forces of any threat from the former warring parties. Unfortunately, there was little to monitor since most of the communications and air defense infrastructure had been destroyed or, according to a U.S. Army SIGINT officer, "intimidated into silence during NATO-sanctioned air strikes conducted in May and August 1995 . . . The loss of access to many of these intelligence sources created a difficult problem for continued monitoring of compliance by the former belligerent parties in the Dayton Peace Accords." By mid-1996, SIGINT in Bosnia had come to an almost complete standstill, since Serbian radio traffic decreased markedly after military operations ended.[46]

Still, senior Clinton administration officials marveled at the agency's ability to garner one "hot" intelligence scoop after another. For example, SIGINT was instrumental in cracking the communications network of the Medellín cartel, revealing the hiding place of its leader, Pablo Escobar, who was killed in December 1993 by the Colombian National Police. In the mid-1990s, NSA produced some incredibly important intelligence about what was transpiring inside the government of Saudi Arabia, including cell phone conversations of senior members of the Saudi royal family talking about high-level government policy.[47] Then on February 24, 1996, NSA intercepted the radio chatter of Cuban fighter pilots as they shot down two unarmed Cessna aircraft, flown by Cuban American pilots belonging to the Miami-based organization Brothers to the Rescue, off the coast of Cuba. The incident led President Clinton to sign the so-called Helms-Burton Act, which made permanent the economic embargo against Cuba, which had been in place unofficially since 1962.[48]

Bad and Worse Choices

Based on NSA's less than stellar performance in Somalia, Haiti, and Bosnia, senior military intelligence officials were demanding immediate improvements in the intelligence support they got from NSA. In all three crises, it turned out that NSA had very little information in its files about the enemy forces facing the U.S. military. During the actual operations, as noted earlier, it was quickly discovered that much of the high-tech SIGINT equipment that NSA and the military brought with them to these less developed countries was poorly suited for the "low-tech" surroundings they were operating in.

And in those cases where there were some communications to intercept, once the enemy fighters in Somalia and Bosnia discovered that NSA and the U.S. military were monitoring their communications, they turned off their radios and reverted to human couriers and intercept-proof telephone landlines.[49] Particularly galling for NSA officials was the fact that in all three operations, HUMINT collected by the CIA and U.S. military intelligence was the primary intelligence source for the U.S. military forces—not SIGINT.[50]

Many senior Pentagon officials, rightly or wrongly, believed that NSA was not giving commanders in the field the intelligence they needed. One reason for this problem was that the older and more experienced NSA analysts who knew more about the needs of these customers had been let go or had resigned as part of the agency's "reduction in force" in the early 1990s.[51]

The long series of crises described above stretched collection resources to the breaking point and diverted personnel and capital away from much-needed modernization programs and infrastructure improvement projects.[52]

As a result, the crucial reform plans that Mike McConnell brought with him when he came to the agency in May 1992 never got implemented. In fact, all indications are that NSA's bureaucratic infarction got worse during McConnell's tenure, leading the agency to make costly mistakes in resource allocation and spending priorities. For example, a 1996 Defense Department inspector general report revealed that in 1991 and 1992 alone, NSA lost eighty-two million dollars' worth of equipment, which it chose to write off on its financial statements rather than find out the fate of.[53]

But what was really killing NSA was the size of the agency's payroll. Although the number of NSA personnel plummeted during McConnell's tenure, the cost of paying those who remained skyrocketed as the agency had to reach deep into its pockets to try to keep its best and brightest from jumping ship and joining the dot-com boom. NSA stripped ever-increasing amounts of money from infrastructure improvement programs and its research and development efforts so that it could meet its payroll. It was left with little money to develop and build the new equipment desperately needed to access international communications traffic being carried by new and increasingly important telecommunications technologies, such as the Internet, cellular telephones, and fiber-optic cables. It was a decision that would, according to a former senior NSA official, "come back and bite us in the ass."[54]

The Minihan Years at NSA: 1996–1999

In February 1996, NSA director McConnell retired. During his tenure, in the opinion of senior agency officials, he simply failed to address the stultifying bureaucracy in NSA's upper ranks and to fully grasp the scope of agency operations, though he was an effective spokesman for NSA in front of administration officials and Congress.[55]

His replacement was the fifty-two-year-old director of DIA, Lieutenant General Kenneth Minihan of the U.S. Air Force. A career intelligence officer but with little operational experience with SIGINT, Minihan was born in Pampa, Texas, on December 31, 1943. After graduating from Florida State University in June 1966, he was commissioned into the air force. As he moved up in rank, he served in a wide variety of intelligence positions, including air force assistant chief of staff, intelligence, from 1994 to 1995; he was the director of DIA from 1995 until being named NSA director in February 1996.[56]

By his own admission, Minihan was chosen because the Pentagon believed he would not only emphasize SIGINT support for the military, but also improve the Pentagon's shaky customer-client relationship with the agency.[57]

Many former senior NSA officials interviewed for this book regard Minihan's tenure at Fort Meade, from 1996 to 1999, as a period fraught with controversy, during which NSA continued to refocus its efforts away from traditional targets and toward new transnational targets, such as narcotics trafficking and international terrorism, and not always with great success. Money, or lack thereof, was a recurring theme during Minihan's term in office. NSA, like every other agency in the U.S. intelligence community, was trying to get more money out of the Clinton White House or Congress, but without much success. CIA director George Tenet admitted, "The fact is that by the mid- to late 1990s American intelligence was in Chapter 11, and neither Congress nor the executive branch did much about it."[58] This led to pitched battles within the intelligence community over which agency would get how much of the money grudgingly allocated by Congress. In November 1998, Minihan, who by this time was a lame duck, made a final plea to the White House and the Pentagon to approve more money for NSA, pointing out that since the end of the Cold War, the agency had lost one third of its manpower and budget and much of its ability to access target communications, and that its antiquated infrastructure was crumbling and desperately in need of repair. He failed, in part because of the widely held view that NSA was being badly mismanaged.[59]

The congressional intelligence oversight committees could not get Minihan or his deputy, Barbara McNamara, to make fundamental reforms or even to send to Congress something as simple as a business plan for the agency. Inaction on the part of the agency's leadership forced Congress to act. In the House Intelligence Committee's May 1998 annual report, the chairman, Porter Goss, announced that his committee had "fenced in," or restricted, the agency's access to a large part of its annual budget because of NSA's continuing intransigence and resistance to reform.[60]

Today, in the opinion of some NSA veterans, Minihan's tenure at the helm of NSA is viewed as having been largely ineffectual. When he produced an agency mission statement in June 1996 titled "National Cryptologic Strategy for the 21st Century," agency staff members were mortified to find it full of vague generalities rather than specifics about how NSA was to meet the increasing challenges it faced.[61]

Efforts by Minihan and his staff to patch up the agency's rocky relationship with the Pentagon largely failed. In March 1997, a full year after he took office, Minihan briefed the senior military leadership on how NSA would improve its SIGINT support for the military. One senior military intelligence official who attended it recalls that Minihan used every current Pentagon buzzword (*asymmetric, paradigm, templates,* etc.) but offered nothing tangible about how things would be improved—other than suggesting that NSA and the military work more closely together.[62]

Yet as the NSA muddled along and one scandal after another rocked the CIA during the mid-1990s, and as the agency's clandestine intelligence capabilities slowly eroded, the Clinton administration came to increasingly treat NSA and its sister intelligence organization, the National Reconnaissance Office, with greater deference, in large part because the SIGINT coming out of NSA was viewed as "cleaner" and less controversial than the material produced by the CIA.[63]

The War on Terrorism

During General Minihan's term, the radical Islamic terrorist group al Qaeda (Arabic for "the base") began appearing on the U.S. intelligence community's radar screen. It was headed by a Saudi multimillionaire and veteran of the 1980s war against the Soviets in Afghanistan named Osama bin Laden, who was then living in exile in the Sudan. The earliest known NSA reporting on bin Laden's activities dates back to 1995 and was based in large part on monitoring the telephone calls coming in and out of his ranch near the Sudanese capital of

Khartoum. For example, the agency intercepted a series of telephone calls congratulating bin Laden on the June 25, 1996, bombing of the Khobar Towers in Dhahran, Saudi Arabia, which killed nineteen American military personnel. (In fact, it was Hezbollah and the Iranian government, not al Qaeda, that had carried out the Khobar Towers attack.)[64]

Despite these successes, NSA was experiencing considerable difficulty monitoring bin Laden. But when he was forced out of the Sudan in mid-1996 by the Sudanese government and moved to Afghanistan, it made SIGINT coverage of his activities significantly easier.[65]

In November 1996, one of bin Laden's operatives in the United States, named Ziyad Khalil, purchased a Inmarsat Compact M satellite telephone and more than three thousand hours of prepaid satellite time from a company in Deer Park, New York, for seventy-five hundred dollars. In a matter of weeks, the sat phone was in the hands of bin Laden in Afghanistan. It was assigned the international telephone number 00873-682-505-331.[66] When NSA was unable to intercept all of the satellite phone traffic, the CIA mounted its own independent SIGINT collection operation. The CIA managed to intercept half of the traffic, and NSA succeeded in getting the rest, but refused to share its take with the CIA.[67]

Over the next two years, NSA's relationship with the CIA deteriorated as officials from the two agencies clashed repeatedly and refused to cooperate with one another on joint SIGINT operations against al Qaeda. During this period, NSA and the CIA independently monitored the telephone conversations of bin Laden and his military operations chief, Mohammed Atef, as they kept in touch with their operatives and sympathizers around the world. Some of these intercepts helped foil a number of bin Laden terrorist plots, including two terrorist attacks on American embassies overseas in 1997 and seven attacks on American diplomatic or military establishments overseas in 1998, among them a planned bombing aimed at American forces stationed at Prince Sultan Air Base, in Saudi Arabia, and the hijacking of an American airliner.[68]

Up until this point, NSA's efforts to monitor bin Laden's activities had been underresourced and desultory. But on August 7, 1998, this changed when al Qaeda operatives bombed the American embassies in Nairobi, Kenya, and Dar es Salaam, Tanzania, killing 224 people (12 of whom were Americans) and injuring thousands more. Overnight, bin Laden became the agency's number-one target. Unfortunately, news reports after the East Africa bombings revealed that NSA was listening to bin Laden's phone conversations. Two months later, in October 1998, bin Laden ceased using the satellite telephone, depriving

NSA and the CIA of their best source of information about what bin Laden and his cohorts were up to.[69]

The Hayden Era at NSA

On February 23, 1999, the Pentagon announced that NSA director Minihan's replacement was to be Major General Michael Hayden of the U.S. Air Force, who was then serving in Seoul as the deputy chief of staff of the United Nations Command and U.S. Forces in Korea. Hayden, age fifty-two, was a veteran intelligence officer who had held a wide variety of high-level intelligence and policy positions over a thirty-two-year career prior to being named NSA director. These included involvement managing intelligence collection operations in the former Yugoslavia during the mid-1990s war in Bosnia, and commanding the Air Intelligence Agency from January 1996 to September 1997. Hayden pinned on his third star and then arrived for his first day of work at Fort Meade on March 26, 1999.[70]

Genial but unprepossessing, Hayden was described by journalist Bob Woodward as "short and balding, with a big head and large-framed eyeglasses—definitely not out of central casting for a TV talk show or a general." But Hayden's qualities had nothing to do with his looks. His subordinates had to learn to pace themselves for the long, grueling days that he put in at the office. He had a reputation for being thoughtful, honest, and forthright and was well known within the U.S. military establishment for his low-key management style and, perhaps more important, his ability to get along with people with temperaments and personalities different from his own. Hayden had just taken over when the United States plunged into another war in the former Yugoslavia, a territory that he knew all too well from his involvement in the mid-1990s conflict. This time, the war was over yet another rebellious Yugoslav province that was seeking its independence—Kosovo.

SIGINT and the War in Kosovo

The three-month war in the Yugoslav province of Kosovo, which lasted from March 24, 1999, to June 10, 1999, pitted the overwhelming might of the combined military forces of the United States and NATO against Slobodan Milošević's overmatched Yugoslavian military. After talks held in Rambouillet, France, to try to negotiate a peaceful settlement of the Kosovo crisis resulted in stalemate, the decision was made to wage a unique kind of war, one conducted from the air only. On March 24, U.S. and NATO warplanes began bombing Yugoslav military positions in Kosovo and throughout Yugoslavia to force the Belgrade government to accept the terms of the Rambouillet Accord. The name given to the U.S. and NATO bombing campaign was Operation Allied Force. Most of NSA's SIGINT effort was focused on collecting as much intelligence as possible about the Yugoslav strategic command-and-control network and air defense system to help the U.S. and allied warplanes win air superiority.

All in all, postwar reporting indicated that NSA performed well during the war, with more than 300,000 Yugoslav telephone calls, 150,000 e-mail messages, and over 2,000 fax messages being intercepted, covering Yugoslav troop movements, force status reports, logistics updates, hospital duty logs, and more. It was a very impressive performance for a three-month conflict, made all the more remarkable by the fact that literally no American soldiers were killed in action.[71]

The 100 Days of Change

Hayden entered the Fort Meade complex in March 1999 determined to make his mark quickly on the agency he had inherited. He flew down to Austin to meet with former NSA director Bobby Ray Inman, who was now teaching at the University of Texas. Inman advised Hayden that the biggest challenge he would face running NSA was obstruction from NSA's senior civilian officials, which Inman had encountered when he ran the agency during the 1970s.[72]

Hayden flew back to Fort Meade and found on his desk a thick report prepared for his predecessor, Minihan, by the NSA Scientific Advisory Board, chaired by retired lieutenant general James Clapper Jr. The Clapper report confirmed many of the findings of the House and Senate intelligence committees, including the conclusions that because the agency did not have a business plan, it was mismanaging its SIGINT collection assets, and that the agency research and development efforts "lacked focus and innovation." A second report from Clapper arrived a few months later, which urged Hayden to retool NSA "organizationally, programically, and technologically." This was followed by an April 9 memo from his director of operations, James Taylor, who told Hayden in no uncertain terms, "The first and most important issue for NSA/CSS is to reform our management and leadership system . . . We have good people in a flawed system."[73]

The Taylor memo was the last straw for Hayden. Clearly his agency was in deeper trouble than he had believed when he took the job, but he needed to know the full extent of the problem. In April 1999, he commissioned two management reviews on the state of NSA; one he assigned to a number of the agency's reform-minded Young Turks, who had chafed at the lack of action under Minihan, while the second report was to be prepared by five outside experts. Both reports, handed to Hayden in October, were scathing, with one concluding that NSA had become "an agency mired in bureaucratic conflict, suffering from poor leadership and losing touch with the government clients it serves." Hayden later told reporters, "The agency has got to make some changes because by standing still, we are going to fall behind very quickly."[74]

Hayden's reformation and modernization plan, "100 Days of Change," hit NSA like a tidal wave on November 10 with an announcement to the entire NSA that "our Agency must undergo change if we are to remain viable in the future." Hayden began by streamlining the agency's labyrinthine management structure, bringing in from the outside a new chief financial officer to try to reform NSA's financial and accounting practices and a veteran air force intelligence officer, Major General Tiiu Kera, to try to improve NSA's tense relations with the Pentagon. Overnight, the agency's top priority became modernization, while its SIGINT mission became the secondary priority. Money was taken from ongoing SIGINT operations and shifted to modernization projects, with particular emphasis on redirecting NSA's SIGINT effort against what Hayden described as the "digital global network." The budget cuts hurt, forcing Hayden to tell his worried employees in January 2000, "I realize the business areas that we decide to disengage from to pay for this transformation will be very important to many of you. I ask you to trust yourselves and your management on the tough calls we must make this winter to survive and prosper as an Agency."[75]

Hayden and his senior managers had hoped that they could keep the massive reengineering of NSA out of the public realm. But these hopes were dashed when, on December 6, reporter Seymour Hersh published an article in the *New Yorker* magazine that blew the lid off NSA's secret, revealing that America's largest intelligence agency was having trouble performing its mission.[76] Hersh's article set off a furious debate within NSA about the difficulties the agency was facing. The considered judgment of many NSA insiders was in many respects harsher and more critical than anything Hersh had written. Diane Mezzanotte, then a staff officer in NSA's Office of Corporate Relations, wrote, "NSA is facing a serious survival problem, brought about by the widespread use of emerging communications technologies and public encryption keys, draconian budget cuts, and an increasingly negative public perception of NSA and its SIGINT operations."[77]

Less than sixty days later, another disaster hit the agency. During the week of January 23, 2000, the main SIGINT processing computer at NSA collapsed and for four days could not be restarted because of a critical software anomaly. The result was an intelligence blackout, with no intelligence reporting coming out of Fort Meade for more than seventy-two hours. A declassified NSA report notes, "As one result, the President's Daily Briefing—60% of which is normally based on SIGINT—was reduced to a small portion of its typical size."[78]

The Switchboard

Located on the strategically important southwestern tip of the Arabian Peninsula, Yemen is one of the poorest and least developed nations in the world. Although the Yemeni government is dedicated to modernizing the nation, the deeply religious Yemeni people remain firmly rooted in the past. For centuries, Dhamar Province, a mountainous region south of Yemen's capital, Sana'a, has been the home of the warlike and rebellious al-Hada tribe. One of its most prominent members was a man named Ahmed Mohammed Ali al-Hada.[79]

Fiercely devoted to the ultraconservative Salafi interpretation of the Koran, al-Hada was steadfastly and vocally opposed to any form of Western influence or presence in the Arab world. Yemeni security officials confirm that al-Hada fought with the mujahideen against the Soviet military in Afghanistan during the 1980s, returning to Yemen in the early 1990s a fully committed jihadi and a member of Osama bin Laden's newly created al Qaeda organization. Both of al-Hada's daughters married al Qaeda operatives. One daughter was married to a senior operative named Mustafa Abdulqader al-Ansari. The other, Hoda, was married to a Saudi named Khalid al-Mihdhar, who on 9/11 would lead the al Qaeda team that crashed a Boeing 757 airliner into the Pentagon.[80]

Al-Hada's principal function within al Qaeda since 1996 had been to serve as a secret communications cutout between bin Laden and his military operations chief, Mohammed Atef, and the organization's operatives around the world. Bin Laden and Atef would call al-Hada's house in Sana'a and give him orders that he was to convey telephonically to al Qaeda's operatives in Europe, Asia, and Africa, and al-Hada would relay back to bin Laden and Atef in Afghanistan the reports he got from the field. Records of bin Laden's satellite phone calls from Afghanistan show that he called al-Hada in Sana'a at least 221 times between May 1996 and the time that the Saudi terrorist leader stopped using his phone in October 1998.[81]

U.S. intelligence first learned about al-Hada and his telephone number from

one of the captured al Qaeda planners of the August 1998 East Africa bombings, a Saudi national named Mohamed Rashed Daoud al-'Owhali, who was arrested by Kenyan authorities on August 12, 1998, five days after the bombing of
the U.S. embassy in Nairobi. Interrogated by a team of FBI agents, al-'Owhali
gave up the key relay number (011-967-1-200-578)—the telephone number of
Ahmed al-Hada.[82]

NSA immediately began intercepting al-Hada's telephone calls. This fortu-
itous break could not have come at a better time for the U.S. intelligence community, since NSA had just lost its access to bin Laden's satellite phone traffic.
For the next three years, the telephone calls coming in and out of the al-Hada
house in Sana'a were the intelligence community's principal window into what
bin Laden and al Qaeda were up to. The importance of the intercepted al-Hada
telephone calls remains today a highly classified secret within the intelligence
community, which continues to insist that al-Hada be referred to only as a "suspected terrorist facility in the Middle East" in declassified reports regarding the
9/11 intelligence disaster.[83]

In January 1999, NSA intercepted a series of phone calls to the al-Hada
house. (The agency later identified Pakistan as their point of origin.) NSA analysts found only one item of intelligence interest in the transcripts of these
calls—references to a number of individuals believed to be al Qaeda operatives,
one of whom was a man named Nawaf al-Hazmi. NSA did not issue any intelligence reports concerning the contents of these intercepts because al-Hazmi and
the other individuals mentioned in the intercept were not known to NSA's analysts at the time. Almost three years later, al-Hazmi was one of the 9/11 hijackers
who helped crash the Boeing airliner into the Pentagon. That al-Hazmi succeeded in getting into the United States using his real name after being prominently mentioned in an intercepted telephone call with a known al Qaeda
operative is but one of several huge mistakes made by the U.S. intelligence community that investigators learned about only after 9/11.[84]

During the summer of 1999, intercepts of Ahmed al-Hada's telephone calls
generated reams of actionable intelligence. In June, the State Department temporarily closed six American embassies in Africa after intercepted calls coming
in and out of al-Hada's house revealed that al Qaeda operatives were in the final
stages of preparing an attack on an unidentified American embassy in Africa.
By early July, intercepted al Qaeda communications traffic had revealed that
bin Laden operatives were preparing another operation, this time in Western
Europe. Two weeks later, more intercepted calls coming from al-Hada's house
indicated that bin Laden was planning to hit a major American "target of op-

portunity" in Albania. As a result, planned trips to Albania by Secretary of State Madeleine Albright and Secretary of Defense William Cohen were hastily canceled.[85]

On a now-ominous note, during that summer intercepted telephone calls coming into al-Hada's home mentioned for the first time a man referred to only as "Khaled." No doubt this was a reference to 9/11 hijacker Khalid al-Mihdhar, who at the time was living in al-Hada's home along with his wife, Hoda. Because this was the first mention of "Khaled" in an al Qaeda intercept, NSA did not report the information, as it could not be determined from the intercept who he was, much less whether he was an al Qaeda operative. After 9/11, investigators learned that a few months after this call, al-Mihdhar caught a flight from Sana'a to Islamabad, Pakistan, then crossed the border into Afghanistan to undergo a special terrorist training course at al Qaeda's Mes Aynak training camp, which was located in an abandoned Russian copper mine outside Kabul. Al-Mihdhar completed the training course and returned to Yemen via Pakistan in early December 1999.[86]

In December 1999, NSA intercepted another series of telephone calls to al-Hada's home in Sana'a, which revealed that an "operational cadre" of al Qaeda operatives intended to travel to Kuala Lumpur, Malaysia, in early January 2000. The transcript of the intercepted call identified only the first names of the team—"Nawaf," "Salem," and "Khalid." Based on the context and wording of the conversation, NSA analysts concluded that "Salem" was most likely the younger brother of "Nawaf," which, as it turned out, was correct. "Salem" was a Saudi national named Salem al-Hazmi, who was the younger brother of Nawaf al-Hazmi. A CIA analyst who reviewed the transcript and accompanying NSA intelligence report surmised that "something more nefarious [was] afoot but did nothing further with the report."[87]

On January 15, 2000, two of the 9/11 hijackers mentioned in the NSA intercept, Khalid al-Mihdhar and Nawaf al-Hazmi, flew into Los Angeles International Airport from Bangkok. Both men used their Saudi passports and visas, issued in their names by the U.S. consulate in Jidda. They spent the next two weeks holed up in an apartment in Culver City, outside Los Angeles, before renting an apartment at 6401 Mount Ada Road in San Diego.[88]

Two months later, on March 20, NSA intercepted a telephone call to al-Hada's house from a man who identified himself only as "Khaled." Unfortunately, because of the technology in use at the time, the agency did not know that the call it was monitoring had originated in the United States. NSA reported some of the contents of the intercepted call, but not all of the details, because the agency's analysts did not think that it was terrorist related. It was not until after the 9/11 attacks that the FBI pulled al-Mihdhar's telephone toll records and confirmed that the anonymous "Khaled" was none other than al-Mihdhar, who was calling his father-in-law from his apartment in San Diego. A 2002 congressional report found that NSA's inability to identify the location of the caller was to prove disastrous because it would have confirmed "the fact that the communications were between individuals in the United States and suspected terrorist facilities overseas."[89]

In May and June 2000, NSA intercepted a number of additional telephone calls to al-Hada's house from the anonymous "Khaled." As before, NSA could not identify the caller or his location. And because the calls dealt mostly with personal matters, the agency did not report the content or even the substance of these conversations. Thanks to the spadework done by the 9/11 Commission, we now know that the purpose of the call was for al-Hada to tell his son-in-law that his wife was expecting their first child. Upon being told by al-Hada of the birth of his son in late May 2000, al-Mihdhar closed his San Diego bank account, transferred the registration of his car to his colleague Nawaf al-Hazmi, and made reservations to fly home to Yemen. He apparently did not bother to tell his boss in Afghanistan, al Qaeda operations chief Khalid Sheikh Mohammed, that he was abandoning his post for purely personal reasons. Al-Mihdhar drove to Los Angeles on June 9 and took Lufthansa Flight 457 from Los Angeles International Airport to Frankfurt the next day. He was not to return to the United States for more than a year.[90]

Despite NSA's successes, it was only a matter of time before al Qaeda finally succeeded. On October 12, 2000, al Qaeda suicide bombers drove a speedboat laden with high explosives into the U.S. Navy destroyer USS *Cole* as it lay at anchor in the port of Aden, Yemen, waiting to be refueled. Seventeen sailors were killed in the blast and another thirty-nine wounded. On the same day that the attack on the *Cole* occurred, NSA issued an intelligence report based on intercepts (most likely calls coming in and out of Ahmed al-Hada's home in Sana'a) warning that terrorists were planning an attack in the region. However, the NSA warning message was not received by consumers until well after the attack had taken place.[91]

CHAPTER 12

Snatching Defeat from the Jaws of Victory

9/11 and the Invasion of Afghanistan

What you are prepared for never happens.
—PENNSYLVANIA DUTCH PROVERB

Zero Hour Is Near

President George W. Bush, who had been inaugurated on January 20, 2001, quickly became a devotee of NSA's intelligence reporting based on the briefings he had received before becoming president.[1] What the president did not know was that the agency was struggling mightily to both modernize its decrepit infrastructure and to meet the varied intelligence needs of its ever-growing clientele in Washington, with NSA analysts admitting, "they had far too many broad requirements (some 1,500 formal ones) that covered virtually every situation and target." Under these adverse conditions, NSA just did not have enough manpower and equipment resources to devote to international terrorism. And although terrorism had been NSA's top priority since the August 1998 East Africa embassy bombings, the agency's director, General Michael Hayden, later admitted that he had at least five other "number one priorities," and was unable to dedicate sufficient personnel and equipment resources to terrorism. The lack of resources available to cover al Qaeda and other terrorist targets was to come back to bite the agency in the months that followed.[2]

Prior to the September 11, 2001, bombings, NSA intercepted a steadily increasing volume of al Qaeda messages indicating that Osama bin Laden was about to launch a major terrorist operation against an American target. In late 2000, NSA intercepted a message in which an al Qaeda operative reportedly boasted over the phone that bin Laden was planning a "Hiroshima" against the United States. Most U.S. intelligence analysts concluded that the threat from al Qaeda was primarily to U.S. military or diplomatic installations overseas, particularly in the Middle East and Persian Gulf.[3]

Beginning in May and continuing through early July 2001, NSA intercepted thirty-three separate messages indicating that bin Laden intended to mount one or more terrorist attacks against U.S. targets in the near future. But the intercepts provided no specifics about the impending operation other than that "Zero Hour was near."[4]

In June, intercepts led to the arrest of two bin Laden operatives who were planning to attack U.S. military installations in Saudi Arabia as well as another one planning an attack on the U.S. embassy in Paris. On June 22, U.S. military forces in the Persian Gulf and the Middle East were once again placed on alert after NSA intercepted a conversation between two al Qaeda operatives in the region, which indicated that "a major attack was imminent." All U.S. Navy ships docked in Bahrain, homeport of the U.S. Fifth Fleet, were ordered to put to sea immediately.[5]

These NSA intercepts scared the daylights out of both the White House's "terrorism czar," Richard Clarke, and CIA director George Tenet. Tenet told Clarke, "It's my sixth sense, but I feel it coming. This is going to be the big one." On Thursday, June 28, Clarke warned National Security Advisor Condoleezza Rice that al Qaeda activity had "reached a crescendo," strongly suggesting that an attack was imminent. That same day, the CIA issued what was called an Alert Memorandum, which stated that the latest intelligence indicated the probability of imminent al Qaeda attacks that would "have dramatic consequences on governments or cause major casualties."[6]

But many senior officials in the Bush administration did not share Clarke and Tenet's concerns, notably Secretary of Defense Donald Rumsfeld, who distrusted the material coming out of the U.S. intelligence community. Rumsfeld thought this traffic might well be a "hoax" and asked Tenet and NSA to check the veracity of the al Qaeda intercepts. At NSA director Hayden's request, Bill Gaches, the head of NSA's counterterrorism office, reviewed all the intercepts and reported that they were genuine al Qaeda communications.[7]

But unbeknownst to Gaches's analysts at NSA, most of the 9/11 hijackers were already in the United States busy completing their final preparations. Calls from operatives in the United States were routed through the Ahmed al-Hada "switchboard" in Yemen, but apparently none of these calls were intercepted by NSA. Only after 9/11 did the FBI obtain the telephone billing records of the hijackers during their stay in the United States. These records indicated that the hijackers had made a number of phone calls to numbers known by NSA to have been associated with al Qaeda activities, including that of al-Hada.[8]

Unfortunately, NSA had taken the legal position that intercepting calls from abroad to individuals inside the United States was the responsibility of the FBI. NSA had been badly burned in the past when Congress had blasted it for illegal domestic intercepts, which had led to the 1978 Foreign Intelligence Surveillance Act (FISA). NSA could have gone to the Foreign Intelligence Surveillance Court (FISC) for warrants to monitor communications between terrorist suspects in the United States and abroad but feared this would violate U.S. laws.[9]

The ongoing argument about this responsibility between NSA and the FBI created a yawning intelligence gap, which al Qaeda easily slipped through, since there was no effective coordination between the two agencies. One senior NSA official admitted after the 9/11 attacks, "Our cooperation with our foreign allies is a helluva lot better than with the FBI."[10]

While NSA and the FBI continued to squabble, the tempo of al Qaeda intercepts mounted during the first week of July 2001. A series of SIGINT intercepts produced by NSA in early July allowed American and allied intelligence services to disrupt a series of planned al Qaeda terrorist attacks in Paris, Rome, and Istanbul. On July 10, Tenet and the head of the CIA's Counterterrorism Center, J. Cofer Black, met with National Security Advisor Rice to underline how seriously they took the chatter being picked up by NSA. Both Tenet and Black came away from the meeting believing that Rice did not take their warnings seriously.[11]

Clarke and Tenet also encountered continuing skepticism at the Pentagon from Rumsfeld and his deputy, Paul Wolfowitz. Both contended that the spike in traffic was a hoax and a diversion. Steve Cambone, the undersecretary of defense for intelligence, asked Tenet if he had "considered the possibility that al-Qa'ida's threats were just a grand deception, a clever ploy to tie up our resources and expend our energies on a phantom enemy that lacked both the power and the will to carry the battle to us."[12]

In August 2001, either NSA or Britain's GCHQ intercepted a telephone call from one of bin Laden's chief lieutenants, Abu Zubaida, to an al Qaeda operative believed to have been in Pakistan. The intercept centered on an operation that was to take place in September. At about the same time, bin Laden telephoned an associate inside Afghanistan and discussed the upcoming operation. Bin Laden reportedly praised the other party to the conversation for his role in planning the operation. For some reason, these intercepts were reportedly never forwarded to intelligence consumers, although this contention is strongly denied by NSA officials.[13] Just prior to the September 11, 2001, bombings, several European intelligence services reportedly intercepted a telephone call that bin Laden made to his wife, who was living in Syria, asking her to return to Afghanistan immediately.[14]

In the seventy-two hours before 9/11, four more NSA intercepts suggested that a terrorist attack was imminent. But NSA did not translate or disseminate any of them until the day after 9/11.[15] In one of the two most significant, one of the speakers said, "The big match is about to begin." In the other, another unknown speaker was overheard saying that tomorrow is "zero hour."[16]

A Day in Hell

On the morning of September 11, 2001, nearly twenty-two thousand NSA employees headed for the gates at Fort Meade to begin their workday, which typically started at seven A.M. They faced delays at the gates because the army had recently restricted public access to the base; security had been drastically tightened because of the recent spate of terrorist threats against U.S. military installations. Only four gates were open full-time (with four more open part-time), which led to long lines of cars waiting for clearance during the morning and afternoon rushes.[17]

There was a second security cordon around what NSA calls the Campus, a massive complex of twenty-six separate buildings patrolled by a 388-man NSA police force, plus an additional forty-nine buildings and warehouses used by NSA in the area surrounding Fort Meade. This was the equivalent of thirty-four hundred four-bedroom homes jammed together into a single office complex. Surrounding these buildings was the largest parking lot in the world.[18]

General Hayden arrived in his office on the eighth floor of the Ops 2B building before seven A.M. The director's office suite was the envy of all NSA employees, with some staff members calling it "The Penthouse" because it was on the top floor. Not only was the suite spacious and well appointed, but the view from Hayden's windows, which faced eastward, was of one of Fort Meade's two tree-shaded eighteen-hole golf courses. As was his penchant, he immediately began going through his e-mails, then turned to the large stack of reports and messages that his executive assistant Cindy Farkus had deposited in his in-box for his perusal.[19]

Elsewhere on the Campus, more than twenty thousand NSA employees were also plowing through their "Read File" of e-mails, cables, reports, and raw intercepts that had come in overnight.

Then at eighty forty-six A.M. on that beautiful Tuesday morning, a Boeing 767 jet, American Airlines Flight 11 out of Boston's Logan International Airport, struck the north side of the North Tower of the World Trade Center between the ninety-fourth and ninety-eighth floors.

Within minutes of the crash, all of the major network television and cable morning news shows had broken into their regularly scheduled broadcasts to show their viewers the first dramatic pictures of the burning North Tower.

Nineteen minutes later, at five past nine A.M., while network news cameras carried the event live, another Boeing 767 commercial jet, United Airlines Flight 175, lazily flew across the television screen and crashed into the South Tower of the World Trade Center. It was obvious then that this was no accident, but the worst terrorist attack on U.S. soil in history. Everything came to a stop as people gathered around TV screens and watched in horror as the Twin Towers collapsed. Those with family or friends in New York City frantically began trying to reach them, only to discover that virtually all of the phone lines along the East Coast of the United States were jammed with calls, quickly causing AT&T's telephone circuits going in and out of New York City to collapse under the strain.[20]

At nine ten a.m., five minutes after the second crash in New York City took place, Colonel Michael Stewart, the army base commander of Fort Meade, ordered that his post be locked down and declared a Threat Condition Delta, the highest force protection alert level in the U.S. military, which is used only in wartime. No one was allowed to enter or leave the base without proof that he or she worked or lived there.

Base public works crews quickly placed rows of three-foot-high concrete barriers in front of all of the closed gates to prevent anyone from ramming their car through one of them. The Maryland State Police closed down a section of Route 32 that ran next to the NSA headquarters complex, which caused a massive traffic jam.[21]

At nine thirty A.M. Hayden ordered that all nonessential NSA personnel be sent home immediately and, as a security precaution, that all remaining, mission-essential personnel be moved out of NSA's two black-glass office towers into the older (and less vulnerable) three-story-high Ops 1 office building next door. He then called his wife, Jeanine, at their quarters on base and asked her to check on their three grown children, all of whom lived or worked in Washington. Before he could explain the reason for his request, he had to hang up the phone as his staff poured into his office with the latest news bulletins.[22]

The planes crashing into the Pentagon and a deserted field in western

Pennsylvania were the final outrages—2,973 Americans were dead, surpassing the death toll at Pearl Harbor on December 7, 1941.[23]

Within minutes of the crash, NSA's internal emergency broadcast system
was activated, and announcements began to be read out over the agency's public address system ordering all nonessential personnel to leave the base immediately. In a matter of minutes, the first of thousands of NSA employees began
leaving the Campus. Within a few hours, the streets of Fort Meade resembled
those of a ghost town.[24]

For the rest of the day, inside the NSA operations buildings a form of controlled chaos reigned. In room 3E099, on the top floor of Ops 1, the duty officer
began calling senior NSA officials who were still at home, on leave, or on the
road on business and ordering them to report back to work immediately. At the
direction of Richard Berardino, the chief of the National Security Operations
Center (NSOC), NSA's watch center, his thirty analysts and reporting officers
began rapidly compiling whatever information they could to brief Hayden and
the agency's senior officials about what had just transpired. Other NSOC
staffers began systematically going back over the past several days' worth of
SIGINT reporting to see if anything had been missed that might have given
any warning of the terrorist attacks. They found nothing.[25]

A now-retired NSA intelligence officer remembered the next twenty-four
hours of his life as "a day in hell." Like all of his colleagues, he sat in on count-
less video and telephone conferences with other senior U.S. and British intelligence officials and attended one staff meeting after another until he reached the
point where he could not remember why he was at the meeting. When he finally
got back to his office, his secretary had a stack of telephone messages that had to
be answered. Then there was a never-ending flow of memos and reports that he
had to read and respond to. At midnight, he decided to leave because he was too
exhausted to think coherently. "How I got home without crashing the car, I don't
know."[26]

Nowhere was the blunt-force trauma inflicted by the 9/11 attacks felt more
deeply than within NSA's one-hundred-man counterterrorism unit, called the
Counterterrorism Product Line, whose leader, Bill Gaches, was well qualified
for the job, having served from 1998 to 2000 as the deputy chief of NSA's Office
of the Middle East and North Africa, where, one of his former analysts recalled,
"terror was king."[27] Hayden later described the state of morale in the NSA counterterrorism office on September 11 as "emotionally shattered." Later that morning, Maureen Baginski, the chief of NSA's Signals Intelligence Directorate,
visited the counterterrorism office and held an impromptu staff meeting, first

taking the time to calm the clearly distressed staff, then urging them to get back to work. Recalling the days of the London blitz, some were busy putting up blackout curtains over the office windows so as to shield their activities from the outside world.[28]

What Hayden and his staff did not know was that messages among al Qaeda officials and sympathizers that had been intercepted by the agency within minutes of the 9/11 attacks were causing a firestorm at the White House and the Pentagon. A number of senior Bush administration officials, including Secretary of Defense Rumsfeld, were convinced that the attacks were the handiwork of Iraqi dictator Saddam Hussein, and not al Qaeda. Tyler Drumheller, then the head of the CIA Clandestine Service division responsible for Europe, noted,

> Within fifteen minutes of the attacks the National Security Agency intercepted a call from an al Qaeda operative in Asia to a contact in a former Soviet republic reporting the "good news" of the attacks in New York and on the Pentagon. [CIA director George J.] Tenet passed that report on to Rumsfeld around midday, but according to notes taken by aides who were with the Secretary of Defense, he characterized the NSA report as "vague" and said there was "no good basis for hanging hat" on the fact that al Qaeda had conducted the assaults.[29]

The intercept that Drumheller referred to, between a known al Qaeda official in Afghanistan and an unidentified person in the former Soviet republic of Georgia, was intercepted by NSA at nine fifty-three A.M., less than fifteen minutes after American Airlines Flight 77 had hit the Pentagon. And despite overwhelming evidence accumulated by the CIA that the hijackers were known al Qaeda operatives, at two forty P.M. Rumsfeld ordered Pentagon officials to immediately begin preparing plans to launch retaliatory air strikes on Iraq. In the days that followed, Rumsfeld and a number of other senior administration officials continued to refuse to accept the fact that the 9/11 attacks had been conducted by Osama bin Laden's operatives. As it turned out, this was a portent of things to come.[30]

The Invasion of Afghanistan

It did not take the Bush administration long to decide where to retaliate for the 9/11 terrorist attacks. At a meeting of the NSC held on the morning of

September 13, 2001, President Bush ordered Secretary of Defense Rumsfeld to begin preparing a plan to attack the Taliban regime in Afghanistan, including a range of options up to and including an actual invasion. The name eventually given to the operation was Enduring Freedom.[31]

Bush's decision to begin preparations for an invasion of Afghanistan put NSA director Hayden in a bind. As of September 2001, NSA's SIGINT coverage of Afghanistan was not particularly good. The agency's SIGINT collection resources had been so tightly stretched prior to 9/11 that it had dedicated only a relatively small amount of its resources to monitoring the communications of the regime in Kabul, since the Taliban was not a big user of radio or other interceptable forms of communications. Other than a dozen or so Soviet-made shortwave radios, the Taliban's military formations used nothing more sophisticated than walkie-talkies and satellite telephones. There was no cell phone service inside Afghanistan, the Internet had been banned by the Taliban regime as "unholy," and the single microwave telephone link between Kabul and Pakistan was so unreliable that it frustrated the NSA intercept operators trying to monitor it as much as it did the Afghan officials who depended on it to communicate with the outside world.[32]

NSA also faced a linguistic shortfall: It had only two or three individuals on staff who could speak the principal languages spoken in the country—Pashto, Dari, Uzbek, and Turkmen. The agency had to rely on decoding the diplomatic messages of countries that maintained embassies in Kabul (the United States had no embassy in Afghanistan), and on intelligence-sharing arrangements with a number of foreign intelligence services.[33]

Completely independent of NSA, the CIA was running a clandestine SIGINT collection effort inside Afghanistan that was slightly more successful than NSA's. In late 1997, the CIA had delivered to the anti-Taliban Northern Alliance forces some off-the-shelf SIGINT intercept equipment, which they used to monitor the radio and walkie-talkie traffic of the Taliban and al Qaeda forces arrayed against them in northern Afghanistan. More equipment was surreptitiously flown in by CIA teams in the summer of 1999. The problem was that prior to 9/11, there was no full-time CIA liaison officer assigned to the Northern Alliance, so the intercepts were picked up by the CIA only sporadically, usually months after the messages were intercepted.[34]

The U.S. military's SIGINT assets were also minimal. The army was slowly in the process of revamping its tactical SIGINT capabilities with new equipment, but until such time as these new systems were fielded, the army's field units were almost completely dependent on NSA's "national systems" for most of the intelligence they got.[35] Linguists were in dreadfully short supply within the U.S. military's SIGINT units because of a lack of recruitment and personnel retention. As of 9/11, the army was missing half of its Arabic linguists, a critical shortfall that obviously could not be rectified overnight and that would have unforeseen consequences in the months that followed.[36]

Right after 9/11, NSA's principal listening post covering the Middle East and Near East, the Gordon Regional Security Operations Center (GRSOC) at Fort Gordon, in Georgia, issued an urgent request for all available Arabic linguists to augment its collection operations. It was just one of many NSA and military SIGINT units making such a request, so as an emergency measure the U.S. Army decided to use Arabic linguists from tactical units based in the United States to augment GRSOC's SIGINT operations. Within weeks, twelve Arabic linguists belonging to the SIGINT company of the Third Armored Cavalry Regiment arrived at Fort Gordon on a 180-day temporary deployment. It turned out that none of the linguists could be used. They did not have the proper security clearances and weren't highly proficient translators. It took almost three months to polygraph all these soldiers and upgrade their language training to the point where they could be used in an operational capacity at GRSOC.[37]

The same problems handicapped the U.S. military's tactical SIGINT units destined for use in Afghanistan. The Defense Language Institute in Monterey, California, did not even begin teaching courses in Pashto and Dari until October 15, 2001, a week after the U.S. invasion of Afghanistan began. At the time of the invasion, only a tiny handful of specially trained Pashto-speaking Green Beret SIGINT collectors assigned to the Fifth Special Forces Group at Fort Campbell, in Kentucky, were up to speed, and they would perform brilliantly inside Afghanistan in the months that followed.[38] But that was all that was available.

The Art of Improvisation

So as in virtually every other world crisis that had preceded this one, NSA was forced to rapidly improvise. Recruiters from NSA, the military, and every other branch of the U.S. intelligence community scoured Fremont, California, which had the largest population of Afghan expatriates in the United States. Weeks after 9/11, several dozen Afghan Americans from the Fremont area had signed contracts for substantial sums of money and had quickly been put on planes to the new front lines in the war on terrorism.[39] Less than two weeks after 9/11, a special Afghanistan Cell was created within the agency's SIGINT Directorate, headed by army lieutenant colonel Ronald Stephens, who was given the thankless job of trying to resurrect overnight NSA's dormant SIGINT collection effort against Afghanistan. Richard Berardino, the head of NSOC, set up a special Afghan Desk on his operations floor to correlate and report to the agency's consumers any intercepts concerning Afghanistan. Teams of NSA and U.S. military linguists and SIGINT collectors and analysts hastily boarded flights at Dulles International Airport and Baltimore-Washington International Airport bound for Uzbekistan, Tajikistan, Kuwait, Turkey, Bahrain, Qatar, and Saudi Arabia to beef up NSA's thin presence in the region. The agency's SIGINT satellites and listening posts were ordered to drop less important targets and instead train their antennae on Afghanistan. NSA, in conjunction with its English, Canadian, and Australian SIGINT partners, was scanning virtually every satellite telephone call coming in and out of Afghanistan, hoping against hope that it might catch Osama bin Laden or one of his lieutenants talking on the phone. The Army's 513th Military Intelligence Brigade hastily sent 200 SIGINT and HUMINT collectors to Kuwait in late September 2001 to augment the 120 SIGINT collectors already there.[40] A navy task force was hurriedly dispatched to the waters off the coast of Pakistan, including a complete marine expeditionary unit, which was essentially a reinforced marine battalion with air support. Aboard one of the ships in that force was a large contingent of U.S. Navy SIGINT collectors, who trained their ship's sophisticated radio intercept antennae on Afghanistan once they came within range.[41]

No matter how many resources, human and technical, the NSA could muster in a few weeks, it could not produce meaningful intelligence about Afghanistan before the beginning of U.S. military operations on October 7, 2001. The CIA worked out a way to fill the intelligence gap by striking a deal with the Northern Alliance officials for SIGINT collection in return for hundreds of thousands of dollars' worth of new and improved SIGINT collection equipment, a deal that would pay huge dividends for the CIA in the weeks that followed.[42]

On Sunday night, October 7, offensive military operations against Afghanistan began with air strikes against thirty-one targets, including major Taliban military units, command posts, communications sites, and early-warning radar and air defense units.[43] Not surprisingly, the Taliban regime's scanty communications system collapsed under the weight of the relentless bombing. In a matter of a couple of hours virtually every communications site and telephone relay facility inside Afghanistan was destroyed, including the telephone switching center at Lataband, twenty-two miles east of Kabul, which connected the capital city with the outside world. A former NSA analyst recalled that from October 7 onward, Mullah Omar and his fellow Taliban leaders could communicate with their military commanders only by satellite telephone, which, of course, NSA could easily intercept.[44]

Even though SIGINT was not much help in finding bin Laden, the quantity and quality of NSA's SIGINT coverage of the Taliban rapidly improved in early October, thanks largely to the commanders' incessant chattering about the most sensitive information over satellite phones and walkie-talkies.[45]

From the time the U.S. air campaign began, one of the top SIGINT targets assigned to NSA was the radio traffic of the Taliban's elite Fifty-fifth Brigade, which was based in a former Afghan army camp at Rishikor, southwest of Kabul. A detachment of the brigade was stationed in the northern Afghan city of Mazar-i-Sharif. Widely considered to be the best combat unit in the Taliban military, the Fifty-fifth Brigade was comprised entirely of foreign fighters, including a large number of Arabs who were members of al Qaeda and had volunteered to fight with the Taliban. The Fifty-fifth Brigade was also an easy target for NSA because unlike other Taliban units it was well equipped with modern radios, walkie-talkies, and satellite phones, many of which were personally paid for by bin Laden. All of the brigade's officers were Arabs, which made monitoring its radio traffic much easier since NSA had plenty of Arabic linguists.[46] This was an instance of SIGINT (employing resources like air force AC-130H Spectre gunships, each of which carried a contingent of Arabic linguists on board) contributing directly to the destruction of a key enemy unit.

One of the Arabic linguists who flew on the Spectre missions recalled, "Every time one of the brigade's commanders went on the air, we quickly triangulated the location of his radio transmission and blasted the shit out of his location with our Gatling gun . . . Once our bird was finished chewing up the enemy positions, there usually were no more radio transmissions heard coming from that location."[47]

The War Ends

By late October 2001, it was clear to U.S. officials that U.S. combat troops were urgently needed on the ground in order to defeat the Taliban and destroy the remnants of al Qaeda in Afghanistan. It was not until October 30, however, that a U.S. Marine Corps MEU operating from ships in the Indian Ocean was ordered by CENTCOM to prepare for deployment to Afghanistan. It would require more than three weeks to assemble and prepare the necessary combat units to execute this order.[48]

Much of the early SIGINT effort was focused on helping the Northern Alliance forces capture the key city of Mazar-i-Sharif in northern Afghanistan. Finally, after two weeks of intense fighting, Mazar-i-Sharif fell to the Northern Alliance on November 10. With the fall of this city, the badly battered Taliban and al Qaeda military forces in northern Afghanistan quickly began to crumble as the Northern Alliance forces drove rapidly southward. Four days later, the Afghan capital of Kabul fell to the Northern Alliance without a fight. Soon after, the remnants of the Taliban military collapsed.

The day that Kabul fell, a radio intercept caught the Taliban's leader, Mullah Omar, broadcasting a message from Kandahar exhorting what was left of his troops to stand and fight, telling them, "I order you to obey your commanders completely and not to go hither and thither. Any person who goes hither and thither is like a slaughtered chicken which falls and dies. Regroup yourselves. Resist and fight . . . This fight is for Islam."[49]

Such exhortations were in vain. Mullah Omar's plea fell on deaf ears as American fighter-bombers decimated what was left of the Taliban and al Qaeda forces fleeing Kabul. But mistakes occurred. On November 13, U.S. warplanes bombed a building in Kabul thought to be a Taliban or al Qaeda headquarters. After the bombs completely leveled the building, a senior military official recalled, "Some cell phone intercepts [contained] some excited or angry exchanges between Taliban and al Qaeda members" indicating that one or more al Qaeda leaders had been killed in the building. U.S. officials later learned that the building housed the Kabul offices of the al-Jazeera television network.[50]

By early December, SIGINT showed that there were few remaining organized Taliban and al Qaeda combat units still operating inside Afghanistan. On the night of December 6–7, Mullah Omar disappeared from Kandahar and was not heard from again for some time. U.S. intelligence later learned that he and his men managed to flee southward across the border into Pakistan, where he remains to this day. The failure of the U.S. military to capture or kill Mullah Omar was to prove to be a major mistake, one that we are still paying for with the lives of our soldiers in Afghanistan.[51]

For the SIGINT personnel in Afghanistan, the fall of Kandahar, the birthplace of the Taliban, meant that the Taliban's ill-conceived attempt at waging a conventional war was over. Despite the failure to capture or kill Mullah Omar, the Bush administration loudly and publicly declared victory. This proved to be a very premature statement. The Taliban not only survived, but has actually thrived in the six years since the invasion of Afghanistan.

The Battle of Tora Bora

This didn't mean that the war was over for the American SIGINTers in Afghanistan. Far from it.

After the fall of Kandahar, teams of Green Beret, Delta Force and Navy SEAL commandos, together with allied Afghan militiamen on the U.S. payroll, began systematically combing the mountainous and sparsely populated southeastern part of the Afghan countryside looking for Osama bin Laden and his fighters. Accompanying them were a half-dozen SIGINT collection teams, who systematically searched the airwaves looking for any sign of bin Laden and his al Qaeda forces.[52]

These SIGINT teams belonged to some of the most secretive units in the U.S. military. There were teams of U.S. Navy Tactical Cryptologic Support operators belonging to Naval Security Group Activity Bahrain, who were assigned to provide SIGINT support to the elite commandos of SEAL Team Six. Working with the operators from the U.S. Army's Delta Force was a squadron of highly skilled SIGINT specialists from the five-hundred-man U.S. Army Security Coordination Detachment (formerly known as the Intelligence Support Activity), based at Fort Belvoir, Virginia, outside Washington, D.C., whose unclassified nickname was Grey Fox.[53]

Bin Laden's whereabouts were not a secret to the Pashtun tribesmen of southeastern Afghanistan. On November 13, he and his forces left the city of Jalalabad in a convoy of Toyota pickup trucks just ahead of advancing American and Northern Alliance forces and moved into prepared defensive positions in the Tora Bora mountains, thirty miles southeast of Jalalabad.[54]

The day after Jalalabad fell, a small CIA Jawbreaker intelligence team called Team Juliet, which was commanded by a Green Beret officer seconded to the CIA, was sent to the city to enlist the help of the Northern Alliance militia commander who had taken control of it, Hazrat Ali. A member of the Pashay tribe from northern Afghanistan, Ali willingly signed on and was instantly put on the CIA payroll to the tune of several hundred thousand dollars in return for his promise to help find and capture or kill bin Laden and his al Qaeda fighters.[55]

It did not take the CIA long to find bin Laden in his new stronghold along the border with Pakistan.[56] The new intelligence prompted the United States to begin a series of major air strikes on Tora Bora on November 30. It also prompted the U.S. Army to immediately begin planning a search-and-destroy operation to root out bin Laden and his fighters. But rather than assigning the mission of destroying the al Qaeda force at Tora Bora to American combat units, General

Tommy Franks and Major General Franklin "Buster" Hagenbeck, commander of the Tenth Mountain Division and the senior army field commander in Afghanistan, decided to give the job to the motley collection of Northern Alliance militiamen in Jalalabad commanded by Ali. This would prove to be a grave military mistake. Ali, as one of his former Green Beret advisers put it, was "a disaster waiting to happen." His troops possessed very little in the way of demonstrable fighting ability. One thing that the CIA and the Green Beret advisers clearly agreed upon was that Ali's ragtag militiamen were going to need substantial American military help if they were to be successful in clearing the Tora Bora mountains of bin Laden's al Qaeda forces. On December 2, a twelve-man Green Beret A-team, designated ODA 572, arrived in Jalalabad to support Ali's attack on Tora Bora. The unit was ordered not to engage in combat operations. Rather, its principal mission was to call in air strikes on al Qaeda positions in the mountains. On board the MH-53 Pace Low helicopters that ferried ODA 572 to Jalalabad was a four-man Green Beret SIGINT team, whose mission was to collect intelligence and locate the source of the al Qaeda radio transmissions, then call in air strikes on the coordinates.[57]

It should come as no surprise that when it came time for Ali's troops to attack the al Qaeda positions, the militia commanders suddenly discovered a large number of different reasons why they could not advance despite repeated entreaties from their Green Beret advisers. Ali's locally recruited Pashtun militiamen were more willing to fight the Northern Alliance troops ferried in by the United States than they were to clear the Tora Bora caves of al Qaeda fighters.[58]

On December 3, a CIA Jawbreaker intelligence team operating near the town of Gardez, in eastern Afghanistan, picked up the first "hard" intelligence that bin Laden was in fact at Tora Bora. A U.S. Army Grey Fox SIGINT team near Gardez intercepted some al Qaeda walkie-talkie radio traffic that confirmed he was personally leading the al Qaeda forces.[59]

Despite the accumulation of evidence from SIGINT, which was confirmed by interrogations of captured al Qaeda personnel after the battle was over, senior Bush administration officials and CENTCOM officers adamantly refused to accept, probably as a matter of political expediency, that bin Laden was ever at Tora Bora. The official view of CENTCOM, as voiced by the command's spokesman, was this: "We have never seen anything that was convincing to us at all that Osama bin Laden was present at any stage of Tora Bora—before, during or after."[60]

But General Franks's version of events does not square with the facts. SIGINT coming out of NSA and intercepts collected by frontline U.S. military intelligence units proved that bin Laden was indeed at Tora Bora. The official history of the U.S. Special Operations Command indicates that U.S. Special Forces continued to collect hard "all-source" intelligence, most of which was coming from SIGINT, that "corroborated" bin Laden's presence at Tora Bora from December 9 through December 14, 2001. Only after December 14 did the trail go dead, the official history indicates.[61]

The most significant intercept of al Qaeda message traffic occurred on December 7, when one of Hazrat Ali's commanders at Tora Bora said, "We have intercepted radio messages from Kandahar to the Al Qaeda forces here, and they ask, 'How is the sheik?' The reply is, 'The sheik [i.e., bin Laden] is fine.' "[62]

But despite repeated and increasingly urgent pleas from Ali's Green Beret advisers, his Afghan militiamen refused to press home their attacks.[63] In retrospect, we should not be surprised that the militiamen, whose motivations were purely mercenary, did not aggressively move in on the Tora Bora cave complex, or that bin Laden and his fighters somehow managed to escape through Ali's lines without being detected. In any case, the evidence is now clear that at some point prior to December 11, 2001, Osama bin Laden and as many as eighteen hundred of his fighters slipped away in the dead of night from the Tora Bora mountains and made their way across the border to the safety of northern Pakistan.[64] Regardless of who is responsible, bin Laden and over a thousand of his fighters managed to escape and are still on the loose today.[65]

Amazingly, despite all the evidence to the contrary, the Pentagon refused to accept the assessments from commanders on the ground that bin Laden was gone. Secretary of Defense Rumsfeld told reporters that he believed that bin Laden had not escaped and was still trapped inside Afghanistan. On what factual basis (if any) Rumsfeld made this claim is not known, but it ran completely contrary to the classified reporting that he and his staff were getting from Afghanistan at the time. This was not the first time that the acerbic secretary of defense was to be proved wrong.[66]

By December 19, even the most optimistic "true believers" at the Pentagon and at CENTCOM headquarters in Tampa, Florida, knew that the Tora Bora operation had been an abysmal failure. Captain Robert Harward, a veteran Navy SEAL and the commander of the elite twenty-three-hundred-man U.S.-coalition Special Forces unit Task Force K-Bar, was quoted as saying after Tora Bora, "All of this had got us nothing. No weapons, no ammunition, nothing."[67]

But we now know that the failure to kill Osama bin Laden and destroy his al Qaeda forces at Tora Bora was a massive strategic blunder by the White House, the Pentagon, and CENTCOM. Today, al Qaeda has reconstituted itself and is back in the business of killing Americans whenever and wherever it can. Author and terrorism expert Peter Bergen neatly sums up the Tora Bora fiasco this way: "Allowing Al Qaeda's leadership to escape from Tora Bora and fight another day has proven to be a costly mistake. And it was only the first of many."[68]

CHAPTER 13

A Mountain out of a Molehill

NSA and the Iraqi Weapons of Mass Destruction Scandal

The greatest derangement of the mind is to believe in something because one wishes it to be so.

— LOUIS PASTEUR

The Hiatus

After the Battle of Tora Bora, there followed a six-month hiatus where the attention of the White House, the U.S. military, and the entire U.S. intelligence community, including NSA, were largely focused on the hunt for Osama bin Laden and the remainder of his al Qaeda forces in Afghanistan and Pakistan.

But while the U.S. military and intelligence community were focused on finding and killing bin Laden, they ignored a new threat that was once again rearing its ugly head—the Taliban. Within a matter of weeks of the end of the Battle of Tora Bora, the Taliban had managed to resurrect themselves across the border in northern Pakistan. After the fall of Kandahar in December 2001, between one thousand and fifteen hundred hard-core Taliban guerrillas, including their one-eyed leader Mullah Mohammed Omar and virtually all of his senior commanders, slipped across the border to the safety of northern Pakistan. No attempt was made by the U.S. Army or the Pakistani military to prevent their exodus from Afghanistan. Thousands more Taliban fighters disappeared into remote mountain hiding places in southern Afghanistan, or returned to their villages to wait to fight another day.[1]

A few weeks later, in mid-January 2002, SIGINT reporting coming out of

NSA revealed that a relatively small number of Taliban military commanders had returned to Afghanistan and were operating along the Afghan-Pakistani border. The intercepts showed that the Taliban had reestablished a crude but effective communications system using satellite telephones, which allowed its field commanders inside Afghanistan to communicate with their superiors in northern Pakistan. Within days of this discovery, small teams of Taliban fighters began launching sporadic mortar and rocket attacks against U.S. military outposts in southern and southeastern Afghanistan, as well as ambushing U.S. Army patrols operating along the Afghan-Pakistani border. By the end of January 2002, U.S. intelligence reporting, including SIGINT, had confirmed that Taliban guerrillas were operating in seven Afghan provinces.[2]

Unfortunately, the reappearance of the Taliban was ignored by the Bush White House, which had already set its sights on Iraq. So beginning in February 2002, and continuing without letup through the summer of 2002, just as Taliban guerrilla attacks were on the rise inside Afghanistan, virtually all CIA and U.S. military intelligence assets (including SIGINT) were withdrawn and sent back to the United States to prepare for the invasion of Iraq. Only a few tactical SIGINT collectors assigned to the small army and marine contingents in Afghanistan remained to keep track of the Taliban and al Qaeda.[3]

Operation Anaconda

The precipitous withdrawal of the CIA and U.S. military intelligence assets could not have come at a worse time. In February 2002, just as the withdrawal of intelligence commenced, a force of three hundred Afghan militiamen plus CIA and Green Beret personnel left the sleepy town of Gardez in southeastern Afghanistan to reconnoiter reported al Qaeda positions in the nearby Shah-i-Kot Valley. They were accompanied by a three-man Green Beret SIGINT team, whose job was to scan the airwaves searching for any sign that the patrol's movements had been detected by al Qaeda forces in the area. Near the village of Zermat, only a few miles from the entrance to the valley, the SIGINT personnel picked up several walkie-talkie radio transmissions by individuals speaking Arabic who were carefully noting the movements of the Green Beret convoy. The gist of one of the intercepted transmissions was: "Where was the convoy headed?" Clearly al Qaeda fighters in the hills were closely monitoring the patrol's movements with the intention of ambushing it if and when the opportunity presented itself. The Green Beret patrol commander prudently ordered the convoy back to the safety of Gardez. It was clear that the enemy was guarding the entrance to the valley.[4]

A few weeks later, in early February, unmanned Predator reconnaissance drones discovered what appeared to be a small concentration of al Qaeda forces in the Shah-i-Kot Valley. But SIGINT indicated that the size of the enemy force might be larger than the drone's imagery indicated, and the intercepts revealed that there were a number of senior al Qaeda commanders operating in the valley, based on the number of satellite telephones detected sending and receiving messages from the valley floor. By mid-February, the rising volume of SIGINT "hits" emanating from the valley indicated that the al Qaeda force there was being reinforced with fresh troops coming across the border. The quantity and quality of the SIGINT, however, left much to be desired, with the desultory number of intercepts indicating that the al Qaeda commanders knew their communications were being monitored.[5]

That month, the commander of U.S. forces in Afghanistan, Major General Franklin Hagenbeck, despite the bitter lessons of Vietnam, began planning a search-and-destroy mission to wipe out the enemy force. Operation Anaconda was supposed to have been a two-day operation using a reinforced brigade of 1,500 troops drawn from the Tenth Mountain Division and the 101st Airborne Division. At the time the operation was being planned, Hagenbeck's staff thought there were only 150 to 200 al Qaeda fighters in the valley. But once the operation began on March 2, 2002, the U.S. forces found themselves locked in a bitter battle with 2,000 entrenched and very determined al Qaeda fighters who would not retreat despite facing a superior force backed by airpower and heavy artillery.[6]

SIGINT could not save the day. Intercepts quickly tailed off because the al Qaeda forces in the Shah-i-Kot Valley "were practicing systematic communications security," which effectively denied American SIGINT operators access to enemy radio traffic. Another major part of the problem was that the SIGINT intercept equipment, designed for use against Soviet forces in Western Europe, was poorly suited for Afghanistan. The mountainous terrain also made SIGINT collection very difficult. Compounding the problem, army SIGINT personnel had to somehow hump their heavy SIGINT intercept equipment up to the tops of the surrounding mountains or hillsides in order to monitor what radio traffic could be picked up.[7]

When Operation Anaconda finally sputtered to its unhappy conclusion on March 18, eight American and three Afghan soldiers were dead and another eighty wounded. Equipment losses were much higher than expected. American commanders claimed that the al Qaeda forces had suffered anywhere from eight hundred to one thousand dead, but no bodies could be found to support these dubious claims. Hagenbeck later asserted that "few bodies had been found because they had been vaporized by the intense bombing by U.S. B-52s."[8]

General Tommy Franks characterized Operation Anaconda as "an absolute and unqualified success."[9] But it was a Pyrrhic victory at best because almost no prisoners were captured, as the al Qaeda fighters preferred to fight to the death. The few documents that were captured offered little in the way of hard information about Osama bin Laden's whereabouts or details of al Qaeda's strength and capabilities. The United States pulled out and the enemy moved back in. Ultimately, nothing had been gained for all the effort.[10]

Hunting al Qaeda

With the end of Operation Anaconda, the focus of the secret intelligence war against al Qaeda shifted to Pakistan, where the NSA's assets were few. Al Qaeda's communications traffic had almost completely disappeared from the airwaves, and decrypted Pakistani military and diplomatic communications did not prove to be a fruitful source of intelligence because the Pakistanis themselves did not seem to know where bin Laden was or what he was up to. The CIA's station in Islamabad, headed by Robert Grenier, had some high-level phone taps and audio surveillance sources targeted against key Pakistani government officials, but it does not appear that these sources were much help either.[11]

Ahmed al-Hada's al Qaeda "switchboard" in Yemen, however, was still up and running. Many of the intercepted telephone calls made through that hub were originating in Pakistan, where the remnants of bin Laden's organization had gone to ground. So, shortly after New Year's Day 2002, NSA, the CIA, and the U.S. military put many of their best SIGINT collection assets into Pakistan to try to locate the source of these al Qaeda phone calls.

But then disaster struck when NSA suddenly lost its access to al-Hada's telephone traffic. The government in Yemen discovered that al-Hada was a member of al Qaeda, and his house was immediately placed under surveillance, which was apparently detected. On the evening of February 13, al-Hada, his wife, their son, and two unidentified men made an attempt to flee. Finally cornered in an alley after a frantic car chase involving Yemeni security personnel, al-Hada's son pulled a grenade from his jacket; the grenade went off in his hand, killing him instantly. The rest got away. With his death, NSA lost its ability to exploit his telephone calls, which was to prove to be an incalculable intelligence loss.[12]

Despite the loss of the "Yemen switchboard," NSA and the CIA managed to find a number of fugitive al Qaeda leaders hiding in Pakistan, but not bin Laden. One of bin Laden's top lieutenants, Abu Zubaida, was arrested in the Pakistani city of Faisalabad on the night of March 27, 2002, after NSA intercepted a number of satellite phone calls, which CIA operatives inside Pakistan used to locate his hideout.[13] Further SIGINT reporting led to the arrest in June in Morocco of al Qaeda's Saudi-born chief of operations, Fowzi Saad al-Obeidi, whose cover name within al Qaeda was Abu Zubair al-Haili.[14] The following month, intercepted phone calls enabled Pakistani security forces to arrest a thirty-three-year-old Kenyan named Sheikh Ahmed Salim Swedan, who was wanted by U.S. authorities for his role in planning the 1998 embassy bombings in Kenya and Tanzania.[15]

On August 27, an NSA listening post intercepted a satellite telephone call placed from somewhere in Karachi, Pakistan, to a known al Qaeda operative. NSA analysts who studied the translation of the phone conversation were not able to deduce much of value.[16] On September 9, on an entirely unrelated matter, Pakistani security forces bagged three Yemenis after an extended exchange of gunfire. One of them was Ramzi bin al-Shibh, who was well known to U.S. intelligence as one of the key al Qaeda planners of the September 11 attack. The call that NSA had monitored coming out of Karachi two weeks earlier had come from his phone. Subsequently, additional al Qaeda phones and laptops were found in Pakistan and eventually turned over to NSA. The telephone numbers and e-mail addresses in the memories of the phones and laptops were downloaded and fed into NSA's burgeoning databases of numbers and addresses of known or suspected al Qaeda members, which were under full-time monitoring. Those telephone numbers or e-mail addresses that were located in the United States were passed to the FBI for investigation.[17]

Then in early November, NSA intercepted al Qaeda's Yemen operations chief as he held a lengthy conversation on his satellite phone while driving through the desert in the so-called Empty Quarter of eastern Yemen. Using the locational data provided by NSA, a CIA unmanned Predator drone was immediately dispatched from Camp Lemonier in Djibouti to the location. The drone quickly found the convoy just where NSA said it would be. The Predator fired a Hellfire missile at the lead vehicle, killing the al Qaeda official instantly. Back at the Pentagon, Secretary of Defense Donald Rumsfeld was furious when he found out that it was the CIA and not the U.S. military who had killed the official. "How did they get the intel?" Rumsfeld demanded from the assembled chiefs of the Pentagon's intelligence agencies. NSA director Michael Hayden admitted that the intelligence had come from NSA. Rumsfeld's reported response was "Why aren't you giving it to us?"[18]

The Focus Shifts to Iraq

In June 2002, NSA and the rest of the U.S. intelligence community turned their attention away from Afghanistan and al Qaeda and toward a new target—Iraq. After U.N. weapons inspectors were forced out of Iraq by Saddam Hussein in December 1988, NSA's ability to collect intelligence there deteriorated rapidly; all of the high-grade Iraqi radio traffic that the agency had been exploiting since Operation Desert Storm in 1991 disappeared from the airwaves. In 1999, there were press reports about how the U.S. and British intelligence communities had used the U.N. weapons inspectors to conduct sensitive SIGINT collection operations inside Iraq, and analysts in NSA's Signals Intelligence Directorate concluded that these had prompted the Iraqis to improve their already superb communications security procedures.[19]

In 1998 and 1999, the Iraqis began shifting most of the Iraqi Republican Guard and Regular Army's radio traffic from the airwaves to a network of one hundred thousand lines of modern fiber-optic cables connecting Baghdad with all of the major command centers of the Iraqi army and air defense forces. The result was that by early 2001, the newly laid fiber-optic cables were depriving NSA of most of the sensitive traffic formerly carried by radio.[20] In February 2001, NSA persuaded the U.S. Air Force and the British Royal Air Force to send fighter-bombers to attack the network as a means of forcing the Iraqis to resume radio communications. But the NSA SIGINT operators subsequently reported that there was not much of significance to listen to coming from within Iraq.[21]

Beyond the diminishing volume of Iraqi radio traffic, Hussein had banned the use of cell phones inside Iraq so as to maintain a tight grip on the flow of information in his country, and only 833,000 Iraqis out of a population of 26 million had telephones. This meant, in effect, that NSA's impressive capability to intercept e-mails and cell phone calls was next to worthless when confronted by the low-tech Iraqi target.[22] Every senior Iraqi military and Republican Guard commander had a Thuraya satellite phone for his personal use, but these insecure phones were rarely used prior to the U.S. invasion in March 2003. After the invasion began, Iraqi commanders stopped using them altogether, knowing that once they activated the phones, they were inviting an air strike or artillery bombardment on their position within a matter of minutes.[23]

So, given the lack of high-level access to Iraqi government, diplomatic, and military communications, the best intelligence NSA was then producing on Iraq came from intercepting and exploiting the thousands of Iraqi commercial and private messages coming in and out of the country by phone and telex every month. NSA was paying particular attention to the telephone calls, faxes, and e-mails between representatives of various Iraqi government ministries and private companies (some of them fronts for the Iraqi government) and a host of foreign companies and individuals in Europe, Asia, and the Middle East.[24]

There had been high expectations among some NSA intelligence analysts that data mining this traffic would produce some hard evidence that Hussein was trying to rebuild his capacity to produce weapons of mass destruction (WMD) and ballistic missiles. These same sorts of commercial intercepts had already produced extremely valuable intelligence concerning Iran's nascent nuclear weapons research and development program.[25]

NSA's commercial intercept program did produce a few successes in Iraq. For example, in the late 1990s SIGINT helped the U.S. government block a number of attempts by foreign companies to violate U.N.-imposed economic sanctions against the country.[26] Intelligence developed by NSA revealed that in August 2002 a French company called CIS Paris helped broker the sale to Iraq of twenty tons of a Chinese-made chemical called HTPB, which was used to make solid fuel for ballistic missiles.[27] SIGINT also helped the U.S. government keep close tabs on which foreign countries (mainly Russia and its former republics) were doing business with Iraq.[28]

The net result was that as of the summer of 2002, NSA's SIGINT coverage of Iraq was marginal at best. The best intelligence material that the agency was producing at the time was on the Iraqi air force and air defense forces, both of whom were heavy users of electronic communications that the agency could easily intercept. But beyond these targets, NSA was experiencing loads of problems monitoring what was going on inside Saddam Hussein's Iraq. SIGINT coverage of the Iraqi Republican Guard and the Regular Army was fair at best. And NSA's intelligence production on Hussein himself, the activities of his senior Ba'ath Party leadership, and the elite Special Republican Guard was practically nonexistent. As Bob Woodward of the *Washington Post* aptly put it, "the bottom line: SIGINT quality and quantity out of Iraq was negligible."[29]

As the fall of 2002 approached and the blistering summer in Washington began to abate, the rhetoric coming out of the White House calling for war with Iraq began to heat up dramatically. Virtually everyone inside the Beltway suspected that war with Iraq was coming. Virtually everyone within the U.S. intelligence community knew that war with Iraq was becoming increasingly inevitable. A senior U.S. military intelligence official who is still on active service ruefully recalled, "You didn't have to be a mind reader to guess what was about to happen. I read the newspapers. I watched the nightly news. I listened carefully to what was being said on the Sunday morning talk shows. I read and reread the classified message traffic. The forces were secretly being mustered and no one thought that we could stop it, even if we wanted to. Everyone I talked to thought that war was inevitable." But as one senior White House official put it, "the deal had not been cinched." Only a few senior White House and Pentagon officials knew that on August 29 President Bush had personally approved the final version of a war plan drawn up by General Franks, the commander of CENTCOM in Tampa, Florida, for the invasion of Iraq.[30]

Bush still had to sell the war to the United Nations, Congress, and, most important, the American people. On September 12, he flew up to New York and addressed the U.N. General Assembly, delivering his indictment of Saddam Hussein, who, he asserted, had proved "only his contempt for the United Nations and for all his pledges. By breaking every pledge, by his deceptions and his cruelties, Saddam Hussein has made the case against himself." The president's speech received polite applause from the assembled world leaders, but fervent approval from American politicians and the U.S. news media.[31]

Hayden Signs Off on the NIE

Distressing today for many former NSA officials is that a short time after President Bush's blistering attack on the Iraqi regime, the agency knowingly and willingly went along with an act that is now widely acknowledged to be one of the saddest moments in U.S. intelligence history. In late September 2002, NSA director Michael Hayden signed off on a CIA-produced National Intelligence Estimate (NIE) on Iraq's WMD program that not only turned out to be wrong in almost all respects, but also served as the principal justification for the Bush administration to lead the United States to war with Iraq.

The Top Secret Codeword NIE was titled *Iraq's Continuing Programs for Weapons of Mass Destruction*. Virtually all its conclusions, major and minor, were later determined to be wrong. When congressional investigators began going through the raw intelligence reporting on which the NIE was ostensibly based, they discovered that there was little factual evidence to support any of the conclusions contained in the document, except for some very dubious reporting by defectors and refugees and extremely unreliable information provided by exile groups like Ahmed Chalabi's Iraqi National Congress. Only the State Department formally dissented from some of the report's conclusions, but its unwillingness to endorse the NIE carried little real weight.[32]

Years after the NIE was issued, Hayden defended his having signed off on the document, telling the members of the Senate's intelligence committee in

2005 that when he reviewed a draft of the NIE in September 2002, his only concern was to assess the use of SIGINT in the estimate, and that he approved the NIE based solely on the fact that the available SIGINT did not contradict the estimate's conclusions. Hayden claimed, "There was nothing in the NIE that signals intelligence contradicted. Signals intelligence ranged from ambiguous to confirmatory of the conclusions in the National Intelligence Estimate."[33]

A year later, Hayden took his campaign to exonerate himself and NSA a step further by asserting that the SIGINT on the Iraqi WMD program was correct, but that the CIA's intelligence analysts who wrote the NIE had gotten the conclusions wrong.[34]

What We Knew and How We Knew It

General Hayden's version of events is somewhat different from the recollections of the small cadre of NSA intelligence analysts who specialized in Iraq and thought that most of the SIGINT at their disposal was ambiguous at best.[35]

Based on a combination of postmortem reports, declassified documents, and interviews with NSA and CIA intelligence officials, the following is what NSA actually knew about the Iraqi WMD program at the time that the NIE was approved, in September 2002.

The Iraqi Nuclear Weapons Program

The NIE stated with "high confidence" that Iraq had reconstituted its nuclear weapons program since the U.N. weapons inspectors had left Iraq in 1998, adding that Iraq "probably will have a nuclear weapon during this decade." According to former NSA and CIA analysts, NSA had collected virtually nothing that came close to confirming this assertion prior to the NIE being issued. The only intercepts that even remotely suggested that the Iraqis were trying to rebuild their capacity to develop and build nuclear weapons were a small number of very low-level e-mails and telexes from 2000 and 2001, involving attempts by Iraqi front companies to buy high-speed balancing machines needed for uranium enrichment.[36]

In his February 5, 2003, presentation to the U.N. Security Council, Secretary of State Colin Powell referred to these intercepts when he said that NSA had evidence "that Iraq front companies sought to buy machines that can be used to balance gas centrifuge rotors. One of these companies also had been involved in a failed effort in 2001 to smuggle aluminum tubes into Iraq."[37]

The problem was that these balancing machines could also have been destined for use in a variety of routine commercial manufacturing operations, which is what the Iraqis claimed they were for. Postwar investigations could not refute Iraq's claim that this equipment was destined for purely civilian purposes. Interviews with former NSA and CIA analysts confirm that there was nothing conclusive in the NSA intercepts collected between 2000 and 2002 to indicate whether these components were destined for use in Iraq's purported nuclear weapons program or for other purposes. A 2005 report on the matter concluded, "Although signals intelligence played a key role in some respects that we cannot discuss in an unclassified format, on the whole it was not useful."[38]

The Iraqi Chemical Weapons Program

Once again, interviews indicate that NSA provided very little usable SIGINT concerning Iraq's alleged chemical weapons program. Most of the intercepts—consisting of low-level faxes, telexes, and e-mails—concerned the attempts of Iraqi front companies in Baghdad and elsewhere in the Middle East to purchase precursor chemicals from a number of companies in Eastern Europe and the former Soviet Union, with much of the SIGINT reporting indicating the chemical purchases were to be used for producing fertilizers, not chemical weapons. The problem was that the reams of intercepted material did not specify for what purpose the chemicals were to be used, so naturally the CIA analysts adopted a worst-case-scenario approach and concluded that the chemical precursors were "most likely" intended for the production of chemical weapons.[39]

Interestingly, the NSA analysts interviewed could not recall that after 1998 the agency ever collected any intelligence information indicating that the Iraqis were developing or had actually produced biological weapons.[40]

The Robb-Silberman committee's findings agree with the recollections of the analysts, concluding, "Signals Intelligence provided only minimal information regarding Iraq's chemical weapons programs and, due to the nature of the sources, what was provided was of dubious quality and therefore of questionable value."[41]

Iraqi Unmanned Drones

The most contentious of the NSA SIGINT material used in the NIE alleged that the Iraqis were developing unmanned drones for the purpose of delivering chemical or biological weapons to targets in the United States. This claim was largely based on an inferential reading by the CIA analysts of a small number of NSA intercepts concerning Iraqi defense contractor Ibn-Firnas's purchase through an Australia-based middleman of mapping software for a prototype drone from a company in Taiwan called Advantech. Indeed, the mapping covered the United States—and the entire rest of the world.[42] Once again, the CIA opted for the worst-case scenario, basing its conclusions on *"analysis of special intelligence."* The phrase "special intelligence" of course refers to SIGINT.[43]

Only after the end of the war did U.S. intelligence experts get to examine prototypes of the Iraqi drone, and they found it incapable of reaching the United States.[44]

The Iraqi Ballistic Missile Program

NSA's analysis of intercepts in 2002 was correct, however, in warning that Iraq was in the process of producing a "large-diameter missile," which meant a regular ballistic missile with booster rockets attached to it that would give the missile a range far in excess of what the United Nations permitted Iraq to have. After the U.S. invasion of Iraq, CIA inspection teams confirmed that two Iraqi ballistic missiles had indeed been flight-tested beyond the 150 kilometers permitted by the United Nations.[45]

Ambiguous Is Our Business

Apart from the missile data, NSA's intelligence analysts had, at best, only "ambiguous" SIGINT intelligence about whether Iraq possessed nuclear, chemical, or biological weapons. Immediately after the NIE was issued, the agency's analysts began to express reservations about their "confidence levels," which caused no fair amount of angst at Fort Meade, especially in General Hayden's office. Hayden later admitted to Congress that he was not pleased by these reservations, which conflicted with his assertion that SIGINT confirmed the NIE's conclusions. NSA's management held firm on this position until Congress started to look at the raw material behind the NIE. Only then did it become clear how skimpy the agency's knowledge was concerning the Iraqi WMD program.[46] According to a former senior CIA official, the NSA intercepts actually revealed that "across the board military expenditures [by the Iraqis] were down massively. We reported that but it was not what the bosses wanted to hear."[47]

By 2007, Hayden, now the director of the CIA, had come full circle. He finally admitted that he, like the rest of the U.S. intelligence community, had been wrong about the nature and extent of Iraq's WMD program, but with a new twist. Hayden told an interviewer from National Public Radio,

> All of the SIGINT I had, when I looked at the key judgments of the National Intelligence Estimate, my SIGINT ranged from ambiguous to confirmatory. And therefore, I was—you know, and ambiguous in our business, I told you, is kind of a state of nature. And so, I was quite comfortable to say, yes, I agree with the NIE. I was comfortable. I was wrong. It turned out not to be true.[48]

The postmortem investigations of the U.S. intelligence community's performance on the Iraqi WMD issue were unsparing in their criticism of NSA. An outside review panel concluded that there was "virtually no useful signals intelligence on a target that was one of the United States' top intelligence priorities."[49]

One now-retired NSA official recalled, "We looked long and hard for any signs that the Iraqis were attempting to smuggle into Iraq equipment needed to build nuclear, chemical, or biological weapons, or precision machinery that was essential to building ballistic missiles or their guidance systems. We just never found a 'smoking gun' that Saddam was trying to build nukes or anything else . . . We did find lots of stuff that was on its face very suspicious, but nothing you could hang your hat on."[50]

The Imperial Hypocrisy

On October 7, 2002, a week after the fateful NIE was published, President Bush gave a speech, now known to history as the "Axis of Evil" speech, that concluded with a now-infamous line: "Facing clear evidence of peril, we cannot wait for the final proof—the smoking gun—that could come in the form of a mushroom cloud."[51]

But Bush's speech was also notable because it based the rationale for war on the allegation that Saddam Hussein had, for many years, aided and abetted "the al Qaeda terrorist network," which shared "a common enemy—the United States of America." This also carried the implication that Iraq had been partly responsible for the 9/11 terrorist attacks.[52]

None of this was based on solid evidence. In fact, what little there was in

NSA's files about a relationship between Hussein's Iraq and al Qaeda was fragmentary, and it did not support the notion that there was a close and longstanding relationship between the Iraqi government and al Qaeda.[53] The one tangible item that NSA did have (which, not surprisingly, the White House and Assistant Secretary of Defense for Policy Douglas Feith immediately fixated on) was a report that a Jordanian-born al Qaeda leader named Abu Musab al-Zarqawi, who would later become the leader of al Qaeda in Iraq during the Iraqi insurgency, had fled to Iran after the U.S. invasion of Afghanistan, then received medical treatment in Iraq in May 2002. Beginning in May 2002, NSA and its foreign partners were monitoring al-Zarqawi's phone calls, and NSA forwarded to Feith's office the intelligence reporting on al-Zarqawi and what little else it had, but at Hayden's insistence, each of the NSA reports started with a disclaimer stating that SIGINT "neither confirms nor denies" that such a link existed.[54]

It wasn't much, but as far as the White House and the Pentagon were concerned, it was more than sufficient evidence—according to Secretary of Defense Rumsfeld, it was "bulletproof" confirmation of the ties between Saddam Hussein's government and al Qaeda, including "solid evidence" that al Qaeda maintained a sizable presence in Iraq. Rumsfeld's allegations were based on NSA intercepts of al-Zarqawi's phone calls to friends and relatives. But according to a U.S. intelligence official, the intercepts "provide no evidence that the suspected terrorist [al-Zarqawi] was working with the Iraqi regime or that he was working on a terrorist operation while he was in Iraq." Nonetheless, the allegations became an article of faith for Bush administration officials.[55]

We Can't Wait for the Politicians

The passage of the Iraq War Resolution by Congress on October 10, 2002, put NSA into high gear. On October 18, General Hayden went on NSA's internal television network to announce that war with Iraq was coming soon and that NSA had to take immediate steps to get ready for the impending invasion. He noted that "a SIGINT agency cannot wait for a political decision" and that weather constraints made it necessary to attack Iraq no later than the end of March 2003.[56]

General Hayden ordered his agency to immediately intensify its SIGINT collection operations against Iraq. The onus of General Hayden's directive fell on the intercept operators, linguists, and intelligence analysts at the Gordon Regional Security Operations Center at Fort Gordon, Georgia, which was NSA's principal producer of intelligence on Iraq. The commander of the Fort Gordon listening post, Colonel Daniel Dailey, was ordered to reinforce his station's SIGINT collection efforts against the complete spectrum of Iraqi military and civilian targets. Most of the intelligence information that Fort Gordon collected in the months that followed was purely military in nature, such as Iraqi Republican Guard maneuvers, flight activity levels for the Iraqi air force, and details of Iraqi air defense reactions to the accelerating number of reconnaissance flights over northern and southern Iraq being conducted by U.S. and British warplanes. In addition, a twenty-nine-person special section was formed at Fort Gordon to concentrate on intercepting and analyzing radio traffic relating to Iraqi WMDs.[57]

Powell's Petard

In mid-January 2003, as the drumbeat for war grew ever louder, intelligence analysts working for Pentagon policy chief Douglas Feith began carefully combing through the SIGINT that NSA had produced about Iraq, looking once again for a "smoking gun" that would provide conclusive proof that Iraq was producing WMDs, as well as evidence that a link existed between Saddam Hussein's Iraq and al Qaeda. Feith was preparing a dossier of intelligence reports that the White House wanted to use to convince the United Nations to support the U.S. government's call for war with Iraq. A former NSA official recalled, "There wasn't much there, and there certainly was no smoking gun, which is what these guys wanted."[58]

To assist Secretary of State Powell in making his U.N. presentation, NSA compiled a complete dossier of all SIGINT reporting and unpublished material taken from the agency's databases that related directly or indirectly to Iraq's WMD programs and alleged links to al Qaeda. An NSA analyst who reviewed the hefty file recalled that the best material the agency had were a few tantalizing taped intercepts of telephone conversations among Iraqi military and Republican Guard officers from 2002 and 2003, suggesting that the Iraqis were engaged in a desperate effort to hide things from the U.N. weapons inspectors who were due to arrive in Iraq soon. But the vague and fragmentary intercepts were devoid of specifics. This, however, did not prevent one senior White House official from telling Newsweek, "Hold on to your hat. We've got it."[59]

When Powell gave his U.N. presentation on the morning of February 5, he had already decided that some of the best intelligence he had to offer came from SIGINT. Although their content may have been ambiguous, he thought the tapes were powerful and made for good presentation—and they were also the kind of material that the Iraqi government could not easily refute.[60]

Powell in the end chose to use only three of the NSA intercepts, all of which were unencrypted telephone calls among Iraqi Republican Guard commanders. All three were chosen because they purportedly showed that Iraqi officials were striving to hide what were believed to be WMDs from U.N. weapons inspectors. But as it turned out, the intercepts were far from conclusive on this point.[61]

The first NSA intercept was of a November 26, 2002, telephone conversation between two senior Iraqi Republican Guard officers. The conversation centered on what was described as a "modified vehicle" that a Republican Guard unit possessed which had previously been "evacuated." The vehicle was from the al-Kindi company, which Powell alleged was "well known" to be involved in the development of WMDs. It turns out that there had been considerable controversy within the U.S. intelligence community about the meaning of this NSA intercept. Before Powell traveled to New York City to give his presentation at the U.N., Vice President Dick Cheney and his staff had strongly argued that the import of the intercept was that the "modified vehicles" that the Iraqis were trying to hide had to be associated with long-range ballistic missiles because that was what al-Kindi historically had specialized in.[62]

But declassified documents show that the State Department argued that because the intercept gave no details about the "modified vehicles," the intercept could only be used to demonstrate that the Iraqis were trying to hide "something" from the returning U.N. weapons inspectors. What they were hiding nobody could say. A former NSA analyst at the time agreed with the State Department's position, saying, "It could have been a souped-up Volkswagen Beetle that they were talking about for all we know." The State Department also disagreed with Cheney and the CIA's conclusion that the "modified vehicles" were most likely associated with long-range ballistic missiles because other portions of the intercept that were not played for the U.N. Security Council indicated that they were used in conjunction with more mundane surface-to-air missiles.[63] Only after Baghdad fell in April 2003 did U.S. intelligence officials learn the truth about what the two Republican Guard officers had been talking about. Captured documents and interrogations of Iraqi officials confirmed that the much ballyhooed "modified vehicles" were actually trailers modified by al-Kindi that carried equipment used by the Iraqi Republican Guard to make hydrogen gas to fill weather balloons, which Iraqi artillery units used to measure wind strength and direction for targeting purposes.[64]

The second intercept that Powell used, dated January 30, 2003, was again a telephone conversation between two Republican Guard officers, where the senior officer ordered the subordinate to "inspect" (not "clean out," as Powell said) portions of the ammunition depot that he commanded. The conversation referred to "forbidden ammunition," but did not indicate that there was any "forbidden ammo" actually at the facility. The order simply was to inspect his depot for anything relating to "forbidden ammo." Powell made much of the fact that the senior officer ordered the subordinate to "destroy the message" after he had carried out the instructions contained therein. But again, there was considerable doubt within the U.S. intelligence community about the actual meaning of this intercepted message. According to a senior government official interviewed by the *Washington Post*, "U.S. intelligence does not know whether there was 'forbidden ammo' at the site where the radio message was received. The tape recording was included in Powell's presentation to show that there was concern such ammo could turn up."[65]

The third message, intercepted "several weeks before" Powell's presentation, in mid-January 2003, was a telephone conversation between two officers of the Second Republican Guard Corps in southern Iraq. The crux of the intercept was that the senior officer on the call told his subordinate to write down the following order: "Remove the expression 'nerve agents' wherever it comes up in the wireless instructions." No copies of the wireless instruction in question were presented by Powell. Taken in isolation, and out of context, the intercept suggested that the Iraqis were trying to hide any references to nerve agents in their files. But as a now-retired State Department intelligence official put it, "We tried to argue to anyone who would listen that this snippet didn't prove anything other than the fact that the Iraqis were trying to purge their files. But no one wanted to listen to our contrarian viewpoint, so we were ignored."[66]

It was not until after the successful conclusion of the U.S. invasion of Iraq that interrogators from the CIA and the U.S. military finally learned what all three of the intercepts were referring to. In the fall of 2002, Hussein, under enormous pressure from the French and Russian governments, agreed to comply with U.N. demands that he let weapons inspectors back into the country. At the same time, he issued an order to his military commanders to destroy any and all records relating to Iraq's previous WMD programs "in order not to give President Bush any excuses to start a war." As the Iraqis hurriedly began sanitizing their records of anything relating to their long-dormant WMD program in advance of the arrival of the U.N. weapons inspectors, a few of the instructions from Baghdad to field commanders were intercepted by NSA and led the intelligence community to conclude that the Iraqis were trying to hide their

WMDs. The Iraqis' attempt to "pretty up" their files so that the inspectors would find nothing that would give the Bush administration a casus belli backfired badly, providing the administration with exactly what Hussein had wanted to avoid at all costs—an excuse to invade Iraq.[67]

But there was a price to be paid for making the intercepts public. NSA had argued strenuously against it, but to no avail. It did not take the Iraqis or al Qaeda in Iraq long to take appropriate countermeasures. Two weeks after Secretary Powell's speech, al Qaeda leader al-Zarqawi suddenly stopped using his cell phone, killing off a vitally important source of intelligence.[68]

Then on March 18, 2003, only a few days before the U.S. invasion of Iraq was to begin, the Iraqi government suddenly switched off all telephone service across Iraq, and the use of satellite and mobile phones was specifically banned by the Iraqi Ministry of the Interior, even by foreign reporters based in Baghdad. This closed off the last low-level sources of SIGINT that were then available to NSA about what was going on inside Iraq.[69]

Conclusions

The performance of the U.S. intelligence community prior to the invasion of Iraq in March 2003 was a complete and unmitigated disaster at all levels. The distinguished British defense correspondent and military historian Max Hastings described the Iraqi WMD intelligence fiasco as "the greatest failure of western intelligence in modern times."[70]

NSA fared better than the CIA and the rest of the U.S. intelligence community in the subsequent congressional investigations, but only because so much of the criticism of the agency's performance was kept secret, including the fact that the fiber-optic network in Iraq had made it impossible for NSA to perform its mission. This was a chilling reminder that changes in telecommunications technology were making it increasingly difficult for NSA to do its job.[71]

CHAPTER 14

The Dark Victory

NSA and the Invasion of Iraq: March–April 2003

Rejoice! We conquer!
—Phidippides, Greek messenger after
Battle of Marathon

The March–April 2003 U.S.-led invasion of Iraq, designated Operation Iraqi Freedom, is a case study of NSA's massive SIGINT collection system mostly performing well, but not completely. But as will be seen in this chapter, the agency's long-standing problem of not being able to quickly and efficiently process, analyze, and disseminate the intelligence that it collected showed up repeatedly in the lead-up to and during the invasion itself. And unfortunately, much of the intelligence NSA produced never made its way to the frontline army and marine field commanders who needed it the most.

NSA'S Iraqi Surge Begins

On Tuesday, February 11, 2003, NSA director Michael Hayden issued a secret directive called a Director's Intent to all NSA components, warning that war with Iraq was near. "I intend to conduct a SIGINT and Information Assurance operation for the Iraq campaign that will meet the combatant commanders' objectives of shock, speed and awe while also providing policy makers information that is actionable and timely. Success will be measured by our ability to limit the conflict geographically, secure regime change in Iraq, and dismantle Iraqi weapons of mass destruction."[1]

Within hours, the agency's sixty thousand military and civilian personnel began implementing long-standing NSA war plans to provide SIGINT support to General Tommy Franks's CENTCOM for the upcoming invasion of Iraq.[2] NSA then sent out classified "war warning" messages to its listening posts covering Iraq, ordering them to immediately ramp up their SIGINT collection efforts.[3] An Iraq Operational Cell was created within the National Security Operations Center (NSOC) in order to manage NSA's SIGINT support for Operation Iraqi Freedom, and from this unit finished intelligence was disseminated in electronic form to cleared intelligence consumers in Washington and the Persian Gulf.[4] In addition, Brigadier General Richard Zahner, NSA's associate deputy director of operations for military support, flew down to CENTCOM headquarters in Florida to coordinate NSA's SIGINT support for General Franks's combat troops.[5]

Hundreds of military reserve and National Guard SIGINT operators and analysts were recalled to active duty. By the beginning of March 2003, 98 percent of all army reserves and 45 percent of all National Guard intelligence units were on active duty either in the United States or in the Persian Gulf. Beginning in January 2003, and continuing right up to the invasion, nearly five hundred army reserve and National Guard personnel, including dozens of Arabic linguists, began arriving by airplane and train at Fort Gordon's Regional SIGINT Operations Center (GRSOC) to reinforce its SIGINT collection and analytic capabilities.[6]

GRSOC's primary task was to thoroughly map the locations and track the activities of Saddam Hussein's seventy-thousand-man Republican Guard. Consisting of six divisions equipped with nine hundred Russian-made T-62 and T-72 tanks, the Republican Guard was nominally headed by Hussein's thirty-six-year-old son, Qusay, although its actual military commander was its chief of staff, Lieutenant General Sayf al-Din Fulayyih Hassan Taha al-Rawi, a staunch Hussein loyalist and competent field commander who had been severely wounded in the 1980s while leading a counterattack against Iranian forces.[7]

NSA wanted GRSOC to monitor 24-7 all radio and satellite telephone traffic coming in and out of the headquarters of the Second Republican Guard Corps at Salman Pak, south of Baghdad, which was commanded by one of the Republican Guard's best field commanders, Lieutenant General Raad Majid al-Hamdani, who was responsible for protecting the southern approaches to Baghdad. Al-Hamdani's corps controlled the Medina Division, at As Suwayrah, thirty-five miles southeast of Baghdad; the Al-Nida Division, at Baquba, thirty-five miles northeast of Baghdad; the Baghdad Division, at Al Kut, one hundred miles southeast of Baghdad; and the Third Special Forces Brigade, at the Al-Rasheed military airfield on the southern outskirts of Baghdad.[8]

NSA's Bad Aibling Station, in southern Germany, would provide SIGINT coverage of the activities of the ten Iraqi combat divisions deployed in northern Iraq. This coverage was deemed essential because CENTCOM planned for the U.S. Army's Fourth Infantry Division to land in Turkey and invade northern Iraq. But the plan was discarded when the Turkish government refused to allow this.[9]

However, NSA's most urgent SIGINT assignment was finding and tracking Iraqi ballistic missile units, which the Iraqis supposedly could use to deliver chemical or biological weapons. NSA simply couldn't come up with intercepts reliably associated with these units.[10]

The U.S. Air Force war planners wanted every detail about the offensive operations of the Iraqi air force's MiG fighters. NSA, however, picked up such limited traffic from enemy airfields that it informed U.S. Air Force war planners that the Iraqi air force's estimated 325 combat aircraft were not flying at all. No U.S. Air Force or coalition aircraft were lost or even damaged in action by Iraqi MiG fighters.

Ever since Operation Desert Shield/Storm in 1990–1991, NSA had closely monitored the Iraqi air defense forces. This coverage was now essential if the first air strikes inside Iraq were to be successful. SIGINT satellites scooped up all microwave relay traffic throughout Iraq. U-2 and RC-135 reconnaissance aircraft equipped with sensitive SIGINT equipment constantly orbited over northern Saudi Arabia and Kuwait, intercepting the communications between Iraqi SAM and antiaircraft gun battery commanders. Right up to the invasion, intercept operators at Fort Gordon and Bad Aibling Station successfully monitored Iraqi radar operators tracking allied aircraft flying training or reconnaissance missions along the Iraqi borders, and NSA intercepted and analyzed the computer-to-computer data traffic between the Iraqi air defense operations center in Baghdad and its subordinate sector operations centers at Taji, Kirkuk, H-3, and Talil air bases. The Iraqi air defense traffic showed that Iraqi radar operators were paying close attention to U.S. Air Force flight activity over Kuwait and Turkey.[11]

NSA was also responsible for helping the CIA and the FBI identify Iraqi agents operating in the United States and abroad who were tasked with launching terrorist attacks on American targets. The name given to this effort was Operation Imminent Horizon. Based in part on material gathered by NSA, on March 5 two diplomats at Iraq's U.N. mission were declared personae non gratae and given forty-eight hours to leave the country.[12]

But Saddam Hussein's Iraq was not the only target that came under closer scrutiny by NSA and its foreign partners after General Hayden signed his war directive. In January 2003, NSA was tasked by the White House to monitor the communications of a surprisingly large number of international organizations, all of whom were key players standing in the way of the Bush adminis-tration's strenuous efforts to convince the world community to join the U.S. and Britain and its so-called Coalition of the Willing in an invasion of Iraq.

NSA and Britain's GCHQ began intercepting all of U.N. Secretary-General Kofi Annan's telephone calls and e-mails, and a special eavesdropping device was surreptitiously planted inside Annan's office suite on the thirty-eighth floor of the U.N. headquarters building in New York City; it recorded all of the private conversations held in his office. The U.S. and British governments were both concerned that Annan was personally opposed to the United Nations' approving a resolution calling for war against Iraq.[13] At the same time, NSA and GCHQ mounted a joint "surge operation" to intensively monitor the communications traffic of governments with seats on the U.N. Security Council in order to deter-mine whether they would vote for the resolution. Included were Chile, Pakistan, Angola, Guinea, Cameroon, and Bulgaria, all of whom were then being inten-sively lobbied to vote with the United States and Britain. A GCHQ linguist named Katherine Gun, who was shocked at what the United States and Britain were up to, confided the details to the British newspaper the *Observer*, which broke the story on March 2. A leak investigation ensued, and Gun was subse-quently fired from her job after she was arrested for violating the Official Secrets Act.[14]

As of January, NSA was also intercepting the communications traffic (calls, e-mails, cables, etc.) of the United Nations' chief weapons inspector, Dr. Hans Blix, and his deputies. According to Bob Woodward of the *Washington Post*, President Bush was convinced that the Swedish diplomat was saying one thing in public and quite another privately in the intercepted UNMOVIC message traffic that Bush, as he interpreted it, was getting from NSA.[15] NSA was also monitoring the telephone calls and e-mails of Dr. Mohamed ElBaradei, the director-general of the United Nations' International Atomic Energy Agency (IAEA), because of the White House's intense dislike of his agency's policies with regard to Iraq, which almost always ran contrary to what the Bush admin-istration wanted.[16]

CENTCOM Prepares

On January 19, 2003, six days after General Hayden ordered NSA to war alert status, General Franks and 350 members of his staff flew to Camp As Sayliyah in Qatar, which was to serve as CENTCOM's forward headquarters for the invasion. Accompanying them was a small team of NSA liaison officials and communicators who became known as the CENTCOM Cryptologic Services Group.

In early March, as the final preparations for the invasion of Iraq were being made, small teams of U.S. Army, Marine Corps, and British SIGINT intercept personnel were secretly deployed, with the help of the Kuwaiti border police, to the Mutla Ridge, the heights that run along the full length of the Kuwaiti border with Iraq, to monitor the activities of the Iraqi army. One marine radio intercept team from the First Radio Battalion was moved up to border post 11 on the Shatt al-Arab waterway to listen to radio traffic coming from Iraqi forces deployed across the way in the port city of Umm Qasr.[17]

One of NSA's highest priorities was to look for any defensive preparations by the Iraqi Regular Army and the Republican Guard in southern Iraq. In January and February, SIGINT indicated that Iraqi forces were making surprisingly few preparations for war, despite the fact that the imminent invasion was front-page news in the United States and Western Europe. Radio intercepts revealed that the Iraqis were not moving any combat units, preparing defensive positions, making logistical preparations, or holding any training exercises. Radio traffic volume remained constant but very light, and the content of the low-level housekeeping radio traffic that NSA could access was amazingly routine.[18]

Through the end of January, no movements by Iraqi Republican Guard units deployed south of Baghdad were detected in SIGINT. It was not until late February that SIGINT began to note the Iraqi army and the Republican Guard hastily redeploying some of their forces. In mid-February, two weak Regular Army infantry brigades were moved to guard Umm Qasr and the massive petroleum production center of Rumailah. Then in late February, SIGINT and satellite reconnaissance detected two Republican Guard divisions—the Adnan Division and the Nebuchadnezzar Division—being hastily moved from their home bases in Mosul and Kirkuk, in northern Iraq, southward toward Saddam Hussein's hometown of Tikrit.[19]

Then an eerie stillness took over the airwaves as the Iraqi military went to near-complete radio silence, which in military parlance is called emission control (EMCON).[20] Even the Iraqi observation posts situated along the border with Kuwait reduced their radio traffic to almost nil. On Tuesday, March 18, only hours before the U.S. invasion was to begin, the Iraqi government switched off all telephone service across the country.[21]

The War Begins with a Bust

At about three P.M. EST on Wednesday, March 19, 2003, the CIA received a FLASH-precedence intelligence message from an agent asset inside Iraq known as Rockstar containing the reported location of Saddam Hussein. CIA director George Tenet immediately informed Secretary of Defense Donald Rumsfeld and his deputy, Paul Wolfowitz, as well as the White House. An hour later, when Rumsfeld and Tenet arrived at the White House for an emergency meeting with President Bush and his senior national security advisers, Tenet stated that Hussein was meeting with his senior commanders at an isolated house in southern Baghdad called the Dora Farms and would remain there for at least several hours. At seven twelve P.M., Bush signed the order to bomb the house and kill Hussein.[22]

A little more than two hours later, at five thirty-three A.M. Baghdad time, March 20, two U.S. Air Force F-117 stealth fighters dropped four two-thousand-pound JDAM "bunker buster" bombs on the Dora Farms complex.

Jubilation broke out throughout the U.S. intelligence community when a few sketchy intercepts of Iraqi civil defense radio traffic indicated that some high-ranking Iraqi government official had been killed. But it turned out that there was no bunker at the Dora Farms, and Saddam Hussein had not been anywhere near the place when the bombs were dropped.[23]

At the exact same moment that the F-117s released their bombs on the Dora Farms, the first of forty-five Tomahawk cruise missiles fired from six U.S. Navy warships in the Persian Gulf and the Red Sea began hitting high-priority Iraqi government buildings and military command posts in and around Baghdad, such as the Ministry of Defense building, the headquarters of the Iraqi Republican Guard, and the compound in east Baghdad that housed the Iraqi intelligence service.

At ten fifteen P.M. EST, President Bush announced on all the major TV networks that the war with Iraq had begun.

The Early Stages of Operation Iraqi Freedom

At six P.M. Baghdad time, March 20, a little more than twelve hours after the Dora Farms attack, the U.S. air campaign against Iraq began. Over the next twenty-four hours, American and British warplanes flew a staggering seventeen hundred combat sorties against hundreds of targets inside Iraq. At the same time, U.S. Navy warships and U.S. Air Force B-52 bombers launched 504 cruise missiles, which systematically took out dozens of Hussein's presidential palaces, military command centers, and large military garrisons in the most heavily defended parts of Iraq, particularly in and around Baghdad itself.[24]

American reporters covering the air assault and cruise missile attacks from their hotel balconies in downtown Baghdad repeatedly used the phrase "shock and awe," popularized by Donald Rumsfeld in 1999, to describe the pyrotechnics. Months later, journalists referred to the initial air campaign attacks as "shucks and awww" when it became clear that the massive (and expensive) air strikes had done only minimal damage to the Iraqi war machine.

NSA, however, was tasked with performing immediate assessments on the effectiveness of the air strikes and cruise missile attacks in taking out the Iraqi air defense system. An air force Arabic linguist recalled that his job was to monitor the known radio frequencies used by Iraqi air defense command posts in southern and central Iraq. One by one, during the predawn hours of March 20, all of the radio frequencies he was monitoring went silent, some in midtransmission, indicating that the fighter-bombers and cruise missiles had done their job. By dawn, SIGINT, including intercepts translated by Arabic linguists aboard U.S. Air Force RC-135 Rivet Joint and U.S. Navy EP-3E Aries reconnaissance aircraft, confirmed that virtually all of the Iraqi air defense system's sector operations centers were out of commission.[25]

In the days that followed, every time an Iraqi radar operator was brave (or foolish) enough to activate his radar system, within minutes the site's radar emissions were detected and located by one of the Rivet Joint or Aries reconnaissance aircraft orbiting over Kuwait, which promptly directed fighter-bombers to destroy the site. By the time Operation Iraqi Freedom was over three weeks later, SIGINT had directly contributed to the destruction of 95 percent of the Iraqi air defense system—which was a remarkable accomplishment by any measure.[26]

SIGINT and the Ground War

At ten fifteen A.M. on March 20, hours after the air campaign began, the Iraqis began sporadically firing their homegrown version of the Russian Scud ballistic missile and Chinese-made Seersucker cruise missiles at U.S. military positions inside Kuwait. Some of these unwieldy and inaccurate missiles were aimed at Camp Commando in northern Kuwait, which was where the marine First Radio Battalion had its main operations site. The missile detonations rocked the camp, but little damage was done. Nonetheless, it shook up the American troops and served to remind them that there was a real war going on just a few miles away.[27]

Shortly after six P.M., an Iraqi patrol boat crossed over from the Iraqi side of the Shatt al-Arab waterway and opened fire on a marine radio intercept team deployed on the Kuwaiti-Iraqi border. At almost exactly the same time, Iraqi mortar fire began falling on the marines position, and the marines spotted Iraqi infantrymen just across the border advancing toward them. The marine SIGINT operators radioed their headquarters and urgently requested covering fire and immediate extraction. While marine artillery units blasted the enemy with massive counter-battery fire, a helicopter flew in and successfully extracted the marine SIGINT team without taking any casualties.[28]

That morning, satellite imagery had indicated that the Iraqis were ready to destroy the huge Rumailah oil field, in southern Iraq. This new intelligence led General Franks to move up the start time of the ground offensive. At nine P.M., hundreds of U.S. and British artillery pieces and missile launchers opened fire on the thin screen of Iraqi border guard posts strung out along the border with Kuwait—and the posts' radios went silent, some in midtransmission, as they were destroyed.[29] After the barrage ended, thousands of American and British tanks, armored personnel carriers, and support vehicles crossed over the border into Iraq. The invasion had begun.

American and British ground troops advanced steadily into the country without any appreciable opposition. In the first twenty-four hours, elements of the U.S. Army's Third Infantry Division advanced one hundred miles, arriving on the outskirts of the city of Nasiriyah by the end of March 21. To the east, the First Marine Division seized the Rumailah oil fields on March 21 and destroyed the Iraqi Fifty-first Mechanized Division by the end of the following day.

Across the border in Kuwait, American and British SIGINT operators were flummoxed by the near total absence of the Iraqi military radio traffic that should have been part of a forceful Iraqi response. Moreover, Iraqi divisions did not move from their peacetime bases, and there was no evidence that Hussein's army had any intention of meeting coalition forces head-on.[30]

The Iraqi army and the Fedayeen Saddam paramilitary forces did not use their radios much to communicate during the initial phases of the invasion. This not only prevented Iraqi forces from coordinating attacks on and mounting resistance to coalition forces—but also degraded the value of SIGINT as a source for intelligence during the first couple of days of the invasion.[31]

In the British sector on the extreme right flank, SIGINT played a relatively small role in the successful taking of the key city of Basra by the British First

Armored Division—by giving the British a very accurate picture of the formidable Iraqi forces facing them.[32]

According to British military officials, high-level strategic intelligence derived from SIGINT on Iraqi military strength and capabilities was hard to come by, but intercepted Iraqi tactical radio traffic proved to be an important source for British field commanders.[33] During the course of the First Armored Division's advance, SIGINT provided some warnings of impending ambushes by Fedayeen Saddam guerrillas as well as information concerning the movements and activities of key Iraqi regime leaders inside Basra itself.[34] But no radio intercepts detected signs that the Shi'ite inhabitants of the city had risen up against Hussein's troops.[35]

The same situation existed in the American sector to the west. One of the more interesting battles where SIGINT played a meaningful role was for Nasiriyah, in southeastern Iraq. With a population of 250,000 people, most of whom were Shi'ites, the city was the linchpin of the Iraqi army's defense of southern Iraq. Garrisoning Nasiriyah was the Iraqi Eleventh Infantry Division, and the city had been reinforced by Ba'ath Party Al Quds militiamen and Fedayeen Saddam guerrillas. Just outside the city was the vitally important Tallil Air Base, which was the headquarters of all air defense forces in southern Iraq. The CIA and U.S. military intelligence believed that the Eleventh Infantry Division would put up minimal resistance since it was comprised primarily of Shi'ite troops who had no love for Saddam Hussein's regime.[36]

But the Iraqis defended the city fiercely. For the next fifteen days, the Iraqi army's Forty-fifth Brigade, bolstered by Al Quds Party militiamen and Fedayeen Saddam guerrillas, fought the numerically superior U.S. Marines to a standstill before finally being overcome. Radio intercepts from the marine Second Radio Battalion on March 26 indicated a buildup of two thousand Iraqi soldiers and Fedayeen Saddam guerrillas who were preparing to launch a counterattack on U.S. Marines trying to clear the city. Marine artillery units immediately hit the Iraqi troops with a barrage of high-explosive antipersonnel shells, killing two hundred and breaking up the planned counterattack before it even began.[37]

The same thing was taking place further to the north in front of the city of Najaf, where Fedayeen Saddam paramilitaries and Al Quds militiamen continued to hold the city against Major General David Petraeus's 101st Airborne Division. SIGINT provided Petraeus with some valuable intelligence about the strength and fighting condition of the Iraqi forces inside the embattled city. This reportedly included intercepted messages from the Iraqi commander of the Najaf civilian militia to Baghdad requesting reinforcements because he and more than one thousand civilian militiamen were surrounded by U.S. troops.[38]

Taking On the Medina Division

The battles between the U.S. Army Third Infantry Division and the Republican Guard Medina Division south of Baghdad in late March and early April 2003 proved to be the decisive events in the war. The importance of defeating the Medina Division was immense. British prime minister Tony Blair had predicted that the impending battle the division would be a "crucial moment" in the war.[39] Even before the invasion began, U.S. military planners had determined that the inevitable battle with the Medina Division would be critical to the successful outcome of the war because it was by far the best Iraqi combat unit guarding the southern approaches to Baghdad. A senior U.S. intelligence officer, who at the time was working in the CENTCOM intelligence shop in Qatar, said, "All roads to Baghdad led through the Medina Division. We had to destroy it to take Baghdad and win the war."[40]

Once the invasion began, every radio transmission and electronic emission coming from the units of the Medina Division was closely monitored by NSA. The SIGINT operators at GRSOC monitored the radio traffic coming in and out of the division's headquarters because of apprehensions created by SIGINT and foreign intelligence reports that the division had already been issued artillery shells filled with either mustard gas or nerve agents.[41] We now know, of course, that Iraq did not have any chemical weapons in its arsenal, so one of the enduring mysteries of Operation Iraqi Freedom is what the source of these wildly inaccurate intelligence reports was.

While NSA kept the intelligence staffs in Kuwait well supplied with the latest intelligence about the Medina Division, the responsibility for providing intelligence support to the U.S. Army's main combat unit on the battlefield, the Third Infantry Division, fell to its own integral intelligence unit, the 103rd Military Intelligence Battalion, which had its own SIGINT collection company. It used a SIGINT collection system called Prophet, which was basically an unarmored Humvee vehicle with two radio intercept personnel sitting in the back, who got their intercepts from a twenty-three-foot-high telescoping antenna mounted on the roof of the vehicle. Prophet intercepts were beamed directly to the 103rd MI Battalion's command center, then sent via satellite to GRSOC, where Arabic linguists translated them and beamed the results back to the Third Infantry Division's analysts in Iraq. But the Third Infantry Division received its complement of Prophet systems only a few weeks before the invasion of Iraq began, meaning that the division's radio intercept operators were still learning how to use the system when the war began.[42]

SIGINT played an important role in the first, abortive attack on the Medina

Division in the Karbala Gap by a force of attack helicopters on the night of March 23–24. That night, the Eleventh Attack Helicopter Regiment, equipped with thirty-two AH-64D Apache attack helicopters, launched a deep airborne strike that was designed to destroy the Second Armored Brigade of the Medina Division, which SIGINT had pinpointed as deployed in defensive positions north of the town of Al Hillal in the Karbala Gap. However, the Iraqis were waiting, and they destroyed one Apache and captured the two pilots. They also damaged the thirty-one other helicopters. Making matters worse, the attack failed to engage, much less destroy, the Medina Division. The U.S. Army's official history of the war describes the abortive attack as "the darkest day" of the war.[43]

On the evening of March 23, SIGINT intercepted ominous messages indicating that the Medina Division had been warned that an attack on its positions was imminent. But once the attack was under way on the morning of March 24, SIGINT operators intercepted dozens of Iraqi radio messages indicating that the Eleventh Attack Helicopter Regiment had indeed flown right into a carefully orchestrated "flak trap."[44] The commander of the U.S. Army's Fifth Corps, Lieutenant General William Wallace, admitted after the war, "We found out, subsequent to the attack, based on some intelligence reports, that apparently both the location of our attack aviation assembly areas and the fact that we were moving out of those assembly areas in the attack was announced to the enemy's air defense personnel by an Iraqi observer, thought to be a major general, who was located someplace in the town of An-Najaf using a cellular telephone. In fact, he used it to speed-dial a number of Iraqi air defenders. As our attack aviation approached the attack positions, they came under intense enemy fire."[45]

Hours after the abortive attack by the Apache helicopters, a trio of army RC-12 Guardrail SIGINT aircraft belonging to the Fifteenth Military Intelligence Battalion, based in Kuwait, flew a special reconnaissance mission over the Karbala Gap looking for the Medina Division and found it positioned around the towns of Karbala, Al Hillal, and Al Haswah. Using the coordinates provided by the Guardrail aircraft, U.S. Army artillery units immediately launched a barrage of lethal multiple-launch rocket system (MLRS) missiles at the Iraqi positions, with COMINT intercepts indicating that the missiles had caused widespread damage.[46]

For the next three days, a ferocious sandstorm brought all operations to a halt. During it, on the night of March 25–26, the Iraqis attempted to move up elements of five Republican Guard divisions to positions south of Baghdad. These moves were quickly detected by SIGINT and other technical sensors, which led to a seemingly never-ending series of air attacks on the Republican

Guards desperately trying to make their way to the front. With the Iraqi air defense system almost completely flattened, American and British fighter-bombers were able to clobber Iraqi military targets with impunity within minutes after SIGINT fingered them. By the end of the war, more than four hundred air strikes on Iraqi military targets had been flown based solely on SIGINT intercepts coming out of NSA.[47]

By March 28, Major General Buford Blount III's Third Infantry Division was ready to take on the Medina Division. The upcoming battle had taken on new importance because on the previous day, SIGINT had picked up the first indications that the Iraqis had moved what were believed to be chemical weapons from a central stockpile site outside Baghdad to the Medina Division. American intelligence analysts at the time strongly believed that the weapons in question were 155-millimeter artillery shells filled with either mustard gas or the nerve agents VX or Sarin.[48] That afternoon, the CENTCOM deputy director of operations in Qatar, Brigadier General Vincent Brooks, confirmed the story, telling reporters, "We have seen indications through a variety of sources . . . [that] orders have been given that at a certain point chemical weapons may be used."[49]

Despite this grave threat, the offensive against the Medina Division in the Karbala Gap proceeded on April 1. By the end of the day, the lead elements of Blount's division had advanced to within fifty kilometers (about thirty miles) of Baghdad. The Iraqis detected the move around their flank almost immediately and reacted as best they could, throwing elements of the Medina Division into the breach to try to slow down the American attack. These Iraqi countermoves were quickly noted by SIGINT and other American intelligence sensors. Fifth Corps commander Lieutenant General William Wallace recalled that his intelligence assets almost immediately detected the Iraqi reaction. "Simultaneous with those reports and that movement, we had UAVs [unmanned aerial vehicles] flying and identifying those formations. That operational maneuver, in my judgment, enabled the operational fires of the coalition to really do some major damage on portions of the Republican Guards. And from that point, over the next twenty-four to thirty-six hours, the number of reports we were getting on destruction of Iraqi armor and artillery formations was dramatically larger than what we had received earlier in the fight."[50]

Blood!

On the afternoon of April 2, as thousands of U.S. troops and hundreds of tanks belonging to General Blount's Third Infantry Division surged through the Karbala Gap, a message from the commander of the Republican Guard Medina Division to his subordinate brigades was intercepted. It contained only three words: "Blood. Blood. Blood." NSA interpreted the message to mean that "blood" was the Iraqi code word for use of chemical or biological weapons. General Jeff Kimmons, CENTCOM's chief of intelligence, agreed with NSA's analysis and so informed General Franks.[51]

The Top Secret SIGINT report from NSA was immediately passed to all senior army and marine commanders in Iraq, who placed their forces on alert. Lieutenant General James Conway, the commander of all Marine Corps forces in Iraq, later recalled, "Everybody that night slept with their [gas] mask in very close proximity, as well as sleeping in your [chemical protection] suit."[52]

Shortly after the intercept was received, three Iraqi missiles impacted near the forward command post of the Fifth Corps in central Iraq, setting off the chemical detection alarms. Though it proved to be a false alarm, it is doubtful that anyone got any sleep that night.[53]

The intercepted message from the commander of the Medina Division caused more than a fair amount of concern in Washington, where Pentagon officials were honestly worried that the Iraqis were about to use their purported stockpile of chemical weapons against the Third Infantry Division. Blount's troops had already crossed the "Red Line," fifty miles outside Baghdad, where U.S. intelligence believed Saddam had authorized his commanders to use chemical weapons against U.S. forces. Senior White House and Pentagon officials quietly informed selected reporters in Washington that "U.S. forces in Iraq have recently intercepted increasing amounts of Iraqi communications that appear to allude to the use of weapons of mass destruction." One unidentified official ominously told a reporter that the intercepts were worrisome because "there are allusions to using special weapons. There seem to be a lot more now."[54]

The Battle for Objective Peach

Unfortunately, perishable SIGINT on Iraqi military activities was not making its way to field commanders. While CENTCOM and the Third Army intelligence staff in Kuwait continued getting the best intelligence available about the strength and capabilities of the Iraqi armed forces from NSA and other national intelligence agencies, it did not filter down to the army division, brigade, and battalion commanders slugging it out with the Iraqis. The Third Infantry's Major Erik Berdy recalled that, despite the excellent intel available, "it still never felt like we had a true picture of who we were fighting, how they were fighting and what their intent was behind it all."[55]

Only after the war did the U.S. military learn that its much-hyped "network centric warfare" electronic communications system, which was supposed to push intelligence down to the commanders on the battlefield in real time, did not work. During key battles, army frontline commanders literally did not know which Iraqi forces they were facing, despite the fact that their superiors in Kuwait did.[56]

A perfect example of this phenomenon was the role SIGINT played in the battle for the strategically important Al-Qa'id Bridge over the Euphrates River, thirty kilometers (about nineteen miles) southwest of Baghdad, on April 2–3. At four thirty P.M. on April 2, a reinforced armored battalion of the Third Infantry Division under the command of Lieutenant Colonel Ernest "Rock" Marcone seized the bridge, which opened Baghdad to attack by the hard-driving Third Infantry, coming up fast from the rear.

Marcone's orders were to hold the bridge until the reinforcements from his brigade arrived. But the relief force had to take a less direct route to the bridge, leading Marcone's force to stick it out overnight in its exposed defensive positions.

Marcone, who had been told the bridge was undefended, recalled later that the "intel picture was terrible . . . I knew there would be Iraqis at the bridge, but I didn't know how many or where." As it turned out, he had no way of knowing that there were thousands of heavily armed Iraqi army soldiers all around him.[57]

At about nine P.M., Marcone was warned by a FLASH-precedence message that SIGINT indicated that the Iraqi Third Special Republican Guard Commando Brigade had just sortied from the Baghdad International Airport, to his north, with orders to attack his position and retake the bridge. Marcone immediately repositioned his forces as best he could in order to face the expected Iraqi infantry counterattack. But what SIGINT and all other intelligence sources missed was that two armored brigades belonging to the Republican Guard Medina and Nebuchadnezzar Divisions, totaling between five thousand and ten thousand men with T-72 tanks, were then converging on Marcone's tightly stretched defensive positions from the south.[58]

Under attack by vastly superior forces during the period beginning at two A.M., Marcone's unit held out against the Iraqi tanks and troops. Despite being repeatedly beaten back and suffering catastrophically heavy casualties, the Iraqi commander continued to press his attack, but Marcone's M1A1 Abrams tanks, with better armor and night vision capability, beat off the Iraqi T-72 tanks. By five thirty A.M., the Tenth Brigade of the Medina Division had ceased to exist as a fighting unit, and radio intercepts revealed that the brigade commander had been killed by an air strike on his command post.

The Bridge over the Diyala Canal

SIGINT proved its value once again on April 7, when the lead elements of the Third Battalion of the Fourth Marine Regiment, First Marine Division, commanded by Lieutenant Colonel Bryan McCoy, prepared to seize another vitally important bridge, over the Diyala Canal, over which the rest of the marine division would cross before driving on into Baghdad.[59] Just as McCoy began his attack, an Arab linguist at GRSOC intercepted messages indicating that Iraqi artillery was preparing to ambush McCoy's force by raining down heavy fire on it.[60]

The reaction was immediate. According to a U.S. Army Intelligence and Security Command account of the action, which deleted all of the salient details of who was involved in the action or where it was transpiring, "An Army strategic group [GRSOC] immediately notified a Marine battalion that it was advancing into the impact zone of an artillery ambush on a bridge. The battalion command [McCoy] immediately redeployed his forces to cross the river at another location."[61] Unfortunately, the move did not take place fast enough. A barrage of Iraqi 155-millimeter artillery shells began falling on his position. Tragically, one of the Iraqi shells scored a direct hit on an armored assault vehicle, killing two marines and wounding four others. But it could have been far worse but for the warning provided by GRSOC.[62]

Los Endos

The capture of the bridges over the Euphrates River and Diyala Canal meant that Baghdad was doomed. Intercepted radio traffic revealed that the decimated Iraqi military was in its death throes, with the few remaining Republican Guard units deployed around Baghdad collapsing almost without a fight. The isolated Iraqi units that tried to stand up to the advancing American forces were quickly destroyed by artillery and air strikes within minutes of their radio operators going on the air. SIGINT revealed that what was left of Saddam Hussein's regime refused to accept the fact that they had been defeated. As late as April 8, the day before Baghdad fell, intercepted Iraqi satellite phone messages showed that

Hussein's son Qusay, the Republican Guard commander, continued to believe that Iraq was winning the war, with Republican Guard commanders telling him of "high American casualties and defeats of the allied forces in various cities."[63]

During the final skirmishes inside Baghdad between the U.S. Army and what was left of the Iraqi Army and Republican Guard, SIGINT was used to find former members of Hussein's government. On April 7, a B-1B bomber dropped four bombs on the al-Saa restaurant in the tony Mansour district of west Baghdad, where intelligence sources indicated Saddam Hussein and two of his sons were meeting. Inspection of the ruins found eighteen dead bodies, all of them unfortunate customers of the restaurant. But Saddam and his sons were not among the casualties. One source suggests that air strikes on Saddam's reported locations were prompted by NSA intercepts of the Thuraya satellite phone used by Saddam Hussein and his key aides. NSA had long been able to locate people using Thuraya satellite telephones by triangulating on the signal emanating from the phone's global positioning system chip. NSA had used this technology to track the movements of al Qaeda terrorists and other high-value targets around the world, even when these individuals were not using their telephones.[64]

Conclusions

Declassified documents and interviews with former U.S. military commanders all generally agree that SIGINT performed well during the three weeks of Operation Iraqi Freedom, in some cases brilliantly, as in the case of the near-complete decapitation of the Iraqi air defense system during the first days of the invasion.

NSA did a superb job of getting its SIGINT product to senior U.S. military commanders as soon as it became available. The Iraq Operational Cell within NSOC at Fort Meade did a remarkable job of packaging and reporting the latest SIGINT coming in from NSA's worldwide network of listening posts designed specifically for the use of field commanders in Iraq through its secure intranet system, known as NSANet. The flood of timely and valuable information in Top Secret/COMINT e-mails from NSA "was almost too much," one senior CENTCOM intelligence officer recalled. "Nobody else in the community gave that kind of service."[65] Virtually all senior American military commanders also praised the quantity, quality, and timeliness of NSA's intelligence production before and during the invasion.[66]

But little has been made public about the fact that Iraqi communications security procedures prior to the invasion were highly effective and denied NSA and the U.S. military SIGINT units access to Iraqi military communications traffic.[67]

Army and marine division commanders in the field and their subordinate brigade and battalion commanders were less than satisfied with SIGINT from NSA and the military intelligence organizations under their command during the invasion. As the desperate and heroic stand of Colonel Marcone's unit at Al-Qa'id Bridge demonstrated, the perennial problem of getting really useful intel to units at the sharp end had yet to be solved.[68] Some of these officers wondered if some sort of "digital divide" accounted for most SIGINT intel going to army and corps commanders and little if any going to division commanders and their subordinates.[69]

Officers lower down on the chain of command, according to a Marine Corps after-action report, "found the enemy by running into them, much as forces have done since the beginning of warfare."[70]

Moreover, according to a U.S. Navy document, once the invasion was under way, NSA's strategic SIGINT collection units in the United States archived 60 percent of the material they collected and never processed (i.e., translated or analyzed) it. The military's tactical SIGINT units taking part in the invasion processed less than 2 percent of the Iraqi messages they intercepted. These are hardly the sorts of numbers one can be proud of if one is an intelligence professional.[71]

Just as in Afghanistan two years earlier, much of the SIGINT collection equipment used by American military intelligence units during the invasion was found to be outdated and unsuited for supporting fast-moving offensive operations.[72] Some of the newly developed collection equipment did not work as advertised. For example, the army's highly touted Prophet tactical SIGINT collection system proved to be fine for short-range target location, but did not perform particularly well when it was tasked with locating Iraqi radio emitters deep behind enemy lines. As a result, many brigade and division commanders reported after the war that they had found themselves completely dependent on NSA's national SIGINT collection assets for locating Iraqi forces, as in the case of the Republican Guard units during the early stages of the invasion.[73]

Severe and persistent shortages of Arabic linguists dogged NSA and the U.S. military's SIGINT collection effort. For example, only half of the linguists assigned to the SIGINT collection unit supporting the 101st Airborne Division during the invasion spoke Arabic. The other half spoke Korean. Since very few of the intelligence community's Arabic linguists could understand the Iraqi dialect, the United States had to turn to a private contractor to hire as quickly and as many translators as possible who could speak the Iraqi dialect. Many of the linguists Titan Corporation recruited on short notice (and at considerable cost to the U.S. government) were Iraqi political refugees living in the United States, Canada, Europe, and Australia or first-generation Americans of Iraqi descent. Olympic speed records were set hiring these individuals, vetting them, and then flying them to Kuwait in time to participate in the invasion.[74]

CHAPTER 15

The Good, the Bad, and the Ugly

SIGINT and Combating the Insurgencies in Iraq and Afghanistan

I don't do quagmires.
—DONALD RUMSFELD, DEPARTMENT OF
DEFENSE TRANSCRIPT

The Repeat Performance

U.S. troops entered Baghdad on April 9, 2003, leading to the immediate collapse of Saddam Hussein's regime. Looting on a massive scale broke out, but U.S. forces did not attempt to stop it. When reporters asked about the escalating level of violence and chaos in Baghdad, Secretary of Defense Donald Rumsfeld made his now-famous comment: "Freedom is untidy."[1]

A flood of books and studies later demonstrated that Rumsfeld viewed the security situation in Iraq through rose-colored glasses. Equally in a state of denial was CENTCOM's General Franks. In what is now widely viewed as one of the most significant blunders in American military history, Rumsfeld and Franks had given little if any thought to how post-Hussein Iraq would be governed. CENTCOM did not even begin reconstruction planning until five months after the fall of Baghdad. But by that time, the Iraqi insurgency was in full swing, and the reconstruction plan was quickly junked in favor of a counterinsurgency plan, which also had not been worked on prior to the fall of Baghdad.[2]

On April 16, Franks cheerfully announced that most U.S. combat forces in Iraq would be withdrawn within sixty days so that they would not "wear out their welcome." Franks's plan called for keeping some thirty thousand U.S. troops there as a peacetime occupation force. As a result, two army divisions that were supposed to be sent to Iraq after the fall of Baghdad were never sent, and on April 21 the Pentagon canceled plans to deploy a third division there. By summer, there were too few U.S. combat troops to secure Baghdad, a teeming city of 4.8 million, or the rest of Iraq. Franks's prescription for disaster had been endorsed by the White House and the Pentagon, and it was a repetition of the same mistake that he and Rumsfeld had made a year earlier in Afghanistan. He declared victory and left the battlefield before the job was finished.[3]

As part of the drawdown of forces, the military began rapidly and drastically reducing its intelligence presence in Iraq, just as it had done a year earlier in Afghanistan. Major General James "Spider" Marks, who had commanded the U.S. military's intelligence effort during Operation Iraqi Freedom, left Iraq in June to return to his former position as commandant of the U.S. Army Intelligence Center at Fort Huachuca, in Arizona. Virtually all of the army's best intelligence units in Iraq left with him, including the entire 513th Military Intelligence Brigade, which had performed so admirably during Operation Iraqi Freedom.[4]

Back in the United States, all of the intelligence staffs and special operations units created to provide intelligence support for the invasion of Iraq, including those at NSA, were disbanded and their personnel returned to their former posts. For example, the Iraq reporting cell within NSA's National Security Operations Center (NSOC) was disbanded on May 2, the day after President Bush declared "Mission Accomplished" on the deck of the aircraft carrier USS *Abraham Lincoln*.[5]

NSA's SIGINT collection assets that had formerly been committed to Iraq were shifted to intercepting the military and diplomatic communications of Iran and Syria. SIGINT coverage of those countries' military and internal security radio traffic turned up nothing to suggest that either Iran or Syria intended anything nefarious. SIGINT also monitored Turkish traffic because of the U.S. concern that Turkey might intervene militarily in northern Iraq to prevent the formation of an independent Kurdish state, anathema to the Turkish government.[6]

Debilitating turf wars broke out between NSA, CENTCOM, and the commander of U.S. forces in Iraq over "who was going to do what to whom," which created all sorts of unnecessary chaos on the ground there.[7]

Coming Prepared for the Wrong War

The first Iraqi insurgent attacks on U.S. forces began within days of the fall of Baghdad, but they were infrequent. However, after President Bush proclaimed

"Mission Accomplished," the number of attacks stepped up dramatically, to six a day by the end of the month. American soldiers began dying, and the press began to question whether Bush's victory declaration might have been a wee bit premature. White House and Pentagon officials dismissed the attacks as the last gasp of "dead-ender" remnants of Saddam Hussein's regime, the work of foreign terrorists aligned with al Qaeda, or the activities of criminal gangs taking advantage of Hussein's downfall.[8]

The leading proponent of this sunny vision of the situation in Iraq, which a retired army general characterized as the "Morning in Iraq Syndrome," was Secretary of Defense Rumsfeld, who breezily told reporters, "In short, the coalition is making good progress."[9] In Baghdad, echoing Rumsfeld, the newly appointed commander of U.S. forces in Iraq, Lieutenant General Ricardo Sanchez, told reporters that the Iraqi insurgency was "strategically and operationally insignificant."[10] The chief of army intelligence in Iraq, Colonel Steven Boltz, went so far as to tell a reporter that the insurgent attacks were "random and it isn't organized and that's a good thing."[11]

But this Panglossian view of things became untenable after suicide bombings in Baghdad and roadside attacks on U.S. forces throughout Iraq jumped 500 percent, to more than thirty a day. By October 2003, 203 American soldiers had died at the hands of Iraqi insurgents, more than all casualties suffered during the invasion of Iraq. After the Baghdad suicide bombings of the Jordanian embassy on August 7 and the U.N. headquarters compound on August 19, the CIA station chief in Baghdad warned Washington that these bombings were symptomatic of the growing strength and deadliness of the Sunni insurgency, but his warning was ignored.[12]

But the equipment that the U.S. military's SIGINT units had brought with them to Iraq during the 2003 invasion proved to be next to useless in an urban counterinsurgency environment. Major Steven Bower, who commanded a company of the 311th Military Intelligence Battalion in northern Iraq, recalled, "As far as SIGINT is concerned, most of our stuff was designed to operate on the military wave band lengths . . . but it doesn't pick up cell phones or a lot of the technology out there. We still picked up some radio traffic and we still got some stuff out of it, but it wasn't as much as we wanted."[13] In 2004, new SIGINT equipment, including the latest version of the army's Prophet tactical SIGINT collection system, called Prophet Hammer, was delivered to every U.S. Army combat division in Iraq. The new version of the Prophet was the army's latest high-tech intelligence collection toy, built specifically for cell phone interception, which everyone in Washington thought was a marvelous improvement.

Designed for use in Europe, the Prophet and Prophet Hammer systems did not work well in the crowded and densely populated cities of Iraq. They were also not designed to cope with the primitive Iraqi signals environment because, as a brigade operations officer with the 101st Airborne Division stationed in northern Iraq pointed out, "at that time there wasn't a lot of mobile phones in use" in Iraq.[14]

So the U.S. Army and Marine Corps were forced to junk much of their expensive SIGINT equipment and spend still more millions replacing it with consumer products—low-tech off-the-shelf radio scanners and other equipment—not really knowing if they would work in Iraq.[15]

And even if SIGINT units could intercept the phone calls of the Iraqi insurgents, the people needed to translate them were not available. Within months of the fall of Baghdad in April 2003, all army division commanders in Iraq began disbanding their SIGINT units and transferring their personnel to fill out Tactical HUMINT Teams that were being formed throughout the country. For example, the Third Infantry Division's commander, Major General Buford Blount, whose division was responsible for garrisoning Baghdad, stripped all of the Arabic linguists out of his division's SIGINT company and transferred them to HUMINT-gathering duties—which of course they were not trained or equipped for. The Arab linguists available were trained only to listen to Arabic communications traffic and transcribe it; they had not been trained to speak the language with any degree of fluency. Moreover, they had no command of the Iraqi dialect, which put them at a severe disadvantage when trying to talk to Iraqis.[16] At the same time, the company's SIGINT equipment, notably Prophet, was parked in the division's motor pool and allowed to gather dust.[17] Much the same thing happened in northern Iraq, which was the operational area of the 101st Airborne Division, commanded by Major General David Petraeus. Many of the Arabic cryptologic linguists assigned to the division's 311th MI Battalion were transferred to HUMINT collection duties, with the division intel officer G-2, Lieutenant Colonel D.J. Reyes, concluding, "The low technology, HUMINT-rich nature of stability operations and support operations mitigated (and at times negated) the effectiveness of our technical intelligence platforms."[18]

Then, in a typical U.S. Army "comedy of errors," its intelligence officers were shocked to discover that many of the cryptologic linguists they had in Iraq could speak Korean, French, Spanish, and other languages—but not Arabic. How they ended up in Iraq in the first place remains a question that army intelligence officials do not seem to want to answer. As of September 2003, many of these "misplaced persons" were still in Iraq doing jobs that had nothing to do with intelligence, such as pulling guard duty, manning traffic checkpoints at base gates, or working as administrative clerks.[19]

The sad result was that by the end of 2003, the U.S. military's SIGINT collection capabilities in Iraq had fallen to such calamitously low levels of accomplishment that some thoroughly pissed-off army division commanders came close to ordering the disbandment of what was left of their SIGINT units completely. The dearth of intelligence being produced by NSA not surprisingly angered many of the senior military commanders in Iraq. A former NSA liaison officer recalled, "There were some very, very unhappy people down in those division headquarters" who were angry about NSA's inability to get them the intelligence they needed.[20]

As if things were not bad enough, when cell phone service was introduced throughout Iraq in the spring and summer of 2004, military SIGINT units discovered that their intercept equipment brought in from the United States was useless against the cell phones that were now being used by the Iraqi insurgents.[21] It was not until the summer of 2004 that the first U.S. Air Force cargo aircraft began landing in Kuwait carrying emergency shipments of hastily purchased replacement cell phone intercept equipment. The equipment was so new that the U.S. Army intelligence personnel accompanying it were literally still reading the operating manuals trying to learn how to use the stuff when the planes touched down.[22]

And even then, the new cell phone intercept equipment being brought into Iraq left much to be desired because it was available only at the brigade level, which meant that little of the SIGINT product from this source made its way down to the battalions slugging it out on the streets of Baghdad and elsewhere in Iraq. The equipment itself was of marginal utility because of technical limitations on what it could hear and its restricted range. A U.S. Army officer who served with the First Cavalry Division in the Shi'ite slum of Sadr City in eastern Baghdad recalled, "I wasn't impressed, though, with how good the cell phone listening capability really was because you could get only one side of the conversation and you had to be within a certain range."[23]

Once cell phone service began to expand, NSA and the military SIGINT units scrambled to find security-cleared linguists who had at least some comprehension of Iraqi dialects, but two resources—the nascent Iraqi army and the national police—were believed to be infiltrated by insurgents. So the recruitment of linguists was handed over to American private sector defense contractors—CACI and Titan Corporation (now part of L-3 Corporation). The candidate linguists who could pass the security clearance requirements were sent not to Iraq but to NSA's Gordon Regional Security Operations Center (GRSOC), where they were immediately put to work in a newly formed operations unit called Cobra Focus, whose sole mission was to translate the cell phone intercepts that were being beamed directly to GRSOC from the Iraqi front lines via satellite.[24]

Monitoring Insurgent Finances and Infiltration

All available evidence indicates that it took NSA a significant amount of time to adapt to the rapidly changing battlefield environment in Iraq. But in the summer of 2003, according to Sergeant Major Kevin Gainey, the head of the Third Infantry Division's all-source intelligence fusion center, "eventually we got signals intelligence (SIGINT) working."[25]

One of NSA's early successes was determining who was providing the Iraqi insurgents with financial and logistical support. In 2003, SIGINT helped the Third Armored Cavalry Regiment destroy an insurgent cell in the town of Rawa in al-Anbar Province that was helping foreign fighters infiltrate into Iraq from neighboring Jordan.[26] Intercepts of telephone calls between insurgent leaders in Iraq and their cohorts in Syria and elsewhere in the Middle East in the summer and fall of 2003 revealed that certain Iraqi insurgent groups were being financed by former members of Saddam Hussein's regime based in Syria and by sympathizers elsewhere in the Arab world. By mid-2004, SIGINT was also providing detailed intelligence concerning the flow of money from Syria that was being used to finance Abu Musab al-Zarqawi's foreign fighters operating in al-Anbar Province. A former NSA intelligence analyst said, "SIGINT showed that Ramadi was the destination for most of the money flowing into Iraq from Syria, Jordan, Lebanon, and Saudi Arabia." President Bush was informed that the flow of money amounted to $1.2 million a month.[27]

Beginning in the summer of 2003, special NSA intercept teams and small U.S. Army SIGINT units at Mount Sinjar, in northern Iraq, and Al Qaim, in western Iraq, kept a quiet vigil on the Syrian border, trying to monitor the flow of foreign fighters seeking to cross over and join al-Zarqawi's al Qaeda in Iraq.[28]

Unfortunately, despite the best efforts of the SIGINT collectors, the vast majority of the foreign fighters managed to successfully evade the U.S. Army units deployed along the border. An army battalion commander stationed on the border in 2003 recalled that they "weren't sneaking across; they were just driving across, because in Arab countries it's easy to get false passports and stuff." Once inside Iraq, most of them made their way to Ramadi, in rebellious al-Anbar Province, which became the key way station for foreign fighters on their way into the heart of Iraq. In Ramadi, they were trained, equipped, given false identification papers, and sent on their first missions. The few foreign fighters who were captured were dedicated—but not very bright. One day during the summer of 2003, Lieutenant Colonel Henry Arnold, a battalion commander stationed on the Syrian border, was shown the passport of a person seeking to enter Iraq. "I think he was from the Sudan or something like that—and under 'Reason for Traveling,' it said, 'Jihad.' That's how dumb these guys were."[29]

Iran was a particularly important target for NSA after the fall of Baghdad. According to a former NSA official, the agency was able to read much of the sensitive communications traffic of Iran's Ministry of Intelligence and Security (MOIS), which gave U.S. intelligence analysts some vivid insights into Iranian policy on Iraq, as well as details of Iranian clandestine intelligence operations inside Iraq. But according to news reports, this extremely sensitive NSA program was badly damaged in the spring of 2004 by none other than America's longtime "expert ally" against Saddam Hussein, Ahmed Chalabi, the leader of the Iraqi National Congress (INC). These reports stated that Chalabi and other senior members of the INC had secretly provided Iranian intelligence officials with details of U.S. political and military plans in Iraq, and NSA intercepts reportedly showed that the head of the INC intelligence organization, Aras Habib, was on the payroll of the Iranian intelligence service. Based on this intelligence information, on May 20, 2004, U.S. troops raided Chalabi's home and the offices of the INC in Baghdad.[30]

Then in early June, news reports in the *New York Times* based on leaks from U.S. intelligence sources indicated that in mid-April, Chalabi himself had told the Baghdad station chief of MOIS that NSA had broken the codes of the Iranian intelligence service. Perhaps not believing Chalabi, the Iranian official reportedly radioed a message to Tehran with the substance of Chalabi's information using the code that NSA had broken. According to the news reports, the Iranians immediately changed their codes, and in a stroke eliminated NSA's best source of information about what was going on inside Iran.[31]

NSA's overall performance during the first year of the war in Iraq has been described by a number of senior military commanders as "disappointing." Among the most serious of the complaints was that NSA overemphasized SIGINT collection directed at Iraq's neighbors Iran and Syria, as well as the internal machinations of the U.S.-backed Iraqi government, at the expense of coverage of the Iraqi insurgency movement.[32]

Fight for Allah! SIGINT and the Battle of Fallujah

SIGINT's first important test in Iraq came in 2004 during the Battle of Fallujah, which pitted thousands of U.S. Marine infantrymen backed by tanks and fighter-bombers against an equally large number of Iraqi insurgents and foreign fighters in a bloody street-by-street battle to decide who controlled the city, which was in the heart of al-Anbar Province, a stronghold of the Sunni insurgency ever since the U.S. invasion of Iraq. Between May 2003 and March 2004, an overextended brigade of the Eighty-second Airborne Division gradually lost control of the city to the Iraqi insurgents and Abu Musab al-Zarqawi's foreign fighters. By November 2003, the security situation in Fallujah had become so precarious that the last remaining units of the Eighty-second had to withdraw, which allowed the insurgents and foreign fighters to control the city, to the consternation of Washington and U.S. military commanders in Baghdad.

In March 2004, the Eighty-second was replaced by the First Marine Division, which was tasked with reasserting control over Fallujah and the rest of al-Anbar Province. The insurgents in Fallujah were well aware of the marines' preparations for a massive conventional assault backed by tanks, artillery, and air strikes. The only question was when.[33]

On March 31, less than two weeks after the marines arrived, a mob in Fallujah killed four American security contractors, mutilated the bodies, and hung them from a bridge for all to see. In response, on April 4 the marines sent in two thousand troops, backed by heavy artillery and air strikes, but the ferocious battle that ensued ended on April 9 when the newly elected Iraqi government; Ambassador L. Paul Bremer III, the chief of the Coalition Provisional Authority (CPA) in Baghdad; and Washington became concerned about unacceptable numbers of civilian casualties caused by the air strikes.[34] After the marines withdrew from Fallujah, the insurgents were once again in control of one of the largest cities in Iraq. The few agents that the marines managed to recruit and infiltrate into Fallujah were never heard from again.[35]

Given the failure of HUMINT, SIGINT and unmanned reconnaissance drones became the principal providers of intelligence about what was going on inside the besieged city. The U.S. Marine SIGINT unit, the Third Radio Battalion, had just arrived in-country and was still trying to learn the terrain and its targets on the fly. By the time it arrived, there were eight thousand marines crammed into a massive tent city, Camp Fallujah. The Marine SIGINTers were confined inside the defensive perimeter of the base, enduring hundred-degree temperatures (except when working in their air-conditioned ops center) as well as frequent rocket and mortar attacks on the base, until they rotated out in October 2004.[36]

During this period, they set about gathering intelligence about the insurgents and quickly discovered that al-Zarqawi's foreign fighters, unlike their more security-conscious Iraqi counterparts, consistently chatted away on their ICOM walkie-talkies and cell phones. Al-Zarqawi's inexperienced fighters were later to pay a terrible price for their lack of communications security.[37]

The marines occasionally used a small armored patrol as bait to get the insurgents chattering on their walkie-talkies and cell phones. A marine infantry commander recalled that "these 'bait and hook' methods worked like a charm" because the SIGINT operators could determine the exact locations where al-Zarqawi's fighters were concentrated in Fallujah. "This is all bad guys," said Captain Kirk Mayfield. "Every sigint [electronic intercept], every humint [informant report] tells us this is where all the foreign fighters hang out."[38]

On September 26, intercepted cell phone calls identified the location of a meeting of senior al-Zarqawi operatives inside the city. An unmanned Predator reconnaissance drone surveyed the target and passed on the coordinates to three fighter-bombers from the aircraft carrier USS *John F. Kennedy*. The air strike destroyed the building and killed everyone inside, including a Saudi named Abu Ahmed Tabouki, one of al-Zarqawi's most senior commanders in Fallujah.[39] Two weeks later, after a Predator identified the house inside Fallujah from which the cell phone calls of another gathering of senior insurgent leaders were originating, two F-16 fighter-bombers were ordered to destroy the house with GBU-38 bombs.[40]

On the night of November 7, ten thousand American troops from the First Marine Division and the army's First Cavalry Division launched the offensive, designated Operation Phantom Fury (Al Fajr), to retake Fallujah.[41] The army and marine troops, supported by tanks, artillery, and air strikes, smashed into the insurgent defenses on the northern outskirts of Fallujah and began inexorably pressing the insurgents back toward the center of the city. Intercepted cell phone calls indicated that the insurgents could not hold back the onslaught. Lieutenant Colonel James Rainey, who commanded one of the army mechanized battalions leading the attack, told an interviewer, "If you've heard any of the enemy radio intercepts, they clearly show that the enemy was panicking and reeling from this attack."[42]

U.S. forces thought they had won the bitter struggle, and intercepted messages from the insurgents such as "It's useless. Fallujah is lost" seemed to confirm that.[43] But the insurgents and foreign fighters inside Fallujah did not quit, falling back before the steadily advancing U.S. forces. The punishment that they took while desperately trying to stem the American advance was horrific. They fought on for eleven more days, until they were finally overwhelmed by the numerically superior marine forces. Hundreds of Iraqi insurgents and foreign fighters had been killed, but the cost in American lives was steep. More than seventy marines died in the fighting for Fallujah, and hundreds more were wounded. The battle may have been won for the moment, but radio intercepts and interrogations of captured fighters revealed that two thousand insurgents, including almost all of al-Zarqawi's senior commanders, had managed to escape from the city *before* the battle. It was the midlevel leadership and their troops who had stayed behind and fought.[44]

After the battle, the army and marine units were ordered to withdraw from the city and turn their positions over to units of the ill-equipped and poorly trained Iraqi army and Iraqi national guard. Within a matter of days, cell phone intercepts showed that al-Zarqawi's foreign fighters and the Sunni insurgents had quickly moved back into Fallujah and had retaken control of the city from the Iraqi forces. Angry marine intelligence officers shared with reporters intercepted telephone calls showing that the insurgents had managed to get through the marine and Iraqi cordon around Fallujah by blending in with the refugees returning to the city. So in the end, the Battle of Fallujah, like Operation Anaconda two years earlier, ended up being nothing more than an illusory and costly victory.[45]

They're Back! The Taliban Resurgence

In Afghanistan, the U.S. military's SIGINT effort, although with a fraction of the size of the resources available in Iraq, continued to improve slowly as time went by. But far too often, an intercept that would have enabled a U.S. unit to take out a medium-value target "using his cell phone to coordinate and call in attacks on coalition forces" had to be called off. With unfortunate frequency, a unit found and engaged the enemy but was forced to withdraw without completing its mission because of a lack of personnel. Trying to run this "secondary" war with manifestly insufficient U.S. forces proved to be an exercise in futility.[46]

Still, U.S. Army SIGINT units in Afghanistan got better at exploiting the Taliban's low-level walkie-talkie traffic. A Green Beret officer put it bluntly: The Taliban were "using simple communications methods . . . This is not the Cold War. We're not using super high-tech stuff to pick up SIGINT and things like that. Once we get on the right frequencies and get a trusted interpreter to translate that for us, it turns out to be a very good tool."[47]

By 2004, most of the major U.S. Army firebases along the fifteen-hundred-mile Afghan-Pakistani border had their own small SIGINT unit, distinguished by the cluster of antennae erupting from the rooftop of the base's barbed-wire-enclosed operations building. The largest were located just outside Kandahar and at Forward Operating Base Salerno, on the outskirts of the border town of Khowst. And all the Green Beret base camps spread throughout southern Afghanistan had small teams of Green Beret and Navy SEAL SIGINT operators providing tactical SIGINT support for Special Forces reconnaissance teams patrolling the region along the Afghan-Pakistani border.[48]

When the radio scanners at one of the firebases picked up traffic from the Taliban's Japanese-made ICOM walkie-talkies (which usually had a range of five miles or less in the rugged terrain), it usually meant that there was a Taliban rocket or mortar team somewhere in the vicinity, clinging to a nearby ridgeline to call in the coordinates of its target to nearby gunners.[49]

At the army firebase at Shkin, in southeastern Afghanistan, the base's SIGINT operators became quite adept at catching Taliban gunners preparing for such attacks. Within minutes of the operators' intercepting the transmissions, artillery fire or air strikes were pummeling the location of the Taliban mortar team. The result was, as an army report notes, that the Taliban was "forced to shift from accurate mortar fire to much less accurate longer range rocket fire from less advantageous firing positions across the border" in Pakistan.[50]

Inside Afghanistan itself, SIGINT was proving to be an increasingly important defensive tool, providing warning of impending Taliban attacks on U.S. Army patrols. Marine Gunnery Sergeant Michael Johnson remembered a helicopter assault during which insurgents were baiting a trap for Afghan forces when they went out on an operation. "We'd intercept communications of their radio communications that they were going to ambush that platoon. Within a minute they had contact."[51]

Beginning in late 2004, U.S. commanders in Afghanistan were gratified to see signs appearing in the battlefield SIGINT they were receiving that some of the Taliban guerrillas operating inside Afghanistan were demoralized and on the run. An anonymous U.S. intelligence officer was quoted as saying, "We actually overheard a Taliban fighter break out into a lament, saying 'Where are you [Mullah] Omar, why have you forsaken us?' "[52]

U.S. military commanders launched their own PR offensive, releasing selected intelligence assessments intended to convince the American public that the Taliban in Afghanistan were all but beaten. First came the chairman of the Joint Chiefs of Staff, General Richard Myers, who described the security situation in Afghanistan as "exceptionally good" during a visit to Kabul. In a meeting with American reporters in Kabul in April 2005, the commander of U.S. forces in Afghanistan, Lieutenant General David Barno, confidently predicted that "the Taliban militia would collapse as a viable fighting force over the next several months," adding that he believed that the Taliban rank and file would accept an amnesty offer from Afghan president Hamid Karzai to lay down their arms and join the Afghan government.[53]

But the spin campaign was already backfiring in late March 2005, when Taliban guerrilla teams once again began surging across the border from their safe havens in northern Pakistan, but this time in numbers never seen before. In a matter of weeks, the security situation inside Afghanistan deteriorated rapidly. The number of attacks on American military installations and Afghan police posts and government offices in southern Afghanistan rose dramatically, as did the number of civilians killed by the Taliban.[54] Intelligence analysts confirmed on the basis of SIGINT intercepts that the number of Taliban guerrilla teams operating inside Afghanistan had also risen dramatically in the previous two months. Moreover, intercepts confirmed that two of the Taliban's best field commanders, Mullah Dadullah and Mullah Brader, had crossed over from Pakistan and were leading large Taliban guerrilla detachments in Kandahar and Zabul Provinces.[55]

By late spring of 2005, large chunks of three important southern Afghan provinces—Kandahar, Uruzgan, and Zabul—were controlled by the Taliban, with the exception of the major cities and a few isolated firebases, which remained in the hands of American forces. When Lieutenant Colonel Don Bolduc's First Battalion, Third Special Forces Group, arrived in Kandahar in June 2005 to take over the responsibility for garrisoning southern Afghanistan, his men found that the U.S. Army unit that they were replacing had done little to prevent the Taliban from consolidating its hold on these three provinces, preferring instead to focus its operations on clearing the areas around the few remaining army firebases in southern Afghanistan. Between January and July 2005, the Taliban, thanks to this complacency, had been allowed to establish permanent base areas in the provinces. It was also furiously reinforcing its forces in these sanctuaries with new guerrilla units infiltrated in from Pakistan and new levies recruited from among sympathetic local tribesmen.[56]

The situation in Zabul Province was particularly grim. A longtime Taliban stronghold, Zabul was so hostile that some American troops referred to it as "Talibanland." Others called it the "Fallujah of Afghanistan," a reference to the Iraqi insurgent stronghold in al-Anbar Province. Patrols from the 173rd Airborne Brigade operating in Zabul were repeatedly attacked by groups of as many as 100 to 150 Taliban fighters. Over and over again, army SIGINT personnel accompanying the 173rd Airborne's patrols picked up heavy volumes of Taliban walkie-talkie traffic closely monitoring their movements and coordinating attacks on their positions. The Taliban suffered heavy casualties, but it was clear that the province had become a far more dangerous place than it had been after the U.S. invasion in 2001.[57]

But no matter how good the SIGINT was, U.S. forces could clear but not hold the ground they took. Take, for example, what happened after a three-day running battle in August 2005 in the Mari Ghar region in the heart of Zabul Province, which pitted more than two hundred Taliban guerrillas against a twelve-man Green Beret team from the First Battalion, Third Special Forces Group commanded by Captain Brandon Griffin, and a sixteen-man detachment of Afghan army troops. When the battle was over, Captain Griffin's team had killed sixty-five guerrillas, losing only one man in return. But no ground had been gained during the battle. Despite three days of near-continuous running battles with the Taliban, Griffin's team had been forced to leave the Mari Ghar region in the hands of the Taliban. It was the same old story—the U.S. Army just had too few troops in Afghanistan to hold anything more than the string of firebases that it occupied throughout the country.[58]

Even worse, tactical SIGINT also showed that the Taliban had morphed from a motley group of insurgents into a heavily armed and well-led guerrilla force, which proved to be insurgents and foreign fighters who, according to a U.S. commander, "were resolute. They stood and fought."[59]

The Surge

Following the Battle of Fallujah in November 2004, the security situation in Iraq continued to deteriorate rapidly as the level of sectarian violence between the country's Sunni and Shi'ite militias steadily mounted and insurgent attacks on U.S. forces shot up. In this savage and unforgiving environment, SIGINT became increasingly vital to U.S. military commanders as the Iraqi insurgents dried up intelligence by closing down (i.e., killing) most of the U.S. military's HUMINT sources. By 2005, SIGINT had once again supplanted HUMINT as the principal source of intelligence for the United States. A postmortem report on the U.S. Army Third Corps's tour of duty in Iraq had this to say about SIGINT's effectiveness:

> Our SIGINT collection was the most spectacular intelligence discipline on the battlefield, as we were able to collect on many targets cued by other intelligence disciplines. Trusted and useful, SIGINT provided an abundance of intelligence on insurgent networks, named persons of interest, and enemy operations. SIGINT is a critical area where continued development of linguists, not only in skill but in numbers, must occur.[60]

Army and marine commanders in Iraq found that SIGINT by itself was only moderately effective at the street level. But when combined with reasonably effective tactical HUMINT gathering, its value soared dramatically. Colonel Emmett Schaill, the deputy commander of the army's First Brigade, Twenty-fifth Infantry Division, which operated in Mosul, in northern Iraq, from September 2004 to June 2005, recalled that SIGINT and unmanned drones played an important supporting role in finding Iraqi insurgents in his sector, but were less important than the HUMINT assets that his brigade developed during its tour in Iraq. Leveraging the intelligence he collected with information from national intelligence agencies like the CIA and NSA, by the end of his tour Schaill was able to lead his brigade to destroy 80 percent of Abu Musab al-Zarqawi's al Qaeda cells in northern Iraq, a fact confirmed by SIGINT intercepts of al Qaeda cell phone traffic.[61]

Even after Schaill's brigade left Mosul and returned home, SIGINT continued to produce valuable intelligence that, working in conjunction with HUMINT and unmanned drones, resulted in heavy insurgent casualties. On August 12, 2005, SIGINT intercepts led U.S. Army Special Forces to an al Qaeda in Iraq hideout outside Mosul. When the firefight was over, three senior al Qaeda in Iraq leaders were dead, including the commander of al Qaeda in Iraq forces in Mosul, Abu Zubayr (aka Mohammed Sultan Saleh), who was killed while wearing a suicide vest packed with explosives.[62]

But SIGINT is an inexact science, especially against an enemy that knows that its communications are almost certainly being monitored. This has meant that American intelligence analysts in Iraq have often not been able to exploit the intercepts they get. Take, for example, a typical "cordon and search" operation launched by a company of U.S. Marines and a battalion of the Iraqi army on June 29, 2005, near the town of Saqlawiyah, an insurgent stronghold in al-Anbar Province. The goal of the operation was to surround the town and conduct a door-to-door search of all houses in certain neighborhoods looking for weapons and insurgents. An army report on the operation recounts, "During the search, a [marine] radio battalion reported picking up insurgent radio traffic that identified individuals by name. The suspected insurgents were instructed to remain in their hideout."

The problem was that the cell phone call that the marines had intercepted did not identify who the insurgents were other than by their first names. Those unfortunates who had those first names were detained—and then released for lack of evidence.[63]

U.S. intelligence officials now candidly admit that the turning point of the war in Iraq occurred in February 2006, when Sunni insurgents bombed a mosque in the city of Samarra, which was one of the holiest shrines for Iraqi Shi'ites. The Samarra bombing unleashed a wave of sectarian fighting that led to unprecedented slaughter in Iraq. All of the progress in winning the "hearts and minds" of Iraqis was swept away, and the carnage dominated the nightly news in the United States. This outburst of violence came at a time when HUMINT in Iraq was, in the words of a commentator, "fairly scarce and usually unreliable." The U.S. military had to depend on SIGINT to help it combat this rising tide of violence.[64]

A February 2006 report notes that an army SIGINT platoon located south of Baghdad was "working miracles and helping us put lots of insurgents into Abu Ghurayb [sic] prison."[65] In July, intelligence generated by the SIGINT platoon assigned to the 506th Regimental Combat Team led to the capture of four of the top ten Iraqi Shi'ite insurgents known to be operating in the unit's area of operations. The commander of the small and overworked team reported that his platoon "continues to exploit and unravel insurgent networks in Eastern Baghdad which is saving American and Iraqi lives every day."[66]

But arguably, SIGINT's greatest single success in Iraq occurred on the evening of June 7, 2006, when al Qaeda in Iraq leader al-Zarqawi and five others were killed by an air strike conducted by two U.S. Air Force F-16 fighter-bombers on al-Zarqawi's safe house five miles north of the city of Baquba. The U.S. military, in celebrating this success, may have gone too far—it revealed and compromised the means used to track al-Zarqawi down, a combination of SIGINT (cell phone interception), HUMINT, and imagery collected by unmanned reconnaissance drones. SIGINT tracked the movements of al-Zarqawi's spiritual adviser, Sheikh Abd al-Rahman, by tapping his cell phone and tracing his movements. HUMINT found the safe house where al-Zarqawi was hiding. And imagery intelligence determined with pinpoint accuracy the coordinates of the house, which was struck by laser-guided bombs dropped by the F-16s.[67]

But as of the end of 2006, SIGINT had "won battles," a now-retired senior Marine Corps officer said, "but it did not get us any closer to winning the war."[68]

It was not until spring of 2007, four years after the U.S. invasion of Iraq, that SIGINT finally hit its stride, producing some of the best intelligence then available to U.S. commanders about the identities and locations of Iraqi insurgents. Concurrent with the beginning of the U.S. Army's "surge" operation in and around Baghdad, SIGINT suddenly became a critically important tool to locate and destroy insurgent cells operating in the Baghdad area and in al-Anbar Province to the west. A large part of the credit for SIGINT's increasing effectiveness was due to the efforts of navy captain Steve Tucker, who since February had held the position of chief of NSA's Cryptologic Services Group (CSG) Baghdad, which was situated in the Al-Faw Palace, west of Baghdad. By the time Tucker arrived, CSG Baghdad had ballooned into NSA's largest overseas liaison organization, consisting of 116 military personnel and NSA civilians in Baghdad and ten locations throughout Iraq. It was responsible for feeding national and tactical-level SIGINT not only to the commander of U.S. forces in Iraq, but also to three division headquarters and twelve brigade staffs, as well as to the headquarters of the secretive Combined Joint Special Operations Task Force, which controlled all U.S. military special forces in Iraq.[69]

But most of the credit for SIGINT's increased effectiveness on the battlefield, according to senior U.S. military and intelligence officials, goes to the new commander of U.S. military forces in Iraq, General David Petraeus, who assumed command of U.S. forces in January 2007. According to sources familiar with U.S. intelligence operations in Iraq, Petraeus, who was acutely aware of the vital importance of intelligence, especially SIGINT, in counterinsurgency warfare, went out of his way to understand how the technology worked, and as a result, made much more effective use of SIGINT against the Iraqi insurgents than his predecessors had.[70]

In part, this was due to the introduction of far more effective equipment like a new intercept system called Prophet Triton, which arrived in Iraq in August 2006 and reportedly revolutionized army SIGINT units' ability to identify and locate the origins of enemy cell phone communications. This system proved to be an extremely valuable intelligence source during the surge counterinsurgency in Baghdad in the summer of 2007.[71] Also arriving on the Iraqi battlefield in 2007 were other newly developed SIGINT collection systems—Cellex, DangerMouse, Searchlite, and SIGINT Terminal Guidance, all of which have improved the U.S. Army's ability to intercept and locate the origins of the cell phone calls of Iraqi insurgents and allied foreign fighters from al Qaeda in Iraq. One of the most advanced of the new systems is an NSA-designed piece of equipment called simply RT-10—but the high-quality intercept intelligence it produces is made available only to selected army and marine commanders and their intelligence staffs.[72]

There have also been some significant changes in tactics that have made SIGINT a more effective tool for field commanders in Iraq. For example, small mobile teams of military SIGINT collectors carrying the newly arrived SIGINT gear now routinely accompany army and marine "door kickers" on missions throughout Iraq. The dangerous job of these teams is to locate the nearby hiding places of Iraqi insurgent fighters so that the patrols they are with can find the bad guys as they talk on their phones. Navy SIGINT teams called Joint Expeditionary SIGINT Terminal Response Units (JESTRs) are assigned to the army brigades in Baghdad tasked with working "the streets to find, fix and finish insurgents."[73]

Another example of a recent positive development has been the successful use of navy SIGINT operators by the elite Navy SEAL team in Iraq, which is permanently based at Camp Dublin, outside Baghdad. The team has its own dedicated Tactical Cryptologic Support team of SIGINT operators, whose job it is to accompany SEAL team members on their combat missions inside Baghdad, protecting them by scanning known enemy frequencies for insurgent threats as well as locating insurgent cell phone emitters so that they can be attacked by the navy special operators.[74] But the work is highly dangerous. On July 6, 2007, one of these navy SIGINT intercept operators, Petty Officer First Class Steven Daugherty, was killed when an improvised explosion device (IED) exploded under his Humvee during an extraction mission inside Sadr City, the sprawling Shi'ite slum in east Baghdad. Also killed in the blast were two other members of SEAL Team Two.[75]

After General Petraeus took command of U.S. forces in Iraq, the army and marines started to use SIGINT in innovative ways to locate Iraqi insurgent IED teams before they could detonate their weapons. Since May 2003, insurgents have launched over eighty-one thousand IED attacks on U.S. and allied forces, killing or wounding thousands of U.S. troops. The U.S. military's efforts to combat the use of IEDs have not been particularly successful; as one senior CENTCOM officer put it, "Hell, we're getting our ass kicked."[76]

From the beginning, Iraqi insurgent IED teams have used spotters equipped with walkie-talkies or cell phones to warn bomb teams when an American convoy is approaching the hidden location of an IED. In order to try to pick up these spotter transmissions, American military convoys in Iraq and patrols in Afghanistan include a Stryker armored vehicle or Humvee with a SIGINT intercept operator who scans the airwaves searching for transmissions from insurgent IED teams targeting the convoy. Since 2005, there have been a growing number of instances where these SIGINT operators, who are sometimes referred to as "convoy riders," have been able to provide advance warning that their convoy is about to be hit by an IED strike.[77]

And as time has gone by and American military commanders have increased their understanding of how the insurgents deploy and use their roadside bombs, SIGINT has become increasingly effective in spotting those emplacing the bombs. Beginning in the summer of 2007, the U.S. Army began using convoys as lures to flush out Iraqi insurgent IED teams so that they could be detected and located by SIGINT sensors.[78]

The results on the battlefield spoke volumes about how valuable the much-improved SIGINT collection and processing effort was to the overall success of the surge. According to one source, SIGINT reporting increased by 200 percent between February 2007 and May 2008, leading to the capture or killing of 600 "high-value" insurgent commanders and the capture of 2,500 Iraqi insurgents and foreign fighters.[79] Between October 2007 and April 2008, one NSA SIGINT Terminal Guidance Unit was credited with generating intelligence that led to the capture or killing of 300 insurgents and a 25 percent drop in IED attacks inside Iraq.[80]

What God Hath Wrought

While the security situation in Iraq has improved markedly over the past year and a half, in Afghanistan the resurgent Taliban has made an impressive comeback.

Going into 2007, U.S. and NATO intelligence analysts admitted that the Taliban controlled most of four key provinces in southern Afghanistan—Helmand, Kandahar, Uruzgan, and Zabul—and that U.S. and NATO forces in the region were losing ground against the ten thousand to fifteen thousand well-armed guerrillas they were facing. The increased number and intensity of Taliban attacks in Afghanistan dismayed many senior officials in the U.S. intelligence community. CIA director Michael Hayden admitted that the Taliban "has become more aggressive than in years past" and is attempting "to stymie NATO's efforts in southern Afghanistan."[81]

The major SIGINT problem in Afghanistan is that apart from satellite phones, the Taliban primarily uses ICOM walkie-talkies. NSA's SIGINT collection resources were long ago overshadowed by low-tech tactical radio intercept gear, such as handheld radio scanners wielded by uncleared Afghan interpreters working for the U.S. Army and detecting enemy surveillance or imminent ambushes of U.S. and NATO forces.[82]

SIGINT faces daunting challenges because the resurgent Taliban has gone on the offensive throughout the country. The struggle in 2007 to create a secure environment in Helmand Province pitted British forces backed by paratroopers from the U.S. Eighty-second Airborne Division against an enemy force that had reached a high not seen since the U.S. invasion of Afghanistan in 2001.[83]

Daily attacks on British and Afghan army positions in the Sangin Valley became the norm, and British patrols into the valley routinely made contact with the Taliban shortly after leaving their increasingly isolated firebases. By early summer, the Taliban forces were inching closer to British defensive positions. In June, U.S. Air Force F-15E fighter-bombers were called in to hit Taliban firing positions around the town of Sangin itself "after intercepting communications chatter revealing their [the Taliban's] position."[84] In early July, a journalist who accompanied British troops assaulting a Taliban stronghold north of Sangin reported that when the troops were attacked by a large enemy force, the unit's translators "constantly scanned radios, listening in to Taliban conversation, and not an hour went by without the promise of an attack. 'The British are walking—get ready,' one intercept said."[85]

Still, thanks in part to SIGINT, the Taliban has suffered severe losses. In May 2007, British commandos killed the Taliban's senior military commander, Mullah Dadullah, a successful operation directly attributable to a systematic effort by British and American SIGINT collectors to track his movements in Helmand Province by monitoring his satellite phone calls and those of his brother Mansour, also a senior Taliban field commander.[86]

But the security situation in Helmand continued to deteriorate as the Taliban became increasingly aggressive in its attacks on understrength British forces, which were largely unable to hold the ground they took from the Taliban. In early December, British and Afghan forces launched an offensive and recaptured the strategically important town of Musa Qa'leh, which had been held by the Taliban since February, but it remained to be seen if it could be held.[87]

The same thing has been happening virtually everywhere else in southern Afghanistan. The Chora District, in Uruzgan Province, for example, is a longtime Taliban stronghold that has consistently defied the best efforts of the Dutch military to reduce it. Intelligence sources, using a combination of HUMINT and SIGINT, confirm that Chora, like many of the surrounding districts, is for all intents and purposes a Taliban base area and sanctuary, with SIGINT confirming that there was a sizable contingent of foreign fighters, mostly Pakistanis, operating in the area. But SIGINT has also confirmed that most of the Taliban guerrillas in the area are now local villagers who remain militarily active all year round instead of retreating to Pakistan before the on-set of winter, as the Taliban has done in the past.[88]

American SIGINT resources have been used to provide the Dutch with air strikes and surveillance, using radio chatter to pinpoint Taliban positions iden-tified by the intercepts. One U.S. Air Force poststrike report notes, "Insurgent communications chatter ceased after the attack."[89]

The military situation in neighboring Kandahar Province, garrisoned by twenty-five hundred Canadian troops, also deteriorated sharply in 2007. By September, the Taliban had retaken all the districts southwest of the city of Kandahar that British and Canadian forces had captured at great cost a year earlier. The inability of the numerically weaker Canadian and Afghan forces to hold on to the territory that they are responsible for led the com-mander of Canadian forces in Kandahar Province, Brigadier General Guy Laroche, to tell reporters that despite efforts to push out the Taliban, "every-thing we have done in that regard is not a waste of time, but close to it, I would say."[90]

SIGINT has also confirmed that the Taliban has expanded its efforts into other, previously quiet provinces, such as Kunar, in the mountainous north-eastern region of Afghanistan. SIGINT has revealed that the Taliban is able to respond rapidly to U.S. and NATO offensives there. During one operation, SIGINT showed that as soon as helicopters deposited U.S. troops on the floor of the Korengal Valley, the Taliban knew they were there and began tracking them. Reporter Sebastian Junger, who accompanied the paratroopers as they moved into the village of Aliabad, recounted, "The platoon radioman has just received word that Taliban gunners are watching us and are about to open fire. Signals intelligence back at the company headquarters has been listening in on the Taliban field radios. They say the Taliban are waiting for us to leave the village before they shoot."[91]

In early November 2007, the Taliban invaded Herat and Farah, in western Afghanistan, both previously quiet provinces that abut the Iranian border. In a mere ten days, Taliban forces captured three districts in Farah without any resistance from the local Afghan police. In neighboring Herat, a series of high-profile attacks on Afghan government forces and police stations sig-naled that the province had become "active."[92]

A sure sign that the military situation in Afghanistan has deteriorated significantly since the beginning of 2007 is the fact that Taliban guerrilla teams are now operating in the provinces surrounding Kabul.[93] Intercepts reveal a dramatic increase in the volume of known or suspected Taliban radio and satellite phone traffic emanating from Ghazni and Wardak Provinces, south of Kabul, and even from within the capital itself since the spring of 2007.[94]

SIGINT, together with other intelligence sources, shows that the Taliban guerrilla forces are becoming larger, stronger, and more aggressive on the battlefield. Intercepts have shown that despite heavy losses among their senior leadership, the Taliban guerrilla teams inside Afghanistan are now led by a new generation of battle-hardened field commanders who have demonstrated unprecedented tenacity and resilience.

The Taliban now possesses a large and robust communications system connecting senior Taliban commanders in northern Pakistan with their guerrilla forces inside Afghanistan. SIGINT indicates that this system has also been used to coordinate the movement of increasing volumes of supplies and equipment from Pakistan into Afghanistan. SIGINT has also provided ample evidence that the Taliban has largely negated the U.S. Army's advantage in superior mobility by carefully monitoring the activities taking place at U.S. and NATO bases in southern Afghanistan. At one isolated American firebase in Zabul Province, intercept operators noted that as soon as a patrol left the base's front gate, there was a spike in Taliban walkie-talkie traffic. "The Americans have just left. They're coming this way. We will need more reinforcements if they approach any closer," one intercepted Taliban radio transmission said.[95] An American soldier serving in Zabul Province wrote a letter home in July 2007 that gives a sense of the problem: "We cannot go anywhere without the [Taliban] being aware of our movements . . . . Their early warning is through the villagers who either by cell phone, satellite phone or ICOM radio inform [Taliban] forces of our movements and the make-up of our convoy."[96]

More than 5,300 people died in Afghanistan in 2007 as a result of increased Taliban attacks, making it the deadliest year since the U.S. invasion of the country in the fall of 2001.[97] The casualty toll for American troops in Afghanistan in 2007 hit 101 dead, a new record surpassing the 93 American troops killed there in 2005. Reports indicate that 87 American troops were killed there in 2006.[98]

Today, the outlook in Afghanistan is grim. In February 2008, Mike McConnell, now the director of national intelligence, told Congress that contrary to the rosier prognosis coming out of the Pentagon, the Taliban now controlled 10 percent of the country, including most of the Pashtun heartland in southern

Afghanistan. Lieutenant General David Barno, who commanded U.S. forces in Afghanistan for twenty-eight months from 2003 to 2005, admitted that the military situation there had deteriorated markedly in recent times, writing in an internal U.S. Army journal that recent developments "in all likelihood do not augur well for the future of our policy goals in Afghanistan."[99]

CHAPTER 16

Crisis in the Ranks

The Current Status of the
National Security Agency

*Secret services are the only real measure of a
nation's political health, the only real
expression of its subconscious.*
                    —JOHN LE CARRÉ, *TINKER, TAILOR,*
                                      SOLDIER, SPY

The Arrival of Keith Alexander

In April 2005, Lieutenant General Mike Hayden stepped down as director of
NSA to become the first deputy director of national intelligence. Then, a year
later, he became the director of the CIA. Meanwhile, on August 1, 2005, a new
director of NSA arrived at Fort Meade. He was fifty-three-year-old Lieutenant
General Keith Alexander, who before coming to NSA had been the U.S.
Army's deputy chief of staff for intelligence since 2003.[1]

A career army intelligence officer, Alexander was born and raised in Syra-
cuse, New York. He graduated from West Point in 1974, then spent the next
twenty years holding a series of increasingly important army intelligence
posts. Alexander served as the director of intelligence of CENTCOM at
MacDill Air Force Base, in Florida, under General Tommy Franks from 1998
to 2001, directing all intelligence operations relating to the invasion of Afghanistan. He was then promoted to be commander of the U.S. Army Intelligence and Security Command at Fort Belvoir, in Virginia, a position he held
from 2001 to 2003.[2]

Explosion

On December 16, 2005, the lead article in the *New York Times*, by James Risen and Eric Lichtblau, was titled "Bush Lets U.S. Spy on Callers Without Courts." The article instantly became a national sensation, revealing the broad outlines of a secret eavesdropping program run by NSA to find al Qaeda operatives, but not many of the specifics. The most explosive aspect of the article was the revelation that for four years NSA had monitored the communications of Americans without obtaining warrants from the Foreign Intelligence Surveillance Court (FISC), which are ordinarily required in order to conduct any form of surveillance inside the United States.[3]

The article produced a firestorm of controversy, further poisoning the already rancorous political environment in Washington, in which the White House and the Republicans, who controlled Congress, were pitted against the Democratic minority. The revelations were particularly embarrassing to CIA director George Tenet and former NSA director Hayden, who had, in a joint appearance five years earlier before the House intelligence committee, stated in unequivocal terms that NSA did not engage in spying on U.S. citizens. Tenet had told the committee, "We do not collect against US persons unless they are agents of a foreign power . . . We do not target their conversations for collection in the United States unless a Foreign Intelligence Surveillance Act (FISA) warrant has been obtained . . . And we do not target their conversations for collection overseas unless Executive Order 12333 has been followed and the Attorney General has personally approved collection." Hayden had described earlier news reports that NSA was engaged in monitoring the communications of U.S. citizens as an "urban myth," and had assured the committee that NSA would assiduously abide by the legal strictures on such activities as contained in 1978's FISA. A little more than a year later, all of these promises would be secretly broken in the aftermath of 9/11.[4]

What We Know

Since that December 2005 *New York Times* article, further information about the nature and extent of the NSA domestic surveillance program has been slow in coming.

It would appear that there are between ten and twelve programs being run by NSA dealing directly in some fashion with the agency's warrantless SIGINT efforts, including at least a half-dozen strictly compartmentalized SIGINT collection, processing, analytic, and reporting projects handling different operational aspects of the problem. For example, there is a special unit located within NSA's Data Acquisition Directorate that is responsible for collecting the vast number of overseas e-mails, personal messaging communications, wire transfers, airplane reservations, and credit card transactions that transit through the United States every day because they are carried over lines owned by American telecommunications companies or Internet service providers. In addition to the five or six compartmented "core" collection and analytic programs, there are another five or six "support" or "rear-end" programs performing research, development, engineering, computer support, and security functions in support of the "front-end" operational units. All of these program units are kept strictly segregated from the NSA SIGINT Directorate's other foreign intelligence collection efforts.[5]

The only one of these NSA programs that the Bush administration has publicly acknowledged is the warrantless eavesdropping program, which the White House labeled in 2005 as the Terrorist Surveillance Program (TSP). All other aspects of NSA's SIGINT collection work that touch on the domestic front have remained unacknowledged. For example, the White House has refused to acknowledge NSA's parallel data-mining program, code-named Stellar Wind, which sifts through vast amounts of electronic data secretly provided by America's largest telecommunications companies and Internet service providers, looking for signs of terrorist activity at home and abroad.

Intense and unwavering secrecy has been the hallmark of these programs since their inception, and even the number of people at NSA headquarters who know the details of the operations has deliberately been kept to a minimum for security reasons. Each of these programs operates from inside its own special "red seal" work center at Fort Meade, meaning that those NSA employees cleared for these specific programs must pass one at a time through a booth containing a retinal or iris scanner and other biometric sensors before they can get inside their operations center.

Interviews with over a dozen former and current U.S. government officials reveal that the number of people within the U.S. government and intelligence community who knew anything about the NSA programs prior to their disclosure by the *New York Times* was very small. The men in the White House who managed the NSA effort, Vice President Dick Cheney and his chief legal counsel, David Addington, strictly regulated who within the U.S. government could have access to information about the eavesdropping programs, restricting clearance to just a select few senior government officials in the White

House and the Justice Department, all of whom were deemed to be "loyal" by Cheney's office, and as such, unlikely to question the programs' legality.[6]

A book by a former senior Justice Department official, Jack Goldsmith, and interviews conducted for this book reveal that a large number of senior officials inside the U.S. government with a "need to know" were deliberately excluded by Cheney's office from having access to information concerning the NSA eavesdropping programs. With the exception of four senior officials, all Justice Department employees were barred from access to details concerning the programs by order of Cheney's office, including Deputy Attorney General Larry Thompson and the Justice Department's Civil and Criminal Divisions.[7] Even the attorney general of the United States himself experienced great difficulty getting essential information about the programs from Cheney's office. Attorney General John Ashcroft, who was one of the few U.S. government officials cleared for access to the programs by the White House, complained in 2004 that "he was barred from obtaining the advice he needed on the program by the strict compartmentalization rules of the WH [White House]."[8] Ashcroft was not alone. Goldsmith noted, "I too faced resistance from the White House in getting the clearance for the lawyers I needed to analyze the program."[9]

Within the U.S. intelligence community, virtually no one was granted access to information about the eavesdropping programs, such as the legal briefs written by White House counsel Alberto Gonzales and Justice Department lawyer John Yoo that justified the program. At the top of the list of people who were *not* permitted to see the Gonzales and Yoo legal briefs were the lawyers in NSA's Office of General Counsel responsible for ensuring that the eavesdropping programs conformed with the law. Goldsmith said, "Before I arrived in O.L.C. [the Justice Department's Office of Legal Counsel], not even NSA lawyers were allowed to see the Justice Department's legal analysis of what NSA was doing." Other senior NSA officials responsible for ensuring the probity of NSA's domestic eavesdropping programs were also denied access to the Gonzales and Yoo legal briefs. In late 2003, two years after the programs began, NSA's inspector general asked for permission to see the Justice Department legal brief authorizing the program, but his request was denied by David Addington.[10]

But of greater importance is that former NSA director Hayden, in trying to defend the legality of the program, has publicly stated that three of NSA's top lawyers assured him in late 2001 that the agency's domestic eavesdropping programs were legal. One has to wonder how NSA's Office of General Counsel could possibly have arrived at this conclusion if the agency's lawyers could not see the documents that served as the legal underpinnings for the programs. Past and present NSA officials interviewed for this book, while refusing to comment specifically on the legality of the agency's domestic eavesdropping programs, confirmed that key NSA operational personnel were never permitted to see these documents, a fact that gave a number of senior NSA officials more than a little cause for concern.[11]

One of the most controversial aspects of the NSA program has been the nagging question of how many people have had their telephone calls and e-mails monitored by NSA since the program commenced after 9/11. The *New York Times'* December 2005 article indicated that the answer was "hundreds, perhaps thousands, of people inside the United States." According to anonymous government officials quoted by the reporters, NSA "eavesdrops without warrants on up to 500 people in the United States at any given time . . . . Overseas, about 5,000 to 7,000 people suspected of terrorist ties are monitored at one time."[12] A *Washington Post* article, citing "two knowledgeable sources," claimed that the number of Americans monitored by NSA was as high as five thousand people between 2001 and early 2006.[13] But U.S. government officials, including Hayden, denied that the number of people being monitored by the agency was anywhere near this large. In an August 2007 interview with the *El Paso Times*, the director of national intelligence, Admiral Mike McConnell, said that the number of NSA eavesdropping targets inside the United States was "100 or less. And then the foreign side, it's in the thousands."[14]

Regardless of the number of American citizens actually monitored since the NSA warrantless eavesdropping program began seven years ago, a number of former NSA officials have expressed concern that the number of targets inside the United States reportedly being monitored appears to be overly large when compared with the actual threat, given that there have been no terrorist attacks in the United States since 9/11, nor any high-profile arrests of al Qaeda "sleeper cells" or operatives. These officials then wonder how so many individuals in the United States could conceivably have been under active surveillance by NSA over the past seven years with virtually no arrests or convictions to show for all the effort.[15]

There is as yet no evidence that the White House used NSA to target the communications of Americans for political purposes. But there are some worrisome signs that the agency's SIGINT reporting may have been misused by some administration officials. In April 2005, a political controversy erupted in Washington when it was learned that the Bush administration's nominee to be the ambassador to the United Nations, John Bolton, had requested from NSA transcripts of intercepted conversations involving or pertaining to other U.S. government officials while he was a senior official at the State Department. NSA admitted that it had made copies of these transcripts, including the names of the American officials involved, available to Bolton.[16] A few weeks later, the magazine *Newsweek* revealed that since January 2004 NSA had received between three thousand and thirty-five hundred requests for transcripts of intercepted communications involving American citizens from various U.S. government departments, four hundred of which came from the State Department. NSA complied with all of these requests. The article indicated that the names of as many as ten thousand Americans were contained in the intercept transcripts turned over to the various U.S. government agencies that had requested them.[17] It was later learned that Bolton, who became the interim ambassador to the United Nations, had personally originated ten requests since January 2004 for unredacted NSA intercept transcripts that mentioned the names of U.S. government officials or American citizens.[18]

Which raises the obvious question of whether the NSA warrantless eavesdropping programs have actually accomplished anything for the billions of dollars spent on them. In justifying the need for the warrantless eavesdropping programs, President Bush, former NSA director Hayden, and other senior administration officials repeatedly stressed that the program had delivered critically important intelligence, but naturally they have provided no details. All Hayden admitted is that the program "has been successful in detecting and preventing attacks inside the United States."[19] By far the strongest defense of the program has come from former vice president Cheney, who in December 2005, while on a visit to Pakistan, told a reporter from CNN that it "has saved thousands of lives."[20]

But to date, the only arrest of an al Qaeda terrorist in the United States that the NSA warrantless eavesdropping program supposedly was involved in was that of Iyman Faris, a thirty-eight-year-old truck driver in Columbus, Ohio, who was caught in March 2003 planning to destroy the Brooklyn Bridge, in New York City. A native of Pakistan but a naturalized American citizen, Faris pleaded guilty to helping al Qaeda plan terrorist attacks in the United States and in October 2003 was sentenced to twenty years in prison.[21]

Former U.S. intelligence officials have confirmed that Faris was identified as an al Qaeda "sleeper" based largely on data provided by NSA. The trail that led to him began just before dawn on January 9, 2003, when Pakistani police stormed a house in the upscale Karachi suburb of Gulshan-i-Maymar that belonged to a senior member of Jamaat-i-Islami, a Pakistani radical Islamic organization. The occupants of the apartment threw two hand grenades at the police. One went off harmlessly. The other failed to detonate because the man who threw it forgot to pull the pin. After a brief struggle, the police arrested and hustled away for interrogation two men—an Egyptian and a Yemeni. Under interrogation, both men admitted to being former al Qaeda fighters in Afghanistan who had fled to Pakistan after the U.S. invasion of that country. CIA and FBI officials who participated in the interrogations of both men in Karachi identified the Egyptian, who told the police his name was Abu Umar, as a senior deputy to Ayman al-Zawahiri, Osama bin Laden's Egyptian-born deputy. The assault on the apartment had resulted from NSA's intercepting satellite phone calls coming into the apartment from al Qaeda operatives throughout the Middle East. Seized in the raid were more than thirty thousand dollars in cash and Abu Umar's satellite phone, which, when its data was downloaded, proved to be a treasure trove of intelligence for the CIA.[22]

From the calling data contained in the phone's memory, NSA was able to determine that a senior al Qaeda leader was operating somewhere in the vicinity of the Pakistani city of Rawalpindi. In February 2003, intercepted e-mails and satellite telephone communications led U.S. and Pakistani security officials to the hideout in Rawalpindi of the al Qaeda mastermind of the 9/11 attacks, Khalid Sheikh Mohammed. At four A.M. on March 1, heavily armed Pakistani security forces burst into Mohammed's hideout and arrested him and another key al Qaeda operative, Mohammed Ahmed al-Hawsawi. A former NSA intelligence analyst confirmed that Faris was identified as an al Qaeda sleeper in the United States based on data downloaded from Khalid Sheikh Mohammed's cell phone and laptop computer seized in the raid.[23]

Despite the identification and arrest of Faris, a number of former U.S. intelligence officials disagree with statements emanating from the White House about the "vital importance" of the NSA warrantless eavesdropping program, believing that these statements grossly overstate its actual accomplishments. Details are admittedly lacking, but a few former intelligence analysts have hinted that the program has been useful in helping stop a number of terrorist attacks overseas, but there appears to be little evidence of major successes against al Qaeda or other terrorist organizations inside the United States since 9/11. When asked for his impression of the value of the eavesdropping program, a recently retired senior CIA official stated, "We spent a ton on the [NSA] program, but got back very little in the way of solid returns . . . I don't think it was worth the money."[24]

Then there is the equally contentious issue of what role America's largest telecommunications companies played in assisting NSA. The first hint that these companies had assisted the agency's warrantless eavesdropping effort appeared in a follow-up December 2005 *Times* article by Eric Lichtblau and James Risen, which reported that "the NSA has gained the cooperation of American telecommunications companies to obtain backdoor access to streams of domes-

tic and international communications." According to the article, this vast
pipeline of raw telephone and e-mail data was being systematically combed by
NSA analysts using the agency's data-mining software "in search of patterns
that might point to terrorism suspects."[25]

In May 2006, the next bombshell hit when *USA Today* revealed that a number of the largest American telecommunications companies, including AT&T,
MCI, and Sprint, had closely collaborated with NSA in the warrantless eavesdropping program. Only Qwest, the nation's fourth-largest telecommunications
company, had refused to participate in the program, despite repeated requests
by NSA. At about the same time, an AT&T technician revealed that the telecommunications giant he worked for had allowed NSA to place eavesdropping
equipment inside its network switching centers in San Francisco and Atlanta,
through which much of America and the world's e-mail traffic passes. This may,
in fact, be the tip of the iceberg, since a number of key American telecommunications companies other than AT&T have refused to answer questions from reporters about whether they too cooperated with NSA's domestic eavesdropping
effort.[26]

Of what little is definitively known about what the telecommunications companies did on behalf of NSA is that they refused to cooperate without a letter
from the U.S. Justice Department assuring them that their efforts on behalf of
NSA were proper and legal. This exact situation had played out fifty-six years
earlier when, in August 1945, NSA's predecessor, the Army Security Agency,
asked America's "Big Three" cable companies to give it access to all international telegraph traffic coming in and out of the United States as part of a Top
Secret program called Shamrock. The U.S. Army knew from the outset that the
program was highly illegal and dangerous, but senior military officials concluded that the risks were worth it to get at the raw traffic.[27] Under extraordinary
pressure from Washington, the cable companies reluctantly agreed to cooperate, but only if the U.S. government would immunize them against any civil or
criminal actions if the operation was uncovered. But back then, the U.S. government could find no way to give the companies the legal protection they were demanding without new legislation, which would have required telling Congress
what they were up.[28]

But unlike this Cold War attempt at domestic eavesdropping, the telecommunications companies this time got what they wanted. Assistant Attorney
General Kenneth Wainstein, testifying before Congress on October 31, 2007,
admitted, "There were letters that went out to these companies that said very
forcefully this is being directed, this is directed by the president, and this has
been deemed lawful at the very highest levels of the government." None of the

letters sent to the companies have been released, but a number of Washington-based attorneys familiar with the matter confirmed that the letters exist and serve as the companies' chief legal defense against the charge that they violated state and federal laws.[29] A Washington-based official representing one of the companies confirmed that his client has in its files almost seven years of accumulated correspondence from the Justice Department assuring the company that its cooperation with NSA was legal and proper, with a new letter arriving from Washington every forty-five days reiterating that the company's work on behalf of the U.S. government continued to be required.[30]

Naturally, the telecommunications companies will neither confirm nor deny their participation in the NSA program, but AT&T and the other companies have repeatedly stated that as a matter of policy they cooperate with all lawful requests made of them by U.S. law enforcement agencies. The companies have furiously fought in the courts attempts by state regulators and private citizens to determine if they improperly provided NSA with calling information for their customers. They have also lobbied intensively, with full White House support, to have Congress immunize them from any civil or criminal liabilities that may have extended from their participation in the NSA domestic eavesdropping program.[31]

But questions have mounted among NSA officials because of the strenuous efforts by the Bush administration to persuade Congress to grant retroactive immunity from both civil suits and criminal prosecution to all of the American telecommunications companies that have participated in NSA's domestic eavesdropping programs. The problem was that until October 2007 the White House would not tell Congress what the companies had done as part of the programs, so Congress was placed in the surreal position of being asked to give complete immunity to the telecommunications companies without knowing what it was that they had done.[32]

Then, to the shock of many, in October 2007 the House and Senate intelligence committees, now controlled by the Democrats, bowed to White House pressure and intense lobbying by the telecommunications companies and, after being given limited access to classified documents concerning the role played by the companies in the NSA domestic eavesdropping effort, approved a proposal to give the companies the full immunity they wanted. The immunity deal was approved by Congress in 2008.[33]

Former NSA officials believe that just as with the ASA Shamrock program of the Cold War, the telecommunications companies knew that what they were doing was illegal from the very beginning. As one NSA retiree put it, "why then would they need immunity if what they did was legal?" After reading a spate of newspaper reports on the subject, a disgusted NSA official said, "They keep trying to give the telecoms a 'Get Out of Jail Free' card. That tells me there is something illegal about what the companies have been doing. [The immunity deal] stinks to high heaven."[34]

But Is It Legal?

Much of the debate since the first New York Times article came out in December 2005 has focused on the legality of the NSA warrantless domestic eavesdropping program. Its legal ramifications are immense and of enormous consequence for every American.

At the center of this debate are a number of still-classified legal briefs written by then–White House legal counsel (and subsequently Attorney General) Alberto Gonzales and Justice Department lawyer John Yoo, which served as the legal rationale and underpinning of the NSA program. Gonzales, who authored one of these Top Secret documents, eventually disclosed that the central argument of his brief, and of Yoo's brief, is that in time of war there are, in his opinion, no restrictions on what the president of the United States can or cannot do in the name of national security. Gonzales's and Yoo's legal briefs essentially argue that the president's expansive wartime powers gave him the authority to bypass the Foreign Intelligence Surveillance Court and order NSA to conduct warrantless surveillance operations without reference to the FISC. In essence, the briefs argue that the president's wartime powers trump the Fourth Amendment of the Constitution, which is supposed to protect Americans against unwarranted searches and seizures. This interpretation of the president's war powers also served as the legal justification for the CIA's highly sensitive counterterrorist intelligence-gathering effort referred to within the U.S. intelligence community solely by the initials "GST."[35]

The problem is that these legal briefs fly in the face of over two hundred years of this nation's constitutional case law, which has found that even in time of war there are indeed constitutional limits on the powers of the presidency. The American Bar Association and a host of prominent American constitutional scholars from all political denominations have argued that there is no court decision or legal precedent that supports President Bush's contention that his constitutional authority allows him to override or disregard an act of Congress or the Constitution. This argument was laid out in a lengthy February 2, 2006, letter to Congress written by fourteen distinguished constitutional law scholars, including Harold Hongju Koh, the dean of Yale Law School, and the former heads of the Stanford and University of Chicago law schools, who wrote,

> The argument that conduct undertaken by the Commander-in-Chief that has some relevance to "engaging the enemy" is immune from congressional regulation finds no support in, and is directly contradicted by, both case law and historical precedent. Every time the Supreme Court has confronted a statute limiting the Commander-in-Chief's authority, it has upheld the statute. No precedent holds that the President, when acting as Commander-in-Chief, is free to disregard an Act of Congress, much less a criminal statute enacted by Congress, that was designed specifically to restrain the President as such.[36]

Interviews reveal that these same concerns are shared by a number of mostly retired NSA officials, some of whom lived through the Church Committee hearings of 1975 on the agency's illegal domestic operations. At the heart of their unease is the fact that many of them just plain don't like spying on Americans, no matter what the stated legal rationale, the predominant feeling being that NSA should remain a strictly foreign intelligence agency and not get caught up in domestic surveillance work. An NSA staffer had this to say in an anonymous e-mail posting sent to a magazine: "It's drilled into you from minute one that you should not ever, ever, ever, under any fucking circumstances turn this massive apparatus on an American citizen. You do a lot of weird shit. But at least you don't fuck with your own people."[37] A retired NSA official, worried about the future ramifications for the agency resulting from the political furor over the its domestic operations, said, "This is just plain cops and robbers stuff . . . This whole thing is a matter for the FBI counter-terrorist types. We shouldn't have anything to do with this at all."[38]

Most of the NSA officials interviewed for this book do honestly believe that the agency's warrantless eavesdropping program and other still-undisclosed NSA intelligence-gathering efforts are a necessary and important component in the fight against al Qaeda. However, a number of them have become increasingly uneasy since that first *New York Times* article about the legality of these programs. One recently retired NSA official wondered why the NSA eavesdropping program could not have been conducted within the strictures of FISA, given the fact that the agency has stated that FISA has in no way hampered its other SIGINT collection operations. For instance, in a March 2005 report to President Bush on the U.S. intelligence community's performance against the Iraqi WMD programs, NSA officials testified that FISA "has not posed a serious obstacle to effective intelligence gathering." It should be noted that at the time that NSA made this statement to the review panel, the agency's secret domestic eavesdropping program, which deliberately bypassed the FISC, had been ongoing for almost three and a half years without the court's knowledge or consent.[39]

Another former senior NSA official was shocked when he read in the newspapers that in May 2006 the Justice Department's Office of Professional Responsibility (OPR) had been forced to shut down an internal investigation into the department's involvement in the NSA eavesdropping program because Vice President Cheney's office had refused to grant the security clearances the investigators needed in order to gain access to documents relating to the program. Only after Michael Mukasey replaced Alberto Gonzales as attorney general in November 2007 did the White House finally relent and grant the security clearances to the OPR investigators.[40]

A small number of NSA officials have been disturbed by the Bush administration loudly and repeatedly arguing that the NSA eavesdropping programs are perfectly legal while at the same time widely using the "state secrets" privilege to quash all lawsuits filed by state regulators and activist groups questioning their legality, contending that any discussion whatsoever in a federal courthouse, even if held in secret, would constitute a threat to the program. Former NSA officials recall that this was the exact same argument used by Nixon administration lawyers during the early 1970s in their unsuccessful effort to prevent the publication of the Pentagon Papers. As it turned out, the publication of the Pentagon Papers caused no meaningful or lasting damage to U.S. national security, but gravely embarrassed the Johnson and Nixon administrations by revealing the tortured path that had led the United States to become involved in the Vietnam quagmire and the mistakes made by the White House in managing the war. This has led many NSA officials to wonder about the legality of these programs. One former senior NSA official whimsically said, "They [the Bush White House] are behaving like they have something to hide rather than something to protect, which scares the shit out of me."[41]

But most disturbing to a number of former and current NSA officials have been the press reports and testimony before Congress by former Justice Department officials revealing that there were significant disagreements between the White House and the Justice Department over the legality of parts of the NSA domestic eavesdropping programs. In May 2007, news reports offered details of an encounter that took place in March 2004 between Justice Department and White House officials at the bedside of Attorney General

John Ashcroft as he lay gravely ill in a room at George Washington University Hospital. What sparked the encounter was Ashcroft deputy James Comey's refusal to reauthorize the NSA domestic eavesdropping program unless substantive changes were made to the underlying authorization order. The White House refused to make the changes and tried to do an end run around Comey by sending White House chief of staff Andrew Card and then–White House legal counsel Gonzales to visit Ashcroft at his bedside and get him to reauthorize the program. Alerted that Card and Gonzales were on their way to see Ashcroft, Comey raced up to the hospital, beating the two White House officials by only a matter of minutes. To his credit, Ashcroft refused to reauthorize the program unless the changes that Comey wanted were made. And to add insult to injury, Ashcroft reminded Card and Gonzales that in his absence, Comey was the attorney general of the United States, leaving unsaid the fact that their attempt at an end run was inappropriate.[42]

After the Comey battle with the White House came out in the press, one currently serving midlevel NSA manager, who was not involved in the warrantless eavesdropping program or related NSA domestic surveillance programs, said, "I wonder what else they're not telling us. It sure as hell doesn't look or smell very good."[43]

A few months later came further revelations that those few Justice Department officials who had been cleared to examine the NSA domestic eavesdropping programs had found the legal justifications for conducting the programs to be at best flawed. The former head of the Justice Department's Office of Legal Counsel, Jack Goldsmith, who reviewed the NSA program in 2003–2004, testified before Congress in October 2007 that he "could not find a legal basis for some aspects of the program," adding, "It was the biggest legal mess I have ever encountered."[44]

Goldsmith's assessment of the legality of the NSA program was confirmed by a number of recent court rulings, including a still-secret March 2007 FISC ruling that found that elements of NSA's domestic eavesdropping effort were illegal. The FISC judge's ruling says, in effect, that certain aspects of NSA's monitoring of foreign communications passing through U.S.-based telephone switching centers and Internet service providers are patently illegal. According to Newsweek, the judge, whose identity remains a secret, concluded "that the [Bush] administration had overstepped its legal authorities in conducting warrantless eavesdropping." As a result, the judge refused to reauthorize the program until such time as it was brought into conformance with FISA.[45]

The Fear of the Unknown

In the end, the fear among a number of retired NSA officers is that the agency's domestic eavesdropping program, in addition to generating much unwanted negative publicity for the agency, almost certainly diverted much-needed manpower and fiscal resources from NSA's foreign-intelligence-gathering mission to what the agency officers generally believe to have been a poorly considered and legally questionable domestic monitoring operation that apparently has produced little in the way of tangible results, despite claims to the contrary from the White House.[46]

Sadly, it seems likely that it will take years before the classified storage vaults are opened and a better understanding of the NSA warrantless eavesdropping program becomes available. Until then, it will be impossible for the American public to fully understand, much less appreciate, the implications of the NSA program and the culture of fear that gave birth to it and continues to sustain it today. Two senior Justice Department officials interviewed for this book, while refusing to provide any specifics, strongly suggested that future public disclosures about the nature and extent of the NSA domestic eavesdropping program will almost certainly raise troubling questions about not only the viability of the program, but also its legality and its overall effectiveness.

But perhaps most troubling of all is the grim acceptance among virtually all of the former and currently serving NSA officials interviewed for this book that, sooner or later, the details of the agency's domestic eavesdropping programs will be disclosed publicly. The concern felt by most of the officials is that the agency, for better or for worse, will bear the brunt of what an NSA retiree called "the frightful harvest" once it becomes known what NSA has done since 9/11. A former NSA official offered this prediction about what the agency is inevitably going to have to face: "There almost certainly will be a host of lawsuits as well as demands for changing existing laws so as to tighten restrictions on what NSA can and cannot do. The pundits will have a field day, and we are going to take it in the pants."[47]

The Uncertain Future

General Keith Alexander inherited an agency in 2005 that was dramatically larger and better funded than that inherited by his predecessor, Mike Hayden. Before the tragic 9/11 terrorist attacks, the thirty-two-thousand-person NSA, with an annual budget of less than four billion dollars, was struggling to transform and modernize itself with only mixed success to show for its efforts.[48] Today, the agency's manpower has topped forty thousand people, and NSA officials indicate that the agency intends to continue with its 2004 project of hiring twelve thousand additional civilian personnel by 2011. NSA's annual budget is now estimated to be in excess of nine billion dollars, having more than doubled in the first five years after the 9/11 terrorist attacks, and press reports indicate that it continues to increase rapidly.[49] If one accepts the publicly reported figures for the size of the U.S. intelligence budget (forty-eight billion dollars as of May 2007), NSA's budget accounts for almost 20 percent of all U.S. intelligence spending, not including the U.S. military's spending on tactical SIGINT programs.[50]

Moreover, the SIGINT empire that NSA controls, known as the U.S. Cryptologic System (USCS), which includes SIGINT personnel assigned to the CIA, the National Reconnaissance Office (NRO), the three military services, and the U.S. Coast Guard, has grown to more than sixty thousand military and civilian personnel since 9/11, making it by far the single largest component of the U.S. intelligence community. NSA is in the process of opening new operations centers in San Antonio, Texas; Denver, Colorado; and Salt Lake City, Utah, which when completed will employ several thousand civilian and military staff.[51] In February 2006, Congress passed an emergency supplemental appropriations bill, which included thirty-five million dollars to immediately expand NSA's huge listening post at Menwith Hill, in northern England, as well as another seven hundred million dollars to construct new operational facilities at the agency's existing intelligence collection stations at Kunia, in Hawaii, and Fort Gordon, in Georgia.[52]

But NSA's power within the U.S. intelligence community is not derived from its massive size and budget, as significant as they may be. Rather, its power stems from the fact that the agency continues to produce the majority of the actionable intelligence coming out of the U.S. intelligence community today. As of 1995, NSA was capable of intercepting the equivalent of the entire collection of the U.S. Library of Congress (one quadrillion bits of information) every three hours, and this figure has increased by several orders of magnitude since 9/11.[53] Prior to the 9/11 disaster, approximately 60 percent of the intelligence contained in the Top Secret *President's Daily Brief*, sent to President Bush every morning, was based on SIGINT coming out of NSA. Today, this number is even higher, as NSA's access to global telecommunications has expanded dramatically since the tragedy.[54]

A number of senior U.S. military officials have recently voiced amazement at both the quantity and the quality of the intelligence that they received from NSA's huge listening post at Fort Gordon, which is now known as NSA/CSS Georgia. One senior U.S. Navy officer who toured the Fort Gordon station in 2006 was stunned by the breadth of the intelligence being produced by the site's intercept operators, linguists, and analysts, including hundreds of linguists speaking ten different dialects of Arabic, as well as Hebrew, Farsi, Pashto and Dari (used in Afghanistan), and the Kurdish dialect spoken in northern Iraq.[55] As one might imagine, the wars in Iraq and Afghanistan dominate much of the SIGINT collection work now being done at Fort Gordon. There was an operations center called Cobra Focus, where many of NSA's best Arabic linguists were producing vitally important intelligence on Iraqi insurgent activities from intercepted cell phone calls relayed to the station via satellite from inside Iraq. Another new operations center, whose cover name is Airhandler, was producing the same kind of intelligence, but concerning Afghanistan. NSA was also running its own highly sophisticated intelligence fusion center inside the operations building called NSA/CSS Geospatial Cell, where agency analysts pulled together all of the SIGINT being collected by the station and other NSA listening posts into a finely tuned written product for the agency's ravenous customers around the world. "I was very impressed," the officer said. "These guys were producing some of the best intelligence available on what the bad guys were up to . . . We were definitely getting our money's worth out of that place."[56]

Other lesser-known NSA success stories include a host of new high-tech collection systems introduced since 9/11 that have allowed the agency to surreptitiously access al Qaeda, Taliban, and Iraqi insurgent telephone, radio, walkie-talkie, e-mail, and text-messaging traffic. For example, one little-known target is the e-mail traffic of known or suspected terrorists; monitoring this traffic is managed by a super-secret NSA office at Fort Meade called Tailored Access Operations (TAO). Working closely with the CIA and other branches of the U.S. intelligence community, TAO identifies computer systems and networks being utilized by foreign terrorists to pass messages. Once these computers have been identified and located, a small group of computer hackers belonging to the U.S. Navy, who call themselves "computer network exploitation operators," assigned to yet another reclusive NSA intercept unit at Fort Meade called the Remote Operations Center (ROC), break into the systems electronically to steal the information contained on the hard drives, as well as monitor the e-mail traffic coming in and out of the computers. Intelligence sources indicate that the TAO/ROC computer search-and-exploitation operations have in a number of instances provided immensely important intelligence about foreign terrorist activities around the world.[57]

Interviews with intelligence officials in Washington suggest that since 9/11 NSA has improved somewhat its sometimes rocky relations with its consumers in Washington and elsewhere around the globe. In the spring of 2001, the position of deputy director for customer relations was created within the agency's SIGINT Directorate to facilitate better communications between NSA and its customers. The first head of this office was Brigadier General Richard Zahner of the U.S. Army.[58] But despite this change, unhappiness has remained. NSA officials contend that since 2001, the ever-increasing number of its customers in Washington has levied conflicting requirements on the agency, whose resolution has necessitated years of often contentious negotiations. Interviews with intelligence officials reveal that there are still widespread complaints about NSA's inability or unwillingness to share information with other government agencies. In particular, FBI officials complain about the lack of cooperation that they have received from NSA since 9/11. The single largest barrier to the free flow of intelligence appears to be the compartmentalized nature of NSA itself, which has prevented an integrated approach to customer relations between NSA and the rest of the U.S. intelligence community.[59]

Problem Areas

Despite the massive budget increases and unfettered operational discretion granted to the agency by the Bush administration since 9/11, General Alexander's NSA remains a deeply troubled organization bedeviled by a host of problems, some of its own making, which pose long-term threats to the agency's viability as the most powerful component of the U.S. intelligence community.

The agency is still spending billions of dollars trying to catch up with the ever-changing and-growing global telecommunications market, and will continue to do so for the foreseeable future. New communications devices, such as the BlackBerry; personal pagers and digital assistants; and, most recently, Skype, the online service that allows people to make low-cost telephone calls through their computers, are all making NSA's job increasingly difficult. Technological changes are taking place so rapidly that even the most stalwart agency defender admits that NSA will have to continue spending ever-increasing sums to try to keep pace. In addition, the wars in Afghanistan and Iraq have forced NSA to spend billions of dollars rebuilding its ability to intercept and locate low-tech walkie-talkie and tactical radio signals, something the agency tried to rid itself of during the late 1990s because NSA officials believed that these were "legacy" skills that would no longer be needed in the twenty-first century.[60]

NSA's constellation of SIGINT satellites in orbit over the earth is in trouble, largely because of foul-ups by program managers at the NRO during the mid-1990s. Faulty satellite designs, constantly changing collection requirements, launch delays, and a few spectacular spacecraft failures have hobbled attempts to put into space a new generation of SIGINT satellites capable of monitoring the kinds of unconventional targets that NSA must now confront. The result has been that over the past decade the agency's SIGINT satellites have not proved to be particularly effective in monitoring insurgent communications traffic in either Iraq or Afghanistan, nor have they been of much use in trying to track down al Qaeda terrorists. Moreover, the enormous amount of time and money needed to redesign and launch the new generation of SIGINT satellites needed to monitor the growing number of cell phone and other personal communications devices is prohibitive.[61]

And despite massive investments in new and costly SIGINT collection technologies since 9/11, NSA is still experiencing a difficult time gaining access to the communications of many of its principal global targets, such as Iran and North Korea, who are increasingly using buried fiber-optic cables to handle important internal communications traffic in lieu of radio. The agency is also finding it increasingly difficult to locate the communications of al Qaeda and other international terrorist organizations, who in recent years have made NSA's job maddeningly difficult by almost completely ceasing to use telephones and radios.[62] A 2005 report to President Bush urged NSA and the rest of the U.S. intelligence community to take more risks, stating, "Regaining signals intelligence access must be a top priority. The collection agencies are working hard to restore some of the access that they have lost; and they've had some successes. And again, many of these recent steps in the right direction are the result of innovative examples of cross-agency cooperation . . . Success on this front will require greater willingness to accept financial costs, political risks, and even human casualties."[63]

This has meant that NSA has had to work, albeit very reluctantly, more closely with its age-old archnemesis, the CIA, in an effort to regain access to these "hard" targets. What outside observers of SIGINT often fail to realize is that in the last fifty years SIGINT has become increasingly dependent on HUMINT for much of its success, leading to what can best be described as a symbiotic relationship between these two intelligence disciplines. Former CIA director John Deutch wrote in the magazine *Foreign Policy*, "Cooperation between human and technical intelligence, especially communications intelligence, makes both stronger. Human sources . . . can provide access to valuable signals intelligence . . . Communications intercepts can validate information provided by a human source."[64]

A few of these extremely risky operations have broken to the surface. In January 1999, the *Boston Globe* and the *Washington Post* revealed that NSA and the CIA had helped to create a covert SIGINT system to aid U.N. weapons inspectors in locating and destroying Iraqi weapons of mass destruction. This clandestine SIGINT collection program began in February 1996 and consisted of commercially available very high frequency (VHF) intercept receivers provided by the CIA being secretly placed inside the U.N. Special Commission (UNSCOM) headquarters at Al-Thawra, in the suburbs of Baghdad. In addition, sophisticated radio scanners hidden inside backpacks were used by the U.N. inspection teams when they operated in the field. This system remained in place until the U.N. weapons inspectors were forced out of Iraq in December 1998.[65] In October 2001, Chinese security officials discovered twenty-seven high-tech listening devices planted throughout a brand-new Boeing 767 that was to serve as the Chinese president's personal aircraft. The security officials even found bugs in the airplane's bathroom and in the headboard of the president's bed. Although the bugging operation was a diplomatic embarrassment, it showed the lengths that the CIA and NSA were willing to go to in order to listen to what the Chinese leader was saying.[66]

But as each of the previous chapters has made clear, historically NSA's Achilles' heel has not been its ability to collect material from around the world. Rather, what has hurt the agency the most has been its inability to process, analyze, and report on the material that it collects. The agency continues to collect far more than it can possibly analyze, and it analyzes more than it actually reports to its customers. In January 2007, NSA director Alexander admitted to Congress that the agency was still experiencing great difficulty coping with the ever-increasing backlog of unprocessed intercepts that were piling up at NSA headquarters at Fort Meade, many of which were intercepts of foreign terrorist message traffic.[67]

Some agency insiders now believe that NSA is only able to report on about 1 percent of the data that it collects, and it is getting harder every day to find within this 1 percent meaningful intelligence. Senior Defense and State Department officials refer to this problem as the "gold to garbage ratio," which holds that it is becoming increasingly difficult and more expensive for NSA to find nuggets of useful intelligence in the ever-growing pile of garbage that it has to plow through. This has raised some questions in the minds of U.S. government officials as to whether all the money being spent on NSA's SIGINT program is a worthwhile investment. Former State Department official Herbert Levin noted, "NSA can point to things they have obtained that have been useful, but whether they're worth the billions that are spent, is a genuine question in my mind."[68]

The Thin Red Line

Today, NSA and the U.S. military's SIGINT units find themselves spread perilously thin. The wars in Iraq and Afghanistan, coupled with the never-ending "global war on terror," continue to eat up the vast majority of NSA's SIGINT collection and processing resources, forcing the agency to give short shrift to many important intelligence targets, such as the former Soviet Union, China, North Korea, Bosnia, and the national narcotics interdiction program. The draining away of resources from North Korea, for example, has been a cause of great concern since 9/11 because the United States admittedly has almost no spies operating there, and from a SIGINT perspective North Korea is an extremely tough target to monitor.[69] The same thing has happened in England since 9/11. The British Parliament's Intelligence and Security Committee in its June 2003 annual report warned that the shift of precious intelligence collection resources from other targets to counterterrorism was creating a dangerous situation, stating, "These reductions are causing intelligence gaps to develop, which may mean over time unacceptable risks will arise in terms of safeguarding national security and in the prevention and detecting of Serious Organised Crime."[70]

NSA has been forced to continue to strip personnel from a number of offices within its SIGINT Directorate at Fort Meade in order to keep its counterterrorism operations going, as well as maintain U.S. and overseas listening posts at full strength. The result has been that the number of complaints from NSA's customers, especially CIA and State Department officials, has risen dramatically in the past several years as more "legacy" targets not connected to the war on terrorism or the insurgencies in Iraq and Afghanistan have suffered for lack of attention and resources.[71] Sources note that NSA's inability to dedicate sufficient resources to monitoring narcotics trafficking in the western hemisphere has forced the small SIGINT organization within the Drug Enforcement Administration (DEA) to largely take over this responsibility.[72] The increasingly important role of the DEA, the CIA, and the military services in the SIGINT field has led, in turn, to the diminishment of NSA's control over the national SIGINT effort. The result has been that NSA has lost somewhat the all-important "centrality of command" that it once enjoyed.[73]

Because of the stress and strain caused by trying to fight three wars simultaneously, there are now persistent and pervasive personnel shortages at NSA
and in the U.S. military SIGINT organizations in virtually every critical specialty. In particular, the agency and the U.S. military have experienced significant problems recruiting and retaining linguists who are fluent enough in the
exotic languages spoken in Iraq and Afghanistan. Attempts by NSA in 2001–
2002 to hire first-generation immigrants living in the United States who speak
Pashto, Urdu, and Dari, the main languages spoken in Afghanistan, immediately ran into roadblocks imposed by the omnipresent security officials, who
forbade their use. An American intelligence officer was quoted as saying,
"NSA cannot get anyone through the background check and vetting process . . . They have created an unachievably high standard for hiring."[74]

The U.S. military's SIGINT units are in even worse shape. The result of declining reenlistment rates and deteriorating morale has been pervasive personnel shortages throughout the military SIGINT components along with a
commensurate decline in unit readiness levels.

Interviews with current and former U.S. military intelligence officials confirm
that the U.S. military's SIGINT system, like the U.S. military as a whole, is deep
in crisis. Resources everywhere are stretched to the limit. Interviews confirm that
the number-one problem facing the military SIGINT system is personnel, or lack
thereof. Over the past six years, frequent and lengthy deployments in Iraq and/or
Afghanistan, coupled with the military's extremely unpopular "stop-loss" policy of
arbitrarily extending terms of service, including those of many SIGINT specialists, such as Arabic linguists, have for all intents and purposes exhausted the military's corps of SIGINT personnel. As a result, attrition rates among military
SIGINT personnel are high and getting worse, with some SIGINT units reporting that more than 50 percent of their first-term recruits are not reenlisting because of the severe hardships associated with repeated tours of duty in Iraq and
Afghanistan. As a result, hundreds of veteran noncommissioned officers and enlisted SIGINT intercept technicians and linguists have chosen to leave the service
because of the strain that frequent deployments are having on their families and
their own mental health. Interviews with over a dozen currently serving military
SIGINT operators reveal that there is one common thread running through their
complaints about current conditions—an all-consuming desire for a sense of nor-
malcy in their lives.[75]

There have also been pervasive equipment shortages to contend with,
brought on by the intensive demands of fighting three wars simultaneously.
These shortages have meant that SIGINT collection equipment has to be kept

in Iraq and Afghanistan, leaving very little for troops to train on upon their return to the United States from their overseas tours of duty. As a result, training and readiness levels of military SIGINT units based in the United States have declined steadily over the past six years. Army and Marine Corps intelligence commanders have confirmed that the equipment in the military's SIGINT units is worn out from nonstop usage in the harsh and unforgiving field environments of Iraq and Afghanistan and is in urgent need of refurbishment or replacement. Moreover, replacement equipment purchases have not kept pace with field losses. Shortages of highly skilled maintenance personnel and spare parts have led to frequent equipment outages at inopportune moments in Afghanistan and Iraq.[76] For example, widespread computer problems meant that the army SIGINT platoon assigned to Forward Operating Base Loyalty in east Baghdad spent the entire month of February 2006 "performing duties not related to their specialty."[77]

These anecdotal conclusions were confirmed by a 2006 report by Major General Barbara Fast, the former commandant of the U.S. Army Intelligence Center at Fort Huachuca, in Arizona, which found that army intelligence specialists were spending more than one year out of every two deployed overseas, and that as a result, reenlistment rates among these specialists, including SIGINT collectors, were falling fast. Many units returning from Iraq were reporting that in addition to being exhausted and short of personnel, they had had to leave behind their equipment, which meant that they had nothing to train with once they got back to the United States. Fast's conclusion was that the intense operations tempo associated with trying to fight three wars simultaneously was "consuming the MI [military intelligence] force."[78]

Searching for a Cure

Today, NSA's modernization programs are, to varying degrees, well over budget and years behind schedule. Recent revelations in the press show that yet another of the agency's hugely expensive modernization programs, Turbulence, has also experienced significant delays and cost overruns, raising doubts within the U.S. intelligence community as to whether it will ever work the way it was originally envisioned. The serious problems being experienced by NSA in bringing this program to fruition prompted intense criticism from members of the Senate intelligence committee during a rare public hearing in March 2007, where they forcefully made clear their concern about where

NSA's transformation efforts were headed, writing, "NSA's transformation program, Trailblazer, has been terminated because of severe management problems, and its successor, Turbulence, is experiencing the same management deficiencies that have plagued the NSA since at least the end of the Cold War."[79]

But these problems may, in fact, be the tip of the iceberg. As strange as it may sound, one of the most urgent problems facing NSA is a severe shortage of electrical power, which threatens to derail the agency's efforts at Fort Meade unless fixed. It will come as no surprise that NSA is a massive consumer of electricity, which, as every American consumer knows, is an increasingly expensive commodity. As of 2000, NSA's annual electricity bill from Baltimore Gas and Electric amounted to twenty-one million dollars. But higher gasoline prices and the continued deterioration of the national electricity grid resulted in NSA's annual bill rising to almost thirty million dollars by 2007.[80] However, the rising cost of electricity is not what is currently strangling NSA. Rather, during the 1990s and post 9/11 era, the agency neglected to build new power generators needed to run the ever-growing number of computers and other high-tech systems that the agency has been buying en masse since 9/11. The situation has become so grave that in many NSA offices at Fort Meade the installation of new computers and data processing systems has been put on hold because there is not enough electricity to run them, and NSA's power grid has become so overtaxed that there have been occasional brownouts of key operational offices for as much as half a day. However, press reports indicate some resistance within the Office of Management and Budget to giving NSA additional funds because the agency has once again failed to provide a detailed accounting of why the money is needed or how it will be spent.[81]

As a result, much of the groundswell of support that NSA once enjoyed inside Congress and the U.S. intelligence community after 9/11 has slowly slipped away as it has become clear that the agency's modernization and reform efforts are not being effectively managed. A former NSA official quoted in a press report said, "Right after Sept. 11 and the ensuing period, I think NSA could have gotten anything they wanted. They lost the support because they didn't handle it properly."[82]

So one of the top items on General Alexander's to-do list today is to try to right the ship and put NSA's internal reforms and modernization efforts back on track, while at the same time increasing the agency's productivity and maintaining its reputation within the U.S. intelligence community. Fixing all of these problems at once will not be easy or cheap. In January 2007, NSA asked Congress for an additional one billion dollars in supplemental funding, and another one billion for 2008. All this was on top of NSA's huge eight-billion-dollar annual budget already approved by Congress.[83]

And yet, despite all the money, resources, and high-level attention being lavished on NSA, there are signs that the agency's "golden days" may be almost over. Agency insiders interviewed for this book understand that following the Bush administration, a greater degree of fiscal austerity and stricter oversight controls will almost certainly return. A now-retired senior NSA official said it best: "I guess we are going to have to go back to the 'bad old days' of doing more with less. It was a great ride while it lasted."[84]

To Live in Perilous Times

NSA in the Obama Administration

The near collapse of the U.S. economy in September–October 2008, followed by the November 4, 2008, election of Barack Obama as the forty-fourth president of the United States, presented a new set of serious problems for NSA's director, Lieutenant General Keith Alexander. The steep downturn of the economy meant that the agency's annual budget submission to Congress had to be completely rewritten to take into account the new climate of fiscal austerity. But it was the president-elect, a former constitutional law professor who had been critical of the Bush administration's domestic eavesdropping programs on the campaign trail, who potentially posed a more serious problem for the agency.

In December 2008, NSA sent classified briefing books to the president-elect and senior members of his national security transition team that explained the agency's mission and capabilities. The documents emphasized that NSA was a completely different organization from the one that existed eight years earlier when George W. Bush had been elected. The empire that NSA commanded had doubled from thirty-two thousand military and civilian personnel in 2001 to more than sixty thousand, and its annual budget has gone from four billion dollars to about ten billion, accounting for roughly 20 percent of all U.S. government spending on foreign intelligence. Billions of dollars had been spent acquiring new hardware and software meant to improve NSA's ability to collect, process, analyze, and report the staggering volume of material intercepted every day. And although there had been costly missteps along the way, this effort was beginning to pay dividends. NSA's intelligence production had rebounded dramatically, and the agency was once again producing much of the best information within the U.S. intelligence community.[1]

The NSA briefing papers emphasized the vital importance of the signals intelligence (SIGINT) produced by the agency since General Alexander had become director in August 2005. NSA's coverage of insurgent e-mails, text messages, and cell phone traffic had been crucial in helping General David Petraeus locate Iraqi insurgent cells operating in and around Baghdad in the spring of 2007, which were then hit by a systematic cyberattack by NSA beginning in May 2007.[2] Then tactical intercept teams belonging to a secretive NSA field unit called the Joint Expeditionary SIGINT Terminal Response Unit (JESTR) helped U.S. military combat units destroy dozens of insurgent cells during the summer and fall of 2007. In Afghanistan, NSA and the U.S. military SIGINT collection efforts against the Taliban were steadily improving. NSA was dedicating more SIGINT collection and analytic resources to monitoring Taliban commanders talking on their cellular and satellite telephones inside Afghanistan and northern Pakistan, and the U.S. military had fielded new airborne and ground-based collection systems that dramatically improved SIGINT coverage of insurgent walkie-talkie communications traffic on Afghan battlefields.

The briefing papers emphasized that these examples were only part of NSA's contribution to the overall national intelligence effort. Several constellations of SIGINT satellites parked in orbit above the earth were providing excellent coverage of a host of key targets, including Iran. More than six hundred intercept operators working for NSA's super-secret Tailored Access Operations office were secretly tapping into thousands of foreign computer systems and accessing password-protected hard drives and e-mail accounts of targets around the world. This highly classified program, known as Stumpcursor, had proved to be critically important during the 2007 surge in Iraq, where it was credited with single-handedly identifying and locating over one hundred Iraqi and al Qaeda insurgent cells in and around Baghdad. Dozens of listening posts hidden inside American embassies and consulates—operated by the joint NSA-CIA SIGINT organization known as the Special Collection Service—were producing excellent intelligence information in areas in Asia, Africa, and the Middle East. Information produced by Green Beret SIGINT teams had been instrumental in helping the Philippine military capture or kill several high-ranking officials of the Muslim extremist group Abu Sayyaf in 2006 and 2007. U.S. Navy SIGINT operators riding on attack submarines were collecting vital intelligence on foreign military forces and international narcotics traffickers as part of a program called Aquador. And the agency was well along in its planning to create a new organization—called United States Cyber Command—that would both attack enemy communications in cyberspace and defend the U.S. telecommunications infrastructure.

But NSA officials still needed to address the agency's controversial domestic eavesdropping programs, which had finally been placed under the control of the Foreign Intelligence Surveillance Court (FISC) in 2007. On July 10, 2008, President Bush had signed into law the Foreign Intelligence Surveillance Act of 1978 Amendments Act of 2008, which granted retroactive immunity from lawsuits to the telecommunications companies who had collaborated with NSA. Obama, then a senator from Illinois, had reluctantly voted for the bill after failing to get the immunity provisions for the telecommunications companies stripped from the legislation. President Bush's director of national intelligence, Admiral Mike McConnell, held a face-to-face meeting with Obama in Chicago in December to try to assuage the president-elect's lingering concerns about the domestic eavesdropping programs. But according to a member of Obama's transition team, when the meeting was over, the president-elect remained troubled by what the agency had done: He was especially concerned with the legality of NSA's domestic spying activities.

After President Obama was inaugurated on January 20, 2009, he and his national security advisers made the decision to focus on the country's more pressing economic problems rather than waste precious political capital by dredging up the misdeeds of the past administration. But on July 10, 2009, the Office of the Director of National Intelligence (DNI) released an unclassified summary of a top-secret report that raised some very serious questions about the legality, effectiveness, and overall value of the NSA domestic eavesdropping programs.[3]

First, the report confirmed that the Justice Department legal briefs written by John Yoo in 2001–2002, which served as the legal predicate for the NSA eavesdropping programs, were filled with so many "serious factual and legal flaws" that they had to be rewritten in their entirety in 2004 in order to bring them into conformance with the law, which raises the obvious question of whether the NSA domestic eavesdropping programs were legal to begin with. Second, the report suggested that the shoddiness of these legal opinions may have jeopardized all of the arrests and/or convictions of terrorist suspects that were based in part on intelligence derived from the NSA eavesdropping. And third, the DNI report cast grave doubts about the claims previously made by former vice president Dick Cheney and NSA director General Michael Hayden about the importance of the NSA domestic eavesdropping to the overall U.S. counterterrorism program. The report revealed that analysts at the National

Counterterrorism Center (NCTC) in McLean, Virginia, could only come up with a few cases where intelligence derived from the NSA eavesdropping programs "may have contributed to a counterterrorism success," and FBI officials stated that the NSA intelligence data "generally played a limited role in the FBI's overall counterterrorism efforts." These were hardly stunning endorsements of the value of the NSA eavesdropping programs given the vast sums of money spent on them to date.

But NSA's eavesdropping programs continue, as evidenced by the revelations that in December 2008 and January 2009, NSA intercepted a dozen or so e-mail messages between a U.S. Army psychiatrist named Major Nidal Malik Hasan and a radical Muslim cleric in Yemen. The messages were examined by FBI agents with the Joint Terrorism Task Force in Washington and deemed not to be sufficiently alarming to warrant further action. On November 5, 2009, Major Hasan killed thirteen of his fellow soldiers at Fort Hood in Texas, and wounded dozens more.

Less than two months later, on Christmas Day 2009, a twenty-three-year old Nigerian named Umar Farouk Abdulmutallab failed to detonate an explosive device sewn into his underwear as his Northwestern Airlines flight from Amsterdam was on final approach to Detroit Metro Airport. In mid-October 2009, NSA intercepted some fragmentary al Qaeda telephone traffic coming from inside Yemen indicating that an unidentified Nigerian was being trained for a planned terrorist attack. On November 18, 2009, Abdulmutallab's father told officials at the U.S. embassy in Abuja, Nigeria, that his son had just sent him text messages from Yemen that showed that the boy had become a jihadi militant. But the analysts at the NCTC somehow failed to connect the reports from the U.S. embassy in Nigeria with the NSA intercepts. So Abdulmutallab's name was not put on the "do not fly" watch list, and he was allowed to board his flight that fateful Christmas morning. As this book goes to print, these unsettling episodes are still under investigation, but both raise a host of troubling questions about who is still being monitored and why, and more importantly, whether the U.S. government's massive security apparatus is capable of identifying impending threats, no matter how much intelligence NSA collects.

January 2010
Washington, D.C.

Acknowledgments

For the past year the National Security Archive in downtown Washington, D.C., has been my home away from home. Without the generous and unstinting support of the archive's director, Tom Blanton, and his staff of dedicated professionals I would not have been able to complete this work. Special thanks go to the archive's general counsel, Meredith Fuchs, and longtime friend Dr. William Burr, both of whom kept me on track and helped me avoid pitfalls in the road.

Three longtime friends and colleagues deserve special thanks for the incredible support they provided me. For the past twenty-five years, Dr. Jeffrey T. Richelson has been a veritable fount of knowledge and wisdom about the U.S. intelligence community, generously providing me with thousands of pages of documents from his collection and pointing me to where more could be found. He is a walking encyclopedia about the U.S. intelligence community. My friend and coauthor Dr. Cees Wiebes did more to push me along than just about anyone else, even if I did not want to go. Every author needs someone like him to keep them honest and their eyes on the prize. And last but not least, I owe a debt of gratitude to my friend and colleague of many years Rosemary Lark, without whom this project would never have been completed.

Over the past twenty-five years, hundreds of individuals freely provided me with documents, leads, and advice. I wish to particularly acknowledge to assistance of the following individuals: Dr. Richard J. Aldrich, Dr. David Alvarez, Joseph S. Bermudez Jr., Dr. Dwayne A. Day, Ralph Erskine, Angela Gendron, Nicky Hager, Seymour M. Hersh, Dr. Robert S. Hopkins, Alf R. Jacobsen, Dr. David Kahn, Miriam A. Kleiman, Dr. Edwin E. Moïse, Dr. Olav Riste, Bill Robinson, Dr. Martin Rudner, Susan Strange, Dr. Athan Theoharis, and Dr. Wesley Wark. Any omissions are purely the fault of the author.

During the past twenty-five years, it has been my pleasure to sit down for lengthy and candid conversations with dozens of former and current officials of the NSA and other agencies of the U.S. intelligence community, many of whom have sadly passed away since I began my research. These men and women helped me sketch out the history of an agency that remains to this day largely invisible, even to those who hold a Top Secret Codeword security clearance. Almost all did so with the understanding that I would not name them, and I have respected their wishes, despite the fact that a number of these individuals have since passed away. Without their help I never would have been able to even begin to understand what NSA does or how important it is.

My heartfelt thanks go to Colonel William J. Williams, USAF (ret.), and his staff at the National Security Agency's Center for Cryptologic History (CCH). The work of the CCH historians runs throughout this history. It is fair to say that this book would not have been possible without them.

And finally, I would also like to extend his most heartfelt thanks to the staff of the National Archives at College Park, Maryland, for helping me conduct my research over the past two decades. I will always remain deeply indebted to the late John E. Taylor, the doyen of military archivists at the National Archives, whose encyclopedic knowledge of the records based on his fifty years at the archives was unparalleled anywhere. His passing in September 2008 at the age of eighty-seven marks the end of an era. The staff of the NARA Library at College Park, especially its amiable head Jeff Hartley, helped me work the CIA's CREST database of declassified documents through many trials and tribulations, and stoically processed the vast amount of declassified documents that I brought to their desks day after day without complaint. They are wonderful people.

My deepest gratitude goes to Peter Ginna, my publisher at Bloomsbury Press, who to his eternal credit took a risk and agreed to publish this book. Michael O'Connor and Pete Beatty did the heavy lifting at Bloomsbury getting this opus ready for publication. Special thanks go to my editor James O. Wade, who performed a Herculean effort to get this manuscript into final form. And last but not least, my agent, Rick Broadhead, worked tirelessly on this project, believing implicitly in the importance of what I was trying to accomplish.

Notes Glossary

AIA	Air Intelligence Agency
ASA	Army Security Agency
CALL	Center for Army Lessons Learned
CCH	Center for Cryptologic History, Fort George G. Meade, Maryland
CNSG	Crane Naval Security Group Archives
DCI	Director of Central Intelligence
DDEL	Dwight D. Eisenhower Library, Abilene, Kansas
DDRS	Declassified Document Retrieval Service
DOCID	Document Identification number
DOD	Department of Defense
FBI	Federal Bureau of Investigations
FOIA	Obtained by Freedom of Information Act request
GPO	Government Printing Office
HCC	Historic Cryptologic Collection, contained in Record Group 457 at the National Archives, College Park, Maryland
HSTL	Harry S. Truman Library, Independence, Missouri
INR	State Department, Bureau of Intelligence and Research
INSCOM	U.S. Army Intelligence and Security Command
JCS	Joint Chiefs of Staff
JFKL	John F. Kennedy Library, Boston, Massachusetts
LBJL	Lyndon Baines Johnson Library, Austin, Texas
NA, CP	National Archives, College Park, Maryland
NARA	National Archives and Records Administration, Washington, D.C.
NIO IIM	National Intelligence Officer Interagency Intelligence Memorandum
NSA OH	NSA Oral History, held by the NSA's Center for Cryptologic History, Fort George G. Meade, Maryland, and obtained through FOIA
PRO	Public Records Office, now National Archives of the United Kingdom, Kew, England
RG-	Record Group
RUMRA	NSA internal designation for the Russian communications target: "RU" = Russia; "M" = Army; "RA" = mainline Morse code circuit
SSA	Signal Security Agency

Notes

PROLOGUE

1. Background and character of Clarke from U.S. Army biographical data sheet, Brigadier General Carter Weldon Clarke, USA (Ret.); interviews with W. Preston Corderman, Frank B. Rowlett, Morton A. Rubin; NSA, oral history, *Interview with Carter W. Clarke*, May 3, 1983; NSA OH-01-74 to NSA OH-14-81, oral history, *Interview with Frank B. Rowlett*, 1976, p. 33, NSA FOIA. See also memorandum, Ohly to McNarney, *Your Proposals with Respect to the Handling of Communications Intelligence and Communications Security*, May 12, 1949, p. 1, RG-330, entry 199, box 97, file: CD 22-1-23, NA, CP; Henry C. Clausen and Bruce Lee, *Pearl Harbor: Final Judgement* (New York: Crown, 1992), p. 24.

2. NSA OH-01-74 to NSA OH-14-81, oral history, *Interview with Frank B. Rowlett*, June 26, 1974, p. 76, NSA FOIA.

3. For the genesis of the SIGINT effort against the USSR in 1943, see Robert Louis Benson and Cecil Phillips, *History of VENONA* (Fort Meade, MD: Center for Cryptologic History, 1995), vol. 1, p. 12, NSA FOIA; Robert Louis Benson and Michael Warner, eds., *VENONA: Soviet Espionage and the American Response, 1939–1957* (Washington, DC: Center for the Study of Intelligence, 1996), p. xiii. For the intense secrecy surrounding the Russian code-breaking effort, see memorandum, Corderman to Taylor, *Draft of "Priorities Schedule,"* March 6, 1943, and memorandum, Taylor to Corderman, *SPSIS 311.5—General—Draft of "Priorities Schedule,"* March 8, 1943, both in RG-457, HCC, box 1432, file: SSS Intercept Priorities, NA, CP; Benson and Phillips, *History of VENONA*, vol. 1, p. 16 and fn27. For the U.S. Navy's parallel SIGINT effort against the Soviet Union, see Naval Communications Activity, *Russian Language Section: July 1943–January 1948*, NSA FOIA via Dr. David Alvarez; Dr. Thomas R. Johnson, *American Cryptology During the Cold War, 1945–1989* (Fort Meade, MD: Center for Cryptologic History, 1995), bk. 1, *The Struggle for Centralization, 1945–1960*, p. 159, NSA FOIA. For the problematic cooperation between the army and navy on the Russian problem, see Thomas L. Burns, *The Origins of the National Security Agency: 1940–1952* (Fort Meade, MD: Center for Cryptologic History, 1990), p. 25, NSA FOIA.

4. SRH-364, *History of the Signal Security Agency, 1939–1945*, vol. 1, p. 139ff, RG-457, entry 9002 Special Research Histories, NA, CP; "Hot Weather Policy," *NSA Newsletter*, June 1956, p. 23; Debbie DuBois, "Those Good Old Days," *NSA Newsletter*, December 1979, p. 7; Jack Gurin, "Dear Old Arlington Hall," *NSA Newsletter*, February 1981, p. 14, all NSA FOIA; "From Coeds to Codewords: How a Girls College Became the Nerve Center for USASA's Global Operations," *Hallmark*, September 1970, p. 8, INSCOM FOIA; "Forty One and Strong: Arlington Hall Station," *INSCOM Journal*, June 1983, pp. 7–12, INSCOM FOIA; U.S. Army Intelligence

and Security Command, *INSCOM and Its Heritage* (Arlington, VA: INSCOM History Office, 1985), Special Historical Series, pp. 137–38, INSCOM FOIA.

5. For keeping the SIGINT effort against the Soviets a secret from the British, see Benson and Phillips, *History of VENONA*, vol. 1, p. 16 and fn27. For details of the British code-breaking effort against the USSR during World War II, including the fact that this operation was kept secret from the United States, see Benson and Phillips, *History of VENONA*, vol. 1, pp. 30–31; Burns, *Origins of the National Security Agency*, p. 25; NSA OH-01-79, oral history, *Interview with Brigadier John H. Tiltman (ret.)*, January 30, 1979, p. 1, NSA FOIA; NSA OH-20-93, oral history, *Interview with Oliver R. Kirby*, June 11, 1993, pp. 10–11, NSA FOIA; handwritten notes labeled "CDR Dunderdale," undated, in OP-20-G organizational file, NSA FOIA.

6. Hallock was one of the first men to excavate the old capital of the Achaemenid civilization at Persepolis in Iran. Recruited into the Signal Security Agency in 1942 because of his linguistic skills, Hallock initially worked on solving Vichy French and German Enigma machine cipher systems before being transferred to the Special Problems Section in 1943. Hallock background from Robert L. Benson, *Introductory History of VENONA* (Fort Meade, MD: Center for Cryptologic History), p. 2; SRH-361, *History of the Signal Security Agency*, vol. 2, *The General Cryptanalytic Problems*, pp. 114, 118, 129, 236, 238, 253, RG-457, entry 9002 Special Research Histories, NA, CP. Hallock was also the author of a number of scholarly books, including *The Chicago Syllabary and the Louvre Syllabary* (Chicago: University of Chicago Press, 1940) and *Persepolis Fortification Tablets* (Chicago: University of Chicago Press, 1969). For details of Hallock's breakthrough, see *Weekly Report for Section B III b9 for Week Ending 1 October 1943*, p. 1; *Weekly Report for Section B III b9 for Week Ending 8 October 1945*, p. 2; *Weekly Report for Section B III b9 for Week Ending 19 November 1945*, p. 1, all in RG-457, HCC, box 1114, file SSA BIII Weekly Reports, NA, CP.

7. David A. Hatch, "Venona: An Overview," *American Intelligence Journal*, vol. 17, nos. 1–2 (1996): p. 72.

8. For change in priorities and expansion of SIGINT effort against neutrals and friendly nations, see memorandum, McCormack to Clarke, *S.S.B. Priorities*, January 26, 1943, RG-457, HCC, box 1432, file: SSS Intercept Priorities, NA, CP; memorandum, Taylor to Clarke and McCormack, *S.S.B. Priorities*, February 3, 1943, RG-457, HCC, box 1432, file: SSS Intercept Priorities, NA, CP; memorandum, Strong to Chief Signal Officer, March 8, 1943, RG-457, HCC, box 1025, file: C/A Solutions, Intercept Evaluations, 1943–44, NA, CP. For not wanting to be bullied after the end of the war, see Lieutenant (j.g.) J. V. Connorton, *The Status of U.S. Naval Communication Intelligence After World War II*, December 17, 1943, p. 9, RG-457, HCC, box 1008, file: Post War Planning Files, NA, CP.

9. For putting distance between the U.S. and British SIGINT efforts, see memorandum, Taylor to Clarke, *Cooperation Between United States Signal Intelligence Service and British Y Service*, April 5, 1943, RG-457, HCC, box 1417, file: Army and Navy COMINT Regulations and Papers, NA, CP. For secrecy of the SIGINT effort against the USSR, see memorandum, Corderman to Taylor, *Draft of "Priorities Schedule,"* March 6, 1943, and memorandum, Taylor to Corderman, *SPSIS 311.5—General—Draft of "Priorities Schedule,"* March 8, 1943, both in RG-457, HCC, box 1432, file: SSS Intercept Priorities, NA, CP.

1: ROLLER-COASTER RIDE

1. Included in the thirty-seven thousand personnel were approximately seventeen thousand assigned to dozens of tactical COMINT collection units stationed overseas. SRH-277, "A Lecture on Communications Intelligence by RADM E.E. Stone, DIRAFSA," p. 12, RG-457, entry 9002 Special Research Histories, NA, CP. For the number of codes and ciphers being exploited in

June 1945, see SSA General Cryptanalytic Branch Organization Chart, June 1, 1945, p. B-2, RG-457, HCC, box 1004, file SSA Organization Charts, NA, CP. For 88,747 diplomatic messages, see "The General Cryptanalytic Branch," in SSA, Annual Report Fiscal Year 1945, *General Cryptanalysis Branch (B-3): July 1944–July 1945*, RG-457, HCC, box 1380, file General Cryptanalysis Branch Annual Report 1945, NA, CP.

2. Memorandum, Adjutant General to Commanding Generals, *Establishment of the Army Security Agency*, September 6, 1945; memorandum, Adjutant General to Chief, Military Intelligence Service, *Establishment of the Army Security Agency*, September 19, 1945; memorandum, Adjutant General to Commanding General, Army Service Forces, *Transfer of Signal Security Agency to Army Security Agency*, September 21, 1945; memorandum, Assistant Chief of Staff, G-2 to Commanding Generals, *Establishment of the Army Security Agency*, November 7, 1945; memo for record, *General Provisions of the Army Security Agency*, May 17, 1946, all in RG-165, entry 421 ABC files, box 269, file: ABC 350.05 (8 Dec 43), sec. 1, NA, CP.

3. SRMN-084, *The Evolution of the Navy's Cryptologic Organization*, p. 9, RG-457, NA, CP.

4. Elliott E. Okins, *To Spy or Not to Spy* (Chula Vista, CA: Pateo Publishing Co., 1985), pp. 150–51; SRH-039, *Unit History, 2nd Army Air Force Radio Squadron, Mobile, April 1945–June 1946*, p. 9, RG-457, entry 9002 Special Research Histories, NA, CP.

5. Oral history, *Interview with Pat M. Holt #1: Years in Journalism*, September 9, 1980, p. 13, U.S. Senate History Office, Washington, DC.

6. SRH-364, *History of SSA*, p. 237, RG-457, entry 9002 Special Research Histories, NA, CP; National Cryptologic School, *On Watch: Profiles from the National Security Agency's Past 40 Years* (Fort Meade, MD: NSA/CSS, 1986), pp. 14–16, NSA FOIA; NSA, oral history, *Interview with Frank B. Rowlett*, 1976, p. 357, NSA FOIA.

7. The overall strength of the combined army and navy COMINT organizations went from 37,000 on duty on VJ Day to only 7,500 men and women at the end of December 1945. The army COMINT organization's command strength went from 10,600 men and women on VJ Day plus 17,000 personnel assigned to tactical intercept units to only 5,000 by the end of December 1945. The navy COMINT organization's staff levels went from 10,051 men and women on duty on VJ Day to only 2,500 personnel on the organization's rolls at the end of December 1945. For the impact of army personnel losses, see ASA, *Summary Annual Report of the Army Security Agency, Fiscal Year 1946*, July 31, 1947, p. 7, INSCOM FOIA; memorandum, Johnston to Assistant Chief of Staff, G-2, *Report of Signal Security Agency and Second Signal Service Battalion Personnel Strength*, December 4, 1945, RG-319, entry 47B Army G-2 Decimal File 1941–1948, box 568, file 320.2 5/1/45–12/31/45 (31 Dec 44), NA, CP; ASA, "Minutes of 38th Staff Meeting Held 4 December 1945 at 1300," in SRMA-011, *SSS/SSA/ASA Staff Meeting Minutes: 25 November 1942–17 February 1948*, pp. 271, RG-457, NA, CP. For the impact of navy personnel losses, see memorandum, Wenger to OP-20, *Report of Progress in OP-20-G During Absence of CNC*, December 5, 1945, Enclosure 1, p. 1, RG-38, CNSG Library, box 114, file 5750/220 OP-20 Memos Covering Various Subjects 1942–45, part 4 of 5, NA, CP; Op-20-A-vb (5 Jan 1946), Serial: 1002P20, memorandum, Chief of Naval Communications to Chief of Naval Operations, *Assistant Chief of Naval Communications for Communications Intelligence—Recommendation for Promotion to the Rank of Commodore, U.S. Navy*, January 7, 1946, p. 1, RG-38, CNSG Library, box 81, file 5420/36 Dyer Board 1945, NA, CP.

8. ASA, *Summary Annual Report of the Army Security Agency: Fiscal Year 1946*, July 31, 1947, pp. 21–22, INSCOM FOIA; SRMA-011, *SSS/SSA/ASA Staff Meeting Minutes*, p. 265, RG-457, NA, CP; memorandum, OP-23 to OP-02, *Future Status of U.S. Naval Communications Intelligence Activities—Comments On*, January 16, 1946; memorandum, Redman to OP-02, *Future Status of U.S. Naval Communications Intelligence Activities*, January 23, 1946; memorandum, Inglis to

OP-02, *Future Status of U.S. Naval Communications Intelligence Activities*, January 25, 1946, all in RG-80, SecNav/CNO Top Secret Decimal File 1944–1947, box 42, file 1946 A8, NA, CP.

9. SSA, "Minutes of 25th Staff Meeting Held 14 August 1945 at 1300," in SRMA-011, *SSS/SSA/ASA Staff Meeting Minutes: 25 November 1942–17 February 1948*, p. 216, RG-457, NA, CP; "Minutes of the Fourteenth Meeting of the Army-Navy Cryptanalytic Research and Development Committee," August 22, 1945, p. 6, RG-38, CNSG Library, box 92, file 5420/169 ANCIB (2 of 2), NA, CP; ASA, *Summary Annual Report of the Army Security Agency: Fiscal Year 1946*, July 31, 1947, p. 24, INSCOM FOIA; NSA OH-15-82, oral history, *Interview with Ann Z. Caracristi*, July 16, 1982, p. 29, NSA FOIA.

10. Copies of these decrypts can be found in the collection of T-series messages in RG-457, HCC, box 521, file Decrypted Diplomatic Traffic: T3101–T3200, NA, CP.

11. Andrew and Leslie Cockburn, *Dangerous Liaison: The Inside Story of the U.S.-Israeli Covert Relationship* (New York: HarperCollins Publishers, 1991), pp. 36–37; NSA-OH-11-82, oral history, *Interview with Captain Wesley A. Wright, USN*, May 24, 1982, p. 66, NSA FOIA.

12. For ASA military targets, see ASA *Descriptive Dictionary of Cryptologic Terms* (Laguna Hills, CA: Aegean Park Press, 1997), pp. 4, 11, 21, 23, 36, 62, 65, 95, 111, 113, 143, 150. For OP-20-G's successes with foreign naval ciphers, see *War Diary Report OP-20-G-4A: 1 September to 1 October 1945*, October 1, 1945, p. 5, RG-38, CNSG Library, file 5750/160, NA, CP; "Minutes of the Sixteenth Meeting of the Army-Navy Cryptanalytic Research and Development Committee," October 17, 1945, p. 11, RG-38, CNSG Library, box 92, file 5420/169 ANCIB (2 of 2), NA, CP; *G4A War Diary Summary for November 1945*, December 4, 1945, p. 1, RG-38, CNSG Library, file 5750/160, NA, CP; *G4A War Diary Summary for May 1946*, June 6, 1946, p. 1, RG-38, CNSG Library, file 5750/160, NA, CP; memorandum, OP-20-3-GY-A to OP-20-3, *Status of Work Report on Spanish, Portuguese, Dutch and French Language Systems*, January 16, 1946, RG-38, CNSG Library, box 22, file 3222/85: Non-Japanese Crypto-Systems Processed—Apr 43–Aug 45 (3 of 3), NA, CP.

13. Memorandum, OP-23 to OP-02, *Future Status of U.S. Naval Communication Intelligence Activities—Comments on*, January 16, 1946, RG-38, CNSG Library, box 114, file 5750/220 OP-20 Memos Covering Various Subjects, 1942–1945 (4 of 5), NA, CP; memorandum, Redman to OP-02, *Future Status of U.S. Naval Communication Intelligence Activities*, January 23, 1946, and memorandum, Inglis to OP-02, *Future Status of U.S. Naval Communications Intelligence Activities*, January 25, 1946, both in RG-80, SecNav/CNO TS, box 42, file 1946 A8, NA, CP.

14. For an example of a Chinese Nationalist military decrypt, see Navy Department, Chief of Naval Operations, *Oriental Communication Intelligence Summary*, April 11, 1946, RG-38, entry 345 Radio Intelligence Summaries 1941–1946, box 122, file 1-30 April 1946 (2 of 2), NA, CP. For decrypted Chinese Communist radio traffic, see Navy Department, Chief of Naval Operations, *Oriental Communication Intelligence Summary*, April 26, 1946, RG-38, entry 345 Radio Intelligence Summaries 1941–1946, box 122, file 1-30 April 1946 (2 of 2), NA, CP.

15. Memorandum, Craig to Acting Deputy Chief of Staff, *Intelligence on Russia*, March 14, 1946, RG-319, entry 154 OPD TS Decimal File 1946–1948, box 75, file P&O 350.05 TS (Section I) Cases 1–44, NA, CP; memorandum, G.A.L. to Hull, *Intelligence on Russia*, March 22, 1946, RG-319, entry 154 OPD TS Decimal File 1946–1948, box 75, file P&O 350.05 TS (Section I) Cases 1–44, NA, CP; memorandum, Starbird to Hull, *Intelligence in Europe*, April 3, 1946, RG-319, entry 154 OPD TS Decimal File 1946–1948, box 75, file P&O 350.05 TS (Section I) Cases 1–44, NA, CP.

16. A heavily redacted version of the BRUSA Agreement was recently released to the author, for which see *British–U.S. Communication Intelligence Agreement*, March 5, 1946, DOCID 3216600, NSA FOIA. See also SRMA-011, *SSS/SSA/ASA Staff Meeting Minutes: 25 November 1942–17 February 1948*, pp. 293, 321, RG-457, NA, CP; *Army-Navy Communication Intelligence Board Organi-*

zational Bulletin No. 1, June 1945, RG-457, HCC, box 1364, NA, CP; *Report to the Secretary of State and the Secretary of Defense* (hereafter *"Brownell Committee Report"*), June 13, 1952, p. 15, NSA FOIA; George F. Howe, "The Early History of NSA," *Cryptologic Spectrum*, vol. 4, no. 2, (Spring 1974): p. 13, DOCID: 3217154, NSA FOIA; Thomas L. Burns, *The Origins of the National Security Agency: 1940–1952* (Fort Meade, MD: Center for Cryptologic History, 1990), pp. 36–37, 52, NSA FOIA.

17. SRMA-011, *SSS/SSA/ASA Staff Meeting Minutes*, p. 257, RG-457, NA, CP; letter, Wenger to Jones, June 4, 1946, RG-38, CNSG Library, box 101, file Miscellaneous June 1945–June 1946, NA, CP.

18. ASA, *Summary Annual Report of the Army Security Agency: Fiscal Year 1947*, February 1950, p. 23, INSCOM FOIA; ASA, *Annual Historical Report, ASA Plans and Operations Section, FY 1950*, p. ii, INSCOM FOIA; SRMA-011, *SSS/SSA/ASA Staff Meeting Minutes: 25 November 1942–17 February 1948*, p. 257, RG-457, NA, CP; Howe, "The Early History of NSA," p. 13, DOCID: 3217154, NSA FOIA; TR/IM 77-02J, TCS 4530-77, CIA, Center for the Study of Intelligence, Intelligence Monograph, *Critique of the Codeword Compartment in the CIA*, March 1977, p. 5, CREST Collection, Document No. CIA-RDP83B00823R000900180001-6, NA, CP; interview, Grant C. Manson.

19. Dr. Thomas R. Johnson, *American Cryptology During the Cold War, 1945–1989*, bk. 1, *The Struggle for Centralization, 1945–1960* (Fort Meade, MD: Center for Cryptologic History, 1995), p. 17, NSA FOIA.

20. Details of Gouzenko's revelations can be found in Memorandum, Hoover to Lyon, *Soviet Espionage Activity*, September 18, 1945, RG-59, Decimal File 1945–1949, box 6648, file 861.20242/9-1845, NA, CP; memorandum, Hoover to Lyon, *Soviet Espionage Activity*, September 24, 1945, RG-59, Decimal File 1945–1949, box 6648, file 861.20242/9-2445, NA, CP; *The Report of the Royal Commission to Investigate the Facts Relating to and the Circumstances Surrounding the Communication by Public Officials and Other Persons in Positions of Trust of Secret and Confidential Information to Agents of a Foreign Power* (Kellock-Taschereau Commission) (Ottawa: Canadian Government Printing Office, 1946).

21. Wenger had held discussions with Captain E. S. Brand, RCN, the director of naval intelligence; Captain George A. "Sam" Worth, RCN, the director of naval communications; and Commander Macdonald concerning future U.S.-Canadian COMINT relations. Letter, Wenger to deMarbois, October 4, 1945, RG-38, CNSG Library, box 101, file Miscellaneous June 1945–June 1946, NA, CP.

22. SD-38092, *Briefing for General Irwin—of Important Happenings in the Intelligence Division for the Period 28 April Through 14 June, 1949*, June 15, 1949, p. 2, RG-319, entry 47A Army G-2 Top Secret Decimal File 1942–1952, box 9, file 014.331 thru 018.2 '49, NA, CP; letter, Cabell to Crean, June 29, 1949. The author is grateful to Bill Robinson in Canada for making a copy of this declassified document available to him. See also letter, Wenger to Jones, November 17, 1949, RG-38, CNSG Library, box 101, file Miscellaneous January 1949–December 1949, NA, CP; letter, Glazebrook to Armstrong, November 18, 1949, RG-59, entry 1561 Lot 58D776 INR Subject File 1945–1956, box 22, file Exchange of Classified Information with Foreign Governments Other than UK, NA, CP; Johnson, *American Cryptology*, bk. 1, p. 18. For the signing of CANUSA in 1949, see IAC 376, Communications Security Establishment, *Canadian SIGINT Security Instructions*, November 2, 1976, p. 2, Canadian Department of National Defense FOIA.

23. Memorandum, McDonald to Secretary of the Air Force et al., *Conversations with British Representatives Concerning British Collaboration with Australia and New Zealand on Communications Intelligence Activities*, January 2, 1948, RG-341, entry 335 Air Force Plans Project Decimal File 1942–1954, box 741-A, file 350.05 England (2 Jan 48), NA, CP; memorandum, Shedden to

Secretary, Defence Committee, *Tripartite Conference at Defence Signals Branch*, September 3, 1953, Series A5954, box 2355, Item 2355/7 Visit of US and UK Representatives to DSB Nov 1952 Tripartite Conference Sept 1953, National Archives of Australia, Canberra, Australia; Johnson, *American Cryptology*, bk. 1, pp. 18–19.

24. Johnson, *American Cryptology*, bk. 1, p. 160.

25. Peter J. Freeman, *How GCHQ Came to Cheltenham* (Cheltenham, U.K.: GCHQ, 2002), p. 9; confidential interview with former GCHQ officer.

26. *British Communications Intelligence*, undated circa early 1946, RG-457, HCC, box 808, file British COMINT, NA, CP. For the size of the London Signals Intelligence Center Russian Section, see *Director's Order No. 77*, September 20, 1945, HW 64/68, PRO, Kew, England; *Number of Staff Employed*, September 30, 1945, HW 14/151, PRO, Kew, England.

27. F. W. Winterbotham, *The Ultra Secret* (London: Weidenfeld and Nicolson, 1974), p. 13.

28. For Alexander, see Michael Smith, *The Spying Game: The Secret History of British Espionage* (London: Politico's, 2003), p. 296. For Morgan, see *British Communications Intelligence*, undated circa early 1946, appendix 1, p. 6, RG-457, HCC, box 808, file British COMINT, NA, CP.

29. *War Diary Summary of G4A for February 1946*, March 5, 1946, p. 1, RG-38, CNSG Library, box 111, file 5750/160 Section War Diaries (3 of 3), NA, CP; *War Diary Summary of G4A for March 1946*, April 9, 1946, p. 1, RG-38, CNSG Library, box 111, file 5750/160 Section War Diaries (3 of 3), NA, CP; *War Diary Summary of G4A for April 1946*, May 6, 1946, p. 1, RG-38, CNSG Library, box 111, file 5750/160 Section War Diaries (3 of 3), NA, CP.

30. Decrypts V-2936, Petropavlovsk to Toyohara, August 10, 1946, RG-38, Translations of Intercepted Enemy Radio Traffic 1940–1946, box 2744, NA, CP; comment to WS BO 17098, Sovetskaya Gavan' Naval Base to Petropavlovsk Naval Base, RUN-17440(N), RUNRA-1, November 15, 1948, RG-38, Translations of Intercepted Enemy Radio Traffic 1940–1946, box 2742, NA, CP. Both reclassified by U.S. Navy.

31. *War Diary Summary of G4A for April 1946*, May 6, 1946, p. 1, RG-38, CNSG Library, box 111, file 5750/160 Section War Diaries (3 of 3), NA, CP; David Alvarez, "Behind Venona: American Signals Intelligence in the Early Cold War," *Intelligence and National Security*, Summer 1999: p. 181.

32. Hugh Denham, "Conel Hugh O'Donel Alexander," *Cryptologic Spectrum*, vol. 4, no. 3 (Summer 1974): p. 31, DOCID: 3217160, NSA FOIA; Smith, *The Spying Game*, p. 296.

33. Confidential interview. For Raven background, see *NSA Newsletter*, May 1954, p. 5, NSA FOIA.

34. For RUMRA decrypts, see RUM-12405, Vienna HQ Central Group of Forces to Moscow Ministry of the Armed Forces, RUMRA-1, intercepted November 15, 1946, solved January 13, 1949; RUM-12410, Moscow to Tbilisi, RUMRA-1, intercepted March 15, 1947, solved January 18, 1949; RUM-12519, Moscow to Kuibyshev: Volga VO, RUMRA-1, intercepted March 21, 1947, solved February 25, 1949; RUM-12000, Moscow to Arkhangel'sk VO, RUMRA-1, intercepted June 24, 1948, solved October 13, 1948; RUM-12293, Tbilisi to Moscow: MVS, RUMRA-1, intercepted October 14, 1947, solved December 6, 1948, all in RG-38, box 2742, NA, CP.

35. *War Diary Summary of G4A for February 1946*, March 5, 1946, p. 1, RG-38, CNSG Library, box 111, file 5750/160 War Diary Sections (3 of 3), NA, CP; *Summary of War Diary for N-51: July 1946*, August 6, 1946, p. 2, RG-38, CNSG Library, box 111, file 5750/160 Section War Diaries (1 of 3), NA, CP; letter, Wenger to Travis, February 15, 1947, RG-38, CNSG Library, box 101, file Miscellaneous November 1951–July 1953, NA, CP.

36. Letter, Currier to Wenger, April 8, 1947, RG-38, Crane CNSG Library, box 101, file Miscellaneous November 1951–July 1953, NA, CP.

37. ASA, *Summary Annual Report of the Army Security Agency: Fiscal Year 1947*, February 1950, p. 45, INSCOM FOIA.

38. See, for example, RUM-12405, Vienna HQ Central Group of Forces to Moscow Ministry of the Armed Forces, RUMRA-1, intercepted November 15, 1946, solved January 13, 1949; RUM-12410, Moscow to Tbilisi, RUMRA-1, intercepted March 15, 1947, solved January 18, 1949; RUM-12519, Moscow to Kuibyshev: Volga VO, RUMRA-1, intercepted March 21, 1947, solved February 25, 1949; RUM-12550, Khabarovsk to Irkutsk, RUMY, intercepted January 15, 1949, solved March 10, 1949, all in RG-38, Translations of Intercepted Enemy Radio Traffic, 1940–1946, box 2739, NA, CP; RUM-11835, Alma Ata: MGB to Directorate of Military Supply, MGB, RUMY, intercepted November 13, 1947, solved September 27, 1948; RUM-11861, Moscow to Arkhangel'sk VO, RUMB, intercepted July 30, 1947, solved September 29, 1948; RUM-11989, Tbilisi to Moscow, intercepted August 6, 1948, solved October 18, 1948; RUM-11992, Tbilisi to Pojly, RUMY, intercepted August 27, 1948, solved October 13, 1948; RUM-12000, Moscow to Arkhangel'sk VO, RUMRA-1, intercepted June 24, 1948, solved October 13, 1948; RUM-12003, Moscow to Alma Ata, intercepted August 23, 1948, solved October 18, 1948; RUM-12087, Moscow to Vorkuta, RUYLA-1, intercepted April 8, 1948, solved October 25, 1948; RUM-12215, Baku to Moscow, RUMY, intercepted September 7, 1948, solved November 18, 1948; RUM-12312, Dal'nij to Moscow: MVS, RUMUC-2, intercepted March 18, 1948, solved December 7, 1948; RUM-12293, Tbilisi to Moscow: MVS, RUMRA-1, intercepted October 14, 1947, solved December 6, 1948; RUM-12320, Khar'kov to Kavkazkaya Station, intercepted October 8, 1948, solved December 15, 1948; RUM-12327, Grozny to Moscow, RUMY, intercepted December 3, 1948, solved December 17, 1948; RUM-12334, Chita to Moscow, RUMY, intercepted September 9, 1948, solved December 20, 1948; RUM-12356, Port Arthur: 39 Army to UKH of MGB, December 31, 1948; RUM-12509, Vladivostok to Moscow, RUMY, intercepted October 14, 1948, solved UNK; RUMI-0622, Riga to Moscow, RUMUA-1A, intercepted December 28, 1946, solved October 12, 1948; RUMI-0625, Tbilisi to Moscow MVS, RUMUA-1, intercepted January 8, 1948, solved October 12, 1948; RUMI-0705, Vienna to Mukachevo, RUMUA-1A, intercepted December 3, 1947, solved December 23, 1948; RUMI-0712, Vienna to Mukachevo, RUMUA-1A, intercepted December 3, 1947, solved December 23, 1948, all in RG-38, Translations of Intercepted Enemy Radio Traffic, 1940–1946, box 2742, NA, CP; V-2936, Petropavlovsk to Toyohara, August 10, 1946, RG-38, Translations of Intercepted Enemy Radio Traffic, 1940–1946, box 2744, NA, CP; RUM-10994, Port Arthur 39 Army to Voroshilov PRIMVO, intercepted March 22, 1948, solved August 19, 1948; RUM-11100, Port Arthur: 39 Army to Voroshilov PRIMVO, intercepted February 20, 1948, solved August 18, 1948; RUM-11107, Voroshilov PRIMVO to Port Arthur 39 Army, intercepted July 7, 1947, solved August 17, 1948; RUM-11059, Yerevan 7 Guards Army to Moscow, intercepted January 9, 1947, solved August 18, 1948, all in RG-38, Translations of Intercepted Enemy Radio Traffic, 1940–1946, box 2745, NA, CP. All of these documents have been reclassified by the U.S. Navy.

39. For examples of Soviet navy cipher solutions, see NI-1-#14928, CinC 5th Fleet to Moscow Naval Headquarters, RUNRA-1, intercepted April 18, 1948, solved March 16, 1949; NI-1-#23815, Vladivostok to Moscow, RUNY, intercepted December 8, 1948, solved April 21, 1949; RUN-16971, Petropavlovsk Naval Base to Sovetskaya Gavan Naval Base, RUNRA-1, intercepted January 16, 1948, solved November 18, 1948, all in RG-38, Translations of Intercepted Enemy Radio Traffic, 1940–1946, box 2739, NA, CP; NI-1 Summary part 2, December 14, 1946; NI-1 Summary, December 26, 1946; NI-1 Summary, March 21, 1947, all in RG-38, Translations of Intercepted Enemy Radio Traffic, 1940–1946, box 2740, NA, CP; RUN-1799, Chief of Staff, Naval Air Forces, Moscow to Chief of Staff, Naval Air Force, Black Sea Fleet, intercepted May 13, 1948, solved December 6, 1948; RUN-16132, Petropavlovsk Naval Base to Sovetskaya Gavan Naval Base, intercepted June 30, 1948, solved November 19, 1948; RUN-18002, Sovetskaya Gavan CinC 7th Fleet to Moscow Naval Hqs, intercepted June 10, 1948, solved December 2, 1948;

RUN-18013, Vladivostok CinC 5th Fleet to Moscow Naval Hqs, intercepted February 13, 1948, solved December 3, 1948; RUN-19962, Vladivostok CinC 5th Fleet to Moscow Naval Hqs, intercepted April 19, 1948, solved December 29, 1948, all in RG-38, Translations of Intercepted Enemy Radio Traffic, 1940–1946, box 2742, NA, CP; RUN-21146, Vladivostok CinC 5th Fleet to Moscow Naval Hqs, intercepted February 4, 1948, solved February 10, 1949, RG-38, Translations of Intercepted Enemy Radio Traffic, 1940–1946, box 2743, NA, CP; RUN-15567, Moscow Naval Headquarters to Sovetskaya Gavan CinC 7th Fleet, intercepted January 30, 1948, solved August 17, 1948; RUN-15702, Moscow Naval Headquarters to CinC 5th Fleet, intercepted August 24, 1948, solved August 31, 1948; RUN-15724, Moscow Naval Headquarters to CinC 5th Fleet, intercepted August 24, 1948, solved September 28, 1948; RUN-15796, Moscow Naval Headquarters to CinC 5th Fleet, intercepted August 25, 1948, solved September 22, 1948, all in RG-38, Translations of Intercepted Enemy Radio Traffic, 1940–1946, box 2744, NA, CP; RUN-15724, Moscow Naval Headquarters to CinC 5th Fleet, intercepted August 24, 1948, solved September 28, 1948; RUN-ARU/T2343, Headquarters Air Force Black Sea to Headquarters Naval Air Force, Moscow, intercepted October 13, 1947, solved September 20, 1948, both in RG-38, Translations of Intercepted Enemy Radio Traffic, 1940–1946, box 2745, NA, CP. All of these documents have been reclassified by the U.S. Navy.

40. RUM-10828, Vozdvizhenka 9th Air Army to Moscow VVS VS, intercepted May 4, 1947, solved August 6, 1948, RG-38, Translations of Intercepted Enemy Radio Traffic, 1940–1946, box 2744, NA, CP; RUM-12083, Moscow: VVS VS to Vienna: 2nd Air Army, RUARA-1, intercepted October 6, 1947, solved October 20, 1948; RUM-12375, Dairen 7 Air Corps to Vozdvizhenka 9th Air Army, RUMUC-2, intercepted December 1, 1947, solved UNK, both in RG-38, Translations of Intercepted Enemy Radio Traffic, 1940–1946, box 2742, NA, CP; RUMI-0505, Tbilisi 11 Air Army to VVS VS, intercepted April 30, 1948, solved August 31, 1948, RG-38, Translations of Intercepted Enemy Radio Traffic, 1940–1946, box 2745, NA, CP. All of these documents have been reclassified by the U.S. Navy.

41. RUAMT-3 was the designation given to the cipher system used by the 9th Air Army at Vozdvizhenka that was being read by the U.S. Army, which usually consisted of messages from air base duty officers reporting on the arrival and departure of aircraft at their base. John Milmore, *#1 Code Break Boy* (Haverford, PA: Infinity Publishing, 2002), pp. 12–13.

42. Johnson, *American Cryptology*, bk. 1, p. 161; Robert Louis Benson and Michael Warner, *Venona: Soviet Espionage and the American Response, 1939–1957* (Washington, DC: Center for the Study of Intelligence, 1996), pp. xxi, 93–104; Desmond Ball and David Horner, *Breaking the Codes: Australia's KGB Network* (Sydney: Allen and Unwin, 1998), p. 203.

43. David A. Hatch and Robert Louis Benson, *The Korean War: The SIGINT Background* (Fort Meade, MD: Center for Cryptologic History, 2000), p. 4.

44. Allen Weinstein and Alexander Vassiliev, *The Haunted Wood* (New York: Random House, 1999), pp. 291–92.

45. Confidential interviews. For the intelligence background to the 1948 Berlin Crisis, see message, SX 2967, HQ EUCOM to CSUSA Washington, DC, April 8, 1948, RG-319, entry 58 Army G-2 Top Secret Messages 1942–1952, box 115, file 1. FR "S" Germany 1-1-48–6-9-48, NA, CP; CIA, information report, *The Current Situation in Berlin and Related Information*, April 30, 1948, CREST Collection, Document No. CIA-RDP83-00415R000800090015-7, NA, CP.

46. Confidential interviews.

47. See, for example, SD-11388, Intelligence Division, U.S. European Command, Air Evaluation Report J-32, *Evaluation of Radio Intercept Reports from Signal Section*, August 17, 1948, RG-319, entry 1041, box 239, file ID No. 960884, NA, CP; SC-8483, U.S. Air Force in Europe, Deputy Chief of Staff, Intelligence, *Estimate of the Situation*, December 1, 1948, p. 12, RG-313, entry 1335

(UD) CINCNELM Top Secret Intelligence Files 1946–1950, box 14, file #29, NA, CP. For the overall importance of the Gehlen Org's SIGINT product, see Kevin C. Ruffner, ed., *Forging an Intelligence Partnership: CIA and the Origins of the BND, 1945–49: A Documentary History* (Washington, DC: CIA History Staff, 1999), vol. II, pp. 105–06, RG-263, CIA Subject Files, box 2, NA, CP; James H. Critchfield, "The Early History of the Gehlen Organization and Its Influence on the Development of a National Security System in the Federal Republic of Germany," in Heike Bungert, Jan G. Heitmann, and Michael Wala, eds., *Secret Intelligence in the Twentieth Century* (London: Frank Cass and Co., 2003), p. 160.

48. TI Item #137, NT-1 Traffic Intelligence, *Unprecedented Coordinated Russian Communications Changes*, November 4, 1948, RG-38, Translations of Intercepted Enemy Radio Traffic, 1940–1946, box 2742, NA, CP (reclassified by the U.S. Navy); National Cryptologic School, *On Watch*, pp. 19–20; Hatch and Benson, *The Korean War*, p. 4; Jeannette Williams and Yolande Dickerson, *The Invisible Cryptologists: African-Americans, WWII to 1956* (Fort Meade, MD: Center for Cryptologic History, 2001), p. 19.

49. National Cryptologic School, *On Watch*, p. 19. See also Hatch and Benson, *The Korean War*, p. 5; Donald P. Steury, "The End of the Dark Era: The Transformation of American Intelligence, 1956," p. 2, paper presented at a conference organized by the Allied Museum, Berlin, April 24, 2006.

50. S/ARU/C735, *Developments in Soviet Cypher [sic] and Signals Security, 1946–1948*, December 1948, RG-38, Translations of Intercepted Enemy Radio Traffic, 1940–1946, box 2739, NA, CP (reclassified by the U.S. Navy); Department of the Army, Pamphlet No. 30-2, *The Soviet Army*, July 1949, p. 41, RG-6, box 107, MacArthur Memorial Library, Norfolk, VA; SRH-277, "A Lecture on Communications Intelligence by Rear Admiral E.E. Stone, DIRAFSA," June 5, 1951, p. 34, RG-457, entry 9002 Special Research Histories, NA, CP; *Brownell Committee Report*, June 13, 1952, pp. 29, 83, NSA FOIA; CIA, CS Historical Paper No. 150, *Clandestine Service History: The Berlin Tunnel Operation: 1952–1956*, August 25, 1967, p. 1, CIA Electronic FOIA Reading Room, Document No. 0001407685, http://www.foia.cia.gov; Defense Intelligence Agency, DDB-1170-3-80, *Warsaw Pact Forces Command, Control, and Communications*, August 1980, pp. 1–2, DIA FOIA; National Cryptologic School, *On Watch*, p. 19; David E. Murphy, Sergei A. Kondrashev, and George Bailey, *Battleground Berlin* (New Haven, CT: Yale University Press, 1997), p. 208; interview, Frank B. Rowlett.

51. *Study of Joint Organizations for the Production of Communications Intelligence and for Security of U.S. Military Communications (Stone Board Report)*, December 27, 1948, part A: Communications Intelligence, p. 5, DOCID: 3187441, NSA FOIA; *Brownell Committee Report*, June 13, 1952, p. 108, NSA FOIA.

52. HQ USAF, AFOIR-SR 322, *Functions of the USAF Security Service*, October 20, 1948, p. 1, AIA FOIA; "35 Years of Excellence," *Spokesman*, October 1983: p. 9, AIA FOIA.

53. USAFSS, *Organizational Development of the USAFSS, 1948–1962*, February 15, 1963, p. 122, AIA FOIA; memorandum, Cabell to Director of Operations et al., *Changes in Personnel and Equipment Priorities for U.S. Air Force Security Service*, December 14, 1949, RG-341, entry 214 Top Secret Cable and Controls Division, box 47, file 2-10500-2-10599, NA, CP.

54. Memorandum, Secretary of Defense to Secretaries of the Army, Navy, and Air Force, *Organization of Cryptologic Activities Within the National Military Establishment*, May 20, 1945, with attachment, RG-330, entry 199 OSD Decimal File 1947–1950, box 97, CD 22-1-23, NA, CP; JCS 2010, *Organization of Cryptologic Activities Within the National Military Establishment*, May 20, 1949, p. 1, RG-341, entry 214, file 2-8100-2-8199, NA, CP.

55. AFSA's fiscal year 1951 budget (all of which came from financial contributions made by the three military services) came to about $23 million, $13.9 million of which was "donated" to

AFSA from ASA's fiscal year 1951 command budget. See *Tentative Plans for FY 1952 Budget of Armed Forces Security Agency—Part I Operating Plans . . . Part II Budget Summary*, April 6, 1950, RG-319, entry 1 (UD) Index to Army Chief of Staff Top Secret Decimal File 1950, box 5, file 040 Armed Forces Security Agency, NA, CP; memorandum, Pace to Director, Armed Forces Security Agency, *Fiscal Year 1951 Financing for AFSA*, June 14, 1950, RG-319, entry 2 (UD) Army Chief of Staff Decimal File 1950, box 552, file 040 AFSA, NA, CP.

56. JCS 2010/10, Report by the Armed Forces Communication Intelligence Advisory Council to the Joint Chiefs of Staff, *Organization of the Armed Forces Security Agency*, September 30, 1949, Enclosure B, p. 47, RG-218, CCS 334 (NSA), sec. 2, NARA FOIA.

57. TS Cont. No. SD-39819, memorandum, Stone to Director of Intelligence, U.S. Army, *Command Responsibility for ASA Fixed Intercept Installations*, March 3, 1950; memorandum for the record, *AFSA Conference with ASA Concerning Policy Questions*, March 1, 1950, both in RG-319, entry 47A G-2 Top Secret Decimal File 1942–1952, box 13, file 676.3 thru 800.2 '50, NARA FOIA.

58. NSA OH-1981-01, oral history, *Interview with Herbert L. Conley*, March 5, 1984, p. 59, partially declassified and on file at the library of the National Cryptologic Museum, Fort Meade, MD.

59. NSA OH-11-82, oral history, *Interview with Captain Wesley A. Wright, USN*, May 24, 1982, p. 75, NSA FOIA.

60. Johnson, *American Cryptology*, bk. 1, p. 184.

61. Williams and Dickerson, *The Invisible Cryptologists*, p. 19.

62. As of 1950, the other members of Jack Gurin's plaintext unit were Olin Adams, Susan Armstrong, James Hones, James Honea, First Lieutenant Justin McCarty, Juliana Mickwitz, Nicholas Murphy, and Constantin Oustinoff. ASA, *ASA Summary Annual Report FY 1948*, p. 33n, INSCOM FOIA; Johnson, *American Cryptology*, bk. 1, p. 169. Gurin background from *NSA Newsletter*, October 1965, p. 13, NSA FOIA; Williams and Dickerson, *The Invisible Cryptologists*, p. 17.

63. *Study of Joint Organizations for the Production of Communications Intelligence and for Security of U.S. Military Communications (Stone Board Report)*, December 27, 1948, part A: Communications Intelligence, p. 16, DOCID: 3187441, NSA FOIA.

64. Memorandum, USCIB to Secretary of Defense, *Atomic Energy Program of the USSR*, May 12, 1949; memorandum for the Secretary of Defense from Admiral Louis Denfield, USN, *Atomic Energy Program of the USSR*, June 30, 1949; memorandum for the Secretary of Defense, *Atomic Energy Program of the USSR*, June 23, 1949, all in RG-330, entry 199 OSD Decimal File 1947–1950, box 61, file CD 11-1-2, NA, CP. For the precipitous decline of AFSA Far Eastern, Chinese, and North Korean missions, see Guy R. Vanderpool, "COMINT and the PRC Intervention in the Korean War," *Cryptologic Quarterly*, vol. 15, no. 2 (Summer 1996): p. 8, NSA FOIA.

65. *Brownell Committee Report*, June 13, 1952, pp. 83–84, NSA FOIA.

66. In lieu of decrypts, the best that the American and British intelligence analysts could do was try to map the Soviet diplomatic radio nets in Europe, the Middle East, and Asia and monitor the flow of communications traffic along them. See, for example, ASA, ID, RU-TAF-GEN-I #24, *Opening of Soviet Legation in Tel Aviv*, August 13, 1948, RG-38, Translations of Intercepted Enemy Radio Traffic, 1940–1946, box 2744, NA, CP; ASA, ID, RU-TAF-GEN-1 #28, *Soviet Operated Diplomatic Radio Links*, December 2, 1948, RG-38, Translations of Intercepted Enemy Radio Traffic, 1940–1946, box 2742, NA, CP; S/ARU/C728, *Soviet Diplomatic W/T Network*, December 9, 1948, RG-38, Translations of Intercepted Enemy Radio Traffic, 1940–1946, box 2739, NA, CP; S/AQP/C61, *Cipher Traffic Between Moscow and Soviet Embassy, New Delhi*, January 3, 1949, RG-38, Translations of Intercepted Enemy Radio Traffic, 1940–1946, box 2742, NA, CP; ASA, ID, RU-TAF-GEN-P #1, *Traffic Analysis Fusion General Periodic #1*, January 12, 1949, RG-38, Translations of Intercepted Enemy Radio Traffic, 1940–1946, box 2742, NA, CP;

S/ARU/C880, *Soviet Diplomatic Wireless Link: Moscow-Oslo*, March 14, 1949, RG-38, Translations of Intercepted Enemy Radio Traffic, 1940–1946, box 2739, NA, CP. All reclassified by the U.S. Navy.

67. T/S/002/103, *Periodic Note—the RUR Networks*, February 12, 1949, RG-38, Translations of Intercepted Enemy Radio Traffic, 1940–1946, box 2739, NA, CP. Reclassified by the U.S. Navy.

68. Benson and Warner, *Venona*, pp. xxiv–xxvi.

69. Of the 206 Russian spies identified by the FBI, 101 had left the United States by 1955 and could not be prosecuted, including 61 Russian officials; 11 had died; 14 were cooperating with the FBI; and 15 were prosecuted. These individuals were Abraham Brothman, Judith Coplon, Klaus Fuchs, Harry Gold, David Greenglass, Valentine A. Gubitchev (Judith Coplon's KGB handler), Miriam Moskowitz, Julius Rosenberg, Ethel Rosenberg, Alfred Slack, Morton Sobell, Jack Soble, Myra Soble, William Perl, and Alger Hiss. This left 77 individuals whom the FBI had investigated but the U.S. Justice Department could not or would not prosecute. Memorandum, Belmont to Boardman, November 27, 1957, pp. 2–3, FBI Venona Files, FBI FOIA Reading Room, Washington, DC.

70. Currie moved to Colombia in 1950 to help that nation liberalize its economy. He remained there for the rest of his life, dying in Bogotá on December 23, 1993, at the age of ninety-one. Memorandum, Belmont to Boardman, February 1, 1956, p. 9, FBI Venona Files, FBI FOIA Reading Room, Washington, DC.

71. Weisband FBI File, Documents No. 65-59095-15, 65-59095-606, and 65-59095-628, FBI FOIA; Howard Benedict, "Book Says U.S. Broke Soviet Code, Implicating Rosenbergs," *Associated Press*, March 3, 1980.

72. *Brownell Committee Report*, pp. 113–14, NSA FOIA; Dr. Thomas R. Johnson, "American Cryptology During the Korean War—A Preliminary Verdict," June 2000, p. 3, paper presented at the 26th Annual Conference of the Society for Historians of American Foreign Relations, June 23, 2000, Toronto, Canada.

73. Woodrow J. Kuhns, ed., *Assessing the Soviet Threat: The Early Cold War Years* (Washington, DC: Center for the Study of Intelligence, 1997), p. 11, n. 39.

74. Memorandum, Hillenkoetter to Executive Secretary, NSC, *Atomic Energy Program of the USSR*, April 20, 1949, p. 46, enclosure to memorandum, Allen to Secretary of the Army et al., *Atomic Energy Program of the USSR*, April 28, 1949, RG-319, 1949–1950 TS, Hot File 091.412, box 165, file 091 Soviet Union, NA, CP; memorandum, Bauman to Assistant Chief of Staff, G-2, *Military Personnel Requirements of AFSA*, June 6, 1950, RG-319, entry 47E Army G-2 Decimal File 1949–1950; memorandum, Brown to Wenger, *Military Personnel Requirements of the Armed Forces Security Agency*, June 7, 1950, RG-319, entry 47E Army G-2 Decimal File 1949–1950, both in box 87, file 320.2 1949–1950 (2 Aug 46), NA, CP; memorandum, Chief, Staff C and D to Assistant Director, Special Operations, *Steps Necessary to Place CIA, Particularly OSO, in a Position to Adequately Fulfill Basic Responsibilities During the Present and Inevitable Future Emergencies*, July 10, 1950, p. 3, CREST Collection, Document No. CIA-RDP84-00499R000700090019-1, NA, CP.

75. Johnson, "A Preliminary Verdict," p. 3.

76. David Halberstam, *The Coldest War* (New York: Random House, 2007), p.1.

2: THE STORM BREAKS

1. This chapter supplements with newly declassified documents the author's previously published detailed examination of the role played by SIGINT in the Korean War, for which see Matthew M. Aid, "U.S. Humint and Comint in the Korean War: From the Approach of War to

the Chinese Intervention," *Intelligence and National Security*, vol. 14, no. 4 (Winter 1999): pp. 17–23; Matthew M. Aid, "American Comint in the Korean War (Part II): From the Chinese Intervention to the Armistice," *Intelligence and National Security*, vol. 15, no. 1 (Spring 2000): pp. 14–49.

2. ASA, *History, Army Security Agency and Subordinate Units, Fiscal Year 1951*, vol. 2, p. 2, INSCOM FOIA; *Report to the Secretary of State and the Secretary of Defense*, June 13, 1952, p. 29, NSA FOIA; Russell "Hop" Harriger, *A Historical Study of the Air Force Security Service and Korea: June 1950–October 1952*, October 2, 1952, p. 4, AIA FOIA; James E. Pierson, *A Special Historical Study: USAFSS Response to World Crises, 1949–1969* (San Antonio, TX: USAFSS Historical Office, 1970), p. 1, AIA FOIA; Richard A. "Dick" Chun, *A Bit on the Korean COMINT Effort*, working notes prepared for the NSA History Office, 1971, DOCID 321697, NSA FOIA; Thomas L. Burns, *The Origins of the National Security Agency: 1940–1952* (Fort Meade, MD: Center for Cryptologic History, 1990), p. 84, NSA FOIA; Dr. Thomas R. Johnson, *American Cryptology During the Cold War, 1945–1989*, bk. 1, *The Struggle for Centralization, 1945–1960* (Fort Meade, MD: Center for Cryptologic History, 1995), p. 39, NSA FOIA; Benson K. Buffham, "The Korean War and AFSA," *The Phoenician*, Spring 2001: p. 7; report, *On the 20th Anniversary of the Korean War: An Informal Memoire by the ORE Korean Desk Officer, Circa 1948–1950*, undated, p. 22, RG-263, entry 17, box 4, file CIA Reporting on ChiComs in Korean War, NA, CP; letter, Morton A. Rubin to author, May 5, 1992. The "North Korean target was ignored" quote is from Jill Frahm, *So Power Can Be Brought into Play: SIGINT and the Pusan Perimeter* (Fort Meade, MD: Center for Cryptologic History, 2000), p. 4.

3. Memorandum, USCIB to Secretary of Defense, May 12, 1949; memorandum, Denfield to Secretary of Defense, *Atomic Energy Program of the USSR*, June 30, 1949, both in RG-330, entry 199 Central Decimal File 1947–1950, box 61, file CD 11-1-2, NA, CP; Russell "Hop" Harriger, *A Historical Study of the Air Force Security Service and Korea: June 1950–October 1952*, October 2, 1952, p. 2, AIA FOIA; historical paper, *The U.S. COMINT Effort During the Korean War: June 1950–August 1953*, January 6, 1954, pp. 2–3, DOCID 3216598, NSA FOIA; interviews, Frank B. Rowlett and Louis W. Tordella. Quote from Frahm, *Power Can Be Brought*, p. 4. Rubin quote from interview with Morton A. Rubin.

4. Historical paper, *The U.S. COMINT Effort During the Korean War: June 1950–August 1953*, January 6, 1954, p. 2, DOCID 3216598, NSA FOIA; Richard A. "Dick" Chun, *A Bit on the Korean COMINT Effort*, working notes prepared for the NSA History Office, 1971, p. 1, DOCID 321697, NSA FOIA; Burns, *Origins*, p. 85; Johnson, *American Cryptology*, bk. 1, p. 39; David A. Hatch and Robert Louis Benson, *The Korean War: The SIGINT Background* (Fort Meade, MD: Center for Cryptologic History, 2000), p. 5; Frahm, *Power Can Be Brought*, p. 4.

5. ASA, Pacific, *ASAPAC Summary Annual Report, FY 1951*, p. 63, INSCOM FOIA; Hatch and Benson, *The Korean War*, p. 8; interviews with Morton Rubin and Clayton Swears.

6. Dr. Thomas R. Johnson, "Signals Intelligence in the Korean War," paper presented at the 26th Annual Conference of the Society for Historians of American Foreign Relations, June 23, 2000, Toronto, Canada; Frahm, *Power Can Be Brought*, pp. 6–7; John Milmore, *#1 Code Break Boy* (Haverford, PA: Infinity Publishing, 2002), pp. 33, 40–41, 47.

7. Johnson, *American Cryptology*, bk. 1, pp. 43, 55; Frahm, *Power Can Be Brought*, p. 7; NSA OH-1999-51, oral history, *Interview with Benson K. Buffham*, June 15, 1999, p. 33, NSA FOIA.

8. Johnson, "Signals Intelligence"; Hatch and Benson, *The Korean War*, p. 9. See also Clay Blair, *The Forgotten War: America in Korea, 1950–1953* (New York: Times Books, 1987), p. 171. Polk quote from April 25, 1991, letter to author from General James H. Polk. Woolnough quote from Senior Officers Debriefing Program, *Oral History of General James K. Woolnough*, vol. 1, p. 31, U.S. Army Military History Institute, Carlisle Barracks, PA.

9. Johnson, *American Cryptology*, bk. 1, p. 43; Dr. Thomas R. Johnson, "American Cryptology During the Korean War—A Preliminary Verdict," June 2000, p. 5, paper presented at the 26th Annual Conference of the Society for Historians of American Foreign Relations, June 23, 2000, Toronto, Canada; Frahm, *Power Can Be Brought*, p. 12; "SIGINT in the Defense of the Pusan Perimeter: Korea 1950," manuscript, date unknown, NSA FOIA; Blair, *Forgotten War*, p. 240.

10. Memorandum, GHQ FEC G-2, Operations Branch to C/S ROK, *JSO/KLO Report No. 17*, 130030K Aug 1950, RG-6, box 14, folder 6, Correspondence: Memoranda/Messageforms, 23 July–August 30, 1950, MacArthur Memorial Library, Norfolk, VA; memorandum, GHQ FEC G-2, Operations Branch to C/S ROK, *JSO/KLO Report No. 19*, August 15, 1950, RG-6, box 14, folder 6, Correspondence: Memoranda/Messageforms, 23 July–August 30, 1950, MacArthur Memorial Library, Norfolk, VA; message, G 10011 KGI, CG, EUSAK REAR to CG EUSAK FORWARD, August 19, 1950, RG-338 Records of the Eighth U.S. Army, entry 116 ACofS, G-2 Outgoing Radio Messages 1950–1951, box 50, file: Comeback Copies—1950, NA, CP; DA TT 3708, Telecon, WASH and CINCFE, August 30, 1950, p. 8, RG-59, Decimal File 1950–1954, box 4268, file: 795.00/8-3050, NA, CP.

11. Memorandum, GHQ FEC G-2, Operations Branch to C/S ROK, *JSO/KLO Report No. 17*, 130030K Aug 1950, RG-6, box 14, folder 6, Correspondence: Memoranda/Messageforms, 23 July–August 30, 1950, MacArthur Memorial Library, Norfolk, VA; SRC-3927, CIA, *Situation Summary*, August 25, 1950, p. 1, President's Secretary's Files, box 211, file: Situation Summary, HSTL, Independence, MO.

12. HQ Eighth U.S. Army Korea, *Appendix No. 1 to Annex A (Intelligence) to Operations Plan 10*, September 10, 1950, pp. 4–5; TS message, Dickey to Davidson, undated but circa September 11, 1950, both in RG-338, Records of Eighth U.S. Army, entry 113, box 44, file 322.1 1950, NA, CP.

13. CIA, *Situation Summary*, August 18, 1950, p. 1, President's Secretary's Files, box 211, file Situation Summary, HSTL, Independence, MO; report, AFSA [deleted]-1230/50, WS-[PKC 321], North Korean, September 14, 1950, NSA FOIA; report, AFSA [deleted]-1305/50, WS-[PKC 360], North Korean, September 14, 1950, NSA FOIA; SRC-4232, CIA, *Situation Summary*, September 15, 1950, p. 2, President's Secretary's Files, box 211, file Situation Summary, HSTL, Independence, MO; SRC-4397, CIA, *Situation Summary*, September 22, 1950, p. 1, President's Secretary's Files, box 211, file Situation Summary, HSTL, Independence, MO; Frahm, *Power Can Be Brought*, p. 13.

14. Milmore, *#1 Code Break Boy*, pp. 57–58.

15. ASA, *History, Army Security Agency and Subordinate Units, FY 1950*, p. 28, INSCOM FOIA; ASA, *History, Army Security Agency and Supporting Units, FY 1951*, vol. 2, pp. 3, 18–22, INSCOM FOIA; Johnson, *American Cryptology*, bk. 1, p. 44; Guy R. Vanderpool, "COMINT and the PRC Intervention in the Korean War," *Cryptologic Quarterly*, vol. 15, no. 2 (Summer 1996): pp. 9–10, NSA FOIA; Hatch and Benson, *The Korean War*, p. 9; Johnson, "Signals Intelligence in the Korean War."

16. CIA, *Situation Summary*, October 27, 1950, p. 3, President's Secretary's Files, box 211, HSTL, Independence, MO; Johnson, *American Cryptology*, bk. 1, pp. 44–45; Vanderpool, "COMINT and the PRC Intervention," pp. 11, 14; Hatch and Benson, *The Korean War*, p. 9.

17. Department of the Army, Assistant Chief of Staff, G-2, Intelligence, *Periodic Intelligence Report on Soviet Intentions and Activities*, July 7, 1950, tab "A," p. 1, RG-319, entry 4 1950 Chief of Staff Top Secret Decimal Files, box 3, 091 Russia Case #5, NA, CP; memorandum for record, November 15, 1950, RG-341, entry 214 file 2-17100-2-17199, NA, CP; Cynthia M. Grabo, "The Watch Committee and the National Indications Center: The Evolution of U.S. Strategic Warnings, 1950–1975," *International Journal of Intelligence and Counterintelligence*, vol. 3, no. 3: p. 367.

18. Interviews with Morton A. Rubin and Louis Tordella. Panikkar's background from K. M. Panikkar, *In Two Chinas: Memoirs of a Diplomat* (London: Allen and Unwin, 1955) and K. M. Panikkar, *An Autobiography* (Madras: Oxford University Press, 1977).

19. Department of State, Office of Intelligence Research, *Current Soviet and Chinese Communist Intentions, No. 1*, August 8, 1950, p. 2, RG-59, entry 1561 Lot 58D776 INR Subject Files 1945–1956, box 17, file: Current Soviet and Chinese Intentions 8-8-50, NA, CP; CIA, *Interim Situation Summary*, September 30, 1950, p. 1, President's Secretary's Files, box 211, file: Situation Summary, HSTL, Independence, MO.

20. SRC-4635, CIA, *Situation Summary*, October 6, 1950, p. 2, President's Secretary's files, box 211, file: Situation Summary, HSTL, Independence, MO.

21. CIA, *Interim Situation Summary*, September 30, 1950, p. 1, President's Secretary's Files, box 211, file: Situation Summary, HSTL, Independence, MO; Vanderpool, "COMINT and the PRC Intervention," p. 14; Hatch and Benson, *The Korean War*, p. 9. See also message no. 792, Moscow to Secretary of State, September 29, 1950, RG-59, Decimal File 1950–1954, box 4298, file: 795A.5/9-2950, NA, CP.

22. Memorandum, McConaughy to Jessup and Rusk, *Credibility of K.M. Panikkar, Indian Ambassador to Communist China*, October 12, 1950, RG-59, entry 399A Office of Chinese Affairs Top Secret Subject Files: 1945–1950, box 18, file: 1950 TS Formosa: August–December, NA, CP.

23. Thomas J. Christensen, "Threats, Assurances, and the Last Chance for Peace," *International Security*, vol. 17, no. 1 (Summer 1992): pp. 151–52; Chen Jian, *China's Road to the Korean War* (New York: Columbia University Press, 1994), pp. 172–77.

24. For the Panikkar warning, see message no. 828, New Delhi to Secretary of State, October 3, 1950, RG-59, Decimal File 1950–1954, box 4268, file: 795.00/10-350, NA, CP; British Embassy, Washington, DC, *Message Received from His Majesty's Chargé d'Affaires, Peking, dated 3rd October, 1950*, RG-59, Decimal File 1950–1954, box 4298, file: 795A.5/10-550, NA, CP; memorandum, Clubb to Merchant, *Chinese Communist Threat of Intervention in Korea*, October 4, 1950, RG-59, entry 399A Office of Chinese Affairs Top Secret Subject Files: 1945–1950, box 18, file: 1950 TS Korea: June–October, NA, CP. See also memorandum, Bolling to Chief of Staff, *U.S. Intelligence Coverage of the Relationship of Communist China to the Korean War from 25 June to 24 November 1950*, May 7, 1951, p. 12, RG-319, entry 1041, ID No. 928809, NA, CP; Bruce W. Bidwell, Col., USA (Ret.), *History of the Military Intelligence Division, Department of the Army General Staff*, 1962, part 7, *Korean Conflict: 25 June 1950–27 July 1953*, p. V-16, OCMH FOIA. For the Dutch warning, see Department of State, *Daily Staff Summary*, October 3, 1950, p. 1, RG-59, entry 3049 Daily Staff Summary 1944-71, box 10, NA, CP; message no. 490, The Hague to Secretary of State, October 3, 1950, Papers of Harry S. Truman, Selected Records Relating to the Korean War, box 7, item no. 18, HSTL, Independence, MO; memorandum, Clubb to Merchant, *General Whitney's Latest Remarks Concerning Chinese Communist Intentions to Intervene in North Korea*, April 22, 1951, p. 2, RG-59, entry 1207 Records of the Office of Chinese Affairs— "P" Files, box 22, file 13p Korea TS, NA, CP.

25. For CIA dismissals of Panikkar warnings, see "Indications of Chinese Intervention in Korea, October 1950–December 1950," p. 1, Exhibit O to CIA Historical Staff, *Study of CIA Reporting on Chinese Intervention in the Korean War: September–December 1950*, October 1955, CIA FOIA; CIA, *Daily Summary #1409*, October 3, 1950, p. 1, CREST Collection, Document No. CIA-RDP78-01617A006100020074-8, NA, CP; CIA, *Weekly Summary*, October 6, 1953, pp. 6, 8, CIA Electronic FOIA Reading Room, Document No. 0001117967, http://www.foia.cia.gov; CIA, *Threat of Full Chinese Communist Intervention in Korea*, October 12, 1950, p. 4, CIA Electronic FOIA Reading Room, Document No. 0000121494, http://www.foia.cia.gov.

26. Chen Jian, *The Sino-Soviet Alliance and China's Entry into the Korean War* (Washington, DC:

Woodrow Wilson International Center for Scholars, Cold War International History Project, 1992), pp. 29–30.

27. John Patrick Finnegan, *Military Intelligence: An Overview, 1885–1987* (Washington DC: Department of the Army, 1998), p. 121, INSCOM FOIA; April 25, 1991, letter to author from General James H. Polk.

28. Memorandum, Smith to President, October 20, 1950, White House Office, National Security Council Staff: Records 1946–61, Executive Secretary's Subject File, box 10, file: Eyes Only (1), Dwight D. Eisenhower Library, Abilene, KS; TS #43933, memorandum, Smith to Deputy Secretary of Defense, *Summary of Intelligence Estimates on Intervention by Chinese Communists in the Korean War (12 October–24 November 1950)*, May 4, 1951, RG-330, entry 199 Central Decimal Files 1951, box 232, file: CD 092 Korea Folder #5 February 1951–April 1951, NA, CP.

29. CIA, *Situation Summary*, October 27, 1950, p. 3, President's Secretary's Files, box 211, file: Situation Summary, HSTL, Independence, MO; Johnson, *American Cryptology*, bk. 1, p. 44; Vanderpool, "COMINT and the PRC Intervention," p. 14.

30. Report, Far East Command, ACS/G-2 *Trends of High Level Washington Estimates on Chinese Communist Intervention*, February 23, 1951, RG-23, MacArthur Memorial Library, Nofolk, VA.

31. Interviews with James Polk, Morton A. Rubin, and Milton Zaslow; Shelley Davis, "New Exhibit Accents the War for Secrets in Korea," *Stars and Stripes*, September 25, 2000; Office of the Secretary of Defense Historical Office, oral history, *Interview with General M.B. Ridgway*, April 18, 1984, pp. 20–21, DoD FOIA Reading Room, Pentagon, Washington, DC. See also Laura Sullivan, "Old Hands Disclose Once-Secret Tales as NSA Opens Exhibit on Korean War," *Baltimore Sun*, September 20, 2000.

32. The best description of the Battle of Unsan is Roy E. Appleman, *South to the Naktong, North to the Yalu* (Washington, DC: OCMH, 1961), pp. 673–81, 689–708.

33. CIA, *Situation Summary*, October 27, 1950, p. 1, President's Secretary's Files, box 211, file: Situation Summary, HSTL, Independence, MO; message, W 95148, DEPTAR WASH DC to CINCFE et al., October 28, 1950, RG-9, box 112, file: DA WX October 1950, MacArthur Memorial Library, Norfolk, VA; message, No. 310, Seoul to Secretary of State, October 29, 1950, RG-59, Decimal File 1950–1954, box 4269, file: 795.00/10-2950, NA, CP; CIA, *Daily Summary #1432*, October 30, 1950, p. 1, CREST Collection, Document No. CIA-RDP78-0617A006100020051-3, NA, CP.

34. Message, GX 26711 KGI, CG EUSAK to CINCFE, October 26, 1950, RG-338 Records of the Eighth U.S. Army, entry 133 AG Section, Security Classified General Correspondence 1950, box 723, file 350.09, NA, CP; message, G 26900 KGI, CG EUSAK to CINCFE, October 30, 1950; message, G 26979 KGI, CG EUSAK to CINCFE, October 31, 1950; and message, GX 27016 KGI, CG EUSAK to CINCFE, October 31, all in RG-338 Records of the Eighth U.S. Army, entry 133 AG Section, Security Classified General Correspondence 1950, box 723, file 350.09, NA, CP.

35. Message, FRU/FEC 1845, October 27, 1950, and message, FRU/FEC 1846, October 27, 1950, both in RG-6, box 14, file: Correspondence, Messageforms, MacArthur Memorial Library, Norfolk, VA. For Willoughby barring the CIA from the POW cages, see letter, White to Tarkenton, October 27, 1950; letter, Ewert to Tarkenton, October 28, 1950; and letter, Ewert to Tarkenton, October 31, 1950, all in RG-338 Records of the Eighth U.S. Army: 1946–1956, Assistant Chief of Staff, G-2, box 55, file: General Willoughby File, NA, CP; message, C-67919, CINCFE TOKYO JAPAN to CG ARMY EIGHT, October 31, 1950, RG-9, box 38, file: Army 8 Out: October 1950, MacArthur Memorial Library, Norfolk, VA.

36. Vanderpool, "COMINT and the PRC Intervention," p. 17.

37. CIA, *Situation Summary*, November 24, 1950, pp. 1–2, President's Secretary's Files, box 211, HSTL, Independence, MO; Vanderpool, "COMINT and the PRC Intervention," p. 18; Cynthia

M. Grabo, *A Handbook of Warning Intelligence*, July 1972, vol. I, p. 18-4, RG-263, CIA Reference Collection, Document No. CIA-RDP80B00829A000800040001-6, NA, CP.

38. Message, WST 268, G-2 GSUSA to SSR TOKYO (Collins to MacArthur Eyes Only), November 11, 1950, p. 2, RG-16A Papers of Major General Courtney Whitney, box 5, folder 14, MacArthur Memorial Library, Norfolk, VA.

39. Message, C 69953, CINCFE TOKYO JAPAN to DA WASH DC, November 28, 1950, RG-6, box 1, folder 11 Correspondence November–December 1950, MacArthur Memorial Library, Norfolk, VA.

40. For lack of SIGINT coverage of the Chinese military prior to the Chinese intervention in Korea, see ASA, *History of the Army Security Agency and Subordinate Units: FY 1951*, vol. 2, pp. 3, 18–22, INSCOM FOIA; Vanderpool, "COMINT and the PRC," p. 9; Hatch and Benson, *The Korean War*, p. 9; Milmore, *#1 Code Break Boy*, p. 65. For lack of Chinese linguists, see ASA, Pacific, *Summary Annual Report, FY 1951*, p. 63, INSCOM FOIA; ASA, *History of the Army Security Agency and Subordinate Units, FY 1951*, vol. 2, p. 8, INSCOM FOIA. Quote about lack of intelligence on Chinese forces from memorandum, Banfill to Commanding General, *Location and Disposition of the CCF in Korea*, December 14, 1950, RG-554, Records of the Far East Command, entry 16 ACofS, G-2 Executive (Coordination) Division General Correspondence Decimal Files, box 23, file 350.09 Book #3, NA, CP.

41. Matthew B. Ridgway, *Soldier* (New York: Harper, 1956), p. 205; *G-2 Briefing Notes for Lt. General Matthew W. Ridgway*, December 26, 1950, pp. 3–4, RG-338, Records of the Eighth U.S. Army 1946–1956, entry 117 EUSAK ACofS, G-2 Intelligence Admin Files 1950–1955, box 51, NA, CP.

42. Johnson, *American Cryptology*, bk. 1, p. 55.

43. *G-2 Briefing Notes for Lt. General Matthew W. Ridgway*, December 26, 1950, pp. 2–3, RG-338, Records of the Eighth U.S. Army 1946–1956, entry 117 EUSAK ACofS, G-2 Intelligence Admin Files 1950–1955, box 51, NA, CP; Special Study Group of the NSA Scientific Advisory Board, *The Potentialities of COMINT for Strategic Warning*, October 20, 1953, appendix 9, COMINT as a Source of Advance Warning in World War II and the Korean Conflict, p. 3, DOCID: 3213594, NSA FOIA; USAFSS History Office, *A Special Historical Study of USAFSS Response to World Crises: 1949–1969*, April 22, 1970, p. 3, AIA FOIA.

44. Memorandum, Pizzi to Commanding General, January 2, 1951, RG-338, Records of the Eighth U.S. Army 1946–1956, entry 118 EUSAK G-2 Action Files, box 58, file G-2 Action Files 1951—vol. 1, NA, CP; Cipher Telegram No. 103, Mao Zedong to Stalin, January 8, 1951, Cold War International History Project, http://www.wilsoncenter.org.

45. Memorandum, Tarkenton to Commanding General, *Intelligence Agencies Available to G-2*, undated but circa January 1951, pp. 2–3, RG-338, Records of the Eighth U.S. Army 1946–1956, entry 118 EUSAK G-2 Action Files, box 58, file G-2 Action File 1951, Book #1, NA, CP; checklist, Tarkenton to C/S, "Notes for the Commanding General," January 16, 1951, pp. 1–2, RG-338, Records of the Eighth U.S. Army 1946–1956, entry 118 EUSAK G-2 Action Files, box 58, file G-2 Action File 1951, Book #1, NA, CP; memorandum, ACofS, G-2/ASA to OCSigO, *Modification of Radio Set AN/CRD-2*, January 19, 1951, RG-319, entry 47E Army G-2 Decimal File 1949–1950, box 177, file 413.44 4/1/50–12/31/50, NA, CP; ASA, *History of the Army Security Agency and Subordinate Units: FY 1951*, vol. 2, pp. 3, 18–22, INSCOM FOIA; Johnson, *American Cryptology*, bk. 1, p. 46.

46. Memorandum, Tarkenton to Assistant Chief of Staff, G2, I Corps et al., *Classified Information for Limited Use*, January 2, 1951, RG-338, Records of the Eighth U.S. Army 1946–1956, entry 117 EUSAK G-2 Intelligence Admin Files 1950–1955, box 53, file Classified Information for Limited Use, NA, CP; message, G-1231, CG EUSAK to CG X CORPS, January 3, 1951, RG-338, Records of the Eighth U.S. Army 1946–1956, entry 133 AG Section, Security Classified General Correspondence 1951, box 785, file 350.09 Jan–Feb, NA, CP.

47. Eighth U.S. Army G-2, "G-2 Brief: Estimate," January 15, 1951, p. 3, RG-338, Records of the Eighth U.S. Army 1946–1956, entry 118 EUSAK G-2 Action Files, box 58, file G-2 Action File 1951, vol. 1, NA, CP; memorandum, Tarkenton to Assistant Chief of Staff, G2, I Corps et al., *Classified Information for Limited Use*, January 14, 1951; memorandum, Tarkenton to Assistant Chief of Staff, G2, I Corps et al., *Classified Information for Limited Use*, January 23, 1951; memorandum, Tarkenton to Assistant Chief of Staff, G2, I Corps et al., *Classified Information for Limited Use*, January 31, 1951, all in RG-338, Records of the Eighth U.S. Army 1946–1956, entry 117 (A1) EUSAK G-2 Intelligence Admin Files 1950–1955, box 53, file Classified Information for Limited Use, NA, CP.

48. Memorandum, Tarkenton to Assistant Chief of Staff, G2, I Corps et al., *Classified Information for Limited Use*, January 29, 1951; memorandum, Tarkenton to Assistant Chief of Staff, G2, I Corps et al., *Classified Information for Limited Use*, February 5, 1951, both in RG-338, Records of the Eighth U.S. Army 1946–1956, entry 117 (A1) EUSAK G-2 Intelligence Admin Files 1950–1955, box 53, file Classified Information for Limited Use, NA, CP.

49. 1st Radio Squadron, Mobile, *First Radio Squadron, Mobile Historical Report: 1 Jan 1951 thru 31 Mar 1951*, pp. 3–4, AIA FOIA; Pierson, *A Special Historical Study*, p. 5; Robert F. Futrell, "A Case Study: USAF Intelligence in the Korean War," in Walter T. Hitchcock, ed., *The Intelligence Revolution: A Historical Perspective* (Washington, DC: Office of Air Force History, 1991), p. 286; John Patrick Finnegan, "The Intelligence War in Korea: An Army Perspective," in Jacob Neufeld and George M. Watson Jr., eds., *Coalition Air Warfare in the Korean War: 1950–1953* (Washington, DC: U.S. Air Force History and Museums Program, 2005), p. 217.

50. Paul Lashmar, "POWs, Soviet Intelligence and the MIA Question," p. 4, presented at the conference The Korean War: An Assessment of the Historical Record, Georgetown University, Washington, DC, July 24–25, 1995.

51. Finnegan, "The Intelligence War," p. 217; confidential interviews.

52. Message, JCS 88180, CHAIRMAN JOINT CHIEFS OF STAFF to CINCFE TOKYO Japan, April 11, 1951, RG-218, JCS Messages Relating to Operations in Korea, box 9, file JCS Outgoing Dispatches 1/3/51–5/31/51, NA, CP.

53. Joseph C. Goulden, *Korea: The Untold Story of the War* (New York: McGraw-Hill, 1982), p. 477.

54. Radio, WST 268, G-2 GSUSA to SSR TOKYO (Collins to MacArthur Eyes Only), November 11, 1950, p. 2, RG-16A Papers of Major General Courtney Whitney, box 5, folder 14, MacArthur Memorial Library, Norfolk, VA.

55. Richard D. McKinzie, *Oral History Interview with Paul H. Nitze*, Northeast Harbor, ME, August 5–6, 1975, pp. 268–69, HSTL, Independence, MO.

56. Handwritten working paper of indications for SIE-1, undated, p. 2, CREST Collection, Document No. CIA-RDP79S01011A000100010028-8, NA, CP; memorandum, Hooker to Nitze, February 28, 1951, RG-59, entry 1568 Policy Planning Staff Records 1947–1953, box 20, file Korea 1951, NA, CP; message, CX 59843, CINCFE TOKYO JAPAN to DEPTAR WASH DC FOR G-2, April 10, 1951, RG-319, entry 58 G-2 Top Secret Cables 1942–1952, box 170, file Japan 3 Jan–31 Aug 51, NA, CP. For breaking of new North Korean codes, see 60th Signal Service Company, *Annual Historical Report, 60th Signal Service Company, Fiscal Year 1951*, pp. 16–17, INSCOM FOIA.

57. Message, GX-3-1440-KGIO, CG EUSAK to CG IX CORPS et al., March 8, 1951, RG-338, Records of the Eighth U.S. Army 1946–1956, entry 220 COMGEN EUSAK Correspondence 1951, box 1638, file March 1951, NA, CP; message, C50802Z, COMNAVFE TOKYO JAPAN to COM7THFLT, April 5, 1951, RG-9, box 57, Radiograms—Incoming Navy (XTS) November 1950–April 1951, MacArthur Memorial Library, Norfolk, VA; HQ Eighth United States Army Korea (EUSAK), Office of the Assistant Chief of Staff, G-2, Intelligence, "Brief Estimate of the Enemy

Situation (Tactical)," April 9, 1951, pp. 4–8, RG-338, Records of the Eighth U.S. Army 1946–1956, entry 124 (A1) EUSAK G-2 Formerly Top Secret Intelligence Reports, box 81, file G-2 Tactical Estimate, NA, CP; message, CX 59843, CINCFE TOKYO JAPAN to DEPTAR WASH DC FOR G-2, April 10, 1951, RG-319, entry 58, box 170, file Japan 3 Jan–31 Aug 51, NA, CP; Eighth Army G-2, "Indications," April 13, 1951, in *Command Report, Eighth United States Army Korea (EUSAK): April 1951*, sec. 2, bk. 3, Part 5, RG-407, Eighth U.S. Army, entry 429, box 1182, NA, CP. See also Blair, *Forgotten War*, pp. 870–71, 873; Roy E. Appleman, *Ridgway Duels for Korea* (College Station, TX: Texas A&M University Press, 1990), p. 507.

58. CIA, Directorate of Intelligence, memorandum, *The Vietnamese Communists Will to Persist*, annex 12, *An Historical Analysis of Asian Communist Employment of the Political Tactics of Negotiations*, August 26, 1966, p. xii–18, CIA Electronic FOIA Reading Room, Document No. 0001169545, http://www.foia.cia.gov; GHQ, UNC/FEC, "Daily Intelligence Summary," No. 3204, June 18, 1951, cited in Eduard Mark, *Aerial Interdiction in Three Wars* (Washington, DC: Center for Air Force History, 1994), pp. 303, 316.

59. The Soviet air force stand-down lasted for nearly two weeks, with entire days going by when there were no signs whatsoever in SIGINT reporting that any Soviet planes were taking off or landing at Soviet military airfields. The eerie silence finally came to an end on May 4, 1951, when radio intercepts confirmed that routine Soviet air force tactical flight activity had resumed. CIA, memorandum, *Cessation of Soviet Far East Tactical Air Activity*, May 12, 1951, p. 1, President's Secretary's Files, box 211, file Situation Summary, HSTL, Independence, MO.

60. TS Cont. No. 2-19203, memorandum, Wilcox to Director of Central Intelligence, *Soviet AOB and Significant Air Developments, 11–17 April 1951, Inclusive*, April 18, 1951, Tab A, p. 1, RG-341, entry 214 Top Secret Cable and Controls Division, box 56, file 2-19200-2-19299, NA, CP; CIA/SIC/N-2M/51, Special Intelligence Estimate No. 2, *Communist Military Forces in the Korean Area*, April 27, 1951, pp. 5, 11, MORI DocID: 1226087, CIA FOIA.

61. Memorandum, Smith to President, *North Korean Army*, July 11, 1951, President's Secretary's Files, box 211, file Situation Summary, HSTL, Independence, MO; Burns, *Origins*, p. 93; Johnson, *American Cryptology*, bk. 1, p. 55; Johnson, "A Preliminary Verdict," p. 9; Milmore, *#1 Code Break Boy*, pp. 116–17.

62. Johnson, "A Preliminary Verdict," p. 10.

63. Burns, *Origins*, pp. 94–95.

3: Fight for Survival

1. Canine background from biographical data sheet, Brigadier General Ralph Julian Canine, September 1946, U.S. Army Center of Military History, Washington, DC; *NSA Newsletter*, January 1954, p. 1, NSA FOIA.

2. Jacob Gurin and [deleted], "Ralph J. Canine," *Cryptologic Spectrum*, vol. 1, no. 1 (Fall 1969): p. 7, DOCID: 3217178, NSA FOIA.

3. Letter, Wenger to Stone, May 13, 1952, RG-38, CNSG Library, box 101, file: MISC November 1951–July 1953, NA, CP; Charles P. Collins, *The History of SIGINT in the Central Intelligence Agency, 1947–1970* (Washington, DC: CIA History Office, October 1971), vol. 2, p. 2; Gurin and [deleted], "Ralph J. Canine," p. 9; U.S. Army Military History Institute, oral history, *Interview with John J. Davis, Lt. General, USA Retired*, 1986, p. 113, Army Center for Military History, Washington, DC.

4. For AFSA's SIGINT problems in Korea, see Thomas L. Burns, *The Origins of the National Security Agency: 1940–1952* (Fort Meade, MD: Center for Cryptologic History, 1990), p. 93, NSA FOIA; memorandum, EUSAK G-2 to Chief of Staff, *Notes for the Commanding General*, January

16, 1951, RG-338, Records of the Eighth U.S. Army 1946–1956, entry 118 EUSAK G-2 Action Files, box 58, file: G-2 Action File, vol. 1, NA, CP; memorandum, G-2 to Commanding General EUSAK, *Intelligence Agencies Available to G-2*, undated, RG-338, Records of the Eighth U.S. Army 1946–1956, entry 118 EUSAK G-2 Action Files, box 58, file G-2 Action File, vol. 1, NA, CP; message, 12/1908Z, Willoughby to ACSI, March 12, 1951, MORI DOCID: 3104676 NSA FOIA; oral history, *Interview with Herbert L. Conley*, March 5, 1984, pp. 73–74, declassified and on file at the library of the National Cryptologic Museum, Fort Meade, MD; Benson K. Buffham, "The Korean War and AFSA," *The Phoenician*, Spring 2001: p. 7. For the nightmarish internal situation at AFSA, see letter, Wenger to Roeder, December 29, 1950, p. 1, RG-38, Crane CNSG Library, box 101, file: Miscellaneous N-RCA, NA, CP; letter, Wenger to Mason, May 19, 1951, RG-38, Crane CNSG Library, box 101, file: Miscellaneous 1950–1951, NA, CP; letter, Mason to Wenger, December 22, 1951, RG-38, Crane CNSG Library, box 101, file: Miscellaneous 1951–1952, NA, CP.

5.   For reorganization of NSA, see AFSA, General Order No. 1, *Staff Assignments*, January 9, 1952, NSA FOIA. For Rowlett's departure, see letter, Wenger to Mason, January 17, 1952, RG-38 CNSG Library, box 101, file MISC 11/51–7/53, NA, CP; NSA oral history, *Interview with Frank B. Rowlett*, 1976, p. 372, NSA FOIA; NSA-OH-11-82, oral history, *Interview with Captain Wesley A. Wright, USN*, May 24, 1982, p. 80, NSA FOIA; Dr. Thomas R. Johnson, *American Cryptology During the Cold War, 1945–1989* (Fort Meade, MD: Center for Cryptologic History, 1995), bk. I: *The Struggle for Centralization, 1945–1960*, p. 93, NSA FOIA.

6.   Burns, *Origins*, pp. 77–78; *Director's Meeting*, October 25, 1951, CREST Collection, Document No. CIA-RDP80B01676R002300070052-5, NA, CP; *Daily Diary*, December 17, 1951, CREST Collection, Document No. CIA-RDP80R01731R0026005300011-9, NA, CP; CIA TS #29771, memorandum, Smith to Executive Secretary, National Security Council, *Proposed Survey of Communications Intelligence Activities*, December 10, 1951, President's Secretary's Files, Box 211, file: Situation Summary, HSTL, Independence, Missouri; ASA, *Annual Historical Report, Army Security Agency: Fiscal Year 1953*, p. 14, INSCOM FOIA; AC of S, G3, ASA, *Annual Historical Report of the Assistant Chief of Staff, G3, Plans, Organization and Training: Fiscal Year 1953*, September 1, 1953, p. 14, INSCOM FOIA. For CIA attitudes toward AFSA's performance, see Ludwell Lee Montague, *General Walter Bedell Smith as Director of Central Intelligence, October 1950–February 1953*, December 1971, vol. 5, p. 54, RG-263, NA, CP; memorandum, Smith to National Security Council, *Report by the Director of Central Intelligence*, April 23, 1952, p. 5, CREST Collection, Document No. CIA-RDP80R01731R001100080027-7, NA, CP.

7.   For Truman's meeting on June 13, 1952, with Smith and Lay, see President Truman's Presidential Appointments Calendar for June 13, 1952, Matthew J. Connelly Files, HSTL, Independence, MO.

8.   Memorandum, Bradley to Lovett, July 17, 1952, RG-218, Bradley CJCS File, box 4, file 334 (A-L1952), NA, CP; memorandum, Samford to Twining, August 6, 1952, RG-341, entry 214, box 66, file 2-24400-2-24499, NA, CP; memorandum, G-2 to Chief of Staff, *Brownell Special Committee Report*, August 7, 1952, RG-319, entry 1 (UD) Army Chief of Staff Top Secret Correspondence, box 11, NA, CP; *Official Diary*, August 7, 1952, p. 2, CREST Collection, Document No. CIA-RDP79-01041A000100020158-9, NA, CP; memorandum, Twining to Secretary of Defense, August 8, 1952, RG-341, entry 214, box 66, file 2-24500-2-24599, NA, CP; memorandum, Howe to Armstrong, October 9, 1952, RG-59, entry 1561 Lot 58D776 INR Subject Files, box 27, file NSA, NA, CP (this document was reclassified by the CIA in 2005); *Official Diary*, October 10, 1952, p. 2, CREST Collection, Document No. CIA-RDP79-01041A000100020105-7, NA, CP; *Official Diary*, October 11, 1952, p. 1, CREST Collection, Document No. CIA-RDP79-01041A000100020104-8, NA, CP; ASA, *Annual Historical Report, Army Security Agency Fiscal Year 1953*, p. 15, INSCOM FOIA.

9. For Truman signing the directive, see President Truman's Presidential Appointments Calendar for October 24, 1952, Matthew J. Connelly Files, HSTL, Independence, MO.

10. Memorandum, President Truman to Secretaries of State and Defense, *Communications Intelligence Activities*, October 24, 1952, CREST Collection, Document No. CIA-RDP77-00389R000100090045-8, NA, CP; NSA, *National Security Agency Organization Manual*, April 19, 1954, chap. 3, p. 1, NSA FOIA; CIA Historical Staff, *Allen Welsh Dulles as DCI*, vol. 2, pp. 157–58, RG-263, NA, CP; ASA, *History of the Army Security Agency and Subordinate Units for Fiscal Year 1953*, vol. 1, pp. 3–4, INSCOM FOIA; ASA, *Annual Historical Report ASA G-3 Fiscal Year 1953*, p. 16, INSCOM FOIA.

4: THE INVENTORY OF IGNORANCE

1. CIA, Office of Current Intelligence, Caesar-1, *"The Doctors' Plot,"* July 15, 1953, p. 13; CIA, Office of Current Intelligence, Caesar-2, *Death of Stalin*, July 16, 1953, pp. 1–2, 11–14; CIA, Office of Current Intelligence, Caesar-4, *Germany*, July 16, 1953, p. 1, all in CIA Electronic FOIA Reading Room, Caesar-Polo-Esau Papers, http://www.foia.cia.gov/cpe.asp.

2. For early HUMINT reporting on the East Berlin riots, see OCI No. 4491A, CIA, Office of Current Intelligence, *Comment on East Berlin Uprising*, June 17, 1953, CIA Electronic FOIA Reading Room, Document No. 0000677387, http://www.foia.cia.gov. For NSA performance, confidential interviews.

3. Dr. Thomas R. Johnson, *American Cryptology During the Cold War, 1945–1989*, bk. 1, *The Struggle for Centralization, 1945–1960* (Fort Meade, MD: Center for Cryptologic History, 1995), p. 227, NSA FOIA.

4. Commission on Organization of the Executive Branch of the Government, *Task Force Report on Intelligence Activities in the Federal Government* (Hoover Commission Report), May 1955, appendix 1, part 1, Report of Survey of National Security Agency, p. 48, CREST Collection, Document No. CIA-RDP86B00269R000900010001-0, NA, CP; Johnson, *American Cryptology*, bk. 1, pp. 228–29; interview with Frank Rowlett.

5. CIA 36337-c, "The Foreign Intelligence Program," February 10, 1954, p. 5, attached to memorandum, Office of Intelligence Coordination to Director of Central Intelligence, *NSC Status Report*, February 17, 1954, CREST Collection, Document No. CIA-RDP80B01676R001100070001-4, NA, CP; Johnson, *American Cryptology*, bk. 1, p. 178. The "very dark" quote is taken from IAC-D-55/4, Intelligence Advisory Committee, *NSC Status Report on the Foreign Intelligence Program*, July 28, 1953, p. 6, CREST Collection, Document No. CIA-RDP80R01731R000800070010-0, NA, CP.

6. CIA, Directorate of Intelligence, RP 77-10141CX, *Probable Soviet Reactions to a Crisis in Poland*, June 1977, pp. 3, 21–22, CIA Electronic FOIA Reading Room, Document No. 0000498549, http://www.foia.cia.gov.

7. "Situation in Hungary," *Current Intelligence Digest*, October 24, 1956, p. 3, CIA Electronic FOIA Reading Room, Document No. 0000119732, http://www.foia.cia.gov; CIA, NSC Briefing, *Hungary*, October 25, 1956, pp. 1–2, CIA Electronic FOIA Reading Room, Document No. 0000119733, http://www.foia.cia.gov; "The Hungarian Situation (as of 0100 EDT)," *Current Intelligence Bulletin*, October 27, 1956, pp. 3–4, 13, CIA Electronic FOIA Reading Room, Document No. 0000119738, http://www.foia.cia.gov; memorandum, Office of Current Intelligence to Deputy Director (Intelligence), *Military Activity Connected with the Hungarian Crisis*, October 27, 1956, CIA Electronic FOIA Reading Room, Document No. 0000119739, http://www.foia.cia.gov; "The Situation in Hungary (as of 0900, 1 November)," *Current Intelligence Weekly Review*, November 1, 1956, pp. 5–6, CIA Electronic FOIA Reading Room, Document No. 0000119766,

http://www.foia.cia.gov. For Bad Aibling monitoring these Russian radio transmissions, see
David Colley, "Shadow Warriors: Intelligence Operatives Waged Clandestine Cold War," *VFW
Magazine*, September 1997.

8. Memorandum, Office of Current Intelligence to Deputy Director (Intelligence), *Military Activity Connected with the Hungarian Crisis*, October 27, 1956, CIA Electronic FOIA Reading Room,
Document No. 0000119739, http://www.foia.cia.gov; "The Situation in Hungary (as of 0900, 1
November)," *Current Intelligence Weekly Review*, November 1, 1956, pp. 5–6, CIA Electronic
FOIA Reading Room, Document No. 0000119766, http://www.foia.cia.gov.

9. "New Large-Scale Mobilization in Israel," *Current Intelligence Bulletin*, October 27, 1956, p. 6,
CREST Collection, Document No. CIA-RDP79T00975A002800070001-3, NA, CP; "Israel Approaching Complete Mobilization," *Current Intelligence Bulletin*, October 28, 1956, p. 5, CREST
Collection, Document No. CIA-RDP79T00975A002800080001-2, NA, CP; message, JCS
91289, Joint Chiefs of Staff to Commander in Chief Strategic Air Command, October 29,
1956, box B206, file Item B-57673, Curtis E. LeMay Papers, Library of Congress; CIA, History
Staff, *Allen Welsh Dulles as Director of Central Intelligence*, vol. 5, p. 12, RG-263, NA, CP; U.S. Department of State, *Foreign Relations of the United States, 1955–57*, vol. 16, *Suez Crisis* (Washington, DC: GPO, 1990), pp. 798–800, 834, 849.

10. John L. Helgerson, *Getting to Know the President: CIA Briefings of Presidential Candidates, 1952–1992* (Washington, DC: Center for the Study of Intelligence, 1996), p. 44.

11. "The Situation in Hungary," *Current Intelligence Weekly Review*, November 8, 1956, p. 8, CIA
Electronic FOIA Reading Room, Document No. 0000119763, http://www.foia.cia.gov.

12. Op-922Y2F/jcr, Ser: 000582P92, memorandum, Chief of Naval Operations to Secretary of
State et al., *Marked Increase Noted in Soviet Submarine Operations Away from Home Waters*, September 22, 1956, p. 2, DDRS; *Watch Committee Report*, undated but circa November 6–7, 1956,
RG-218 JCS, Chairman's File, Adm. Radford 1953–1957, box 47, file ME 1956, NA, CP; Johnson, *American Cryptology*, bk. 1, p. 235.

13. TS #141612-e, IAC-D-55/12, *Annual Report to the National Security Council on the Status of the
Foreign Intelligence Program (as of 30 June 1957)*, September 3, 1957, p. 2, CREST Collection,
Document No. CIA-RDP79R00961A000300110011-1, NA, CP.

14. Historical Division, Joint Chiefs of Staff, *Summary Study of Nine Worldwide Crises*, Tab 7: Hungarian Crisis, October 1956, September 25, 1973, p. 2, DoD FOIA Reading Room, Document
No. 984-4, Pentagon, Washington, DC; Johnson, *American Cryptology*, bk. 1, p. 235.

15. Johnson, *American Cryptology*, bk. 1, p. 239.

16. *NSA Newsletter*, December 1968, p. 3; *NSA Newsletter*, November 1977, p. 8, both NSA FOIA.

17. John Prados, *The Soviet Estimate* (New York: Dial Press, 1982), pp. 41–43; interview with former
senior intelligence official.

18. Johnson, *American Cryptology*, bk. 1, p. 107.

19. Commission on Organization of the Executive Branch of the Government, *Task Force Report on
Intelligence Activities in the Federal Government*, appendix 1, part 1, "Report of Survey of the National Security Agency," May 1955, p. 18, CREST Collection, Document No. CIA-RDP86B00269-R000900010001-0, NA, CP; "Response of USCIB to *Report on Intelligence Activities in the Federal
Government Prepared for the Commission on Organization of the Executive Branch of the Federal Government by the Task Force on Intelligence Activities*," undated but circa June–July 1955, p. 2,
DDRS; "Staff D Comments on Part I of Clark Report," undated but circa July 1955, pp. 7–8,
CREST Collection, Document No. CIA-RDP78S05450A000100150023-8, NA, CP; CSM No.
374, CIA, Office of Research and Reports, current support memorandum, *Soviets Plan Extensive
High-Capacity Microwave Systems*, March 29, 1956, CIA Electronic FOIA Reading Room, Document No. 0000234174, http://www.foia.cia.gov; CIA/RR IM-444, CIA, Office of Research and

Reports, *Intelligence Memorandum: Major Telecommunications Goals of the Soviet Sixth Five Year Plan (1956–60)*, January 9, 1957, p. 15, CREST Collection, Document No. CIA-RDP79-T00935-A000400210004-4, NA, CP; U.S. Air Force Security Service, *History of COMINT Collection Operations: Fiscal Year 1958*, no date but circa 1959, pp. 14, 32, AIA FOIA; James S. Lay, *History of the United States Intelligence Board*, Part 2, sec. P, Summary of USIB Annual Reports to the NSC, no date, p. 194, CREST Collection, Document No. CIA-RDP79M00098A000200020001-7, NA, CP; Johnson, *American Cryptology*, bk. 1, p. 231; David A. Hatch, "Quis Custodiet Ipsos Custodes?," *Cryptologic Almanac*, February 2003, p. 2, NSA FOIA.

20. The two best sources for details of the U-2 program are Gregory W. Pedlow and Donald E. Welzenbach, *The CIA and the U-2 Program: 1954–1974* (Washington, DC: CIA History Staff, Center for the Study of Intelligence, 1998); and Chris Pocock, *The U-2 Spyplane: Toward the Unknown: A New History of the Early Years* (Atglen, PA: Schiffer Military History, 2000).

21. Johnson, *American Cryptology*, bk. 1, p. 175.

22. SAPC 6081, memorandum, [deleted] to Project Director of Operations, *NSA Support for AQUATONE*, May 9, 1956, CREST Collection, Document No. CIA-RDP33-02415A000100100074-7, NA, CP. Quote from the "Cold War 101" chapter, p. 49, of the Jack M. Gallimore home page at http://www.aipress.com/jackmem/.

23. Memorandum, ELINT Staff Officer to Special Assistant to the Director for Planning and Coordination, *Review of Implementation of CIA Responsibilities Under Technological Capabilities Panel*, July 11, 1957, CREST Collection, Document No. CIA-RDP61S00750A000400050014-6, NA, CP; NSA, 3/0/TALCOM/8-59, *Status of Siberian Air Defense District Installations as of* [deleted], December 1, 1959, p. 2, CREST Collection, Document No. CIA-RDP78T05439A000500070004-9, NA, CP; CHAL-0914, *Situation Estimate for Project Chalice: Fiscal Years 1961 and 1962*, March 14, 1960, pp. 1–2, CREST Collection, Document No. CIA-RDP33-02415A000200420002-0, NA, CP; TCS-7519-60-b, *Accomplishments of the U-2 Program*, May 27, 1960, p. 6, CREST Collection, Document No. CIA-RDP33-02415A000100070007-5, NA, CP. See also Pedlow and Welzenbach, *CIA and the U-2 Program: 1954–1974*, p. 101; Pocock, *U-2 Spyplane*, p. 48.

24. Paul L. Allen, "Pusk Bad News for Spy Crews," *Tucson Citizen*, November 23, 1998.

25. The story of the Powers shootdown has been extensively covered in a number of books and articles, such as Michael R. Beschloss, *Mayday* (New York: Harper and Row, 1986). For the Russian version of the U-2 shootdown incident, see Anatoliy Lokuchaev, "Okhota v Stratosfere," *Aviatsiya i Kosmonavtika*, no. 4 (2000): p. 17.

26. For SIGINT identification of ICBM construction activity at Plesetsk, see *Utilization of Aerial Reconnaissance to Determine the Status of the Soviet ICBM Threat*, September 8, 1959, p. 8, CREST Collection, Document No. CIA-RDP92B01090R002600270002-9, NA, CP; TCS No. 5819-59, Tab C, *USSR Targets for Highest Priority Collection*, 1959, p. 1, CREST Collection, Document No. CIA-RDP92B01090R002600270004-7, NA, CP; memorandum, Reber to Deputy Director (Plans), *ARC Recommendations for Future Targets as of 14 April 1960*, April 14, 1960, CREST Collection, Document No. CIA-RDP61S00750A000600150007-1, NA, CP; Deployment Working Group of the Guided Missiles and Astronautics Intelligence Committee, *Soviet Surface-to-Surface Missile Deployment*, Tab I-P-1, October 1, 1962, p. 18, CREST Collection, Document No. CIA-RDP78T04757A000300010003-3, NA, CP; Johnson, *American Cryptology*, bk. 1, p. 175. For Norwegian detection of signals coming from Plesetsk, see Rolf Tamnes, *The United States and the Cold War in the High North* (Oslo: ad Notam forlag AS, 1991), p. 135. For a description of the construction of the Plesetsk launch site based on Russian materials, see Steven J. Zaloga, *Target America* (Novato, CA: Presidio Press, 1993), pp. 150–51.

27. Johnson, *American Cryptology*, bk. 1, p. 183.

28. CHAL-1088-60, *The Future of the Agency's U-2 Capability*, July 16, 1960, p. 6, CREST Collection,

Document No. CIA-RDP62B00844R000200160034-9, NA, CP; letter, Prettyman et al. to Mc-Cone, February 27, 1962, p. 1, CIA Electronic FOIA Reading Room, Document No. 0000009451, http://www.foia.cia.gov; memorandum for the record, *Board of Inquiry—Francis Gary Powers*, March 20, 1962, CREST Collection, Document No. CIA-RDP80B01676R002200070001-2, NA, CP; Johnson, *American Cryptology*, bk. 1, p. 183; Beschloss, *Mayday*, pp. 30, 37, 356–57.

29. Letter, Prettyman et al. to McCone, February 27, 1962, p. 1, CIA Electronic FOIA Reading Room, Document No. 0000009451, http://www.foia.cia.gov; memorandum, Blanchard to Director of Central Intelligence, *Technical Analysis of Powers U-2 Incident*, February 27, 1962, pp. 3–4, CREST Collection, Document No. CIA-RDP80B01676R002200030001-6, NA, CP; Johnson, *American Cryptology*, bk. 1, p. 183.

30. Memorandum for the record, *Board of Inquiry—Francis Gary Powers*, March 20, 1962, p. 2, CREST Collection, Document No. CIA-RDP80B01676R002200020001-7, NA, CP.

5: THE CRISIS YEARS

1. $654 million SIGINT budget figure from *Memorandum of Discussion at the 473rd Meeting of the National Security Council*, January 5, 1961, in U.S. Department of State, *Foreign Relations of the United States, 1961–1963*, vol. 25, *Organization of Foreign Policy; Information Policy; United Nations; Scientific Matters* (Washington, DC: GPO, 2001), located at http://www.state.gov/r/pa/ho/frus/kennedyjf/xxv/index.htm, NSA's personnel figures from Dr. Thomas R. Johnson, *American Cryptology During the Cold War, 1945–1989*, bk. 2, *Centralization Wins, 1960–1972* (Fort Meade, MD: Center for Cryptologic History, 1995), p. 293, NSA FOIA; U.S. House of Representatives, Appropriations Committee, *Military Construction Appropriations for 1964*, 85th Congress, 1st session, 1963, p. 487; U.S. Army Military History Institute, oral history, *Lt. General John J. Davis, USA (Ret.)*, 1986, p. 136, U.S. Army Center of Military History, Washington, DC. CIA personnel and budget figures from report, *CIA Activity Inventory*, undated but circa 1963, p. 3, RG-263, entry 36, box 8, file 726, NA, CP.

2. Memorandum, Secretary of Defense to Executive Secretary, National Security Council, August 17, 1960, DDRS; *The Joint Study Group Report on Foreign Intelligence Activities of the United States Government*, December 15, 1960, pp. 35–36, ASANSA, Matters Received Since January 1961, box 1, Dwight D. Eisenhower Library, Abilene, KS.

3. Frost background from "Vice Admiral Laurence H. Frost Is New Director," *NSA Newsletter*, December 1, 1960, p. 2; "Admiral Laurence H. Frost, 74, Dies," *NSA Newsletter*, June 1977, p. 4, both NSA FOIA; "Vice Adm. Laurence Frost, 74, Dies, Former National Security Agency Chief," *Washington Post*, May 26, 1977.

4. Interviews with Frank Rowlett, Louis Tordella, confidential sources; NSA OH-1983-14, oral history, *Interview of Dr. Howard Campaigne*, June 29, 1983, pp. 124–25, partially declassified and on file at the library of the National Cryptologic Museum, Fort Meade, MD.

5. Johnson, *American Cryptology*, bk. 2, p. 294.

6. After leaving B Group in 1964, Shinn served as the NSA representative on a number of interdepartmental committees, including the Watch Committee. He died on December 11, 1968, at the age of fifty-eight. Shinn's background from his obituary at *NSA Newsletter*, January 1969, p. 7, NSA FOIA.

7. William D. Gerhard, *In the Shadow of War (To the Gulf of Tonkin)*, Cryptologic History Series, Southeast Asia (Fort Meade, MD: Center for Cryptologic History, 1969), p. 29, NSA FOIA; Robert J. Hanyok, *Spartans in Darkness: American SIGINT and the Indochina War, 1945–1975*, U.S. Cryptologic History, series 6, vol. 7 (Fort Meade, MD: Center for Cryptologic History, 2002), p. 73, NSA FOIA. For information about the North Vietnamese direction of the Viet

Cong insurgency derived from SIGINT, see SNIE 10-62, *Communist Objectives, Capabilities, and Intentions in Southeast Asia,* annex: Communist North Vietnam's Military Communications Nets and Command Structures in Laos and South Vietnam, February 21, 1962, CIA Electronic FOIA Reading Room, Document No. 0001166399, http://www.foia.cia.gov, draft memorandum for the president, *Covert Operations Against North Vietnam,* attached to memorandum, McNamara to Chairman, Joint Chiefs of Staff, January 3, 1963, RG-200, entry 13230A Records of Robert S. McNamara, box 119, file Reading File January 1963, NA, CP.

8.   Hanyok, *Spartans in Darkness,* pp. 146–47. For the switch to KTB, see David W. Gaddy, ed., *Essential Matters: A History of the Cryptographic Branch of the People's Army of Viet-Nam, 1945–1975* (Fort Meade, MD: Center for Cryptologic History, 1994), pp. 111–12. See also Seymour M. Hersh, *The Price of Power: Kissinger in the Nixon White House* (New York: Summit Books, 1983), p. 74n; James L. Gilbert, *The Most Secret War: Army Signals Intelligence in Vietnam* (Fort Belvoir, VA: Military History Office, U.S. Army Intelligence and Security Command, 2003), p. 18; Robert J. Hanyok, "Book Review: James L. Gilbert, The Most Secret War: Army Signals Intelligence in Vietnam," *Intelligence and National Security,* Summer 2004: p. 395.

9.   Oral history, *Interview with Dr. Ray S. Cline,* May 21, 1983, p. 21, LBJL, Austin, TX.

10.   Memorandum, Lansdale to O'Donnell, *Possible Courses of Action in Vietnam,* September 13, 1960, in *U.S. Department of Defense Pentagon Papers,* U.S. House of Representatives ed., 1971, pp. 1307–09; *Memorandum of Conference with President Kennedy,* February 23, 1961, National Security Files, Chester V. Clifton Series, Conferences with the President, vol. I, JFKL, Boston, MA; *Annual Historical Report, 3rd Radio Research Unit, Fiscal Year 1961,* vol. 2, p. 8, INSCOM FOIA; Gerhard, *In the Shadow,* p. 29; 509th Radio Research Group, *When the Tiger Stalks No More: The Vietnamization of SIGINT: May 1961–June 1970,* 1970, pp. 5, 7, INSCOM FOIA.

11.   Gerhard, *In the Shadow,* pp. 30–31; 509th Radio Research Group, *When the Tiger Stalks No More: The Vietnamization of SIGINT: May 1961–June 1970,* 1970, pp. 6, 11, INSCOM FOIA; Johnson, *American Cryptology,* bk. 2, p. 502; *The Pentagon Papers,* Senator Gravel ed., vol. 2 (Boston: Beacon Press, 1975), pp. 641–42; John D. Bergen, *Military Communications: A Test for Technology* (Washington, DC: U.S. Army Center of Military History, 1986), p. 388.

12.   HQ Third Radio Research Unit, *Annual Historical Report, 3rd Radio Research Unit, Fiscal Year 1961,* vol. 1, pp. 1–2, and vol. 2, p. 2, INSCOM FOIA; *Annual Historical Report, 3rd Radio Research Unit, Fiscal Year 1962,* vol. 1, pp. 1–2, INSCOM FOIA; *Annual Historical Report, 3rd Radio Research Unit, Fiscal Year 1963,* vol. 3, tab 28, INSCOM FOIA; Donald B. Oliver, "Deployment of the First ASA Unit to Vietnam," *Cryptologic Spectrum,* vol. 10, nos. 3–4 (Fall/Winter 1991), NSA FOIA; Johnson, *American Cryptology,* bk. 2, p. 503. The stamp in the medical records is from Gilbert, *Most Secret War,* p. 7.

13.   Gilbert, *Most Secret War,* p. 8.

14.   *Report on General Taylor's Mission to South Vietnam,* November 3, 1961, sec. 7, Intelligence, p. 3, National Security File, Country File: Vietnam, Report on Taylor Mission—November 1961, box 210, JFKL, Boston, MA; extract from memorandum #273, no subject, November 26, 1961, p. 9, Record #195503, Item #3671510005, George J. Veith Collection, Vietnam Archive, Texas Tech University, Lubbock, TX; *Pentagon Papers,* Gravel ed., vol. 2, pp. 439, 656–57.

15.   Memorandum, Helms to Director of Central Intelligence, *Meeting with the Attorney General of the United States Concerning Cuba,* January 19, 1962, National Security Archive, Washington, DC; memorandum, Lansdale to Special Group (Augmented), *Review of Operation Mongoose,* July 25, 1962, National Security Archive, Washington, DC; Director of Central Intelligence, *Report to the President's Foreign Intelligence Advisory Board on Intelligence Community Activities Relating to the Cuban Arms Build-Up: 14 April Through 14 October 1962,* December 1962, p. 4, National Security Files: Countries: Cuba, box 61, JFKL, Boston, MA. For an excellent overall description and collec-

tion of declassified documents relating to Operation Mongoose, see Lawrence Chang and Peter Kornbluh, eds., *The Cuban Missile Crisis, 1962: A National Security Archive Documents Reader* (New York: New Press, 1992).

16. JCSM-272-62, memorandum, Lemnitzer to Secretary of Defense, April 10, 1962, p. 1, National Security Archive, Washington, DC.

17. Memorandum, Lansdale to Distribution List, *Program Review by the Chief of Operations, Operation Mongoose*, January 18, 1962, RG-59, Central Decimal File, 737.00/1-2062, NA, CP; memorandum, Helms to Director of Central Intelligence, *Meeting with the Attorney General of the United States Concerning Cuba*, January 19, 1962, National Security Archive, Washington, DC; memorandum, Tidwell to Deputy Director (Intelligence) and Deputy Director (Plans), *Intelligence Support on Cuba*, March 6, 1962, CIA Electronic FOIA Reading Room, Document No. 0001161975, http://www.foia.cia.gov; memorandum for the record, Brig. Gen. Lansdale, *Meeting with President, 16 March 1962*, March 16, 1962, National Security Archive, Washington, DC; Director of Central Intelligence, *Report to the President's Foreign Intelligence Advisory Board on Intelligence Community Activities Relating to the Cuban Arms Build-Up: 14 April Through 14 October 1962*, December 1962, pp. 4–5, National Security Files: Countries: Cuba, box 61, JFKL, Boston, MA; Johnson, *American Cryptology*, bk. 2, pp. 320, 322.

18. Moody's background from memorandum, John D. Roth, U.S. Civil Service Commission to Department and Agency Incentive Awards Officers, *1971 Federal Woman's Award*, February 2, 1971, CREST Collection, Document No. CIA-RDP84-00313R000100250007-7, NA, CP; *NSA Newsletter*, March 1971, pp. 4–5; *NSA Newsletter*, April 1972, p. 5; *NSA Newsletter*, May–June 1974, p. 7; *NSA Newsletter*, January 1976, p. 10; *NSA Newsletter*, February 1977, p. 4, all NSA FOIA. For Moody taking command of NSA's Cuban operations in July 1961, see Johnson, bk. 2, *American Cryptology*, p. 322.

19. Memorandum, Tidwell to Deputy Director (Intelligence) and Deputy Director (Plans), *Intelligence Support on Cuba*, March 6, 1962, p. 2, CIA Electronic FOIA Reading Room, Document No. 0001161975, http://www.foia.cia.gov; Draft: vol. 4, chap. 2: The Cuban Missile Crisis, JFK Assassination Records, CIA Miscellaneous Files, box 7, Document No. 104-10302-10026, NA, CP; Director of Central Intelligence, *Report to the President's Foreign Intelligence Advisory Board on Intelligence Community Activities Relating to the Cuban Arms Build-Up: 14 April Through 14 October 1962*, December 1962, p. 8, National Security Files: Countries: Cuba, box 61, JFKL, Boston, MA.

20. Memorandum, Lansdale to Distribution List, *Program Review by the Chief of Operations, Operation Mongoose*, January 18, 1962, RG-59, Central Decimal File, 737.00/1-2062, NA, CP.

21. ASA, *Annual Historical Summary, U.S. Army Security Agency: Fiscal Year 1962*, p. 3, INSCOM FOIA.

22. Dr. Thomas R. Johnson, *American Cryptology During the Cold War, 1945–1989*, bk. 3, *Retrenchment and Reform, 1972–1980* (Fort Meade: Center for Cryptologic History, 1995), p. 84, NSA FOIA; U.S. Senate, Select Committee to Study Governmental Operations, *Final Report of the Select Committee to Study Government Operations with Respect to Intelligence Activities, Supplementary Detailed Staff Reports on Intelligence Activities and the Rights of Americans*, bk. 2, 94th Congress, 2nd session 1976, pp. 744–45, 773; U.S. House of Representatives, Government Operations Committee, *Interception of Nonverbal Communications by Federal Intelligence Agencies*, 94th Congress, 1st and 2nd sessions, 1976, pp. 104, 110–11.

23. Memorandum, Lansdale to Special Group (Augmented), *Progress OPERATION MONGOOSE*, July 11, 1962, pp. 3–4, Church Committee Files, RG-233, NA, CP; Director of Central Intelligence, *Report to the President's Foreign Intelligence Advisory Board on Intelligence Community Activities Relating to the Cuban Arms Build-Up: 14 April Through 14 October 1962*, December 1962, pp. 16, 33, National Security Files: Countries: Cuba, box 61, JFKL, Boston, MA; SC No. 12160/62-KH,

untitled CIA report on the agency's intelligence collection effort against Cuba, December 1962, p. 4, CREST Collection, Document No. CIA-RDP66B00560R000100100176-0, NA, CP; Chang and Kornbluh, *Cuban Missile Crisis*, p. 42. Details of the USS *Oxford's* background and mission from Julie Alger, *A Review of the Technical Research Ship Program: 1961–1969*, undated, pp. 7, 16, 88, NSA FOIA; *USS Oxford (AG-159) Technical Research Ship History*, undated, p. 1, Ships Histories Division, Naval Historical Center, Washington, DC. For Castro's negative reaction to the presence of the USS *Oxford* off Cuba, see "Castro Says a U.S. Ship Violated Cuban Waters," Associated Press, February 23, 1962. A copy of this AP dispatch, carried in the February 23, 1962, edition of the *Buffalo Evening News*, can be found at http://members.tripod.com/~USS _OXFORD/seastories.html.

24. Director of Central Intelligence, *Report to the President's Foreign Intelligence Advisory Board on Intelligence Community Activities Relating to the Cuban Arms Build-Up: 14 April Through 14 October 1962*, December 1962, p. 19, National Security Files: Countries: Cuba, box 61, JFKL, Boston, MA.

25. Headquarters United States Air Force, Assistant Chief of Staff for Intelligence, *Revisions and Additions to S-25-62, Aerospace Forces Based in Cuba*, supplement to annex 1, sec. 1, November 1, 1962, pp. 44–48, National Security Archive, Washington, DC; Arms Control and Disarmament Agency, SC No. 08088/63-KH, *The 1962 Soviet Arms Build-Up in Cuba*, 1963, p. 1, CREST Collection, Document No. CIA-RDP78T05439A000300130013-4, NA, CP; CIA, SC 03387/64, DD/I staff study, *Cuba 1962: Khrushchev's Miscalculated Risk*, February 13, 1964, pp. 24–25, RG-263, entry 82, box 35, MORI DocID: 120333, NA, CP; Johnson, *American Cryptology*, bk. 2, p. 323.

26. Memorandum, Lansdale to Special Group (Augmented), *Operation Mongoose Progress*, July 11, 1962, pp. 3–4, JFK Assassination Records, HSCA (RG-233), NA, CP; memorandum, OP-922Y to Secretary of the Navy, *Navy Participation in Increased SIGINT Program for Cuba*, July 19, 1962, in *NSA and the Cuban Missile Crisis: Document Archive of Declassified Files from the Cuban Missile Crisis*, http://www.nsa.gov/cuba.

27. CIA, Office of Research and Reports, CIA/RR EP 60-73-S4, *Electronics Facilities in Cuba*, November 1960, CREST Collection, Document No. CIA-RDP79T01049A002100090001-8, NA, CP; CIA, Office of Research and Reports, CIA/RR CB 62-65, *Current Support Brief: Possible Use of Military Microwave Network in Cuba for Command-Control Purposes*, November 2, 1962, CREST Collection, Document No. CIA-RDP79T01003A001300200001-4, NA, CP; Arms Control and Disarmament Agency, SC No. 08088/63-KH, *The 1962 Soviet Arms Build-Up in Cuba*, 1963, p. 78, CREST Collection, Document No. CIA-RDP78T05439A000300130013-4, NA, CP; CIA/ORR, SC 03387/64, DD/I staff study, *Cuba 1962: Khrushchev's Miscalculated Risk*, February 13, 1964, map following p. 24, RG-263, entry 82, box 35, MORI DocID: 120333, NA, CP; CIA, Office of Research and Reports, CIA/RR CB 65-8, *Intelligence Brief: Cuba Plans New Nationwide High-Capacity Microwave System*, January 1965, CIA Electronic FOIA Reading Room, http://www .foia.cia.gov.

28. Thomas N. Thompson, *USAFSS Performance During the Cuban Crisis*, vol. 1, *Airborne Operations, April–December 1962* (San Antonio, TX: USAFSS Historians Office, no date), pp. 4–6, AIA FOIA; Victor Marchetti and John D. Marks, *The CIA and the Cult of Intelligence* (New York: Laurel, 1980), p. 262.

29. Message, 191653Z, DIRNSA to CNO, July 19, 1962, and memorandum, OP-922Y to Secretary of the Navy, *Navy Participation in Increased SIGINT Program for Cuba*, July 19, 1962, both in *NSA and the Cuban Missile Crisis: Document Archive of Declassified Files from the Cuban Missile Crisis*, http://www.nsa.gov/cuba; memorandum, Harris to Chief of Operations, *Operation Mongoose, End of Phase I*, July 23, 1962, p. 5, JFK Assassination Records, JFK Library Files, box 23, file Special Group (Augmented) Meetings, Record No. 176-10011-10063, NA, CP.

30. The USS *Oxford's* operations area (OPAREA) was very small, consisting of a one-hundred-

mile-long "racecourse track" along the northern coast of Cuba between 82 degrees west longitude and 83 degrees west longitude and running roughly along latitude 23.11 degrees north to 23.20 degrees north. The OPAREA was subdivided into five zones, numbered one through five, each twenty miles in length, that ran from just east of Havana to just west of the port of Mariel. Message, 191653Z DIRNSA to CNO, July 19, 1962, and memorandum, OP-922Y to Secretary of the Navy, *Navy Participation in Increased SIGINT Program for Cuba,* July 19, 1962, both in *NSA and the Cuban Missile Crisis: Document Archive of Declassified Files from the Cuban Missile Crisis,* http://www.nsa.gov/cuba; *Ship's History: USS Oxford (AG-159) for CY 1962,* January 25, 1963, Ships Histories Division, Naval Historical Center, Washington, DC; *Deck Log: USS Oxford (AG-159),* entries for period July 16, 1962, through July 31, 1962, Ships Histories Division, Naval Historical Center, Washington, DC; Thomas N. Thompson, *USAFSS Performance During the Cuban Crisis,* vol. 2, *Ground Based Operations, October–December 1962* (San Antonio, TX: USAFSS Historians Office, no date), p. 38, AIA FOIA. For monitoring the Cuban microwave radio-relay system, see Bill Baer, "USNS Joseph E. Muller, TAG-171," undated, http://www.asa.npoint.net/baer01.htm.

31. *USS Oxford Deck Log,* entry for July 31, 1962, Ships Histories Division, Naval Historical Center, Washington, DC. For the Cuban perception of the *Oxford*'s mission off Havana, see Fabián Escalante, *The Secret War: CIA Covert Operations Against Cuba: 1959–62* (Melbourne: Ocean Press, 1995), pp. 138, 185.

32. Johnson, *American Cryptology,* bk. 2, p. 341; "Lieutenant General Gordon A. Blake, USAF, Is Appointed Director, NSA," *NSA Newsletter,* August 1, 1962, p. 2; "Lt. General Gordon A. Blake to Retire on May 31," *NSA Newsletter,* May 1965, p. 5; "In Memoriam: Lt. Gen. Gordon A. Blake, Former Director," *NSA Newsletter,* November 1997, p. 2, all NSA FOIA.

33. NSA OH-1984-7, oral history, *Interview with Lt. General Gordon A. Blake,* April 19, 1984, p. 49, NSA FOIA.

34. Johnson, *American Cryptology,* bk. 2, p. 341; memorandum for the record, *Luncheon Meeting with Assistant Secretary of Defense John H. Rubel,* April 9, 1963, p. 2, RG-263, CIA Reference Collection, Document No. CIA-RDP80B01676R003000020015-3, NA, CP; NSA OH-1984-7, oral history, *Interview with Lt. General Gordon A. Blake,* April 19, 1984, p. 98–99, NSA FOIA; "Lt. General Gordon A. Blake to Retire on May 31," *NSA Newsletter,* May 1965, p. 5, NSA FOIA.

35. SC No. 11649/62, memorandum, [deleted] to [deleted] (O/IG), *Ballistic Missile Shipments to Cuba,* November 16, 1962, CREST Collection, Document No. CIA-RDP70T00666R000100140006-4, NA, CP; SC No. 11655/62, memorandum, [deleted] to Inspector General, *Total Cargo Tonnage Moved to Cuba by Soviet Ships, 26 July–30 September,* November 16, 1962, CREST Collection, Document No. CIA-RDP70T00666R000100140007-3, NA, CP; SC No. 11664/62, memorandum, [deleted] to [deleted] (O/IG), *DIA and NSA Reporting on the Cuban Arms Build-Up,* November 16, 1962, CREST Collection, Document No. CIA-RDP70T00666R000100140005-5, NA, CP. Quote from director of Central Intelligence, *Report to the President's Foreign Intelligence Advisory Board on Intelligence Community Activities Relating to the Cuban Arms Build-Up: 14 April Through 14 October 1962,* December 1962, p. 40, National Security Files: Countries: Cuba, box 61, JFKL, Boston, MA.

36. National Indications Center, *The Soviet Bloc Armed Forces and the Cuban Crisis: A Chronology: July–November 1962,* June 18, 1963, p. 1, CIA Electronic FOIA Reading Room, Document No. 0001161985, http://www.foia.cia.gov; Arms Control and Disarmament Agency, SC No. 08088/63-KH, *The 1962 Soviet Arms Build-Up in Cuba,* 1963, p. 8, CREST Collection, Document No. CIA-RDP78T05439A000300130013-4, NA, CP.

37. For SIGINT reporting on the surge in Soviet shipping traffic to Cuba, see the following NSA reports: message, "Unusual Number of Soviet Passenger Ships en Route to Cuba," July 24, 1962; message, "Possible Reflections of Soviet/Cuban Trade Adjustments Noted in Merchant

Shipping," July 31, 1962; message, "Further Unusual Soviet/Cuban Trade Relations Recently Noted," August 7, 1962; message, "Status of Soviet Merchant Shipping to Cuba," August 23, 1962; message, "Further Information on Soviet/Cuban Trade," August 31, 1962, all in *NSA and the Cuban Missile Crisis: Document Archive of Declassified Files from the Cuban Missile Crisis*, http://www.nsa.gov/cuba. For CIA analysis of the SIGINT reporting on Soviet shipping to Cuba, see memorandum, Assistant Director, Research and Reports, to Deputy Director (Intelligence), *Further Analysis of Bloc and Western Shipping Calling at Cuban Ports*, September 11, 1962, CIA Electronic FOIA Reading Room, Document No. 0000307720, http://www.foia.cia.gov; appendix 1, enclosure to OP-922N memo to SECDEF Ser SSO/00323 of 26 Oct 1962, in Chief of Naval Operations, *The Naval Quarantine of Cuba, 1962*, Post '46 Command File, box 10, Operational Archives, Naval Historical Center, Washington, DC; National Indications Center, *The Soviet Bloc Armed Forces and the Cuban Crisis: A Discussion of Readiness Measures*, July 15, 1963, p. 4, RG-263, entry 82, box 28, MORI DocID: 107300, NA, CP.

38. Steven Zaloga, "The Missiles of October: Soviet Ballistic Missile Forces During the Cuban Missile Crisis," *Journal of Soviet Military Studies*, vol. 3, no. 2 (June 1990): p. 315.

39. SC No. 11664/62, memorandum, [deleted] to [deleted] (O/IG), *DIA and NSA Reporting on the Cuban Arms Build-Up*, November 16, 1962, p. 1, CREST Collection, Document No. CIA-RDP70T00666R000100140005-5, NA, CP; CIA, Inspector General, *Inspector General's Survey of Handling of Intelligence Information During the Cuban Arms Build-Up*, November 20, 1962, pp. 8–9, CREST Collection, Document No. CIA-RDP80B01676R001800060005-4, NA, CP.

40. John A. McCone, *Memorandum on Cuba*, August 20, 1962, p. 1, RG-263, entry 25, box 1, folder 5, NA, CP.

41. Memorandum for the file, *Discussion in Secretary Rusk's Office at 12 o'Clock, 21 August 1962*, August 21, 1962, RG-263, entry 25, box 1, NA, CP; *Memorandum of the Meeting with the President*, August 22, 1962, RG-263, entry 25, box 1, NA, CP; memorandum, *Soviet MRBMs in Cuba*, October 31, 1962, p. 1, RG-263, entry 25, box 1, NA, CP.

42. NSA, COMINT report, *Status of Soviet Merchant Shipping to Cuba*, August 23, 1962, in *NSA and the Cuban Missile Crisis: Document Archive of Declassified Files from the Cuban Missile Crisis*, http://www.nsa.gov/cuba. See also CIA, TDCS-3/520,583, information report, *Arrival of Soviet Ships and Prefabricated Concrete Forms*, August 23, 1962, CIA Electronic FOIA Reading Room, Document No. 0001264810, http://www.foia.cia.gov.

43. CIA, TDCS-3/651,139, information report, *Arrival of Men and Equipment at the Ports of Trinidad and Casilda*, August 24, 1962, CIA Electronic FOIA Reading Room, Document No. 0001264817, http://www.foia.cia.gov.

44. SC-08458-62, memorandum, Cline to Acting Director of Central Intelligence, *Recent Soviet Military Activities in Cuba*, September 3, 1962, pp. 1–2, RG-263, entry 25, box 1, folder 11, NA, CP; Historical Division, Joint Chiefs of Staff, *Summary Study of Nine Worldwide Crises*, Tab 4: Cuban Missile Crisis, October–November 1962, September 25, 1973, p. 2, DoD FOIA Reading Room, Document No. 984-4, Pentagon, Washington, DC.

45. Memorandum, Assistant Director, Research and Reports, to Deputy Director (Intelligence), *Further Analysis of Bloc and Western Shipping Calling at Cuban Ports*, September 11, 1962, CIA Electronic FOIA Reading Room, Document No. 0000307720, http://www.foia.cia.gov.

46. Thomas R. Johnson and David A. Hatch, *Synopsis of the Cuban Missile Crisis* (Fort Meade, MD: Center for Cryptologic History, May 1998), p. 1.

47. Johnson, *American Cryptology*, bk. 2, p. 332.

48. The *Omsk* arrived at the port of Casilda on September 8, 1962, and the *Poltava* arrived at the port of Mariel on September 15, 1962. The *Poltava* returned to Russia, and by mid-October 1962 it was on its way back to Cuba carrying twenty-four R-14 intermediate range ballistic mis-

siles, but the U.S. blockade of Cuba was imposed. The ship and the missiles in its hold never reached Cuba. Zaloga, "Missiles of October," p. 316; General Anatoli I. Gribkov and General William Y. Smith, *Operation Anadyr: U.S. and Soviet Generals Recount the Cuban Missile Crisis* (Chicago: Edition Q, 1994), pp. 45–46; Dino A. Brugioni, *Eyeball to Eyeball: The Inside Story of the Cuban Missile Crisis* (New York: Random House, 1990), p. 545.

49. Gribkov and Smith, *Operation Anadyr*, pp. 29, 34, 39.

50. SC No. 08172/62, memorandum, Guthe to INR/RSB, *Soviet Military Technicians Abroad*, September 20, 1962, pp. 1–2, CREST Collection, Document No. CIA-RDP70T00666R000100140020-8, NA, CP.

51. USAFSS History Office, *A Special Historical Study of the Production and Use of Special Intelligence During World Contingencies: 1950–1970*, March 1, 1972, p. 52, declassified through FOIA by the National Security Archive, Washington, DC.

52. NSA, COMINT report, "*Cuban MIGs Scramble on Two U.S. Navy Patrol Planes*," September 11, 1962, in *NSA and the Cuban Missile Crisis: Document Archive of Declassified Files from the Cuban Missile Crisis*, http://www.nsa.gov/cuba.

53. Johnson and Hatch, *Synopsis*, pp. 4–5.

54. NSA, COMINT report, "New Radar Deployment in Cuba," September 19, 1962, in *NSA and the Cuban Missile Crisis: Document Archive of Declassified Files from the Cuban Missile Crisis*, http://www.nsa.gov/cuba.; Headquarters, U.S. Marine Corps, Marine Corps Emergency Actions Center, *Summary of Items of Significant Interest for the Period 200701–210700 September 1962*, p. 3, National Security Archive, Washington, DC; Arms Control and Disarmament Agency, SC No. 08088/63-KH, *The 1962 Soviet Arms Build-Up in Cuba*, 1963, p. 81, CREST Collection, Document No. CIA-RDP78T05439A000300130013-4, NA, CP; Johnson, *American Cryptology*, bk. 2, p. 323.

55. Message, OUT76318, Director to [deleted], September 13, 1962, CIA Electronic FOIA Reading Room, Document No. 0000242399, http://www.foia.cia.gov.

56. Message, OUT77481, Director to [deleted], September 17, 1962, CIA Electronic FOIA Reading Room, Document No. 0000242402, http://www.foia.cia.gov.

57. NSA, COMINT report, *Further Information on Cargo Shipments to Cuba in Soviet Ships*, September 25, 1962, in *NSA and the Cuban Missile Crisis: Document Archive of Declassified Files from the Cuban Missile Crisis*, http://www.nsa.gov/cuba.

58. Arms Control and Disarmament Agency, SC No. 08088/63-KH, *The 1962 Soviet Arms Build-Up in Cuba*, 1963, p. 6, CREST Collection, Document No. CIA-RDP78T05439A000300130013-4, NA, CP. These intercepts are also referenced in Defense Intelligence Agency, *Use of the Intelligence Product*, undated but circa 1963, CREST Collection, Document No. CIA-RDP68B00255-R000300010009-0, NA, CP.

59. John A. McCone, *Memorandum of Mongoose Meeting Held on Thursday, October 4, 1962*, October 4, 1962, p. 2, RG-263, entry 25, box 1, file 41, NA, CP; Thomas A. Parrott, memorandum for record, *Minutes of Meeting of the Special Group (Augmented) on Operation MONGOOSE, 4 October 1962*, October 4, 1962, pp. 2–3, National Security Archive, Washington, DC. Both documents were released in full in 1994 and 1997 respectively. In one of those laughable attempts at rewriting history, in 2004 the CIA released into its CREST database of declassified documents new versions of the documents, which this time were heavily redacted. The excised content includes all mentions of the National Reconnaissance Office, Vice President Lyndon Johnson's participation in the meeting, and all discussion of covertly mining Cuban harbors, for which see "4 October (Thursday)," CREST Collection, Document No. CIA-RDP80B01676R001700180033-1, NA, CP.

60. Director of Central Intelligence, *Report to the President's Foreign Intelligence Advisory Board on Intelligence Community Activities Relating to the Cuban Arms Build-Up: 14 April Through 14 October 1962*, December 1962, p. 35, National Security Files: Countries: Cuba, box 61, JFKL, Boston, MA.

61. NSA, COMINT report, *Intercept of Probable Cuban Air Defense Grid Tracking*, October 10, 1962, in *NSA and the Cuban Missile Crisis: Document Archive of Declassified Files from the Cuban Missile Crisis*, http://www.nsa.gov/cuba.; Arms Control and Disarmament Agency, SC No. 08088/63-KH, *The 1962 Soviet Arms Build-Up in Cuba*, 1963, p. 81, CREST Collection, Document No. CIA-RDP78T05439A000300130013-4, NA, CP; Johnson, *American Cryptology*, bk. 2, p. 323.

62. CIA/ORR, SC 03387/64, DD/I staff study, *Cuba 1962: Khrushchev's Miscalculated Risk*, February 13, 1964, p. 25, RG-263, entry 82, box 35, MORI DocID: 120333, NA, CP; Headquarters, U.S. Marine Corps, Marine Corps Emergency Actions Center, *Summary of Items of Significant Interest for the Period 200701–210700 September 1962*, p. 3, National Security Archive, Washington, DC; Johnson and Hatch, *Synopsis*, pp. 4–5.

63. NSA, COMINT report, *Further Information on Cargo Shipments to Cuba in Soviet Ships*, October 11, 1962, in *NSA and the Cuban Missile Crisis: Document Archive of Declassified Files from the Cuban Missile Crisis*, http://www.nsa.gov/cuba.

64. CIA, memorandum, *Probable Soviet MRBM Sites in Cuba*, October 16, 1962, p. 1, RG-263, entry 25, box 1, folder 46, NA, CP; memorandum, Lundahl to Director of Central Intelligence, *Additional Information—Mission 3101*, October 16, 1962, pp. 1–3, RG-263, entry 25, box 1, folder 50, NA, CP.

65. For details of how the San Cristóbal area was designated as a possible missile-launching site to be investigated by a U-2 overflight, see excerpt from memorandum, Lehman to Director of Central Intelligence, *CIA Handling of the Soviet Buildup in Cuba, 1 July–16 October 1962*, November 14, 1962, pp. 23–26, RG-263, entry 25, box 1, folder 36, NA, CP. In another of those sadly too frequent instances of the CIA declassification personnel reclassifying previously declassified material in the post-9/11 era, in 2004 the CIA released to the CREST database at the National Archives another version of this document, which this time was heavily redacted, for which see CREST Collection, Document No. CIA-RDP80B01676R001700180076-4, NA, CP.

66. Memorandum for the record, *MONGOOSE Meeting with the Attorney General*, October 16, 1962, National Security Archive, Washington, DC.

67. Confidential interview.

68. NSA OH-1982-20, oral history, *Interview with Harold L. Parish*, October 12, 1982, p. 3, declassified and on file at the library of the National Cryptologic Museum, Fort Meade, MD; NSA OH-1983-17, oral history, *Interview with Paul Odonovich*, August 5, 1983, pp. 123–127, declassified and on file at the library of the National Cryptologic Museum, Fort Meade, MD; Johnson, *American Cryptology*, bk. 2, pp. 326–27.

69. Johnson, *American Cryptology*, bk. 2, p. 327.

70. Guided Missile and Astronautics Intelligence Committee, *Joint Evaluation of Soviet Missile Threat in Cuba, 2100 Hours*, October 18, 1962, p. 1, RG-263, entry 25, box 1, folder 61, NA, CP; Guided Missile and Astronautics Intelligence Committee, *Joint Evaluation of Soviet Missile Threat in Cuba, 2000 Hours*, October 19, 1962, p. 2, RG-263, entry 25, box 1, folder 65, NA, CP; Johnson, *American Cryptology*, bk. 2, p. 325.

71. CIA, National Indications Center, *The Soviet Bloc Armed Forces and the Cuban Crisis: A Chronology: July–November 1962*, June 18, 1963, p. 40, CIA Electronic FOIA Reading Room, Document No. 0001161985, http://www.foia.cia.gov; Timothy Naftali and Philip Zelikow, eds., *The Presidential Recordings: John F. Kennedy*, vol. 2 (New York: W. W. Norton, 2001), pp. 520, 582.

72. NSA OH-1983-17, oral history, *Interview with Paul Odonovich*, August 5, 1983, pp. 127–28, declassified and on file at the library of the National Cryptologic Museum, Fort Meade, MD; Johnson and Hatch, *Synopsis* p. 9.

73. Johnson, *American Cryptology*, bk. 2, p. 329.

74. Two weeks later, on November 4, the NSA cryptanalysts discovered that the same messages

that were being passed on both teletype links were also being transmitted simultaneously by the Russian navy's very low frequency (VLF) radio broadcast facility at Kudma, outside the city of Gorki. NSA concluded that neither of the radio links was providing communications support for the Soviet missile units in Cuba, suggesting that either the Kudma VLF radio transmission station or the Soviet Strategic Rocket Forces' primary high frequency radio transmitter facility at Perkushkovo, outside Moscow, was performing this function. Headquarters United States Air Force, Assistant Chief of Staff for Intelligence, *Revisions and Additions to S-25-62, Aerospace Forces Based in Cuba*, supplement to annex 1, sec. 1, November 1, 1962, p. 32a, National Security Archive, Washington, DC; Arms Control and Disarmament Agency, SC No. 08088/63-KH, *The 1962 Soviet Arms Build-Up in Cuba*, 1963, pp. 78–79, CREST Collection, Document No. CIA-RDP78T05439A000300130013-4, NA, CP; NPIC/R-1047/63, photographic interpretation report, *Soviet Communications Facilities in Cuba*, January 1963, CREST Collection, Document No. CIA-RDP78B04560A001000010081-8, NA, CP.

75. Johnson, *American Cryptology*, bk. 2, p. 329.

76. National Indications Center, *The Soviet Bloc Armed Forces and the Cuban Crisis: A Chronology: July–November 1962*, June 18, 1963, p. 48, CIA Electronic FOIA Reading Room, Document No. 0001161985, http://www.foia.cia.gov.

77. CIA, DD/I staff study, *The Soviet Missile Base Venture in Cuba*, February 17, 1964, p. 90, CIA Electronic FOIA Reading Room, Caesar-Polo-Esau Papers, http://www.foia.cia.gov/cpe.asp.

78. Johnson, *American Cryptology*, bk. 2, p. 329; message, 230750Z, USN-22 to DIST NOVEMBER WHISKEY/ALPHA, SIGINT Readiness Bravo, Owen, Spot Report No. 4, October 23, 1962; message, 230910Z, USN-22 to NOVEMBER WHISKEY/ALPHA, SIGINT Readiness Bravo, Owen, Spot Report No. 5, October 23, 1962, both in *NSA and the Cuban Missile Crisis: Document Archive of Declassified Files from the Cuban Missile Crisis*, http://www.nsa.gov/cuba. See also Philip Zelikow and Ernest May, eds., *The Presidential Recordings: John F. Kennedy*, vol. 3 (New York: W. W. Norton, 2001), p. 184.

79. CIA, memorandum, *The Crisis: USSR/Cuba*, October 24, 1962, p. i, CIA Electronic FOIA Reading Room, Document No. 0000725840, http://www.foia.cia.gov; memorandum for the director, *Your Briefings of the NSC Executive Committee*, November 3, 1962, p. 1, RG-263, entry 25, box 2, folder 109, NA, CP; National Indications Center, *The Soviet Bloc Armed Forces and the Cuban Crisis: A Chronology: July–November 1962*, June 18, 1963, p. 52, CIA Electronic FOIA Reading Room, Document No. 0001161985, http://www.foia.cia.gov; National Indications Center, *The Soviet Bloc Armed Forces and the Cuban Crisis: A Discussion of Readiness Measures*, July 15, 1963, p. 14, RG-263, entry 82, box 28, MORI DocID: 107300, NA, CP; Zelikow and May, *Presidential Recordings*, vol. 3, p. 184.

80. The eight ships that SIGINT indicated had reversed course were the freighters *Yuri Gagarin, Klimovsk, Poltava, Dolmatova, Metallurg Kurako, Urgench, Fizik Vavilov*, and *Krasnograd*. CIA, memorandum, *The Crisis: USSR/Cuba*, October 25, 1962, p. II-1, CIA Electronic FOIA Reading Room, Document No. 0000725841, http://www.foia.cia.gov; CIA, *Background Material for 24 October*, sec. 3, Soviet Shipping to Cuba, CREST Collection, Document No. CIA-RDP80B01676-R001800010015-8, NA, CP; CIA, DD/I staff study, *The Soviet Missile Base Venture in Cuba*, February 17, 1964, p. 89, CIA Electronic FOIA Reading Room, Caesar-Polo-Esau Papers, http://www.foia.cia.gov/cpe.asp.

81. Robert F. Kennedy, *Thirteen Days: A Memoir of the Cuban Missile Crisis* (New York: W. W. Norton, 1969), p. 60.

82. Johnson, *American Cryptology*, bk. 2, p. 329.

83. Zelikow and May, *Presidential Recordings*, vol. 3, p. 184.

84. National Indications Center, *The Soviet Bloc Armed Forces and the Cuban Crisis: A Discussion of Readiness Measures*, July 15, 1963, p. 10, CIA Electronic FOIA Reading Room, Document No. 0001161983, http://www.foia.cia.gov.

85. Norman Klar, *Confessions of a Code Breaker (Tales From Decrypt)* (privately published, 2004), pp. 137–38; Zelikow and May, *Presidential Recordings*, vol. 3, p. 185.

86. Chief of Naval Operations, *The Naval Quarantine of Cuba, 1962*, p. 49, Post '46 Command File, box 10, Operational Archives, Naval Historical Center, Washington, DC.

87. CIA, memorandum, *The Crisis: USSR/Cuba*, October 24, 1962, pp. 3–4, CIA Electronic FOIA Reading Room, Document No. 0000725840, http://www.foia.cia.gov; CIA, memorandum, *The Crisis: USSR/Cuba*, October 25, 1962, pp. 2–3, CIA Electronic FOIA Reading Room, Document No. 0000725841, http://www.foia.cia.gov; CIA, *Background Material for 24 October*, pp. 2–3, CREST Collection, Document No. CIA-RDP80B01676R001800010015-8, NA, CP; memorandum for the director, *Your Briefings of the NSC Executive Committee*, November 3, 1962, p. 1, RG-263, entry 25, box 2, folder 109, NA, CP; Chief of Naval Operations, *The Naval Quarantine of Cuba, 1962*, pp. 49–50, Post '46 Command File, box 10, Operational Archives, Naval Historical Center, Washington, DC; Zelikow and May, *Presidential Recordings*, vol. 3, pp. 185, 187.

88. Chief of Naval Operations, *The Naval Quarantine of Cuba, 1962*, pp. 49–50, Post '46 Command File, box 10, Operational Archives, Naval Historical Center, Washington, DC.

89. CIA, memorandum, *The Crisis: USSR/Cuba*, October 25, 1962, pp. 2–3, CIA Electronic FOIA Reading Room, Document No. 0000725841, http://www.foia.cia.gov; CIA, *Background Material for 25 October*, CREST Collection, Document No. CIA-RDP80B01676R001800010016-7, NA, CP; memorandum for the file, *Executive Committee Meeting 10/25/62—10:00 a.m.*, October 25, 1962, CREST Collection, Document No. CIA-RDP80B01676R001900100027-4, NA, CP; National Indications Center, *The Soviet Bloc Armed Forces and the Cuban Crisis: A Discussion of Readiness Changes*, July 15, 1963, p. 15, RG-263, entry 82, box 28, MORI DocID: 107300, NA, CP; Zelikow and May, *Presidential Recordings*, vol. 3, p. 235.

90. CIA, memorandum, *The Crisis: USSR/Cuba*, October 26, 1962, pp. 2–4, CIA Electronic FOIA Reading Room, Document No. 0000725842, http://www.foia.cia.gov; Zelikow and May, *Presidential Recordings*, vol. 3, p. 287.

91. United Nations General Assembly, Document A/5266, October 22, 1962, p. 2; memorandum for the file, *Meeting of the NSC Executive Committee, 26 October 1962, 10:00 A.M.*, October 26, 1962, p. 2, CREST Collection, Document No. CIA-RDP80B01676R001900100009-4, NA, CP.

92. Zelikow and May, *Presidential Recordings*, vol. 3, p. 290.

93. Chief of Naval Operations, *OPNAV 24 Hour Resume of Events, 300000 to 310000 Oct 62*, October 31, 1962, Operational Archives Branch, Naval Historical Center, Washington, DC; Commander Service Force U.S. Atlantic Fleet, *Cuban Quarantine Operations*, December 31, 1962, p. 4, Operational Archives Branch, Naval Historical Center, Washington, DC; memorandum, OP-03 to CNO, *Compilation of Lessons Learned/Deficiencies Noted as a Result of the Cuban Operation*, February 20, 1963, p. 12, National Security Archive, Washington, DC. See also Kennedy, *Thirteen Days*, p. 86; Raymond L. Garthoff, *Reflections on the Cuban Missile Crisis* (Washington, DC: Brookings Institution, 1987), pp. 56–57n; Ernest R. May and Philip D. Zelikow, eds., *The Kennedy Tapes: Inside the White House During the Cuban Missile Crisis* (Cambridge, MA: Harvard University Press, 1997), p. 444.

94. NSA OH-1982-20, oral history, *Interview with Harold L. Parish*, October 12, 1982, p. 6, declassified and on file at the library of the National Cryptologic Museum, Fort Meade, MD.

95. CIA, memorandum, *The Crisis: USSR/Cuba*, October 27, 1962, pp. 3–5, CIA Electronic FOIA Reading Room, Document No. 0000725843, http://www.foia.cia.gov; CIA, *Background Material for 27 October*, CREST Collection, Document No. CIA-RDP80B01676R001800010026-6, NA, CP; Zelikow and May, *Presidential Recordings*, vol. 3, pp. 356–57.

96. Regarding the August 30 and September 8, 1962, U-2 incidents, see IDEA 0887, memorandum, McMahon to Cunningham, *Mission 127*, September 12, 1962, CREST Collection, Document No. CIA-RDP33-02415A000300150009-2, NA, CP; memorandum, Lehman to Director of Central Intelligence, *CIA Handling of the Soviet Buildup in Cuba, 1 July–16 October 1962*, November 14, 1962, p. 12, CREST Collection, Document No. CIA-RDP80B01676R001700180076-4, NA, CP.

97. CIA, memorandum, *The Crisis: USSR/Cuba*, October 28, 1962, pp. I-1–I-2, CIA Electronic FOIA Reading Room, Document No. 0000725844, http://www.foia.cia.gov; National Indications Center, *The Soviet Bloc Armed Forces and the Cuban Crisis: A Discussion of Readiness Changes*, July 15, 1963, p. 15, RG-263, entry 82, box 28, MORI DocID: 107300, NA, CP; Brugioni, *Eyeball to Eyeball*, pp. 460, 491. Joint Chiefs of Staff briefing on U-2 intercept from JCS Historical Division, *Notes Taken from Transcripts of Meetings of the Joint Chiefs of Staff, October–November 1962, Dealing with the Cuban Missile Crisis*, notes made in 1976 and typed in 1993, p. 22, National Security Archive, Washington, DC; Johnson, *American Cryptology*, bk. 2, p. 329.

98. NSA OH-1982-20, oral history, *Interview with Harold L. Parish*, October 12, 1982, p. 7, declassified and on file at the library of the National Cryptologic Museum, Fort Meade, MD; Johnson, *American Cryptology*, bk. 2, p. 330. For another version of these events, see Seymour Hersh, "Was Castro out of Control in 1962?," *Washington Post*, October 11, 1987.

99. CIA, memorandum, *The Crisis: USSR/Cuba*, October 31, 1962, p. 1, CIA Electronic FOIA Reading Room, Document No. 0000725847, http://www.foia.cia.gov; CIA, memorandum, *The Crisis: USSR/Cuba*, annex: Evidence on Possibility Cubans May Be Manning SA-2 SAM Sites in Cuba, November 1, 1962, CIA Electronic FOIA Reading Room, Document No. 0001161977, http://www.foia.cia.gov; memorandum for the file, *NSC Executive Committee Record of Action, November 1, 1962, 10:00 AM Meeting No. 16*, November 1, 1962, p. 1, CREST Collection, Document No. CIA-RDP80B01676R002600090022-3, NA, CP; CIA, memorandum, *The Crisis: USSR/Cuba*, November 2, 1962, p. 2, CIA Electronic FOIA Reading Room, Document No. 0000725850, http://www.foia.cia.gov; memorandum by McGeorge Bundy, *NSC Executive Committee Record of Action, November 2, 1962, 11:00 AM, Meeting No. 17*, November 2, 1962, CREST Collection, Document No. CIA-RDP80B01676R002600090021-4, NA, CP; Arms Control and Disarmament Agency, SC No. 08088/63-KH, *The 1962 Soviet Arms Build-Up in Cuba*, 1963, pp. 81–82, CREST Collection, Document No. CIA-RDP78T05439A000300130013-4, NA, CP; NSA OH-1982-20, oral history, *Interview with Harold L. Parish*, October 12, 1982, p. 6, declassified and on file at the library of the National Cryptologic Museum, Fort Meade, MD.

100. CIA, memorandum, *The Crisis: USSR/Cuba*, October 28, 1962, pp. 3–4, CIA Electronic FOIA Reading Room, Document No. 0000725844, http://www.foia.cia.gov; CIA, DD/I staff study, *The Soviet Missile Base Venture in Cuba*, February 17, 1964, p. 109, CIA Electronic FOIA Reading Room, Caesar-Polo-Esau Papers, http://www.foia.cia.gov/cpe.asp.

101. CIA, memorandum, *The Crisis: USSR/Cuba*, October 29, 1962, p. IV-1, CIA Electronic FOIA Reading Room, Document No. 0000725845, http://www.foia.cia.gov; CIA, *Background Material for 29 October*, p. IV-1, CREST Collection, Document No. CIA-RDP80B01676R001800010029-3, NA, CP; memorandum for the record, October 29, 1962, CREST Collection, Document No. CIA-RDP80B01676R001800010029-3, NA, CP; John A. McCone, *Memorandum of Meeting of Executive Committee of the NSC, Tuesday, October 30, 1962, 10:00 a.m.*, October 30, 1962, pp. 1–2, CREST Collection, Document No. CIA-RDP80B01676R001900100009-4, NA, CP; CIA, memorandum, *The Crisis: USSR/Cuba*, annex: Evidence of Cuban Instructions for *Demonstrations, Sabotage Operations in Latin America*, November 1, 1962, p. 1, CIA Electronic FOIA Reading Room, Document No. 0000725849, http://www.foia.cia.gov; CIA, memorandum, *The Crisis: USSR/Cuba*, November 2, 1962, p. 3, CIA Electronic FOIA Reading Room, Document No. 0000725850, http://www.foia.cia.gov.

102. Memorandum, Lehman to Director of Central Intelligence, *CIA Handling of the Soviet Buildup in Cuba, 1 July–16 October 1962*, November 14, 1962, p. 1, CREST Collection, Document No. CIA-RDP80B01676R001700180076-4, NA, CP; confidential interview. See also Director of Central Intelligence, *Report to the President's Foreign Intelligence Advisory Board on Intelligence Community Activities Relating to the Cuban Arms Build-Up: 14 April Through 14 October 1962*, December 1962, p. 27, National Security Files: Countries: Cuba, box 61, JFKL, Boston, MA. Quote from SC No. 12160/62-KH, untitled CIA report on the agency's intelligence collection effort against Cuba, December 1962, p. 5, CREST Collection, Document No. CIA-RDP66B00560R000100100176-0, NA, CP; Office of the Secretary of Defense Historical Office, *History of the Strategic Arms Competition: 1945–1972*, part 2, March 1981, p. 615, DoD FOIA Reading Room, Pentagon, Washington, DC.

103. Johnson, *American Cryptology*, bk. 2, p. 317.

6: ERRORS OF FACT AND JUDGMENT

1. This argument is forcefully made in William B. Bader, "From Vietnam to Iraq: Pretext and Precedent," *International Herald Tribune*, August 27, 2004.

2. The tragic history of the CIA and the Pentagon's efforts to insert agents and then commando teams into North Vietnam between 1958 and 1968 is detailed in Sedgwick D. Tourison Jr., *Secret Army, Secret War* (Annapolis, MD: Naval Institute Press, 1995); Kenneth Conboy and Dale Andradé, *Spies and Commandos* (Lawrence: University Press of Kansas, 2000). McNamara quote from W. Thomas Johnson, "Notes of the President's Meeting with Senator Dirksen and Congressman Ford," January 30, 1968, p. 8, Tom Johnson's Notes of Meetings, box 2, file January 30, 1968, LBJL, Austin, TX.

3. Memorandum, Forrestal to President, *Vietnam*, December 11, 1963, p. 1, Top Secret, Douglas Pike Collection, Vietnam Archive, Texas Tech University, Lubbock, TX; Tourison Jr., *Secret Army, Secret War*, pp. 73–112; Richard H. Schultz Jr., *The Secret War Against Hanoi* (New York: HarperCollins Publishers, 1999), pp. 31–40; Conboy and Andradé, *Spies and Commandos*, pp. 81–100; Robert J. Hanyok, "Skunks, Bogies, Silent Hounds and the Flying Fish: SIGINT and the Gulf of Tonkin Mystery, 2–4 August 1964," *Cryptologic Quarterly*, vol. 19, no. 4–vol. 20, no. 1 (Winter 2000–Spring 2001): p. 8, November 2005 NSA Gulf of Tonkin document release.

4. NSA OH-17-93, oral history, *Interview of Milton S. Zaslow*, September 14, 1993, pp. 33–34, November 2005 NSA Gulf of Tonkin document release.

5. Memorandum, Tordella to Fubini, "[deleted] Operations," November 23, 1964, p. 1, November 2005 NSA Gulf of Tonkin document release; Hanyok, "Skunks, Bogies," p. 10.

6. USIB-S-34.1/9, memorandum, Carroll to Chairman, U.S. Intelligence Board, *Ad Hoc Committee Report and Recommendations Relating to Disclosure of US SIGINT Successes Against North Vietnam*, June 13, 1964, pp. 1–2, DDRS. For an example of the kind of SIGINT NSA was producing at the time about North Vietnam's growing military involvement in the insurgencies in South Vietnam and Laos, see National Indications Center, memorandum, Denny to Watch Committee, *Recent Infiltration of PAVN Personnel into Northern South Vietnam*, July 24, 1964, p. 1, DDRS.

7. Memorandum for the record, *Briefing of CIA Subcommittee of House Armed Services Committee—4 August 1964—9:00 a.m.*, August 18, 1964, p. 13, CREST Collection, Document No. CIA-RDP82R00025R000400160001-4, NA, CP.

8. For SIGINT on increasing resolve of North Vietnamese navy, see Hanyok, "Skunks, Bogies," pp. 9–10; spot report, 2/O/VHN/R03-64, *Significant Increase in Activity of North Vietnamese Naval Communications*, June 8, 1964, November 2005 NSA Gulf of Tonkin document release. For re-

sults of OPLAN 34A raids, see Tourison Jr., *Secret Army, Secret War*, pp. 114–28; Conboy and Andradé, *Spies and Commandos*, pp. 101–15; Marolda and Fitzgerald, *United States Navy*, p. 397.

9. Edwin E. Moïse, *Tonkin Gulf and the Escalation of the Vietnam War* (Chapel Hill: University of North Carolina Press, 1996), p. 51.

10. *Desoto* was actually an acronym based on the name of the first destroyer to conduct one of these patrols, the USS *DeHaven*, with *Desoto* standing for "DeHaven Special Operations Off Tsingtao." CINCPAC, *1964 Command History*, pp. 366–67. The author is grateful to Dr. Edwin E. Moïse of Clemson University for making a copy of this document available. See also Edward J. Marolda and Oscar P. Fitzgerald, *The United States Navy and the Vietnam Conflict: From Military Assistance to Combat, 1959–1965* (Washington, DC: Naval Historical Center, 1986), p. 393. For the Navy SIGINT detachment on each Desoto destroyer, see Dr. Thomas R. Johnson, *American Cryptology During the Cold War, 1945–1989* (Fort Meade, MD: Center for Cryptologic History, 1995), bk. 2, *Centralization Wins, 1960–1972*, p. 515, NSA FOIA; oral history, *Interview with Captain Frederick M. Frick*, January 8, 1996, p. 5, Oral History Project, Vietnam Archive, Texas Tech University, Lubbock, TX.

11. CINCPAC, *1962 Command History*, p. 44, CINCPAC FOIA; CINCPAC, *1963 Command History*, pp. 56–57, CINCPAC FOIA; CINCPAC, *1964 Command History*, p. 367; "The Gulf of Tonkin Incident," *Cryptolog*, February–March 1975: p. 8, November 2005 NSA Gulf of Tonkin Release; National Cryptologic School, *On Watch: Profiles from the National Security Agency's Past 40 Years* (Fort Meade, MD: NSA/CSS, 1986), p. 43, NSA FOIA; Wyman H. Packard, *A Century of U.S. Naval Intelligence* (Washington, DC: GPO, 1996), p. 114.

12. Memorandum for the record, *Chronology of Events Relating to DESOTO Patrol Incidents in the Gulf of Tonkin on 2 and 4 August 1964*, August 10, 1964, p. 1, November 2005 NSA Gulf of Tonkin document release; CINCPAC, *1964 Command History*, pp. 367–68; U.S. Senate, Foreign Relations Committee, *The U.S. Government and the Vietnam War: Executive and Legislative Roles and Relationships*, part 2, 1961–1964, 98th Congress, 2nd session, 1984, p. 284.

13. Description of the *Maddox* from *Jane's Fighting Ships 1955–1956* (New York: McGraw-Hill, 1956), p. 412. For the choice of the *Maddox* based on space on the 0-1 deck, see Don Tuthill, "Tonkin Gulf 1964," *Naval Intelligence Professionals Quarterly*, vol. 4, no. 1 (Winter 1988): p. 19.

14. Hanyok, "Skunks, Bogies," pp. 6–7; message, DIRNAVSECGRUPAC 012345Z Aug 64, DIRNAVSECGRUPAC to Distribution, "Gulf of Tonkin Desoto Patrol," August 1, 1964, November 2005 NSA Gulf of Tonkin document release; Moïse, *Tonkin Gulf*, p. 53. For Herrick and Ogier being generally briefed about OPLAN 34A, but not told about the dates and times of planned raids, see Moïse, *Tonkin Gulf*, p. 60; Delmar C. Lang, Lt. Col., USAF, *Chronology of Events of 2–5 August 1964 in the Gulf of Tonkin*, October 14, 1964, November 2005 NSA Gulf of Tonkin document release.

15. Norman Klar, *Confessions of a Code Breaker (Tales from Decrypt)* (privately published, 2004), p. 163.

16. Message, DIRNAVSECGRUPAC 180013Z Jul, DIRNAVSECGRUPAC to DIRNSA et al., "Aug Desoto Patrol," July 18, 1964, November 2005 NSA Gulf of Tonkin document release; message, DIRNSA P214/0054, 2119122Z, DIRNSA to Distribution List, "Surface Surveillance (Desoto Patrol)," July 21, 1964, November 2005 NSA Gulf of Tonkin document release; message, DIRNSA P214/0078, 241805Z, DIRNSA to [deleted], July 24, 1964, November 2005 NSA Gulf of Tonkin document release. See also Moïse, *Tonkin Gulf*, pp. 52–55; Klar, *Confessions*, pp. 163–64; Captain Norman Klar, USN (Ret.), "How to Help Start a War," *Naval History*, August 2002, p. 42.

17. Marolda and Fitzgerald, *United States Navy*, p. 410.

18. Unless otherwise stated, all times given in this chapter are in Gulf of Tonkin time, which the U.S. military referred to as "Golf" or "G" time, and which is eleven hours ahead of Eastern Daylight Time in Washington.

19. For details of the patrol boat attack on North Vietnam, see Marolda and Fitzgerald, *United States Navy*, p. 409. For San Miguel intercept, see message, 310922Z, USN 27 to QUEBEC/QUEBEC, "DRV Naval Communications Reflect 'Enemy' Incursion, 31 July 1964," July 31, 1964, November 2005 NSA Gulf of Tonkin document release.

20. Marolda and Fitzgerald, *United States Navy*, p. 411.

21. Marolda and Fitzgerald, *United States Navy*, p. 411. For North Vietnamese radar surveillance of the *Maddox*, see message, 010546Z, USN 27 to DIST QUEBEC/QUEBEC, "Possible Reflection Desoto Patrol Noted DRV Naval Communications," August 1, 1964, November 2005 NSA Gulf of Tonkin document release.

22. Message, 011924Z Aug 64, USN-27 to Dist Quebec/Mike, "DRV Navy May Attack Desoto Patrol," August 1, 1964, November 2005 NSA Gulf of Tonkin document release; Hanyok, "Skunks, Bogies," p. 13.

23. Message, 012152Z Aug 64, USN-27 to Dist Quebec/Mike, "DRV Navy May Attack Desoto Patrol," August 1, 1964, November 2005 NSA Gulf of Tonkin document release. See also Marolda and Fitzgerald, *United States Navy*, pp. 411–12; Edwin E. Moïse, "Tonkin Gulf: Reconsidered," in William B. Cogar, *New Interpretations in Naval History: Selected Papers from the Eighth Naval History Symposium* (Annapolis, MD: Naval Institute Press, 1989), pp. 305–06. For intercepts, see "The 'Phantom Battle' That Led to War," *U.S. News & World Report*, July 23, 1984, p. 59.

24. CINCPAC, *1964 Command History*, p. 368; Marolda and Fitzgerald, *United States Navy*, pp. 412–13.

25. CINCPAC, *1964 Command History*, p. 368; Marolda and Fitzgerald, *United States Navy*, p. 414; Moïse, *Tonkin Gulf*, pp. 73–74.

26. Message, DIRNSA B205/981-64, 020302Z Aug 64, DIRNSA to COMSEVENTHFLEET, "Possible Planned Attack by DRV Navy on Desoto Patrol," August 2, 1964, p. 1, November 2005 NSA Gulf of Tonkin document release; memorandum, Hughes to the Secretary, *Incident Involving Desoto Patrol*, August 2, 1964, November 2005 NSA Gulf of Tonkin document release; Hanyok, "Skunks, Bogies," pp. 13–14.

27. Marolda and Fitzgerald, *United States Navy*, pp. 414–15; Moïse, *Tonkin Gulf*, p. 74.

28. The torpedo intercept can be found in message, 020635Z Aug 64, USN-414T to USN-27, August 2, 1964, November 2005 NSA Gulf of Tonkin document release. For issuing of CRITIC message, see Johnson, *American Cryptology*, bk. 2., p. 516; Hanyok, "Skunks, Bogies," p. 14.

29. Marolda and Fitzgerald, *United States Navy*, p. 414; "The 'Phantom Battle,'" *U.S. News & World Report*, pp. 59, 63; Moïse, "Tonkin Gulf: Reconsidered," p. 306; Moïse, *Tonkin Gulf*, pp. 73–76.

30. Marolda and Fitzgerald, *United States Navy*, p. 415; "The 'Phantom Battle,'" *U.S. News & World Report*, p. 59.

31. National Cryptologic School, *On Watch: Profiles from the National Security Agency's Past 40 Years* (Fort Meade, MD: NSA/CSS, 1986), p. 45. NSA FOIA.

32. Lyndon Baines Johnson, *The Vantage Point: Perspectives of the Presidency, 1963–1969* (New York: Holt, 1971), p. 113; Christopher Andrew, *For the President's Eyes Only* (New York: HarperCollins Publishers, 1995), pp. 317–18; "The 'Phantom Battle,'" *U.S. News & World Report*, p. 60; U.S. Department of State, *Foreign Relations of the United States, 1964–1968*, vol. 1, *Vietnam 1964* (Washington, DC: GPO, 1992), pp. 590–97.

33. Transcript of telephone call between Johnson and McNamara, August 3, 1964, 10:20 A.M., tape WH6408.03, Recordings of Telephone Conversations—White House Series, Recordings and Transcripts of Conversations and Meetings, LBJL, Austin, TX; U.S. Department of State, *Foreign Relations*, vol. 1, pp. 598–99, 603; "The 'Phantom Battle,'" *U.S. News & World Report*, pp. 60–61.

34. Message, DIRNSA 021268Z, DIRNSA to OSCAR VICTOR ALPHA, "SIGINT Readiness

Bravo Lantern Established," August 2, 1964, November 2005 NSA Gulf of Tonkin document release; Johnson, *American Cryptology*, bk. 2, p. 516; Hanyok, "Skunks, Bogies," p. 18.

35. Hanyok, "Skunks, Bogies," p. 19.

36. Moïse, *Tonkin Gulf*, p. 75.

37. Hanyok, "Skunks, Bogies," p. 20; oral history, *Interview with Captain Frederick M. Frick*, January 8, 1996, p. 10, Oral History Project, Vietnam Archive, Texas Tech University, Lubbock, TX.

38. Johnson, *American Cryptology*, bk. 2, p. 518. See also U.S. Senate, Foreign Relations Committee, *The Gulf of Tonkin, the 1964 Incidents*, 90th Congress, 2nd session, 1968, pp. 67–68; CINCPAC, *1964 Command History*, p. 369; Marolda and Fitzgerald, *United States Navy*, p. 423; *Pentagon Papers*, Gravel ed., vol. 5, p. 325; Anthony Austin, *The President's War* (New York: J. B. Lippincott Co., 1971), p. 277.

39. Marolda and Fitzgerald, *United States Navy*, pp. 423–24; *Pentagon Papers*, Gravel ed., vol. 5, p. 325; Moïse, "Tonkin Gulf: Reconsidered," p. 308.

40. Johnson, *American Cryptology*, bk. 2, p. 518; "The 'Phantom Battle,'" *U.S. News & World Report*, p. 61.

41. U.S. Senate, Foreign Relations Committee, *The Gulf of Tonkin, the 1964 Incidents*, 90th Congress, 2nd session, 1968, pp. 33, 40.

42. National Cryptologic School, *On Watch*, p. 46.

43. Marolda and Fitzgerald, *United States Navy*, p. 426; National Cryptologic School, *On Watch*, pp. 46–47.

44. Johnson, *American Cryptology*, bk. 2, p. 518; Hanyok, "Skunks, Bogies," p. 22.

45. U.S. Senate, Foreign Relations Committee, *The Gulf of Tonkin, the 1964 Incidents*, 90th Congress, 2nd session, 1968, pp. 34–35; Moïse, *Tonkin Gulf*, p. 113; Marolda and Fitzgerald, *United States Navy*, pp. 426–27; *Pentagon Papers*, Gravel ed., vol. 5, p. 325; John Galloway, *The Gulf of Tonkin Resolution* (Rutherford, NJ: Fairleigh Dickinson University Press, 1972), pp. 290–91.

46. Over the next three hours (seven forty-one to ten forty P.M.), three separate surface contacts were tracked by the radar operators of the *Maddox* and the *Turner Joy*. Herrick concluded that the "skunks" had to be North Vietnamese torpedo boats, since the contacts were moving at speeds in excess of thirty knots.

47. Johnson, *American Cryptology*, bk. 2, p. 520; Marolda and Fitzgerald, *United States Navy*, p. 437; "The 'Phantom Battle,'" *U.S. News & World Report*, p. 61; Moïse, "Tonkin Gulf: Reconsidered," p. 308.

48. Marolda and Fitzgerald, *United States Navy*, p. 437.

49. Marolda and Fitzgerald, *United States Navy*, p. 434; "The 'Phantom Battle,'" *U.S. News & World Report*, pp. 62–63.

50. Marolda and Fitzgerald, *United States Navy*, pp. 437–40; *Pentagon Papers*, Gravel ed., vol. 5, p. 326; "The 'Phantom Battle,'" *U.S. News & World Report*, p. 63.

51. Marolda and Fitzgerald, *United States Navy*, p. 440; *Pentagon Papers*, Gravel ed., vol. 5, p. 327; U.S. Senate, Foreign Relations Committee, *The U.S. Government and the Vietnam War: Executive and Legislative Roles and Relationships*, part 2, 1961–1964, 98th Congress, 2nd session, 1984, pp. 290–91.

52. National Cryptologic School, *On Watch*, p. 49.

53. "The 'Phantom Battle,'" *U.S. News & World Report*, pp. 62–63; National Cryptologic School, *On Watch*, p. 48; U.S. Senate, Foreign Relations Committee, *The U.S. Government and the Vietnam War: Executive and Legislative Roles and Relationships*, part 2, 1961–1964, 98th Congress, 2nd session, 1984, pp. 291–92.

54. U.S. Senate, Foreign Relations Committee, *The U.S. Government and the Vietnam War: Executive and Legislative Roles and Relationships*, part 2, 1961–1964, 98th Congress, 2nd session, 1984, p. 292; *Pentagon Papers*, Gravel ed., vol. 5, p. 327.

55. Marolda and Fitzgerald, *United States Navy*, p. 441; *Pentagon Papers*, Gravel ed., vol. 5, p. 327; "The 'Phantom Battle,'" *U.S. News & World Report*, p. 63.

56. U.S. Department of State, *Foreign Relations of the United States, 1964–1968*, vol. 1, *Vietnam 1964* (Washington, DC: GPO, 1992), p. 609; U.S. Senate, Foreign Relations Committee, *The U.S. Government and the Vietnam War: Executive and Legislative Roles and Relationships*, part 2, 1961–1964, 98th Congress, 2nd session, 1984, p. 292.

57. Electrical report, 2/O/VHN/T10-64, DIRNSA to OSCAR/VICTOR ALPHA, *DRV Naval Entity Reports Losses and Claims Two Enemy Aircraft Shot Down*, August 4, 1964, 2242G, November 2005 NSA Gulf of Tonkin document release; Hanyok, "Skunks, Bogies," p. 25.

58. Moïse, "Tonkin Gulf: Reconsidered," p. 313.

59. Johnson, *American Cryptology*, bk. 2, p. 520.

60. Moïse, *Tonkin Gulf*, p. 197.

61. Oral history, *Interview with Dr. Ray S. Cline*, May 31, 1983, p. 33, LBJL, Austin, TX.

62. Hanyok, "Skunks, Bogies," p. 32.

63. Confidential interviews.

64. Electrical report, 2/O/VHN/T10-64, DIRNSA to OSCAR/VICTOR ALPHA, *DRV Naval Entity Reports Losses and Claims Two Enemy Aircraft Shot Down*, August 4, 1964, 2242G, November 2005 NSA Gulf of Tonkin document release; Hanyok, "Skunks, Bogies," p. 33.

65. Hanyok, "Skunks, Bogies," p. 34.

66. Ibid., pp. 34–35.

67. U.S. Senate, Foreign Relations Committee, *The U.S. Government and the Vietnam War: Executive and Legislative Roles and Relationships*, part 2, 1961–1964, 98th Congress, 2nd session, 1984, p. 292; "The 'Phantom Battle,'" *U.S. News & World Report*, p. 63.

68. Transcript of conversation between Sharp and Burchinal, 5:23 PM EDT 4 August 1964, in *Gulf of Tonkin Transcripts*, pp. 36–37, Document No. 751, DoD FOIA Reading Room, Pentagon, Washington, DC. See also Marolda and Fitzgerald, *United States Navy*, pp. 441–42; *Pentagon Papers*, Gravel ed., vol. 5, p. 327; U.S. Senate, Foreign Relations Committee, *The U.S. Government and the Vietnam War: Executive and Legislative Roles and Relationships*, part 2, 1961–1964, 98th Congress, 2nd session, 1984, pp. 292, n42, 295–96.

69. Marolda and Fitzgerald, *United States Navy*, p. 442.

70. Transcript of conversation between Sharp and Burchinal, 5:39 PM EDT 4 August 1964, in *Gulf of Tonkin Transcripts*, pp. 41–42, Document No. 751, DoD FOIA Reading Room, Pentagon, Washington, DC.

71. U.S. Senate, Foreign Relations Committee, *The U.S. Government and the Vietnam War: Executive and Legislative Roles and Relationships*, part 2, 1961–1964, 98th Congress, 2nd session, 1984, p. 296.

72. *Pentagon Papers*, Gravel ed., vol. 5, p. 327; National Cryptologic School, *On Watch*, pp. 49–50.

73. *Pentagon Papers*, Gravel ed., vol. 5, p. 327.

74. U.S. Senate, Foreign Relations Committee, *The U.S. Government and the Vietnam War: Executive and Legislative Roles and Relationships*, part 2, 1961–1964, 98th Congress, 2nd session, 1984, p. 296.

75. U.S. Senate, Foreign Relations Committee, *The U.S. Government and the Vietnam War: Executive and Legislative Roles and Relationships*, part 2, 1961–1964, 98th Congress, 2nd session, 1984, pp. 296–97.

76. NSA, William Gerhard and Jeanne Renee Jones, *Interview with Lt. General Gordan A. Blake, USAF (Ret.)*, June 5, 1972, p. 5, November 2005 NSA Gulf of Tonkin document release.

77. Memorandum for the record, *Meeting in the Cabinet Room, the White House, 10:45 a.m., 19 September 1964*, September 19, 1964, pp. 1–3, CREST Collection, Document No. CIA-RDP80B01676-R001400050041-9, NA, CP.

78. Johnson, *American Cryptology*, bk. 2, p. 522; transcript, oral history, *Interview with George Ball I*, July 8, 1971, p. 14, LBJL, Austin, TX.
79. Moïse, "Tonkin Gulf: Reconsidered," p. 320.
80. "The 'Phantom Battle,'" *U.S. News & World Report*, pp. 63–64.
81. Hanyok, "Skunks, Bogies," p. 39.
82. Johnson, *American Cryptology*, bk. 2, p. 522.
83. Hanyok, "Skunks, Bogies," p. 3.
84. Oral history, *Interview with Dr. Ray S. Cline*, May 31, 1983, p. 27, LBJL, Austin, TX.
85. Johnson, *American Cryptology*, bk. 2, p. 523.

7: THE WILDERNESS OF PAIN

1. Robert J. Hanyok, *Spartans in Darkness: American SIGINT and the Indochina War, 1945–1975*, U.S. Cryptologic History, series 6, vol. 7 (Fort Meade, MD: Center for Cryptologic History, 2002), p. 461, NSA FOIA.
2. Hanyok, *Spartans in Darkness*, p. 149.
3. CIA quote from CIA, interim report, *Intelligence Warning of the Tet Offensive in South Vietnam*, April 8, 1968, p. 2, CIA Electronic FOIA Reading Room, Document No. 0000097712, http://www.foia.cia.gov. See also memorandum, Rostow to the President, September 6, 1968, National Security Archive, Washington, DC.
4. State Department, INR briefing note, *North Vietnam: Ashmore and Baggs Given Aide Memoire*, April 9, 1968, p. 1, RG-59, Harriman Files, Lot 71D 461, NND 979509, box 7, NA, CP; NSA, *Technical SIGINT Report 002-92, NSA Correlation Study—POW/MIA*, August 21, 1992, p. 16, RG-46, Records of the U.S. Senate, Senate Select Committee on POW/MIA Affairs, NA, CP; confidential interviews.
5. The GDRS unit controlling infiltration into the south was known as Military Region 559 or Transportation Group 559 (because it was created in May 1959). It started life with only five hundred people but over time grew to forty to fifty thousand military and civilian personnel organized into sixteen units called Binh Trams, each of which controlled infiltration activities in its own sector. CIA, Office of Current Intelligence, SC No. 00642/64, *Special Report: Viet Cong Infiltration into Northern South Vietnam*, October 23, 1964, pp. 3–5, MORI Doc ID: 8460, CIA FOIA; ASA, *Annual Historical Report USASA Fiscal Year 1965*, pp. 308–09, via Dr. Jeffrey T. Richelson; Dr. Thomas R. Johnson, *American Cryptology During the Cold War, 1945–1989*, bk. 2, *Centralization Wins, 1960–1972* (Fort Meade, MD: Center for Cryptologic History, 1995), pp. 500, 539, NSA FOIA.
6. CIA, Office of Current Intelligence, SC No. 05780/64, intelligence memorandum, *Communist Military Posture and Capabilities Vis-a-Vis Southeast Asia*, December 31, 1964, p. 4, Larry J. Berman Collection, Vietnam Archive, Texas Tech University, Lubbock, TX; CIA, Office of Current Intelligence, SC No. 00682/65, intelligence memorandum, *Communist Troop Movements in Laos*, January 13, 1965, p. 1, Larry J. Berman Collection, Vietnam Archive, Texas Tech University, Lubbock, TX; CIA, Office of Current Intelligence, SC No. 00989/65, intelligence memorandum, *Report of Viet Cong Terrorist Plans Against US Installations*, February 12, 1965, p. 2, LBJL, Austin, TX; CIA, Office of Current Intelligence, SC No. 04209/64, intelligence memorandum, *Possible PAVN Tactical Command Headquarters in South Vietnam*, March 31, 1965, pp. 1–2, Larry J. Berman Collection, Vietnam Project Archive, Texas Tech University, Lubbock, TX; CIA, Directorate of Intelligence, memorandum, *The Matter of Communist Intentions Re: South Vietnam*, April 1, 1965, p. 1, RG-263, entry 35, box 11, folder 1, NA, CP; State Department, INR, *Vietnam: 1961–1968 as Interpreted in INR's Production*, special annex 1, 1969, pp. 1–3, National

Security Archive, Washington, DC; oral history, *Interview with Dean Rusk II*, September 26, 1969, p. 5, LBJL, Austin, TX; Hanyok, *Spartans in Darkness*, pp. 109–10.

7. "Operation Starlight: A Sigint Success Story," *Cryptologic Spectrum*, vol. 1, no. 3. (Fall 1971): pp. 9–11, DOCID: 3217148, NSA FOIA; Johnson, *American Cryptology*, bk. 2, p. 530; James L. Gilbert, *The Most Secret War: Army Signals Intelligence in Vietnam* (Fort Belvoir, VA: Military History Office, U.S. Army Intelligence and Security Command, 2003), pp. 35–36. For the military aspects of Operation Starlight, see Brigadier General Edwin H. Simmons, USMC (Ret.), *The U.S. Marines: The First Two Hundred Years, 1775–1975* (New York: Viking Press, 1976), p. 211.

8. Hanyok, *Spartans in Darkness*, p. 305.

9. Johnson, *American Cryptology*, bk. 2, p. 530.

10. Hanyok, *Spartans in Darkness*, p. 306.

11. Ibid., p. 149.

12. CIA, Office of Current Intelligence, SC No. 03777/66, intelligence memorandum, *Evidence of Continuing Vietnamese Communist War Preparations*, January 24, 1966, p. 4, CIA Electronic FOIA Reading Room, Document No. 0000621146, http://www.foia.cia.gov; untitled CIA draft estimate with supporting documents, undated but circa June 1966, RG-263, entry 36, HRP 89-2/00443, box 11, file 777A, NA, CP.

13. Jim Lairson, "8th RRU: Phu Bai 1965–66," http://www.npoint.net/maddog/8thin65.htm.

14. William E. LeGro, "The Enemy's Jungle Cover Was No Match for the Finding Capabilities of the Army's Radio Research Units," *Vietnam*, June 1990, pp. 14, 18–19.

15. 6994 Security Squadron, letter, "360 Reconnaissance Missions in Quang Tri Province," September 3, 1966, in *History, 360th Reconnaissance Squadron: July–September 1966*, Microfilm Roll No736, frame 1695, Air Force Historical Research Agency, Maxwell Air Force Base, AL; Project Corona Harvest, *USAF Reconnaissance Operations in Support of Operations in Southeast Asia: January 1, 1965–March 31, 1968*, p. 11, Air Force Historical Research Agency, Maxwell Air Force Base, AL.

16. SI-TS-61/PL-4, memorandum, Carroll to Secretary of Defense, *Release of COMINT Pertaining to Gulf of Tonkin Incidents of 2 and 4 August 1964*, December 13, 1967, November 2005 NSA Gulf of Tonkin document release; Johnson, *American Cryptology*, bk. 2, p. 539; Hanyok, *Spartans in Darkness*, pp. 307–08.

17. Memorandum, Rostow to President with Attachment, *Situation in the DMZ, 13 October 1966*, October 13, 1966, Larry J. Berman Collection, Vietnam Archive, Texas Tech University, Lubbock, TX; memorandum, [deleted] to Chief, Far East Area, *The Communist Buildup in Northern South Vietnam*, November 4, 1966, pp. 1–2, CREST Collection, Document No. CIA-RDP78S02149R000200280007-2, NA, CP; CIA, Directorate of Intelligence, intelligence memorandum, *The Communist Buildup in Northern South Vietnam*, November 4, 1966, pp. 1–2, Larry J. Berman Collection, Vietnam Archive, Texas Tech University, Lubbock, TX; Hanyok, *Spartans in Darkness*, p. 306.

18. CIA, Directorate of Intelligence, SC No. 01393/67, intelligence memorandum, *The Communist Buildup in South Vietnam's Northern I Corps*, May 11, 1967, p. 1, Larry J. Berman Collection, Vietnam Archive, Texas Tech University, Lubbock, TX; memorandum, Rostow to President, May 12, 1967, Larry J. Berman Collection, Vietnam Archive, Texas Tech University, Lubbock, TX; memorandum, Ginsburgh to Rostow, *Possible Attack on Con Thieu*, May 12, 1967, p. 1, Larry J. Berman Collection, Vietnam Archive, Texas Tech University, Lubbock, TX.

19. State Department, INR, *Vietnam: 1961–1968 as Interpreted in INR's Production*, special annex 1, 1969, p. 6, National Security Archive, Washington, DC; General Bruce Palmer Jr., *The 25-Year War: America's Military Role in Vietnam* (Lexington: University Press of Kentucky, 1984), p. 79; Bruce E. Jones, *War Without Windows* (New York: Vanguard Press, 1987), pp. 136–37.

20. Military Assistance Command Vietnam, *Operations in the Cambodia/Laos/SVN Tri-Border Area*, circa January 1968, p. 1 passim, NSF: Vietnam, LBJL, Austin, TX; James E. Pierson, *USAFSS Response to World Crises, 1949–1969* (San Antonio, TX: USAFSS Historical Office, 1970), pp. 102–03, AIA FOIA; John D. Bergen, *Military Communications: A Test for Technology* (Washington, DC: U.S. Army Center of Military History, 1986), pp. 247–49; Don E. Gordon, "Private Minnock's Private War," *International Journal of Intelligence and Counterintelligence*, vol. 4, no. 2 (Summer 1990): pp. 204–05; Johnson, *American Cryptology*, bk. 2, p. 560; Hanyok, *Spartans in Darkness*, p. 317.

21. State Department, INR, *Vietnam: 1961–1968 as Interpreted in INR's Production*, special annex 1, 1969, pp. 1, 6, National Security Archive, Washington, DC; Johnson, *American Cryptology*, bk. 2, pp. 539–40; Hanyok, *Spartans in Darkness*, pp. 111–12. For Binh Tram 8 communications in Vinh, see CIA, Directorate of Intelligence, TCS 15240/71, "Imagery Analysis Service Notes," March 26, 1971, p. 3, CREST Collection, Document No. CIA-RDP78T04759A009900010012-6, NA, CP; Lewis Sorley, *A Better War* (New York: Harcourt Brace and Company, 1999), p. 218.

22. Hanyok, *Spartans in Darkness*, p. 113.

23. Ibid., pp. 114–16; confidential interviews.

24. Palmer quote from ASA, *The Army's Program for Command Supervision of Readiness: Command Presentation by United States Army Security Agency*, September 9, 1969, p. 25, copy of which is in the files of the U.S. Army Center of Military History, Washington, DC. For SIGINT successes, see U.S. Army Vietnam (USARV), *Evaluation of U.S. Army Combat Operations in Vietnam*, vol. 2, annex A—Intelligence, April 25, 1966, pp. A-12-2–A-12-3, Vietnam Archive, Texas Tech University, Lubbock, TX; SI-TS-61/PL-4, memorandum, Carroll to Secretary of Defense, *Release of COMINT Pertaining to Gulf of Tonkin Incidents of 2 and 4 August 1964*, December 13, 1967, November 2005 NSA Gulf of Tonkin document release; Johnson, *American Cryptology*, bk. 2, p. 543.

25. HQ ASA, *Historical Summary of the U.S. Army Security Agency, Fiscal Years 1968–1970*, p. 61, INSCOM FOIA. The "SIGINT with their orange juice" quote is from U.S. Senate, *Final Report of the Select Committee to Study Government Operations with Respect to Intelligence Activities*, 94th Congress, 2nd session, bk. 1, 1975, p. 27.

26. Palmer, *25-Year War*, pp. 63, 167. For a classified version of this thesis, see General Bruce Palmer Jr., "US Intelligence and Vietnam," *Studies in Intelligence*, vol. 28, no. 5 (special ed., 1984): p. 42, CIA Electronic FOIA Reading Room, Document No. 0001433692, http://www.foia.cia.gov.

27. Johnson, *American Cryptology*, bk. 2, p. 565.

28. Confidential interviews; David Fulghum and Terence Maitland, *The Vietnam Experience: South Vietnam on Trial, Mid-1970 to 1972* (Boston: Boston Publishing Co., 1984), p. 127.

29. Confidential interviews with a number of senior U.S. Army and Marine Corps commanders who served in Vietnam. Abrams quote from Gilbert, *Most Secret War*, p. 1; U.S. Army Military History Institute, oral history 87-17, *Interview with General Frederick J. Kroesen, USA, Retired*, vol. 1, 1987, p. 84, U.S. Army Center of Military History, Washington, DC.

30. CIA, Directorate of Intelligence, intelligence memorandum, SC No. 08753/67, *A Review of the Situation in Vietnam*, December 8, 1967, p. IV-2, CIA Collection, Vietnam Archive, Texas Tech University, Lubbock, TX; message, 140014Z DEC 67, JCS to CINCPAC, December 14, 1967, Larry J. Berman Collection, Vietnam Archive, Texas Tech University, Lubbock, TX; Johnson, *American Cryptology*, bk. 2, p. 561; Hanyok, *Spartans in Darkness*, p. 320.

31. Hanyok, *Spartans in Darkness*, pp. 320–21.

32. Interim report, *Intelligence Warning of the Tet Offensive in South Vietnam*, April 8, 1968, p. 3, CIA Electronic FOIA Reading Room, Document No. 0000097712, http://www.foia.cia.gov;

exhibit 518, "Treatment of Indications in Finished Intelligence: NSA," November 30, 1982, in 82 CIV 7913, *General William C. Westmoreland v. Columbia Broadcasting System, Inc. et al.*, U.S. District Court for the Southern District of New York; Hanyok, *Spartans in Darkness*, p. 326.

33. CIA, memorandum, *Comments on Saigon Embassy Telegram 16107, 5 January 1968*, January 5, 1968, p. 1, CREST Collection, Document No. CIA-RDP80R01720R000500090106-7, NA, CP; State Department, Director of INR, intelligence note, Hughes to the Secretary, *Continuing Communist Military Deployments in Northern South Vietnam*, January 6, 1968, pp. 1–2, Larry J. Berman Collection, Vietnam Archive, Texas Tech University, Lubbock, TX; CIA, intelligence memorandum, *The Enemy Threat to Khe Sanh*, January 10, 1968, pp. 2–3, CREST Collection, Document No. CIA-RDP85T00875R001100070001-8, NA, CP; memorandum, Rostow to the President, *Tet Ceasefire*, January 19, 1968, p. 1, 109th Quartermaster Company Collection, Vietnam Archive, Texas Tech University, Lubbock, TX.

34. CIA, interim report, *Intelligence Warning of the Tet Offensive in South Vietnam*, April 8, 1968, p. 7, CIA Electronic FOIA Reading Room, Document No. 0000097712, http://www.foia.cia.gov; ASA, *Historical Summary of U.S. Army Security Agency and Subordinate Units, FY 1968–1970*, 1971, p. 77, INSCOM FOIA.

35. Exhibit 518, "Treatment of Indications in Finished Intelligence: NSA," November 30, 1982, in 82 CIV 7913, *General William C. Westmoreland v. Columbia Broadcasting System, Inc. et al.*, U.S. District Court for the Southern District of New York; Hanyok, *Spartans in Darkness*, p. 326. "Ubiquitous and unmistakable" quote from Johnson, *American Cryptology*, bk. 2, p. 562.

36. 2/O/VCM/R32-68, report, *Coordinated Vietnamese Communist Offensive Evidenced in South Vietnam*, January 25, 1968, NSA FOIA.

37. Palmer, "US Intelligence and Vietnam," pp. 55, 57.

38. CIA, SC No. 07250/68, *Warning of the Tet Offensive*, undated but circa April 1968, p. 7, Larry J. Berman Collection, Vietnam Archive, Texas Tech University, Lubbock, TX.

39. Westmoreland cable cited in Hanyok, *Spartans in Darkness*, p. 326.

40. Exhibit 518, "Treatment of Indications in Finished Intelligence: NSA," November 30, 1982, in 82 CIV 7913, *General William C. Westmoreland v. Columbia Broadcasting System, Inc. et al.*, U.S. District Court for the Southern District of New York; Johnson, *American Cryptology*, bk. 2, p. 563.

41. CIA, SC No. 07250/68, *Warning of the Tet Offensive*, undated but circa April 1968, pp. 7–8, Larry J. Berman Collection, Vietnam Archive, Texas Tech University, Lubbock, TX.

42. David Parks, *Bien Hoa Air Base: Tet '68*, http://www.vspa.com/bien-hoa-tet-68.htm.

43. Oral history, *Interview with Daniel O. Graham*, May 24, 1982, p. 15, LBJL, Austin, TX.

44. Harold P. Ford, *CIA and the Vietnam Policymakers: Three Episodes, 1962–1968* (Washington, DC: Center for the Study of Intelligence, 1998), p. 116.

45. CIA, interim report, *Intelligence Warning of the Tet Offensive in South Vietnam*, April 8, 1968, p. 3, CIA Electronic FOIA Reading Room, Document No. 0000097712, http://www.foia.cia.gov. In 2005, the CIA declassified another version of this document, which deleted the substance of this paragraph, for which see CREST Collection, Document No. CIA-RDP80R01720R000100080001-8, NA, CP.

46. Johnson, *American Cryptology*, bk. 2, p. 562; Ford, *CIA*, p. 116; Hanyok, *Spartans in Darkness*, p. 331.

47. Hanyok, *Spartans in Darkness*, p. 333.

48. Message, MAC 01430, GENERAL WESTMORELAND COMUSMACV to ADMIRAL SHARP CINCPAC, January 20, 1968, attached to memorandum, Rostow to President, January 30, 1968, 109th Quartermaster Company Collection, Vietnam Archives, Texas Tech University, Lubbock,

TX. See also Don Oberdorfer, *Tet!* (New York: Da Capo Press, 1984), pp. 110–11; Jones, *War Without Windows*, p. 168; John L. Plaster, *SOG: The Secret Wars of America's Commandos in Vietnam* (New York: Simon and Schuster, 1997), p. 179.

49. Theodore Lukacs, *Focus on Khe Sanh*, Southeast Asia Cryptologic History Series (Fort Meade, MD: Center for Cryptologic History, December 1969), pp. 4, 6, NSA FOIA; Johnson, *American Cryptology*, bk. 2, p. 561.

50. Johnson, *American Cryptology*, bk. 2, p. 562.

51. Oral history, *Interview with Daniel O. Graham*, May 24, 1982, p. 21, LBJL, Austin, TX.

52. The best all-around history of the tragic U.S. involvement in Cambodia remains William Shawcross's epic *Sideshow: Kissinger, Nixon and the Destruction of Cambodia* (New York: Simon and Schuster, 1979). The military aspects of the Cambodia invasion are well covered in Keith William Nolan, *Into Cambodia: Spring Campaign, Summer Offensive, 1970* (Novato, CA: Presidio Press, 1970).

53. Johnson, *American Cryptology*, bk. 2, p. 573.

54. Hanyok, *Spartans in Darkness*, pp. 363–64.

55. Johnson, *American Cryptology*, bk. 2, p. 574.

56. Dr. Thomas R. Johnson, *American Cryptology During the Cold War, 1945–1989*, bk. 3, *Retrenchment and Reform, 1972–1980* (Fort Meade, MD: Center for Cryptologic History, 1995), p. 1, NSA FOIA; Hanyok, *Spartans in Darkness*, pp. 420–21.

57. Message, CIA/OCI/WHIZ 741006, "Communist Combat and Command Units Move Closer to Saigon," October 6, 1974, CREST Collection, Document No. CIA-RDP78S01932A000 100100011-5, NA, CP; message, CIA/OCI/WHIZ 741112, "North Vietnamese 308th Division May Move South," November 12, 1974, CREST Collection, Document No. CIA-RDP78S01932 A000100110010-5, NA, CP; message, CIA/OCI/WHIZ 741214, "Vietnam Military Situation," December 14, 1974, CREST Collection, Document No. CIA-RDP78S01932A000100190027-9, NA, CP; Johnson, *American Cryptology*, bk. 3, p. 3; Hanyok, *Spartans in Darkness*, pp. 429–30.

58. U.S. Intelligence Board Watch Committee, *Watch Report: Draft—Submitted for USIB Approval*, February 5, 1975, CREST Collection, Document No. CIA-RDP93T01468R001000400011-3, NA, CP; National Indications Center, *Draft Watch Report for Watch Committee Consideration*, February 18, 1975, CREST Collection, Document No. CIA-RDP93T01468R00100040022-1, NA, CP.

59. Johnson, *American Cryptology*, bk. 3, p. 5; Hanyok, *Spartans in Darkness*, pp. 432–34.

60. Johnson, *American Cryptology*, bk. 3, p. 6; Hanyok, *Spartans in Darkness*, p. 436.

61. DCI briefing for House Foreign Affairs Subcommittee, *The Situation in Cambodia*, March 10, 1975, pp. 1–3, DDRS; Johnson, *American Cryptology*, bk. 3, p. 9; Hanyok, *Spartans in Darkness*, p. 437.

62. CIA, Directorate of Intelligence, intelligence memorandum, *The Situation in Indochina (as of 1600 EST) No. 1*, April 3, 1975, CREST Collection, Document No. CIA-RDP86T00608R0 00200060001-4, NA, CP; CIA, Directorate of Intelligence, intelligence memorandum, *The Situation in Indochina (as of 1600 EST) No. 14*, April 16, 1975, CREST Collection, Document No. CIA-RDP79T00865A002500420001-9, NA, CP; Johnson, *American Cryptology*, bk. 3, pp. 9–10; Hanyok, *Spartans in Darkness*, pp. 439–41.

63. Letter, Carver to Schlesinger, April 23, 1975, CREST Collection, Document No. CIA-RDP 80R01720R000400110002-0, NA, CP; DCI briefing for 24 April NSC Meeting, *The Situation in Vietnam*, April 24, 1975, pp. 1–2, CREST Collection, Document No. CIA-RDP79R01142A 002100010004-8, NA, CP.

64. Johnson, *American Cryptology*, bk. 3, pp. 11–12; Hanyok, *Spartans in Darkness*, pp. 442–44.

65. Johnson, *American Cryptology*, bk. 3, p. 15.

8: Riding the Whirlwind

1. Dr. Thomas R. Johnson, *American Cryptology During the Cold War, 1945–1989*, bk. 2, *Central-ization Wins, 1960–1972*, p. 293, and bk. 3, *Retrenchment and Reform, 1972–1980*, p. 21 (Fort Meade, MD: Center for Cryptologic History, 1995), NSA FOIA. See also U.S. House of Representatives, Appropriations Committee, *Department of Defense Appropriations for 1972*, 92nd Congress, 1st session, part 3, 1971, p. 536; U.S. House of Representatives, Appropriations Committee, *Department of Defense Appropriations for 1975*, 93rd Congress, 2nd session, part 1, 1974, p. 598; U.S. House of Representatives, Appropriations Committee, *Department of Defense Appropriations for 1975*, 93rd Congress, 2nd session, part 3, 1974, pp. 340, 663; U.S. Senate, Select Committee to Study Governmental Operations with Respect to Intelligence Activities, *Final Report*, 94th Congress, 2nd session, bk. 1, 1976, p. 340.
2. William Reed and W. Craig Reed, "Thirteen Days: The Real Story," *Troika Magazine*, 2001, http://www.troikamagazine.com/network/13days.html.
3. OPNAVINST S3270.1, *Employment and Operating Policy for the U.S. Navy HFDF Nets*, May 18, 1984, pp. 2–4, U.S. Navy FOIA; OPNAVINST 02501.5E, *Cryptologic Tasks Assigned to Fleet Commanders in Chief*, June 24, 1969, p. 3, U.S. Navy FOIA; NSGINST C3270.2, *Bullseye System Concept of Operations*, June 30, 1989, p. 3, via Dr. Jeffrey T. Richelson; NWP-5, *Naval Cryptologic Operations*, pp. 3-3–3-4, U.S. Navy FOIA; *1984 Annual History Report for the Headquarters Naval Security Group Command*, June 5, 1985, sec. 10, item 10.2.1, COMNAVSECGRU FOIA; Desmond Ball, "The U.S. Naval Ocean Surveillance Information System—Australia's Role," *Pacific Defence Reporter*, June 1982, pp. 45–46.
4. The seven technical research ships were the USS *Oxford* (AGTR-1), the USS *Georgetown* (AGTR-2), the USS *Jamestown* (AGTR-3), the USS *Belmont* (AGTR-4), the USS *Liberty* (AGTR-5), the USNS *Private Jose F. Valdez* (T-AG-169), and the USNS *Joseph E. Muller* (T-AG-171). "Technical research ship" section in *History of COMINT Operations: 1917–1959*, undated, RG-38, CNSG Library, box 104, file 5750/89, NA, CP; "Seaborne SIGINT Stations," *Cryptologic Milestones*, issue 5 (May 1965): p. 2, NSA FOIA; message, JCS 5338, "*Contingency Planning for TRS Operations*," November 6, 1965, DoD FOIA Reading Room, Document No. 845, Pentagon, Washington, DC; Julie Alger, *A Review of the Technical Research Ship Program, 1961–1969*, undated, NSA FOIA; Johnson, *American Cryptology*, bk. 2, p. 315; Wyman H. Packard, *A Century of U.S. Naval Intelligence* (Washington, DC: GPO, 1996), p. 114.
5. Confidential interviews. See also U.S. Senate, Armed Services Committee, *Department of Defense Authorization for Appropriations for Fiscal Year 1994*, 103rd Congress, 1st session, part 7, 1993, pp. 452, 456.
6. For building spy satellites to monitor the Soviet ABM program, see Committee on Overhead Reconnaissance, TCS-0108-66, *Agenda for COMOR-M-390*, November 16, 1966, p. 3, CREST Collection, Document No. CIA-RDP79B01709A000100010029-0, NA, CP; letter, Helms to Vance, November 21, 1966, CREST Collection, Document No. CIA-RDP79B01709A000 600060006-5, NA, CP; memorandum, Land and Killian to Hornig, December 15, 1966, CREST Collection, Document No. CIA-RDP79B01709A000600060004-7, NA, CP. For the intelligence effort against the ABM, see Frank Eliot, "Moon Bounce ELINT," *Studies in Intelligence*, Spring 1967; pp. 63–64, RG-263, entry 27, NA, CP; Edward Tauss, "Foretesting a Soviet ABM System," *Studies in Intelligence*, Winter 1968: pp. 22–23, RG-263, entry 27, NA, CP; David S. Brandwein, "Interaction in Weapons R&D," *Studies in Intelligence*, Winter 1968: pp. 18–19, RG-263, entry 27, NA, CP; Donald C. Brown, "On the Trail of Hen House and Hen Roost," *Studies in Intelligence*, Spring 1969, pp. 11–19, RG-263, entry 27, box 16, NA, CP; Gene Poteat, "Stealth, Countermeasures, and ELINT, 1960–1975," *Studies in Intelligence*, vol. 42, no. 1

(1998): pp. 53–54, 57–58, RG-263, NA, CP. Copley quote from "John O. Copley: Developing Early Signals Intelligence Programs," in Robert A. McDonald, ed., *Beyond Expectations— Building an American National Reconnaissance Capability: Recollections of the Pioneers and Founders of National Reconnaissance* (Bethesda, MD: American Society for Photogrammetry and Remote Sensing, 2002), p. 79.

7. Harvest was retired from use at NSA in 1976. "Harvest: NSA's Ultra High-Speed Computer," *Cryptologic Milestones*, issue 13 (November 1968): pp. 2–3, NSA FOIA; Sam Snyder, "Age of the Computer," *NSA Newsletter*, November 1977, p. 15.

8. Johnson, *American Cryptology*, bk. 2, p. 368, NSA FOIA.

9. CIA, Report, *The Long-Range Plan of the Central Intelligence Agency*, August 31, 1965, p. 29, CREST Collection, Document No. CIA-RDP82M00311R000100350001-3, NA, CP; Richard M. Bissell Jr., *Review of Selected NSA Cryptanalytic Efforts*, February 18, 1965, p. 1.

10. The author is grateful to Dr. Jeffrey T. Richelson for providing a copy of this report. See also memorandum, Wheelon to DD/S&T, *Advanced Planning Progress Report*, May 26, 1965, p. 4, CREST Collection, Document No. CIA-RDP71B00822R000100110007-9, NA, CP; CIA, *External Reviews of the Intelligence Community*, December 1974, p. 10, CREST Collection, Document No. CIA-RDP87B01034R000700230001-3, NA, CP.

11. See, for example, CIA, memorandum, *Areas Highly Suspected to Contain Soviet ICBM Launching Facilities*, February 21, 1962, CREST Collection, Document No. CIA-RDP78T05449A 000200010001-0, NA, CP; Deployment Working Group of the Guided Missiles and Astronautics Intelligence Committee, *Soviet Surface-to-Surface Missile Deployment*, October 1, 1962, tab 1, p. 5, CREST Collection, Document No. CIA-RDP78T04757A000300010003-3, NA, CP; Guided Missiles and Astronautics Intelligence Committee, *Preliminary Analysis of Missile- or Space-Associated Facilities at Emba, USSR*, March 1963, pp. 4–6, CREST Collection, Document No. CIA-RDP78T05449A000200270001-2, NA, CP; CIA, memorandum, *Rocket Engine Test Facility, Perm, USSR*, September 28, 1964, CREST Collection, Document No. CIA-RDP78T05929 A000200010025-1, NA, CP.

12. Memorandum, SC No. 03292/61, *Guided Missile Task Force Comments on AFCIN Concept Papers on Soviet Missile Deployment*, February 14, 1961, CREST Collection, Document No. CIA RDP70T00666R000100130027-2, NA, CP; memorandum for the file, *Nuclear Test Ban Treaty*, March 5, 1963, in Department of State, *Foreign Relations of the United States 1961–1963*, vol. 7, *Arms Control and Disarmament* (Washington, DC: GPO, 1995); National Intelligence Estimate No. 11-2A-63, *The Soviet Atomic Energy Program*, July 2, 1963, p. 6, CIA Electronic FOIA Reading Room, Document No. 0000843188, http://www.foia.cia.gov; NIE 11-11-66, *Impact of a Threshold Test Ban Treaty on Soviet Military Programs*, May 25, 1966, p. 11, CIA Electronic FOIA Reading Room, Document No. 0000239460, http://www.foia.cia.gov.

13. CIA, Photographic Intelligence Center, PIC/JR-1023/61, *Microwave Stations Within a 100-Kilometer Radius of Moscow*, June 1961, CREST Collection, Document No. CIA-RDP78T04751 A000100010025-7, NA, CP; Economic Intelligence Committee, Subcommittee on Electronics and Telecommunications, EIR SR-6, *Economic Intelligence Report: Status of High-Capacity Communications in the Soviet Bloc*, October 1962, pp. 2–4, CREST Collection, Document No. CIA-RDP79S01100A000100110007-1, NA, CP; CIA, Office of Research and Reports, CIA/RR EP 65-68, *Prospects and Problem Areas for the Development of Telecommunications in the European Satellites, 1964–75*, August 1965, CREST Collection, Document No. CIA-RDP79T01049A003100 130001-2, NA, CP. Quote from Albert D. Wheelon, "And the Truth Shall Keep You Free: Recollections by the First Deputy Director for Science and Technology," *Studies in Intelligence*, Spring 1995: p. 75, CIA Electronic FOIA Reading Room, Document No. 0000752314, http://foia.cia .gov. "Reestablish COMINT access" quote from memorandum, Wheelon to DD/S&T, *Advanced*

Planning Progress Report, May 26, 1965, p. 6, CREST Collection, Document No. CIA-RDP71B00822R000100110007-9, NA, CP.

14. Carter background from biographical data sheet, Lt. General Marshall S. Carter, USA; "Commander, Diplomat, Executive Ends Distinguished Military Career," *NSA Newsletter*, July 1969, p. 4, NSA FOIA.

15. David Wise and Thomas B. Ross, *The Invisible Government* (New York: Vintage Books, 1974), p. 198; David C. Martin, *Wilderness of Mirrors* (New York: Harper and Row, 1980), p. 118; Doris M. Condit, *History of the Office of the Secretary of Defense*, vol. 2, *The Test of War, 1950–1953* (Washington, DC: GPO, 1988), p. 484; Dino Brugioni, *Eyeball to Eyeball: The Inside Story of the Cuban Missile Crisis* (New York: Random House, 1990), pp. 85–86; Bruce Lambert, "Marshall Carter, 83, Intelligence Official and Marshall Aide," *New York Times*, February 20, 1993.

16. Johnson, *American Cryptology*, bk. 2, p. 358.

17. "Poisoned the atmosphere" quote from Johnson, *American Cryptology*, bk. 2, p. 359.

18. Memorandum, Duckett to D/DCI/NIPE, *DCI Report on the Community to the President's Foreign Intelligence Advisory Board*, September 1968, pp. 3–4, CREST Collection, Document No. CIA-RDP71R00140A000100050001-0, NA, CP; memorandum, ASA/D/DCI/NIPE to Bross, *SIGINT Collection Requirements*, December 2, 1969, p. 1, CREST Collection, Document No. CIA-RDP80B01138A000100080014-1, NA, CP; "Information Support to Intelligence Production: The Reality and the Dream," *Cryptologic Spectrum*, vol. 10, no. 4 (Fall 1980): p. 4, NSA FOIA; Scott D. Breckinridge, *The CIA and the U.S. Intelligence System* (Boulder, CO: Westview Press, 1986), p. 58.

19. "U.S. Electronic Espionage: A Memoir," *Ramparts*, August 1972, pp. 43–44; Chet Flippo, "Can the CIA Turn Students into Spies?," *Rolling Stone*, March 11, 1976, p. 30.

20. CIA, Directorate of Intelligence, CAESAR XXXVIII, intelligence report, *Soviet Policy and the 1967 Arab-Israeli War*, March 16, 1970, pp. 3–4, CIA Electronic FOIA Reading Room, http://www.foia.cia.gov/cpe.asp; William D. Gerhard and Henry W. Millington, *Attack on a Sigint Collector, the U.S.S. Liberty* (Fort Meade, MD: Center for Cryptologic History, 1981), p. 1, NSA FOIA.

21. Gerhard and Millington, *Attack*, pp. 2–3.

22. CIA, Directorate of Intelligence, CAESAR XXXVIII, intelligence report, *Soviet Policy and the 1967 Arab-Israeli War*, March 16, 1970, p. 5, CIA Electronic FOIA Reading Room, http://www.foia.cia.gov/cpe.asp.

23. Gerhard and Millington, *Attack*, pp. 2–3.

24. USAFSS History Office, *A Special Historical Study of the Production and Use of Special Intelligence During World Contingencies: 1950–1970*, March 1, 1972, pp. 95, 97, declassified through FOIA by the National Security Archive, Washington, DC.

25. *Briefing Notes for Director of Central Intelligence Helms for Use at a White House Meeting*, May 23, 1967, CREST Collection, Document No. CIA-RDP80R01580A001021000I-5, NA, CP; message, 231729Z, DIRNSA to JCS/Joint Reconnaissance Center, May 23, 1967, NSA FOIA; USAFSS History Office, *A Special Historical Study of the Production and Use of Special Intelligence During World Contingencies: 1950–1970*, March 1, 1972, pp. 97–98, declassified through FOIA by the National Security Archive, Washington, DC; Gerhard and Millington, *Attack*, p. 3; Johnson, *American Cryptology*, bk. 2, p. 428; J. L. Freshwater [William K. Parmenter], "Policy and Intelligence: The Arab-Israeli War," *Studies in Intelligence*, Winter 1969, CREST Collection, Document No. CIA-RDP79T01762A000500040020-8, NA, CP.

26. Message, ADP/224-67, DIRNSA to JCS, "Diversion of USS Liberty," May 23, 1967, NSA FOIA; Gerhard and Millington, *Attack*, pp. 5, 13; Johnson, *American Cryptology*, bk. 2, p. 429. For U.S. Army Communications Support Unit, see Department of the Army, Asst Chief of Staff for Force Development, *Active Army Troop List*, part 4, June 1968, p. 3, copy in U.S. Army Center of Military History Library, Washington, DC.

27. Gerhard and Millington, *Attack*, pp. 10–12; Fleet Air Reconnaissance Squadron Two, *Aviation Historical Summary: Fleet Air Reconnaissance Squadron Two (VQ-2): 1 Jan 1967 to 31 Dec 1967*, March 4, 1969, p. 4, U.S. Navy FOIA.

28. USAFSS History Office, *A Special Historical Study of the Production and Use of Special Intelligence During World Contingencies: 1950–1970*, March 1, 1972, pp. 97–98, declassified through FOIA by the National Security Archive, Washington, DC.

29. Ibid., p. 98.

30. "U.S. Electronic Espionage," pp. 43–44.

31. Oral history, *Interview with Philip Merrill*, January 22, 1997, Foreign Affairs Oral History Collection, Association for Diplomatic Studies and Training, Library of Congress, Washington, DC.

32. The description of this incident is taken from "Kagnew Station, Asmara, Eritrea," undated, http://www.cdstrand.com/areas/kagnew.htm.

33. Gerhard and Millington, *Attack*, p. 3.

34. "Arab States-Israel," *President's Daily Brief*, June 5, 1967, CIA Electronic FOIA Reading Room, Document No. 0000382247, http://www.foia.cia.gov; memorandum for the record, *Walt Rostow's Recollections of June 5, 1967*, November 17, 1968, National Security File, NSC Histories, Middle East Crisis, vol. 3, LBJL, Austin, TX; Gerhard and Millington, *Attack*, p. 3.

35. CIA, Office of Current Intelligence, memorandum, *The Arab-Israeli War: Who Fired the First Shot*, June 5, 1967, pp. 1–2, National Security File, Country File: Middle East Crisis, Situations Reports, LBJL, Austin, TX; memorandum for the record, *Walt Rostow's Recollections of June 5, 1967*, November 17, 1968, p. 2, National Security File, NSC Histories, Middle East Crisis, vol. 3, LBJL, Austin, TX.

36. Crispin Aubrey, *Who's Watching You? Britain's Security Services and the Official Secrets Act* (London: Penguin Books, 1981), p. 142.

37. David Leigh, *The Frontiers of Secrecy* (London: Junction Books, 1980), p. 191; Duncan Campbell, "Crisis in the Gulf 3: Inside Story: Under U.S. Eyes; The West Has a Hidden Advantage over Iraq," *Independent*, September 30, 1990.

38. For the number of Soviet supply flights, see CIA, Directorate of Intelligence, ESAU XXXIX, intelligence report, *Annex: The Sino-Soviet Dispute on Aid to North Vietnam (1965–1968)*, November 25, 1968, p. 63n, CIA Electronic FOIA Reading Room, http://www.foia.cia.gov/cpe.asp; NIE 11-6-84, *Soviet Global Military Reach*, November 1984, p. 129, CIA Electronic FOIA Reading Room, Document No. 0000278544, http://www.foia.cia.gov.

39. NSA OH-15-80, oral history, *Interview with Robert L. Wilson*, May 6, 1980, p. 10, NSA February 2007 USS Liberty Release.

40. "Arab States-Israel," *President's Daily Brief*, June 7, 1967, CIA Electronic FOIA Reading Room, Document No. 0000382249, http://www.foia.cia.gov; "Arab States-Israel," *President's Daily Brief*, June 9, 1967, CIA Electronic FOIA Reading Room, Document No. 0000382251, http://www.foia.cia.gov.

41. The best single account of the Israeli attack on the USS *Liberty* remains James M. Ennes Jr., *Assault on the Liberty* (New York: Random House, 1979). The Israeli version of events is contained in Hirsh Goodman and Zeev Schiff, "The Attack on the Liberty," *Atlantic Monthly*, September 1984, pp. 78–84. For the SIGINT aspects of the *Liberty* incident, see Gerhard and Millington, *Attack*, pp. 18, 26; 2nd Radio Battalion, FMF, *Command Chronology, 2nd Radio Battalion, FMF: January 1, 1967–June 30, 1967*, U.S. Marine Corps Historical Center, Quantico, VA. The literature on whether the Israeli attack was an accident or deliberate is voluminous and getting larger every day. See, for example, Reverdy S. Fishel, "The Attack on the Liberty: An 'Accident'?," *Journal of Intelligence and Counterintelligence*, vol. 8, no. 3 (Fall 1995): p. 349.

42. CIA, intelligence memorandum, *The Israeli Attack on the USS Liberty*, June 13, 1967, p. 3, CIA Electronic FOIA Reading Room, Document No. 0001359216, http://www.foia.cia.gov.

43. Ibid.; USAFSS History Office, *A Special Historical Study of the Production and Use of Special Intelligence During World Contingencies: 1950–1970*, March 1, 1972, p. 102, declassified through FOIA by the National Security Archive, Washington, DC.

44. For Kosygin's June 10, 1967, message, see message, Kosygin to Johnson, June 19, 1967, National Security File, Head of State Correspondence, USSR, Washington-Moscow "Hot Line" Exchange, LBJL, Austin, TX. See also Lyndon Baines Johnson, *The Vantage Point: Perspectives of the Presidency: 1963–1969* (New York: Holt, 1971), p. 302; L. Wainstein, *Some Aspects of the U.S. Involvement in the Middle East Crisis, May–June 1967* (Washington, DC: Institute for Defense Analysis, 1968), p. 123, DoD FOIA Reading Room, Pentagon, Washington, DC. Helms quote from Robert M. Hathaway and Russell Jack Smith, *Richard Helms as Director of Central Intelligence: 1966–1973* (Washington, DC: CIA History Staff, 1993), p. 142. For NSA being placed on alert, see Gerhard and Millington, *Attack*, p. 4.

45. Letter, Carroll to Helms, August 28, 1967, CREST Collection, Document No. CIA-RDP79 B00972A000100070003-1, NA, CP; SC No. 10088/67, memorandum, *Large-Scale Soviet Military Exercise [deleted]*, undated but circa late August 1967, CREST Collection, Document No. CIA-RDP79B00972A000100070001-3, NA, CP; TCS 95801/75, K. F. Spielmann Jr., *The Evolution of Soviet Strategic Command and Control and Warning, 1945–72* (Washington, DC: Institute for Defense Analysis, 1975), p. 271, National Security Archive, Washington, DC.

46. Robert E. Newton, *The Capture of the USS Pueblo and Its Effect on SIGINT Operations*, vol. 7 Special Series, Crisis Collection (Fort Meade: Center for Cryptologic History, 1992), p. 11, DOCID 3075778, NSA FOIA; U.S. House of Representatives, Armed Services Committee, *Hearings Regarding Inquiry into the U.S.S. Pueblo and EC-121 Incidents*, 91st Congress, 1st session, 1969, p. 636; U.S. House of Representatives, Armed Services Committee, H.A.S.C. No. 91-12, *Report of Inquiry into the U.S.S. Pueblo and EC-121 Plane Incidents*, 91st Congress, 1st session, 1969, pp. 1632–33; Trevor Armbrister, *A Matter of Accountability: The True Story of the Pueblo Affair* (New York: Coward-McCann, 1970), pp. 82–85.

47. Newton, *USS Pueblo*, p. 12; historical fact sheet, USS Banner (AGER-1), Ships Histories Division, Naval Historical Center, Washington, DC. For a description of the Sod Hut, see Dan Hearn, "A Career Built on SIGINT," *American Intelligence Journal*, Spring/Summer 1994: p. 68. "Least unsuitable" quote from Armbrister, *Matter of Accountability*, pp. 85–86.

48. Commander-in-Chief, Pacific, *CINCPAC Command History 1966*, vol. 1, pp. 89–90; Commander-in-Chief, Pacific, *CINCPAC Command History 1968*, vol. 4, pp. 230–31, sanitized copies of both at U.S. Army Center of Military History, Washington, DC; Packard, *U.S. Naval Intelligence*, p. 115; Vice Admiral Edwin B. Hooper, USN (Ret.), *Mobility, Support, Endurance: A Story of Naval Operational Logistics in the Vietnam War, 1965–1968* (Washington, DC: Naval History Division, 1972), pp. 220–21; Joseph F. Bouchard, "Use of Naval Force in Crises: A Theory of Stratified Crisis Interaction," vol. 1 (Ph. D. diss., Stamford University, 1989), p. 331.

49. U.S. House of Representatives, Armed Services Committee, *Hearings Regarding Inquiry into the U.S.S. Pueblo and EC-121 Incidents*, 91st Congress, 1st session, 1969, pp. 636–38; U.S. House of Representatives, Armed Services Committee, H.A.S.C. No. 91-12, *Report of Inquiry into the U.S.S. Pueblo and EC-121 Plane Incidents*, 91st Congress, 1st session, 1969, pp. 1646–49; Hooper, *Mobility, Support, Endurance*, pp. 222–25.

50. The most detailed description of all aspects of the USS *Pueblo*'s mission and seizure by the North Koreans can be found in Newton, *USS Pueblo*, p. 3. See also Commander-in-Chief, Pacific, *CINCPAC Command History 1968*, vol. 4, p. 229, Operational Archives, Naval Historical Center, Washington, DC; *Central Intelligence Bulletin*, January 23, 1968, p. 4, CIA Electronic FOIA Reading Room, Document No. 0000265983, http://www.foia.cia.gov.

51. U.S. House of Representatives, Armed Services Committee, *Hearings Regarding Inquiry into the*

U.S.S. Pueblo and EC-121 Incidents, 91st Congress, 1st session, 1969, pp. 692, 698; U.S. House of Representatives, Armed Services Committee, Report No. 91-12, *Report of the Special Subcommittee on the U.S.S. Pueblo: Inquiry into the U.S.S. Pueblo and EC-121 Incidents*, 91st Congress, 1st session, 1969, pp. 1654–56. CIA memo quote from memorandum, Smith to Director of Central Intelligence, *JRC Monthly Reconnaissance Schedule for January 1968*, January 2, 1968, CIA Electronic FOIA Reading Room, Document No. 0001458144, http://www.foia.cia.gov.

52. CIA, *The Pueblo Incident: Briefing Materials for Ambassador Ball's Committee*, February 5, 1968, p. 1, CIA Electronic FOIA Reading Room, Document No. 0000267787, http://www.foia.cia.gov.

53. Letter, Goldberg to President of U.N. Security Council, January 25, 1968, in *Department of State Bulletin*, February 12, 1968, pp. 195–96.

54. Johnson, *American Cryptology*, bk. 2, p. 439.

55. For TV pictures of the NSA documents, see Newton, pp. 122–23; Johnson, *American Cryptology*, bk. 2, p. 448. For the North Korean book containing NSA documents, see *Les actes d'agression declares de l'imperialisme U.S. contre le peuple coreen* (Pyongyang: Éditions en Langues Étrangères, 1968).

56. CIA, Directorate of Intelligence, intelligence memorandum, *Pueblo Sitrep No. 14*, January 28, 1968, p. 3, CIA Electronic FOIA Reading Room, Document No. 0000230614, http://www.foia.cia.gov; SC 13455/69, memorandum, Clarke to Assistant Deputy Director for Intelligence, *Senator Russell's Remarks on Soviet Exploitation of USS Pueblo*, January 3, 1969, p. 3, CREST Collection, Document No. CIA-RDP79B00972A000100430001-3, NA, CP; confidential interview.

57. For SIGINT sources drying up, see final draft, *SIGINT 101 Seminar Course Module*, 2002, NSA FOIA. For NSA damage assessment, see "Notes of Meeting," January 24, 1968, in U.S. Department of State, *Foreign Relations of the United States, 1964–1968*, vol. 29, *Korea* (Washington, DC: GPO, 1999).

58. U.S. Army Military History Institute, Oral History 73-2, *Interview with General Charles H. Bonesteel III, USA Retired*, vol. 1, 1973, pp. 345–46, U.S. Army Center of Military History, Washington, DC.

59. Johnson, *American Cryptology*, bk. 2, pp. 455–57; HQ ASA, *Historical Summary of the U.S. Army Security Agency, FY 1968–1970*, pp. 73–74, INSCOM FOIA; CIA, memorandum, *DCI Briefing for Congressional Leaders: Soviet Troop Movements*, August 23, 1968, p. Troops-1, CIA Electronic FOIA Reading Room, Document No. 0000677561, http://www.foia.cia.gov; memorandum, Hendrickson to Chairman, Strategic Warning Working Group, *Rapid Readout and Reporting of Imagery for Warning and Indications Intelligence Purposes*, September 26, 1969, p. 1, CREST Collection, Document No. CIA-RDP79B01709A002200100006-2, NA, CP; CIA, Directorate of Intelligence, intelligence memorandum, ESAU XLIV, *Czechoslovakia: The Problem of Soviet Control*, January 16, 1970, p. 14, CIA Electronic FOIA Reading Room, http://www.foia.cia.gov/cpe.asp; James H. Polk, "Reflections on the Czechoslovakian Invasion, 1968," *Strategic Review*, vol. 5, no. 5: p. 31; interview, James H. Polk.

60. Confidential interviews. For an early example of the material being produced by the Moscow listening post, see CIA, *The President's Intelligence Checklist*, October 18, 1962, p. 8, JFKL, Boston, MA.

61. Johnson, *American Cryptology*, bk. 2, p. 473; oral history, *Interview with David J. Fischer*, March 6, 1998, Foreign Affairs Oral History Collection, Association for Diplomatic Studies and Training, Library of Congress, Washington, DC.

62. Memorandum, Taylor to Deputy Director for Intelligence, *Indications of Soviet Intent to Invade Czechoslovakia*, August 22, 1968, CREST Collection, Document No. CIA-RDP79B00972A0

00100240004-1, NA, CP; Memorandum, Karl to Smith, *DDCI Memo on Handling of Indications Traffic*, August 23, 1968, CREST Collection, Document No. CIA-RDP79B00972A000 100240003-2, NA, CP; memorandum, Hendrickson to Chairman, Strategic Warning Working Group, *Rapid Readout and Reporting of Imagery for Warning and Indications Intelligence Purposes*, September 26, 1969, p. 1, CREST Collection, Document No. CIA-RDP79B01709A002200 100006-2, NA, CP; Johnson, *American Cryptology*, bk. 2, p. 458.

63. Johnson, *American Cryptology*, bk. 2, p. 459; Polk, "Reflections on the Czechoslovakian Invasion, 1968," p. 32; interview, General James H. Polk.

64. Robert J. Hanyok, *Spartans in Darkness: American SIGINT and the Indochina War, 1945–1975*, U.S. Cryptologic History, series 6, vol. 7 (Fort Meade, MD: Center for Cryptologic History, 2002), pp. 156–60.

65. In April 1972, *Washington Post* columnist Jack Anderson revealed that NSA had been able to read the most sensitive South Vietnamese military and diplomatic communications for a number of years, for which see Anderson, "U.S. Is Forced to Spy on Saigon," *Washington Post*, April 30, 1972; Seymour M. Hersh, *The Price of Power: Kissinger in the Nixon White House* (New York: Summit Books, 1983), p. 183n.

66. U.S. Department of State, *Foreign Relations of the United States, 1964–1968*, vol. 7, *Vietnam: September 1968–January 1969* (Washington, DC: GPO, 2003); Daniel Schorr, "The Secret Nixon-LBJ War," *Washington Post*, May 28, 1995. See also Bui Diem with David Chanoff, *In the Jaws of History* (Boston: Houghton Mifflin, 1987), p. 244.

67. Oral history, *Interview with Arthur B. Krim*, April 7, 1983, p. 22, Austin, TX.

68. For CIA taps on Thieu's office, see Frank Snepp, *Decent Interval* (New York: Random House, 1977), pp. 15, 294; Thomas Powers, *The Man Who Kept the Secrets: Richard Helms and the CIA* (New York: Pocket Books, 1979), p. 252.

69. Memorandum, CIA to Rostow and Rusk, *President Thieu's Views Regarding the Issues Involved in Agreeing to a Bombing Halt*, October 26, 1968, p. 1, CIA Electronic FOIA Reading Room, Document No. 0000576096, http://www.foia.cia.gov.

70. Memorandum, Rostow to President, October 29, 1968, p. 1, National Security File: Walt Rostow Files, File: Richard Nixon—Vietnam, LBJL, Austin, TX.

71. H. R. Haldeman, *The Haldeman Diaries: Inside the Nixon White House* (New York: G. P. Putnam's Sons, 1994), p. 567; Douglas Watson, "Houston Says NSA Urged Break-Ins," *Washington Post*, March 3, 1975; transcript, Cartha D. "Deke" DeLoach Oral History Interview 1, January 11, 1991, pp. 19–20, LBJL, Austin, TX.

9: Tragedy and Triumph

1. Dr. Thomas R. Johnson, *American Cryptology During the Cold War, 1945–1989* (Fort Meade, MD: Center for Cryptologic History, 1995), bk. 2, *Centralization Wins, 1960–1972*, pp. 293, 297, NSA FOIA.

2. *DCI Remarks to PFIAB*, January 13, 1982, p. 1, CREST Collection, Document No. CIA-RDP84B00049R001102660009-2, NA, CP; Dr. Thomas R. Johnson, *American Cryptology During the Cold War, 1945–1989* (Fort Meade, MD: Center for Cryptologic History, 1995), bk. 3, *Retrenchment and Reform, 1972–1980*, p. 21, NSA FOIA.

3. HQ ASA, *Annual Historical Summary of the U.S. Army Security Agency, FY 1971*, p. 61, INSCOM FOIA; HQ ASA, *Annual Historical Summary of the U.S. Army Security Agency, FY 1972*, p. 47, INSCOM FOIA; "U.S. Electronic Espionage: A Memoir," *Ramparts*, August 1972, p. 50; Tad Szulc, "The NSA—America's $10 Billion Frankenstein," *Penthouse*, November 1975, p. 194.

4. Johnson, *American Cryptology*, bk. 3, p. vii.

5. U.S. House of Representatives, Select Committee on Intelligence, *U.S. Intelligence Agencies and Activities: The Performance of the Intelligence Community*, 94th Congress, 2nd session, part 2, 1975, p. 646; Seymour M. Hersh, *The Price of Power: Kissinger in the Nixon White House* (New York: Summit Books, 1983), p. 207.

6. Johnson, *American Cryptology*, bk. 3, p. 487.

7. The official NSA history of this incident can be found in Thomas P. Ziehm, *The National Security Agency and the EC-121 Shootdown*, vol. 3, Special Series, Crisis Collection (Fort Meade: Center for Cryptologic History, 1989), NSA FOIA. See also Fleet Air Reconnaissance Squadron One, *Fleet Air Reconnaissance Squadron One 1969 Command History*, 1970, p. 7, Navy FOIA; Capt. Don East, USN, "A History of U.S. Navy Fleet Air Reconnaissance: Part One, the Pacific and VQ-1," *Hook*, Spring 1987: pp. 29–30; CTMCM Jay R. Brown, "Kamiseya Update P-2," *NCVA Cryptolog*, Spring 1995: p. 23; "ELINT Techniques 'Pirate' Radar Data," *Aviation Week & Space Technology*, February 21, 1972, p. 40.

8. U.S. House of Representatives, Armed Services Committee, HASC No. 91-12, *Report of the Special Subcommittee on the USS Pueblo: Inquiry into the U.S.S. Pueblo and EC-121 Plane Incidents*, 91st Congress, 1st session, July 28, 1969, pp. 1675, 1680.

9. Johnson, *American Cryptology*, bk. 2, p. 466.

10. James E. Pierson, *USAFSS Response to World Crises, 1949–1969* (San Antonio, TX: USAFSS Historical Office, 1970), p. 35, AIA FOIA; Johnson, *American Cryptology*, bk. 2, p. 466.

11. Seymour M. Hersh, *The Price of Power: Kissinger in the Nixon White House* (New York: Summit Books, 1983), pp. 69–70, 73–74; confidential interview.

12. Johnson, *American Cryptology*, bk. 2, p. 477.

13. Memorandum with attachments, Hughes to President, July 16, 1969, p. 1, Nixon Presidential Materials, White House Central Files/Subject Files, box 7, file FG 13-11/A NSA (7/16/69), NA, CP; "Vice Admiral Noel Gayler, USN Becomes Agency's New Director," *NSA Newsletter*, August 1969, p. 3, NSA FOIA.

14. Hersh, *Price of Power*, p. 208.

15. Johnson, *American Cryptology*, bk. 2, p. 478.

16. Confidential interviews.

17. Loch K. Johnson, *A Season of Inquiry: Congress and Intelligence* (Chicago: Dorsey Press, 1988), p. 83.

18. Mike Frost and Michel Gratton, *Spyworld* (Toronto: Doubleday Canada, 1994), pp. 45–76.

19. See, for example, CIA, Directorate of Intelligence, intelligence report, *The Politburo and Soviet Decision Making*, April 1972, CIA Electronic FOIA Reading Room, Document No. 0001024724, http://www.foia.cia.gov; CIA, Directorate of Intelligence, *The SALT I Agreements and Future Soviet Weapons Programs: A Framework for Analyzing Soviet Decisionmaking*, October 1972, CIA Electronic FOIA Reading Room, Document No. 0000969878, http://www.foia.cia.gov.

20. John M. McConnell, "The Evolution of Intelligence and the Public Policy Debate on Encryption," p. 151, Seminar on Intelligence, Command and Control, Center for Information Policy Research, Harvard University School of Government, January 1997.

21. Jack Anderson, "CIA Eavesdrops on Kremlin Chiefs," *Washington Post*, September 16, 1971; McConnell, "The Evolution of Intelligence and the Public Policy Debate on Encryption."

22. Memorandum, Kissinger to President, *Moscow Politics and Brezhnev's Position*, May 22, 1972, Secret/Sensitive, Nixon Presidential Materials, NA, CP.

23. Hersh, *Price of Power*, p. 547; David Kahn, "Big Ear or Big Brother?," *New York Times Magazine*, May 16, 1976, p. 62; "Eavesdropping on the World's Secrets," *U.S. News & World Report*, June 26, 1978, p. 47; Walter Andrews, "Kissinger Allegedly Withheld Soviet Plan to Violate SALT I," *Washington Times*, April 6, 1984; Bill Gertz, "CIA Upset Because Perle Detailed Eavesdropping," *Washington Times*, April 19, 1987.

24. NIO IIM 76-030J, interagency intelligence memorandum, *Implications for US-Soviet Relations of Certain Soviet Activities*, June 1976, p. 7, CIA Electronic FOIA Reading Room, Document No. 0000283807, http://www.foia.cia.gov. See also "The Microwave Furor," *Time*, March 22, 1976.

25. Memorandum with attachments, Scowcroft to President, Nixon Presidential Materials, White House Central Files/Subject Files, box 7, file FG 13-11/A NSA (7/24/72), NA, CP; "Lt. Gen. Samuel C. Phillips, USAF Becomes Agency's Seventh Director," *NSA Newsletter*, June 1972, p. 4, NSA FOIA.

26. Johnson, *American Cryptology*, bk. 3, p. 89, NSA FOIA.

27. Interviews with Walter G. Deeley and Charles R. Lord; NSA OH-09-97, oral history, *Interview with Bobby Ray Inman*, June 18, 1997, p. 12, NSA FOIA.

28. Allen background from biographical data sheet, Lt. General Lew Allen, Jr., U.S. Air Force Office of Public Affairs.

29. Poker-face comments from confidential interview. Snider quote from L. Britt Snider, "Unlucky Shamrock: Recollections from the Church Committee's Investigation of NSA," *Studies in Intelligence*, Winter 1999–2000, unclassified ed.: p. 44.

30. U.S. Senate, *Hearings Before the Select Committee to Study Governmental Operations with Respect to Intelligence Activities*, 94th Congress, 1st session, vol. 6, pp. 4–46.

31. For details of the missions and capabilities of these SIGINT satellite systems, see Christopher Anson Pike, "Canyon, Rhyolite and Aquacade: U.S. Signals Intelligence Satellites in the 1970s," *Spaceflight*, vol. 37 (November 1995): p. 381; Jonathan McDowell, "U.S. Reconnaissance Satellite Programs, Part 2, Beyond Imaging," *Quest*, vol. 4, no. 4 (1995): p. 42; Major A. Andronov, "American Geosynchronous SIGINT Satellites," *Zarubezhnoye Voyennoye Obozreniye*, no. 12 (1993): pp. 37–43. For NSA's emphasis on SIGINT collection from space in the 1970s, see William E. Odom, *Fixing Intelligence for a More Secure America* (New Haven, CT: Yale University Press, 2003), p. 120; Loch K. Johnson, *Secret Agencies: U.S. Intelligence in a Hostile World* (New Haven, CT: Yale University Press, 1996), p. 178.

32. William Drozdiak, "A Suspicious Eye on U.S. 'Big Ears': Europeans Fear Listening Posts Eavesdrop on Their Businesses," *Washington Post*, July 24, 2000.

33. A description of the mission and capabilities of the Rhyolite satellite can be found in Pike, "Canyon, Rhyolite and Aquacade," pp. 381–82; McDowell, "U.S. Reconnaissance Satellite Programs, Part 2," 1995, p. 42; Angelo Codevilla, *Informing Statecraft: Intelligence for a New Century* (New York: Free Press, 1992), pp. 115–16. Wheelon quote from Albert D. Wheelon, "Technology and Intelligence," *Technology and Society*, January 2004, pp. 4–5.

34. U.S. Pacific Fleet, *Command History of the Commander in Chief U.S. Pacific Fleet: CY 1979, 1980*, p. 32, CINCPACFLT FOIA; Jeffrey T. Richelson, *The U.S. Intelligence Community*, 3rd ed. (Boulder, CO: Westview Press, 1995), pp. 204–05; Ivan Amato, *Pushing the Horizon* (Washington, DC: GPO, 1998), p. 202; Anthony Kenden, "U.S. Reconnaissance Satellite Programs," *Spaceflight*, vol. 20, no. 7 (1978): pp. 257–58; Philip J. Klass, "Aircraft Ocean Surveillance Role Studied," *Aviation Week & Space Technology*, May 8, 1972, p. 26; "Navy Ocean Surveillance Satellite Depicted," *Aviation Week & Space Technology*, May 24, 1976, p. 25; "Expanded Ocean Surveillance Effort Set," *Aviation Week & Space Technology*, July 10, 1978, pp. 22–23; "NASA Souvenir Spills Navy Satellite Secrets," *Aviation Week & Space Technology*, October 22, 1984, p. 20; Major A. Andronov, "The U.S. Navy's 'White Cloud' Spaceborne ELINT System," *Zarubezhnoye Voyennoye Obozreniye*, no. 7, 1993: pp. 57–60.

35. Christopher Ford and David Rosenberg, *The Admiral's Advantage: U.S. Navy Operational Intelligence in World War II and the Cold War* (Annapolis, MD: Naval Institute Press, 2005), p. 62.

36. U.S. Senate, *Final Report of the Select Committee to Study Governmental Operations with Respect to Intelligence Activities*, 94th Congress, 2nd session, bk. 1, 1976, p. 85; *CIA: The Pike Report* (London: Spokesman Books, 1977), p. 141.

37. United States European Command, *Historical Report 1973*, 1974, p. 295, National Security Archive, Washington, DC; U.S. House of Representatives, Select Committee on Intelligence, *U.S. Intelligence Agencies and Activities: The Performance of the Intelligence Community*, 94th Congress, 2nd session, part 2, 1975, pp. 678–81; William Colby and Peter Forbath, *Honorable Men* (New York: Simon and Schuster, 1978), pp. 434–35; confidential interviews.

38. TS 204127, memorandum, *Proficiency of Egyptian Air Force and Air Defense Personnel*, July 13, 1973, CREST Collection, Document No. CIA-RDP75B00380R000200050087-4, NA, CP.

39. Memorandum, National Security Council Staff to Kissinger, *Indications of Arab Intentions to Initiate Hostilities*, circa May 1973, Nixon Presidential Materials Project, Henry Kissinger Office Files, box 135, file Rabin/Kissinger (Dinitz) 1973 Jan–July (2 of 3), NA, CP; Intelligence Community Staff, *The Performance of the Intelligence Community Before the Arab-Israeli War of October 1973: A Preliminary Post-Mortem Report*, December 1973, CIA Electronic FOIA Reading Room, Document No. 0001331429, http://www.foia.cia.gov; U.S. House of Representatives, Select Committee on Intelligence, *U.S. Intelligence Agencies and Activities: The Performance of the Intelligence Community*, 94th Congress, 1st session, part 2, 1975, pp. 658–59, 680–81; *Pike Report*, pp. 143, 147; Marvin L. Kalb and Bernard Kalb, *Kissinger* (Boston: Little, Brown, 1974), p. 454; Henry Kissinger, *Years of Upheaval* (Boston: Little, Brown, 1982), p. 475; Daniel O. Graham, *Confessions of a Cold Warrior* (Fairfax, VA: Preview Press, 1995), p. 77; "Eavesdropping," *U.S. News & World Report*, p. 47.

40. Intelligence Community Staff, *The Performance of the Intelligence Community Before the Arab-Israeli War of October 1973: A Preliminary Post-Mortem Report*, December 1973, p. i, CIA Electronic FOIA Reading Room, Document No. 0001331429, http://www.foia.cia.gov; U.S. House of Representatives, Select Committee on Intelligence, *U.S. Intelligence Agencies and Activities: The Performance of the Intelligence Community*, 94th Congress, 1st session, part 2, 1975, pp. 658–59, 680–81; *Pike Report*, pp. 143, 147.

41. Norman Klar, *Confessions of a Code Breaker (Tales from Decrypt)* (privately published, 2004), p. 280.

42. Intelligence Community Staff, *The Performance of the Intelligence Community Before the Arab-Israeli War of October 1973: A Preliminary Post-Mortem Report*, December 1973, p. i, CIA Electronic FOIA Reading Room, Document No. 0001331429, http://www.foia.cia.gov; Richard W. Shyrock, "The Intelligence Community Post-Mortem Program, 1973–1975," *Studies in Intelligence*, RG-263, NA, CP.

43. U.S. House of Representatives, Select Committee on Intelligence, *U.S. Intelligence Agencies and Activities: The Performance of the Intelligence Community*, 94th Congress, 1st session, part 2, 1975, pp. 658–59, 680–81; *Pike Report*, pp. 143, 147.

44. Allen quote from Douglas F. Garthoff, *Directors of Central Intelligence as Leaders of the U.S. Intelligence Community: 1946–2005* (Washington, DC: Center for the Study of Intelligence, 2005), pp. 117–18.

45. Klar's background from Klar, *Confessions*, his obituary, *Washington Post*, April 4, 2005.

46. Klar, *Confessions*, pp. 279–80; interview with Norman Klar.

47. For Nixon's 1972 order for SIGINT coverage of terrorism, see U.S. Department of Justice, *Report on Inquiry into CIA-Related Electronic Surveillance Activities*, June 30, 1976, p. 31. For SIGINT successes, see Robert J. Hanyok, "The First Round: NSA's Efforts Against International Terrorism in the 1970s," *Cryptologic Almanac*, November–December 2002, NSA FOIA; Klar, *Confessions*, p. 289. For monitoring Arafat, see, for example, memorandum,

Palestinian Involvement in US-Iranian Dispute, November 21, 1979, p. 1, CREST Collection, Document No. CIA-RDP81B00401R000500130031-2, NA, CP.

48. "Angola: After Independence," in CIA, *Weekly Review*, November 21, 1975, pp. 2–3, CIA Electronic FOIA Reading Room, Document No. 0000126975, http://www.foia.cia.gov; U.S. Intelligence Board, *National Intelligence Bulletin*, November 26, 1975, p. 12, CIA Electronic FOIA Reading Room, Document No. 0000098693, http://www.foia.cia.gov; NIO IIM 76-004C, interagency intelligence memorandum, *Soviet and Cuban Aid to the MPLA in Angola from March Through December 1975*, January 24, 1976, p. i, CIA Electronic FOIA Reading Room, Document No. 0000681964, http://www.foia.cia.gov; interagency intelligence memorandum, *Soviet and Cuban Aid to the MPLA in Angola During January 1976*, February 3, 1976, p. 3, CIA Electronic FOIA Reading Room, Document No. 0000307945, http://www.foia.cia.gov; interagency intelligence memorandum, *Soviet and Cuban Aid to the MPLA in Angola During February 1976*, March 26, 1976, pp. 2–4, CIA Electronic FOIA Reading Room, Document No. 0000681967, http://www.foia.cia.gov; CIA, Directorate of Intelligence, *Soviet and Cuban Intervention in the Angolan Civil War*, March 1977, p. 22, CIA FOIA Electronic Reading Room, http://www.foia.cia.gov; CIA, National Foreign Assessment Center, *The Cuban Military Establishment*, April 1979, pp. 1–3, CREST Collection, Document No. CIA-RDP80T00942A000900030001-2, NA, CP.

49. CIA, *The Situation in Lebanon*, March 30, 1976, CREST Collection, Document No. CIA-RDP85T00353R000100260020-6, NA, CP; George Bush, memorandum for the record, April 10, 1976, CIA Electronic FOIA Reading Room, Document No. 0000191281, http://www.foia.cia.gov; NIO IIM 76-015, interagency intelligence memorandum, *Israeli-Syrian Hostilities*, April 12, 1976, CIA FOIA; CIA, SC No. 07362/76, intelligence memorandum, *Lebanon Evacuation Situation Report No. 2*, June 18, 1976, CREST Collection, Document No. CIA-RDP83M00171R001800080031-7, NA, CP.

50. ASA Detachment, Southern Command, *Annual Historical Report, USASA Detachment, Southern Command Fiscal Year 1975*, 1976, p. 1 passim, INSCOM FOIA; 408th ASA Company (Brigade Support), *Annual Historical Report, 408th Army Security Agency Company (Brigade Support), Fiscal Year 1975*, 1976, pp. 1, 5, INSCOM FOIA.

51. Confidential interview.

52. HQ 470th Military Intelligence Group, *Historical Report Annual Supplement: 1 October 1977–30 September 1978*, appendix T, DCI Letter of Commendation, INSCOM FOIA; John Dinges, *Our Man in Panama* (New York: Random House, 1990), pp. 81–83; Manuel Noriega and Peter Eisner, *America's Prisoner: The Memoirs of Manuel Noriega* (New York: Random House, 1997), p. 60; Seymour M. Hersh, "Panama Strongman Said to Trade in Drugs, Arms and Illicit Money," *New York Times*, June 12, 1986; Stephen Engelberg and Jeff Gerth, "Bush and Noriega: Their 20-Year Relationship," *New York Times*, September 28, 1988; *Congressional Record—Senate*, February 21, 1978, p. 3972. For Travis Trophy going to the 470th Military Intelligence Group, see *NSA Newsletter*, October 1978, p. 6, NSA FOIA.

53. OSP-13-76T, polygraph examination report, November 10, 1976; File No. ZG000265, report of investigation, February 14, 1977, both in Canton Song 1 dossier, INSCOM FOIA. The army investigation into what was described as the "Singing Sergeants" case was first brought to public light in Hersh, "Panama Strongman."

54. OSP-13-76T, polygraph examination report, November 10, 1976; witness statement, November 11, 1976, both in Canton Song 1 dossier, INSCOM FOIA; File CE 76-245-03, report of investigation, December 7, 1977, Canton Song 2 dossier, INSCOM FOIA.

55. Engelberg and Gerth, "Bush and Noriega." See also Dinges, *Our Man in Panama*, pp. 83–84; Frederick Kempe, *Divorcing the Dictator: America's Bungled Affair with Noriega* (New York: G. P. Putnam's Sons, 1990), p. 28.

56. For congressional oversight committees being briefed on the case and asked not to do anything, see *Congressional Record—Senate*, February 21, 1978, p. 3972.

57. Inman background from NSA OH-09-97, oral history, *Interview with Bobby Ray Inman*, June 18, 1997, NSA FOIA; biographical data sheet, Vice Admiral Bobby Ray Inman, U.S. Navy Office of Public Affairs.

58. Johnson, *American Cryptology*, bk. 2, p. 190.

59. Confidential interviews.

60. Memorandum, Requirements & Evaluation Staff to Assistant Comptroller, Requirements & Evaluation, *The CIA/NSA Relationship*, August 20, 1976, CREST Collection, Document No. CIA-RDP79M00467A002400030009-4, NA, CP.

61. For NSA's $1.3 billion budget, see memorandum, [deleted] to C/M&AS, *Annual Defense Report*, March 8, 1977, p. 275, CREST Collection, Document No. CIA-RDP80-00473A000600100011-7, NA, CP. See also Elaine Sciolino, "An Operator for the Pentagon," *New York Times*, December 17, 1993; Barton Gellman and Bob Woodward, "Analyst with a Nonpartisan Touch," *Washington Post*, December 17, 1993.

62. NSA OH-09-97, oral history, *Interview with Bobby Ray Inman*, June 18, 1997, p. 18, NSA FOIA.

63. James G. Hudec, "Provision of Cryptologic Information to the Congress," *Cryptologic Spectrum*, vol. 11, no. 3 (Summer 1981): pp. 12–13, NSA FOIA.

64. NSC, *Report on Presidential Review Memorandum/NSC-11: Intelligence Structure and Mission*, February 23, 1977, p. 15, Department of State FOIA; memorandum, [deleted] to [deleted], *Intelligence Community Deficiencies—PRM-11*, February 28, 1977, CREST Collection, Document No. CIA-RDP79M00095A000100030020-9, NA, CP; DCI/IC 77-4657, Intelligence Community Staff, *1977 Director of Central Intelligence Report on the Intelligence Community*, March 1977, pp. 23–24, CREST Collection, Document No. CIA-RDP83M00171R002100110007-6, NA, CP.

65. Memorandum, [deleted] to C/M&AS, *Annual Defense Report*, March 8, 1977, pp. 276–77, CREST Collection, Document No. CIA-RDP80-00473A000600100011-7, NA, CP; memorandum, Vice Admiral Bobby R. Inman, USN, to Special Assistant, Office of the Secretary of Defense, *Transition Coordination*, December 9, 1980, p. 4, via Dr. Jeffrey T. Richelson; Bob Woodward, *Veil: The Secret Wars of the CIA, 1981–1987* (New York: Simon and Schuster, 1987), pp. 71–72.

66. Foreword of Admiral Stansfield Turner, USN (Ret.), to David D. Newsom, *The Soviet Brigade in Cuba: A Study in Political Diplomacy* (Bloomington: Indiana University Press, 1987), p. ix.

67. Memorandum, Vice Admiral Bobby R. Inman, USN, to Special Assistant, Office of the Secretary of Defense, *Transition Coordination*, December 9, 1980, sec. 8, Modernization Objectives; Johnson, *American Cryptology*, bk. 3, pp. 196–97, NSA FOIA. For NSA opposition to APEX, see memorandum, SA to the DCI for Compartmentation to Director of Central Intelligence, *APEX—NSA Issue Paper*, December 2, 1980, CREST Collection, Document No. CIA-RDP85T00788R000100150003-5, NA, CP; memorandum, SA to the DCI for Compartmentation to Director of Central Intelligence, *APEX—Navy Issue Paper*, December 3, 1980, CREST Collection, Document No. CIA-RDP85T00788R000100150002-8, NA, CP; memorandum, Chairman, DCI Committee on Compartmentation, to Deputy Director of Central Intelligence, *DCI Committee on Compartmentation Final Report*, July 27, 1981, CREST Collection, Document No. CIA-RDP85T00788R000100070023-2, NA, CP.

68. Confidential interview.

69. Mark Urban, *UK Eyes Alpha* (London: Faber and Faber, 1996), p. 6; confidential interviews.

70. Memorandum, Levi to the President, January 6, 1976, p. 1, DDRS; Jack Anderson, "Project Aquarian: Tapping the Tappers," *Washington Post*, December 2, 1980.

71. Prime was released from prison in March 2001. For Prime's background and details of his

espionage on behalf of the USSR, see D. J. Cole, *Geoffrey Prime: The Imperfect Spy* (London: Robert Hale, 1998); Richard J. Aldrich, "GCHQ and Sigint in Early Cold War, 1945–1970," in Matthew M. Aid and Cees Wiebes, eds., *Secrets of Signals Intelligence During the Cold War and Beyond* (London: Frank Cass, 2001), pp. 91–92. For damage done by Prime, see Urban, *UK Eyes Alpha*, p. 6; Philip Taubman, "U.S. Aides Say British Spy Gave Soviet Key Data," *New York Times*, October 24, 1982; Jon Nordheimer, "British Spy Hurt the U.S., Mrs. Thatcher Declares," *New York Times*, November 12, 1982.

72. Defense Panel on Intelligence, *Report of the Defense Panel on Intelligence*, January 1975, p. 8, partially declassified and obtained by FOIA, by National Security Archive, Washington, DC; Commission on the Organization of the Government for the Conduct of Foreign Policy ("Murphy Commission"), *Report of the Commission on the Organization of the Government for the Conduct of Foreign Policy*, vol. 7 (Washington, DC: GPO, 1975), p. 26; CIA, *Intelligence Community Experiment in Competitive Analysis: Soviet Strategic Objectives: An Alternative View: Report of Team "B"*, December 1976, p. 9, RG-263, NA, CP.

73. Richard Pearson, "Computer Pioneer Seymour Cray Dies," *Washington Post*, October 6, 1996.

74. Castro background from biographical data sheet, Lawrence Castro, NSA Coordinator for Homeland Security Support, http://www.itoc.usma.edu/workshop/2002/documents/Castro_Bio.htm.

75. William R. Corson, Susan B. Trento, and Joseph J. Trento, *Widows* (New York: Crown Publishers, 1989), p. 94.

76. Memorandum, Director, Program Assessment Office, to Assistant Deputy Director for Operations, National Security Agency, *Project HOOFBEAT*, August 26, 1980, p. 1, CREST Collection, Document No. CIA-RDP83M00171R001100150001-9, NA, CP.

77. Examples of SIGINT reporting on Iran after the February 1979 revolution can be found in CIA, National Foreign Assessment Center, memorandum, *Status of Iranian Armed Forces*, November 7, 1979, CREST Collection, Document No. CIA-RDP81B00401R000500030017-9, NA, CP; CIA, memorandum, *Impact of US Severance of Diplomatic Ties with Iran*, November 30, 1979, CREST Collection, Document No. CIA-RDP81B00401R000500130030-3, NA, CP; CIA, National Foreign Assessment Center, memorandum, *Iranian Military Readiness*, December 7, 1979, CREST Collection, Document No. CIA-RDP81B00401R000500030012-4, NA, CP; CIA, memorandum, *Current Situation in Iran*, December 31, 1979, CREST Collection, Document No. CIA-RDP81B00401R000500100019-9, NA, CP; CIA, National Foreign Assessment Center, memorandum, *Iran: Growing Leftist Influence Among Minorities*, January 1980, CREST Collection, Document No. CIA-RDP81B00401R000500160018-4, NA, CP; CIA, National Foreign Assessment Center, memorandum, *Iran: Decline in Air Force Capability*, May 1980, CREST Collection, Document No. CIA-RDP81B00401R000500030011-5, NA, CP. For Rhyolite satellite collection on Iran, confidential interviews.

78. CIA, *The Vietnam-Cambodia Conflict*, March 8, 1978, CIA Electronic FOIA Reading Room, Document No. 0000690153, http://www.foia.cia.gov; Johnson, *American Cryptology*, bk. 3, p. 255.

79. CIA, *Alert Memorandum: China-Vietnam*, January 5, 1979, pp. 1–2, CREST Collection, Document No. CIA-RDP81B00080R001400010002-4, NA, CP.

80. CIA, NSC briefing, *Indochina: China/Vietnam*, February 18, 1979, CREST Collection, Document No. CIA-RDP83B00100R000100030014-8, NA, CP; CIA, Strategic Warning Staff, *Monthly Report to the Director of Central Intelligence*, March 29, 1979, CIA Electronic FOIA Reading Room, Document No. 0000789481, http://www.foia.cia.gov; CIA, National Foreign Assessment Center, *The Sino-Vietnamese Border Dispute*, April 1979, CIA Electronic FOIA Reading Room, Document No. 0000789482, http://www.foia.cia.gov. See also Brian Toohey and Marian Wilkinson, *The Book of Leaks* (Sydney: Angus and Robertson Publishers, 1989), p. 134; Rear Admiral James B. Linder, USN (Ret.), and Dr. A. James Gregor, "The Chinese Communist Air

Force in the 'Punitive' War Against Vietnam," *Air University Review*, vol. 32, no. 6 (September/October 1981): p. 77.

81. Toohey and Wilkinson, *Book of Leaks*, pp. 134–35; Desmond Ball, "Over and Out: Signals Intelligence in Hong Kong," *Intelligence and National Security*, vol. 11, no. 3 (July 1996): pp. 479–80.

82. Confidential interviews with former NSA officials; Gloria Duffy, "Crisis Mangling and the Cuban Brigade," *International Security*, vol. 18, no. 1 (Summer 1983): p. 71. For navy SIGINT aircraft operating from Guantánamo and Florida, see U.S. Sixth Fleet, *1979 Sixth Fleet Command History*, p. III-7; U.S. Sixth Fleet, *1980 Sixth Fleet Command History*, p. III-6, both in Operational Archives, Naval Historical Center, Washington, DC.

83. Confidential interviews. See also Raymond Bonner, *Weakness and Deceit: U.S. Policy and El Salvador* (New York: Times Books, 1984), p. 263.

84. David Binder, "Soviet Brigade: How the U.S. Traced It," *New York Times*, September 13, 1979.

85. Memorandum, Brzezinski to President, *NSC Weekly Report #98*, May 25, 1979, p. 1, NSC Files, Jimmy Carter Presidential Library, Atlanta, GA.

86. CIA, interagency intelligence memorandum, Memorandum to Holders, *Updated Report on Soviet Ground Forces Brigade in Cuba*, September 18, 1979, p. 2, RG-263, entry 82, box 33, MORI DocID: 14459, NA, CP; Stansfield Turner, *Secrecy and Democracy: The CIA in Transition* (New York: Harper and Row Publishers, 1985), pp. 230–31; Robert M. Gates, *From the Shadows* (New York: Simon and Schuster, 1996), p. 155; Don Oberdorfer, "Chapter I: 'Brigada': Unwelcome Sight in Cuba," *Washington Post*, September 9, 1979; Binder, "Soviet Brigade," *New York Times*.

87. Newsom, *Soviet Brigade in Cuba*, pp. vii–xii.

88. CIA, interagency intelligence memorandum, Memorandum to Holders, *Updated Report on Soviet Ground Forces Brigade in Cuba*, September 18, 1979, pp. 2–4, RG-263, entry 82 (A1), box 33, MORI DocID: 14459, NA, CP; *White Paper on the Presence of Soviet Troops in Cuba*, September 28, 1979, pp. 2–3, NSC Files, Jimmy Carter Presidential Library, Atlanta, GA.

89. Memorandum, PB/NSC Coordinator to Director of Central Intelligence, *"Leak" on Soviet Brigade*, October 5, 1979, CREST Collection, Document No. CIA-RDP81B00401R002400100010-7, NA, CP.

90. For an excellent monograph on the U.S. intelligence community's coverage of events leading up to the Soviet invasion of Afghanistan, see Douglas J. MacEachin, *Predicting the Soviet Invasion of Afghanistan: The Intelligence Community's Record* (Washington, DC: Center for the Study of Intelligence, April 2002). MacEachin served as the CIA's deputy director for intelligence from 1993 to 1995.

91. TCS 3267-79, interagency intelligence memorandum, *Soviet Options in Afghanistan*, September 27, 1979, p. 6, CIA Electronic FOIA Reading Room, Document No. 0000267105, http://www.foia.cia.gov.

92. CIA, interagency intelligence memorandum, *The Soviet Invasion of Afghanistan: Implications for Warning*, October 1980, p. 9, CIA Electronic FOIA Reading Room, Document No. 0000278538, http://www.foia.cia.gov.

93. TCS 3267-79, interagency intelligence memorandum, *Soviet Options in Afghanistan*, September 27, 1979, pp. 6–7, CIA Electronic FOIA Reading Room, Document No. 0000267105, http://www.foia.cia.gov; CIA, interagency intelligence memorandum, *The Soviet Invasion of Afghanistan: Implications for Warning*, October 1980, pp. 10, 13, CIA Electronic FOIA Reading Room, Document No. 0000278538, http://www.foia.cia.gov; Johnson, *American Cryptology*, bk. 3, p. 252; MacEachin, *Predicting the Soviet Invasion*, p. 13.

94. CIA, interagency intelligence memorandum, *The Soviet Invasion of Afghanistan: Implications for Warning*, October 1980, pp. 17–19, CIA Electronic FOIA Reading Room, Document No. 0000278538, http://www.foia.cia.gov; MacEachin, *Predicting the Soviet Invasion*, pp. 19–20.

95. Memorandum, Turner to National Security Council, *Alert Memorandum on USSR-Afghanistan*, September 14, 1979, CIA Electronic FOIA Reading Room, Document No. 0000267104, http://www.foia.cia.gov.

96. CIA, interagency intelligence memorandum, *The Soviet Invasion of Afghanistan: Implications for Warning*, October 1980, pp. 19–20, CIA Electronic FOIA Reading Room, Document No. 0000278538, http://www.foia.cia.gov; MacEachin, *Predicting the Soviet Invasion*, p. 21.

97. Lt. General William J McCaffrey, USA (Ret.), *A Review of Intelligence Performance in Afghanistan*, April 9, 1984, p. 8, CREST Collection, Document No. CIA-RDP86B00269R001100100003-5, NA, CP.

98. Ibid., p. 9.

99. CIA, *DDCI Notes*, January 2, 1980, CREST Collection, Document No. CIA-RDP81B00401R00 0600230018-5, NA, CP; Lt. General William J McCaffrey, USA (Ret.), *A Review of Intelligence Performance in Afghanistan*, April 9, 1984, p. 10, CREST Collection, Document No. CIA-RDP86 B00269R001100100003-5, NA, CP; Willis C. Armstrong et al., "The Hazards of Single-Outcome Forecasting," in H. Bradford Westerfield, ed., *Inside the CIA's Private World* (New Haven, CT: Yale University Press, 1995), p. 254; Gates, *From the Shadows*, p. 133; MacEachin, *Predicting the Soviet Invasion*, p. 33.

100. CIA, Afghan Task Force, intelligence memorandum, *The Buildup of Soviet Forces in Afghanistan Since 29 November*, December 28, 1979, CREST Collection, Document No. CIA-RDP81B00 401R000600230019-4, NA, CP; CIA, *DDCI Notes*, January 2, 1980, p. 2, CREST Collection, Document No. CIA-RDP81B00401R000600230018-5, NA, CP; Lt. General William J McCaffrey, USA (Ret.), *A Review of Intelligence Performance in Afghanistan*, April 9, 1984, p. 11, CREST Collection, Document No. CIA-RDP86B00269R001100100003-5, NA, CP. For the Russian perspective, see Valerie I. Ablazov, "VVS Sovetskoy Armii v perviy god voiny," undated, http://www.airwar.ru/history/locwar/afgan/vvs/vvs.html.

101. CIA, interagency intelligence memorandum, *The Soviet Invasion of Afghanistan: Implications for Warning*, October 1980, CIA Electronic FOIA Reading Room, Document No. 0000278538, http://www.foia.cia.gov.

102. Johnson, *American Cryptology*, bk. 3, p. 254.

103. "CRYPTOLOG Interviews NSA Employee Gene Becker," *Cryptolog*, Spring 1996: p. 19.

104. Johnson, *American Cryptology*, bk. 3, p. vii.

10: DANCING ON THE EDGE OF A VOLCANO

1. "Gen. Faurer Named as NSA Director," *Washington Post*, March 11, 1981; "Director Completes Distinguished Career," *NSA Newsletter*, April 1985, p. 3, NSA FOIA.

2. NSA OH-09-97, oral history, *Interview with Bobby Ray Inman*, June 18, 1997, p. 5, NSA FOIA; interview with Charles R. Lord; confidential interviews.

3. National Cryptologic School, *On Watch: Profiles from the National Security Agency's Past 40 Years* (Fort Meade, MD: NSA/CSS, 1986), p. 91, NSA FOIA.

4. Bob Woodward, *Veil: The Secret Wars of the CIA, 1981–1987* (New York: Simon and Schuster, 1987), p. 88; H. D. S. Greenway and Paul Quinn-Judge, "CIA Chief Voices Final Hopes and Fears," *Boston Globe*, January 15, 1993; confidential interviews.

5. CIA, interagency intelligence assessment, *Ramifications of Planned US Naval Exercise in the Gulf of Sidra: 18–20 August 1981*, August 10, 1981, p. 1, DDRS.

6. *1981 Command History, USS Caron*, pp. 1–3, Ships Histories Division, Naval Historical Center, Washington, DC; David C. Martin and John Walcott, *Best Laid Plans* (New York: Harper and Row, 1988), p. 72; Daniel P. Bolger, *Americans at War* (Novato, CA: Presidio Press, 1988), p. 179.

7. Confidential interviews; Jay Peterzell, *Reagan's Secret Wars* (Washington, DC: Center for National Security Studies, 1984), p. 69; Woodward, *Veil*, pp. 165–67, 409; Martin and Walcott, *Best Laid Plans*, pp. 72–73.

8. Raymond Bonner, *Weakness and Deceit: U.S. Policy and El Salvador* (New York: Times Books, 1984), p. 263; Woodward, *Veil*, pp. 164, 229, 251; Steven Emerson, *Secret Warriors* (New York: G. P. Putnam's Sons, 1988), pp. 87–88; Raymond Tate, "Worldwide C3I and Telecommunications," p. 37, Seminar on Command, Control, Communications and Intelligence, Center for Information Policy Research, Harvard University, 1980; Joan Edwards, "Reagan's Charges 'Total Untruths,' Ex-CIA Man Says," *Toronto Globe and Mail*, June 29, 1984; David Johnston and Michael Wines, "Intelligence Material on Sandinistas Is Said to Have Involved Lawmakers," *New York Times*, September 15, 1991; Scott Shane and Tom Bowman, "Catching Americans in NSA's Net," *Baltimore Sun*, December 15, 1995.

9. For RC-135 missions, see Dick van der Aart, *Aerial Espionage* (Shrewsbury, UK: Airlife Publishing, 1984), pp. 93, 154–57; Captain Rosa Pasos, "Report on Military Aggression Against Nicaragua by U.S. Imperialism," in Marlene Dixon, ed., *On Trial: Reagan's War Against Nicaragua* (San Francisco: Synthesis Publications, 1985), p. 49; Marlise Simons, "Nicaragua Lists U.S. 'Violations' in Bitter Reply to Reagan Speech," *New York Times*, May 2, 1983; Todd Ensign, "Viewpoints: The First Refusal of Military Duty over Nicaragua," *Newsday*, July 7, 1987; "Spying Over Nicaragua Revealed," *Washington Times*, July 10, 1987. For C-130 SIGINT missions, see Dr. Dennis F. Casey and Msgt. Gabriel G. Marshall, *A Continuing Legacy: USAFSS–AIA, 1948–2000: A Brief History of the Air Intelligence Agency and Its Predecessor Organizations* (San Antonio, TX: Headquarters Air Intelligence Agency, History Office, 2000), p. 28. Fred Hiatt, "U.S. Said Planning More Exercises for Latin America: One Site to Be El Salvador," *Washington Post*, October 26, 1984. For use of SIGINT to target AC-130 gunships, see transcript, "The Pentagon Turned Its Back on Them," *60 Minutes*, May 21, 1995.

10. Commander-in-Chief, Atlantic, *Command History, U.S. Atlantic Command 1982*, 1983, p. XVI-1, U.S. Joint Forces Command FOIA; Office of Naval Intelligence, *Command History, Naval Intelligence Command for 1982*, 1983, p. 1, ONI FOIA; *Command History USS Deyo for 1982*, February 28, 1983, p. 1; *Command History USS Caron for 1982*, 1983, both in Ships Histories Division, Naval Historical Center, Washington, DC; "U.S. Vessel on Alert for Cuban Arms Shipments," *Los Angeles Times*, February 24, 1982; Richard Halloran, "US Destroyer Monitors Activity in Area of Salvador and Nicaragua," *New York Times*, February 25, 1982; Richard Halloran, "U.S. Says Navy Surveillance Ship Is Stationed Off Central America," *New York Times*, February 25, 1982; "Judging Spies and Eyes," *Time*, March 22, 1982, p. 22; James LeMoyne with David C. Martin, "High-Tech Spycraft," *Newsweek*, March 22, 1982, p. 29.

11. Confidential interviews with former CIA officials. See also "Haig Hints at New Talks with Cuba on Salvador," *Globe and Mail*, March 15, 1982; "New Report on El Salvador Lacks Evidence for Charges," Dow Jones News Service, March 22, 1982.

12. CIA, Directorate of Intelligence, *El Salvador: Guerrilla Capabilities and Prospects over the Next Two Years*, appendix E, "External Support: The Cuba-Nicaragua Pipeline," October 1984, p. 37, CIA Electronic FOIA Reading Room, Document No. 0000761619, http://www.foia.cia.gov.

13. The best book by far on the shootdown of KAL 007 remains Seymour Hersh, *The Target Is Destroyed* (New York: Random House, 1986).

14. Confidential interviews with NSA analysts and U.S. Air Force intercept operators involved in the KAL 007 incident; *History of the 6920th Electronic Security Group: 1 July–31 December 1983*, vol. 1, March 31, 1984, AIA FOIA; 6920th Electronic Security Group, *1983 Travis Trophy Submission for Misawa AB, Japan*, undated but circa 1984, AIA FOIA. See also Philip Taubman, "U.S. Had Noticed Activity by Soviet," *New York Times*, September 14, 1993.

15. Hersh, *Target*, pp. 57–61.

16. Oral history, *Interview with George P. Shultz*, December 18, 2002, p. 13, Ronald Reagan Presidential Oral History Project, Miller Center, University of Virginia, Charlottesville.

17. For the text of Secretary Shultz's comments, see "Secretary's News Briefing, September 1, 1983," *Department of State Bulletin*, October 1983, pp. 1–2. For press reporting on intelligence revelations stemming from Shultz's briefing, see David Shribman, "Side Effect: Peek at U.S. Intelligence Abilities," *New York Times*, September 2, 1982; George C. Wilson, "Electronic Spy Network Provided Detailed Account," *Washington Post*, September 2, 1983; Walter S. Mossberg and Gerald F. Seib, "U.S. Response Gives Glimpse of Ability to Track Russian Military Activities," *Wall Street Journal*, September 2, 1983.

18. Robert M. Gates, *From the Shadows* (New York: Simon and Schuster, 1996), p. 267. It was not until September 11, 1983, ten days after the shootdown, that the State Department released a full transcript of the NSA intercept tape, which confirmed that Major Osipovich had repeatedly tried to warn KAL 007 to no effect. Michael Getler, "Soviet Fired Gun Toward Jet, New Analysis Shows," *Washington Post*, September 12, 1983; Paul Mann, "U.S. Admits Soviets Fired Cannon Shots," *Aviation Week & Space Technology*, September 19, 1983, p. 25.

19. Reagan's televised address to the nation can be found at Ronald Reagan, "Address to the Nation on the Soviet Attack on a Korean Civilian Airliner," September 5, 1983, http://www.reagan.utexas.edu/archives/speeches/1983/90583a.htm. Ambassador Kirkpatrick's presentation to the U.N. can be found at "Ambassador Kirkpatrick's Statement, U.N. Security Council, September 6, 1983," in *Department of State Bulletin*, October 1983, pp. 8–11. The transcript of the three extracts from the NSA tape that Ambassador Kirkpatrick played can be found at "U.S. Intercepts Soviet Fighter Transmissions," *Aviation Week & Space Technology*, September 12, 1983, pp. 22–23.

20. Gates, *From the Shadows*, p. 268.

21. Alvin A. Snyder, *Warriors of Disinformation* (New York: Arcade Publishing, 1995); Alvin A. Snyder, "Flight 007: The Rest of the Story," *Washington Post*, September 1, 1996.

22. Raymond L. Garthoff, *The Great Transition: American-Soviet Relations and the End of the Cold War* (Washington, DC: Brookings Institution, 1994), pp. 119–20.

23. Interview with Walter G. Deeley; NSA OH-09-97, oral history, *Interview with Bobby Ray Inman*, June 18, 1997, p. 11, NSA FOIA

24. Confidential interviews with NSA analysts. A caustic analysis of the performance of the Soviet air defense system can be found in "Special Analysis: USSR: The Shootdown," *National Intelligence Daily*, September 7, 1983, p. 2, RG-263, entry 42, box 69, NA, CP; NI IIM 85-10008, CIA, interagency intelligence memorandum, *Air Defense of the USSR*, December 1985, p. 13, CIA Electronic FOIA Reading Room, Document No. 0000261292, http://www.foia.cia.gov. See also William L. Norton, *Briefing on the Re-Organization of Soviet Air and Air Defense Forces* (Falls Church, VA: E-Systems Melpar Division, 1984), pp. 29–33, paper presented at the Strategy 84 Conference, Washington, DC, March 12, 1984; Richard Halloran, "Soviet's Defenses Called Inflexible," *New York Times*, September 18, 1983; Walter Pincus, "The Soviets Had the Wrong Stuff," *Washington Post*, September 18, 1983; Dusko Doder, "Soviets Said to Remove Air Officers," *Washington Post*, October 5, 1983; Bill Gertz, "Soviet 007 Tape Revealing," *Washington Times*, August 15, 1992.

25. HQ 22nd Marine Amphibious Unit, *Command Chronology: 1–31 May 1983*, June 7, 1983, part 3, p. 1, Marine Corps Historical Center, Quantico, VA; message, Beirut 05379, AMEMBASSY BEIRUT to SECSTATE WASHDC, May 6, 1983, Department of State Electronic FOIA Reading Room, Document No. 83BEIRUT05379, http://www.foia.state.gov; message, Beirut 05381, AMEMBASSY BEIRUT to AMEMBASSY AMMAN, May 6, 1983, Department of State Electronic FOIA Reading Room, Document No. 83BEIRUT05381, http://www.foia.state.gov.

26. Confidential interviews with former senior CIA officials. See also Martin and Wolcott, *Best Laid Plans*, pp. 105, 133; R. W. Apple Jr., "U.S. Knew of Iran's Role in Two Beirut Bombings," *New York Times*, December 8, 1986; Stephen Engelberg, "U.S. Calls Iranian Cleric Leading Backer of Terror," *New York Times*, August 27, 1989; "New Evidence Ties Iran to Terrorism," *Newsweek*, November 15, 1999, p. 7.

27. Jack Anderson, "U.S. Was Warned of Bombing at Beirut Embassy," *Washington Post*, May 10, 1983; Jack Anderson, "Syria Supported Terrorism, Say U.S., Britain," *Newsday*, November 7, 1986; Apple, "U.S. Knew."

28. The intercept quote is taken from Civil Action No. 01-2094 (RCL), memorandum opinion, May 30, 2003, *Deborah D. Peterson v. Islamic Republic of Iran*, p. 12, U.S. District Court for the District of Columbia. For background of Musawi, his organization, and its relationship with the Iranian government, see CIA, Directorate of Intelligence, *The Terrorist Threat to US Personnel in Beirut*, January 12, 1984, CIA Electronic FOIA Reading Room, Document No. 0000256547, http://www.foia.cia.gov; CIA, Directorate of Intelligence, *Lebanon: The Hizb Allah*, September 27, 1984, CIA Electronic FOIA Reading Room, Document No. 0000256558, http://www.foia.cia.gov; memorandum for the DCI, *Iranian Support for International Terrorism*, November 22, 1986, CIA Electronic FOIA Reading Room, Document No. 0000258607, http://www.foia.cia.gov. For September 27, 1983, NSA warning message, see James P. Stevenson, *The $5 Billion Misunderstanding: The Collapse of the Navy's A-12 Stealth Bomber Program* (Annapolis, MD: Naval Institute Press, 2001), p. 39n.

29. For a rendition of all the intelligence and security failings surrounding the October 23, 1983, bombing of the U.S. Marine barracks in Beirut except for the NSA warning message, see *Report of the DoD Commission on Beirut International Airport Terrorist Act, October 23, 1983 (Long Commission)* (Washington, DC: GPO, 1983).

30. Message, 230725Z OCT 83, CIA to [deleted], October 23, 1983, CIA Electronic FOIA Reading Room, Document No. 0000805432, http://www.foia.cia.gov; message, 230822Z OCT 83, CIA to [deleted], October 23, 1983, CIA Electronic FOIA Reading Room, Document No. 0000805431, http://www.foia.cia.gov.

31. For SIGINT aircraft orbiting the Mediterranean, see U.S. Sixth Fleet, *1984 Sixth Fleet Command History*, 1985, p. IV-58, Operational Archives, Naval Historical Center, Washington, DC. For Marine SIGINT operations, confidential interviews, as well as "Marines Thumb Noses at Local Marksmen," *Globe and Mail*, December 15, 1983.

32. Confidential interviews.

33. "Director Completes Distinguished Career," *NSA Newsletter*, April 1985, p. 3, NSA FOIA; Robert C. Toth, "Security Agency Chief Said Forced out of Office," *Washington Post*, April 19, 1985; George C. Wilson, "Reagan to Name Army General as NSA Director," *Washington Post*, April 20, 1985; David Burnham, "Move into World of Computer Nets by Intelligence Unit Raises Doubt," *New York Times*, June 27, 1985; Bill Gertz, "Superseded General Expected to Resign," *Washington Times*, February 22, 1988.

34. For the brief but intense fight over the selection of Odom to be NSA director, see Douglas F. Garthoff, *Directors of Central Intelligence as Leaders of the U.S. Intelligence Community: 1946–2005* (Washington, DC: Center for the Study of Intelligence, 2005), pp. 167–68.

35. Odom background from biographical data sheet, Lt. General William E. Odom, Department of the Army, Office of Public Affairs; "New Director Named," *NSA Newsletter*, July 1985, p. 2, "View from the Top," *NSA Newsletter*, November 1987, pp. 6–8, both NSA FOIA; Wilson, "Reagan to Name"; Charles R. Babcock, "Professorial Director NSA Suddenly in Spotlight," *Washington Post*, May 31, 1986; Emerson, *Secret Warriors*, p. 81.

36. Woodward quote from Woodward, *Veil*, p. 450.

37. NSA OH-09-97, oral history, *Interview with Bobby Ray Inman*, June 18, 1997, p. 6, NSA FOIA.
38. For details of the Wobensmith case, see Stephen Engelberg, "A Career in Ruins in Wake of Iran-Contra Affair," *New York Times*, June 3, 1988.
39. NSA OH-09-97, oral history, *Interview with Bobby Ray Inman*, June 18, 1997, p. 7, NSA FOIA.
40. Confidential interviews with former CIA officials.
41. Because of the public revelation of Chalet's existence in June 1979, the Byeman designation for the system was changed from Chalet to Vortex, or VO. In 1987, the Vortex system was again renamed Mercury, or MC. Angelo Codevilla, *Informing Statecraft: Intelligence for a New Century* (New York: Free Press, 1992), p. 116; Christopher Anson Pike, "Canyon, Rhyolite and Aquacade: U.S. Signals Intelligence Satellites in the 1970s," *Spaceflight*, vol. 37 (November 1995): p. 383; Jonathan McDowell, "U.S. Reconnaissance Satellite Programs, Part 2, Beyond Imaging," *Quest*, vol. 4, no. 4 (1995): p. 42. For the codename Mercury, see Craig Covault and Joseph C. Anselmo, "Titan Explosion Destroys Secret 'Mercury' SIGINT Satellite," *Aviation Week & Space Technology*, August 17, 1998, p. 28.
42. For Vortex monitoring of Soviet forces in Afghanistan, confidential interviews. For monitoring SS-24 ICBM communications, see Major A. Andronov, "American Geosynchronous SIGINT Satellites," *Zarubezhnoye Voyennoye Obozreniye*, no. 12 (1993): pp. 37–43. For Vortex generating intelligence on Chernobyl and the Pavlograd explosion, see Jeffrey T. Richelson, *The U.S. Intelligence Community*, 3rd ed. (Boulder, CO: Westview Press, 1995), pp. 172, 179; Jeffrey T. Richelson, *America's Space Sentinels: DSP Satellites and National Security* (Lawrence: University of Kansas Press, 1999), p. 153; "Soviet Missile-Motor Plant Shut by Explosion, Pentagon Says," *Washington Post*, May 18, 1988; Peter Almond and Paul Bedard, "Explosion Deals Serious Setback to New Soviet ICBMs," *Washington Times*, May 18, 1988.
43. Details of Pelton's espionage on behalf of the Soviet Union derived from his interrogation by the FBI can be found in FBI Special Agent David E. Faulkner, affidavit in support of complaint, December 20, 1985, in CRIMINAL No. HM85-0621, *United States of America v. Ronald William Pelton*, U.S. District Court for the District of Maryland. The best general description of the Pelton case is in Thomas B. Allen and Norman Polmar, *Merchants of Treason* (New York: Dell Publishing, 1988), pp. 255–67.
44. For details of the Ivy Bells operation, see Sherry Sontag and Christopher Drew, *Blind Man's Bluff* (New York: Public Affairs, 1998), pp. 158–83; Michael Dobbs, "KGB Chief Details U.S. Spy Operation," *Washington Post*, September 3, 1988; Norman Polmar, "How Many Spy Subs," *Naval Institute Proceedings*, December 1996, p. 87. For the Russian perspective, see Nikolai Brusnitsin, *Openness and Espionage* (Moscow: Military Publishers House, 1990), pp. 13–14; N. Burbiga, "A Fishy Day at the CIA," *Izvestia*, March 1, 1994. See also Angelo M. Codevilla, "Pollard Was No Pelton," *Forward (N.Y.)*, December 8, 2000, http://www.jonathanpollard.org/2000/120800.htm.
45. Interview with Charles R. Lord; confidential interviews with former NSA officials. For damage done by Pelton generally, see Woodward, *Veil*, pp. 448–51. For loss of the data from the Moscow listening posts, see Mike Frost, *Spyworld* (Toronto: Doubleday Canada, 1994), pp. 245–52; "Alleged Radio Intelligence Operations from US Embassy in Moscow," *BBC Summary of World Broadcasts*, March 31, 1980. For the tree stump operation, see "US Espionage Activities in USSR: Two CIA Agents Detected," *BBC Summary of World Broadcasts*, March 28, 1980; "Izvestiya on Alleged Espionage Operations by US Diplomats," *BBC Summary of World Broadcasts*, March 29, 1980.
46. Indictment, December 20, 1985, in CRIMINAL No. HM85-0621, *United States of America v. Ronald William Pelton*, U.S. District Court for the District of Maryland, Baltimore, Maryland.
47. Richard Whittle, "Libya Jets Intercept U.S. Plane," *Dallas Morning News*, January 15, 1986.
48. Message, JCS 280015Z Feb 86, JCS to multiple recipients, February 28, 1986, JCS FOIA; Command Historian 6916th Electronic Security, *History of the 6916th Electronic Security Squadron:*

1 January–30 June 1986, 1986, vol. 2, tab 36, AIA FOIA; *1986 Command History, USS Caron*, 1987, p. 1, Ships Histories Division, Naval Historical Center, Washington, DC; confidential interview. See also Joseph S. Bermudez, "Libyan SAMs and Air Defenses," *Jane's Defence Weekly*, May 17, 1986, p. 880; Seymour M. Hersh, "Target Qaddafi," *New York Times Magazine*, January 22, 1987, p. 71; Capt. Don East, USN, "The History of U.S. Naval Airborne Electronic Reconnaissance: Part 2, the European Theater and VQ-2," *Hook*, Summer 1987: p. 42.

49. Confidential interviews; U.S. Sixth Fleet, *1986 Sixth Fleet Command History*, 1987, p. III-6, Operational Archives, Naval Historical Center, Washington, DC; George C. Wilson, "Alert Brings Out Libyan Military's Weaknesses," *Washington Post*, January 9, 1986; "Gadaffi's men fear getting lost," *Jane's Defence Weekly*, January 18, 1986, p. 43.

50. George C. Wilson, "U.S. Planes Retaliate for Libyan Attack," *Washington Post*, March 25, 1986.

51. Woodward, *Veil*, pp. 444–45; Oliver R. North and William Novak, *Under Fire: An American Story* (New York: HarperCollins Publishers, 1991), p. 216; Bob Woodward and Patrick E. Tyler, "U.S. Shows Spy Systems' Capabilities," *Washington Post*, April 15, 1986; Bob Woodward, "Intelligence 'Coup' Tied Libya to Blast," *Washington Post*, April 22, 1986; Leslie H. Gelb, "How Libya Messages Informed U.S.," *New York Times*, April 23, 1986; Rick Atkinson, "Bomb Suspect Sent to Germany," *Washington Post*, May 24, 1996; "Trial Begins in the 1986 Bombing of Berlin Disco," *Seattle Times*, November 18, 1997.

52. Frank Greve, "Spying on Libya Yields Information Bonanza," *Houston Chronicle*, May 18, 1986.

53. Hersh, "Target Qaddafi," p. 74.

54. W. O. Studeman, "The Philosophy of Intelligence," p. 105, Seminar on Intelligence, Command and Control, Center for Information Policy Research, Harvard University, December 1991.

55. Stephen Engelberg, "Head of National Security Agency Plans to Retire," *New York Times*, February 23, 1988; Molly Moore, "Odom to Resign as Head of NSA," *Washington Post*, February 23, 1988; Gertz, "Superseded General."

56. Studeman background from biographical data sheet, RADM William Oliver Studeman, Department of the Navy, Office of Public Affairs, October 1, 1987; "Agency Welcomes New Director RADM William O. Studeman," *NSA Newsletter*, September 1988, p. 2, NSA FOIA.

57. John Barron, *Breaking the Ring: The Rise and Fall of the Walker Family Spy Network* (New York: Avon Books, 1987), pp. 196–97.

58. Confidential interviews.

59. Mark Urban, *UK Eyes Alpha* (London: Faber and Faber, 1996), p. 111; Bernard E. Trainor, "Bush Bars Normal Ties Now; Beijing Is Warned," *New York Times*, June 9, 1989; Daniel Williams and David Holley, "China Hard-Liners Appear in Control," *Los Angeles Times*, June 9, 1989; "Communications Vacuumed: Satellite Intelligence Provides Key to Bush China Decision," *Communications Daily*, June 12, 1989, p. 5; "Reign of Terror," *Newsweek*, June 19, 1989, p. 14. See also the declassified morning intelligence summaries for the secretary of state, examples of which are at http://www.seas.gwu.edu/nsarchive/NSAEBB16/documents.

60. Oral history, *Interview with Warren Zimmermann*, December 10, 1996, Foreign Affairs Oral History Collection, Association for Diplomatic Studies and Training, Library of Congress, Washington, DC.

61. For the deterioration of U.S. relations with Panama, see Seymour M. Hersh, "Our Man in Panama: The Creation of a Thug," *Life*, March 1990, pp. 81–93. For intelligence efforts in Panama prior to the U.S. invasion, see U.S. Army Intelligence and Security Command, *Annual Historical Report INSCOM Fiscal Year 1990*, 1991, pp. 41–42, INSCOM FOIA. Also, confidential interviews. For quote concerning elimination of SOUTHCOM and CIA HUMINT sources, see Captain Brian J. Cummins, USA, *National Reconnaissance Support to the Army* (Fort Leavenworth, KS: U.S. Army Command and General Staff College, 1994), p. 101.

62. Department of the Army, Office of the Deputy Chief of Staff for Intelligence, *Annual Historical Review: 1 October 1989 to 30 September 1990*, 1991, p. 4-52, National Security Archive, Washington, DC; *Command Chronology, Marine Support Battalion, for the Period 1 July–31 December 1989*, 1990, enclosure 4; *Command Chronology 2nd Radio Battalion for the Period 1 July–31 December 1989*, 1990, enclosure 2, pp. 1, 4, both in Marine Corps Historical Center, Quantico, VA; "Just Cause," *Insight*, January–March 1990, pp. 11–13, AIA FOIA; Technical Sergeant. Mark Harlfinger, "Flight Operations End at 94th IS," *Spokesman*, May 1997, p. 23, AIA FOIA. For creation of a Panama Cell at NSA, see W. O. Studeman, "The Philosophy of Intelligence," p. 109, Seminar on Intelligence, Command and Control, Center for Information Policy Research, Harvard University, December 1991.

63. Cummins, *National Reconnaissance Support*, pp. 104–05. For more concerning NSA's attempts at tracking Noriega, see Christopher Andrew, *For the President's Eyes Only* (New York: HarperCollins Publishers, 1995), p. 514; Bill Gertz, "NSA Eavesdropping Was Vital in Panama," *Washington Times*, January 10, 1990.

64. Patrick E. Tyler, "U.S. Commander Decries Leak on Panamanian Invasion," *Washington Post*, February 27, 1990; Cummins, *National Reconnaissance Support*, pp. 104–05.

65. Dr. Thomas R. Johnson, *American Cryptology During the Cold War, 1945–1989*, bk. 3, *Retrenchment and Reform, 1972–1980* (Fort Meade: Center for Cryptologic History, 1995), p. 21, NSA FOIA. For the seventy-five thousand NSA personnel figure, see declaration of Dr. Richard W. Gronet, Director of Policy, National Security Agency, June 14, 1989, in CIV. No. HM87-1564, *Ray Lindsey v. National Security Agency/Central Security Service*, p. 5, U.S. District Court for the District of Maryland.

66. Confidential interviews.

67. Bob Drogin, "NSA Blackout Reveals Downside of Secrecy," *Los Angeles Times*, March 13, 2000.

68. Memorandum, Vice Admiral Bobby R. Inman, USN, to Special Assistant, Office of the Secretary of Defense, *Transition Coordination*, sec. 8, Modernization Objectives, December 9, 1980, NSA FOIA; Codevilla, *Informing Statecraft*, p. 124; Loch K. Johnson, *Secret Agencies: U.S. Intelligence in a Hostile World* (New Haven, CT: Yale University Press, 1996), p. 21.

11: Troubles in Paradise

1. This era in NSA's history is covered in greater detail in Matthew M. Aid, "The Time of Troubles: The US National Security Agency in the Twenty-first Century," *Intelligence and National Security*, vol. 15, no. 3 (Autumn 2000): pp. 1–32.

2. David Y. McManis, "Technology, Intelligence, and Control," p. 20, Seminar on Intelligence, Command and Control, Center for Information Policy Research, Harvard University, February 1993.

3. The literature on Operations Desert Shield/Storm is substantial. The most detailed official accounts of the war can be found in: United States Central Command, *Operation Desert Shield/Desert Storm: Executive Summary*, July 11, 1991, p. 1, National Security Archive, Washington, DC; Department of Defense, *Conduct of the Persian Gulf War: Final Report to Congress* (Washington, DC: GPO, April 1992); Brigadier General Robert H. Scales Jr., USA, *Certain Victory: The U.S. Army in the Gulf War* (Washington, DC: Brassey's, 1994). The conduct of the air campaign is detailed in Dr. Thomas A. Keaney and Dr. Eliot A. Cohen, eds., *Gulf War Air Power Survey* (Washington, DC: GPO, 1993), 5 vols. The best all-around books on the war are Rick Atkinson, *Crusade: The Untold Story of the Persian Gulf War* (New York: Houghton Mifflin, 1993); Michael R. Gordon and General Bernard E. Trainor, *The General's War* (Boston: Little, Brown, 1995). The Saudi perspective on the war can be found in HRH General Khaled bin Sultan, *Desert Warrior* (New York: HarperCollins Publishers, 1995).

4. NSA's successes and failings in Operation Desert Storm are detailed in David A. Hatch, *Shield and Storm: The Cryptologic Community in the Desert Operations*, vol. 5, Special Series, Crisis Collection (Fort Meade: Center for Cryptologic History, 1992). SIGINT's success against the Iraqi air defense system from Department of Defense, *Conduct of the Persian Gulf War* (Washington, DC: GPO, 1992), pp. 12, 150, 154, 164; Keaney and Cohen, *Gulf War Air Power*, vol. 2, part 1, pp. 77–82, vol. 4, p. 182, and vol. 5, part 2, pp. 51, 190; Scales, *Certain Victory*, p. 178; Richard G. Davis, *On Target: Organizing and Executing the Strategic Air Campaign Against Iraq* (Washington, DC: Air Force History and Museums Program, 2002), p. 152.

5. Final draft, *SIGINT 101 Seminar Course Module*, 2002, NSA FOIA. McConnell quote from letter, McConnell to Senator Sam Nunn with enclosure, April 28, 1992, p. 6, NSA FOIA.

6. Monograph, *John F. Stewart Jr. and the Vigilant Eye of the Storm* (Fort Huachuca, AZ: History Office, U.S. Army Intelligence Center and Fort Huachuca, no date), p. 18.

7. bin Sultan, *Desert Warrior*, p. 399; Mark Urban *UK Eyes Alpha* (London: Faber and Faber, 1996), p. 170; David A. Fulghum, "Yugoslavia Successfully Attacked by Computers," *Aviation Week & Space Technology*, August 23, 1999, p. 31.

8. Keaney and Cohen, *Gulf War Air Power*, summary vol., p. 98.

9. Brigadier General John F. Stewart, Jr., *Operation Desert Storm. The Military Intelligence Story: A View from the G-2, 3rd U.S. Army*, April 1991, p. 6, INSCOM FOIA; U.S. Army Intelligence and Security Command, *Annual Historical Review, U.S. Army Intelligence and Security Command (INSCOM): Fiscal Year 1991*, appendix K, 1992, p. 29, INSCOM FOIA; Daniel F. Baker, "Deep Attack: A Military Intelligence Task Force in Desert Storm," *Military Intelligence Professional Bulletin*, October–December 1991, p. 39; Lt. Colonel Richard J. Quirk, III, USA, *Intelligence for the Division: A G2 Perspective* (Carlisle Barracks, PA: U.S. Army War College, 1992), p. 307; Major Raymond E. Coia, USMC, *A Critical Analysis of the I MEF Intelligence Performance in the 1991 Persian Gulf War* (Quantico, VA: Marine Corps Command and Staff College, 1995), p. 6; Major Robert H. Taylor, USA, *Heavy Division Organic Signals Intelligence (SIGINT): Added Value or Added Baggage* (Fort Leavenworth, KS: School of Advanced Military Studies, U.S. Army Command and General Staff College, 1996), p. 24; Lt. Colonel John J. Bird, USA, *Analysis of Intelligence Support to the 1991 Persian Gulf War: Enduring Lessons* (Carlisle Barracks, PA: U.S. Army War College, Strategic Studies Institute, 2004), pp. 7–8. For Iraqi communications security being more thorough than the Soviets' during the Cold War, see Barbara Starr, "Measuring the Success of the Intelligence War," *Jane's Defence Weekly*, April 20, 1991, p. 636.

10. Keaney and Cohen, *Gulf War Air Power*, vol. 1, part 2, p. 270. McManis quote from David Y. McManis, "Technology, Intelligence, and Control," p. 31, Seminar on Intelligence, Command and Control, Center for Information Policy Research, Harvard University, February 1993.

11. U.S. Senate, Armed Services Committee, *Department of Defense Authorization for Appropriation, FY 1992 and FY 1993*, part 2, 102nd Congress, 1st session, 1991, p. 19; Scales, *Certain Victory*, pp. 222, 237, 251; Gordon and Trainor, *General's War*, p. 365; Taylor, *Heavy Division* p. 24; Colonel John Patrick Leake, *Operational Leadership in the Gulf War: Lessons from the Schwarzkopf-Franks Controversy*, undated, http://www.cfcsc.dnd.ca/irc/amsci/024.html.

12. According to Defense Department records, the Iraqis fired forty-two Scud missiles at Israel, targeting Tel Aviv, Haifa, and the Israeli nuclear reactor and weapons facility at Dimona in the Negev Desert. OGA-1040-23-91, Defense Intelligence Agency, *Defense Intelligence Assessment: Mobile Short-Range Ballistic Missile Targeting in Operation DESERT STORM*, November 1, 1991, p. 1, partially declassified and on file at the National Security Archive, Washington, DC; Captain Brian J. Cummins, USA, *National Reconnaissance Support to the Army* (Fort Leavenworth, KS: U.S. Army Command and General Staff College, June 1994), pp. 69–70.

13. Defense Intelligence Agency, OGA-1040-23-91, *Defense Intelligence Assessment: Mobile Short-Range*

Ballistic Missile Targeting in Operation DESERT STORM, November 1, 1991, p. 7, partially declassified and on file at the National Security Archive, Washington, DC; Cummins, *National Reconnaissance Support,* p. 70.

14. Confidential interviews with a number of U.S. Army and Marine Corps division, brigade, and regimental commanders conducted between 1992 and 1995. For "sanitization" problems, see Office of the Assistant Secretary of Defense (Command, Control, Communication and Intelligence), Intelligence Program Support Group, *Final Report: Operation Desert Shield/Desert Storm Intelligence Dissemination Study,* 1992, p. 4–15, DoD Electronic FOIA Reading Room. See also Anthony H. Cordesman and Abraham R. Wagner, *The Lessons of Modern War,* vol. 4, *The Gulf War* (Boulder, CO: Westview Press, 1996), p. 296.

15. Use of Iraqi Americans in the military for SIGINT service from anonymous letter, "Army Linguists," *Soldiers,* August 2001, http://www.army.mil/Soldiers/aug2001/feedback.html. The secret hiring of three hundred Kuwaitis from U.S. Army Intelligence and Security Command, *Annual Historical Review, U.S. Army Intelligence and Security Command (INSCOM): Fiscal Year 1991,* appendix K, 1992, p. 31, INSCOM FOIA. Quote from Brigadier General John F. Stewart, Jr., USA, *Operation Desert Storm: The Military Intelligence Story: A View from the G-2 3rd U.S. Army,* April 1991, p. 22, INSCOM FOIA

16. Major William E. David, USA, *Modularity: A Force Design Methodology for the Force XXI Divisional Military Intelligence Battalion* (Fort Leavenworth, KS: School of Advanced Military Studies, U.S. Army Command and General Staff College, 1995), pp. 18–19.

17. U.S. House of Representatives, Permanent Select Committee on Intelligence, Report No. 101-1008, *Report by the Permanent Select Committee on Intelligence,* 101st Congress, 2nd session, January 2, 1991, p. 9.

18. Defense Department, Office of the Inspector General, Report No. 96-03, *Final Report on the Verification Inspection of the National Security Agency,* February 13, 1996, p. 2, DOD FOIA.

19. NSA/CSS, report of the Director's Task Force on Organizational and Procedural Dysfunction, *Bureaucracy and NSA: Management's Views,* March 1991, pp. 1–2, NSA FOIA.

20. This conclusion came through loud and clear in a March 1992 report to the director of the CIA, which held NSA out to be a model of what the U.S. intelligence community should have been aspiring to, stating, "NSA's control and influence over almost all aspects of the SIGINT discipline offers a sense of cohesion, focus and accountability that would be advantageous to invest in." ICS-4548/92, memorandum, Imagery Blue Ribbon Task Force to Director of Central Intelligence, *Transmittal of Report Regarding Restructuring the Imagery Community,* March 6, 1992, p. 11, MOR DocID: 924226, CIA FOIA.

21. President George H. W. Bush, "Remarks at a Presentation Ceremony for the National Security Agency Worldwide Awards in Fort Meade, Maryland," May 1, 1991, http://csdl.tamu.edu/bushlibrary/papers/1991/91050101.html.

22. U.S. Senate, Select Committee on Intelligence, *Report Together with Additional and Minority Views: Appropriations for Fiscal Year 1994 for Intelligence Activities,* 103rd Congress, 2nd session, July 28, 1993, p. 4; memorandum, Studeman to All Employees, *Farewell,* April 8, 1992, p. 1, NSA FOIA; "A Visit with the Deputy Director," *NSA Newsletter,* November 1990, p. 2, NSA FOIA.

23. Confidential interviews.

24. Cummins, *National Reconnaissance Support,* p. 5.

25. Memorandum, Studeman to All Employees, *Farewell,* April 8, 1992, NSA FOIA.

26. Memorandum, Taylor to DIRNSA, *Thoughts on Strategic Issues for the Institution,* April 9, 1999, p. 3. The author is grateful to Dr. Jeffrey T. Richelson for making available a copy of this document.

27. SOV 91-10039X, CIA, Directorate of Intelligence, *The Implications of a Breakup of the USSR:*

Defense Assets at Risk, September 1991, CIA Electronic FOIA Reading Room, Document 0000499575, http://www.foia.cia.gov.

28. Confidential interview.

29. "Third Party Nations: Partners and Targets," *Cryptologic Quarterly*, vol. 7, no. 4 (Winter 1989): p. 17, DOCID: 3221078, NSA FOIA.

30. Confidential interviews.

31. McConnell background from biographical data sheet, Rear Admiral John Michael McConnell, Department of the Navy, Office of Public affairs, August 1, 1991; "Agency Welcomes New Director Vice Admiral John Michael McConnell," *NSA Newsletter*, August 1992, p. 2, NSA FOIA.

32. For McConnell's recollections of this time period, see John M. McConnell, "The Role of the Current Intelligence Officer for the Chairman of the Joint Chiefs of Staff," Seminar on Intelligence, Command and Control, Center for Information Policy Research, Harvard University, August 1994.

33. Lawrence Wright, "The Spymaster," *New Yorker*, January 21, 2008, p. 44.

34. Letter, McConnell to Senator Sam Nunn with enclosure, April 28, 1992, p. 5, NSA FOIA.

35. "NSA Plans for the Future," *NSA Newsletter*, January 1993, p. 4, NSA FOIA; Department of Defense, Office of the Inspector General, Report No. IR 96-03, *Final Report on the Verification Inspection of the National Security Agency*, February 13, 1996, p. 6. "Not warmly embraced" quote from John M. McConnell, "The Evolution of Intelligence and the Public Policy Debate on Encryption," p. 153, Seminar on Intelligence, Command and Control, Center for Information Policy Research, Harvard University, January 1997.

36. This period at NSA is detailed in Aid, "Time of Troubles." For the decline in the size of the budget and personnel of the U.S. intelligence community, see Charlie Allen, Assistant Director of Central Intelligence for Collection, PowerPoint presentation, "Intelligence Community Overview for Japanese Visitors from Public Security Investigation Agency," June 22, 1998, http://cryptome .org/cia-ico.htm, "Statement for the Record by Lt. General Michael V. Hayden, USAF, Director NSA/CSS Before the Joint Inquiry of the Senate Select Committee on Intelligence and the House Permanent Select Committee on Intelligence," October 17, 2002, p. 6. "One of the side effects" quote from U.S. Senate, Report No. 107-351, and U.S. House of Representatives, Report No. 107 792, report of the U.S. Senate Select Committee on Intelligence and U.S. House Permanent Select Committee on Intelligence, *Joint Inquiry into Intelligence Community Activities Before and After the Terrorist Attacks of September 11, 2001*, 107th Congress, 2nd session, December 2002 (declassified and released in July 2003), p. 76.

37. Major Harold E. Bullock, USAF, *Peace by Committee: Command and Control Issues in Multinational Peace Enforcement Operations* (Maxwell Air Force Base, AL: School of Advanced Airpower Studies, 1994), pp. 9–10; Norman L. Cooling, "Operation Restore Hope in Somalia: A Tactical Action Turned Strategic Defeat," *Marine Corps Gazette*, September 2001, p. 92. "Somalis from salami" quote from Robert F. Baumann, Lawrence A. Yates, and Versalle F. Washington, *"My Clan Against the World": US and Coalition Forces in Somalia, 1992–1994* (Fort Leavenworth, KS: Combat Studies Institute Press, 2003), p. 48.

38. For the Marine Corps radio battalion detachment SIGINT operations in Somalia, see I Marine Expeditionary Force, *I MEF Command Chronology 1992*, sec. 2, pp. 22–23, passim, Marine Corps Historical Center, Quantico, VA. For examples of the SIGINT collected from Aideed's militia, see U.S. Army Intelligence and Security Command, *Annual Command History, U.S. Army Intelligence and Security Command (INSCOM): Fiscal Year 1993*, 1994, p. 35, INSCOM FOIA; trial transcript, April 23, 2001, in 98 Cr. 1028, *United States of America v. Usama bin Laden et al.*, pp. 4458–59, U.S. District Court for the Southern District of New York. For Travis Trophy award, see press release, "1st Radio Battalion Wins NSA's Director's Trophy for 1993," Headquarters U.S. Marine

Corps, Division of Public Affairs, May 4, 1994; "Honoring the Best of the Best," *NSA Newsletter*, July 1994, p. 3, NSA FOIA.

39. U.S. Army Intelligence and Security Command, *Annual Command History, U.S. Army Intelligence and Security Command (INSCOM): Fiscal Year 1994*, 1995, p. 32, INSCOM FOIA; Air Intelligence Agency, *History of the Air Intelligence Agency: 1 January–31 December 1994*, vol. 1, pp. 30–31, AIA FOIA; Lt. Commander Darren Sawyer, USN, "JTF JIC Operations: Critical Success Factors," *Military Intelligence Professional Bulletin*, April–June 1995, p. 11; "704th MI Brigade," *Military Intelligence Professional Bulletin*, April–June 1996; "23rd IS Thrives in Joint Environment," *Spokesman*, October 1995, p. 20, AIA FOIA; Lt. Col. Bob Butler, "23rd IS Inactivation Ceremony," *Spokesman*, August 1996, p. 5, AIA FOIA; George J. Church, "Destination Haiti," *Newsweek*, September 26, 1994, p. 23; Scott Shane and Tom Bowman, "America's Fortress of Spies," *Baltimore Sun*, December 3, 1995.

40. CALL, *Operation Uphold Democracy Initial Impressions: Haiti D-20 to D+40*, vol. 1, December 1994, p. 93; CALL, *Operation Uphold Democracy Initial Impressions: Haiti D-20 to D+40*, vol. 2, April 1995, p. 175, both in the library of CALL, Fort Leavenworth, KS. See also 2nd Lt. Tania Chacho, "XVII Airborne CMISE Support in Haiti," *Military Intelligence Professional Bulletin*, April–June 1995, pp. 14–17.

41. "Yugoslavia: Army Fails to Ease Tension," *National Intelligence Daily*, April 2, 1991, p. 9, CIA Electronic FOIA Reading Room, Document No. 0000372387, http://www.foia.cia.gov. Zimmermann quote from oral history, *Interview with Warren Zimmermann*, December 10, 1996, Foreign Affairs Oral History Collection, Association for Diplomatic Studies and Training, Library of Congress, Washington, DC. For Zimmermann's account of his time in Belgrade, see Warren Zimmermann, "The Last Ambassador: A Memoir of the Collapse of Yugoslavia," *Foreign Affairs*, March/April 1995, pp. 2–21; Warren Zimmermann, *Origins of a Catastrophe: Yugoslavia and Its Destroyers—America's Last Ambassador Tells What Happened and Why* (New York: Crown, 1996).

42. Confidential interview. See message, DCI Interagency Balkan Task Force to members, *Task Force Information*, December 29, 1992, CIA Electronic FOIA Reading Room, http://www.foia.cia.gov; Major William P. Clappin, USA, *Moving Signals Intelligence from National Systems to Army Warfighters at Corps and Division* (Fort Leavenworth, KS: U.S. Army Command and General Staff College, June 5, 1998), p. 34. For SIGINT targeting of Bosnian Serb air defense systems, see Tim Ripley, "Operation Deny Flight," *World Air Power Journal*, vol. 16 (Spring 1994): pp. 19–20; Dylan Eklund, "The Reconnaissance Squadron," *Air World International*, November 1995, p. 36; Chris Pocock, "U-2: The Second Generation," *World Air Power Journal*, vol. 28 (Spring 1997): p. 94.

43. Urban, *UK Eyes Alpha*, p. 216; Tim Ripley, *Operation Deliberate Force* (Lancaster, U.K.: Center for Defence and International Security Studies, 1999), p. 64; Paul Quinn-Judge, "Serbs Called Low on Fuel, Options," *Boston Globe*, June 1, 1995, p. 1; Karsten Prager, "Message from Serbia," *Time*, July 17, 1995.

44. Walter Pincus, "U.S. Sought Other Bosnia Arms Sources," *Washington Post*, April 26, 1996; James Risen, "Iran Paid Bosnian Leader, CIA Says," *Los Angeles Times*, December 31, 1996.

45. Robert C. Owens, Col., USAF, *Deliberate Force: A Case Study in Effective Air Campaigning* (Maxwell Air Force Base, AL: School of Advanced Airpower Studies, 1988), pp. 8-14–8-16; Fleet Air Reconnaissance Squadron Six, *Command History Fleet Air Reconnaissance Squadron Six for CY 1995*, enclosure 1, 1996, p. 3, Navy FOIA; "Operation Deliberate Force," *World Air Power Journal*, vol. 24 (Spring 1996): pp. 24, 28.

46. Office of the Under Secretary of Defense for Acquisition and Technology, *Report of the Defense Science Board Task Force on Improved Application of Intelligence to the Battlefield: May–July 1996*, July

1996, p. 49, DoD FOIA; Clappin, *Moving Signals Intelligence*, p. 34; Major Kathleen A. Gavle, USA, *Division Intelligence Requirements for Sustained Peace Enforcement Operations* (Fort Leavenworth, KS: School of Advanced Military Studies, U.S. Army Command and General Staff College, 2000), pp. 16–17. For a few examples of SIGINT success stories in the post–Dayton Peace Accords period, see Rick Atkinson, "GIs Signal Bosnians: Yes, We're Listening," *Washington Post*, March 18, 1996; Rick Atkinson, "Warriors Without a War," *Washington Post*, April 14, 1996.

47. Seymour M. Hersh, *Chain of Command: The Road from 9/11 to Abu Ghraib* (New York: Harper Collins Publishers, 2004), pp. 324–30.

48. John M. Goshko, "Transcripts Show Joking Cuban Pilots," *Washington Post*, February 28, 1996; Barbara Crossette, "U.S. Says Cubans Knew They Fired on Civilian Planes," *New York Times*, February 28, 1996; Mabell Dieppa, "Basulto: U.S. Conspired with Cuba," *Miami Herald*, January 18, 1997. For intelligence coverage of the Cuban reaction to the shootdown incident, see "Cuba: Casting Shootdown as Bilateral Issue," *National Intelligence Daily*, February 27, 1996, CIA Electronic FOIA Reading Room, Document No. 0000957791, http://www.foia.cia.gov; "Cuba: Handling Aftermath of Shootdown," *National Intelligence Daily*, February 29, 1996, CIA Electronic FOIA Reading Room, Document No. 0000957792, http://www.foia.cia.gov; "Cuba: Behind the Shootdown," *National Intelligence Daily*, March 2, 1996, CIA Electronic FOIA Reading Room, Document No. 0000957793, http://www.foia.cia.gov.

49. For radio scanner usage in Haiti, see CALL, *Operation Uphold Democracy Initial Impressions: Haiti D-20 to D+40*, December 1994, vol. 1, p. 93; CALL, *Operation Uphold Democracy Initial Impressions: Haiti D-20 to D+40*, April 1995, vol. 2, p. 175, both in the library of CALL, Fort Leavenworth, KS. For Bosnia, see Larry K. Wentz, ed., *Lessons from Bosnia: The IFOR Experience* (Washington, DC: National Strategic Studies Institute, 1997), p. 105.

50. This conclusion is drawn from a review of a large number of declassified "lessons learned" reports currently on file at CALL, in Fort Leavenworth, KS, as well as unclassified papers written by army intelligence officers for the U.S. Army Command and Staff College at Fort Leavenworth. The most incisive of these studies is David W. Becker, *Coming in from the Cold War: Defense Humint Services Support to Military Operations Other than War* (Fort Leavenworth, KS: U.S. Army Command and General Staff College, 2000).

51. Confidential interviews; Alfred Monteiro, Jr., "Mustering the Force: Cryptologic Support to Military Operations," *Defense Intelligence Journal*, vol. 4, no. 2 (Fall 1995): pp. 75–76; General Accounting Office, NSIAD-96-6, *Personnel Practices at CIA, NSA and DIA Compared with Those of Other Agencies*, March 1996, p. 5.

52. Confidential interviews.

53. Defense Department, Office of the Inspector General, Report No. 96-03, *Final Report on the Verification Inspection of the National Security Agency*, February 13, 1996, p. 2, DOD FOIA.

54. U.S. House of Representatives, Permanent Select Committee on Intelligence, *IC21: Intelligence Community in the 21st Century*, 104th Congress, 1st session, 1996, pp. 120–21; Commission on the Roles and Capabilities of the United States Intelligence Community, *Preparing for the 21st Century: An Appraisal of U.S. Intelligence* (Washington, DC: GPO, 1996), p. 125. "Bite us in the ass" quote from confidential interview.

55. Confidential interviews.

56. Minihan background from USAF biography, Lt. General Kenneth A. Minihan, U.S. Air Force, Office of Public Affairs, September 1995; "Agency Welcomes New Director, Lt. General Kenneth A. Minihan," *NSA Newsletter*, April 1996, p. 2, NSA FOIA; R. Jeffrey Smith, "Military Men Named to Top Intelligence Posts," *Washington Post*, January 25, 1996; Tom Bowman, "Air Force General to Head NSA," *Baltimore Sun*, January 25, 1996; "Minihan Biography," *Spokesman*, June 1993, p. 9, AIA FOIA.

57. NSA OH-1999-21, oral history, *Interview with Lt. General Kenneth A. Minihan, USAF (Ret.)*, March 8, 1999, p. 1, NSA FOIA.

58. George Tenet, *At the Center of the Storm: My Years at the CIA* (New York: HarperCollins Publishers, 2007), p. 108.

59. Minihan's "pitch" for more money is contained in Lt. General Ken Minihan, USAF, DIR-540, *NSA/CSS Position Report*, November 9, 1998, NSA FOIA.

60. U.S. House of Representatives, Permanent Select Committee on Intelligence, Report 105-508, *Intelligence Authorization Act for Fiscal Year 1999*, 105th Congress, 2nd session, May 5, 1998, pp. 9–11; Walter Pincus, "Panel Ties NSA Funds to Changes at Agency," *Washington Post*, May 7, 1998; interview with John Millis.

61. NSA/CSS, "National Cryptologic Strategy for the 21st Century," June 1996, NSA FOIA; confidential interviews.

62. Confidential interview. Minihan's briefing is contained in Lt. General Ken Minihan, USAF, DIR-152, PowerPoint presentation, "NSA Integration with Military Operations," March 13, 1997, NSA FOIA.

63. Frank J. Cilluffo, Ronald A. Marks, and George C. Salmoiraghi, "The Use and Limits of U.S. Intelligence," *Washington Quarterly*, vol. 25, no. 1 (Winter 2002): p. 62.

64. Bill Gertz, "Bin Laden's Several Links to Terrorist Units Known," *Washington Times*, August 23, 1998. See also Bill Gertz, *Breakdown: How America's Intelligence Failures Led to September 11* (Washington, DC: Regnery Publishing, 2002), pp. 7, 9. The Gertz 1998 article specifically cites NSA SIGINT intercepts for the intelligence about these phone calls. The 2002 book does not. For Alexandria, VA, indictment, see FBI, press release and attached indictment, June 21, 2001, http://www.fbi.gov/pressrel/pressrel01/khobar.htm.

65. Confidential interviews.

66. Trial transcript, May 1, 2001, in 98 Cr. 1028, *United States of America v. Usama bin Laden et al.*, pp. 5287–92, U.S. District Court for the Southern District of New York; Nick Fielding and Dipesh Gadhery, "The Next Target: Britain?," *Sunday Times*, March 24, 2002. See also government exhibits 48 and 321, attached to trial transcript, April 4, 2001, in *United States of America v. Usama bin Laden et al.*

67. Anonymous [Michael Scheuer], "How *Not* to Catch a Terrorist," *Atlantic Monthly*, December 2004, p. 50.

68. Confidential interviews; DCI Counterterrorist Center, *Bin Laden Preparing to Hijack US Aircraft and Other Attacks*, December 4, 1998, CIA Electronic FOIA Reading Room, Document No. 0001110635, http://www.foia.cia.gov; Walter Pincus and Vernon Loeb, "CIA Blocked Two Attacks Last Year," *Washington Post*, August 11, 1998; "Islam Rising," *Atlantic Monthly*, February 17, 1999, http:www.theatlantic.com/unbound/bookauth/ba990217.htm; "Terrorism Directed at America," ERRI Daily Intelligence Report, February 24, 1999, http://www.emergency.com/1999/bnldn-pg.htm; Walter Pincus, "CIA Touts Successes in Fighting Terrorism," *Washington Post*, November 1, 2002.

69. For NSA designating al Qaeda its top target in the aftermath of the East Africa bombings, see U.S. Senate, Report No. 107-351, and U.S. House of Representatives, Report No. 107-792, report of the U.S. Senate Select Committee in Intelligence and U.S. House Permanent Select Committee on Intelligence, *Joint Inquiry into Intelligence Community Activities Before and After the Terrorist Attacks of September 11, 2001*, 107th Congress, 2nd session, December 2002 (declassified and released in July 2003), p. 377. The 9/11 Commission identified a specific *Washington Times* article as having alerted bin Laden to the fact that NSA was monitoring his phone calls. The article in question was Martin Sieff, "Terrorist Is Driven by Hatred for U.S., Israel," *Washington Times*, August 21, 1998. See National Commission on Terrorist Attacks upon the United States, *The 9/11 Commission*

Report: Final Report of the National Commission on Terrorist Attacks upon the United States (New York: W. W. Norton, 2004), p. 127. The 9/11 Commission's assertion that it was this article that alerted bin Laden that his phone was being tapped is disputed, for which see Glenn Kessler, "File the Bin Laden Phone Leak Under 'Urban Myths'," *Washington Post*, December 22, 2005.

70. Vernon Loeb, "General Named to Head NSA," *Washington Post*, February 25, 1999; "DIRNSA's Desk" and "Agency Welcomes New Director Lieutenant General Michael V. Hayden," *NSA Newsletter*, May 1999, pp. 3–4, NSA FOIA. A very readable rendition of Hayden's days in the former Yugoslavia in the mid-1990s can be found in Michael V. Hayden, "Warfighters and Intelligence: One Team—One Fight," *Defense Intelligence Journal*, vol. 4, no. 2 (Fall 1995): pp. 17–30.

71. U.S. Naval Academy, PowerPoint presentation, "Information Warfare Information Operations," undated, http://prodevweb.prodev.usna.edu/SeaNav/ns310/Web%20Documents/ppt%20docs/iwlesson.ppt.

72. Confidential interview.

73. NSA Scientific Advisory Board, Panel on Conventional Collection, *Report to the Director NSA/CSS*, March 9, 1999, NSA FOIA; NSA Scientific Advisory Board, Panel on Digital Network Intelligence (DNI) (formerly "C2C"), *Report to the Director*, June 28, 1999, NSA FOIA; memorandum, Taylor to DIRNSA, *Thoughts on Strategic Issues for the Institution*, April 9, 1999, p. 3. The author is grateful to Dr. Jeffrey T. Richelson for making available a copy of this document.

74. NSA/CSS, New Enterprise Team (NETeam) recommendations, *The Director's Work Plan for Change*, October 1, 1999, NSA FOIA; NSA/CSS, external team report, *A Management Review for the Director, NSA*, October 22, 1999, NSA FOIA.

75. DIRgram-00, "100 Days of Change," November 10, 1999; DIRgram-01, "Change, Candor, and Honesty," November 15, 1999; DIRgram-02; "Our New Executive Leadership Team," November 16, 1999; DIRgram-05, "Expanded Role for Our Executive Director," November 19, 1999; DIRgram-06, "Deputy Chief Central Security Service," November 22, 1999; DIRgram-07, "Getting Our Financial House In Order," November 23, 1999; DIRgram-08, "Bringing In Outside Help," November 24, 1999; DIRgram-11, "Major Dollar Decisions," December 1, 1999; DIRgram-28, "Resuming the Journey," January 3, 2000, all NSA FOIA; NSA/CSS, *Transition 2001*, December 2000, p. 19. The author is grateful to Dr. Jeffrey T. Richelson for making a copy of this document available. Hayden announcement quote from "DIRNSA's Desk," *NSA Newsletter*, January 2000, p. 3, NSA FOIA.

76. Seymour M. Hersh, "The Intelligence Gap: How the Digital Age Left Our Spies out in the Cold," *New Yorker*, December 6, 1999.

77. Diane Mezzanotte, *Infocentricity and Beyond: How the Intelligence Community Can Survive the Challenge of Emerging Technologies, Shrinking Budgets, and Growing Suspicions* (Newport, RI: Naval War College, 2000), p. 2.

78. NSA/CSS, *Transition 2001*, December 2000, p. 33. See also John McWethy, "Major Failure: NSA Confirms Serious Computer Problem," ABC News, January 29, 2000; Walter Pincus, "NSA System Inoperative for Four Days," *Washington Post*, January 30, 2000; Walter Pincus, "NSA System Crash Raises Hill Worries," *Washington Post*, February 2, 2000; Laura Sullivan, "Computer Failure at NSA Irks Intelligence Panels," *Baltimore Sun*, February 2, 2000.

79. For the widespread practice by Yemeni tribesmen of taking hostages in order to obtain political or economic concessions from the Yemeni government, see Director of Central Intelligence, National Intelligence Estimate 94-33/11, *Global Humanitarian Emergencies, 1995*, vol. 2, December 1994, p. 16, CIA Electronic FOIA Reading Room, Document No. 0000619031, http://www.foia.cia.gov.

80. Details of al-Hada's background from confidential interviews with U.S. and Yemeni intelligence officials.

81. Government exhibits 48 and 321, attached to trial transcript, April 4, 2001, in 98 Cr. 1028, *United States of America v. Usama bin Laden et al.*, U.S. District Court for the Southern District of New York. See also Fielding and Gadhery, "The Next Target: Britain?"; Rohan Gunaratna, *Inside Al Qaeda: Global Network of Terror* (New York: Berkley Books, 2003), p. 188.

82. Al-'Owhali was extradited to the United States to stand trial for murder. In 2001, he and three other defendants were convicted of murder and sentenced to life in prison without parole. He is currently serving his life sentence at the ADX Florence Supermax prison.

83. For use of the phrase "suspected terrorist facility in the Middle East," see U.S. Senate, Report No. 107-351, and U.S. House of Representatives, Report No. 107-792, report of the U.S. Senate Select Committee on Intelligence and U.S. House Permanent Select Committee on Intelligence, *Joint Inquiry into Intelligence Community Activities Before and After the Terrorist Attacks of September 11, 2001*, 107th Congress, 2nd session, December 2002 (declassified and released in July 2003), pp. 155–57. For general examination of the role played by al-Hada, see Michael Isikoff and Daniel Klaidman, "The Hijackers We Let Escape," *Newsweek*, June 10, 2002, p. 6.

84. U.S. Senate, Report No. 107-351, and U.S. House of Representatives, Report No. 107-792, report of the U.S. Senate Select Committee on Intelligence and U.S. House Permanent Select Committee on Intelligence, *Joint Inquiry into Intelligence Community Activities Before and After the Terrorist Attacks of September 11, 2001*, 107th Congress, 2nd session, December 2002 (declassified and released in July 2003), p. 11.

85. "Citing Threats, Britain Joins U.S. in Closing Embassies in Africa," CNN, June 25, 1999; David Phinney, "Fund-Raising for Terrorism," ABC News, July 9, 1999; John McWethy, "U.S. Tries to Get Bin Laden," ABC News, July 9, 1999; Barbara Starr, "Bin Laden's Plans," ABC News, July 16, 1999.

86. U.S. Senate, Report No. 107-351, and U.S. House of Representatives, report No. 107-792, report of the U.S. Senate Select Committee on Intelligence and U.S. House Permanent Select Committee on Intelligence, *Joint Inquiry into Intelligence Community Activities Before and After the Terrorist Attacks of September 11, 2001*, 107th Congress, 2nd session, December 2002 (declassified and released in July 2003), p. 11; National Commission, pp. 156–57.

87. U.S. Senate, Report No. 107-351, and U.S. House of Representatives, Report No. 107-792, report of the U.S. Senate Select Committee on Intelligence and U.S. House Permanent Select Committee on Intelligence, *Joint Inquiry into Intelligence Community Activities Before and After the Terrorist Attacks of September 11, 2001*, 107th Congress, 2nd session, December 2002 (declassified and released in July 2003), pp. 12, 143–44; 9/11 Commission, *9/11 Commission Report*, pp. 181, 353.

88. 9/11 Commission, *9/11 Commission Report*, pp. 215–18.

89. Justice Department, Office of the Inspector General, *Special Report: A Review of the FBI's Handling of Intelligence Information Related to the September 11 Attacks*, chap. 5, part B, "Hazmi and Mihdhar in San Diego," sec. 3, Hazmi and Mihdhar's Communications, November 2004 (released Jan. 2006); U.S. Senate, Report No. 107-351, and U.S. House of Representatives, Report No. 107-792, report of the U.S. Senate Select Committee on Intelligence and U.S. House Permanent Select Committee on Intelligence, *Joint Inquiry into Intelligence Community Activities Before and After the Terrorist Attacks of September 11, 2001*, 107th Congress, 2nd session, December 2002 (declassified and released in July 2003), pp. 16–17, 157.

90. U.S. Senate, Report No. 107-351, and U.S. House of Representatives, Report No. 107-792, report of the U.S. Senate Select Committee on Intelligence and U.S. House Permanent Select Committee on Intelligence, *Joint Inquiry into Intelligence Community Activities Before and After the Terrorist Attacks of September 11, 2001*, 107th Congress, 2nd session, December 2002 (declassified and released in July 2003), pp. 135, 157; 9/11 Commission, *9/11 Commission Report*, p. 222.

91. Bill Gertz, "NSA's Warning Arrived Too Late to Save the Cole," *Washington Times*, October 25, 2000.

12: SNATCHING DEFEAT FROM THE JAWS OF VICTORY

1. Dr. David A. Hatch, *Presidential Transition 2001: NSA Briefs a New Administration* (Fort Meade, MD: Center for Cryptologic History, 2004), NSA FOIA. The author is grateful to Dr. Jeffrey T. Richelson for making a copy of this report available.

2. NSA analysts quote from Joint Inquiry Staff, House Permanent Select Committee on Intelligence and Senate Permanent Select Committee on Intelligence, Eleanor Hill, Staff Director, *Joint Inquiry Staff Statement: Hearing on the Intelligence Community's Response to Past Terrorist Attacks Against the United States from February 1993 to September 2001*, October 8, 2002. Hayden comment from "Statement for the Record by Lt. General Michael V. Hayden, USAF, Director NSA/CSS Before the Joint Inquiry of the Senate Select Committee on Intelligence and the House Permanent Select Committee on Intelligence," October 17, 2002.

3. U.S. Senate, Report No. 107-351, and U.S. House of Representatives, Report No. 107-792, report of the U.S. Senate Select Committee on Intelligence and U.S. House Permanent Select Committee on Intelligence, *Joint Inquiry into Intelligence Community Activities Before and After the Terrorist Attacks of September 11, 2001*, 107th Congress, 2nd session, December 2002 (declassified and released in July 2003), p. 8; James Risen and Stephen Engelberg, "Failure to Heed Signs of Change in Terror Goals," *New York Times*, October 14, 2001.

4. Joint Inquiry Staff, House Permanent Select Committee on Intelligence and Senate Permanent Select Committee on Intelligence, Eleanor Hill, Staff Director, Joint Inquiry Staff, *Joint Inquiry Staff Statement*, part 1, September 18, 2002, p. 20; "Statement for the Record by Lt. General Michael V. Hayden, USAF, Director NSA/CSS Before the Joint Inquiry of the Senate Select Committee on Intelligence and the House Permanent Select Committee on Intelligence," October 17, 2002, p. 4; U.S. Senate, Report No. 107-351, and U.S. House of Representatives, Report No. 107-792, report of the U.S. Senate Select Committee on Intelligence and U.S. House Permanent Select Committee on Intelligence, *Joint Inquiry into Intelligence Community Activities Before and After the Terrorist Attacks of September 11, 2001*, 107th Congress, 2nd session, December 2002 (declassified and released in July 2003), pp. 7, 203. See also Bob Woodward, *State of Denial: Bush at War, part 3* (New York: Simon and Schuster, 2006), p. 50; James Risen, "In Hindsight, CIA Sees Flaws That Hindered Efforts on Terrorism," *New York Times*, October 7, 2001.

5. Mary Dejevsky, "US Forces on High Alert After Threat of Attack," *Independent*, June 23, 2001; Walter Pincus, "CIA Touts Successes in Fighting Terrorism," *Washington Post*, November 1, 2002.

6. U.S. Senate, Report No. 107-351, and U.S. House of Representatives, Report No. 107-792, report of the U.S. Senate Select Committee on Intelligence and U.S. House Permanent Select Committee on Intelligence, *Joint Inquiry into Intelligence Community Activities Before and After the Terrorist Attacks of September 11, 2001*, 107th Congress, 2nd session, December 2002 (declassified and released in July 2003), p. 7; National Commission on Terrorist Attacks upon the United States, *The 9/11 Commission Report: Final Report of the National Commission on Terrorist Attacks upon the United States* (New York: W. W. Norton, 2004), p. 257; Woodward, *State of Denial*, p. 50.

7. Woodward, *State of Denial*, pp. 50–51; confidential interviews.

8. U.S. Senate, Report No. 107-351, and U.S. House of Representatives Report No. 107-792, report of the U.S. Senate Select Committee on Intelligence and U.S. House Permanent Select Committee on Intelligence, *Joint Inquiry into Intelligence Community Activities Before and After the Terrorist Attacks of September 11, 2001*, 107th Congress, 2nd session, December 2002 (declassified and released in July 2003), p. 36.

9. Joint Inquiry Staff, House Permanent Select Committee on Intelligence and Senate Permanent Select Committee on Intelligence, Eleanor Hill, Staff Director, *Joint Inquiry Staff Statement: Hearing on the Intelligence Community's Response to Past Terrorist Attacks Against the United States from February 1993 to September 2001*, October 8, 2002; 9/11 Commission, *9/11 Commission Report*, pp. 87–88.

10. Confidential interview with senior NSA official, 2003.

11. Woodward, *State of Denial*, p. 51; George Tenet, *At the Center of the Storm: My Years at the CIA* (New York: HarperCollins Publishers, 2007), p. 154; Pincus, "CIA Touts Successes."

12. Tenet, *At the Center*, p. 154.

13. "The Proof They Did Not Reveal," *Sunday Times*, October 7, 2001; "Early Warnings: Pre-Sept. 11 Cautions Went Unheeded," ABCNews, February 18, 2002.

14. Raymond Bonner and John Tagliabue, "Eavesdropping, U.S. Allies See New Terror Attack," *New York Times*, October 21, 2001; Neil A. Lewis and David Johnston, "Jubilant Calls on Sept. 11 Led to FBI Arrests," *New York Times*, October 28, 2001.

15. U.S. Senate, Report No. 107-351, and U.S. House of Representatives, Report No. 107-792, report of the U.S. Senate Select Committee on Intelligence and U.S. House Permanent Select Committee on Intelligence, *Joint Inquiry into Intelligence Community Activities Before and After the Terrorist Attacks of September 11, 2001*, 107th Congress, 2nd session, December 2002 (declassified and released in July 2003), p. 32.

16. The existence of these intercepts was first disclosed in Rowan Scarborough, "Intercepts Foretold of 'Big Attack,'" *Washington Times*, September 22, 2001. Details of these messages are contained in James Risen and David Johnston, "Agency Is Under Scrutiny for Overlooked Messages," *New York Times*, June 20, 2002; Walter Pincus and Dana Priest, "NSA Intercepts on Eve of 9/11 Sent a Warning," *Washington Post*, June 20, 2002; Scott Shane and Ariel Sabar, "Coded Warnings Became Clear Only in Light of Sept. 11 Attacks," *Baltimore Sun*, June 20, 2002.

17. For 22,000 NSA employees, see Advanced Infrastructure Management Technologies (AIMTech) report, *Integrated Solid Waste Management Plan: Fort George G. Meade, Maryland*, January 2002, p. 29. The report reveals that 44 percent of the 50,075 persons working at Fort Meade (i.e., 22,000 personnel) worked for NSA. The tightened security restrictions at Fort Meade were publicly announced on August 15, 2001, for which see Steve Vogel, "Region's Army Posts to Restrict Public Access," *Washington Post*, August 15, 2001.

18. The size of the NSA Campus and number of buildings from "Keeping NSA Clean," *NSA Newsletter*, June 1994, p. 8; "Drawing Down for the Future: NSA Consolidates Its Resources," *NSA Newsletter*, August 1994, pp. 8–9; "Facilities Maintenance: A Look at Building Management," *NSA Newsletter*, February 1995, p. 9, all NSA FOIA. The size of NSA's security force from "Protective Services Celebrates 10th Anniversary," *NSA Newsletter*, October 1996, p. 8, NSA FOIA. "Largest parking lot in the world" from Gary W. O'Shaughnessy, "The Structure and Missions of Air Force Intelligence Command," p. 50, Seminar on Intelligence, Command and Control, Center for Information Policy Research, Harvard University, August 1994.

19. 1st Lt. Breton Lewellen, "Medina Regional SIGINT Operations Center Strengthens Joint Missions," *Spokesman*, February 1999, p. 8, AIA FOIA.

20. Confidential interviews.

21. Tom Pelton, "Terrorism Strikes America: Baltimore Travelers Get Left in the Lurch," *Baltimore Sun*, September 12, 2001; Col. Michael J. Stewart, "Community Urged to Be Patient, Strengthen Resolve," *Soundoff*, September 20, 2001.

22. General Michael V. Hayden, Deputy Director of National Intelligence, address to the National Press Club, "What American Intelligence and Especially the NSA Have Been Doing to Defend the Nation," January 23, 2006; General Michael V. Hayden, Director of the Central Intelligence

Agency, address at the Duquesne University Commencement Ceremony, May 4, 2007, Pittsburgh, PA.

23. The casualties included more than 2,600 dead in the World Trade Center, 125 in the Pentagon, and the 246 passengers and crew members of the four commercial aircraft.

24. Stephanie Desmon, "Frightened Parents, Confusion Prompt Schools to Close Early," *Baltimore Sun*, September 12, 2001; confidential interviews with NSA staff members.

25. Confidential interview. For thirty analysts and reporters at NSOC, see Bob Woodward, *Plan of Attack* (New York: Simon and Schuster, 2004), p. 215.

26. Confidential interview.

27. A biography for Gaches, who since February 2006 has held the position of assistant administrator for intelligence and analysis at the Transportation Security Administration, can be found at http://www.tsa.gov/who_we_are/people/bios/bill_gaches_bio.shtm.

28. "Statement for the Record by Lt. General Michael V. Hayden, USAF, Director NSA/CSS Before the Joint Inquiry of the Senate Select Committee on Intelligence and the House Permanent Select Committee on Intelligence," October 17, 2002, p. 2.

29. Tyler Drumheller, *On the Brink* (New York: Carroll and Graf Publishers, 2006), pp. 36–37.

30. David Martin, "Plans for Iraq Attack Began on 9/11," CBS News, September 4, 2002, http://www.cbsnews.com/stories/2002/09/04/september11/main520830.shtml.

31. 9/11 Commission, *9/11 Commission Report*, pp. 331–32.

32. Sharon Gaudin, "The Terrorist Network," *Network World*, November 26, 2001; Paul Kaihla, "Weapons of the Secret War," *Business 2.0 Magazine*, November 2001; "Taliban Outlaws Net in Afghanistan," Reuters, July 17, 2001; a confidential interview.

33. For general state of NSA's capabilities against Afghanistan, confidential interviews. For lack of linguists at NSA who could speak the languages spoken in Afghanistan, see U.S. Senate, Report No. 107-351, and U.S. House of Representatives Report No. 107-792, report of the U.S. Senate Select Committee on Intelligence and U.S. House Permanent Select Committee on Intelligence, *Joint Inquiry into Intelligence Community Activities Before and After the Terrorist Attacks of September 11, 2001*, 107th Congress, 2nd session, December 2002 (declassified and released in July 2003), p. 336.

34. Confidential interview with former CIA official. See also Steve Coll, "Flawed Ally Was Hunt's Best Hope," *Washington Post*, February 23, 2004.

35. Stephen P. Perkins, "Projecting Intelligence, Surveillance, and Reconnaissance in Support of the Interim Brigade Combat Team," in Williamson Murray, ed., *Army Transformation: A View from the Army War College* (Carlisle, PA: U.S. Army War College, 2001), p. 290; John F. Berry, "The 513th Military Intelligence Brigade in Support of Operation Enduring Freedom," *Military Intelligence Professional Bulletin*, April–June 2002, p. 4; Major Michael C. Kasales, U.S. Army, "The Reconnaissance Squadron and ISR Operations," *Military Review*, May–June 2002, pp. 53–56.

36. Colonel Brian L. Tarbet, Utah ARNG, and Lt. Colonel Ralph R. Steinke, USA, "Linguists in the Army: Paradise Lost or Paradise Regained?," *Military Intelligence Professional Bulletin*, October–December 1999, p. 6. For the 50 percent shortfall of Arabic linguists, see U.S. General Accounting Office, GAO-02-375, *Foreign Languages: Human Capital Approach Needed to Correct Staffing and Proficiency Shortfalls*, January 2002, p. 7.

37. Lt. Colonel Lisa C. Bennett, USA, *Increasing Intelligence Support to the Long War* (Carlisle Barracks, PA: U.S. Army War College, 2007), pp. 3–4.

38. Harold E. Raugh, Jr., "The Origins of the Transformation of the Defense Language Program," *Applied Language Learning*, vol. 16, no. 2 (2006): pp. 3–5; PowerPoint presentation, "98G Cryptologic Linguist Locations by Language," 2002. This unclassified document, which formerly resided on the Web site of the U.S. Army's Personnel Command, has since been removed.

39. Confidential interview. For Fremont serving as a recruiting ground for Afghan language teachers for the U.S. Army, see Clifford F. Porter, *Asymmetrical Warfare, Transformation, and Foreign Language Capability* (Fort Leavenworth, KS: Combat Studies Institute Press, 2003), p. 11.

40. Berry, "513th Military Intelligence Brigade," p. 4. For NSA teams leaving from BWI airport for the Middle East, see Laura Sullivan, "National Security Agency Retreats into Secrecy Shell," *Baltimore Sun*, November 3, 2001.

41. Confidential interviews.

42. Confidential interview.

43. Benjamin S. Lambeth, *Air Power Against Terror: America's Conduct of Operation Enduring Freedom* (Santa Monica, CA: Rand Corporation, 2005), p. xvi.

44. "Air Raid Cuts Afghan Capital Telephone Network," Reuters, October 14, 2001; Rahimullah Yusufzai, "Taliban Command Structure Crumbles," *News: Jang*, December 3, 2001; confidential interview.

45. Confidential interviews.

46. For importance of the Fifty-fifth Brigade, see Ali A. Jalali, "Afghanistan: The Anatomy of an Ongoing Conflict," *Parameters*, vol. 31, no. 1 (Spring 2001): p. 89; "Pentagon Sets Sights on Taliban's Elite Brigade 55," AFP, October 15, 2001; Rory McCarthy, Helen Carter, and Richard Norton-Taylor, "The Elite Force Who Are Ready to Die," *U.K. Guardian*, October 27, 2001; Daniel Eisenberg, "Secrets of Brigade 055," *Time*, October 29, 2001; Romesh Ratnesar, "Into the Fray," *Time*, October 29, 2001.

47. Confidential interview.

48. *Unclassified Documents from Marine Task Force 58's Operations in Afghanistan: Forming: 27 October to 5 November 2001*, February 2002, http://www.strategypage.com/articles/tf58/forming.asp.

49. " 'No More Retreat,' Taleban Troops Told," BBC, November 13, 2001, http://news.bbc.co.uk/1/hi/world/south_asia/1654256.stm.; William Branigin, "Afghan Rebels Seize Control of Kabul," *Washington Post*, November 14, 2001; Jonathan Steele, "Stand and Fight, Fleeing Taliban Told," *U.K. Guardian*, November 14, 2001.

50. Vernon Loeb and Bradley Graham, "Special Forces Block Traffic in Search for bin Laden," *Washington Post*, November 15, 2001.

51. Confidential interviews. See also "Omar 'Disappears' as Taliban Surrender Ends," Reuters, December 7, 2001.

52. For SIGINT teams searching for bin Laden, see confidential interviews with former military intelligence officers; Michael Smith, *Killer Elite: The Inside Story of America's Most Secret Special Operations Team* (London: Weidenfeld & Nicolson, 2006), pp. 224–25.

53. Open source discussion of the mission and functions of Grey Fox can be found in Peter Beaumont, " 'Grey Fox' Closes in on Prize Scalp: Saddam," *U.K. Observer*, June 22, 2003; Rowan Scarborough, "Agencies United to Find Bin Laden," *Washington Times*, March 15, 2004. For mentions of the U.S. Army Security Coordination Detachment, see Defense Department, Under Secretary of Defense for Personnel and Readiness, *Defense Manpower Requirements Report for Fiscal Year 2006*, July 2005, p. 65; "USATST Recruiting Effort," *Fort Huachuca Scout*, September 19, 2002, p. 6.

54. Philip Smucker, "How bin Laden Got Away," *Christian Science Monitor*, March 4, 2002.

55. U.S. Special Operations Command, *U.S. Special Operations Command History: 1987–2007* (MacDill Air Force Base, FL: USSOCOM History Office, 2007), p. 94.

56. Charles H. Briscoe, Richard L. Kiper, James A. Schroeder, and Kalev I. Sepp, *U.S. Army Special Operations in Afghanistan* (Boulder, CO: Paladin Press, 2006), p. 213; U.S. Special Operations Command, *Special Operations Command History*, p. 93.

57. Briscoe, Kiper, Schroeder, and Sepp, *Army Special Operations*, pp. 214–15. The mission of the Green Beret SIGINT team from confidential interview.

58. Michael R. Gordon and Eric Schmitt, "U.S. Force May Search Tora Bora for bin Laden," *New York Times*, December 19, 2001.

59. Confidential interviews. See also Rory McCarthy, "Radio Picks Up Voice of bin Laden," *U.K. Observer*, December 16, 2001.

60. Barton Gellman and Thomas E. Ricks, "U.S. Concludes Bin Laden Escaped at Tora Bora Fight," *Washington Post*, April 17, 2002.

61. U.S. Special Operations Command, *Special Operations Command History*, p. 98. See also Peter Bergen, "War of Error: How Osama bin Laden Beat George W. Bush," *New Republic*, October 22, 2007.

62. Patrick Healy and Farah Stockman, "Taliban Flee Kandahar," *Boston Globe*, December 8, 2001.

63. Armando J. Ramirez, *From Bosnia to Baghdad: The Evolution of US Army Special Forces from 1995–2004* (Monterey, CA: Naval Postgraduate School, 2004), p. 65.

64. Tony Karon, "Why the Bad Guys Get Away in Afghanistan," *Time*, January 8, 2002.

65. Confidential interviews. See also James Risen and Dexter Filkins, "Qaeda Fighters Said to Return to Afghanistan," *New York Times*, September 10, 2002; Evan Thomas, "The Ongoing Hunt for Osama bin Laden," *Newsweek*, September 3, 2007.

66. Steve Vogel, "Rumsfeld Doubts Bin Laden Escaped," *Washington Post*, January 17, 2002.

67. Mark Mazzetti, "On the Ground: How Special Ops Forces Are Hunting al Qaeda," *U.S. News & World Report*, February 17, 2002.

68. Bergen, "War of Error."

13: A MOUNTAIN OUT OF A MOLEHILL

1. Bradley Graham, "Unfinished Business in Proxy War," *Washington Post*, January 6, 2002; Tony Karon, "Why the Bad Guys Get Away in Afghanistan," *Time*, January 8, 2002; Rory McCarthy, "Fighters Who Slipped Through the Net," *U.K. Guardian*, February 13, 2002; William R. Hawkins, "What Not to Learn from Afghanistan," *Parameters*, vol. 32, no. 2 (Summer 2002): p. 30.

2. Confidential interviews with NSA and U.S. military intelligence officials; Battalion Landing Team 3/6, 26th Marine Expeditionary Unit, *Command Chronology for Period 1 July 2001–28 February 2002*, sec. 2, March 1, 2002, p. 16, Marine Corps Historical Center, Quantico, VA. For confirmation by Defense Department officials that the U.S. military was continuing to detect Taliban usage of satellite telephones, see also Jim Garamone, "Central Command Can Call More Troops If Needed," American Forces Press Service, January 25, 2002. For resumption of Taliban attacks in southern Afghanistan, see "Afghan Fighters Seal Border Crossing," Associated Press, January 11, 2002; Richard Lacayo, "The Deadly Hunt," *Time*, January 14, 2002; Eric Schmitt, "U.S. Says Tribal Leaders Balk at Aiding Search for Taliban," *New York Times*, January 17, 2002; Tim McGirk, "Where Danger Lurks," *Time*, January 27, 2002; Philip Smucker, "After Tora Bora, US Hunts Alone," *Christian Science Monitor*, January 28, 2002.

3. Barton Gellman and Dafna Linzer, "Afghanistan, Iraq: Two Wars Collide," *Washington Post*, October 22, 2004. For withdrawal of the 513th Military Intelligence Brigade and its SIGINT units, see John F. Berry, "The 513th Military Intelligence Brigade in Support of Operation Enduring Freedom," *Military Intelligence Professional Bulletin*, April–June 2002; Spc. Leslie Pearson, "Longtime Reservist Recalls Two-Year Activation," *Mirage*, vol. 1, 4th Quarter ed. (2003): p. 17; "513th Military Intelligence Brigade," *Mirage*, vol. 1, 4th Quarter ed. (2003): p. 20; confidential interviews.

4. Sean Naylor, *Not a Good Day to Die: The Untold Story of Operation Anaconda* (New York: Berkley Books, 2005), pp. 41–42.

5. Naylor, *Not a Good Day*, p. 75; Rowan Scarborough, "Military Officers Criticize Rush to Use Ground Troops," *Washington Times*, March 7, 2002; Richard T. Cooper, Geoffrey Mohan, and Rone Tempest, "Fierce Fight in Afghan Valley Tests U.S. Soldiers and Strategy," *Los Angeles Times*, March 24, 2002; confidential interview.

6. The best single description of Operation Anaconda and its aftermath can be found in Naylor, *Not a Good Day*.

7. Bruce D. MacLachlan, Lt. Colonel, U.S. Marine Corps, *Operational Art in the Counter-Terror War in Afghanistan* (Newport, RI: Naval War College, 2002), p. 17; Stephen Biddle, *Afghanistan and the Future of Warfare: Implications for Army and Defense Policy* (Carlisle, PA: Strategic Studies Institute, November 2002), pp. 20, 31; oral history, *Interview with Major Jason Warner*, third interview, August 21, 2007, p. 8, Combat Studies Institute, Fort Leavenworth, KS.

8. Accounts of Operation Anaconda differ markedly as to whether the operation was a success or a failure. For a generally rosy assessment see Dr. Richard Kugler, *Operation Anaconda in Afghanistan: A Case Study of Adaptation in Battle* (Washington, DC: National Defense University, Center for Technology and National Security Policy, 2007). Critical assessments of U.S. military performance during Operation Anaconda can be found in Naylor, *Not a Good Day*; Bradley J. Armstrong, *Rebuilding Afghanistan: Counterinsurgency and Reconstruction in Operation Enduring Freedom* (Monterey, CA: U.S. Naval Postgraduate School, 2003), p. 7; Lt. Commander Todd Marzano, USN, *Criticisms Associated with Operation Anaconda: Can Long-Distance Leadership Be Effective?* (Newport, RI: Naval War College, October 23, 2006); Scarborough, "Military Officers Criticize Rush"; Elaine Grossman, "Was Operation Anaconda Ill-Fated from the Start? Army Analyst Blames Afghan Battle Failings on Bad Command Set-up," *Inside the Pentagon*, July 29, 2004, p. 1; Elaine Grossman, "Anaconda: Object Lesson in Poor Planning or Triumph of Improvisation?," *Inside the Pentagon*, August 12, 2004, p. 1.

9. "Prepared Statement of General Tommy R. Franks, Commander, U.S. Central Command Before the U.S. Senate Armed Services Committee," July 31, 2002, p. 6; General Tommy Franks (USA, Ret.), *American Soldier* (New York: Regan Books, 2004), p. 379.

10. Confidential interviews with U.S. Army officers involved in the operation. See also Paul Haven, "Top General in Afghanistan Says al-Qaida and Taliban Forces Are Trying to Regroup in East," Associated Press, March 20, 2002; Anthony Lloyd, "Marines Start Sub-Zero Hunt for al-Qaeda," *U.K. Times*, April 17, 2002; Rick Scavetta, "Military Interrogators in Afghanistan Use Detective Work in Mental Chess Game," *Stars and Stripes*, April 30, 2002.

11. Confidential interviews.

12. Ibid.

13. Karl Vick and Kamran Khan, "Raid Netted Top Al Qaeda Leader," *Washington Post*, April 2, 2002; Aftab Ahmad, "Osama in Faisalabad?," *The Nation* (Lahore ed.), April 8, 2002, FBIS-NEW-2002-0408; Ijaz Hashmat, "US Intercepted Satellite Phone Message That Led to Raid in Faisalabad," *Khabrain*, April 9, 2002, FBIS-NES-2002-0409.

14. Jonathan Fowler, "Al-Zarqawi Used Swiss Cell Phone," Associated Press, November 25, 2004.

15. Rory McCarthy and Julian Borger, "Secret Arrest of Leading al-Qaida Fugitive," *U.K. Guardian*, September 4, 2002.

16. Jason Burke, "Brutal Gun Battle That Crushed 9/11 Terrorists," *U.K. Observer*, September 15, 2002; Nick Fielding, "Phone Call Gave Away Al Qaida Hideout," *U.K. Sunday Times*, September 15, 2001; Rory McCarthy, "Investigators Question Key September 11 Suspect," *U.K. Guardian*, September 16, 2002; Nick Fielding, "War on Terror: Knocking on Al-Qaeda's Door," *U.K. Sunday Times*, September 22, 2002.

17. Confidential interview. See also James Risen and Eric Lichtblau, "Bush Lets U.S. Spy on Callers Without Courts," *New York Times*, December 16, 2005.

18. For killing of al-Harethi, see "U.S. Kills al-Qaeda Suspects in Yemen," Associated Press, November 5, 2002. For Hayden-Rumsfeld interchange, see Dana Priest and Ann Scott Tyson, "Bin Laden Trail 'Stone Cold,'" *Washington Post*, September 10, 2006.

19. Colum Lynch, "US Used UN to Spy on Iraq, Aides Say," *Boston Globe*, January 6, 1999; Barton Gellman, "Annan Suspicious of UNSCOM Probe," *Washington Post*, January 6, 1999; Bruce W. Nelan, "Bugging Saddam," *Time*, January 18, 1999; Seymour M. Hersh, "Saddam's Best Friend," *New Yorker*, April 5, 1999, pp. 32, 35; David Wise, "Fall Guy," *Washingtonian*, July 1999, pp. 42–43.

20. Charles Duelfer, Special Advisor to the Director of Central Intelligence, *Comprehensive Report of the Special Advisor to the DCI on Iraqi WMD*, vol. 1, chap. 2, September 30, 2004, pp. 108–09, CIA Electronic FOIA Reading Room, Document No. 0001156395, http://www.foia.cia.gov; Bill Gertz, "China Fortifying Iraq's Air-Defense System," *Washington Times*, February 20, 2001.

21. Charles Aldinger, "Western Warplanes Hit Iraqi Defenses," Reuters, August 8, 2001.

22. Mohammed Hayder Sadeq and Sabah al-Anbaki, "Cell Phone Service Is Spotty, But Reception Is Great," *USA Today*, March 3, 2005; Yaroslav Trofimov and Sarmad Ali, "Iraq's Cellphone Battle," *Wall Street Journal*, July 21, 2005.

23. Kevin M. Woods et al., *Iraqi Perspectives Project: A View of Operation Iraqi Freedom from Saddam Hussein's Senior Leadership* (Norfolk, VA: U.S. Joint Forces Command, 2006), p. 129.

24. Confidential interviews.

25. Joe Trento, "Pakistan & Iran's Scary Alliance," National Security News Service, August 15, 2003, http://www.storiesthatmatter.org/index.php?option'com_content&task'view&id'48&Itemid'29.

26. "Sanction Busting," *Newsweek*, December 31, 1990, p. 4. See also Director of Central Intelligence, *Annual Report on Intelligence Community Activities*, August 22, 1997, http://www.cia.gov.

27. Bill Gertz, "French Connection Armed Saddam," *Washington Times*, September 8, 2004.

28. Bill Gertz, *Betrayal* (Washington, DC: Regnery Publishing, 1999), p. 283.

29. Memorandum, *Intelligence and Analysis on Iraq: Issues for the Intelligence Community*, July 29, 2004, p. 5, CIA Electronic FOIA Reading Room, Document No. 0001245667, http://www.foia.cia.gov.; Commission on the Intelligence Capabilities of the United States Regarding Weapons of Mass Destruction, *Report to the President of the United States* (Washington, DC: GPO, March 31, 2005), p. 15. Woodward quote from Bob Woodward, *Plan of Attack* (New York: Simon and Schuster, 2004), p. 217.

30. Rowan Scarborough, "U.S. Rushed Post-Saddam Planning," *Washington Times*, September 3, 2003.

31. President George W. Bush "President's Remarks at the United Nations General Assembly," New York City, September 12, 2002, http://www.whitehouse.gov.

32. NIE 2002-16HC, *Iraq's Continuing Programs for Weapons of Mass Destruction*, October 2002, p. 7, CIA Electronic FOIA Reading Room, Document No. 0001075566, http://www.foia.cia.gov.

33. U.S. Senate, Select Committee on Intelligence, *Nomination of Lt. General Michael V. Hayden, USAF, to Be Principal Deputy Director of National Intelligence*, 109th Congress, 1st session, April 14, 2005, p. 17.

34. U.S. Senate, Select Committee on Intelligence, *Nomination of General Michael V. Hayden, USAF, to Be the Director of the Central Intelligence Agency*, 109th Congress, 2nd session, May 18, 2006, p. 103.

35. Confidential interviews.

36. U.S. Senate, Select Committee on Intelligence, *Report on the U.S. Intelligence Community's Prewar Intelligence Assessments on Iraq*, 108th Congress, 2nd session, July 7, 2004, p. 20; confidential interviews.

37. Colin L. Powell, "Remarks to the United Nations Security Council," New York City, February 5, 2003, http://www.state.gov/secretary/former/powell/remarks/2003/17300.htm.

38. U.S. Senate, Select Committee on Intelligence, *Report on the U.S. Intelligence Community's Prewar Intelligence Assessments on Iraq*, 108th Congress, 2nd session, July 7, 2004, p. 139; Charles Duelfer, Special Advisor to the Director of Central Intelligence, *Comprehensive Report of the Special Advisor to the DCI on Iraqi WMD*, vol. 1, Nuclear Section, September 30, 2004, p. 36, CIA Electronic FOIA Reading Room, Document No. 0001156442, http://www.foia.cia.gov.

39. U.S. Senate, Select Committee on Intelligence, *Report on the U.S. Intelligence Community's Prewar Intelligence Assessments on Iraq*, 108th Congress, 2nd session, July 7, 2004, p. 203; confidential interviews.

40. Confidential interviews.

41. Commission on the Intelligence Capabilities of the United States Regarding Weapons of Mass Destruction, *Report to the President of the United States* (Washington, DC: GPO, March 31, 2005), pp. 113, 130.

42. U.S. Senate, Select Committee on Intelligence, *Report on the U.S. Intelligence Community's Prewar Intelligence Assessments on Iraq*, 108th Congress, 2nd session, July 7, 2004, pp. 227–29; Charles Duelfer, Special Advisor to the Director of Central Intelligence, *Comprehensive Report of the Special Advisor to the DCI on Iraqi WMD*, vol. 2, September 30, 2004, pp. 49–50, CIA Electronic FOIA Reading Room, Document No. 0001156442, http://www.foia.cia.gov.

43. NIE 2002-16HC, *Iraq's Continuing Programs for Weapons of Mass Destruction*, October 2002, p. 7, CIA Electronic FOIA Reading Room, Document No. 0001075566, http://www.foia.cia.gov.

44. U.S. Senate, Select Committee on Intelligence, *Report on the U.S. Intelligence Community's Prewar Intelligence Assessments on Iraq*, 108th Congress, 2nd session, July 7, 2004, p. 139; U.S. Senate, Select Committee on Intelligence, *Report on Postwar Findings About Iraq's WMD Programs and Links to Terrorism and How They Compare with Prewar Assessments*, 109th Congress, 2nd session, September 8, 2006, p. 59. See also Dafna Linzer and John J. Lumpkin, "Experts Doubt U.S. Claim on Iraqi Drones," Associated Press, August 24, 2003; Bradley Graham, "Air Force Analysts Feel Vindicated on Iraqi Drones," *Washington Post*, September 26, 2003.

45. U.S. Senate, Select Committee on Intelligence, *Report on the U.S. Intelligence Community's Prewar Intelligence Assessments on Iraq*, 108th Congress, 2nd session, July 7, 2004, p. 219 and appendix B, p. 430; U.S. Senate, Select Committee on Intelligence, *Report on Postwar Findings About Iraq's WMD Programs and Links to Terrorism and How They Compare with Prewar Assessments*, 109th Congress, 2nd session, September 8, 2006, p. 58.

46. Confidential interviews. Hayden comment from U.S. Senate, Select Committee on Intelligence, *Nomination of General Michael V. Hayden, USAF, to Be the Director of the Central Intelligence Agency*, 109th Congress, 2nd session, May 18, 2006, pp. 110, 119.

47. Joe Trento, "The Price of Cooking the CIA Books," National Security News Service, June 2, 2003, http://www.storiesthatmatter.org/index.php?option=com_content&task=view&id=53& Itemid=29.

48. Transcript of interview of Hayden by C-SPAN's Brian Lamb, April 15, 2007, https://www.cia .gov/cia/public_affairs/press_release/2007/pr041707.htm.

49. Commission on the Intelligence Capabilities of the United States Regarding Weapons of Mass Destruction, *Report to the President of the United States* (Washington, DC: GPO, March 31, 2005), p. 157.

50. Confidential interview.

51. A transcript of Bush's "Axis of Evil" speech can be found at http://www.whitehouse.gov/news/ releases/2002/10/20021007-8.html.

52. Ibid.

53. Confidential interview.

54. U.S. Senate, Select Committee on Intelligence, *Nomination of General Michael V. Hayden, USAF, to Be the Director of the Central Intelligence Agency*, 109th Congress, 2nd session, May 18, 2006, p. 32; Senator Carl Levin, "Nomination of General Michael V. Hayden," *Congressional Record*, May 25, 2006 (Senate), pp. S5298–S5301; U.S. Senate, Select Committee on Intelligence, *Report on Postwar Findings About Iraq's WMD Programs and Links to Terrorism and How They Compare With Prewar Assessments*, 109th Congress, 2nd Session, September 8, 2006, pp. 86–87, 109.

55. Warren P. Strobel, Jonathan S. Landay, and John Walcott, "Dissent over Going to War Grows Among U.S. Government Officials," *Miami Herald*, October 7, 2002; Dana Milbank, "For Bush, Facts Are Malleable," *Washington Post*, October 22, 2002. For telephone intercepts, see Julian Borger, "White House Exaggerating Iraqi Threat," *U.K. Guardian*, October 9, 2002.

56. Woodward, *Plan of Attack*, p. 214.

57. Confidential interviews. For the twenty-nine-man section concentrating on Iraqi WMD, confidential interviews and Capt. Mark Choate, "Knowing Is Half the Battle," *INSCOM Journal*, vol. 26, no. 2 (2003 Almanac): p. 13.

58. Confidential interviews.

59. Michael Hirsh and Michael Isikoff, "No More Hide and Seek," *Newsweek*, February 10, 2003, p. 44.

60. Confidential interview.

61. Powell's presentation and accompanying graphics, including the Iraqi intercepts, can be found in "U.S. Secretary of State Colin Powell Addresses the U.N. Security Council," February 5, 2003, http://www.whitehouse.gov/news/releases/2003/02/20030205-1.html.

62. U.S. Senate, Select Committee on Intelligence, *Report on the U.S. Intelligence Community's Prewar Intelligence Assessments on Iraq*, 108th Congress, 2nd session, July 7, 2004, p. 429, appendix B.

63. U.S. Senate, Select Committee on Intelligence, *Report on the U.S. Intelligence Community's Prewar Intelligence Assessments on Iraq*, 108th Congress, July 7, 2004, p. 423, appendix A, and p. 429, appendix B.

64. See also Karen DeYoung and Walter Pincus, "U.S. Hedges on Finding Iraqi Weapons," *Washington Post*, May 29, 2003; Barton Gellman, "Iraq's Arsenal Was Only on Paper," *Washington Post*, January 7, 2004.

65. Dana Priest and Walter Pincus, "Bin Laden–Hussein Link Hazy," *Washington Post*, February 13, 2003.

66. Confidential interview with former State Department official.

67. Woods et al., *Iraqi Perspectives Project*, pp. 93–94.

68. Fowler, "Al-Zarqawi."

69. "Iraq Shuts Down Phone Network to Thwart CIA Eavesdropping," Associated Press, March 19, 2003.

70. Max Hastings, "The Iraq Intelligence Fiasco Exposes Us to Terrible Danger," *U.K. Guardian*, September 20, 2004.

71. Information concerning NSA's performance in the Iraqi WMD scandal was deleted in toto from the final report of the Senate intelligence committee on the U.S. intelligence community's performance prior to the invasion of Iraq, for which see U.S. Senate, Select Committee on Intelligence, *Report on the U.S. Intelligence Community's Prewar Intelligence Assessments on Iraq*, 108th Congress, 2nd session, July 7, 2004, pp. 264–65.

14: The Dark Victory

1. NSA/CSS, Office of the Director, "Director's Intent," February 11, 2003, partially declassified and on file at the National Security Archive, Washington, DC.

2. Bob Woodward, "The Foreign Policy Questions John Kerry Would Not Answer," *Manchester Union Leader*, October 26, 2004. For sixty thousand military and civilian personnel belonging to NSA, National Guard Bureau, *National Guard Assistant Program (NGAP) Position Description: Mobilization Assistant to the Deputy Chief, Central Security Service, National Security Agency*, September 1, 2003. This document has since been removed from the National Guard Bureau Web site, from which it was downloaded in 2003.

3. Confidential interview.

4. Director of Central Intelligence, *The 2003 Annual Report of the United States Intelligence Community*, July 2004, sec. Support to Operation Iraqi Freedom.

5. Confidential interview.

6. Capt. Mark Choate, "Knowing Is Half the Battle," *INSCOM Journal*, vol. 26, no. 2 (2003 Almanac): pp. 13–15.

7. Amatzia Baram, "The Republican Guard: Outgunned and Outnumbered, but They Never Surrender," *U.K. Guardian*, March 25, 2003.

8. For the order of battle of the Second Republican Guard Corps, see NIE 99-04, National Intelligence Council, *Iraqi Military Capabilities Through 2003*, April 1999, p. 4, CIA Electronic FOIA Reading Room, Document No. 0001261421, http://www.foia.cia.gov; Charles Duelfer, Special Advisor to the Director of Central Intelligence, *Comprehensive Report of the Special Advisor to the DCI on Iraqi WMD*, vol. 1, September 30, 2004, p. 94, CIA Electronic FOIA Reading Room, Document No. 0001156395, http://www.foia.cia.gov.

9. For Bad Aibling Station, see Choate, "Knowing," p. 20. For ten Iraqi divisions deployed in northern Iraq, see Stephen T. Hosmer, *Why the Iraqi Resistance to the Coalition Invasion Was So Weak* (Santa Monica, CA: Rand Corporation, 2007), p. 42.

10. Confidential interview.

11. Confidential interview.

12. Choate, "Knowing," p. 20. For the expulsion of the two Iraqi diplomats in New York, see John McWethy, "Iraq's Attack Network (Operation Imminent Horizon)," ABC News, March 5, 2003.

13. Confidential interviews. See also Ed Johnson, "Former Cabinet Member: British Intelligence Spied on Annan," Associated Press, February 26, 2004; Patrick E. Tyler, "Ex-Aide to Blair Says the British Spied on Annan," *New York Times*, February 27, 2004; Glenn Frankel, "Britain Accused of Spying on Annan Before Iraq War," *Washington Post*, February 27, 2004; Todd Richissin and Scott Shane, "West's Spies Listening in on U.N.'s Annan," *Baltimore Sun*, February 27, 2004.

14. Martin Bright, Ed Vulliamy, and Peter Beaumont, "Revealed: US Dirty Tricks to Win Vote on Iraq War," *U.K. Observer*, March 2, 2003.

15. Chaka Ferguson, "Woodward: Media Should Have Been More Critical of Iraq Intelligence," Associated Press, July 9, 2004.

16. Dafna Linzer, "IAEA Leader's Phone Tapped," *Washington Post*, December 12, 2004.

17. Scott R. Gourley, "MEU (SOC)," *Special Operations Technology*, vol. 2, issue 6, September 13, 2004, www.special-operations-technology.com/article.cfm?DocID=606.

18. Confidential interviews.

19. Confidential interviews. See also Kevin M. Woods et al., *Iraqi Perspectives Project: A View of Operation Iraqi Freedom from Saddam Hussein's Senior Leadership* (Norfolk, VA: U.S. Joint Forces Command, 2006), p. 103, http://handle.dtic.mil/100.2/ADA446305; Bradley Graham, "Republican Guard Troops Moved Nearer to Baghdad," *Washington Post*, February 28, 2003.

20. Michael R. Gordon and General Bernard E. Trainor, *Cobra II* (New York: Pantheon Books, 2006), p. 165.

21. "Iraq Shuts Down Phone Network to Thwart CIA Eavesdropping," Associated Press, March 19, 2003.

22. The description of the events leading up to the Dora Farms attack is drawn from Barton Gellman and Dana Priest, "CIA Had Fix on Hussein," *Washington Post*, March 20, 2003; Elisabeth Bumiller and David Johnston, "Surprise Strike at Outset Leaves Urgent Mystery: Who Was Hit?," *New York Times*, March 21, 2003; Bob Woodward, "Attack Was 48 Hours Old When It 'Began,'" *Washington Post*, March 23, 2003.

23. James Kitfield, "Army's Race to Baghdad Exposes Risks in Battle Plan," *National Journal*, March 28, 2003, p. 9.

24. Michael T. Mosely, "Operation Iraqi Freedom—by the Numbers," U.S. Central Command Air Force, April 30, 2003, p. 15, http://www.globalsecurity.org/military/library/report/2003/uscentaf_oif_report_30apr2003.pdf.

25. Confidential interview.

26. Tech. Sgt. Kristina Brown, "New Leadership Takes Over 70th IW," *Spokesman*, April 2004, AIA FOIA.

27. Gregg K. Kakesako, "Isle Marines Return from Iraq Conflict," *Honolulu Star-Bulletin*, June 10, 2003, http://starbulletin.com/2003/06/10/news/story4.html.

28. Gourley, "MEU (SOC)."

29. Confidential interview.

30. Confidential interviews.

31. Confidential interviews.

32. Woods et al., *Iraqi Perspectives Project*, p. 105.

33. Confidential interviews.

34. "14th Signal Regiment (Electronic Warfare) Operations in Southern Iraq," *The Rose and Laurel*, 2003, p. 104.

35. Confidential interview.

36. 3rd Infantry Division, *Operation Iraqi Freedom: 3rd Infantry Division (Mechanized) "Rock of the Marne" After Action Report*, Operational Overview Section, Battle for Tallil, March 21, 2003, final draft, 2003, Army FOIA.

37. Major Walker M. Field, USMC, "Marine Artillery in the Battle of An Nasiriyah," *Field Artillery*, November–December 2003, p. 29.

38. Oral history, *Interview with Major Steven Bower*, Combat Studies Institute, Fort Leavenworth, KS, October 30, 2006, p. 7; oral history, *Interview with Major Nicole Stanford*, Combat Studies Institute, Fort Leavenworth, KS, May 4, 2007, p. 7.

39. Julian Borger, "The Crucial Moment; US Must Defeat Elite Iraqi Troops," *U.K. Guardian*, March 25, 2003.

40. Confidential interview. For the importance placed on defeating the Medina Division by army planners, see Kitfield, "Army's Race to Baghdad."

41. Dana Priest and Walter Pincus, "Havens Offered to Defectors," *Washington Post*, March 22, 2003; Walter Pincus, "Evidence on Hussein Detailed," *Washington Post*, March 24, 2003; David E. Sanger, "Officials Fear Iraqis Plan to Use Gas," *New York Times*, March 25, 2003.

42. Corey Pein, "The Tech Fix," *Metro Spirit*, June 20, 2006, http://metrospirit.com.

43. Col. Gregory R. Fontenot, U.S. Army, Ret., *On Point: The United States Army in Operation Iraqi Freedom* (Fort Leavenworth, KS: Center for Army Lessons Learned, 2004), p. 89.

44. Sig Christenson, "Flight into Ambush," *San Antonio Express-News*, March 21, 2004, http://www.mysanantonio.com/news/military/stories/MYSA21.01A.Longbow_1_0321.7d24b3c.html.

45. Transcript, *Fifth Corps Commander Live Briefing from Baghdad*, May 7, 2003, http://www.de fenselink.mil/transcripts/transcript.aspx?transcriptid=2573.

46. For the Guardrail mission over the Karbala Gap, confidential interviews. For the artillery strike on the Medina Division, see Colonel Theodore J. Janosko and Lt. Colonel Robert G. Cheatam Jr., "The Sound of Thunder: VCA in Operation Iraqi Freedom," *Field Artillery Journal*, September–October 2003, p. 36.

47. Col. James Poss, "Intelligence Family Made NTI Successful," *Spokesman*, July 2003, AIA FOIA. This article was pulled from the AIA Web site at some point after its publication in 2003.

48. Bernard Weinraub, "Army Reports Iraq Is Moving Toxic Arms to Its Troops," *New York Times*, March 28, 2003.

49. "Rumsfeld Warns Syria," *Chicago Sun-Times*, March 28, 2003.

50. Interview, Lt. General William Scott Wallace, "The Invasion of Iraq," PBS, *Frontline*, February 26, 2004, http://www.pbs.org/wgbh/pages/frontline/shows/invasion/interviews/wallace.html.

51. "Blood. Blood. Blood." quote from General Tommy Franks (USA, Ret.), *American Soldier* (New York: Regan Books, 2004), p. 515. See also H.A.S.C. No. 108-15, U.S. House of Representatives, Armed Services Committee, *Operation Iraqi Freedom: Operations and Reconstruction*, 108th Congress, 1st session, July 10, 2003, p. 79; Rick Atkinson, Peter Baker, and Thomas E. Ricks, "Confused Start, Decisive End," *Washington Post*, April 13, 2003.

52. Interview, Lt. General James Conway, "The Invasion of Iraq," PBS, *Frontline*, February 26, 2004, http://www.pbs.org/wgbh/pages/frontline/shows/invasion/interviews/conway.html.

53. James Kitfield, "March on Baghdad Brings Mix of Power, Flexibility," *National Journal*, April 4, 2003.

54. Bob Drogin, "Iraqi 'Chatter' Threatens Use of Chemicals," *Los Angeles Times*, April 3, 2003.

55. Oral history, *Interview with Major Erik Berdy*, January 20, 2006, p. 17, Combat Studies Institute, Fort Leavenworth, KS.

56. Confidential interviews.

57. Greg Grant, "Network Centric Blind Spot: Intelligence Failed to Detect Massive Iraqi Counterattack," *Defense News*, September 12, 2005, p. 1.

58. Gordon and Trainor, *Cobra II*, p. 352; David Talbot, "How Technology Failed in Iraq," *Technology Review*, November 2004.

59. The most detailed coverage of the incident at the Diyala Canal bridge can be found in John Koopman, "The Compound," *San Francisco Chronicle*, November 14, 2003.

60. Confidential interview.

61. Choate, "Knowing," p. 20. SIGINT's role in preventing this ambush is also obliquely referred to in Lt. General Keith B. Alexander, Headquarters, Department of the Army, Deputy Chief of Staff, G-2, U.S. Senate, statement before the Armed Services Committee, *Hearings on Fiscal Year 2005 Joint Military Intelligence Program (JMIP) and Army Tactical Intelligence and Related Activities (TIARA)*, 108th Congress, 2nd session, April 7, 2004, p. 21.

62. John Koopman, "Iraq, Not Friendly Fire, Killed Marines, U.S. Says," *San Francisco Chronicle*, April 10, 2003.

63. Lt. General Keith B. Alexander, Headquarters, Department of the Army, Deputy Chief of Staff, G-2, Statement before the U.S. Senate Armed Services Committee, *Hearings on Fiscal Year 2005 Joint Military Intelligence Program (JMIP) and Army Tactical Intelligence and Related Activities (TIARA)*, U.S. Senate, 108th Congress, 2nd session, April 7, 2004, p. 21; oral history, *Interview with Major Christopher Carter*, Combat Studies Institute, Fort Leavenworth, KS, June 28, 2006, p. 19; Bernard Weinraub, "U.S. Military Says It Hears Hussein Son Calling Shots," *New York Times*, April 8, 2003.

64. Fred Kaplan, "Smart Bombs, Dumb Targets," *Slate*, December 16, 2003, http://www.slate .com/id/2092759/.

65. Confidential interview.
66. Poss, "Intelligence Family."
67. Confidential interview.
68. Confidential interviews.
69. Confidential interviews. See also U.S. Marine Corps, Major J. P. Myers, Enduring Freedom Combat Assessment Team, PowerPoint presentation, "Intelligence Operations in Operation Iraqi Freedom," slide 13, August 2003, https://www.mccdc.usmc.mil.
70. U.S. Marine Corps, Enduring Freedom Combat Assessment Team, PowerPoint presentation, briefing to MORS, "Information Management Issues Emerging from USMC Experience in Operation Iraqi Freedom," slide 16, October 28, 2003, http:www.mors.org/meetings /c2_2003/Exner.pdf.
71. Department of the Navy, Office of Naval Research, BAA #07-008, presentation, "Command and Control Systems (C2 and CS), Programmic Issues," January 29, 2007, http:www.onr.navy .mil/sci_tech/31/docs/c2cs_Fy08_industry_day_academia.pdf.
72. U.S. Marine Corps, Major J. P. Myers, Enduring Freedom Combat Assessment Team, Power-Point presentation, "Intelligence Operations in Operation Iraqi Freedom," slide 19, August 2003, https://www.mccdc.usmc.mil.
73. Oral history, *Interview with Major Steven Bower*, October 30, 2006, p. 7, Combat Studies Institute, Fort Leavenworth, KS.
74. Oral history, *Interview with Major Kris Arnold*, April 1, 2005, p. 7, Combat Studies Institute, Fort Leavenworth, KS; confidential interviews.

15: The Good, the Bad, and the Ugly

1. Sean Loughlin, "Rumsfeld on Looting in Iraq: 'Stuff Happens,'" CNN, April 12, 2003.
2. Oral history, *Interview with Colonel James Boozer*, January 24, 2006, p. 5, Combat Studies Institute, Fort Leavenworth, KS.
3. Warren P. Strobel and John Walcott, "Post-war Planning Non-Existent," Knight Ridder Newspapers, October 17, 2004; Michael R. Gordon, "The Strategy to Secure Iraq Did Not Foresee a 2nd War," *New York Times*, October 19, 2004.
4. "513th Military Intelligence Brigade," *Mirage*, vol. 1, Fourth Quarter ed. (2003): p. 20; Dr. Donald P. Wright and Col. Timothy R. Reese, *On Point II: Transition to the New Campaign* (Fort Leavenworth, KS: Combat Studies Institute Press, 2008), p. 193.
5. Oral history, *Interview with Major Ronald Beadenkopf*, November 15, 2006, p. 9, Combat Studies Institute, Fort Leavenworth, KS.
6. Confidential interviews.
7. Oral history, *Interview with Major Ronald Beadenkopf*, November 15, 2006, p. 4, Combat Studies Institute, Fort Leavenworth, KS.
8. Douglas Jehl, "U.S. Withdraws a Team of Weapons Hunters from Iraq," *New York Times*, January 8, 2004.
9. "Rumsfeld Blames Iraq Problems on 'Pockets of Dead-Enders,'" *USA Today*, June 18, 2003.
10. Michael Keane, "The Guerrilla Advantage in Iraq," *Los Angeles Times*, November 18, 2003.
11. Anthony Shadid, "Two U.S. Soldiers Killed in Iraqi Baath Bastion," *Washington Post*, May 28, 2003.
12. Eric Schmitt, "New Spy Gear Aims to Thwart Attacks in Iraq," *New York Times*, October 23, 2003; David Rieff, "Blueprint for a Mess," *New York Times*, November 2, 2003.
13. Oral history, *Interview with Major Steven Bower*, October 30, 2006, p. 8, Combat Studies Institute, Fort Leavenworth, KS.

14. Michael J. Gearty, "Lessons Learned: Task Force Sentinel Freedom OEF/OIF," *Military Intelligence Professional Bulletin*, October–December 2003; CALL, *Initial Impressions Report: Operations in Samarra, Iraq: Stryker Brigade Combat Team 1, 3rd Brigade, 2nd Infantry*, December 2004, p. 38, CALL, Fort Leavenworth, KS; oral history, *Interview with Major Chris Budihas*, January 31, 2006, p. 12, Combat Studies Institute, Fort Leavenworth, KS.

15. Oral history, *Interview with Major Ronald Beadenkopf*, November 15, 2006, p. 6, Combat Studies Institute, Fort Leavenworth, KS.

16. Confidential interviews.

17. 3rd Infantry Division, *Operation Iraqi Freedom: 3rd Infantry Division (Mechanized) "Rock of the Marne" After Action Report*, 2003, p. 15, Army FOIA.

18. D.J. Reyes, "Intelligence Battlefield Operating System Lessons Learned: Stability Operations and Support Operations During Operation Iraqi Freedom," *Military Intelligence Professional Bulletin*, January–March 2004.

19. For Korean linguists, see oral history, *Interview with Major Greg Ford*, May 23, 2007, p. 8, Combat Studies Institute, Fort Leavenworth, KS. Joe Bauman, "Long Iraq Stay Irks Utahns," *Salt Lake City Deseret Morning News*, September 8, 2003; Anne O'Donnell, "The Translator Crisis," *New Republic*, December 22, 2003. For Serbo-Croatian linguists with the First Armored Division, confidential interview.

20. Kendall G. Gott, ed., *Eyewitness to War: The US Army in Operation AL FAJR: An Oral History*, vol. 1 (Fort Leavenworth, KS: Combat Studies Institute Press, 2006), p. 3; oral history, *Interview with Major Ronald Beadenkopf*, November 15, 2006, pp. 3–5, Combat Studies Institute, Fort Leavenworth, KS.

21. CALL, *Initial Impressions Report: Operations in Mosul, Iraq, Stryker Brigade Combat Team 1, 3rd Brigade, 2nd Infantry Division*, December 21, 2004, pp. 68, 75, CALL, Fort Leavenworth, KS.

22. Confidential interview.

23. Oral history, *Interview with Lt. Colonel David Seigel*, October 5, 2006, p. 6, Combat Studies Institute, Fort Leavenworth, KS.

24. Confidential interviews. For the formation of Cobra Focus, Collin Agee, Deputy Chief of Staff, G-2, "PowerPoint presentation, Army Intelligence Transformation," given at Association of the U.S. Army (AUSA) Annual Conference, "Actionable Intelligence Panel," October 26, 2004. The slides accompanying this presentation were removed from the AUSA Web site at some point after 2004.

25. Oral history, *Interview with Sergeant Major Kevin Gainey*, December 9, 2005, p. 9, Combat Studies Institute, Fort Leavenworth, KS.

26. Wright and Reese, *On Part II*, p. 222.

27. Confidential interview; Thomas E. Ricks, *Fiasco: The American Military Adventure in Iraq* (New York: Penguin Press, 2006), pp. 408–09.

28. Confidential interviews; oral history, *Interview with Major Greg Ford*, May 23, 2007, p. 9, Combat Studies Institute, Fort Leavenworth, KS; Lt. Colonel Robert P. Whalen, Jr., "Everything Old Is New Again: Task Force Phantom in the Iraq War," *Military Review*, May–June 2007, pp. 31–35.

29. Oral history, *Interview with Major Thomas Neemeyer*, December 2, 2005, p. 8, Combat Studies Institute, Fort Leavenworth, KS; oral history, *Interview with Lt. Colonel Henry A. Arnold*, October 21, 2005, p. 15, Combat Studies Institute, Fort Leavenworth, KS.

30. Confidential interviews; Scott Wilson, "Chalabi Aides Suspected of Spying for Iran," *Washington Post*, May 22, 2004; Rupert Cornwell, "Chalabi Falls from Grace as US Spy Row Erupts," *U.K. Independent*, June 3, 2004.

31. James Risen and David Johnston, "Chalabi Reportedly Told Iran That U.S. Had Code," *New*

York Times, July 2, 2004; David Johnston and James Risen, "Polygraph Testing Starts at Pentagon in Chalabi Inquiry," *New York Times*, June 3, 2004.

32. Confidential interviews.

33. The background on the Battle of Fallujah can be found in Colonel John R. Ballard, "Lessons Learned from Operation AL FAJR: The Liberation of Fallujah," presented at the 10th Annual Command and Control Research and Technology Symposium: The Future of C2, April 6, 2005, pp. 4–5.

34. A detailed description of the first Battle of Fallujah can be found in U.S. Army National Ground Intelligence Center, *Complex Environments: Battle of Fallujah I, April 2004*, March 6, 2006, https://www.wikileaks.org/leak/fallujah.pdf.

35. Oral history, *Interview with Captain Natalie Friel*, July 28, 2006, p. 6, Combat Studies Institute, Fort Leavenworth, KS.

36. Karen Blakeman, "Marine's Wry Joke: Iraq Isn't Like Hawai'i," *Honolulu Advertiser*, May 18, 2004; William Cole, "Marines Recall Their Time in Iraq," *Honolulu Advertiser*, July 22, 2004.

37. Confidential interviews.

38. Oral history, *Interview with Lt. General Richard F. Natonski*, April 5, 2007, p. 4, Combat Studies Institute, Fort Leavenworth, KS; Toby Harnden, "This Is Where the Foreign Fighters Hang Out," *U.K. Daily Telegraph*, November 10, 2004.

39. Dr. Rebecca Grant, *The War of 9/11: How the World Conflict Transformed America's Air and Space Weapon* (Washington, DC: Air Force Association, 2005), p. 39; Thom Shanker and Eric Schmitt, "Terror Command in Falluja Is Half Destroyed, U.S. Says," *New York Times*, October 12, 2004.

40. Colonel Terri Meyer, USCENTAF/A2, PowerPoint presentation, "Operational ISR in the CENTCOM AOR," December 7, 2004.

41. The story of the second Battle of Fallujah is detailed in Matt M. Matthews, *Operation AL FAJR: A Study in Army and Marine Corps Joint Operations* (Fort Leavenworth, KS: Combat Studies Institute, 2006).

42. "Interview, Lt. Colonel James Rainey," April 19, 2006, in Gott, *Eyewitness to War*, vol. 1, p. 119.

43. Oral history, *Interview with Lt. Colonel John Reynolds*, March 14, 2006, p. 12, Combat Studies Institute, Fort Leavenworth, KS.

44. Oral history, *Interview with Lt. Colonel John Reynolds*, March 14, 2006, p. 24, Combat Studies Institute, Fort Leavenworth, KS.

45. Gordon Trowbridge, "Ready or Not, Civilians to Return to Fallujah Within Days," *Air Force Times*, December 20, 2004.

46. Oral history, *Interview with Gunnery Sergeant Michael Johnson*, February 10, 2006, pp. 16–17, Cold War Oral History Project, John A. Adams '71 Center for Military History and Strategic Analysis, Virginia Military Institute, VA.

47. Oral history, *Interview with Captain Brandon Griffin*, July 24, 2006, p. 11, Combat Studies Institute, Fort Leavenworth, KS.

48. Oral history, *Interview with Master Sergeant Michael Threatt*, September 20, 2006, p. 20, Combat Studies Institute, Fort Leavenworth, KS; confidential interviews.

49. Oral history, *Interview with Captain Paul Toolan*, July 24, 2006, p. 8, Combat Studies Institute, Fort Leavenworth, KS.

50. CALL, *Operation OUTREACH Newsletter*, No. 03-27, October 2003 Section: Afghanistan Counter-Mortar Predictive Analysis, p. 20.

51. Oral history, *Interview with Gunnery Sergeant Michael Johnson*, February 10, 2006, pp. 14–15, Cold War Oral History Project, John A. Adams '71 Center for Military History and Strategic Analysis, Virginia Military Institute, VA.

52. Tim McGirk, "The Taliban on the Run," *Time*, April 4, 2005.

53. U.S. Senate, Armed Services Committee, Vice Admiral Lowell E. Jacoby, USN, Director, Defense Intelligence Agency, statement for the record, "Current and Projected National Security Threats to the United States," March 17, 2005, p. 9; Sayed Salahuddin, "Afghanistan's Taliban Just Won't Go Away," Reuters, April 7, 2005; N. C. Aizenman, "General Predicts Taliban's Demise," *Washington Post*, April 17, 2005; Carlotta Gall, "U.S. Training Pakistani Units Fighting Qaeda," *New York Times*, April 27, 2005.

54. Carlotta Gall, "As Winter Ends, Afghan Rebels Step Up Attacks," *New York Times*, April 3, 2005; Carlotta Gall, "Afghan Rebels Step Up Attacks, Killing 9 Near Pakistani Border," *New York Times*, May 6, 2005; Nick Meo, "In Afghanistan, the Taliban Rise Again for Fighting Season," *U.K. Independent*, May 15, 2005; Carlotta Gall, "Despite Years of U.S. Pressure, Taliban Fight On in Jagged Hills," *New York Times*, June 4, 2005; N. C. Aizenman, "Violence Linked to Taliban Swells in Afghanistan," *Washington Post*, June 9, 2005.

55. Confidential interview. See also Daniel Cooney, "2 Taliban Leaders May Be Directing Battle in Afghanistan," Associated Press, June 24, 2005.

56. Sean D. Naylor, "The Waiting Game: A Stronger Taliban Lies Low, Hoping the U.S. Will Leave Afghanistan," *Armed Forces Journal International*, February 2006; Pete Boisson, "Punishment in Syahchow, Afghanistan, 25 July 2005," in William G. Robertson, ed., *In Contact! Case Studies from the Long War* (Fort Leavenworth, KS: Combat Studies Institute Press, 2006), pp. 101–23.

57. For an example of coordinated Taliban attacks on units of the 173rd Airborne Brigade in Zabul Province in the summer of 2005, including Taliban use of walkie-talkies, see Pfc. Jon H. Arguello, "Paratroopers Deal Blow to Taliban in Remote Valley," Army News Service, May 9, 2005; Paul Wiseman, "Taliban on the Run but Far from Vanquished," *USA Today*, July 26, 2005; Catherine Philp, "They Expected an Easy Ride, Then the Enemy Struck Back," *U.K. Times*, July 30, 2005; Scott Baldauf, "Small US Units Lure Taliban into Losing Battles," *Christian Science Monitor*, October 31, 2005; Scott Patsko, "Sergeant Risks Own Life to Protect His Men," *Lorain (OH) Morning Journal*, November 11, 2005.

58. The only detailed publicly available description of the Battle of Mari Ghar can be found in Sean D. Naylor, "The Battle of Mari Ghar," *Army Times*, June 26, 2006.

59. Oral history, *Interview with Captain Brandon Griffin*, July 24, 2006, p. 11, Combat Studies Institute, Fort Leavenworth, KS; oral history, *Interview with Captain Paul Toolan*, July 24, 2006, p. 9, Combat Studies Institute, Fort Leavenworth, KS; quote from oral history, *Interview with Lt. Colonel Don Bolduc*, July 26, 2006, p. 8, Combat Studies Institute, Fort Leavenworth, KS. See also Naylor, "The Waiting Game."

60. Lieutenant General Thomas F. Metz, Colonel William J. Tait, Jr., and Major J. Michael McNealy, "OIF II: Intelligence Leads Successful Counterinsurgency Operations," *Military Intelligence Professional Bulletin*, July–September 2005.

61. Oral history, *Interview with Colonel Emmett Schaill*, January 24, 2007, p. 14, Combat Studies Institute, Fort Leavenworth, KS.

62. Capt. Kevin Stemkaamp, PowerPoint presentation, *1st Brigade, 25th Infantry Division, Stryker Brigade Combat Team OIF III (Sep 04–Sep 05)*, March 9, 2006.

63. "IIF Recover Weapons, Detainees," *Advisor*, July 2, 2005, p. 11, http://www.mnstci.iraq.centcom.mil.

64. Department of Defense "Bloggers Roundtable" with Major General Rick Lynch, USA, Commanding General, Multinational Division Center, via teleconference from Iraq, *Operation Marne Husky*, August 16, 2007, http:www.defenselink.mil./dodcmsshare/BloggerAssets/2007-08/Lynch_081607_transcript.pdf. "Fairly scarce" quote from "Blogger Call: MG Rick Lynch, CDR 3rd ID," the Q and O Blog, August 16, 2007, http://www.qando.net/details.aspx?entry=6690.

65. "Special Troops Battalion, 2 Bde, FOB Kalsu, Iraq," *Lonestar News*, February 15, 2006, p. 1.

66. CAPT Brian Gellman, "From Dagger 6," in *Dagger News*, July 2006, p. 1, http://www.506infantry.org/pdf/506rct/jul_dagger_news.pdf.

67. Hamza Hendawi and Jim Krane, "Deputy Unwittingly Led Troops to al-Zarqawi," Associated Press, June 8, 2006; Sean D. Naylor, "Inside the Zarqawi Takedown," *Defense News*, June 12, 2006; "Cell Phone Tracking Helped Find al-Zarqawi," CNN, June 10, 2006, http://www.cnn.com/2006/WORLD/meast/06/09/iraq.al.zarqawi.

68. Confidential interviews. See also Captain Daniel J. Smith, USN, *Intelligence Gathering in a Counterinsurgency* (Carlisle, PA: U.S. Army War College, 2006), p. 15.

69. The commanding officer of CSG Baghdad from September 2005 to May 2006 was Commander Stone Davis, USN. From May 2006 to February 2007, the chief of CSG Baghdad was Captain Dennis M. Pricolor, USN. Captain Steve Tucker, USN, was chief of CSG Baghdad from February 2007 to May 2008. For Tucker's background, see "Local Soldier Returns from Iraq, Is Awarded Bronze Star," *Morgan County News (TN)*, July 12, 2008.

70. Confidential interviews with senior U.S. military officials. See also Rear Amiral Edward H. Deets III, "Individual Augmentee," *InfoDomain*, Fall 2007, p. 23, www.netwarcom.navy.mil/pao/infodomain/006-InfoDomain%20fall%202007%20On-Line.pdf; Rear Admiral Ned Deets III, Vice Commander, Naval Network Warfare Command, PowerPoint presentation, "Readiness to Fight: Our Shift Forward," November 8, 2007.

71. David A. Fulghum, "Technology Will Be Key to Iraq Buildup," *Aviation Week & Space Technology*, January 14, 2007; Capt. Angela Johnson and Capt. Tim Crowe, "Triton Signals Intelligence Collection System Proves Critical Tool," *Fort Lewis (WA) Northwest Guardian*, June 14, 2007; Association of the U.S. Army, Torchbearer National Security Report, *Key Issues Relevant to Army Intelligence Transformation*, July 2007, p. 10.

72. Confidential interviews. See also Deets, "Individual Augmentee," p. 23.

73. Deets, "Readiness to Fight." Deets, "Individual Augmentee," p. 23; Raymond T. Odierno, Nicole F. Brooks, and Francesco P. Mastracchio, "ISR Evolution in the Iraqi Theater," *Joint Forces Quarterly*, issue 50 (2008): p. 54.

74. Deets, "Individual Augmentee," p. 23.

75. Naval Special Warfare Group 2, press release, "Navy SEAL and Two Combat Support Sailors Killed in Iraq," July 9, 2007; "Barstow Navy Man Killed by Iraq Bomb," Associated Press, July 10, 2007.

76. Rick Atkinson, "The Single Most Effective Weapon Against Our Deployed Forces," *Washington Post*, September 30, 2007.

77. Confidential interviews.

78. Commanding General MNF(I) General David H. Petraeus, *Multi-National Force—Iraq Counterinsurgency Guidance*, June 13, 2007, http://www.airforce.forces.gc.ca/CFAWC/Contemporary_Studies/2007/2007-Jun/2007-06-06_MNF-I_COIN_Guidance-Summer_2007_v7_e.asp.

79. "Local Soldier Returns from Iraq, Is Awarded Bronze Star," *Morgan County News (TN)*, July 12, 2008.

80. Frank Graham, "Branch's Service in Iraq Earns Bronze Star," *North Platte (NE) Bulletin*, August 27, 2008.

81. Confidential interviews with American, British, Canadian, and Dutch intelligence officers; General Michael V. Hayden, USAF, Director, Central Intelligence Agency, statement for the record, U.S. Senate, Armed Services Committee, "The Current Situation in Iraq and Afghanistan," November 15, 2006, p. 3.

82. Oral history, *Interview with Major Jason Warner*, third interview, August 21, 2007, p. 8, Combat Studies Institute, Fort Leavenworth, KS.

83. Confidential interview.

84. "June 18 Airpower Summary: Strike Eagles Watch Over Troops," *Air Force Print News*, June 19, 2007, http://www.af.mil/news/story.asp?id=123057754.

85. Tim Albone, "Medic! Man Down! Under Fire with British Troops in a Taliban Ambush," *U.K. Sunday Times*, July 8, 2007.

86. Michael Smith, "SBS Behind Taliban Leader's Death," *U.K. Sunday Times*, May 27, 2007.

87. Taimoor Shah, "NATO Seeks to retake Taliban Haven," *New York Times*, December 8, 2007.

88. Confidential interviews. See also Ahto Lobjakas, "Afghan Diary, Part 4: 'You Can Go from Being Smiled At to Being Shot At,'" Radio Free Europe/Radio Liberty report, September 21, 2007, http://www.rferl.org/content/article/1078732.html.

89. "June 17 Airpower Summary: Fighting Falcon Provides Show of Force," *Air Force Print News*, June 18, 2007, http://www.af.mil/news/story.asp?id=123057615; "June 18 Airpower Summary," *Air Force Print News*.

90. Christie Blatchford, "Canadian Troops Forced to Start from Scratch," *Globe and Mail*, August 31, 2007. See also "Operation Groundhog Day: The Final Assault on a Stubborn Enemy," *U.K. Independent*, September 23, 2007.

91. Les Neuhaus, "NATO Soldier Killed in Offensive Against Taliban in Afghanistan," *Stars & Stripes*, October 25, 2007. For SIGINT, see Sgt. 1st Class Jacob Caldwell, "Company Works to Flush Out Taliban During 'Rock Avalanche,'" American Forces Press Service, October 31, 2007; Sebastian Junger, "Into the Valley of Death," *Vanity Fair*, January 2008.

92. Pervaiz Iqbal Cheema, "Testing NATO's Determination," *Lahore Post*, November 11, 2007, http://thepost.com.pk/OpinionNews.aspx?dtlid=128142&catid=11.

93. John Ward Anderson, "Emboldened Taliban Reflected in More Attacks, Greater Reach," *Washington Post*, September 25, 2007.

94. Confidential interviews.

95. Denis D. Gray, "U.S. Troops Patrol Gray Afghan World, Watched by Taliban," Associated Press, April 8, 2007.

96. "MacGyver," Letter, July 27, 2007, http://blogs.thestate.com/bradwarthensblog/files/27_jul_2007_anp_operations1.pdf.

97. Noor Khan, "Taliban Surrounded in Kandahar Fight," Associated Press, October 31, 2007.

98. Jason Straziuso, "Deaths Mark Grim Afghan, Iraq Milestones," Associated Press, November 10, 2007.

99. Lt. General David W. Barno, U.S. Army Ret., "Fighting 'The Other War': Counterinsurgency Strategy in Afghanistan, 2003–2005," *Military Review*, September–October 2007, p. 43.

16: CRISIS IN THE RANKS

1. NSA/CSS, NSA Public and Media Affairs, press release, "NSA/CSS Welcomes LTG Keith B. Alexander, USA," July 30, 2005.

2. Keith background from biographical data sheet, Lt. General Keith B. Alexander, Department of the Army, Office of Public Affairs; biography, LTG Keith B. Alexander, USA, http://www.nsa.gov/about/about00022.cfm.

3. James Risen and Eric Lichtblau, "Bush Lets U.S. Spy on Callers Without Courts," *New York Times*, December 16, 2005; Eric Lichtblau and James Risen, "Eavesdropping Effort Began Soon After Sept. 11 Attacks," *New York Times*, December 18, 2005.

4. George J. Tenet, "SIGINT in Context," *Defense Intelligence Journal*, vol. 9, no. 2 (Summer 2000): pp. 9–12; Lt. Gen. Michael V. Hayden, USAF, "Background on NSA: History, Oversight, Relevance for Today," *Defense Intelligence Journal*, vol. 9, no. 2 (Summer 2000): pp. 13–26; "Statement

for the Record of NSA Director Lt. General Michael V. Hayden, USAF Before the House Permanent Select Committee on Intelligence," April 12, 2000.

5. Confidential interviews. A detailed examination of the wide range of data being collected by NSA can be found in Siobhan Gorman, "NSA's Domestic Spying Grows as Agency Sweeps Up Data," *Wall Street Journal*, March 10, 2008.

6. Confidential interviews.

7. Confidential interviews with senior Justice Department officials; Eric Lichtblau, "Debate and Protest at Spy Program's Inception," *New York Times*, March 30, 2008; Dan Eggen, "White House Secrecy on Wiretaps Described," *Washington Post*, October 3, 2007.

8. Robert S. Mueller, III, "RSM Program Log," Wednesday, March 10, 2004, entry, p. 1, attached to David Johnston and Scott Shane, "Notes Detail Visit to Ashcroft's Hospital Room," *New York Times*, August 16, 2007.

9. Jack Landman Goldsmith, prepared statement, "Preserving the Rule of Law in the Fight Against Terrorism," U.S. Senate, Judiciary Committee, October 2, 2007.

10. Jeffrey Rosen, "Conscience of a Conservative," *New York Times Magazine*, September 9, 2007.

11. Confidential interviews.

12. Risen and Lichtblau, "Bush Lets U.S. Spy."

13. Barton Gellman, Dafna Linzer, and Carol D. Leonnig, "Surveillance Net Yields Few Suspects," *Washington Post*, February 5, 2006.

14. Chris Roberts, "Transcript: Debate on the Foreign Intelligence Surveillance Act," *El Paso Times*, August 22, 2007.

15. Confidential interviews.

16. Douglas Jehl, "Senator Asks U.N. Nominee to Explain His Security Requests," *New York Times*, April 14, 2005.

17. Mark Hosenball, Periscope, "Spying—Giving Out U.S. Names," *Newsweek*, May 2, 2005.

18. Katherine Shrader, "Bolton Requested 10 Names in Spy Reports," *Associated Press*, June 27, 2005.

19. Attorney General Alberto Gonzales and General Michael Hayden, Principal Deputy Director for National Intelligence, press briefing, December 19, 2005, http:www.whitehouse.gov/news/releases/2005/12/20051219-1.html.

20. Richard W. Stevenson and Adam Liptak, "Cheney Defends Eavesdropping Without Warrants," *New York Times*, December 21, 2005.

21. Risen and Lichtblau, "Bush Lets U.S. Spy." Connection to Khalid Sheikh Mohammed from confidential interview.

22. "Two Al Qaeda Suspects Arrested in Karachi," *Dawn (Pakistan)*, January 10, 2003; Syed Saleem Shahzad, "Pakistani Backlash to FBI Raids," *Asia Times*, January 15, 2003; Jason Burke, "Shots in the Dark Against an Unknown Enemy," *U.K. Observer*, February 16, 2003.

23. Confidential interviews; Kevin Johnson and Jack Kelly, "Terror Arrest Triggers Mad Scramble," *USA Today*, March 2, 2003; Rory McCarthy and Jason Burke, "Endgame in the Desert of Death for the World's Most Wanted Man," *U.K. Observer*, March 9, 2003; Kevin Whitelaw, "A Tightening Noose," *U.S. News & World Report*, March 17, 2003.

24. Confidential interview.

25. Eric Lichtblau and James Risen, "Spy Agency Mined Vast Data Trove, Officials Report," *New York Times*, December 24, 2005.

26. John Markoff and Scott Shane, "Documents Show Link Between AT&T and Agency in Eavesdropping Case," *New York Times*, April 13, 2006; John Markoff, "U.S. Steps into Wiretap Suit Against AT&T," *New York Times*, April 29, 2006; Leslie Cauley, "NSA Has Massive Database of America's Phone Bills," *USA Today*, May 11, 2006; John O'Neill and Eric Lichtblau, "Qwest's Refusal of NSA Query Is Explained," *New York Times*, May 12, 2006.

27. NSA OH-01-74 to NSA OH-14-81, oral history, *Interview with Frank B. Rowlett*, 1976, pp. 357–61, NSA FOIA; NSA OH-02-79 thru 04-79, oral history, *Interview with Dr. Abraham Sinkov*, May 1979, p. 84, NSA FOIA

28. U.S. Senate, *Final Report of the Select Committee to Study Governmental Operations with Respect to Intelligence Activities*, 94th Congress, 2nd session, bk. 3, pp. 767–69; letter, Barsby to Corderman, October 9, 1945, and letter, Abzug to McKay, in U.S. House of Representatives, Government Operations Committee, *Interception of Nonverbal Communications by Federal Intelligence Agencies*, 94th Congress, 1st and 2nd sessions, 1976, pp. 208, 210; L. Britt Snider, "Unlucky Shamrock: Recollections from the Church Committee's Investigation of NSA," *Studies in Intelligence*, Winter 1999–2000, unclassified ed., pp. 50–51. For the army's abortive attempts to get legislation passed that would have provided legal protection to the cable companies, see memorandum, Russell to Larkin, *Proposed Bill to Amend Section 605 of the Communications Act of 1934 in Order to Increase the Security of the United States, and for Other Purposes*, March 13, 1948, p. 1, CREST Collection, Document No. CIA-RDP57-00384R001000070061-9, NA, CP; memorandum, Clarke to Forrestal, December 13, 1947, RG-330, Entry 199 OSD Decimal File 1947–1950, box 105, file: CD 24-1-1, NA, CP; letter, Carville to Martin, June 1948, CREST Collection, Document No. CIA-RDP57-00384R001000070088-0, NA, CP; ASA, *Annual Report, Plans and Operations Section (AS-23) FY 1948*, p. 24, INSCOM FOIA.

29. Eric Lichtblau, "Key Senators Raise Doubts on Eavesdropping Immunity," *New York Times*, November 1, 2007; confidential interviews.

30. Confidential interviews.

31. Scott Shane, "Attention in NSA Debate Turns to Telecom Industry," *New York Times*, February 11, 2006.

32. Katherine Shrader, "Bush Seeks Legal Immunity for Telecoms," Associated Press, September 5, 2007; Eric Lichtblau, "Immunity Crucial in Talks on Eavesdropping Rules," *New York Times*, October 10, 2007.

33. For an example of McConnell's impassioned pleas for granting retroactive immunity to the telecommunications companies, see Mike McConnell, "A Key Gap in Fighting Terrorism," *Washington Post*, February 15, 2008.

34. Confidential interview.

35. U.S. Department of Justice, *Legal Authorities Supporting the Activities of the National Security Agency Described by the President*, January 19, 2006; Attorney General Alberto Gonzales and General Michael Hayden, Principal Deputy Director for National Intelligence, press briefing, December 19, 2005. For CIA programs, see Dana Priest, "Covert CIA Program Withstands New Furor," *Washington Post*, December 30, 2005.

36. Letter, February 2, 2006, http://www.eff.org/files/filenode/nsaspying/FISA_AUMF_replyto DOJ.pdf.

37. "Wiretap Mystery: Spooks React," Defensetech.org, December 20, 2005, http://www.defensetech.org/archives/002032.html.

38. Confidential interview.

39. Commission on the Intelligence Capabilities of the United States Regarding Weapons of Mass Destruction, *Report to the President of the United States* (Washington, DC: GPO, March 31, 2005), p. 375.

40. Devlin Barrett, "Security Issue Kills Domestic Spying Inquiry," Associated Press, May 10, 2006.

41. Confidential interviews.

42. The Comey incident was first revealed in Eric Lichtblau and James Risen, "Justice Deputy Resisted Parts of Spy Program," *New York Times*, January 1, 2006. See also David Johnston, "Pres-

ident Intervened in Dispute over Eavesdropping," *New York Times*, May 16, 2007; Dan Eggen and Paul Kane, "Gonzales Hospital Episode Detailed," *Washington Post*, May 16, 2007.

43. Confidential interview.

44. Eggen, "White House Secrecy."

45. Michael Isikoff and Mark Hosenball, "Behind the Surveillance Debate," *Newsweek*, August 1, 2007; Greg Miller, "Court Puts Limits on Surveillance Abroad," *Los Angeles Times*, August 2, 2007.

46. Siobhan Gorman, "NSA Has Higher Profile, New Problems," *Baltimore Sun*, September 8, 2006.

47. Confidential interviews.

48. Gorman, "NSA Has Higher Profile."

49. Ariel Sabar, "Want to Be a Spy? NSA Is Hiring," *Baltimore Sun*, April 10, 2004; Stephen Barr, "NSA Makes No Secret of Stepped-Up Recruitment Effort," *Washington Post*, April 22, 2004; "A Good Spy Is Hard to Fund," *U.S. News & World Report*, November 22, 2004; "Spy Agency to Undergo Major Changes," Associated Press, November 12, 2005; Gorman, "NSA Has Higher Profile"; Siobhan Gorman, "Budget Falling Short at NSA," *Baltimore Sun*, January 17, 2007; confidential interviews.

50. As of 2005, the size of the U.S. intelligence budget was forty-four billion dollars, for which see Scott Shane, "Official Reveals Budget for U.S. Intelligence," *New York Times*, November 8, 2005. In May 2007, Congress approved a forty-eight-billion-dollar intelligence budget, for which see Walter Pincus, "House Panel Approves a Record $48 billion for Spy Agencies," *Washington Post*, May 4, 2007.

51. Sheila Hotchkin, "NSA Will Let Its Dollars Do the Talking," *San Antonio Express-News*, April 16, 2005; Mike Soraghan and Aldo Svaldi, "NSA Moving Some Workers, Operations to Denver Area," *Denver Post*, January 24, 2006; Robert Gehrke, "Key Spy Agency Expands to Utah," *Salt Lake Tribune*, February 2, 2006; Amy Choate, "NSA Seeks Linguists at BYU to Staff Utah Center," *Salt Lake City Deseret Morning News*, February 24, 2006.

52. "Emergency War Supplemental Hides Millions," UPI, February 20, 2006.

53. Scott Shane and Tom Bowman, "America's Fortress of Spies," *Baltimore Sun*, December 3, 1995.

54. NSA/CSS, *Transition 2001*, December 2000, p. 33. The author is grateful to Dr. Jeffrey T. Richelson for making a copy of this document available.

55. There are twenty-two distinct Arabic dialects spoken in the Muslim countries of North Africa and the Middle East, each marked by subtle differences in vocabulary, verb usage, and pronunciation.

56. Confidential interviews. For languages spoken by linguists at Fort Gordon, see Joseph Gunder, "Tongue Sharpening: GCL Helps Cryptologists Brush Up Before Shipping Out," *InfoDomain*, Summer 2007, p. 10.

57. Confidential interviews. For a brief description of the work performed by NSA's TAO, see Rowan Scarborough, *Sabotage: America's Enemies Within the CIA* (Washington, DC: Regnery Publishing, 2007), p. 161; U.S. Army War College, *Information Operations Primer: Fundamentals of Information Operations*, November 2006, pp. 88–89. A description of the work performed by the navy's computer network exploitation operators at Fort Meade is contained in MILPERSMAN 1306-980, *Navy Interactive ON-NET (ION) Computer Network Exploitation (CNE) Operator Certification Program*, May 29, 2007; MILPERSMAN 1306-981, *Navy Interactive ON-NET (ION) Computer Network Exploitation (CNE) Trainer Certification Program*, May 29, 2007.

58. Technical Document 3131, *SPAWAR Systems Center San Diego Command History 2001*, March 2002, p. 41, http://www.spawar.navy.mil/sti/publications/pubs/td/3131/td3131.pdf.

59. Memorandum, Zenker to Joint Tactical SIGINT Architecture (JTSA) Working Group, *Quarterly Meeting Minutes–December 2001*, December 31, 2001. This document has since been reclassified and removed from the Internet site where the author originally found it.

60. NSA/CSS, *Transition 2001*, December 2000, p. 19. Shane Harris, "Internet Devices Threaten NSA's Ability to Gather Intelligence Legally," *National Journal*, April 10, 2006; Richard Willing, "Growing Cellphone Use a Problem for Spy Agencies," *USA Today*, August 2, 2007; confidential interview.

61. Loren B. Thompson, PowerPoint presentation, "ISR Lessons of Iraq," Defense News ISR Integration Conference, November 18, 2003, http://www.lexingtoninstitute.org/docs/435.pdf.

62. Confidential interviews.

63. Commission on the Intelligence Capabilities of the United States Regarding Weapons of Mass Destruction, *Report to the President of the United States* (Washington, DC: GPO, March 31, 2005), p. 16.

64. U.S. House of Representatives, Permanent Select Committee on Intelligence, *IC21: Intelligence Community in the 21st Century*, 104th Congress, 1st session, 1996, p. 189; U.S. House of Representatives, Permanent Select Committee on Intelligence, Report 104-578, *Intelligence Authorization Act for Fiscal Year 1998*, 105th Congress, 1st session, June 18, 1997, p. 18; Philip H. J. Davies, "Information Warfare and the Future of the Spy," *Information Communication and Society*, vol. 2, no. 2 (Summer 1999); Warren P. Strobel, "The Sound of Silence?," *U.S. News & World Report*, February 14, 2000; John Deutch and Jeffrey H. Smith, "Smarter Intelligence," *Foreign Policy*, January–February 2002.

65. Colum Lynch, "US Used UN to Spy on Iraq, Aides Say," *Boston Globe*, January 6, 1999; Barton Gellman, "Annan Suspicious of UNSCOM Probe," *Washington Post*, January 6, 1999; Bruce W. Nelan, "Bugging Saddam," *Time*, January 18, 1999; Seymour M. Hersh, "Saddam's Best Friend," *New Yorker*, April 5, 1999, pp. 32, 35; David Wise, "Fall Guy," *Washingtonian*, July 1999, pp. 42–43.

66. John Pomfret, "China Finds Bugs on Jet Equipped in U.S.," *Washington Post*, January 19, 2002.

67. Bill Gertz and Rowan Scarborough, "Inside the Ring," *Washington Times*, January 12, 2007.

68. Loch K. Johnson, *Secret Agencies: U.S. Intelligence in a Hostile World* (New Haven, CT: Yale University Press, 1996), p. 21; Robert D. Steele, *Improving National Intelligence Support to Marine Corps Operational Forces: Forty Specific Recommendations*, September 3, 1991, p. 5, http://www.oss.net/Papers/reform. Quote from interview, Herbert Levin, March 5, 1994, Foreign Affairs Oral History Collection, Association for Diplomatic Studies and Training, Arlington, VA.

69. David E. Sanger, "What Are Koreans Up To? U.S. Agencies Can't Agree," *New York Times*, May 12, 2005.

70. Parliamentary Intelligence and Security Committee, CM 5837, *Annual Report 2002–2003*, June 2003, p. 20.

71. Confidential interviews.

72. Confidential interviews.

73. NSA's loss of "centrality of command" was reflected for the first time in the 1994 edition of the agency's principal SIGINT operating policy document, *U.S. Signals Intelligence Directive 1*, which states, "Certain SIGINT collection and processing activities, specifically designated by the Director of Central Intelligence (DCI) as essential and integral to activities conducted under the authority of NSCID No. 5 [U.S. Espionage and Counterintelligence Activities Abroad], are specifically exempted by NSCID No. 6 [Signals Intelligence] from the control of DIRNSA/Chief, CSS (DIRNSA.CHCSS)." NSA/CSS, United States Signals Intelligence Directive 1 (USSID 1), *SIGINT Operating Policy*, June 13, 1994, p. 4, NSA FOIA.

74. Rowan Scarborough, "Lack of Fluency in Islamic Languages Impedes U.S.," *Washington Times*, July 2, 2007.

75. Confidential interviews. See also Lt. Colonel Stephen K. Iwicki, "CSA's Focus Area 16: Actionable Intelligence," *Military Intelligence Professional Bulletin*, January–March 2005, p. 51.

76. Confidential interviews.

77. 1LT Brian Noble, "SIGINT," *Dagger News*, February 2006, p. 2, http://www.506infantry.org/pdf/506rct/feb_dagger_news.pdf.

78. Major General Barbara Fast, Commander, USAIC&FH, US Army Geospatial Intelligence, PowerPoint presentation, presented at Geospatial Intelligence Defense Conference, May 15, 2006.

79. NSA/CSS, director's message, "Media Scrutiny on TURBULENCE," February 19, 2007, NSA FOIA; Siobhan Gorman, "Costly NSA Initiative Has Shaky Takeoff," *Baltimore Sun*, February 11, 2007; Siobhan Gorman, "NSA Program Draws Congress' Ire," *Baltimore Sun*, March 28, 2007; Alice Lipowicz, "Hard Sell: NSA's Tech Reorg Faces Uphill Road to Win Over Critics," *Washington Technology*, June 11, 2007.

80. NSA's twenty-one-million-dollar electricity bill in 2000 from Dana Roscoe, "NSA Hosts Special Partnership Breakfast," *NSA Newsletter*, p. 4, NSA FOIA. For thirty-million-dollar electricity bill in 2007, confidential interview.

81. Siobhan Gorman, "NSA Electricity Crisis Gets Senate Scrutiny," *Baltimore Sun*, January 26, 2007; Siobhan Gorman, "Power Supply Still a Vexation for the NSA," *Baltimore Sun*, June 24, 2007.

82. Gorman, "NSA Has Higher Profile."

83. Gorman, "Budget Falling Short."

84. Confidential interview.

AFTERWORD

1. The information contained in the following pages is derived from a more detailed treatment of the subject contained in Matthew M. Aid, "The Troubled Inheritance: The National Security Agency and the Obama Administration," in Loch K. Johnson, ed., *The Oxford Handbook of National Security Intelligence* (New York: Oxford University Press, 2010), 242–256.

2. Shane Harris, "The Cyberwar Plan," *National Journal*, November 14, 2009, 18–24.

3. Offices of Inspector General of the Department of Defense, Department of Justice, Central Intelligence Agency, National Security Agency, and Office of the Director of National Intelligence, Report No. 2009-0013-AS, *Unclassified Report on the President's Surveillance Program*, July 10, 2009, located at http://www.dni.gov/electronic_reading_room.htm.

Index